THEGREENGUIDE
French Riviera

House in Île de Porquerolles © Monika Lewandowska/iStockphoto.com

THEGREENGUIDE **FRENCH RIVIERA**

Editor	Clive Hebard
Principal Writer	Steven Durose
Production Manager	Natasha G. George
Cartography	Stéphane Anton, John Dear
Photo Editor	Yoshimi Kanazawa
Photo Researcher	Regina Wolek
Interior Design	Chris Bell
Layout	Michelin Apa Publications Ltd.
	Anna Gatt, John Heath
Cover Design	Chris Bell, Christelle Le Déan
Cover Layout	Michelin Apa Publications Ltd.

Contact Us

The Green Guide
Michelin Travel and Lifestyle
One Parkway South
Greenville, SC 29615
USA
www.michelintravel.com
michelin.guides@us.michelin.com

Michelin TravelPartner
Hannay House
39 Clarendon Road
Watford, Herts WD17 1JA
UK
℘01923 205240
www.ViaMichelin.com
travelpubsales@uk.michelin.com

Special Sales

For information regarding bulk sales,
customized editions and premium sales,
please contact our Customer Service
Departments:
USA   1-800-432-6277
UK   01923 205240
Canada 1-800-361-8236

HOW TO USE THIS GUIDE

PLANNING YOUR TRIP

The blue-tabbed PLANNING YOUR TRIP section at the front of the guide gives you **ideas for your trip** and **practical information** to help you organise it. You'll find tours, practical information, a host of outdoor activities, a calendar of events, information on shopping, sightseeing, kids' activities and more.

INTRODUCTION

The orange-tabbed INTRODUCTION section explores the French Riviera's **Nature** and geology. The **History** section spans 1500 BC through the Revolution to the modern day. The **Art and Culture** section covers architecture, art, literature and music, while the **Region Today** delves into the modern French Riviera.

DISCOVERING

The green-tabbed DISCOVERING section describes Principal Sights by region, featuring the most interesting local **Sights**, **Walking Tours**, nearby **Excursions**, and detailed **Driving Tours**. Admission prices shown are normally for a single adult.

ADDRESSES

We've selected the best hotels, restaurants, cafes shops, nightlife and entertainment to fit all budgets. See the Legend on the cover flap for an explanation of the price categories. See the back of the guide for an index of where to find hotels and restaurants.

Sidebars

Throughout the guide you will find blue, peach and green-colored text boxes with lively anecdotes, detailed history and background information.

🍃 A Bit of Advice 🍃

Green advice boxes found in this guide contain practical tips and handy information relevant to your visit or to a sight in the Discovering section.

STAR RATINGS★★★

Michelin has given star ratings for more than 100 years. If you're pressed for time, we recommend you visit the ★★★, or ★★ sights first:

★★★	**Highly recommended**
★★	**Recommended**
★	**Interesting**

MAPS

- Principal Sights map.
- Region maps.
- Maps for major cities and villages.
- Local tour maps.

All maps in this guide are oriented north, unless otherwise indicated by a directional arrow. The term "Local Map" refers to a map within the chapter or Tourism Region. A complete list of the maps found in the guide appears at the back of this book.

PLANNING YOUR TRIP

INTRODUCTION TO THE FRENCH RIVIERA

CONTENTS

DISCOVERING THE FRENCH RIVIERA

Welcome to the French Riviera

The French Riviera stretches along the Mediterranean coast in southeastern France between the Italian border and the Rhône Valley. It's an amazingly diverse region of sunny beaches and prestigious ports, as well as dramatic mountain peaks and *villages perchées*, the Medieval hilltowns perched atop secluded escarpments and headlands. Aside from its natural beauty, visitors will also discover a rich artistic, cultural and architectural heritage from Roman times and the Middle Ages through the Belle Époque to the present day.

Îles des Embiez

©Camille Moirenc/Hemis/Photoshot

TOULON & AROUND (pp98–125)

The oft-overlooked city of Toulon at the western edge of the French Riviera is well worth a stop for its historic harbour, naval museum and restored old town. The surrounding villages produce some of the finest wines and olive oils in the south, while the region's coastal paths and isolated beaches offer a sunny retreat from the summer crowds, especially around the Îles des Embiez.

HYÈRES, THE GOLDEN ISLANDS AND THE MASSIF DES MAURES (pp126–169)

For those who dream of unspoiled islands, sandy beaches and chic resorts, this Eden-like stretch of the Riviera won't disappoint. The natural beauty of the Maures Massif and the Golden Islands has been fiercely protected from over-development. And even after the summer crowds of St-Tropez and Hyères have disappeared, the Provençal-style fishing villages, tropical parks and gardens, eccentric villas and Belle Époque palaces make for pleasant sightseeing.

Île de Porquerolles

©Luca Chiartano/Dreamstime.com

Cotignac

S. Sauvignier/MICHELIN

INLAND PROVENCE (pp170–195)

Far from the showy splendour and busloads of tourists found on the coastal resorts, the villages, valleys and prehistoric monuments of Inland Provence are given to peaceful exploration. The 12C Abbaye du Thoronet is worth a detour of its own, while wine collectors won't want to miss the organic vineyards around Brignoles. Aups and Cotignac remain two of the most charming spots in the region, along with the cave dwellings of Villecroze.

Esterel Massif viewed from Fréjus
©Guillaume Besnard/Fotolia.com

FRÉJUS & THE ESTEREL MASSIF *(pp196–225)*

The most Provençal area of the French Riviera is known for its unspoilt forests and red rock hills of the Massif de l'Esterel, while the lively twinned towns of Fréjus and St-Raphaël attract visitors who prefer a more discreet resort experience to its beaches. History *aficionados* won't want to miss the impressive Gallo-Roman remains found in and around Fréjus or the archaeology museum in St-Raphaël.

CANNES & THE GRASSE REGION *(pp226–292)*

Don't forget to pack your bathing suit and sunglasses! The most popular beaches on the French Riviera are found in the dynamic resort towns of Cannes, Antibes and Juan-les-Pins, while the hills further inland are home to the world-famous perfume-making town of Grasse and its surrounding perched villages. The fashionable palace hotels and private yachts are in surprising contrast to the Provençal-style villages with their shady squares and ancient churches, making this an ideal place to experience both worlds. And if you're interested in exploring the region's exceptional artistic heritage, don't miss the cutting-edge galleries and museums of Mougins, Vallauris and Antibes.

NICE, THE RIVIERA & MONACO *(pp293–357)*

This glamorous stretch of the Riviera features the glittering Principality of Monaco, with its Belle Époque casino and oceanographic institute; the bustling city of Nice, known for its colourful Carnival parades, old town market, and world-class art collections; and Menton, with its exotic gardens and Cocteau museum. While cruising between them on the scenic corniche roads, visitors will find more tranquil coastal paths along Cap Ferrat and Cap d'Ail, and amazing views from the perched villages of Èze and Ste-Agnès, Europe's highest coastal village.

Rock cliffs of La Colmiane
©Michel Megret/Robert Harding

THE PRE-ALPS OF NICE *(pp358–397)*

The most dramatic landscape on the French Riviera is found in the hinterlands above Nice, where the sunny Mediterranean meets the snow-covered Alps. The rocky peaks and deep river valleys attract hikers, rock climbers, rafters and mountain bikers in summer, as well as skiers in winter. The Mercantour National Park, which shares a border with Italy, offers glimpses of rare flora and fauna, as well as prehistoric engravings in the Vallée des Merveilles. Sturdy shoes and reliable maps are a must!

Promenade des Anglais and Hôtel Negresco, Nice
©Romain Cintract/Hemis/Photolibrary

Michelin Driving Tours

1 VAR COASTLINE AND THE GOLDEN ISLANDS

Round tour of 146mi/235km starting from Toulon

The city of Toulon should be visited in the local tradition, in other words at a leisurely pace, taking time to explore the intricate streets shaded by centuries-old plane trees. After dropping by the lively marché Lafayette and choosing a few fresh vegetables and mouthwatering local treats, set out to discover "the most beautiful harbour" on the Riviera, passing by Pointe du Fort Balaguier and Cap Sicié. Nestled between land and sea, Sanary and Bandol, and their islands of Bendor and Embiez, will seduce you with their heavenly setting. Further on, the perched villages of Le Castellet, Beausset and Evenos compose the perfect picture of Provençal bliss. Next, admire the harbour from atop Mont Faron. Continue to the bird sanctuary at La Londe for an escape to the tropics. Treat yourself to a stay on the gorgeous islands of Port-Cros and Porquerolles; the underwater sightseeing trail offers incomparable views of the sea's fauna and flora for divers and snorkellers. A tour of the Mine de Cap-Garonne at Le Pradet is the perfect way to round off your outing.

2 LE HAUT-VAR

Round tour of 152mi/245km starting from Draguignan

This itinerary will take you across the upper stretches of the Var Valley, with its rolling wooded countryside dotted with old abbeys and remarkable sites: Tourtour nestling on the crest of a hill overlooking olive groves; Cotignac perched precariously on a cliff; Villecroze and Seillans enhanced by hardened volcanic ash rock formations; Entrecasteaux, whose château is graced by gardens attributed to Le Nôtre. You'll be surprised by the diversity of the villages and towns you encounter. Some clearly enjoy perpetuating local tradition while others promote a more dynamic artisan culture. Don't miss the colourful markets offering truffles, goat's cheese or olives, depending on the season, and the restaurants, where you will be served tasty regional cuisine pleasantly seasoned with aromatic herbs.

3 LE MASSIF DES MAURES

Round tour of 171mi/275km starting from Fréjus

Far away from the coast and its bustling crowd, this tour will take you through refreshingly cool forests of cork oak and the pretty Gratteloup arboretum, where eucalyptus, chestnut, maple, cedar and juniper trees exude their intoxicating aroma. Visit the superb Domaine du Rayol, laid out at the turn of the 20C, and discover regional arts and crafts: the cork industry in Gonfaron; *marrons glacés* in Collobrières; pipe-making and carpet weaving in Cogolin. The hill villages of Ramatuelle, Grimaud and Gassin command **panoramic views** of the coast, as do the Moulins de Paillas. Before taking a swim in one of the many sheltered rocky inlets, you may want to settle on the terrace of the Sénéquier in St-Tropez alongside the rich and famous or you may prefer to browse among the market stalls in the old port in the hope of chancing upon a fake Picasso...

4 MASSIF DE L'ESTEREL AND THE FAYENCE REGION

Round tour of 177mi/285km starting from Cannes

Whatever the season, this itinerary will prove an enchanting experience on many counts: the rich, luxuriant vegetation, the chirping of the cicadas, the delicately fragrant mimosa blossoms, the warm embrace of the sun and the red rock of the Esterel heights. Running between La Napoule and Agay, the Corniche d'Or offers stunning **views** of the sea.

You'll find it hard to resist the charms of St-Raphaël, a lively seaside resort, and Fréjus, with its exceptional Roman and military heritage, not to mention Fréjus-Plage, which boasts the longest sandy beach on the Riviera. Further inland, the Fayence area will introduce you to a host of perched villages huddled on mountain slopes, dominated by vestiges of their medieval citadels: Caillan, Fayence, Tourrettes, Seillan, Tanneron and Auribeau-sur-Siagne.

5 FRAGRANCES AND COLOURS OF THE PRE-ALPS

Round tour of 134mi/215km
starting from Grasse

The Pre-Alps of Provence, extending to the foot of the Alpine range and cut across by steep ravines, offer a delightful combination of colours and fragrances, where the heady smells of olive and cypress trees vie with the more subtle scent of rose, jasmin, oleander and violet. Grasse's reputation is built on flowers, so don't miss the International Museum of Perfume and the different *parfumeries* explaining the secrets of the trade. The entrance to the Gorges du Loup is the perfect place to stop and admire the hill village of Gourdon, jealously guarding its abyss, and the Caussols Plateau, a curiously barren stretch of land riddled with chasms. After observing the geological formations in the caves of St-Vallier and St-Cézaire, continue to St-Paul-de-Vence, a typical medieval village known for its crafts and world-class art gallery, and to the delightful hamlet of Tourrettes-sur-Loup, where terraced violet fields have been cultivated from generation to generation. The Baou of St-Jeannet dominating the Var River is a sheer rocky cliff popular among seasoned climbers. Lastly, the coastal road stretching between Cagnes-sur-Mer and Antibes offers pretty **views** of the Baie des Anges and access to a number of contemporary art museums.

6 L'ARRIÈRE-PAYS NIÇOIS

Round tour of 168mi/270km
starting from Nice

This driving tour will provide you with a fascinating selection of natural sites and architectural riches: quaint perched villages, chapels decorated by famous painters or unknown artists from the Middle Ages, steep cliffs overlooking gorges echoing with the swirling of crystal-clear waters and lush forests rustling with the sounds of local fauna. Running alongside the lower Var Valley, bordered to the west by the Baou of St Jeannet, approach the heights to the rear of Nice, dominated by Mont Chauve. After driving through Aspremont, Levens and Duranus, take an hour or two to admire the breathtaking Vésubie Gorges. From there, brace yourself for the long series of steep hairpin bends leading up to the Madone d'Utelle sanctuary, a popular place of pilgrimage, and the nearby belvedere commanding a splendid **panorama** of the Alpes-Maritimes and the Mediterranean. Proceeding upstream along the Vésubie River towards Col de Turini, gateway to the vast Forêt de Turini, stop at Bollène-Vésubie, precariously nestling on a mountain slope. On reaching L'Authion, go round to Pointe des Trois-Communes and feast your eyes on the sweeping landscape. Continue towards the Gorges of Piaon. After the curious Notre-Dame-de-la-Menour Chapel, with its two-storey Renaissance façade, head for Sospel, springing from its verdant setting, and visit its fortified bridge and imposing Maginot Line fort. Drive through several passes before rejoining Lucéram Valley, famed for its heritage museums and religious artworks. Finally, three belvederes, each home to a small village, Berre, Falicon and Tourrettes, will complete your tour of the Nice hinterland.

7 THE CORNICHES OF THE RIVIERA

Round tour of 155.5mi/250km starting from Nice.

If you have seen Hitchcock's thriller *To Catch a Thief,* then you will know that it is advisable to hug the road winding its way between Nice and Monte-Carlo as closely as possible. This route, which features a series of vertiginous viewpoints, goes past some of the prettiest spots on the Côte d'Azur. Set out from Villefranche, famous not only for its Chapelle St-Pierre decorated by Jean Cocteau, but also for its pretty harbour and succulent seafood dishes. Follow the Grande Corniche up to Roquebrune, with forays downhill to Beaulieu (Villa Kérylos), St-Jean-Cap-Ferrat (Villa Rothschild and Villa Santo Sospir) and Èze, the muse of philosopher Frédéric Nietzsche, clinging to its rocky spur, where a tour of artists' workshops can be pleasantly rounded off by a visit to the Jardin Exotique. Enjoy the **view** from the Vistaero before descending towards Roquebrune with its medieval castle and venerable olive tree believed to be more than 1,000 years old. After Menton and the Cocteau Museum, the road will take you through the perched villages of Ste-Agnès, Europe's highest coastal village, Peille and Peillon, where steep alleyways *(calades)* lead to chapels adorned with fine frescoes.

When and Where to Go

WHEN TO GO
SEASONS

The **tourist season** on the French Riviera lasts virtually all year round. **Winter months** are characterised by a mild, sunny climate and are ideal for those seeking to avoid the peak tourist season. However, some hotels, restaurants and attractions are closed between November and February. **Spring** and **autumn** can sometimes bring heavy rainfall and the infamous *mistral* wind, but neither overshadows the magnificent display of flora in full bloom at these times. **Summer** is of course the best season for bathing and working up a suntan, not to mention taking part in the energetic nightlife. Traffic on the coast is, however, always very congested during this period; it can also be difficult to find accommodation, so it's advisable to book well in advance, particularly in August.

WEATHER FORECASTS
Recorded report
♦ for the Alpes-Maritimes: ℘08 92 68 02 06
♦ for the Var: ℘08 92 68 02 83
♦ for conditions at sea: ℘08 92 68 08 77
♦ for the region: ℘08 92 68 00 00
♦ for the mountains: ℘08 92 68 04 04

Online weather reports
♦ www.meteo.fr
♦ www.meteo123.com

Road conditions
♦ www.ViaMichelin.com (itineraries and updates)
♦ snow and avalanche reports: ℘08 92 68 10 20

WHAT TO PACK

As little as possible! Cleaning and laundry services are available everywhere. Most personal items can be replaced at reasonable cost. Try to pack everything into one suitcase and a tote bag. Porter help may be in short supply, while new purchases will add to the original weight. Take an extra tote bag for packing new purchases, shopping at the market, carrying a picnic, etc. Be sure luggage is clearly labelled and old travel tags removed. Do not pack medication in checked luggage, but keep it in your carry-on. **Tourist Information Centres – The Michelin Guide France** gives the addresses and telephone numbers of the Tourist Information Centres (*Syndicats d'Initiative*) to be found in most large towns and many tourist resorts. They can supply large-scale town maps, timetables and information on local entertainment, accommodation, sports and sightseeing.

WHERE TO GO
WEEKEND BREAKS

Two itineraries for those who want to spend a long weekend in the Riviera:

NICE

Day 1	Visit the seafront and the Vieille Ville in the morning, then Cimiez and a museum or gallery.
Day 2	Spend the morning in **Monaco**★★★, then drive up to **Èze** ★★ and or along to **Cap Ferrat**★ via the corniche roads.
Day 3	Drive up to the **Gorges de la Vésubie**★★★, with a detour to the **Madone d'Utelle Panorama**★★★ for **views** across the whole of the Alps-Maritimes region, returning via **Sospel**★.

CANNES

Day 1	Visit the Marché, Le Suquet and the port in the morning, with lunch, sunbathing and shopping on the Croisette.
Day 2	Drive to **Antibes**★★ via the **Cap**★ to stroll around the **Old Town**★, followed by a tour of **St-Paul-de-Vence**★★, returning via **Grasse**★ and **Mougins**★.
Day 3	Drive along the **Corniche de l'Esterel**★★★ to **St-Raphaël**, then visit the Roman remains at **Fréjus**★.

ONE-WEEK ITINERARY

For a seven-day visit, make Nice your base for the first three days. Visit the Old Town and its world-class museums, then the towns along the Corniche roads from Villefranche up to Menton for the best **views**, including an evening in Monte-Carlo.
Head west to Antibes and Cannes for the next three days, with time for a trip to the Île des Lérins, an afternoon at the beaches of Juan-les-Pins and a drive up the Loup Valley to St-Paul-de-Vence or Gourdon. Use the last day to drive the scenic Corniche de l'Esterel, with a detour to St-Tropez if the traffic isn't too bad, or to Le Thoronet to escape the heat and crowds.

View of the Massif de l'Esterel

J. Malburet/MICHELIN

Promenade des Anglais, Nice

TWO-WEEK ITINERARY

Two weeks on the French Riviera will allow you time to explore each area in-depth, to enjoy the many opportunities for watersports or hiking, or to visit the museums or explore the ancient churches off-season. To the one-week itinerary add a day in the hinterlands of Nice, hiking in the Mercantour to see the Vallée des Merveilles or rafting down the Roya Valley. Add an extra day for shopping in the artisan villages of Èze, Vence or Valbonne, or the fashionable boutiques of Monaco or Cannes. The remaining two days can be spent diving in the Îles de Porquerolles or hiking along the nature trails at Port Cros, with a guided tour of the historic naval harbour at Toulon and a drive up to Mont Faron for exceptional **panoramic views**.

THEMED TOURS
FOREST PARKS

All along the Alpes-Maritimes coast there are islands of greenery *(parcs forestiers départementaux)* provided for walkers of all abilities.

- **Parc de la Grande-Corniche** in Èze (access from Col d'Èze on the Grande Corniche)
- **Parc de Vaugrenier** (access by RN 7 between Antibes and Marina Baie des Anges)

- **Parc de la Vallée de la Brague** (at the eastern end of Biot village)
- **Parc du San Peyre** (from La Napoule towards A 8 motorway and a left turn onto Route du Cimetière), a former look-out post (alt. 430ft/131m), which offers a superb **panorama** of Cannes Bay
- **Parc de la Pointe de l'Aiguille** (car park on D 6098 at the edge of Théoule)
- **Route Historique des Hauts-Lieux de Provence** – A circuit from St-Maximin-la-Ste-Baume via Draguignan and Les Arcs to Fréjus returning along the coast to Toulon, organised by an association at the Office de Tourisme, 83460 Les Arcs-sur-Argens, ✆04 94 73 37 30.
- **Route des Côtes de Provence**

SCENIC VIEWS
Riviera Caves

The limestone region of the Pays Grassois (especially the Caussols Plateau) features many interesting geological features dating from different periods – the caves *(grottes)* at St-Cézaire (✆ *see GRASSE p245*), the gigantic limestone crevices such as the original caves consisting of a succession of natural dams *(gours)* including the Grotte de Baume Obscure (✆ *see ST-VALLIER-DE-THIEY p250*). The **Grottes de Villecroze** near

Draguignan (*see VILLECROZE p178*) are formed of tufa (hardened volcanic ash). Other caves, which are accessible with adequate equipment and some technical knowledge, belong in the caving category (*see p23*). People with no caving experience can get an idea of the activity in the first section (about 39ft/12m) of the **Embut de Caussols** (*embut* is the Provençal word for swallowhole).

Military Fortifications of the Alpes-Maritimes

The strategic significance of the frontier zone in the southeast was developed in 1880 by Sérés de Rivières. The project was completed and improved in 1929 by its integration into the Maginot Line, which defended the eastern frontier from Dunkirk to Menton. It offers a fascinating insight into military architecture in the 19C and 20C. Some of the buildings have been disarmed, restored and are accessible to visitors:

- **Fort de Ste-Agnès**
  (*see MENTON p349*)
- **Fort du Barbonnet**
  (*see Forêt de TURINI p380*)
- **Fort Suchet (19C)**, the only one that can be visited
  (*see Forêt de TURINI p380*)
- **Fort St-Roch** (*see SOSPEL p382*)

Other forts make pleasant destinations for walks with fine **views**.

Visitors should bear in mind that although the buildings of the Maginot Line appear to be in good condition, they may conceal indoor wells or dangerous passages. Some properties are private, as they have been acquired by individuals.

In the highly strategic sector of L'Authion, near Col de Turini (*see Forêt de TURINI p380*), several structures designed by Sérés de Rivières have survived and can be reached by the loop road encircling the massif:

- Fort des Mille-Fourches
- La Forca
- Redoute des 3 Communes (1897), the first building constructed using reinforced concrete.

From Mont Chauve d'Aspremont (*see NICE p296*) there is a brilliant **view** of the whole coast under clear skies. On the summit (2,802ft/854m) is a Sérés de Rivières fort with a monumental southern façade, typical of the period; it is occupied by the Service des Télécommunications. Mont Chauve de Tourette is visible further north, capped by a fort from a similar period.

The section near Col de Tende, which was Italian from 1860 to 1947, is an impressive example of the Italian defence system. The central fort is set on top of the col and approached by the narrow road, which branches off by the entrance to the road tunnel. The interior (*difficult access*) was self-sufficient in supplies.

On the Track of Macaron

The old rail bed of one of the dismantled sections of the pinecone train (*train des pignes*), which linked Toulon to St-Raphaël from early in the 20C to 1950, is open to walkers. Although the track and stations have mostly disappeared, works of art and some stations (Carqueiranne) have survived. The tunnels are often used by walkers as short cuts, providing unusual and surprising glimpses of the Maures coast.

Beware Snakes!

Avoid moving rocks and wear sturdy walking boots when hiking through scrubland. If you are bitten, go straight to the nearest hospital; do not attempt to remove the poison yourself. To ward off a snake, simply stamp your feet or make a loud noise.

What to See and Do

OUTDOOR FUN
BOAT TRIPS

There are regular ferries to the Île de Bendor, Île des Embiez, Îles d'Hyères and Îles de Lérins, and also boat trips from the following resorts:

Bandol
- Les Embiez to Toulon via Cap Sicié, Gare Maritime (*04 94 32 51 41*), Cassis and the Calanque d'En-Vau via La Ciotat – whole day to the Château d'If and Le Frioul – underwater exploration with l'Aquascope (Cie Atlantide)

Sanary
- Îles des Embiez to Toulon Anchorage and Cap Sicié to Calanques de Cassis

Le Lavandou
- Île du Levant

Cavalaire
- Îles d'Hyères

St-Tropez
- Îles d'Hyères

Ste-Maxime
- Les Issambres, Port-Grimaud (navettes), Baie des Cannebiers

Ste-Maxime
- St-Tropez (shuttle) to Îles d'Hyères

Cannes
- Îles de Lérins – excursion to St-Tropez and Monaco on a catamaran

Juan les Pins
(departure from Ponton Courbet)
- Underwater viewing cruise off Cap d'Antibes

Nice
- La Riviera

Menton
- The Riviera to Monaco (with and without stopping)

Toulon
- La Seyne-sur-Mer, Les Sablettes, Tamaris, St-Mandrier *(navettes)*. Harbours of Toulon

St-Raphaël
- St-Tropez
- Îles de Lérins

SAILING

Most of the seaside resorts on the French Riviera, from Lecques to Menton, have well-equipped marinas, making this coast arguably the best in France for sailing. Although nearly every port has moorings with good facilities, the enthusiasm for sailing is such that enormous marinas have been constructed with extensive services to satisfy even the most exacting yachtsman. Ports providing over 1,000 berths are Bandol, Toulon, Hyères (Port-St-Pierre), La Londe (Port Miramar), Le Lavandou, St-Raphaël (Ste-Lucia), Cannes (Pierre Canto and the Vieux Port), St-Laurent-du-Var and Antibes (Port-Vauban), which is the largest to date.

Another great place for sailing and other watersports is Mandelieu-La-Napoule, which has six ports (*www.mandelieu.com*).

There are sailing clubs which provide lessons in most resorts; during the summer it is possible to hire craft with or without a crew.

Further information is available from each port authority and from the **Fédération Française de Voile** (*17 rue Henri-Bocquillon, 75015 Paris; *01 40 60 37 00; www.ffvoile.org*).

SCUBA DIVING

There are many clubs providing scuba diving lessons. The main centres are Bendor (Centre Padi is one of the largest in Europe), Le Pradet (Garonne beach), Giens (La Tour Fondue), Sanary, Cavalaire, Ramatuelle (L'Escalet), St-Tropez, Ste-Maxime,

Cannes marina

© Monika Lewandowska/iStockphoto.com

St-Raphaël, Mandelieu-La-Napoule, Cannes and Villefranche.

A brochure listing all the local clubs is available from **La Maison du Tourisme du Golfe de St-Tropez** in Gassin (*℘04 94 43 42 10; www.st-tropez-lesmaures.com*). Excursions to explore Mediterranean flora and fauna are provided by the Domaine du Rayol (*℘04 98 04 44 01; www.domainedurayol.org*) and the Parc National de Port-Cros (*www.portcrosparcnational.fr*).

The **Fédération Française d'Études et de Sports Sous-Marins** (*24 Quai de Rive-Neuve, 13007 Marseille; ℘04 91 33 99 31; www.ffessm.fr*) is an umbrella organisation, comprising 100 local clubs, which publishes a comprehensive yearbook covering all underwater activities in France. Information is also available from the **Comité Régional des Sports Sous-Marins de la Côte d'Azur** (*875 chemin des charrettes, Cuers; ℘04 94 00 40 71; www.ffessmcotedazur.fr*).

Maritime archaeology

The coves of the Maures and the Esterel on the Var coast and the clear water around the Îles d'Hyères invite you to discover the charm of the Mediterranean (*La Grande Bleue*) and the silent underwater world.

Over the centuries, the volume of marine traffic, has turned the seabed into a museum of shipwrecks – about 100 ships and upwards of 20 aircraft have sunk along this coast. Most of them are lying in more than 65ft/20m of water, accessible only to experienced divers who are members of specialist clubs. Other wrecks, lying in more shallow waters, can easily be visited by amateurs. Information about underwater centres near such wrecks is available from the Fédération des Sports Sous-marins in Marseille.

The wrecks of the Provençal coast and their history are described in *Naufrages en Provence* by J-P Joncheray.

UNDERWATER FISHING

The abundance of creeks along the coast should satisfy all demands. This sport is strictly regulated; the essential regional regulations are given below. Underwater fishing is forbidden in certain areas of the coastline from early November to the beginning of March. It is essential to check with the local maritime authority – *Var, 244 Avenue de l'Infanterie-de-Marine, Toulon ℘04 94 46 92 00 and Alpes-Martimes, 22 Quai Lunel, Nice ℘04 92 00 41 50.*

Some areas are out of bounds to fishing all year round – south coast

Exploring the underwater world

of St-Mandrier Peninsula, part of Porquerolles Island, Port-Cros Island and its neighbouring islets. There are underwater nature reserves, marked by buoys, near Golfe-Juan, Beaulieu and Roquebrune-Cap-Martin. Villefranche harbour is a protected area. Underwater anglers must comply with general fishing regulations and bear in mind that in the Mediterranean Sea:

-   it is illegal to catch or fish for grouper and oysters (for mother-of-pearl)

-   it is illegal to fish for sea urchins from 1 May to 30 September

-   it is illegal to pursue or catch marine mammals (dolphins, porpoises), even without intending to kill them

-   the minimum size of catch is 4.7in/12cm (except for sardines, anchovies), 7.1in/18cm for crayfish

-   whatever the circumstances, it is illegal to be in possession of both diving equipment and an underwater gun

Underwater safety

Enthusiasm for exploring the superb underwater landscape of the Riviera should not blind amateur divers to the need to observe certain regulations:

-   never go diving alone, nor after eating a heavy meal, nor after drinking alcohol or fizzy drinks, or when tired

-   avoid shipping lanes and areas used by windsurfers

-   when signalling for help, make it known that it is a diving accident so that the rescuers can prepare a decompression chamber, which is the only effective aid in the case of diving accidents, even minor ones.

SEA FISHING

In Sanary, in the Cogolin Marina and in Ste-Maxime visitors may hire out boats and professional fishermen for sea fishing trips or join a sea fishing party (usually in summer from 6am to 10am). Contact the local tourist offices for more information.

OTHER SEASIDE ACTIVITIES

The long stretches of the Var coast, consisting of beaches where the *mistral* blows, have become some of the most popular locations in the Mediterranean for those who enjoy riding the waves on a **sail board** (windsurfing) or a **funboard**. Almanarre beach on the west side of the Giens peninsula has become a mecca for funboarders and has played host to the World Championships. More technical skill is required on other beaches such as Six-Fours-les-Plages and the two sides of Cap Nègre. For a different view of their favourite beaches, holidaymakers can indulge in a spot of **parascending**: flying over the water below a parachute towed by a motorboat.

The aim is to stay in the air for as along as possible and as high as possible. Instruction in this sport is available on nearly all the organised beaches, where there is enough wind.

Jet-skiing is practiced on certain stretches of coast, which have been carefully chosen and are not accessible from the land. Although offering a guaranteed adrenalin rush, it is, however, strictly regulated:

- machines must be 164yd/ 150m apart
- machines may operate only during the day
- machines may operate between 328yd/300m outside the channels and up to 1 nautical mile
- pilots must hold a proficiency certificate.

Most of the large resorts offer jet-ski rentals by the hour or the half day. It is also possible to hire sea canoes in Salins d'Hyères and certain resorts on the Var coast. Motor vessels are forbidden within 328yd/300m of the shore (except in the access channels) and must not exceed 5 knots in certain restricted areas (Îles d'Hyères, Îles de Lérins and Villefranche harbour). Elsewhere the top speed is 10 knots.

COASTAL WALKS

Before the late 20C building boom the famous Customs Path ran all along the Riviera coast; some particularly picturesque sections still survive and have been developed by the Coastal Conservation Service (*Conservatoire du Littoral*).

There are several signed country footpaths along the Var coast, of which about ten, from Bandol to St-Aygulph, are described in a topoguide published by the **Fédération Française de la Randonnée Pédestre** (*www.ffrandonnee.fr*).

HIKING

A network of waymarked paths covers the region described in this guide. **GR (Grande Randonnée) paths**, which are fully open only from the end of June to early October, are for experienced hikers accustomed to mountain conditions.

- **GR 5:** the oldest and most majestic, which terminates in Nice after crossing Europe; the last section from Nice to St-Dalmas-Valdeblore passes through Aspremont, Levens, the Vésubie gorge and Madone d'Utelle.
- **GR 52:** from St-Dalmas-Valdeblore to Menton via Le Boréon, La Vallée des Merveilles, Turini Forest, Sospel.
- **GR52A:** among the peaks in the eastern part of the Parc National du Mercantour beyond the Col de Tende.

Jet skis

© Rocky Reston/Bandu/Dreamstime.com

Other paths, open all year, for walkers of all levels of competence:

- **GR 4:** from Grasse via Gréolières and Entrevaux to the Verdon Gorge.
- **GR 51:** nicknamed "the Mediterranean balcony", from Castellar (east of Menton) to Col de la Cadière (Esterel) providing **panoramic views** of the coast from the first ridge.
- **GR 510:** entirely in the Alpes-Maritimes region, from Breil-sur-Roya via Sospel, Villars-sur-Var, Puget-Rostand, Roquestéron, St-Auban and Escragnolles to St-Cézaire-sur-Siagne, discovering another valley dotted with hill villages at each stage of the 10-day hike.
- **GR 9:** from Signes through the Massif des Maures to St-Pons-les-Mûres.
- **GR 99:** from Toulon through the Brignolais country to the Verdon Gorge.
- **GR 90:** the shortest, from Le Lavandou through the Massif des Maures to Notre-Dame-des-Anges, where it meets the GR 9.

Topo-guides for the **Grandes Randonnées** (long hikes) and **Petites Randonnées** (short hikes) are published by the Fédération Française de la Randonnée Pédestre – *Comité National des Sentiers de Grande Randonnée, 64 r. du Dessous-des-Berges, 75013 Paris; ℘01 44 89 93 90*. Alternatively, contact the **Comité départemental de randonnée pédestre des Alpes-Maritimes**, Maison des associations – *4 avenue de Verdun, Cagnes-sur-Mer; ℘04 93 20 74 73, http://cdrp06.org* or the **Comité départementale de randonnée pédestre du Var**, L'Hélianthe, *rue Emilie-Ollivier, Toulon; ℘04 94 42 15 01; http://cdrp83.fr*. The Conseil Général des Alpes-Maritimes publish three hiking guides as part of its **RandOxygène** series covering various altitudes and coastal paths. They are available by calling ℘04 97 18 79 16 or visiting www.randoxygene.org.

NATURE PARKS

Wildlife – Parc National du Mercantour

Mercantour National Park, the most recently-established National State Park in France, was created in 1979 and covers an area of 169,267 acres/68,500ha in the Alpes-Maritimes and Alpes-de-Haute-Provence *départements* (encompassing 22 and 6 *communes* respectively).

Until 1947, the park was a hunting ground for Italian kings and extended over both sides of the Alps; it has been twinned since 1987 with the Italian Argentera Nature Park, with which it shares a 20.5mi/33km border.

These two organisations are in charge of introducing and monitoring animal species across this protected region. In this way, ibexes which have wintered in the Argentera arrive to spend the summer months in the Mercantour, while wild sheep *(mouflons)* do the opposite.

The Mercantour is a high, mountainous park, with terraces from 1,640–10,312ft/500–3,143m in altitude, offering breathtaking **views** of natural amphitheatres, glacial valleys and deep gorges.

It contains a rich variety of flora; over 2,000 species have been counted there, including **Saxifraga florulenta**, one of the park's emblems. All types of vegetation are present, from olive trees to rhododendrons and gentians, making for a splendid display of colour in the spring.

Fauna includes some chamois, ibexes and mouflons, various deer and smaller mammals such as hares, ermines and marmots. Feathered members of this community include black grouse, ptarmigans and birds of prey. The reintroduction of the bearded vulture was successfully achieved in the summer of 1993. For the first time in France since 1942, wolves have returned from Italy of their own accord to live in the park.

The 373mi/600km of footpaths laid out within the park's boundaries enable tourists to discover the park

Ibex, Parc National du Mercantour
© jm/Fotolia.com

on foot. These include the **GR5** and the **GR52A** 🚲, or the Mercantour **panoramic** footpath, which crosses the Vallée des Merveilles, as well as footpaths at L'Authion, Le Boréon and Madone de Fenestre.

This guide describes the regions of the Vésubie and Merveilles valleys, the Authion Massif and Turini Forest. 🚲*Mountain bikes are not allowed in the central area of the park.*

OTHER PARKS

The old royal hunting ground of the Sardinian monarchy extended until the Second World War over the two slopes of the Mercantour and the Marguareis. Since then the Italian section has been administered as a nature reserve with an active policy dedicated to the conservation of species and habitats. Two large natural parks have been created: **Parco dell'Argentera**, the largest, and Alta Valle Pesio, further east. Together with the Parc du Mercantour, they have conducted a campaign for the reintroduction of endangered species – the bearded vulture and the ibex. In the Parco dell'Argentera there are many "royal" botanical paths easily accessible to hikers from the French side of the border by the frontier passes – Col de la Lombarde

and Col de Tende. From the latter pass two paths *(each about 3hr)* follow the peaks towards Rocca dell'Abisso (9,039ft/2,755m – west) and Cima di Pepino (7,661ft/2,335m – east).

The **Alta Valle Pesio** park, in the Marguareis, is the wildest and least easy to reach from France. Hikers should branch into the northeast route from Limone-Piemonte or go up the valley from Savone.

The Vermenagna Valley, which extends from Col de Tende to the Cuneo Plain, still reveals its strong Provençal roots; Provençal spectacles *(Roumiage de Provenço)* are held in the Grana Valley in July. The district's specialities include a famous cheese, Castelmagno, and handmade cutlery, such as the Vernantino pocket knife.

Parco Naturale Regionale dell'Argentera
Corso Dante Livio Bianco 5 – 12010 Valdieri (CN) 📞39 171 97 397.

Parco Naturale Regionale Alta Valle Pesio e Tanaro
Via Sta Anne 34 – 12013 Chiusa Pesia (CN) 📞39 171 73 40 21.

Tourist office in Limone-Piemonte
Via Roma (CN) 📞39 171 92 101.

GOLF

There are dozens of golf courses spread across the region, many of them open to non-members. The most attractive courses lie along the western coast of the Riviera.

- **Fédération française de golf (FFG)** – 68 r. Anatole France, 92300 Levallois-Perret 📞 01 41 49 77 00 www.ffgolf.org.
- **Comité départemental du Var** – Maison départementale des sports L'Hélianthe r. Émile-Ollivier 83000, Toulon 📞 04 94 03 78 08. www.cd83golf.com.
- **Section départementale des Alpes-Maritimes** – Maison régionale des sports, Esterel Gallery BP 21,809 bis blvd. des Écureuils, 06210 Mandelieu 📞 04 92 97 46 96 www.cdgolf06.com.

HORSE RIDING

- **Comité National de Tourisme Équestre** Parc équestre, Lamotte-Beuvron, 📞 02 54 94 46 80. www.tourisme-equestre.fr or www.ffe.com. This service produces an annual guide (in French) called "Tourisme et loisirs équestres en France".

- **Comité Régional de Tourisme Équestre Pays d'Azur** Immeuble le Weldom, 2 rte de Nice, 06650 Le Rouret, 📞 06 81 58 84 70. http://cheval.d.azur.crte.free.fr.

Exploring the Border on Horseback This is an original way of exploring the Massif du Mercantour. There is a waymarked route on the **Franco Italian Natural Spaces Equestrian Itinerary** (Itinéraire Équestre des Espaces Naturels Franco-Italiens – Itinerario Equestre degli Soazi Naturali Franco-Italiani) from St-Martin-Vésubie through the Italian parks – Argentera and Alta Valle Pesio – to Certosa di Pesio; there are 10 staging posts with facilities for riders and their mounts. Practical information is available from the Parc du Mercantour and the Parco dell'Argentera information offices (see Hiking p19).
The Parc du Mercantour publishes a brochure containing various bridle routes and staging posts in the Argentera and Mercantour highlands.

WINTER SPORTS

It is only a short distance (less than 2hr by car) from the coast to a range of winter sports stations:

- La Colmiane-Valdeblore
- La Gordolasque-Belvédère
- Boréon-St-Martin-Vésubie
- Turini-Camp d'Argent
- Peïra-Cava
- Gréolières-les-Neiges
- L'Audibergue

There are cross-country skiing runs near La Haute-Roya – La Brigue (alt. 2,953ft/900m) and Tende-Val Casterino (alt. 4,921ft/1,500m). The proximity of the Italian ski resort, Limone-Piemonte, which can be reached by rail, means that many types of snow sport are available. Visit www.randoxygene.org for details of RandoNeige itineraries published by the Conseil Général des Alpes-Maritimes.

MOUNTAINEERING

Mountaineers can choose from a wide variety of different terrains, from the Pre-Alps of Nice to the rockfaces of the Verdon Gorge. Guided excursions in rock-climbing, mountaineering, rambling, downhill skiing and cross-country skiing are organised by:

- the **Club Alpin Français – Section du Var** 41 rue Charles-Poncy, 83000 Toulon 📞 04 94 62 19 16 http://clubalpin.toulon.online.fr

- the **Club Alpin Français – Section des Alps-Maritimes**
  14 Avenue Mirabeau, 06000 Nice
  ☎04 93 62 59 99
  www.cafnice.org

- the **Association des Guides et Accompagnateurs des Alpes Méridionales**
  Roquebillière
  ☎04 93 03 44 30
  St-Martin-Vésubie
  ☎04 93 03 26 60

- **Bureau des Guides de la Côte d'Azur**
  71 Blvd. de la Rocade,
  06250 Mougins
  ☎04 93 58 68 25/06 09 55 80 67
  www.altitude06.com

- **Bureau des guides du Mercantour**
  Pl. du marché
  St-Martin-Vésubie
  ☎04 93 03 31 32

VIA FERRATA

A combination of climbing, mountaineering and hiking, via ferrata is practiced across a handful of sites in the region.

Sites

At Col de la Colmiane, the **baus de la Frema** course (⨀see St-Martin-Vésubie p376), provides a great introduction, while more experienced enthusiasts will enjoy the Baus (2 246m/7368ft), with **views** of the Massif de Mercantour.

At **Lantosque**, the via ferrata passes through a rocky jungle of vegetation and down the narrow Canyon du Riou and up the Gorges de la Vésubie (⨀see Vallée de La Vésubie p374). The "Comtes de Lascaris" circuit includes two sites: **Tende** and **Peille** (see below).

La Ciappéa at **La Brigue** is a particularly demanding course overhanging deep caves.

Lastly, the **via souterrata** in Caille, at the foot of the Audibergue, near Grasse, offers a circuit including two sinkholes.

The Conseil général des Alpes-Maritimes produces a "**Rando Via Ferrata**" guide available from tourist offices and **www.randoxygene.org**.

CAVING

The Var has many original sites. The Siou Blanc Plateau includes chasms and potholes for amateurs. Among these is the deepest pothole in the region (1,148ft/350m).

The Grotte de Mouret, near Draguignan, is useful for practice. In the Alpes-Maritimes, both the Pays Grassois and the Caussols Plateau offer many opportunities for seasoned cavers. The legendary

Massif du Marguareis

©De Agostini/Photoshot

23

Massif du Marguareis (northeast of Tende), the site of the exploits of the potholer Michel Siffre in the 1960s, is still a paradise for the experienced caver. This immense chalky plateau is peppered with sinkholes and vertiginous rockfaces overhanging the Italian slopes, and contains deep chasms (more than 2,953ft/900m). Information available from:

♦ **Comité Départemental de Spéléologie du Var**
l'Hélianthe, rue Émile-Olivier, 83000 Toulon
℘04 94 31 29 43
www.cdspeleo83.fr

♦ **Comité Départemental de Spéléologie des Alpes-Maritimes**
809 blvd. des Ecureuils, Mandelieu
℘04 92 97 46 85
http://cds06.ffspeleo.fr

♦ Speleology divisions of the **Club Alpin Français** in Nice or Toulon.

WATERSPORTS

Canoeing

Some of the rivers in the Alpes-Maritimes can be explored by canoe throughout the year but the best time is in spring. In any season beware of sudden floods caused by heavy rain upstream. The most attractive stretches of river are to be found just inside the boundaries of the Mercantour or near St-Martin-Vésubie. Shooting rapids excursions through gorges accompanied by experts are organised by the Toulon division of the Club Alpin Français. Those offering the best services are awarded the title **Point-Canoë-Nature** by the **Fédération Française de Canoë-Kayak** (87 Quai de la Marne, 94340 Joinville-le-Pont; ℘02 48 89 39 89; www.ffcanoe.asso.fr).
Comité régionale de la canoë-kayak PACA – 50 ave. du 11-novembre, Antibes 04 93 34 08 65, www.canoe-paca.fr.

Canyoning

The most attractive stretches of water in the Alpes-Maritimes for this activity, which combines rock-climbing, potholing and swimming in running water, are to be found within the Parc du Mercantour and in St-Martin-Vésubie. There are also two exceptional sites in the valley of the **Haute-Roya** near Saorge – **La Maglia** (through caves) and **La Bendola** (two days in the water). Canyoning is strictly forbidden in the central part of the Parc du Mercantour.
Between St-Martin-Vésubie and its confluence with the Var, the **River Vésubie** offers a variety of canyons – Duranus, L'Imberguet, La Bollène

Canyoning, Verdon Gorges

Canoeing on Lac de Saint-Croix, Verdon

© Jan Minea/iStockphoto.com

and Gourgas, which is technically demanding.

The **Estéron**, an eastern tributary of the Var, provides classic stretches in exceptional settings between Roquestéron and St-Auban.

The network of rivers in the Var provides many opportunities for canyoning, with 11 authorised sites of varying difficulty suitable for all levels of competence. The **Destel Gorge**, between **Caramy** and **Carcès**, the lower stretches of the **Jabron** (downstream of **Trigance**) and the **Pennafort Gorge** are suitable for beginners. Seillans-la-Cascade, the Nartuby and the Destéou in the Maures demand greater skill. At all times of the year there is a risk of sudden increases in the volume of water following a storm upstream and a sudden release of retained water. Canyoning trips with guides are organised by the Toulon branch of the Club Alpin Français.

The **"Clues et Canyons" guide** published by the Conseil Général des Alpes-Maritimes *(www.randoxygene. org)*, available from tourist offices throughout the Alpes-Maritimes, is essential reading.

Lakes

The largest lake in the Estérel, **Lac de St-Cassien** (430ha/1 062 acres) not only supplies electricity and water to the eastern Var and water for fire-fighting aircraft, but also has a nature reserve at the west end with a reed-bed, where more than 150 species of wintering migratory seabird have been recorded.

There are facilities for windsurfing and pedalo – tuition at the base and equipment for hire from the open-air cafés along the sometimes steep banks; motorised vessels are forbidden.

- ◆ **Aviron St-Cassien-Club Inter communal du pays de Fayence**
  Lieu-dit Biançon
  83440 Montaurous
  ℘04 94 39 88 64/04 93 42 20 91

The **Lac de Carcès** (247 acres/100ha) is a reservoir formed by a dam and fed by the River Argens. There is a pleasant wooded road along the eastern bank; the opposite bank, more rural, is much-used by fishermen. Canoeing in kayaks is permitted.

Game Fishing

Local and national fishing regulations apply to fishing in lakes (Carcès and St Cassien) and in rivers (Gapeau, Réal Martin, Argens, Roya, Bévéra, etc.). It is also advisable to join the Association de Pêche et de Pisciculture in the area in question by paying the annual fees appropriate to the form of fishing

Pushing Pedals from Sea to Sea

EuroVelo is a venture funded by the European Union and about 60 local organisations in 22 countries. Visit **www.EuroVelo.org** to find out about the 12 cycling routes that will eventually trace more than 37,282mi/60,000km throughout Europe. Routes include Moscow to Galway, Ireland, and another from northern Norway to the tip of Sicily. The Mediterranean route traces the coastline from Cadiz, Spain, to Athens, via the French Riviera and Monaco.

practised and then by buying a daily permit from an authorised vendor. Trout fishing is permitted from the 2nd Saturday in March to the 3rd Sunday in September; pike fishing is allowed only between 31 January and 15 April. Fishing for common grayling in the Siagne is banned year round. Up-to-date information available from:

- **Fédération Départementale du Var**
  𝒞 04 94 69 05 56
  www.fedepechevar.com

- **Fédération Départementale des Alpes-Maritimes**
  𝒞 04 93 72 06 04
  www.peche-cote-azur.com

- **Fédération national de pêche en France**
  17 r. Bergère, Paris
  𝒞 01 48 24 96 00,
  www.federationpeche.fr,
  which provides information on fishing regulations.

CYCLING AND MOUNTAIN BIKING

The diversity of the inland terrain and the network of cycle tracks along the coast and in the massifs of the Esterel and the Maures make mountain biking a popular sport in this region.

Many organisations, hotels and clubs hire out mountain bikes and provide details of local cycle tracks. Lists of suppliers are also available from local tourist offices.

Main Railway Stations

Antibes, Bandol, Cagnes-sur-Mer, Cannes, Hyères, Juan-les-Pins and St-Raphaël hire out various types of bicycle, which can be returned to a different station.

The regulations concerning admission to the Parc du Mercantour apply also to cyclists. The Conseil Général des Alpes-Maritimes publish the **Rando VTT** guide containing 30 routes across the region (available at www.rando xygene.org).

The **Comité Départemental du Tourisme du Var** publishes a leaflet covering more than 20 signed routes for cyclists, including:

- Roof of the Var (*Toit du Var*) (43mi/70km)
- Bauxite Road (*Route de la Bauxite*) (50mi/80km)
- North face of the Maures (*l'Ubac des Maures*) (50mi/80km)
- Maures chestnut woods (*Châtaigneraies des Maures*) (56mi/90km)

One of the most famous mountain biking events in Europe is the Roc d'Azur at Ramatuelle with a height difference of nearly 656ft/200m (31mi/50km long) (see Calendar of Events p35).

- **Comité Départemental de Cyclotourisme des Alpes-Maritimes:** 2 Blvd. Settimelli Lazare, 06230 Villefranche-sur-Mer
  𝒞 04 93 01 81 85
  www.cyclotourisme06-ffct.org

- **Comité Départemental de Cyclotourisme du Var:**
  L'Hélianthe, Rue Émile-Ollivier, 83000 Toulon
  𝒞 04 94 36 04 09
  www.cyclotourisme83-ffct.org

- **Fédération Française de Cyclotourisme:** 12 rue Louis-Bertrand, 94207 Ivry-sur-Seine Cedex.
  ℘01 56 20 88 87
  www.ffct.org

AERIAL SPORTS

Hang-gliding, parachuting and ultra-light craft
There are about 20 suitable sites for parachuting, hang-gliding *(vol libre)* and ultra-light craft *(planeur ultra léger motorisé)*.

- **Envol de Provence:** 7 Ave du Cheval Blanc, 83870 Signes
  ℘04 94 90 86 13 or 06 07 28 93 41
  www.envol-parapente.com

- **Fédération Française de Vol Libre:** 4 rue de Suisse, 06000 Nice
  ℘04 93 88 62 89
  www.ffvl.fr

- **Fédération Française de Planeur Ultra-Léger Motorisé:** 96bis rue Marc-Sangnier, 94700 Maisons-Alfort
  ℘05 49 81 74 43
  www.ffplum.com

Gliding
The main gliding centre, which is run by the **Association Aéronautique Provence-Côte d'Azur**, is near Fayence, where aerological conditions are exceptional. It has become the leading gliding centre in Europe and has contributed to the rapid development of glider aerobatics. Each year champions from all over the world demonstrate their skill at the *open de france de planeur*.

- **Association Aéronautique Provence-Côte d'Azur**
  83440 Fayence
  ℘04 94 76 00 68.
  www.aapca.net.

ACTIVITIES FOR KIDS 👫
For a change from the beach, on cloudy days there are many attractions all along the riviera, including leisure pools and animal parks. In this guide, sights of particular interest to children are indicated with a kids symbol (👫). Some attractions offer discount fees for children.

LEISURE POOLS

- **Parc Nautique Niagara**
  Route du Canadel, 83310 La Môle
  ℘04 94 49 58 87
  www.parcniagara.com
- **Aquasplash**
  RN7, 06600 Antibes
  ℘04 93 33 49 49
  www.marineland.fr
- **Aqualand Fréjus**
  RN98, 83600 Fréjus
  ℘04 94 51 82 51
  www.aqualand.fr
- **Aqualand**
  559 Chemin Départemental, 83270 St-Cyr-sur-Mer
  ℘04 94 32 08 32
  www.aqualand.fr

ANIMAL PARKS

- **Sanary-Bandol** – Zoo
- **Toulon** – Zoo du Mont-Faron
- **La Londe-les-Maures** – Jardin d'Oiseaux Tropicaux (🔎 *see HYÈRES p130*)
- **Gonfaron** – Village des Tortues (🔎 *see Massif des MAURES p147*)
- **Fréjus** – Zoo
- **Antibes** – La Jungle des Papillons, La Petite Ferme, le Golf Adventureland and Marineland
- **Monaco** – Jardin Animalier

SPAS AND WELLNESS
Spas and wellness facilities are found across the region, including: **Antibes** (fitness), **Bandol** (thalassotherapy), **Hyères** (fitness), **St-Raphaël** ("thalasports"), **Fréjus** (thalassotherapy), **Île des Embiez** (balneotherapy).

- **Syndicat national de thalasso-thérapie** – ℘ 02 40 11 72 35.
  www.thalassofederation.com.

◆ The tiny resort of **Berthemont-les-Bains** (*see Vallée de La Vésubie p374*), treatsrespiratory and articular disorders (℘04 93 03 47 00, www.valvital.fr).

◆ **Confédération nationale des exploitants thermaux** – 1 r. Cels, 75014 Paris, ℘ 01 53 91 05, www.france-thermale.org.

SHOPPING

Most of the larger shops are open Mondays to Saturdays from 9am to 6.30 or 7.30pm, and some chain stores now open on Sundays in Nice. Smaller, individual shops may close during the lunch hour. Food shops – grocers, wine merchants and bakeries – are generally open from 8am to 6.30 or 7.30pm; some open on Sunday mornings. Many food shops close between noon and 2pm and on Mondays. Bakery and pastry shops sometimes close on Wednesdays. Hypermarkets usually open until 9pm or later. Those travelling to the USA cannot import plant products or fresh food, including fruit, cheeses and nuts. It is acceptable to carry tinned products or preserves.

RECOVERING VALUE ADDED TAX

There is a Value Added Tax in France (TVA) of 19.6% on almost every purchase (some foods and books are subject to a lower rate). However, non-European visitors who spend more than 175€ in any one participating store can get the VAT amount refunded. Usually, you fill out a form at the store, showing your passport. Upon leaving the country, you submit all forms to customs for approval (they may want to see the goods, so if possible, don't pack them in checked luggage). The refund is usually paid directly into your bank or credit card account, or it can be sent by mail. Big department stores catering to tourists provide special services to help you; be sure to mention that you plan to seek a refund before you pay for goods (no refund is possible for tax on services). If you are visiting two or more countries within the European Union, you submit the forms only on departure from the last EU country. The refund is worthwhile for those visitors who would like to buy fashion, furniture or other fairly expensive items, but remember, the minimum amount must be spent in a single shop (though not necessarily on a single day).

Market day in Lorgues

PROVENÇAL MARKETS

Provençal markets, fragrant with thyme, tarragon, lavender and garlic, are part of the traditional image of the South of France.

A list of traditional craft markets where the products of the Var region are sold, is published annually by the **Chambre des Métiers** *(BP 69 – 83402 Hyères Cedex; ℘04 94 21 00 57; www.cm-alpesmaritimes.fr)*.

As a rule, during the summer season stalls selling fruit and vegetables and craftwork can be found in even the smallest villages. They typically open at about 8am or 9am, and finish at lunchtime or about 1pm.

The most picturesque and lively markets of the Var and the days on which they are held are listed in the table opposite.

CRAFTS AND SOUVENIRS

In high season many villages and resorts organise courses on local arts and crafts – painting on porcelain in Le Cannet, weaving and woodwork in the Cannes district and regional cuisine in St-Martin-Vésubie. Certain villages are designated "Ville et Métiers d'Art" such as Biot, Cagnes-sur-Mer, Fréjus, Ollioules and Vallauris. For more information on these, call ℘01 48 88 26 56 or visit www.vma.asso.fr.

REGIONAL SPECIALITIES

The main areas where craftwork and local produce can be bought by visitors from the producers are shown on the map – Specialities & Vineyards (℘see pp66–67).

Further information on specialist products:

Sweets

Confiserie des Gorges du Loup, Le Pont-du-Loup, 06140 Tourrettes-sur-Loup. ℘04 93 59 32 91.
You will also find nougat in Roquebrune-sur-Argens and honey in Bandol, Cotignac or the Massif du Tanneron.

PROVENÇAL MARKETS	
Aups	Wednesdays, Saturdays
Bargemon	Thursdays
Le Beausset	Fridays (fair)
Bormes-les-Mimosas	Wednesdays
Brignoles	Saturdays
Callas	Tuesdays, Saturdays
Cogolin	Wednesdays, Saturdays (fair)
La Croix-Valmer	Sundays
Draguignan	Wednesdays, Saturdays
Fayence	Tuesdays, Thursdays (fair)
Fréjus	Wednesdays, Saturdays (fair)
La Garde	Tuesdays, Saturdays (fair)
Grimaud	Thursdays (fair)
Hyères	Tuesdays, Thursdays (fair)
Le Lavandou	Thursdays
Lorgues	Tuesdays
Le Luc	Fridays
Ramatuelle	Thursdays, Sundays (fair)
St-Tropez	Tuesdays, Saturdays (fair)
Ste-Maxime	Thursdays (fair)
Toulon	daily
Tourtour	Tuesdays, Saturdays
Trans-en-Provence	Sundays
Villecroze	Thursdays (fair)

Candied fruit

J.L. Gallo/ MICHELIN

Biot glasses

S. Sauvignier/ MICHELIN

- **Marrons glacés and preserved chestnuts**
  Nouvelle Confiserie Azuréenne, Boulevard Koenig, Collobrières
  ℘04 94 48 07 20.
  www.confiserieazureenne.com.

Glassware
Verrerie de Biot in Biot, where it is possible to watch master glassblowers at work.

Perfume
Scents for the home or body are made in Grasse, Èze and Gourdon.

Ceramics
Biot, Vallauris, and Salernes (&see AUPS p178) specialise in pottery as well as ceramics.

Santon Fairs in the Var

Clay figures (santons) became popular during the French Revolution, when many churches were closed. A craftsman in Marseille decided to market these figurines so that people could set up nativity scenes at home. The term comes from the Provençal santoun, meaning "little saint". Originally, these statuettes were confined to religious or biblical themes, but they have come to represent traditional aspects of the region (arts, crafts, folklore, animals).

Liqueur de Lérina
This drink is made on the Îles de Lérins, by the monks of the Abbaye St-Honorat.

Leather
The sandale tropézienne is the model that has been made by the same company since 1927 (&see ST-TROPEZ p159).

WINE TASTING

Wine Cooperative Cellars
The **Côte de Provence wine road** wends its way through the vineyards; wine cellars open for tastings are usually indicated on roadside signs (look for dégustation). To organise tours and tastings of particular wines, contact these organisations:

- **Vins de Bandol**
  La Maison des Vins du Bandol, 22 allée Alfred-Vivien, 83150 Bandol
  ℘04 94 29 45 03.
  http://maisondesvins.free.fr.

- **Coteaux varois**
  La Maison des Vins Coteaux Varois, inside the Abbaye Royale de la Celle, 83170 La Celle. ℘04 94 69 33 18. www.visitvar.fr. The Coteaux Varois AOC is spread out over 28 communes around Brignoles, and Sainte-Baume to Bessillons.

- **Côtes-de-Provence**
  La Maison des vins des Côtes de Provence, RN 7, 83460 Les Arcs-sur-Argens. ℘04 94 99 50 20. www.cotes-de-provence.com. This is the most popular wine of the Provence-Alpes-Côte d'Azur region. There are three vineyards on Île de Porquerolles producing an AOC (Appellation d'Origine Contrôlée) Côte de Provence wine. All offer wine tasting sessions:
- Domaine de l'Île, the oldest
- Domaine Perzinsky
- Domaine Courtade.

Other Côte de Provence wines are made in Les Arcs, Draguignan (organic wine), Fréjus, Gassin (&see

RAMATUELLE p156), Le Luc (organic wine) and Lorgues. This Maison des Vins also offers classes on wine tasting.

♦ **Vins de Bellet**
Syndicat des vignerons de Bellet, 06200 St-Roman-de-Bellet
℘04 93 37 81 57
www.vinsdebellet.com
Vin de Bellet is produced on the hillsides behind Nice around St-Romain-de-Bellet; it is on sale in the cellars, which are open to the public; further information from the Nice tourist office.

♦ **Domaine de Lauzade**
Route de Toulon, 83340 Le Luc
℘04 94 60 72 51
www.lauzade.com
Tastings of Provençal wines Mon–Sat morning.

♦ **La Cave du Moulin**
50 Avenue Mallet, 06250 Mougins
℘04 92 92 06 88
Oenologie courses and wine tasting.

Wine Courses

Although most vineyards offer wine tasting sessions, only a few have professional courses, where you can learn more about local wines. Try the addresses below or contact your local *Maison des vins* for more details:

♦ **Maison des vins des Côtes-de-Provence** – RN 7, Les Arcs-sur-Argens. ℘04 94 99 50 10. www.vinsdeprovence.com.
♦ **Domaine de Lauzade** – rte de Toulon, 83340 Le Luc. ℘04 94 60 72 51. www.lauzade.com. Daily tasting sessions of Provençal wines.
♦ **La Cave de Mougins** – 50 ave. Charles-Mallet. Mougins-Village. ℘04 92 28 06 11. Introductions to oenology

Vallauris pottery

S. Sauvignier/ MICHELIN

COOKING CLASSES

The Comité Régional du Tourisme Provence-Côte d'Azur (*www.decouverte-paca.fr*) provides information on cooking classes throughout the region and publishes an annual brochure on local gastronomy, *Terre de Saveurs*.

♦ **Lenôtre Côte d'Azur**
63 rue d'Antibes, Cannes.
℘04 97 06 67 62. www.lenotre.fr.
Classes for children, teens and adults on everything from pastries to perfectly prepared vegetables.

SUMMER AÏOLI FESTIVALS IN THE VAR	
8–11 July	Châteauvieux
8 August	Mazaugues
9 August	Entrecasteaux (one of the largest)
12–15 August	La Motte-du-Var
12–15 August	La Celle
12–16 August	Collobrières
14–16 August	Ampus
20–22 August	Solliès-Ville
26–28 August	Fayence
(Reserve and pay entrance fees at the local tourist office).	

SIGHTSEEING
TOURIST TRAINS

The single-track main railway line between Nice and Cuneo in Italy crosses the old County of Nice, passing through Peille, L'Escarène, Sospel, Breil-sur-Roya, Fontan-Saorge, St-Dalmas-de-Tende, Tende, Vievola and finally, Limone in Italy. The track was built from 1920 onwards and incorporates some spectacular engineering feats as it twists and turns through the tortuous mountain landscapes. The **views** are particularly wonderful between L'Escarène and Sospel and between Breil and Tende along the rugged gorges of the River Roya. On the Italian side of the border, the line descends less steeply down to Cuneo through the charming Vermegnagna Valley. The frequent service enables skiers to reach the Massif du Mercantour and spend the day skiing in the Italian winter sports resort of Limone-Piemonte. There are at least four daily return services to and from Nice-Ville station, but check the schedule carefully, download from the website. For timetable information: ℘08 91 70 30 00; www.ter-sncf.com/Regions/paca/fr.

The **Train des Merveilles** is a scenic tourist train between Nice and Tende that runs daily July–October through Sospel, Peille, Breil-sur-Roya and La Brigue. The winter service, known as the **Train des Neiges Castérino**, runs weekends January–March. For times and ticket information, visit www.trainstouristiques-ter.com.

Provençal Railway

The famous pine-cone train (**Train des Pignes**) is named after the pine cones which were once used as fuel to stoke the engines. It runs between Nice and Digne-les-Bains (93mi/150km) passing through Puget-Théniers, Entrevaux, Annot and St-André-les-Alpes. The single track was constructed from 1890 to 1911 and comprises 60 remarkable feats of engineering – metal bridges, viaducts, tunnels (one of which is 2.3mi/3.5km long).

It is a relic of a vast regional network which once served the whole inland area from Toulon to Draguignan. The journey, 2hr by train, 3hr by omnibus, passes through five valleys often difficult to reach by car.

All year round it is possible to take the train to Lac de Castillon, the Verdon Gorges and the winter sports stations in the Alpes-Maritimes *département*. From Plan-du-Var there is a service to the walking country in the Vésubie Valley. In summer the Alpazur service runs from Nice as far as Grenoble and there is a tourist steam train on the Puget-Théniers section. There are wayside halts at which walkers can leave or rejoin the train at the beginning and end of a day's hike.

Chemins de Fer de Provence: Gare du Sud, 4 rue Alfred-Binet, 06000 Nice. ℘04 97 03 80 80. www.trainprovence. com. Also: Station/Gare, Avenue P.-Sémard, 04000 Digne-les-Bains. ℘04 92 31 01 58.

FROM THE AIR

Several companies organise aerial sightseeing, including hang-gliding, para-gliding and kite-surfing:

- **Envol de Provence** – 7 ave du Cheval Blanc, Signes. ℘04 94 90 86 13 or 06 07 28 93 41. www.envol-parapente.com.
- **Fédération Française de Vol Libre** – 4 rue de Suisse, 06000 Nice. ℘04 97 03 82 82. www.ffvl.fr.
- **Association Aéronautique Provence-Côte d'Azur** – Aérodrome, Fayence-Tourrettes. ℘04 94 76 00 68. www.aapca.net.
- **Fédération Française de Vol à Voile** – 29 rue de Sèvres, 75006 Paris. ℘01 45 44 04 78. www.ffvv.org.

For helicopter sightseeing and transfers:
- **Héli Air Monaco** – ave. des Ligures. ℘00 377 92 05 00 50 www.heliairmonaco.com
- **Héli Sécurité** – Grimaud. ℘04 94 55 59 99 www.helicopter-saint-tropez.com.

BOOKS

*Travels through France and Italy –
Tobias Smollett (1766).*
Seasoned grumbler, Tobias
Smollett wrote this travel journal
on his journey through France
and Italy, complaining bitterly
about the service, inns and people
at every stop... except Nice. Not
surprisingly, there is now a rue
Smollett, just off place Garibaldi.

Les Misérables – Victor Hugo (1862).
An historic look at the slave-galley
days of Toulon from the point of
view of the convict Jean Valjean,
who spent 19 years in the Bagne of
Toulon for stealing bread to feed
his starving family.

*Tender is the Night – F. Scott Fitzgerald
(1934).* Inspired by the Boston art
collectors Gerald and Sara Murphy,
as well as by his own wife, Zelda,
Fitzgerald's classic story of
Americans adrift on the French
Riviera describes the slow demise
of Dick Diver, a psychiatrist, who
marries his patient, Nicole.

The Rock Pool – Cyril Connolly (1936).
Originally rejected by publishers in
England on grounds of obscenity,
this book examines the decadent
side of the expatriate community
in Juan-les-Pins and Antibes.

*Bonjour Tristesse (Hello Sadness) –
Françoise Sagan (1954).* A classic of
French literature, the heroine,
Cécile, is a precocious 17-year-old
(the author's age when she wrote
the story), who grapples with her
widowed father's second marriage
and her own coming-
of-age on the Esterel Coast.

Letters from Colette – Colette. (1980).
The letters of this renowned
French author document the
change in St-Tropez from a
secluded, peaceful fishing
village, where artists and
writers would retreat to
a glitzy tourism destination.

Voices in the Garden – Dirk Bogarde (1981).
The British actor, who resided in
Grasse for many years during the
latter part of his life, wrote this

fascinating novel about a
middle-aged couple living on
the Riviera, whose life
is irrevocably changed after
meeting a young English tourist
and his girlfriend and offering
them hospitality in
their sumptuous villa.

*The Garden of Eden – Ernest Hemingway
(1986).* This story, published after the
author died, unfolds on the Riviera
and involves a young writer, his
glamorous wife and the pressures
of a destructive love triangle.

*Maigret on the Riviera – Georges
Simenon (1988).* Only mildly distracted
by the balmy weather and lush
vegetation, the famous, pipe-
smoking Inspector Jules Maigret
must discover how an inoffensive,
down-at-heel Australian came to
be murdered in this idyllic setting.

Perfume – Patrick Süskind (1989).
A dramatic thriller set in the
18C perfume-making industry
of Grasse.

*Artists and their Museums on the Riviera
– Barbara Freed, Alan Halpern; Harry
Abrams (1998).* A useful paperback
guide for exploring the art
museums in the region, placing
the artists and their work in
context.

*Art-Sites France: Contemporary Art &
Architecture Handbook – Sidra Stich
(1999).* Invaluable for those interested
in contemporary artwork, this
book covers the whole of France
with detailed descriptions of
galleries, museums, film and video
centres, specialised bookstores,
sculpture parks and many
architectural sites.

*Once Upon a Time: The Story of Princess
Grace, Prince Rainier and Their Family –
J. Randy Taraborrelli (2003).*
A biography of the Monégasque
Royal family, which starts with the
history of the principality vis-à-vis
the life of Grace Kelly and finally,
Monaco today.

FILMS

Max in Monaco (1913).
A silent comedy, featuring Max Linder, is set in the Principality of Monaco.

Fleur d'Amour (1927).
Maurice Vandal portrays the formerly "hot" district of "Chicago" in Toulon.

À Propos de Nice (1929).
Jean Vigo's classic focused on the contrast between holidaymakers loafing around on the beach in Nice and the working-class districts.

César (1936).
The colourful pre-war setting of Toulon appears in this locally-made Marcel Pagnol film with Provençal actor Raimu (⊙ see COGOLIN p157).

Les Visiteurs du Soir (1942).
Tourrettes-sur-Loup was the Medieval setting for Marcel Carné's period drama.

Les Démons de l'Aube (1945).
Yves Allégret's film set in the Var is about the Provençal landings in the Second World War.

To Catch a Thief (1955).
The impressive drops of the Grande Corniche provided a marvellous backdrop (before urban development changed the look of Monaco) in this thriller by Alfred Hitchcock starring Cary Grant and Grace Kelly.

And God Created Woman (1956).
Roger Vadim launched both Brigitte Bardot and St-Tropez with this provocative film.

The Collector (1967).
Eric Rohmer's love triangle takes place in a vacation villa in St-Tropez.

Le Gendarme de St-Tropez (1964).
The absurd side of the glitzy St-Tropez lifestyle is shown in six episodes of this celebrated comedy detective series.

Monte Carlo or Bust! (1969).
A comedy set in 1920s Monte Carlo, starring Tony Curtis, Dudley Moore, Peter Cook and Eric Sykes.

La Nuit Àméricaine (1973).
Partly filmed at the Studios de la Victorine, François Truffaut's movie used several locations, including Nice and the Vésubie Valley.

Herbie Goes to Monte Carlo (1977).
The comic adventures of the *Love Bug* throughout the world had to include an episode in Monaco, starring Dean Jones.

La Cage aux Folles (1978).
The original version of this comedy is set within a transvestite club in St-Tropez.

Festival in Cannes (2002).
An insider look at the movie industry from the international film festival in Cannes by Ron Silver.

Ocean's Twelve (2004).
The Monte Carlo Casino is the high-stakes setting for this drama starring George Clooney, Brad Pitt, Matt Damon, Julia Roberts, Catherine Zeta-Jones and Vincent Cassel.

Heartbreaker (2010).
Alex breaks up relationships for a living. Hired by a father unhappy at his daughter's impending wedding, he scours the luxurious hot spots of Monaco bent on seduction. Starring Vanessa Paradis and Romain Duris.

Kiss and Tell (2010).
A woman on holiday in the South of France meets her ideal man and has a shot-gun wedding. Once back home, their idyllic life takes a turn for the worst.

Brigitte Bardot in And God Created Woman (1956)

©STARSTOCK/Photoshot

Calendar of Events

FÊTES, FESTIVALS & SPORTING EVENTS

JANUARY

Barjols – Festival of St Marcel, celebrated since 1350.
Bormes-les-Mimosas – Mimosalia mimosa festival.
Valbonne – Grape and Olive Festival (last weekend).
Monaco – International Circus Festival. *www.montecarlofestival.mc*
Monaco and hinterlands – Monte-Carlo Rally (end of the month).

27 JANUARY

Monaco (La Condamine) – Festival of St Dévote. A torchlight procession, symbolic burning of a boat and fireworks to honour the patron saint. *www.visitmonaco.com*

FEBRUARY

Menton – Lemon Festival.
Villefranche-sur-Mer – Flowered Naval Parade.

TWO WEEKS AROUND SHROVE TUESDAY (MARDI GRAS)

Nice – Carnival and Flower Festival *(Batailles de Fleurs)*. *www.nicecarnival.com*

EVENING OF GOOD FRIDAY

Roquebrune-Cap-Martin – Evening Procession of the Entombment of Christ. Reenacted annually since the time of the White Penitents, with snail-shell candles and symbols of the Passion carried by costumed participants.

EASTER SUNDAY AND MONDAY

Vence – Provençal Folklore Festival. A joyous village festival commemorating their resistance to the Huguenot siege during the Wars of Religion of 1592.

THIRD SUNDAY AFTER EASTER

Fréjus – Bravade St-François. A popular costumed military processional through town in honour of the patron St-Francis-de-Paul, who saved the town from the Plague.

MARCH

Golfe-Juan – Reenactment of Napoleon's landing (first weekend).
Gonfaron – Donkey festival (last weekend): procession and blessing.
Nice (Cimiez) – Feast of the Gourds (with dried and painted gourds) (end of the month).
Nice – Arrival of the Paris–Nice Cycling Race.

APRIL

Monaco – Printemps des arts. The Spring Arts Festival celebrating the latest in theatre, dance and music: *www.printempsdesarts.com* (through May).
Monaco, Nice – International Tennis Tournament (one week).
Mouans-Sartoux – Honey Festival (last Sunday).

MAY

Cannes – International Film Festival. ✆ 05 45 61 66 00 (reserved for professionals). *www.festival-cannes.com*

Lemon Festival, Menton

©Sean Nel/Bigstockphoto.com

35

Parade at Nice Carnival

Fréjus – Bravade St-François (third Sunday after Easter)

Grasse – Rose Festival (penultimate weekend). A 3-day cut-rose festival with a market, concerts and rose competition: *www.ville-grasse.fr/exporose*

La Garde-Freinet – Seasonal bird migration festival

Monaco – Formula One Grand Prix in the centre of Monaco. *www.formula1.com*

Nice (Cimiez) – La Fête des Mai. The oldest folk festival in Nice, with dancing and picnics in the Cimiez gardens (weekends). *www.nicetourisme.com*

LATE MAY TO MID-JULY

Toulon – Music Festival and International Music Competition (wind instruments)

JUNE

Levens – Lou Festin d'Aqui. Nissart and Occitan contemporary music festival. One Saturday in the month.

St-Tropez – Spanish Procession (Bravades) (15th). A colourful Provençal festival and procession honouring the town's patron saint since the 15C. *www.ot-saint-tropez.com*

EARLY JULY TO LATE SEPTEMBER (EVEN YEARS)

Vallauris – Biennial International Festival of Ceramic Art. *www.vallauris-golfe-juan.fr*

JULY

Cannes (Le Suquet) – Musical evenings featuring famous virtuosos and young talent. *www.palaisdesfestivals.com*

Cap d'Antibes (La Garoupe) – Seamen's Festival. Barefoot procession of seamen carries the gilded statue of Notre-Dame de la Garoupe from the cathedral in Antibes to the chapel in La Garoupe.

Vence – Fête de la Conque. Traditional music festival (first weekend) with concerts and a village-wide country-style buffet: *http://pagesperso-orange.fr/locepon*

Villefranche-sur-Mer – Feast of St Peter, fishermen's festival (first weekend)

Tende – Feast of St Eligius, patron saint of muleteers (second Sunday).

FIRST FORTNIGHT IN JULY

Sospel – Les Baroquiales festival of baroque art. ☏04 93 04 12 55. *www.lesbaroquiales.org*

SECOND FORTNIGHT IN JULY

Abbaye du Thoronet – Medieval music festival. ☏04 93 52 26 38

Îles des Embiez – Les Voix du Gaou: salsa, rock, soul, reggae, Raï, etc. *www.voixdugaou.com.*

Juan-les-Pins-Antibes – World Jazz Festival. *www.jazzajuan.fr*

Nice (Cimiez: Amphitheatre) – Jazz in Nice: ☏04 93 87 16 28 *www.nicejazzfestival.fr*

Ramatuelle – Classical Music Festival. ☏04 98 12 64 00.

Toulon – Jazz Festival. ☏04 94 09 71 00. *www.jazzatoulon.com*

JULY AND AUGUST

Abbaye du Thoronet – Medieval and Traditional Music Festival. *www.musique-medievale.fr*

Cotignac – Open-air Cinema Festival (evenings). "Toiles du Sud" take place at the Théâtre du Rocher. *www.lestoilesdusud.fr*

Nice – Musicalia, free world music concerts.

St-Tropez – Music, Dance & Theatre Festival at the Château de la Moutte (evenings). *www.lesnuits duchateaudelamoutte.com*

Vence – Les Nuits du Sud: world music festival.

AUGUST

Barjols – Leatherwork Fair (17–18th)

Bendor – Fishermen's Festival (15th)

Entrecasteaux – Chamber Music Festival: ☏04 94 04 44 83.

Fréjus – Grape Festival (first Sunday). Celebration of the first grapes harvested, with tastings and traditional dancing, followed by a special mass. *www.frejus.fr*

Grasse – Jasmine Festival (first weekend). Flowered float parade and fireworks. *www.ville-grasse.fr/jasminade*

Grimaud – Wool Festival (Ascension Day). With sheep shearing contests, market and village feast. *www.mairie-grimaud.fr*

Hyères – Festival'Hyères, a three-week music festival on the beachfront. *www.festivalhyeres.fr*

Menton – Chamber Music Festival: some 13 concerts are held in front of the Church of St-Michel).

Roquebrune-Cap-Martin – Passion Procession through the old village streets (5th).

Vallauris – Pottery Festival (13th).

Villeneuve-Loubet – Shingle Castle Competition (third Sunday). Castle building competition with the "galets" from the beach, followed by fireworks show. *www.villeneuveloubet.fr*

FIRST FORTNIGHT IN AUGUST

Ramatuelle – Theatre Festival ☏04 94 79 20 50. *www.festivalderamatuelle.com*

SEPTEMBER

Cannes – Royal Regattas (last week). *www.regatesroyales.com*

Fayence – Aoïlis festival.

Many villages – Michaelmas Celebrations (29th) **Monaco** – Vintage Car Rally (third weekend).

Peille – Folk Festival *Festin des Baguettes* in honour of a young dowser-shepherd, who during a drought found water with a diving rod made from an olive branch (first weekend).

Throughout France – Heritage Days (third weekend). All listed historic buildings throughout France are open to the public during the weekend of the Fête du Patrimoine: *www.journeesdu patrimoine.culture.fr*

Royal Regattas, Cannes

©Serge Villa/Dreamstime.com

OCTOBER

Collobrières – Chestnut Festival
(last three Sundays).
Local produce market, activities
for children and chestnut products
to celebrate the harvest.
www.collobrieres-tourisme.com

Fréjus – Roc'Azur: mountain biking
races (beginning of the month).

Gonfaron – Chestnut Festival.
Grilled chestnuts and a market
of local products made from
chataignes (chestnuts).
www.journal.gonfaron.net

La Garde-Freinet – Chestnut
Festival (last two Sundays).

Ollioules – Olive Festival (first
weekend).

Roquebrune-sur-Argens –
Honey Festival (first weekend).

St-Tropez – Les Voiles de St-Tropez
sailing race (beginning of October).

Vence – Folk festival of music, dancing
(beginning of the month).

NOVEMBER

Cannes – International dance festival
(odd years).

Monaco – Monaco's National Day (19th).

Taradeau – New wine festival
(third Sunday).

DECEMBER

Bandol – Wine Festival (first Sunday).

Lucéram – The Shepherds' Christmas
Offering and Provençal Mass.

Vallée de la Roya – Santon Festival
(Nativity scenes).

Know Before You Go

USEFUL WEBSITES

www.ambafrance-us.org

The French Embassy in the USA has a
website providing basic information
(geography, demographics, history),
a news digest and business-related
information. It offers special pages
for children, and pages devoted to
culture, language study and travel,
as well as links to other selected
French sites (regions, cities, ministries).

www.fngi.fr

Federation of Licenced Tour Guides.
Membership of over 700 guides
working in 32 languages.

www.franceguide.com

The French Government Tourist
Office/Maison de la France site is
packed with practical information
and tips for those travelling to France.
The home page has a number of
links to more specific guidance (for
American or Canadian travellers,
for example) or to the FGTO's
London pages.

www.FranceKeys.com

This sight has plenty of practical
information for visiting France.

www.ukinfrance.fco.gov.uk

The official website of the UK
Embassy in France.

www.visiteurope.com

The European Travel Commission
provides useful information on
travelling to and around 39 EU and
European countries, and includes links
to some commercial booking services
(e.g. vehicle hire), rail schedules,
weather reports and more.

VIRTUAL RIVIERA

Here are a few selected websites
devoted to the Côte d'Azur:

www.beyond.fr

Beyond the French Riviera is a
site in English with lots of links,
information on places, sports, history,
accommodation and more; practical
and comprehensive.

www.provenceweb.fr

Provence on the Web includes an
on-line magazine with featured

villages, upcoming events, recipes and touring suggestions (thematic tours, bike tours and others) for surfers.

www.rivieratimes.com
The online edition for the monthly English newspaper *The Riviera Times* includes the latest news, classified ads and a link to the sister newspaper, *The Monaco Times*.

http://riviera.angloinfo.com
AngloINFO is a popular website for the English-speaking expatriate community along the Côte d'Azur. It includes a directory of local businesses and organisations, particularly those run by or catering for English speakers, plus lively community Forums.

www.riviera-reporter.com
This is the website for the monthly printed English magazine *Riviera Reporter*. It has archived articles that are helpful for both visitors and English-speaking locals on the Riviera.

TOURIST OFFICES
Information from **France on Call**:
℘(514) 288-1904.

INTERNATIONAL

Australia – New Zealand
Sydney
Level 13, 25 Bligh Street,
Sydney, New South Wales 2000
℘(02) 9231 5244
Fax: (02) 9221 8682

Canada
Montreal
1981 Avenue McGill College,
Suite 490, Montreal PQ H3A 2W9
℘(514) 288-2026
Fax: (514) 845 4868

Eire
10 Suffolk Street, Dublin 2
℘(353) 16 790 813

South Africa
P.O. Box 41022, Craig Hall 2024
℘(011) 880 8062
Fax: (011) 770 1666

United Kingdom
London
Lincoln House, 300 High Holborn,
London WC1 V7JH
℘(0207) 061 6639
Fax: (020)7493 6594

United States
East Coast – New York
444 Madison Avenue,
16th Floor, NY 10022-6903
℘(212) 838-7800
Fax: (212) 838-7855

Mid West – Chicago
676 North Michigan Avenue,
Suite 3360, Chicago, IL 60611-2819
℘(312) 751-7800
Fax: (312) 337-6339

West Coast – Los Angeles
9454 Wilshire Boulevard,
Suite 715,
Beverly Hills, CA 90212-2967
℘(310) 271-6665
Fax: (310) 276-2835

LOCAL/REGIONAL

Visitors may also contact local tourist offices for more detailed information and to receive brochures and maps. The addresses and telephone numbers of tourist offices for individual towns in this guide are located in that town's listing after the symbol ⬛.

Below, the addresses are given for local tourist offices of the *départements* and *régions* covered in this guide.

Comité Régional du Tourisme de Provence-Alpes-Côte d'Azur
10 Pl. de la Joliette, Les Docks,
Atrium 10.5, BP 46214
13567 Marseille, Cedex 02
℘04 91 56 47 00
www.tourismepaca.fr

Comité Régional du Tourisme Riviera-Côte d'Azur
55 Promenade des Anglais,
BP 602, 06011 Nice Cedex 1
℘04 93 37 78 78
www.cotedazur-tourisme.com

Comité Départemental du Tourisme du Var

1 Boulevard de Strasbourg,
83093 Toulon
℘04 94 18 59 60
www.visitvar.fr

Office de Tourisme et des Congrès de la Principauté de Monaco

2A Boulevard des Moulins,
98000 Monaco
℘04 93 50 60 88
www.visitmonaco.com

Parc Naturel National du Mercantour

23 rue d'Italie, 06000 Nice
℘04 93 16 78 88
www.parc-mercantour.com

Parc Naturel National de Port-Cros

Castel Ste-Claire, Rue Ste-Claire,
83400 Hyères
℘04 94 12 82 30
www.portcrosparcnational.fr

Fédération Nationale des Comités Départementaux de Tourisme

2 rue Linois, 75015 Paris
℘01 45 75 62 16
www.fncdt.net

Tourist Information Centres

The Michelin Guide France gives the addresses and telephone numbers of the Tourist Information Centres (*Syndicats d'Initiative*) to be found in most large towns and many tourist resorts. They can supply large-scale town plans, timetables and information on local entertainment, accommodation, sports and sightseeing.

INTERNATIONAL VISITORS
DOCUMENTS

Passport

Nationals of countries within the European Union entering France need only a national identity card (a passport for UK nationals). Nationals of other countries must be in possession

DUTY-FREE ALLOWANCES	
Spirits (whisky, gin, vodka, etc.)	2.6gal/10l
Fortified wines (vermouth, port, etc.)	5.2gal/20l
Wine (not more than 60 sparkling)	23.7gal/90l
Beer	29gal/110l
Cigarettes	800
Cigarillos	400
Cigars	200
Smoking Tobacco	2.2lb/1kg

of a valid national passport. In case of loss or theft, report to your embassy or consulate and the local police.

Visa

No entry visa is required for Canadian, US or Australian citizens travelling as tourists and staying for up to 90 days, except for students planning to study in France. If you think you may need a visa, apply to your local French Consulate. US citizens are advised to consult www.travel.state.gov for entry requirements, security and other information including contact numbers of US embassies and consulates. In an emergency call the **Overseas Citizens Services**: ℘1-888-407-4747 (℘1-202-501-4444 *from overseas*).

CUSTOMS

In the UK, **HM Revenue & Customs** (*www.hmrc.gov.uk*) publishes *A Guide for Travellers* on customs regulations and duty-free allowances. **US citizens** should view *Tips for Traveling Abroad* online (*travel.state.gov/travel/tips/brochures/brochures_1225.html*) for general information on visa requirements, customs regulations, medical care, etc. There are no customs formalities for holidaymakers bringing their caravans into France for a stay of less than six months. No customs document is necessary for pleasure boats and outboard motors

EMBASSIES AND CONSULATES IN FRANCE

Australia	Embassy	4 rue Jean-Rey, 75015 Paris ℘01 40 59 33 00. www.france.embassy.gov.au
Canada	Embassy	35 avenue Montaigne, 75008 Paris ℘01 44 43 29 00. www.international.gc.ca
Eire	Embassy	4 rue Rude, 75016 Paris ℘01 44 17 67 00. www.embassyofireland.fr
New Zealand	Embassy	7 rue Léonard-de-Vinci, 75016 Paris ℘01 45 00 24 11. www.nzembassy.com/france
South Africa	Embassy	59 quai d'Orsay, 75007 Paris ℘01 53 59 23 23. www.afriquesud.net
UK	Embassy	35 rue du Faubourg St-Honoré, 75008 Paris ℘01 44 51 31 00. http://.ukinfrance.fco.gov.uk/en
	Consulate	16 bis rue d'Anjou, 75008 Paris ℘01 44 51 31 00
	Consulate	353 boulevard du Président Wilson, 33073 Bordeaux ℘05 57 22 21 10
USA	Embassy	2 avenue Gabriel, 75008 Paris ℘01 43 12 22 22. http://france.usembassy.gov
	Consulate	2 rue St-Florentin, 75001 Paris. ℘01 43 12 22 22

for a stay of less than six months but the registration certificate should be kept on board. Americans can bring home, tax-free, up to US$ 800 worth of goods (limited quantities of alcohol and tobacco products); Canadians up to CND$ 750; Australians up to AUS$ 900 and New Zealanders up to NZ$ 700. Persons living in a member state of the European Union are not restricted with regard to purchasing goods for private use.

HEALTH

First aid, medical advice and chemists' night service are provided by chemists/drugstores (*pharmacie*), identified by the green cross sign. Since the recipient of medical treatment in French hospitals or clinics must pay the bill, it is advisable to take out comprehensive insurance coverage. Nationals of non-EU countries should check with their insurance companies about policy limitations. Reimbursement can then be negotiated with the insurance company according to the policy held.

All prescription drugs should be clearly labelled and it is recommended you carry a copy of the prescription. **British and Irish citizens**, if they are not already in possession of an **EHIC** (European Health Insurance Card), should apply for one before travelling. The card entitles UK residents to free or reduced-cost medical treatment. Apply at UK post offices call: ℘0845 606 2030 or visit www.ehic.org. uk. You pay upfront but can reclaim most of the money (*see website for details*). **Americans** concerned about travel and health may contact the International Association for Medical Assistance to Travelers, which can also provide details of English-speaking doctors in different parts of France: ℘(716) 754-4883. www.iamat.org. **The American Hospital of Paris** is open 24hr for emergencies as well as consultations, with English-speaking staff (*63 Blvd. Victor Hugo, 92200 Neuilly sur Seine; ℘01 46 41 25 25; www.american-hospital.org*). The hospital is accredited by major insurance companies. **The British Hospital** is just outside Paris in Levallois-Perret (*3 r. Barbès;*

☎01 46 39 22 22; www.british-hospital.org). This facility is registered as a charity in the UK and provides English-speaking medical staff to the British community in France.

ACCESSIBILITY
The sights described in this guide that are easily accessible to people of reduced mobility are indicated by the symbol &. Many of France's historic buildings, including musems and hotels, have limited or no wheelchair access. Older hotels tend to lack lifts (elevators). Tourism for All UK (☎0845 124 9971; www.tourismforall.org.uk) publishes some handy information about accessibility, which is also available from French disability organisations such as **Association des**

Paralysés de France (17 bd Auguste Blanqui, 75013 Paris; ☎01 40 78 69 00; www.apf.asso.fr). Useful information on transport, holidaymaking and sports associations for the disabled is available from French-language website: www.handicap.fr. In the UK, www.radar.org.uk is a good source of info and support and US website www.access-able.com provides information for mature travellers or those with special needs, including lists of experienced travel agents and useful internet links. The **Michelin Guide France** and **Michelin Camping & Caravanning France** both indicate hotels and campsites with facilities suitable for travellers with physical disabilities.

Getting There and Getting Around

BY PLANE
The French domestic network operates frequent services from Paris (Charles de Gaulle and Orly), covering the whole country. The main holiday destinations in the south of France are Nice, Marseille, Toulon and Monaco. **Air France** is the leading airline for domestic flights but there are also flights available on the European carrier, **easyJet**.
Direct flights from the UK can be booked with **easyJet**, **British Airways**, **British Midland** and **Ryanair**. There are transfer buses to town terminals and to rail stations. The **RER-B** regional rail links to the centre of Paris from both Roissy and Orly. There are also package tour flights with a rail or coach link-up. Information, brochures and timetables are available from airlines and travel agents.

- **easyJet**
  ☎08 25 08 25 08 *within France*
  www.easyjet.com
- **British Airways**
  ☎0870 8509 850 *from England*
  ☎0825 825 040 *from France*
  www.britishairways.com
- **British Midland**
  ☎0870 6070 222 *from England*
  ☎01 55 69 83 06 *from France*
  www.flybmi.com
- **Air France**
  ☎0 820 820 820 *within France*
  www.airfrance.com
- **Ryanair**
  ☎08 92 55 56 66 *within France*
  www.ryanair.com
- **BMI Baby**
  ☎08 90 71 00 81 *within France*
  www.bmibaby.com
- **Aéroports de Paris**
  ☎08 36 681 515
  www.adp.fr
- **Aéroport de Nice-Côte d'Azur**
  ☎04 89 88 98 28
  www.nice.aeroport.fr
- **Aéroport international de Toulon-Hyères**
  ☎0825 01 83 87
  www.toulon-hyeres.aeroport.fr

BY SEA
FROM THE UK OR IRELAND

There are numerous **cross-Channel services** from the United Kingdom and Ireland. To choose the most suitable route between your port of arrival and your destination use the **Michelin Tourist and Motoring Atlas France**, **Michelin map 726** (which gives travel times and mileages) or **Michelin Local maps** from the 1:200 000 series.

BY TRAIN/RAIL

Eurostar runs via the Channel Tunnel between London St Pancras and Paris in 3hr *(bookings and information ℘08432 186 186 in the UK; ℘00 (0)1233 617 575 from outside the UK; www.eurostar.co.uk)*. In Lille and Paris it links to the high-speed rail network **(TGV)**, which covers most of the country and has recently been extended to the South of France *(for details call ℘0836 676 869)*. The main towns served by the TGV network are Lyon, Avignon, Valence, Montpellier, Aix-en-Provence and Marseille. As far as the Riviera is concerned, there are 6–8 trains leaving daily from Paris-Gare de Lyon for Nice station, running roughly between 8am and 10.30pm (night train). The fastest schedule takes 5hr.

Eurail *(www.eurail.com)* offers travel passes that may be purchased by residents of countries outside the European Union. In the US, contact your travel agent.
⊘*Tickets must be validated (composter) by using the orange automatic date-stamping machines at the platform entrance (⊘failure to do so may result in a fine).*

Eurailpass, **Flexipass** and **Saverpass** are three of the travel passes which may be purchased by residents of countries outside the European Union. In the US, contact your travel agent or Rail Europe *(44 South Broadway, White Plains, NY 10601; ℘1-800-622-8600)* or **Europrail International** *(℘1 888*

P&O Ferries	In the UK: ℘08716 645 645. In France: ℘0825 120 156 www.poferries.com
Norfolk-line	In the UK: ℘0844 847 5042 Outside the UK: ℘+44 208 127 8303 www.norfolkline-ferries.co.uk
Brittany Ferries	In the UK: ℘0871 244 0744 In France: ℘08 25 82 88 28 In Ireland: ℘021 427 7801 www.brittany-ferries.com
Irish Ferries	In the UK: ℘08717 300 400 In Ireland: ℘0818 300 400 In France: ℘01 70 72 03 26 In the US: ℘(772) 563 2856 www.irishferries.com
Seafrance	In the UK: ℘0871 423 7119 In France: ℘0825 082 505 www.seafrance.com

667 9731; www.europrail.net). If you are a European resident, you can buy an individual country pass if you are not a resident of the country you are buying it for. In the UK, contact Europrail *(179 Piccadilly, London W1V OBA; ℘0990 848 848)*. Information on schedules can be obtained on websites for these agencies and the **SNCF**, respectively: www.raileurope.com, www.voyages-sncf.com. At the SNCF site, you can book ahead, pay with a credit card, and receive your ticket in the mail at home free of charge (seven days minimum before leaving in the case of foreign countries, four days for France).

☺ Practical Information ☺

The French railway company SNCF operates a telephone information, reservation and prepayment service in English from 7am to 10pm (French time). In France call ℘08 36 35 35 39 *(when calling from outside France, drop the initial 0)*.

TGV Méditerranée

In June 2001, former President of the Republic, Jacques Chirac, officially inaugurated France's southern high-speed rail link, bringing Provence within three hours of Paris and six of London. The streamlined blue and silver train now reaches Marseille after a mere 3hr, leaving from Paris. The 12-year campaign to complete the route followed by the TGV Méditerranée was fraught with difficulties. Besides the opposition shown by local residents, there were a number of geographical, architectural and ecological constraints. Considerable care was taken to preserve the natural environment and to avoid disturbing protected species. Moreover, new bridges and viaducts had to be built with local stone in order to blend in with the surrounding landscape. Indeed, on the journey from Valence to Marseille you will see no fewer than 23 bridges! Today the line carries over 60,000 passengers every day.

The line travels from Paris–Lyon-Saint Exupéry Airport, Paris–Valence, Paris–Avignon, Paris–Aix-en-Provence, Paris–Marseille, Paris–**Toulon**, Paris–**Hyères**, Paris–**Fréjus**, Paris–**Nice**, Paris–Nîmes, Paris–Montpellier, Paris–Béziers and Paris–Perpignan.

The trains provide a very good service to passengers: more legroom, a central luggage rack, an area set aside for bicycles, family and disabled facilities, telephone booths, plug sockets for European 2-pin plugs (first class), a wide range of light snacks or meals and even a free newspaper with your breakfast in first class.

DISCOUNTS

There are numerous **discounts** available when you purchase your tickets in France, from 25–50% below the regular rate. These include discounts for using senior cards and youth cards (the nominative cards with a photograph must be purchased beforehand), and lower rates for 2–9 people travelling together (no card required, advance purchase necessary).

There is a limited number of discount seats available during peak travel times, but the best discounts are available during off-peak periods.

- **Line no 1**
  Marseille, Toulon, Hyères
- **Line no 2**
  Marseille, Toulon,
  Les Arcs-Draguignan
- **Line no 3**
  Les Arcs, Draguignan, Fréjus,
  St-Raphaël, Cannes, Nice
- **Line no 4**
  Mandelieu, Cannes, Nice,
  Ventimiglia
- **Line no 5A**
  Nice, Breil-sur-Roya, Cueno, Torino
- **Line no 6**
  Marseille, Toulon, Nice,
  Ventimiglia
- **Line Grasse-Cannes**
  Grasse, Le Bosquet, Cannes, Nice

From July to September the **Carte Isabelle** is an unlimited day-pass between Fréjus and Vintimille, Cannes and Grasse, and Nice and Tende.

BY COACH/BUS

- **Eurolines (London)**
  4 Cardiff Road, Luton, Bedfordshire
  LU1 1PP. ℰ08717 818 181.
  www.eurolines.co.uk.
- **Eurolines (Paris)** ℰ08 92 89 90 91.
  www.eurolines.fr.
- **www.eurolines.com**
  The international website with information about travelling all over Europe by coach (bus).

BY CAR

The area covered in this guide is easily reached by main motorways and national routes. **Michelin map 726** indicates the main itineraries, as well as alternative routes for avoiding heavy traffic during busy holiday periods, and gives estimated travel times. The latest Michelin route-planning service is available on the Internet: **www.ViaMichelin.com**. Travellers can calculate a precise route using such options as shortest route, route avoiding toll roads, Michelin-recommended route, as well as gain access to tourist information (hotels, restaurants, attractions). The service is available on a pay-per-route basis or by subscription. Roads are very busy during holiday periods (particularly weekends in July and August) and to avoid traffic congestion it is advisable to follow the recommended secondary routes (signposted as *Bison Futé – itinéraires bis*). The motorway network includes rest areas *(aires d'autoroute)* and petrol/gas stations, usually with restaurant and shopping malls attached, about every 25mi/40km, so that long-distance drivers have no excuse not to stop for a rest every now and then.

DOCUMENTS

Driving licence

For British drivers unaccustomed to driving on the right, extra care will be needed. Road signs generally use easy-to-understand international visual symbols instead of words. When driving in France, EU nationals must have their own valid **national driving licence**. Travellers from other EU countries and North America can drive in France with a valid national or home-state **driving licence**. An **international driving licence** is useful because the information on it appears in nine languages (keep in mind that traffic officers are empowered to fine motorists). A permit is available (US $15) from the **National Automobile Club** *(1151 East Hillsdale Blvd., Foster City, CA 94404; ℘650-294-7000; www.nationalautoclub.com)*; or contact your local branch of the **American Automobile Association**

(www.aaa.com). All drivers must also have with them the vehicle's **registration papers** and a current **insurance certificate**. The originals of all documents are required. Copies are not acceptable.

INSURANCE

Many motoring organisations offer accident insurance and breakdown service schemes for members. Check with your current insurance company regarding cover while abroad. If you plan to hire a car using your credit card, check with the company, which may automatically provide liability insurance (and thus save you having to pay the cost for optimum coverage).

ROAD REGULATIONS

The minimum driving age is 18. Traffic drives on the right. All passengers must wear **seat belts**. Children under the age of 10 must ride in the back seat. Headlights must be switched on in poor visibility and at night; use side-lights only when the vehicle is stationary. In the case of a **breakdown**, a red warning triangle or hazard warning lights are obligatory, as well as a luminous jacket. In the absence of stop signs at intersections, cars must **yield to the right**. Traffic on main roads outside built-up areas (priority indicated by a yellow diamond sign) and on roundabouts has right of way. Vehicles must stop when the lights turn red at road junctions and may filter to the right only when indicated by an amber arrow. The regulations on **drinking and driving** (limited to 0.50g/l) and **speeding** are strictly enforced, usually by an on-the-spot fine.

Speed Limits

Although liable to modification, these are as follows:

- Toll motorways *(autoroutes)* 80mph/130kph (68mph/110kph when raining);

RENTAL CARS – RESERVATIONS IN FRANCE		
Avis France:	☏ 0820 05 05 05 (UK)	www.avis.fr
Europcar:	☏ 0825 35 83 58 (UK)	www.europcar.com
Budget France:	☏ 0825 00 35 64 (UK)	www.budget.com
Hertz France:	☏ 0825 861 861 (UK)	www.hertz.com
SIXT:	☏ 0820 00 74 98 (UK)	www.e-sixt.com
CITER:	☏ 0825 16 12 20 (UK)	www.citer.fr
Thrifty:	☏ 01494 751 500 (UK)	www.thrifty.com
Nova Car Hire:	☏ 0800 018 6682 (UK)	www.novacarhire.com

- Dual carriageways and motorways without tolls 68mph/110kph (62mph/100kph when raining);
- Other roads 56mph/90kph (50mph/80kph when raining) and in towns 31mph/50kph;
- Outside lane on motorways during daylight, on level ground and with good visibility – minimum speed limit of 50mph/80kph.

Parking Regulations

In town there are zones where parking is either restricted or subject to a fee; tickets should be obtained from the ticket machines *(horodateurs)* and displayed inside the windscreen on the driver's side; failure to do so may result in a fine or towing.

Tolls

In France, most motorway sections are subject to a toll *(péage)*. You can pay in cash or with a credit card (Visa, MasterCard).

CAR RENTAL

There are car rental agencies at airports, railway stations and in large towns. Drivers must be over 21; between ages 21–25, drivers are required to pay an extra daily fee; some companies allow drivers under 23 only if the reservation has been made through a travel agent. It is relatively expensive to hire a car in France; Americans in particular will notice the difference.

MOTORHOME RENTAL

Worldwide Motorhome Rentals

Offers fully equipped camper vans for hire.

☏ 888- 519-8969 *US toll-free*
☏ 530-389-8316 *outside the US*
Fax 530-389-8316
www.mhrww.com

PETROL/GASOLINE

French service stations dispense:

- *sans plomb 98* (super unleaded 98)
- *sans plomb 95* (super unleaded 95)
- *diesel/gazole* (diesel)
- *GPL* (LPG).

For US citizens: gasoline is more expensive in France than in the USA. Prices are listed on signboards on the motorways; it is usually cheaper to fill up after leaving the motorway; check hypermarkets on the outskirts of town. You can pay at the pump using credit/debit cards.

Where to Stay and Eat

WHERE TO STAY
FINDING A HOTEL

Turn to the **Addresses** within individual sight listings for descriptions and prices of typical places to stay **(Stay)** with local flair. The key on the front cover flap of the guide explains the symbols and abbreviations used in these sections. The French Riviera offers a wide array of accommodation options, from simple bed and breakfasts (known as *gîtes* or *maisons d'hôte*) in charming villages to palatial hotels overlooking the Mediterranean.

Prices tend to rise in proximity to the beaches and in the larger cities such as Nice, Cannes, Toulon and Monte Carlo, while some of the best deals can be found in the smaller perched villages and quiet country inns in the hinterlands.

For an even greater selection, use the **Michelin Guide France**, with its famously reliable star-rating system and hundreds of establishments all over France.

Book ahead! The French Riviera is a very popular holiday destination. For further assistance, **Loisirs Accueil** is a booking service that has offices in some French *départements* – contact tourism offices for further information. A guide to good-value, family-run hotels, **Logis et Auberges de France**, is available from the French tourist office, as are lists of other kinds of accommodation such as hotel-châteaux, bed-and-breakfasts, etc. **Relais et Châteaux** provides information on booking in luxury hotels with character: 15 rue Galvani, 75017 Paris; ℘08 25 323 232.

Economy Chain Hotels

If you need a place to stop en route, these can be useful, as they are inexpensive (around 45€ for a double room) and generally located near the main road. While breakfast is available,

there may not be a restaurant; rooms are small, with a television and bathroom. Central reservation numbers:

- **Akena** ℘01 69 84 85 17 www.hotels-akena.com
- **B&B** ℘01 72 36 51 06 www.hotel-bb.com
- **Etap Hotel** ℘0892 688 900 www.etaphotel.com
- **Hotel Formula 1** ℘0892 685 685 www.hotelformule1.com
- **Accor Hotels** ℘0825 88 00 00 www.accorhotels.com/fr
- **Villages Hôtel** ℘03 80 60 92 70 www.villages-hotel.com

The chain hotels listed below are slightly more expensive (from 58€) and offer a few more amenities and services. Central reservation numbers:

- **Campanile** ℘01 64 62 59 70 www.campanile.com
- **Etap** ℘0892 688 900 www.etaphotel.com
- **Ibis** ℘0892 686 686 www.ibishotel.com

COTTAGES, BED & BREAKFASTS

The **Maison des Gîtes de France** is an information service on self-catering accommodation on the French Riviera (and the rest of France). *Gîtes* usually take the form of a cottage or apartment decorated in the local style, where visitors can make themselves at home, or bed and breakfast accommodation *(chambres d'hôtes)*, which consists of a room and breakfast at a reasonable price. Contact the Gîtes de France office in Paris (℘01 49 70 75 75; www.gites-de-france.com) or their representative in the UK, **Brittany Ferries** (see p43). You can also contact the local tourist offices, which may have lists of available properties and local bed and breakfast establishments.

HOSTELS, CAMPING

To obtain an **International Youth Hostel Federation card** (there is no age requirement, and a senior card is available, too), you should contact the IYHF in your own country

Caravanning

© Robert Paul van Beets/Bigstockphoto.com

for information and membership applications *(US ℰ1 301 495 1240*; UK *ℰ01629 592 700*; Australia *ℰ61 2 9283 7195)*. There is a booking service online *(www.hihostels.com)*, which you may use to reserve rooms as far as six months in advance.

There are two main youth hostel *(auberges de jeunesse)* associations in France, the **Ligue Française pour les Auberges de Jeunesse** *(67 r Vergniaud, 75013 Paris; ℰ01 44 16 78 78; www.auberges-de-jeunesse.com)* and the **Fédération Unie des Auberges de Jeunesse** *(27 r. Pajol, 75018 Paris; ℰ01 44 89 87 27; www.fuaj.org)*.

The Féderation's informative website provides an online booking service. There are numerous officially graded **campsites** with varying standards of facilities on the French Riviera.

The **Michelin Camping & Caravanning France** guide lists a selection of camp sites. The area is popular with campers in the summer months, so it is wise to book in advance.

WHERE TO EAT

A selection of places to eat **(Eat)** in the different locations covered in this guide can be found in the **Addresses** appearing in the *Discovering The French Riviera* section. The key at the back of the book explains the symbols and abbreviations used in the Addresses. We have highlighted an array of eating places primarily for their atmosphere, location and regional delicacies. Prices indicate the average cost of a starter, main dish and dessert for one person. Use the red-cover **Michelin Guide France**, with its well-known star-rating system and hundreds of establishments throughout France, for an even greater choice. If you would like to experience a meal in a highly rated restaurant from **The Michelin Guide**, be sure to book ahead.

A number of associations aim to promote good-quality, often local and independent businesses throughout France. **Sites remarquables du goût** *(www.sitesremarquablesdugout. com)* organise activities such as walks and cookery courses and their logo will help you identify a restaurant that contributes to the preservation of local or artisan products and customs. **Bistrot des Pays** *(www. bistrotdepays.com)* are open all year and located in villages of fewer than 2,000 inhabitants, making a vital contribution to local economies and the social life of rural communities. In the countryside, restaurants usually serve lunch between noon and 2pm and dinner between 7.30 and 10pm. It is not always easy to find something in between those two mealtimes, as the "non-stop" restaurant is still a rarity in the provinces. However, a hungry traveller can usually get a sandwich (often a filled baguette) in a café, and ordinary hot dishes may be available in a brasserie. Throughout France, the culture leans more towards sitting and eating than grabbing a sandwich on the go, so plan ahead.

Useful Words and Phrases

Sights

	Translation
Abbey	Abbaye
Belfry	Beffroi
Bridge	Pont
Castle	Château
Cemetery	Cimetière
Chapel	Chapelle
Church	Église
Cloisters	Cloître
Convent	Couvent
Courtyard	Cour
Fountain	Fontaine
Garden	Jardin
Gateway	Porte
Hall	Halle
House	Maison
Lock (Canal)	Écluse
Market	Marché
Monastery	Monastère
Museum	Musée
Park	Parc
Port/harbour	Port
Quay	Quai
Ramparts	Remparts
Square	Place
Statue	Statue
Street	Rue
Tower	Tour
Town Hall	Mairie
Windmill	Moulin

On the Road

	Translation
Car Park	Parking
Driving Licence	Permis de conduire
East	Est
Garage (For Repairs)	Garage
Left	Gauche
Motorway/Highway	Autoroute
North	Nord
Parking Meter	Horodateur
Petrol/Gas	Essence
Petrol/Gas Station	Station essence
Right	Droite
South	Sud
Toll	Péage
Traffic Lights	Feu tricolore
Tyre	Pneu
West	Ouest
Wheel Clamp	Sabot
Zebra Crossing	Passage clouté

Shopping

	Translation
Baker's	Boulangerie
Bank	Banque
Big	Grand
Butcher's	Boucherie
Chemist's	Pharmacie
Closed	Fermé
Cough Mixture	Sirop pour la toux
Cough Sweets	Cachets pour la gorge
Entrance	Entrée
Exit	Sortie
Fishmonger's	Poissonnerie
Grocer's	Épicerie
Newsagent, Bookshop	Librairie
Open	Ouvert
Post Office	Poste
Pull	Tirer
Push	Pousser
Shop	Magasin
Small	Petit
Stamps	Timbres

Common Words

	Translation
Hello/Good Morning	Bonjour
Goodbye	Au revoir
Excuse Me	Excusez-moi
Please	S'il vous plaît
Thank You	Merci
Yes/No	Oui/Non
I Am Sorry	Pardon
How	Comment
Why	Pourquoi
When	Quand
Today	Aujourd'hui
Tomorrow	Demain
Yesterday	Hier

MENU READER

La Carte	The Menu

ENTRÉES / STARTERS

Crudités	Raw vegetable salad
Terrine de lapin	Rabbit terrine (pâté)
Frisée aux lardons	Curly lettuce with bacon bits
Escargots	Snails
Cuisses de grenouille	Frog's legs
Salade au crottin	Goat cheese on a bed of lettuce

PLATS (VIANDES) / MAIN COURSES (MEAT)

Bavette à l'échalote	Sirloin with shallots
Faux filet au poivre	Sirloin with pepper sauce
Côtes d'agneau	Lamb chops
Filet mignon de porc	Pork filet
Blanquette de veau	Veal in cream sauce
Nos viandes sont garnies	Our meat dishes are served with vegetables

PLATS (POISSONS, VOILAILLE) / MAIN COURSES (FISH, FOWL)

Filets de sole	Sole fillets
Dorade aux herbes	Sea bream with herbs
Saumon grillé	Grilled salmon
Coq au vin	Chicken in red wine sauce
Poulet de Bresse rôti	Free-range roast chicken from the Bresse
Omelette aux morilles	Wild-mushroom omelette

PLATEAU DE FROMAGES / SELECTION OF CHEESES

DESSERTS / DESSERTS

Tarte aux pommes	Apple pie
Crème caramel	Cooled baked custard with caramel sauce
Sorbet: trois parfums	Sorbet: three flavours

BOISSONS / BEVERAGES

Bière	Beer
Eau minérale (gazeuse)	(Sparkling) mineral water
Une carafe d'eau	Tap water (no charge)
Vin rouge, vin blanc, rosé	Red wine, white wine, rosé
Jus de fruit	Fruit juice

MENU ENFANT / CHILDREN'S MENU

Jambon	Ham
Steak haché	Ground beef
Frites	French fried potatoes

Basic Information

BUSINESS HOURS

National museums and art galleries are closed on Tuesdays; municipal museums are generally closed on Mondays. Shop hours are usually Monday to Saturday 10am to 6pm. In smaller towns, shops may also close for lunch and off-season. Churches, especially in secluded areas or small villages, are often only opened for services or on request.

DISCOUNTS

Significant discounts are available for senior citizens, students, under 25-year-olds, teachers and groups for public transportation, museums and monuments plus some leisure activities such as films (at certain times of day). Bring student or senior cards with you, and bring along some extra passport-size photos for discount travel cards.

The **International Student Travel Conference** (www.istc.org), global administrator of the International Student and Teacher Identity Cards, is an association of student travel organisations around the world. ISTC members collectively negotiate benefits with airlines, governments and providers of other goods and services for the student and teacher community, both in their own country and around the world. The non-profit association sells international ID cards for students, youngsters under the age of 25 and teachers (who may get discounts on museum entrances, for example).

The ISTC is active in a network of international education and work exchange programes. The corporate headquarters address is:

- Herengracht 479,
  1017 BS Amsterdam,
  The Netherlands
  ℘31 20 421 28 00
  Fax 31 20 421 28 10.

ELECTRICITY

The electric current is 220 Volts/50Hz. Circular two-pin plugs are the rule. Adapters and converters (for hairdryers, for example) are best bought before you leave home. If you have a rechargeable device, read the instructions carefully. Sometimes these items only require a plug adapter, in other cases you must use a voltage converter.

EMERGENCIES

Police:	17
SAMU (Paramedics):	15
Fire (Pompiers):	18

INTERNET ACCESS

Internet access is often easiest to find in hotels in larger towns such as Nice, Monaco, Cannes and Antibes, where WiFi is becoming standard (often free) and dial-up access is virtually nonexistent. These towns have many wireless hotspots in cafés, bars and libraries, as well as a few internet cafés for those travelling without a computer. The villages and mountain valleys inland have less reliable access; always call hotels or local tourist offices to confirm in advance.

🏛 Museum Passes 🏛

The Comité Régional du Tourisme Riviera Côte d'Azur has three different museum passes available: City of Nice Pass (municipal museums), Museums of Menton pass (eight sights in and around Menton), and the French Riviera Museum Pass, which offers unlimited free priority access to museums, monuments and gardens on the Riviera from Fréjus to Menton. For more information contact any of the tourist offices within the region, or visit **www.guideriviera.com**.

You can look online at **www.easy internetcafe.com** to find your nearest internet café.

MAIL/POST

Main post offices open Monday to Friday 8am to 7pm, Saturday 8am to noon. Smaller branch post offices generally close at lunchtime between noon and 2pm, and at 4pm.

Postage via airmail:
- UK: letter (20g) 0.70€
- North America: letter (20g) 0.85€
- Australia, NZ: letter (20g) 0.85€

Stamps are also available from news agents and *bureaux de tabac*. Stamp collectors should ask for *timbres de collection* in any post office.

MEDIA

With a large Anglophone expatriate population living on the Côte d'Azur year-round in addition to the seasonal tourists, there are several news sources available in English.

NEWSPAPERS

Local print media in English include the bi-monthly *Riviera Reporter* magazine, the monthly *Riviera Times* newspaper, and the *Var Village Voice*. Newsstands in major towns carry the daily editions of the *International Herald Tribune*, the *Financial Times* and the London *Times* the day they are printed. Other newspapers often arrive on the Riviera a day later.

RADIO

Riviera Radio

Feeling pangs for your native language? Desperately seeking an English-speaking doctor or nanny? Looking for rented accommodation? Riviera Radio is the answer to all your problems. The only 100% English-speaking radio in the area, it broadcasts on FM *(106.5 in the Alpes-Maritimes, 106.3 in Monte-Carlo; ℘00 377 97 97 94 94 from France)* and covers the stretch of coastline running

between St-Tropez and the Italian resort of San Remo. This Monaco-based radio station provides useful tips for tourists and residents alike, and presents a great many regular programmes: business and financial news, local traffic and weather reports, guide to English-speaking films in VO *(Version Originale)*, job offers, updated news bulletins in conjunction with the BBC World Service, calendar of major fairs and conferences, etc. One of Riviera Radio's most popular features is their weekday morning Community Chest *(9.20am)*, when listeners call in to buy or sell miscellaneous items.

TELEVISION

French channels Canal+ and Arte often air American and British programmes in their original language, however most English-speaking residents and hotels subscribe to satellite for channels such as BBC and CNN.

MONEY
CURRENCY

There are no restrictions on the amount of currency visitors can take into France. Visitors carrying a lot of cash are advised to complete a currency declaration form on arrival because there are restrictions on currency export.

Notes and coins

Since January 2002, the **euro** is the official currency of France and other participating EU Member States. One euro is divided into 100 cents, or *centimes*. Franc notes can be exchanged only at the Banque de France (until 2012).

BANKS

Banks are open from 9am to noon and 2pm to 4pm while branches are closed either on Monday or Saturday. Banks close early on the day before a bank holiday. A passport is necessary as identification when cashing traveller's cheques in banks. Commission charges vary and hotels usually charge more than banks for cashing cheques. One of the most economical ways to use your money in France is by using **ATM/cash machines** to obtain cash directly from your bank account or to use your credit cards to get cash advances. Be sure to remember your 4-digit PIN: you will need it to use cash dispensers and to pay with your card in most shops, restaurants, etc. ATM code pads are numeric; use a telephone pad to translate a letter code into numbers. Visa is the most widely accepted credit card, followed by MasterCard; other cards (Diners Club, Plus, Cirrus) are also accepted in most cash machines. American Express is more often accepted in premium establishments.

Most places post signs indicating the cards they accept; if you don't see such a sign and want to pay with a card, ask before ordering or making a selection. Cards are widely accepted in shops, hypermarkets, hotels and restaurants, at tollbooths and in petrol stations. If your card is lost or stolen in France, call one of the following 24-hour hotlines:

American Express ℰ 01 47 77 72 00

Visa ℰ 08 36 69 08 80

MasterCard/Eurocard ℰ 01 45 67 84 84

Diners Club ℰ 01 49 06 17 50

You must report any loss or theft of credit cards or traveller's cheques to the local police, who will issue you with a certificate (useful proof to show the issuing company).

PUBLIC HOLIDAYS

There are 11 public holidays in France. In addition, there are other religious and national festival days, and local saints' days, etc. On all these days, museums and monuments may vary their hours of admission.

In addition to the usual school holidays at Christmas and in spring and summer, there are long mid-term

1 January	New Year's Day (Jour de l'An)
March/April	Easter Day and Easter Monday (Pâques)
1 May	May Day (Fête du Travail)
8 May	VE Day (Fête de la Libération)
Thurs 40 days after Easter	Ascension Day (Ascension)
7th Sun–Mon after Easter	Whit Sunday and Monday (Pentecôte)
14 July	France's National Day (Fête de la Bastille)
15 August	Assumption (Assomption)
1 November	All Saint's Day (Toussaint)
11 November	Armistice Day (Fête de la Victoire)
25 December	Christmas Day (Noël)

breaks (ten days to two weeks) in February and early November.

SMOKING

Smoking is banned inside all public spaces, including hotel rooms, bars, and clubs, since January 2008. It is still permitted on outdoor café terraces and in specially-built fumoirs.

TELEPHONES
PUBLIC TELEPHONES

Most public phones in France use pre-paid phone cards (télécartes), rather than coins. Some telephone booths accept credit cards (Visa, MasterCard/Eurocard). Télécartes (50 or 120 units) can be bought in post offices, branches of France Télécom, bureaux de tabac (cafés that sell cigarettes) and newsagents and may be used to make calls in France and abroad. Calls can be received at phone boxes where the blue bell sign is shown; the phone will not ring, so keep your eye on the small digital screen.

INTERNATIONAL DIALLING CODES (00 + code) 🖉			
Australia	61	**New Zealand**	64
Canada	1	**United Kingdom**	44
Eire	353	**United States**	1

NATIONAL CALLS

French telephone numbers have ten digits. Paris and Paris region numbers begin with 01; 02 in northwest France; 03 in northeast France; 04 in southeast France and Corsica; 05 in southwest France.

INTERNATIONAL CALLS

To call France from abroad, dial the country code (33) + 9-digit number (omit the initial 0). When calling abroad from France dial 00, then dial the country code followed by the area code and number of your correspondent.
International information: US/Canada: 00 33 12 11
International operator: 00 33 12 + country code
Local directory assistance: 12

TO USE YOUR PERSONAL CALLING CARD	
AT&T	🖉 0-800 99 00 11
Sprint	🖉 0-800 99 00 87
MCI	🖉 0-800 99 00 19
Canada Direct	🖉 0-800 99 00 16

MOBILE/CELL PHONES

In France these have numbers that begin with 06 and 07. Two-watt (lighter, shorter reach) and eight-watt models are on the market, using the Orange, Bouygtel or SFR networks. *Mobicartes* are prepaid phone cards that fit into mobile units. Mobile phone rentals (delivery or airport pickup provided):
World Cellular Rentals: www.worldcr.com

WHEN IT IS NOON IN FRANCE, IT IS	
3am	in Los Angeles
6am	in New York
11am	in Dublin
11am	in London
7pm	in Perth
9pm	in Sydney
11pm	in Auckland

In France "am" and "pm" are not used but the 24-hour clock is widely applied.

TIME

France is one hour ahead of Greenwich Mean Time (GMT). Even though the Prime Meridian (0°) passes through Spain and France, both countries use the mean solar time of 15 degrees east (Central European Time) rather than 0 degrees (GMT).

TIPPING

Since a service charge is automatically included in the price of meals and accommodation in France, any additional tipping is up to the visitor, generally small change, and generally not more than 5%. Hairdressers are usually tipped 10–15%.

As a rule, prices for hotels and restaurants as well as for other goods and services are significantly less expensive in the French regions than in Paris.

Restaurants usually charge for meals in two ways: a *forfait* or *menu*, that is a fixed price menu with two to three courses, sometimes a small pitcher of wine, all for a set price, or *à la carte*, the more expensive way, with each course ordered separately.

Cafés have very different prices, depending on where they are located. The price of a drink or a coffee is cheaper if you stand at the counter (*comptoir*) than if you sit down (*salle*) and sometimes it is even more expensive if you sit outdoors (*terrace*). In some big cities, prices go up after 10pm in the evening.

CONVERSION TABLES

Weights and Measures

	🇺🇸	🇬🇧	
1 kilogram (kg) 6.35 kilograms 0.45 kilograms	**2.2 pounds (lb)** 14 pounds 16 ounces (oz)	**2.2 pounds** 1 stone (st) 16 ounces	*To convert kilograms to pounds, multiply by 2.2*
1 metric ton (tn)	**1.1 tons**	**1.1 tons**	
1 litre (l) 3.79 litres 4.55 litres	**2.11 pints (pt)** 1 gallon (gal) 1.20 gallon	**1.76 pints** 0.83 gallon 1 gallon	*To convert litres to gallons, multiply by 0.26 (US) or 0.22 (UK)*
1 hectare (ha) **1 sq kilometre (km²)**	**2.47 acres** 0.38 sq. miles (sq mi)	**2.47 acres** 0.38 sq. miles	*To convert hectares to acres, multiply by 2.4*
1 centimetre (cm)	**0.39 inches (in)**	**0.39 inches**	*To convert metres to feet, multiply by 3.28; for kilometres to miles, multiply by 0.6*
1 metre (m)	**3.28 feet (ft) or 39.37 inches** **or 1.09 yards (yd)**		
1 kilometre (km)	**0.62 miles (mi)**	**0.62 miles**	

Clothing

Women	🇪🇺	🇺🇸	🇬🇧
	35	4	2½
	36	5	3½
	37	6	4½
Shoes	38	7	5½
	39	8	6½
	40	9	7½
	41	10	8½
	36	6	8
	38	8	10
Dresses	40	10	12
& suits	42	12	14
	44	14	16
	46	16	18
	36	6	30
	38	8	32
Blouses &	40	10	34
sweaters	42	12	36
	44	14	38
	46	16	40

Men	🇪🇺	🇺🇸	🇬🇧
	40	7½	7
	41	8½	8
	42	9½	9
Shoes	43	10½	10
	44	11½	11
	45	12½	12
	46	13½	13
	46	36	36
	48	38	38
Suits	50	40	40
	52	42	42
	54	44	44
	56	46	48
	37	14½	14½
	38	15	15
Shirts	39	15½	15½
	40	15¾	15¾
	41	16	16
	42	16½	16½

Sizes often vary depending on the designer. These equivalents are given for guidance only.

Speed

KPH	10	30	50	70	80	90	100	110	120	130
MPH	6	19	31	43	50	56	62	68	75	81

Temperature

Celsius (°C)	0°	5°	10°	15°	20°	25°	30°	40°	60°	80°	100°
Fahrenheit (°F)	32°	41°	50°	59°	68°	77°	86°	104°	140°	176°	212°

To convert Celsius into Fahrenheit, multiply °C by 9, divide by 5, and add 32.
To convert Fahrenheit into Celsius, subtract 32 from °F, multiply by 5, and divide by 9.
NB: Conversion factors on this page are approximate.

Villefranche-sur-Mer
© Enrico De Vita/iStockphoto.com

The Region Today

LIFE ON THE RIVIERA
THE COAST

A Holiday Destination – Visitors seeking fashionable and elegant resorts can choose between the hustle and bustle of Cannes and Monte-Carlo or the quieter and more discreet setting of Hyères, Beaulieu, Menton, Cap Ferrat or Cap Martin. Those longing for the rush of a big city with all its amusements will undoubtedly turn to Nice. Lively St-Tropez attracts a large number of summer visitors, while anyone seeking a little solitude should head for the isolated rocky inlets along the coast. Wherever you stay, the Riviera offers a full range of hotels catered to every budget. Architectural styles vary widely on the Riviera, although small country houses built in Provençal rustic style, with pink or ochre-coloured façades and overhanging red-tiled roofs, definitely set the tone. Most towns and villages, and many former grand houses play host to exotic gardens that are a pleasure to visit all year round. Many magnificent parks offer fine **views** from their terraces, where the unique light and colour of the Mediterranean come to life.

The coastline is heavily built-up, particularly towards the east, and some towns are even built over the water, such as the lake town of Port-Grimaud, the Cogolin Marina, the marine city of Port-la-Galère and Fontvieille in Monaco.

Ambitious building projects, some of them totally out of proportion, have sprung up on all sides; a great number of private properties have appeared at the water's edge, although the public has right of access all along the coast. Anyone looking for deserted coastlines should head west to the Hyères region.

Ports and Fishing – The naval port of Toulon is in a league of its own on its popular recreational coast. Cannes, Monaco and Antibes are long-established pleasure boat ports: beautiful yachts with polished wood and gleaming steelwork lie at anchor in their bays or are moored along the quaysides.

Fishing on the Riviera is confined to the coast and as the catch is insufficient for the area, it has to be supplemented by shipments from the Atlantic.

Rather than large fishing ports, the coast is dotted with small harbours. Bandol, St-Tropez, St-Raphaël and Villefranche-sur-Mer have adapted to the demands of tourists and equipped themselves with moorings for pleasure boats.

For some years now the Nice region has made efforts to modernise the fishing industry and increased the number of boats in use. This has been achieved through the use of very large running nets known as *lamparos* and *seinches* and the construction of fish canneries.

The Markets – Most of the coastal towns have their own open-air markets where, to the colourful banks of flowers, fresh produce and stalls of gleaming fish, are added the noisy bustle and the warmth of the local accents of buyers and sellers, creating a true Côte d'Azur scene.

INLAND

The interior reveals the last vestiges of what was once a rough and precarious way of life: valleys and hill slopes terraced with stone walls retaining small strips of soil for growing cereals or two or three rows of vines and a few olive and almond trees.

The *garrigue*, where small flocks of sheep and goats are put to graze, form a sharp contrast with the fertile valleys and irrigated plains of the lowlands and the coast, where cereals, early vegetables and flowers are harvested and vines and fruit trees flourish. The lonely villages clinging to solitary ridges and small farms lying abandoned among their terraced walls bear little resemblance to the market towns of the plains, spread along the main roads, or to the farms *(mas)* scattered in the midst of large cultivated areas.

At the centre of most villages is a small square *(cours)* shaded by plane trees round a fountain. This is where the cafés are to be found, always full in this region. Many villages seem unoccupied, but very often shutters remain closed to keep out the heat and insects.

21ST CENTURY

While the museums, old town markets, quaint perched villages and sandy beaches keep the continuous influx of tourists occupied for most of the year, the Riviera economy doesn't solely depend on tourism, an industry vulnerable to international politics and economic slumps. Nice, Monaco and Cannes have invested heavily to become important business travel destinations, hosting conferences and trade shows year round, and Toulon continues to develop its thriving port, while technology and research centres have been booming throughout the region.

The French Riviera will always preserve and promote its colourful history and natural beauty, but in the 21C it has shrugged off its sleepy resort reputation to embrace a dynamic and international identity.

POPULATION

The population of the French Riviera was just 200,000 in 1860, growing to 1.8 million residents today, with a 3% growth rate since 1990, more than twice the national average. Over 90% of this population is concentrated around the coastal cities of Menton, Nice, Antibes, Cannes, Hyères, Fréjus and Toulon. International residents make up 12% of the population, with half of them coming from the European Union and almost 45% from North Africa.

LIFESTYLE

The French Riviera lifestyle is perfectly summed up as *Art de Vivre*, or the Art of Living. Everything from the lush Mediterranean landscape to the sundrenched Provençal cuisine contributes to the overall sense of people living the good life… and taking the time to enjoy it. The region runs at the leisurely pace typical of Latin countries, where afternoon siestas and Sunday boules games around the village square with a glass of chilled rosé or pastis are still common.

RELIGION

Like much of France, Catholicism is the most widespread religion on the French Riviera, with Catholic churches, chapels, abbeys and monasteries found throughout the region. Other religions, including Judaism, Islam and Christian faiths such Protestantism and Russian Orthodoxy are also represented here, often with architecturally fascinating places of worship, thanks to the large international communities from North Africa, Russia, northern Europe and the Middle East.

LOCAL GOVERNMENT

The French Riviera is made up of 316 *communes* (town, village or city) and two administrative *départements* (the Var and the Alpes-Maritimes), within the larger Provence-Alpes-Côte-d'Azur (PACA) region. This guide covers the Riviera from Bandol to Menton, including the mountainous inland regions of the Provençal Tableland, the Pre-Alps of Grasse and the high country north of Nice. Also covered in this guide is Monaco, a small principality on the Riviera surrounded by the Alpes-Maritimes. Adjacent regions described in the Michelin Green Guides are *Provence* and *French Alps*.

Since the early 1980s, the government of the French Republic has decentralised its legislative authority, so that each *commune*, *département* and *région* now has its own locally elected council and mayor or president.

Nice is the *prefecture*, or administrative capital, for the Alpes-Maritimes, while Toulon is the *préfecture* for the Var. Since 2008, both Nice and Toulon elected mayors from the Union for a Popular Movement (UMP), the party of President Nicolas Sarkozy.

INDUSTRY

Economic activities on the French Riviera have evolved significantly over the centuries, from shipping and fishing to farming and wine-making. The first major shift happened in the 18C with the arrival of the first tourists. Since the 1970s, the region has evolved into a region focused on technology, science, and international business.

TOURISM

The French Riviera is second only to Paris for tourism. It represents 6% of French tourist activity (€4billion in spending), with between 60,000 and 600,000 visitors present on the Rivieria at any one time, around 52% of them from outside France. A third of all tourists stay in Nice. One in five visitors is a business traveller, and today the region is home to the largest concentration of conference and trade show facilities in Europe. In addition to an attractive setting and enviable climate, the region is ultimately successful because of its highly developed infrastructure and accommodation for all budgets. The pleasure ports of the French Riviera are the largest in Europe, hosting 50% of the world's yachts and cruise ships each year.

CRAFTS

Many craftworkers have moved into the old inland villages, which they have often restored with care, producing traditional objects using age-old methods.

Biot – The production of large earthenware jars in Biot goes back to the days of the Phoenicians. In the Middle Ages Biot was an important centre for ceramics and it was not until the 19C that it was eclipsed by Vallauris. There are several modern workshops specialising in traditional earthenware jars, pottery, ornamental stoneware and metalwork.

Since the 1960s Biot has owed a growing international reputation to its glass craftsmanship. By visiting a glass workshop you can see how the various pieces are made using early techniques. Exhibits include carafes, bottles, glasses, small oil lamps and traditional Provençal jugs with long spouts (calères, ponons) for drinking without touching the vessel with the lips.

Vallauris – Ceramics from Vallauris enjoy a worldwide reputation. In 1947, Pablo Picasso came to work in a studio in the town and attracted a crowd of followers. Nowadays it is difficult to distinguish between the mass-produced pot and the handmade article.

Many of the potters – whether they use old methods (wood firing) or new techniques – produce attractive work, including glazed kitchenware (tureens, bowls, jugs), handsome stoneware, various glazed or unglazed articles and clay pipes. Besides pottery, many other interesting activities have been introduced, including the production of hand-crafted puppets, handsome furniture and decorative sculpture made from olive wood, colourful painted chests and cupboards, fine hand-woven linen and furnishings.

Tourrettes-sur-Loup – Tourrettes has been revived by its crafts industry. It was an important weaving town in the Middle Ages and renewed its connection with this craft after the Second World War, becoming a renowned centre for hand-woven fabrics. The weavers produce very high-quality goods in small quantities.

Several of the workshops in the winding streets offer a varied range of cloth: reproductions of old Provençal fabrics, shot material for the high fashion market or furnishings, and hand-woven ties.

Tourrettes is also home to a number of potters making earthenware sheep using a Mexican process, engraving in vivid enamels, painters and sculptors of olive wood.

AGRICULTURE

Cut Flowers – Alphonse Karr (⟲ see ST-RAPHAËL p208), a political refugee living in Nice before the annexation, is generally credited with founding the flower trade on the Riviera. With the help of an associate, Karr began growing flowers in large quantities and had the idea of sending bunches of fresh violets and small packets of mixed seed to Paris. From these modest beginnings the trade in cut flowers and mimosa has developed considerably owing to irrigation and hothouses.

Hill Villages

The Riviera's first inhabitants built their strongholds on isolated hills. Many old villages can still be seen perched like an eagle's nest on hilltops or set on the flank of a hill; some are practically deserted, while others have been restored, such as the villages of Gourdon, Èze, Utelle and Peille. For centuries the peasants built their villages in this way, at a distance from their lands and water supplies, and surrounded them with ramparts.

This was a wise precaution against the Saracen pirates and mercenaries, who stalked the area from the Middle Ages through to the 18C. Greater security, better communications and the development of farming techniques in the 19C ended this isolation. Villages began to expand in the plains, sometimes doubling in size, and country dwellers were able to live on the land they cultivated and build their houses there.

These secluded villages are picturesque to visit. Built with stones from the hillsides, they seem to blend in with the countryside. The winding streets and alleyways *(calades)*, which are steeply sloped and only to be traversed on foot, are paved with flagstones or cobbles, intersected by tortuous stairways and crossed overhead by vaults and arches. Sometimes arcades follow one another at ground level, affording the passer-by shelter from the sun and rain.

The houses, roofed with curved clay tiles, have high narrow fronts, worn by the centuries. They buttress each other and often surround a church or château, which dominates the village. Old nail-studded doors, wrought-iron hinges and bronze knockers still adorn the more prosperous residences.

Some of these villages, now inhabited by craftworkers and artists, are still enclosed by ramparts, with a fortified gate as the main entrance.

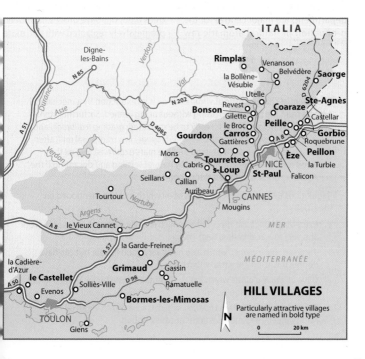

HILL VILLAGES

Particularly attractive villages are named in bold type

0   20 km

Flowers and Scented Plants of the Grasse Region – The two main flower crops of this area are roses and jasmine. The May tea-rose is the same as that grown in the east but the Mediterranean variety has a fine scent. Jasmine is of the large flowering variety, which has been grafted onto jasmine officinalis. It is a particularly costly and delicate plant, which flowers from the end of July to the first winter frosts.

The orange blossom used for perfume is obtained from the bitter fruit tree, known as the Seville orange *(bigaradier)*. Orange-flower water is made from direct distillation. The cherry laurel, eucalyptus and cypress are distilled both for their essence and for *eau de toilette*. Mimosa is used for the production of essence by extraction.

Sweet basil, clary (sage), tarragon, melissa or balm mint, verbena, mignonette, peppermint and geranium all yield products used in perfumery, confectionery and pharmaceuticals. Scented plants include wild lavender, aspic, thyme, rosemary, sage, etc.

Le Bar-sur-Loup, Golfe-Juan, Le Cannet and Vallauris, as well as Seillans (Var department) are major centres for the production of natural aromatic raw materials, although Grasse is number one in this domain.

This luxury industry, which caters mostly to the export market, is supplemented by the synthetic perfume industry. The French perfume industry's exports exceed €5.9 billion, the most important customers being the United States, Japan, Germany and the United Kingdom.

First Vegetables – After North Africa, Spain and Italy, the region of Toulon and Hyères provides the first seasonal vegetables and fruit. The Var is noted for cherries from Solliès-Pont and peaches from the region around Fréjus.

Olive Trees and Oils – Traditionally the northernmost place where olive trees (the symbol of Southern agriculture) are grown is also the limit of the Midi or South of France.

Production of olive oil in the region accounts for more than two-thirds of that of the whole country, and is spread throughout the Var, around Draguignan and Brignoles, and in the Bévéra and Roya valleys. Following the frosts of 1956, when nearly a quarter of the olive trees died, the olive groves have been progressively replanted with two more

How to Recognise a Good Olive Oil

The essential characteristic of virgin olive oil is its extraction by a mechanical process from the first cold pressing without being refined. Six further steps are necessary before the oil is ready to be marketed: grading *(calibrage)* and washing in cold water *(lavage)*, crushing *(broyage)* in a traditional mill, after which the resulting paste is pressed on fibre mats *(scourtins)*. The oil thus obtained is purified by centrifuge (or by natural settling and decanting if the traditional process is followed throughout).

Regulations define several categories of oil which must be mentioned on the label:

- Extra-virgin oil *(huile vierge extra)*, which is easily digested, has most flavour and very low acidity (less than 1%)

- Virgin oil *(huile vierge)*, which also has a very good flavour but can have double the acidity of extra-virgin oil

- Olive oil *(huile d'olive)*, which has an acceptable taste for local cooking but fairly high acidity (about 3%)

- Refined oil *(huile d'olive lampante)*, which is mixed with virgin oil as its acidity (nearly 4%) makes it unfit for consumption.

Bouillabaise

S. Sauvignier/MICHELIN

hardy species: the **aglandau** and the **verdale**. There are many other varieties, with flavours which vary according to the soil and the date of harvest.

Traditionally, several varieties are grown in one olive grove. Harvest is from the end of August, depending on the area; table olives are picked by hand, while those destined for milling are shaken off the tree and collected in nets.

Around Nice, shaking *(gaulage)* is always used. Olives from Nyons *(tanches)* are the only ones to be designated AOC (*Appellation d'origine contrôlée* – of guaranteed quality).

The **belgentiéroise** olive, harvested at the end of August, can be eaten within the month; the **grossane** is a fleshy black, salted olive; the **salonenque** is a green variety also known as *olive des Baux*.

The **cailletier**, or little Nice olive, is stored in brine for six months before being eaten. All of these can be eaten as an apéritif or made into oil.

SHIPPING

Toulon is the largest commercial shipping port on the French Riviera and also serves as the largest naval base in France. It's the primary port for shipments of cargo and passengers to Corsica.

There is a smaller commercial shipping port in Nice, although regional shipping activity consists mainly of cruise ships, ferries and pleasure yachts.

FISHING

Most of the fishing along the French Riviera is done on a small *artisanale* scale for local consumption, much as it has for centuries. Despite its relatively small contribution to the region's economy, it nevertheless touches many coastal communities, where fishing has been an important way of life for the locals for many generations.

TECHNOLOGY

The high-tech industry has grown significantly since the 1970s, encouraged by the establishment of science parks such as Sophia-Antipolis, near Valbonne. Today, information technology and telecommunication represent €4.2million in annual revenue, and biotechnology and chemical research (cosmetics, scents, flavourings) account for another €2.1million annually. Aerospace research and development have also grown in importance, both in the public and private sectors, while Toulon has begun investing in naval technology tied to national defence.

FOOD AND DRINK

The main features of Provençal cooking are garlic and frying in oil (preferably olive oil). Garlic has inspired many poets, who have called it the "Provençal truffle", the "divine condiment" and even "man's friend"! Olive oil is used wherever butter would be used further north. "A fish lives in water and dies in oil" according to a local proverb.

Bouillabaisse – This is the most celebrated of Provençal dishes. The classic *bouillabaisse* consists of the "three fishes": scorpion fish *(rascasse)*, red gurnet and conger eel. Several other kinds of fish and shellfish are usually added – it is essential that the fish be freshly caught and cooked in good-quality olive oil. The seasoning is just as important: salt, pepper, onion, tomato, saffron, garlic, thyme, bay leaves, sage, fennel and orange peel. Sometimes a glass of white wine or brandy gives the final flavour to the broth, which is poured onto thick slices of bread.

Aïoli – *Aïoli* – a mayonnaise made with olive oil, strongly flavoured with crushed garlic – is another Provençal speciality. Comparing the northern variety of mayonnaise with *aïoli*, Frédéric Mistral, a 19C writer and defender of Provençal culture, dismissed it as insipid "jam". *Aïoli* is served with fish, *hors-d'œuvres*, or with *bourride* (a soup of angler fish, bass and whiting, etc.), among many other dishes.

Fish – One of the Mediterranean's tastiest fish is the red mullet *(rouget)*, which the famous gastronome, Brillat-Savarin, called the "woodcock of the sea", probably because gourmets cook it without first scaling or cleaning it. The *loup* (local name for bass) grilled with fennel or vine shoots is another delicious dish. *Brandade de morue* is a purée of pounded cod mixed with olive oil, some garlic cloves and truffle slices.

Aromatic herbs – Considered with garlic and olive oil to be one of the basics of Southern cooking, aromatic herbs, cultivated or growing naturally on sunny hillsides, perfume gardens or found in markets, form an essential part of local cuisine. Known as *herbes de Provence,* the mixture includes **savory** *(sarriette),* used to flavour goats' and ewes' milk cheeses; **thyme** *(thym)* cooked with most vegetables and also grilled meat; **basil** *(basilic);* **sage** *(sauge),* **wild thyme** *(serpolet);* **rosemary** *(romarin),* which is good for the digestion; **tarragon** *(estragon);* **juniper** *(genièvre),* used to

flavour game; **marjoram** *(marjolaine);* and **fennel** *(fenouil)*. It is used in many dishes and can, according to taste, be a main constituent or just a trace.

Thirteen desserts – Provençal tradition presents diners at Christmas with 13 desserts (representing Christ and the 12 Apostles): raisins, dried figs, walnuts, hazelnuts, almonds, grapes on the vine, apples, pears, black nougat (made with honey), *fougasse* (a sort of savoury brioche), prunes stuffed with almond paste, melons stored in straw and dry cakes flavoured with orange blossom.

At Epiphany, a **galette des rois** is served in the form of a brioche filled with almond paste and topped with a paper crown, which goes to whoever finds the china figurine in their slice.

Wines – Vines have been cultivated in Provence since Antiquity.

Rosé wines, their glowing colour achieved by a special process using a particular type of black grape, are increasingly popular; pleasant and fruity to the palate, they go well with any dish.

White wines are generally dry in character but have a good bouquet and are an excellent accompaniment to shellfish and Mediterranean fish.

There is a wide variety of full-flavoured **red wines**: full-bodied or subtle and delicate depending on whether they come from Bandol or the southern slopes of the Maures or, on the other hand, from the Argens Valley or St-Tropez.

The most popular wines are from the region of Bandol, Ollioules, Pierrefeu, Cuers, Taradeau and La Croix-Valmer, from the Niçois area and particularly the wines of Bellet, La Gaude, St-Jeannet and Menton (℗*see Planning Your Trip: Wine Tasting and Regional Produce*).

SPECIALITIES FROM NICE

Niçois cuisine, a lively expression of the character of Nice, is inspired by the cooking of Provence and Liguria in Italy.

The narrow streets of Old Nice, clustered at the foot of the castle hill, overflow with opportunities to try the best-known specialities as well as seasonal variations. Two well-known examples are **onion tart** *(pissaladière)*, garnished with a thick anchovy sauce *(pissala)* and black Nice olives, and **salade niçoise**, a tasty combination of local tomatoes, cut into four, lettuce leaves, radishes, green and red peppers, spring onions, hard-boiled eggs and Nice olives, garnished with anchovy fillets and basil leaves then moistened with olive oil. As a tasty snack, try the large chickpea flour pancake *(socca),* divided into portions and accompanied by a small glass of local wine *(pointu)*; it is sold around place St-François.

At lunchtime recharge your batteries for more sightseeing with a round sandwich *(pan bagnat* or soaked bread) containing tuna, tomatoes, lettuce, onions, anchovies and olives, moistened with olive oil and flavoured with garlic. Salad, soup or omelette may accompany a marinade of young fish *(poutina)*, which are caught with the permission of the local authorities between Antibes and Menton in February. During the rest of the year gourmets may console themselves with a **fish soup** *(soupe aux poissons de roche)*, which also contains little crabs *(favouilles)*.

The evening menu may be enlivened by a slice of **suckling pig** *(porchetta)* stuffed with herbs and its own offal, served with a mixed salad *(salade de mesclun* in the local dialect) composed of 14 types of young salad plant picked in the area. The dishes on offer in the tiny village restaurants inland include stuffed courgette or squash blossoms *(fleurs de courgette farcies)*; a vegetable stew *(ratatouille)* made of tomatoes, aubergine or eggplant *(aubergines)*, peppers and courgettes (zucchinis) gently cooked in oil and water; shell-shaped pasta *(gnocchi)* made of wheat and potato flour and served with a thick meat sauce *(daube)*; deep-fried pastry parcels *(barbajouan* – Uncle John) filled with rice, squash, garlic, onion and cheese; a stockfish dish known as **estocaficada** (👉 *see right*). The convivial family dish, known as **soupe au pistou**, is a vegetable soup to which is added

Pissaladière
©Tips Images

an unctuous concoction of basil, garlic, tomatoes and olive oil.

For dessert there is a sweet tart *(tourte de blettes)* garnished with chopped chard leaves, pine kernels and currants. Halfway through Lent the pastry cooks' windows display small sweet pastry cushions known as **ganses**. A cake flavoured with orange-flower water *(fougasse)* is sold all year round; in Monaco it is decorated with aniseed in the national colours of red and white. Resist the midday heat with a glass of crushed ice flavoured with mint *(gratta queca)*.

Estocaficada – This is the local version of the stockfish of Marseille, known to old hands as "estocafic". To fillets of stockfish (dried cod), flaked with a fork and lightly browned, are added peeled and de-seeded tomatoes, the tripe of the stockfish cut into strips, chopped olives and bouquets of herbs, including fennel, marjoram, parsley, thyme, bay and savory. The dish is braised for three to four hours and generously laced with brandy *(la brande)*. When the liquor has reduced to a level which only the vigilance of the cook can determine, a good measure of stock is added to the pot.

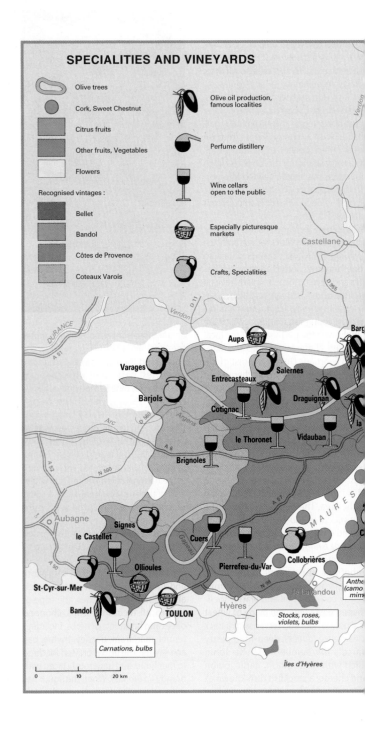

SPECIALITIES AND VINEYARDS

Olive trees

Cork, Sweet Chestnut

Citrus fruits

Other fruits, Vegetables

Flowers

Recognised vintages :

Bellet

Bandol

Côtes de Provence

Coteaux Varois

Olive oil production, famous localities

Perfume distillery

Wine cellars open to the public

Especially picturesque markets

Crafts, Specialities

Castellane

DURANCE

Verdon

Verdon

Barg

Aups

Varages

Salernes

Entrecasteaux

Barjols

Cotignac

Draguignan

le Thoronet

Vidauban

la

Brignoles

Arc

Argens

MAURES

Aubagne

Signes

le Castellet

Cuers

Collobrières

Ollioules

Pierrefeu-du-Var

St-Cyr-sur-Mer

Anthe (camo mim

Bandol

TOULON

le Lavandou

Hyères

Stocks, roses, violets, bulbs

Carnations, bulbs

Îles d'Hyères

0   10   20 km

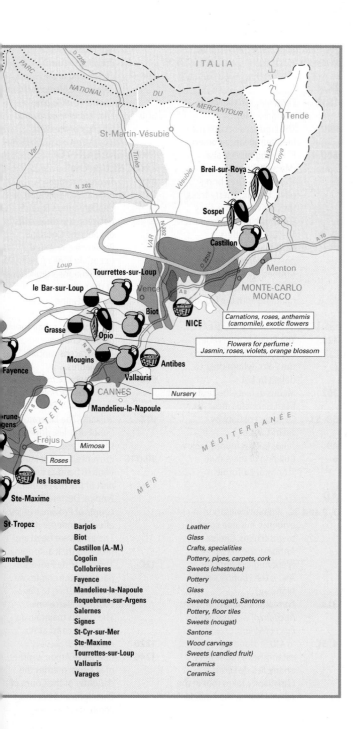

Carnations, roses, anthemis (camomile), exotic flowers

Flowers for perfume :
Jasmin, roses, violets, orange blossom

Nursery

Mimosa

Roses

Barjols	Leather
Biot	Glass
Castillon (A.-M.)	Crafts, specialities
Cogolin	Pottery, pipes, carpets, cork
Collobrières	Sweets (chestnuts)
Fayence	Pottery
Mandelieu-la-Napoule	Glass
Roquebrune-sur-Argens	Sweets (nougat), Santons
Salernes	Pottery, floor tiles
Signes	Sweets (nougat)
St-Cyr-sur-Mer	Santons
Ste-Maxime	Wood carvings
Tourrettes-sur-Loup	Sweets (candied fruit)
Vallauris	Ceramics
Varages	Ceramics

History

Events in italics indicate milestones in history.

BC

1500   Engravings in the Vallée des Merveilles.

900   The Ligurians occupy the Mediterranean seaboard.

600   Founding of Massalia (Marseille) by the Phocaeans. They bring olive, fig, nut, cherry trees, the cultivated vine; they substitute money for barter.

5–4C   The Greek settlers in Marseille introduce trading posts: Hyères, St-Tropez, Antibes, Nice and Monaco. The Celts invade Provence, mingling with the Ligurians.

GALLO-ROMAN PROVENCE

122   The Romans intervene to protect Marseille from the Celts, whom they defeat in 124.

102   Marius defeats the Teutons from Germania, near Aix.

58–51   Conquest of Gaul by Julius Caesar.

49   Julius Caesar founds Fréjus.

6   Building of the Alpine Trophy at La Turbie.

AD

1, 2 and 3C   Roman civilisation in evidence in some coastal towns (Fréjus, Cimiez, Antibes); the Via Aurelia (Ventimiglia-Brignoles-Aix) is the country's main highway.

313   *Constantine grants Christians freedom of worship by the Edict of Milan.*

4, 5C   In 410 St-Honorat establishes a monastery on the Îles de Lérins. Christianity takes root in the coastal towns, then inland.

5, 6C   Vandals, Visigoths, Burgundians, Ostrogoths and Franks invade Provence in turn.

496   *Clovis, King of the Franks, defeats the Alemanni from Germania at Tolbiac.*

800   *Charlemagne is crowned Emperor of the West.*

PROVENCE UP TO THE "REUNION"

843   *Treaty of Verdun* regulates the division of Charlemagne's Empire between the three sons of Louis the Debonair. Provence is restored to Lothair (one of Charlemagne's grandsons) at the same time as Burgundy and Lorraine.

855   Provence is made a kingdom by Lothair for his son, Charles.

884   The Saracens capture the Maures.

962   *Restoration of the Western Empire as the Holy Roman Empire under Otto I.*

974   William "The Liberator", Count of Arles, drives out the Saracens.

10, 11C   Provence, after passing from hand to hand, is finally made part of the Holy Roman Empire. Despite this, the counts of Provence enjoy effective independence. The towns are freed and proclaim their autonomy.

12C   The comté de Provence passes to the comtes de Toulouse, then to the counts of Barcelona. The counts maintain an elaborate court at Aix.

1226   *Accession of St Louis.*

1246   Charles of Anjou, brother of St Louis, marries the daughter of the Count of Barcelona and becomes comte de Provence.

The Wars of Religion – 1562–98

This is the name given to a 36-year-long crisis marked by complex political and religious conflicts. During the latter half of the 16C, the French monarchy was in poor shape to withstand the looming hegemony of Spain, with political life in chaos and the national debt reaching incredible dimensions. The firm stand on religion taken by Spain and Italy on the one hand and by Protestant countries on the other was missing in the France of Catherine de' Medici's regency, where both parties jostled for favour and a policy of appeasement prevailed.

The nobility took advantage of the situation, seeking to bolster their power base in the provinces and under cover of religion, to grasp the reins of government. The Catholic League was formed by the Guise and Montmorency families, supported by Spain and opposed by the Bourbon, Condé and Coligny factions, Huguenots all, with English backing.

Though historians distinguish eight wars separated by periods of peace or relative tranquillity, the troubles were continuous: in the country, there were endless assassinations, persecutions and general lawlessness, and the royal court was split by intrigue and *volte-faces*. Actual warfare, threatened ever since the Amboise Conspiracy, began at Wassy in 1562, following a massacre of Protestants. The names of Dreux, Nîmes, Chartres, Longjumeau, Jarnac, Montcontour, St-Lô, Valognes, Coutras, Arques, Ivry follow in bloody succession.

The Peace of St-Germain in 1570 demonstrated a general desire for reconciliation, but only two years later came the St Bartholomew's Day Massacre.

The States General were convened at Blois on the request of the supporters of the League, who were opposed to the centralisation of power in royal hands. Fearful of the power enjoyed by Henri duc de Guise, head of the Catholic League and the kingdom's best military commander, King Henri III had him assassinated in the château de Blois one cold morning in December 1588, only to be cut down himself by a fanatical monk the following year.

This left the succession open for the Huguenot Henri de Navarre, the future Henri IV. By formally adopting the Catholic faith in 1593 and promulgating the Edict of Nantes in 1598, this able ruler succeeded in rallying all loyal Frenchmen to his standard, putting at least a temporary end to the long-drawn-out crisis.

254	Landing of St Louis at Hyères on return from the seventh Crusade.
295	Charles II establishes the village and port of Villefranche.
308	Overlordship of Monaco is bought from the Genoese by a member of the Grimaldi family.
343–82	Queen Jeanne becomes comtesse de Provence. Plague decimates the population.
388	Nice hands itself over to the comte de Savoie.
419	Nice is officially ceded to the duc de Savoie.
1434	René of Anjou, "Good King René", becomes comte de Provence. He sets up court in Aix and helps revive the economy of the region.
1481	Charles of Maine, nephew of René of Anjou, bequeaths Provence (except Nice, which belongs to Savoie) to Louis XI.
1486	Reunion of Provence with France ratified by the "Estates" of Provence (assembly of representatives of the three orders); Provence attached to the Kingdom "as one principal to another".

1489 The independence of Monaco is recognised by regional powers, Provence and the comté de Nice, both of whom attempt to increase the population with favourable immigration incentives.

PROVENCE AFTER THE "REUNION"

1501 Establishment of Parliament at Aix (Parliament of Provence), sovereign court of justice, which later claims certain political prerogatives.

1515 *Accession of François I.*

1524 During the wars between François I (1515–45) and Emperor Charles V, Provence is invaded by Imperial forces.

1536 Invasion of Provence by Emperor Charles V.

1539 Edict of Villers-Cotterêts decrees French as the language for all administrative laws in Provence.

1543 Nice besieged by French and Turkish troops.

1562–98 *Wars of Religion. Promulgation of the Edict of Nantes.* Henri IV builds the first military port in Toulon.

1622 Louis XIII visits Provence.

1639 Richelieu establishes the French Royal Navy, with the a fleet in Toulon.

1643–1715 *Reign of Louis XIV.*

1691 Nice taken by the French.

1696 France returns Nice to Savoie.

1707 Invasion of Provence by Prince Eugene of Savoie.

1718 Comté de Nice becomes part of the newly created Kingdom of Sardinia.

1720 The great plague decimates the population of Provence.

1746 Austro-Sardinian offensive is broken at Antibes. Austrian War of Succession.

1787 Reunion of the "Estates" of Provence.

1789 *The French Revolution.*

REVOLUTION–EMPIRE

1790 Provence divided into three *départements*: Bouches-du-Rhône, Var, Basses-Alpes. Wealthy French aristocrats buy property in Nice.

1793 Siege of Toulon, in which Bonaparte distinguishes

The French Revolution

The French Revolution, which opened up the continent of Europe to democratic ideas, was the culmination of a long crisis that had paralysed the Ancien Régime.

Hastened along by the teachings of Enlightenment philosophers as much as the inability of a still essentially feudal system to adapt itself to new social realities, the Revolution broke out following disastrous financial mismanagement and the emptying of the state's coffers. In 1789, the commoners created the National Assembly, stormed the Bastille prison, abolished artistocratic and church privileges (night of 4 July) and proclaimed the Rights of Man. The royal family tried to flee in 1791 and after being captured were tried as traitors and guillotined in 1793.

The main events unfolded in Paris but their repercussions were felt throughout France and Europe. In 1792, the French Revolutionary Army captured Nice, which had been under Sardinian rule (to whom it would return 1814–60). In 1793, a counter-revolution broke out in several southern cities, including Toulon, where Royalists handed the city to a Anglo-Spanish fleet. The Revolutionary Army laid siege to Toulon for four months, ultimately driving the British out under the command of the young artillery commander, Napoleon Bonaparte, who was then promoted to Brigadier General.

9C print depicting the Siege of Toulon in 1793

himself. Nice is reunited with France.

1799 On 9 October, Bonaparte lands at St-Raphaël on his return from Egypt.

1804 *Coronation of Napoleon.* The Riviera economy suffers from his Continental Blockade. Completion of the **Grande Corniche** from Nice to Menton.

1814 *Abdication of Napoleon at Fontainebleau, 6 April.* Embarkation of Napoleon at St-Raphaël, 28 April, for the Island of Elba. The comté de Nice is restored to the King of Sardinia.

1815 Landing of Napoleon at Golfe-Juan, 1 March. He reaches Paris in record time by crossing the Alps. *Battle of Waterloo, 18 June.*

19TH CENTURY
THE DEVELOPMENT OF THE FRENCH RIVIERA

In the 19C, the French Riviera was slowly transformed from the isolated, impoverished and somewhat unwelcoming corridor between Provence and Italy into a chic resort destination. Early travel guides by Tobias Smollett *(Travels through France and Italy)* and Stephen Liégeard (*La Côte d'Azur*) offered glowing descriptions of flowering gardens and sparkling blue seas, but the popularity of the region really took off after the Brit-

ish Lord Brougham and Queen Victoria began visiting on a regular basis for the curative climate. Aristocrats and royal courts from Europe and Russia were first to build their palaces along the coast in Cannes, Nice and Monaco, where the casino was booming. The arrival of the railway in 1864 brought the affluent bourgeoisie and famous artists, many of whom shocked locals by sunbathing and swimming in the Mediterranean. By the turn of the century the French Riviera was an internationally renowned resort for the rich and famous.

1830 *Accession of Louis-Philippe.*

1832 The duchesse de Berry lands at Marseille, hoping to raise Provence in favour of a legitimist restoration.

1834 Ex-Chancellor Lord Brougham "discovers" Cannes.

1852-1870 *Reign of Napoleon III.*

1860 Comté de Nice restored to France.

1865 Roquebrune and Menton, who declared their independence from Monaco in 1848, become part of France.

1865 The railway links Marseille to Nice, reaching Monaco in 1868.

1878 Opening of the Monte-Carlo Casino. Development of the winter tourist season of the Riviera.

American troops landing East of Toulon, August 1944

1887	The journalist Stephen Liégeard coins the phrase, "Côte d'Azur", or Azure Coast.
late 19C	Artists such as Paul Signac establish the St-Tropez School of Painting.

20TH CENTURY
THE SUMMER SEASON DEBUTS

In the late 19th and early 20C, most of the tourism on the French Riviera was still reserved for the winter months. Ski resorts began appearing in the snowy mountains above Nice as early as 1909. The summer season, popularised by American artists and writers, officially launched in 1931, when hotels and resorts remained open throughout the year and Coco Chanel made sunbathing fashionable. In France, the first paid vacations made the French Riviera accessible for the average worker.

After WWII, the French Riviera's infrastructure grew exponentially, with high-speed trains, highways and an international airport opening up the region to the mass tourism that the region enjoys to this day.

1911	First Monte Carlo Rally
1914–18	Many village populations depleted by the First World War.
1920	Moyenne Corniche built.
1931	Resorts open in summer.
1940	The Italians occupy Menton.
1942	The Germans invade the Free Zone. The scuttling of the French Fleet in Toulon harbour.
1944	Liberation of Provence.

ALLIED LANDING IN PROVENCE (1944)

Operation "Dragon" – This was an extension of operation "Overlord", which had liberated Normandy three months earlier. At a critical moment in the battle of Normandy the Allies landed on the coast of Provence, fortified by the Germans under the name "Südwall" with the American 7th Army under **General Patch**, of which the French Ist Army (composed mostly of African soldiers) formed the principal part.

"Nancy a le torticolis" (Nancy has a stiff neck) – This laconic message, broadcast on the BBC on the evening of 14 August to announce the landings in Provence, raised the hopes of the Resistance groups which had been on alert since the projected landings reported on 6 June 1944. Between June and August, the dropping of arms by parachute was stepped up, notably in the *pouvadous* (dry and stony moors); these arms were destined for the Maquis (Resistance) in the Maures, the Alps, Bessillon and Ste-Baume. In the early hours of 15 August, airborne Anglo-American troops were dropped around Le Muy to take control of the strategic communications route, RN 7. The village of **La Motte** became the first Provençal village to be liberated. At the same time, French commandos from Africa landed at Cap Nègre and Esquillon Point, while American Special Forces attacked the Îles d'Hyères. Thus protected, the main army, assembled on 2,000 ships, including 250 warships, landed at 8am on the beaches of Cavalaire, St-Tropez,

Le Dramont and the Esterel. Despite a rapid advance, the two sectors were still separated at the end of the day by pockets of German resistance at St-Raphaël and Fréjus, which fell only the following day. On 16 August the B Army under General De Lattre landed at Cavalaire Bay and in the gulf of St-Tropez and, having relieved the Americans, attacked the defences of Toulon.

General Montsabert outflanked the town to the north to fall on Marseille. After the fall of Hyères and Solliès, Toulon was reached on 23 August, but fighting continued until 28 August with the surrender of the St-Mandrier peninsula. On the same day, after five days of fighting, Marseille was liberated.

To the east, the Americans of the First Special Force advanced to the Alpes-Maritimes to back up the Resistance forces and drive the Germans back into the Italian Alps: Nice fell on 30 August and Menton on 6 September. In the hinterland, the Massif de l'Authion, transformed into an entrenched camp by the Germans, was the site of hard fighting for 8 months. L'Authion was overcome on 13 April 1945, Saorge on 18 April, but Tende was liberated only on 5 May, three days before the General Armistice! Provence had been liberated in less than 15 days. The Allies pursued the Germans, who retreated up the Rhône Valley; the 1st French Army under De Lattre de Tassigny effected a link-up with the 2nd Amoured Division under Leclerc in Côte d'Or south of Châtillon-sur-Seine.

1946 First International Film Festival in Cannes.

Since 1946 Development of the summer tourist trade on the Riviera.

1947 Upper valley of the Roya incorporated into France.

1960–63 Modern art flourishes in the region with the New Realism and the School of Nice artists.

1970 International technology park opens at Sophia Antipolis, near Valbonne.

1980 The Provençal Motorway (A 8) links the Rhône and Italian networks.

1989 Law passed to strengthen measures against forest fires.

1989 The **TGV** (*train à grande vitesse* – high-speed train) arrives on the Riviera.

August 1994 Celebration of the 50th anniversary of the Liberation of Provence.

1996 A high-speed boat service (NGV) between Nice and Corsica.

21ST CENTURY

2000 The naval base at the Toulon Arsenal becomes home to the French nuclear-powered aircraft carrier, the *Charles De Gaulle*.

June 2001 The *TGV Méditerranée* is inaugurated, reducing the Paris–Marseille trip to three hours.

April 2005 Prince Albert succeeds his father, Prince Ranier III, who died after ruling the Principality of Monaco for 57 years.

2007 Construction completed on the first line of the Nice tramway.

2008 Thales Alenia Space, in the Centre spatial de Cannes Mandelieu, becomes the biggest employer in the Alpes-Maritimes.

2009 Planning begins for the new LGV PACA high-speed train linking Marseille to Nice, for 2020.

2010 Creation of the Métropole Nice Côte d'Azur, responsible for the joint management of economic, development and transport issues in 46 communes, including Cagnes-sur-Mer, Cap Ferrat and Mercantour.

2011 Launch of Auto Bleue, the world's first large-scale self-service electric hire car service in Nice.

Art and Culture

ABC OF ARCHITECTURE

Roman Era

LA TURBIE – The Alpine Trophy (1stC BC)

This monument was erected in homage to Augustus' victory in the Alps. Damaged and despoiled over the years, it was finally restored by the architect Formigé in the 1930s.

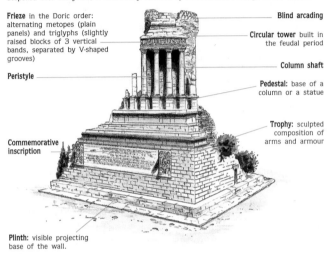

Frieze in the Doric order: alternating metopes (plain panels) and triglyphs (slightly raised blocks of 3 vertical bands, separated by V-shaped grooves)

Peristyle

Commemorative inscription

Plinth: visible projecting base of the wall.

Blind arcading

Circular tower built in the feudal period

Column shaft

Pedestal: base of a column or a statue

Trophy: sculpted composition of arms and armour

Early Christian Era

FRÉJUS – Interior of the baptistery (5C)

This is one of the few edifices from the Early Christian Era visible in the region. Some parts date from the Roman Era. An early 20C restoration restored the building to its former appearance.

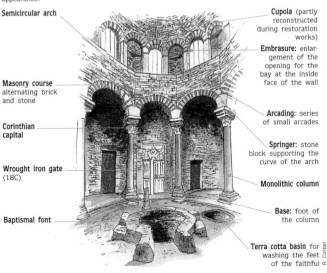

Semicircular arch

Masonry course alternating brick and stone

Corinthian capital

Wrought iron gate (18C)

Baptismal font

Cupola (partly reconstructed during restoration works)

Embrasure: enlargement of the opening for the bay at the inside face of the wall

Arcading: series of small arcades

Springer: stone block supporting the curve of the arch

Monolithic column

Base: foot of the column

Terra cotta basin for washing the feet of the faithful

R. Corbel

Religious architecture

LE THORONET – Ground plan of the abbey church (11C)

Because it did not serve a parish, the church in Thoronet does not have a central doorway. The rounded east end is typical of the region of Provence, in contrast to the flat chevet usually preferred by the Cistercian order.

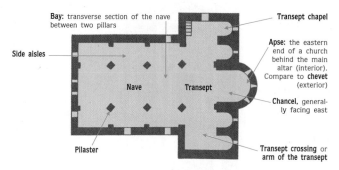

Bay: transverse section of the nave between two pillars

Transept chapel

Apse: the eastern end of a church behind the main altar (interior). Compare to **chevet** (exterior)

Side aisles

Nave   **Transept**

Chancel, generally facing east

Pilaster

Transept crossing or **arm of the transept**

Cross-section of a Romanesque Provençal church

The right and left-hand sides of the drawing show two main variations of this type of church.

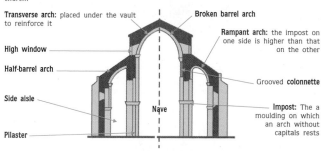

Transverse arch: placed under the vault to reinforce it

Broken barrel arch

Rampant arch: the impost on one side is higher than that on the other

High window

Half-barrel arch

Grooved colonnette

Side aisle

Nave

Impost: The a moulding on which an arch without capitals rests

Pilaster

GRASSE – Doorway of the Chapelle de l'Oratoire (14C)

The Gothic doorway and windows of this chapel were recovered from the old Franciscan church. In 1851, they were moved to this chapel, set on a hill in the old town centre.

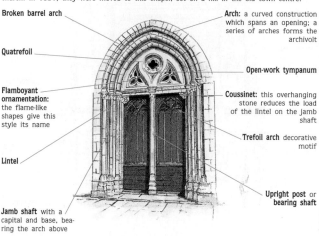

Broken barrel arch

Arch: a curved construction which spans an opening; a series of arches forms the archivolt

Quatrefoil

Open-work tympanum

Flamboyant ornamentation: the flame-like shapes give this style its name

Coussinet: this overhanging stone reduces the load of the lintel on the jamb shaft

Trefoil arch decorative motif

Lintel

Upright post or **bearing shaft**

Jamb shaft with a capital and base, bearing the arch above

R. Corbel

NICE – Cathédrale Sainte-Réparate (17C)

Sainte-Réparate was originally a chapel, built in the 13C. The current Baroque façade and ground plan are the work of the local architect Jean-André Guilbert.

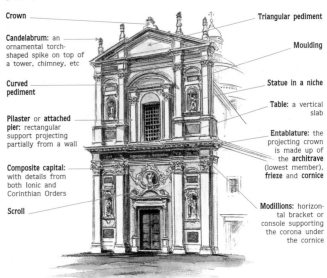

Crown

Candelabrum: an ornamental torch-shaped spike on top of a tower, chimney, etc

Curved pediment

Pilaster or **attached pier:** rectangular support projecting partially from a wall

Composite capital: with details from both Ionic and Corinthian Orders

Scroll

Triangular pediment

Moulding

Statue in a niche

Table: a vertical slab

Entablature: the projecting crown is made up of the **architrave** (lowest member), **frieze** and **cornice**

Modillions: horizontal bracket or console supporting the corona under the cornice

LES ARCS – Altar screen of the Sainte-Roseline chapel (early 16C)

Baroque altar screens in Nice and the surrounding region are mostly made of coloured marbles and stucco; gilded wood is more common on the other side of the Var.

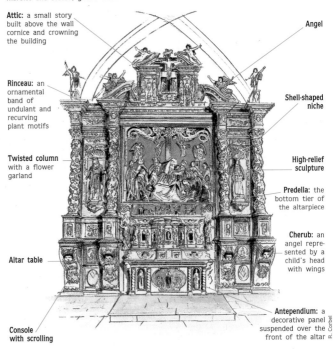

Attic: a small story built above the wall cornice and crowning the building

Rinceau: an ornamental band of undulant and recurving plant motifs

Twisted column with a flower garland

Altar table

Console with scrolling

Angel

Shell-shaped niche

High-relief sculpture

Predella: the bottom tier of the altarpiece

Cherub: an angel represented by a child's head with wings

Antependium: a decorative panel suspended over the front of the altar

R. Corbel

Traditional architecture

SAINT-TROPEZ – Houses on the harbour

The houses typically found in a village on the Riviera, known in France as the Côte d'Azur, are narrow and high, packed together along the waterfront or the winding streets of a hillside town; they are enlivened by colourful façades.

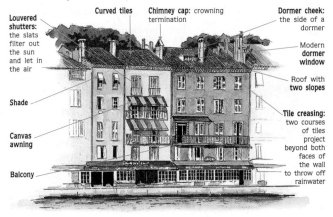

Louvered shutters: the slats filter out the sun and let in the air

Curved tiles

Chimney cap: crowning termination

Dormer cheek: the side of a dormer

Modern **dormer window**

Roof with **two slopes**

Shade

Canvas awning

Tile creasing: two courses of tiles project beyond both faces of the wall to throw off rainwater

Balcony

LE VIEUX-CANNET – Campanile

Campaniles appeared in the 16C, atop bell towers or belfries. Of various sizes, some are quite elaborate.

Metal frame withstands wind

Masonry course: the height of the regular rows is variable

Ressaut (projecting part)

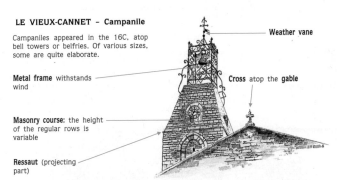

Weather vane

Cross atop the **gable**

LORGUES – Fontaine de la Noix (1771)

Each town or village has one or more fountains, whether a simple spigot or a sculpted, dated monument.

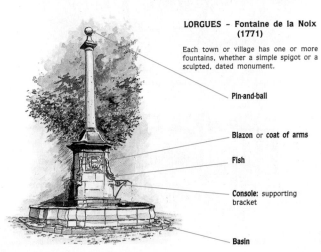

Pin-and-ball

Blazon or **coat of arms**

Fish

Console: supporting bracket

Basin

R. Corbel

Seaside architecture

HYÈRES – Villa Tunisienne (1884)

Seaside architecture of the 19C was inspired by Moorish culture. Chapoulart, the architect who designed the Villa Mauresque in Hyères, built this variation on the theme for himself, with a patio. Previously, it was also known as the "Algerian Villa".

Crenellations: made of crenels (notches) and merlons

Rosette: round pattern with a floral motif

Projecting pointed arch

Denticulated merlons

Interlace

Ceramic ornamentation

Multifoil arch

Meshrebeeya: lattice screen

Fore part of the building, projecting from the façade and as high as the main building

Balustrade: railing with balusters

MONTE-CARLO – Game room in the casino (late 19C)

Monte-Carlo grew up around the casino, which typifies the eclectic style of seaside architecture at the end of the 19C. The luxurious decoration inside echoes the elaborate ornamentation on the outside.

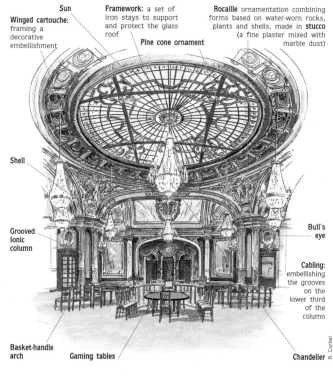

Sun

Winged cartouche: framing a decorative embellishment

Framework: a set of iron stays to support and protect the glass roof

Pine cone ornament

Rocaille ornamentation combining forms based on water-worn rocks, plants and shells, made in **stucco** (a fine plaster mixed with marble dust)

Shell

Grooved Ionic column

Bull's eye

Cabling: embellishing the grooves on the lower third of the column

Basket-handle arch

Gaming tables

Chandelier

R. Corbel

Military architecture

ANTIBES – Fort Carré (16C)

The ramparts of Antibes were demolished in 1895. All that remains is this fort, completed in 1585; the bastion design is a precursor of the star bastion defensive system developed by Vauban in the century following.

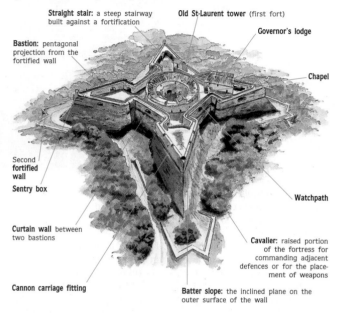

Straight stair: a steep stairway built against a fortification

Old St-Laurent tower (first fort)

Governor's lodge

Bastion: pentagonal projection from the fortified wall

Chapel

Second fortified wall

Sentry box

Watchpath

Curtain wall between two bastions

Cavalier: raised portion of the fortress for commanding adjacent defences or for the placement of weapons

Cannon carriage fitting

Batter slope: the inclined plane on the outer surface of the wall

Contemporary architecture

SOPHIA ANTIPOLIS – Commercial building (1978)

The buildings in the Valbonne business park were constructed beginning in 1970. They have been designed to fit into the natural shape of the landscape. Some are equipped to use solar energy.

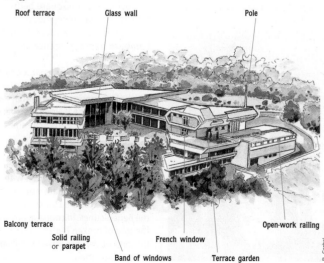

Roof terrace

Glass wall

Pole

Balcony terrace

Solid railing or parapet

French window

Band of windows

Terrace garden

Open-work railing

R. Corbel

HISTORY OF ARCHITECTURE

The Riviera enjoys an incredibly rich art and architectural heritage, dating from Antiquity right up to the present day. Whether you're exploring the alleyways of picturesque perched villages or strolling along the coast, you'll find every major architectural movement reflected in this region.

GALLO-ROMAN REMAINS

Provence and particularly the Riviera have enjoyed a high level of prosperity since Roman times. As later generations took the materials used by the Romans to construct their own new buildings, only a few fragments of this ancient civilisation have survived. Despite this fact, in the districts of Fayence, Fréjus and St-Raphaël, Roman canals are still being used to carry water to this day! The Roman ruins at Cimiez (see NICE p296) are extensive and consist of one of the best preserved bath complexes in southern Europe. Fréjus (see FRÉJUS p200) still boasts an impressive restored arena and fascinating traces of a Roman harbour.

The Alpine Trophy at La Turbie (see LA TURBIE p317) is of special interest; it is one of the few such Roman trophies still in existence. Buildings from the Merovingian and Carolingian periods include the baptistry at Fréjus and the chapels of

Remains of the Roman aqueduct in Fréjus

E. Baret/MICHELIN

Abbaye du Thoronet

©David Lloyd/Dreamstime.com

Notre-Dame-de-Pépiole and La Trinité at St-Honorat de Lérins

ROMANESQUE PERIOD

In the 12C an architectural renaissance in Provence led to the construction of dozens of churches. The Romanesque style here is more eclectic than innovative, resulting not in large buildings, such as those in Burgundy, but rather unpretentious churches, remarkable for the bonding of their evenly-cut stones with fine mortar work.

The churches are plain outside, with austere façades broken only by powerful buttresses. The square belfry and the east end are sometimes decorated with applied blind arcades, known as **Lombard bands**, evidence of a north Italian influence.

On entering, the visitor is struck by the simplicity and austerity of the interior, which often consists of a single nave and a shallow transept. If aisles form part of the plan, the apse ends in a semicircle flanked by two apsidal chapels.

The interesting abbey of Le Thoronet (see Le THORONET p183) contains a church of the Cistercian Order with the wide transept and bare appearance characteristic of the churches built by the Benedictines. In contrast, however, the roof of broken barrel vaulting and the semicircular apse show the influence of local craftsmen.

GOTHIC TO BAROQUE

There are few Gothic buildings in the region. Provençal Gothic is a transitional style which depends heavily on Romanesque traditions. The best examples of this style can be found in the powerful groined vaulting in Grasse and the remarkable cloisters at Fréjus.

In the 15C, Good King René brought numerous Italian craftsmen to Provence. But although Provençal painting was influenced by the Renaissance, the architecture remained largely unaffected. Most churches in the comté de Nice are based on Romanesque, Piedmontese, Genoese models. Façades are adorned with pediments, niches and statues; inside, the architectural lines are often concealed by highly ornate altarpieces, panelling and baldaquin. The façade of the Lascaris palace (1648–80) and the colossal order (upright structural members spanning over two storeys) of the former Sénat de Nice, are a display of wealth and power, as are the regular lines and porticoes of place Garibaldi (1782–92), which structures the extension of the city along the road to Turin.

MODERN PERIOD

The 19C showed little originality and Baroque continued to be favoured for new constructions and restorations. The Romanesque-Byzantine style was employed in the church of Notre-Dame-de-la-Victoire-de-Lépante, St-Raphaël, the neo-Gothic style on the west front of the church at Cimiez and the neo-Romanesque style for Monaco's cathedral. Slightly later, the Casino in Monte-Carlo and the Hôtel Negresco in Nice were designed in an ostentatious style borrowed from the Belle Epoque (c 1900). Examples of 20C works include the church of Ste-Jeanne-d'Arc in Nice, the country church of St-Martin-de-Peille and the Chapelle du Rosaire des Dominicaines in Vence (also known as the Chapelle Matisse). The Fondation Maeght in St-Paul, the Musée Marc-Chagall in Nice and the striking property development of the Baie des Anges Marina in Villeneuve-Loubet or

Baroque-style house (1890),
Place l'Île-de-Beauté, Nice

E. Baret/MICHELIN

Port-Grimaud are other fine examples of modern architecture.

ART
PAINTING
Primitives

From the middle of the 15C to the middle of the 16C a school of painting, at first purely Gothic, then influenced by the Italian Renaissance, flourished in the comté de Nice. It is best-known through the works of **Louis Bréa** and **Durandi**. Bréa has been described as the "Provençal Fra Angelico", praise justified by the sincerity and sobriety of his brushwork and his gift for stressing the humanity of his subjects. However, his simplicity is a far cry from the mysticism of Fra Angelico, and his colours and dull tones lack the sparkle of the great Italian genius.

These Provençal artists worked mainly for the Penitent brotherhoods, which explains why their paintings are scattered in many churches and pilgrim chapels. They can be seen in Nice (where Bréa's brother Antoine and nephew François are represented), Gréolières, Antibes, Fréjus, Grasse and Monaco.

During the same period, the humblest churches of the comté de Nice were decorated with the most striking mural paintings. There are still fine examples in Coaraze, Venanson, Lucéram, Saorge and Notre-Dame-des-Fontaines, where Renaissance Primitive **Giovanni Canavesio**, working beside **Jean Baleison**, created Gothic-inspired works of exceptional quality.

The Classical Period

The 17C and 18C were marked by the work of the Parrocles, the Van Loos, Joseph Vernet and Hubert Robert. It is **Fragonard**, however, who is the pride of Provence. Rakish scenes were his favourites; he painted them with great enthusiasm and exquisite style. He often used the light-filled landscapes and flowering gardens around his native town of Grasse as a background to his jubilant party scenes.

Modern Painting

At the end of the 19C, numerous artists, representing the main trends in modern painting, were fascinated by the radiant light of the Mediterranean South of France.

Impressionism

The return of **Cézanne** to Provence (1881) was followed by many Impressionists such as **Berthe Morisot** (Nice),

Love Letter *(c. 1770)*
by Jean-Honoré Fragonard

Monet (Antibes) and **Renoir** (Cagnes), who sought to portray the subtle effects of light on Mediterranean landscapes. Monet's works marked the first appearance of the Riviera in painting: "I fence and wrestle with the sun" (letter from Monet to Rodin, January 1888).

Amphorae

From ancient times, the Provençal coasts have been plied by merchant ships, often of imposing size (more than 98ft/30m long) and heavily laden (up to 8,000 amphorae, or two-handled jars). The problems of manoeuvring these heavy boats with oar, sail and a lack of knowledge of the reefs led to innumerable shipwrecks. The wrecks salvaged with their cargoes of amphorae bear witness to the busy commercial exchanges between the regions producing these goods and consumers in urban centres. Navigation took place between April and September, when the weather conditions were most favourable. Foodstuffs such as wine, oil and fish were also transported.

The cargo on these boats was arranged at right angles to the keel; the pointed ends of the amphorae were wedged in place by the branches of trees, and the empty spaces between their necks were filled with the next row, thus assuring the whole cargo was stable. Some holds contained up to four levels of amphorae. Some fascinating examples are on display on the Ile Ste-Marguerite.

Regulations concerning underwater archaeological finds:

All cultural goods from the sea (amphorae, etc.) found on public property belong to the State. Therefore, anyone diving who finds any archaeological remains must leave them in place and untouched.

In the event of objects being brought up by chance (e.g. in nets), it is forbidden to dispose of them and the find should be reported to the nearest Affaires Maritimes within 48hr. Offenders are dealt with in the High Courts.

Lastly, as a small consolation, divers who have declared a find of a wreck or archaeological remains could benefit from a reward fixed by the government.

They mark a turning point in his career and, starting with his "series", he subsequently devoted himself to variations of light on the same subject. Renoir spent the last years of his life in Cagnes, painting flowers and fruits, landscapes and the people of the South.

Impressionism gave birth to a new school, **Pointillism**, a method of painting created by **Seurat**, which consisted of dividing shades into tiny dots of pure colour, distributed so as to intensify the effect of light.

Paul Signac, Seurat's disciple, established himself in St-Tropez in 1898 and many of his friends followed him, namely Manguin, Bonnard and Matisse.

Fauvism

Matisse and Dufy, who had settled in Nice, reacted against Impressionism and, through their use of pure and brill-iant colours, juxtaposed in simplified forms and perspectives, tried to express not just the fleeting sensation evoked by the spectacle of nature but the very thoughts and emotions of the artist.

Contemporary Movements

Picasso, co-founder with Braque of Cubism – an art concerned above all with form – was in his turn seduced by the Riviera and lived in Vallauris in 1946, then in Cannes and finally in Mougins.

Pierre Puget (1620–94)

This native of Marseille was one of the greatest French sculptors of the 17C. He began by carving the prows of ships and later developed huge carved poops. During a journey in Italy, he developed his many talents by working as a pupil of Pietro da Cortona.

After the fall of Fouquet, his patron, he established himself away from Versailles and was appointed director of Toulon harbour by Colbert, who thought well of him. Jealousy and conspiracy soon brought him into disgrace, so he threw himself into the embellishment of Toulon. His best-known works are the atlantes supporting the balcony of Toulon Town Hall and the *Milo of Croton*, which is exhibited in the Louvre in Paris. Puget's Baroque style could express power, movement and pathos.

Braque spent his last years painting in Le Cannet, while **Fernand Léger**, another Cubist painter, lived in Biot.

Dunoyer de Segonzac was tireless in his portrayal of St-Tropez.

Chagall found the light and flowers of Vence a marvellous stimulus to his multicoloured dreams.

Detail of Port St-Tropez by Paul Signac

©Photo Scala, Florence/Musee de l'Annonciade

Pablo Picasso in his studio at Vallauris in 1957

Other artists, such as **Kandinsky** in La Napoule, **Cocteau** in Menton, **Van Dongen** in Cannes, **Magnelli** in Grasse and **Nicolas de Staël** in Antibes, although not spending much time in the region, nevertheless left an indelible impression. At the same time in Nice in the 1960s a group of artists including **Arman**, **César**, Dufrêne, Hains, **Klein**, Raysse, Rotella, Spoerri, Tinguely and Villeglé formed the **Nouveau Réalisme** movement, later by Niki de Saint Phalle, Deschamps and Christo. They were reacting against **Abstraction**, which was the prevailing artistic trend after the war, and experimented with new approaches to reality, making use of objects found in the modern industrial and consumer world. Alongside these innovators were the members of the **Nice School**, who each sought their own vision (**Ben**, Bernar Venet, Sacha Sosno); and **Bernard Pagès** and **Claude Viallat**, who, closely linked to the theories of Conceptual Art, led to the creation of the Support-Surface movement in the 1970s *(for more on contemporary movements see NICE – Musée d'Art Moderne et d'Art Contemporain p307).*

LITERATURE

The region's fine climate and natural beauty, which so appealed to artists throughout the centuries, has also worked their magic on writers and poets from around the world. Tobias Smollett, whose *Travels Through Italy and France* was published in 1766, was an early visitor, who helped put the Riviera on the literary map. In the second half of the 19C, the area acquired its second name when French author Stephen Liégeard published his guide to the Provençal coast called *La Côte d'Azur.*

By now, the tide of visiting authors had become a flood. Some came for the sake of their health, others to escape unhappy marriages or persecution, or heavy taxes, and still more for the way of life. These literary refugees include some of the art's greatest names: D.H. Lawrence, James Joyce, Vladimir Nabokov, Berthold Brecht, Katherine Mansfield, W.B. Yeats, Graham Greene, Anthony Burgess, W. Somerset Maugham, Aldous Huxley, H.G. Wells, Ernest Hemingway, F. Scott Fitzgerald, Dorothy Parker and James Thurber.

For some, the Riviera provided a comfortable place in which to write about distant lands and the list of titles written along this stretch of coastline is vast. Others, such as F. Scott Fitzgerald in his tragic *Tender is the Night* (1934), were inspired by the people and landscapes they found there.

Not all the writers who flocked to the Riviera were foreign, however. Jean Cocteau arrived on the Côte d'Azur at a young age, spending much of his life around Menton, while Colette lived in St-Tropez for 10 years in the 1920s and 1930s.

CINEMA

The Riviera's association with moving pictures is almost as long as the history of film itself. In 1895, the pioneering brothers Auguste and Louis Lumière shot several of their first works in and around their summer residence, the Villa du Clos des Plages in La Ciotat, including *L'Arrivée d'un Train en Gare de La Ciotat* (The Arrival of a Train at La Ciotat Station), which so alarmed early audiences. The seaside town's cinematic credentials don't stop there; the Eden Theatre, which opened soon after, is the world's oldest-surviving movie theatre. During the early decades of the 20C, the "seventh art" put down firm roots in the Riviera, with stars and directors alike lured by the light, the climate and the way of life. The Victorine, the area's first film studio, opened in Nice in 1919, around the same time as Hollywood was setting up shop. Its acquisition, six years later, by Hollywood director Rex Ingram established it as the focus of the burgeoning European film industry.

The launch of an international film festival in Cannes in 1946, originally planned for 1939, served to confirm the Riviera's place in the cinematic universe and heralded a "golden era" for film-making in the region. The following decades produced US and French classics such as Alfred Hitchcock's *To Catch A Thief* (1956) starring Cary Grant and Grace Kelly, while Roger Vadim's *Et Dieu... créa*

la femme of the same year catapulted both Brigitte Bardot and the fishing port of St-Tropez into the limelight.

Since the 1970s, increasing competition from other parts of Europe – particularly after the fall of Communism in eastern Europe from the late 1980s – has helped to create a more challenging era. However, the industry's leading lights still flock to Cannes each May for the festival; more than 300 of them have added their handprint and signature to the Pavement of the Stars in front of the Palais des Festivals since its inception in 1985. Nice's Victorine studio still attracts international as well as local stars.

MUSIC

Though eclipsed by a starrier literary and cinematic heritage, the Riviera has a musical tradition, too. The *gaboulet-tambourin*, a cross between a flute and a tambourine thought to date from the 13C, is an intrinsic element of the local traditional songs and dances, in particular the *farandole*. On the classical side, Nice's Opera opened in 1776, and hosted many of the south's most famous concerts; the lyric society of Nice was founded in the 19C, and still organises private concerts as well as weekly open-air free concerts in the Albert 1er garden.

Cannes Film Festival

In 1939, Jean Zay, the French Minister of Fine Arts, founded the International Film Festival at Cannes, which was chosen for its sunny climate.

The inauguration, planned for September, was cancelled when the Second World War broke out. The real launch of the festival took place on 20 September 1946 in the former Casino Municipal near the Old Port; the festival returned to this site 40 years later at the time of the inauguration of the Nouveau Palais des Festivals in 1983.

In 1949 the festival moved to the Palais de la Croisette (demolished in 1988). In spite of its suspension in 1948 and 1950 for financial reasons and an interruption in May 1968, the fame of the festival has grown over the years, with a star-studded jury presided over by celebrities.

During the 10 days of the event, several competitions take place: the *Selection Officielle* (competing for the prestigious **Palme d'Or**); *Hors-Compétition* (not in competition); *Semaine de la Critique* (critics' picks); *Quinzaine des Réalisateurs* (film directors' programme); *Caméra d'Or* (first films); *Un Certain Regard* (independent productions). The great media interest generated by the festival offers a unique springboard for the films screened at the event, including both mainstream and fringe productions.

Nature

TOPOGRAPHY
A LANDSCAPE OF CONTRASTS
Coastline
Extending from Bandol to Menton, the Riviera landscape is extremely varied (☙ see The Coast p91). The sheltered inlets between the red rock promontories of the Esterel differ markedly from the great sweeping bays and flat shores which gently punctuate the coastline; while elsewhere on the coast, such as at Cap Sicié, mountains plunge steeply into the sea, sheer as a wall.

Relief
Inland, the countryside is just as varied. The fertile plains and foothills of Provence are covered by typically Mediterranean vegetation dotted with barren, rugged heights like those to the north of Toulon. The mountain masses of the Maures, which rise to no more than 2,600ft/800m, are crisscrossed by valleys and ravines and covered with fine forests of cork oak and chestnut; the Esterel massif is dominated by the outline of Mont Vinaigre and the peaks of Pic de l'Ours and Pic du Cap Roux. The country behind Cannes and Nice is one of undulating hills stretching to the Pre-Alps of Grasse, where gorges have been cut into the plateaux and the mountain chains are split by rifts (clues), particularly in Haute-Provence.

Behind the Riviera the peaks of the Pre-Alps of Nice rise to more than 6,560ft/2,000m, while further to the north and northeast the true Alpine heights tower over the Italian border.

Climate
The winter months are relatively warm on the Nice coast (the average temperatures for January in Nice are max 55°F/13°C; min 39°F/4°C), although the icy air of the ski slopes is less than two hours away by car; in summer the coast is fairly hot in contrast to the exhilarating coolness of the mountain resorts.

Vegetation
The forest of Turini, with its centuries-old beeches and firs, has a northern feel; the woods of the Maures and the Esterel are more typically southern, carpeted with their cork oaks and pines, periodically ravaged by forest fires. The wild scrub and underbrush of the mountain maquis contrast starkly with the orderly rows of the orange and lemon groves of the plains; in many western areas, lavender and thyme grow wild in vast cultivated fields of flowers; in the pre-Alps of Nice, the palm trees, agaves and cacti of the coast merge into the firs and larches of the highlands.

Baie de Briande, St-Tropez Peninsula

E. Baret/MICHELIN

Activity

The coastline is extremely busy in summer, with the busiest roads, largest towns and best-equipped resorts concentrated there. Inland, however, there is peace and quiet, even complete solitude, with sleepy towns and old villages perched like eagles' nests high up on the hillsides.
(see HILL VILLAGES p358).

Economy

Nice is the coast's tourist capital and the centre of a thriving high-tech industry. The busy flower trade and the production of perfume exist side by side with new research centres dealing with oceanography and data processing.

Land of the Sun

The region is united, of course, by one common factor – the Mediterranean climate. Here, the sun shines almost continually (2,725 hours annually in Nice compared to 1,465 hours in London). Except in high summer, outlines are sharpened and natural features acquire an architectural aspect in the clear air. The shining blue of the sea and sky blends with the green of the forests, the silver-grey of the olive trees, the red porphyry rock and the white limestone.

TERRAIN

Provence was formed from two mountain systems: one very old – the Maures and the Esterel – the other much younger – the Provençal Pyrenean ranges and the Pre-Alps.

The Maures

This crystalline mountain mass spreads from the River Gapeau in the west to the Argens Valley in the east, and from the sea in the south to a long depression in the north, beyond which are the limestone peaks of the Pre-Alps. Long low parallel ranges, covered with fine forests which have not escaped recent forest fires, make up the Maures Massif; the highest point is La Sauvette (556ft/779m).

The Esterel

Separated from the Maures by the lower Argens Valley, the Esterel, has also been eroded by time and therefore lies at a low altitude. Its highest peak is Mont Vinaigre at 2,027ft/618m. The deep ravines cut into its sides and its jagged crests dispel any impression of mere hills. The Esterel, like the Maures, was once entirely covered with forests of pine and cork oak but these have been periodically ravaged by forest fires.

Shrubs and bushes grow beneath the trees (tree heathers, arbutus, lentisks and lavender), while scrub (maquis) covers the open ground. In spring the red and white flowers of the cistus, yellow mimosa and broom, and white heather and myrtle form a brilliant floral patchwork.

Provençal Ranges

These short limestone chains, arid and rugged, rise to heights of 1,200–3,500ft/400–1,150m. Of Pyrenean origin with a highly complex structure, they do not have the continuity of those of Alpine origin such as the Southern Pre-Alps. The most southerly peaks, just north of Toulon, are the Gros Cerveau (1,407ft/429m), which is bisected by the Ollioules gorges, Mont Faron (1,778ft/542m), which dominates the town; and Le Coudon; Montagne de la Loube rises 17.4mi/28km to the north. Between the ranges are fertile valleys, where the traditional crops of cereals, vines and olives are cultivated.

Maritime Alps and Mercantour

To the northeast, the horizon is dominated by a vast mountainous mass (alt. 4,922–9,515ft/1,500–2,900m), which is dissected by the upper valleys of the Var, Tinée, Vésubie and Roya. On the Italian border these mountains meet the great crystalline massif, Le Mercantour, the peaks of which exceed 9,842.5ft/3,000m.

Pre-Alps

This region contains a large part of the Southern Pre-Alps. Between the River Verdon and River Var the **Pre-Alps of**

River Loup

Grasse are formed by a series of parallel east-west chains, with altitudes varying between 3,609–5,249ft/1,100–1,600m, which are frequently indented by wild and narrow rifts *(clues)*.

The **Pre-Alps of Nice** rise from the coast in tiers to a height of 3,281ft/1,000m, affording a wide variety of **views** inland from Nice and Menton. These ranges, which are Alpine in origin, run north-south before abruptly changing direction to finish up parallel with the coast.

Provençal Tableland

From Canjuers plateau to the Vence pass, the Pre-Alps are rimmed with a tableland of undulating limestone plateaux, similar to the *causses*, through which water penetrates into rifts that feed resurgent streams like the Siagne. The gorge carved out by the River Loup is very picturesque.

Below lies a **depression** or "lowland", where the towns of Vence, Grasse and Draguignan are situated. Beyond the River Argens, the depression extends east down the river to Fréjus and west towards Brignoles; the main axis, however, is southwest to Toulon to the northern slopes of the Maures and Le Luc basin.

RIVERS

Mediterranean rivers are really torrents and their volume, which varies considerably from a mere trickle to a gushing flood, is governed by melting snow, rainfall and evaporation, depending on the season.

The lack of rain and the intense evaporation of the summer months reduce the rivers to dribbles of water along their stony beds.

In spring and autumn the rains fall suddenly and violently, and even the smallest streams are immediately filled with rushing water.

The flow of the Argens varies from 60–132,000gal/3–600m^3 a second and that of the Var from 17–5,000m^3/3,790 to over a million gallons. At the height of its spate the Var is more than half a mile wide and the stain of its muddy waters can be seen in the sea as far away as Villefranche on the far side of Nice.

The water level of rivers in limestone regions is always uneven. Rains seep into the ground through numerous fissures to reappear often a considerable distance away as large springs gushing out from the sides of valleys. Some of the springs rise in riverbeds, such as the gushers *(foux)*, which cause the River Argens to flood. Most of the rivers with torrential rates of flow transport material but the River Argens is the only one to have built up an alluvial plain comparable to those of the Languedoc coast. All the torrential rivers have created beautiful valleys, deep gorges (the Loup and the Siagne gorges) or rifts (*clues* – the Clue de Gréolières), which are among the attractions of inland Provence.

CAVES AND CHASMS

In contrast to the region's deeply dissected green valleys, such as the gorges of the Loup and the Siagne, the Caussols plateau (*see ST-VALLIER-DE-THIEY p250*) rolls away to the far horizon, stony and deserted, a typical karst relief. The dryness of the soil is due to the calcareous nature of the rock, which absorbs rain like a sponge.

Water Infiltration

Rainwater, charged with carbonic acid, dissolves the carbonate of lime found in the limestone. Depressions, which are usually circular in shape and small in size, known as **cloups** or **sotchs**, are then formed. The dissolution of the limestone rocks, containing large quantities of salt or gypsum, produces a rich soil particularly suitable for growing crops; when the *cloups* increase in size they form large, closed depressions known as **dolines**. Where rainwater infiltrates deeply through the countless fissures in the plateau, the hollowing out and dissolution of the calcareous layer produces wells or natural chasms, which are called **avens**. Little by little, the chasms grow, lengthen and branch off, communicating with each other and enlarging into caves.

Le Boréon in the upper valley of Vésubie

E. Baret/MICHELIN

Underground Rivers

The infiltrating waters finally produce underground galleries and collect to form a more or less swiftly flowing river. The river widens its course and often changes level, to fall in cascades. Where the rivers run slowly, they form lakes above natural dams known as **gours**, which are raised layer by layer by deposits of carbonate of lime. The dissolution of the limestone also continues above water-level in these subterranean galleries: blocks of stone fall from the roof and domes form, the upper parts pointing towards the surface of the earth. When the roof of the dome wears thin it may cave in, disclosing the cavity from above and opening the chasm.

THE COAST

The mainly rocky coastline reflects the different types of mountain and plateau to be found inland, emerging as cliffs and rocks where they meet the sea.

The Toulon Coast

This highly indented section of the coast provides well-sheltered harbours, Bandol and Sanary bays and the outstanding port of Toulon. The stretches of almost vertical cliffs are interrupted by some fine beaches.

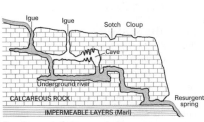

Development of a resurgent spring

The Maures Coast

Between Hyères and St-Raphaël, the Maures Massif meets the sea and the coastal scenery offers charming sites and enchanting **views**.

The Giens Peninsula, formerly an island, is now joined to the mainland by two sandy isthmuses. Nearby are the Hyères islands, densely covered with vegetation, and the Fréjus plain, once a wide bay but now filled by alluvial deposits brought down by the Argens. Characteristic also of this particular section of the coast are great promontories such as Cap Bénat and the St-Tropez Peninsula, narrow tongues of land such as Cap Nègre and Cap des Sardinaux, and wide bays like the Bormes harbour and the gulf of St-Tropez.

The Esterel Coast

The red porphyry rocks of the Esterel Massif, steep and rugged, form a striking contrast with the blue of the sea. Along this stretch of coast the mountains thrust great promontories into the sea, between inlets *(calanques)* and small bays. Offshore, the surface of the sea is scattered with thousands of rocks and small, green moss-covered islets, while submerged reefs can be seen beneath the clear water. The Corniche d'Or (*see Massif de l'ESTEREL p213*) is internationally reputed for its breathtaking scenery, superb **viewpoints** and resorts.

The Antibes Coast

Once again the vista changes between Cannes and Nice. The shore is no longer eaten away by the sea; it is flat and opens into wide bays. On this smooth, unbroken coast, the Cap d'Antibes peninsula is the sole promontory.

The Riviera Proper

From Nice to Menton the Alps plunge abruptly into the sea. Here, the coastline forms a natural terrace, facing the Mediterranean but isolated from its hinterland. Cap Ferrat and Cap Martin are the two main promontories along this stretch of coast. The term Riviera, which has already passed into the language of geography, is applied to this type of coastline. A triple roadway has been cut over the steep slopes, lined with villas and terraced gardens.

THE MEDITERRANEAN SEA

The Mediterranean is Europe's bluest sea. The shade – cobalt blue to artists – comes from the clarity of the water. Visitors soon realise that the colour often changes depending on the nature of the sky, the light, the seabed and the depth of water so that at times the "blue Mediterranean" is opal or a warm grey.

The Water

The temperature of the water, governed on the surface by the sun's heat, is constant (55.4°F/13°C) from 650–13,000ft/200–4,000m downwards, whereas in the Atlantic it drops from 57.2–35°F/14–2°C. This is an important factor in the climate, for the sea cools the air in summer and warms it in winter. Rapid evaporation makes the water noticeably more salty than that of the Atlantic. The waves are small, short and choppy; storms come and go quickly.

The Tides

Tides are almost non-existent (about 10in/25cm). Sometimes when the wind is very strong the tide may reach as much as 3ft/1m. These levels are markedly different from the tides of the Atlantic or from the tides of 40–50ft/13–15m round Mont-St-Michel, off the Normandy coast. This relative tidal stability has resulted in the Mediterranean being chosen as the base level for all French altitudes.

The Provençal coastline drops sharply into water that becomes relatively deep a short distance from the shore. Between Nice and Cap Ferrat soundings indicate a depth of 3,281ft/1,000m about half a mile out.

THE SEASONS

A Superb Climate

Crowds come flocking in summer and the tourist season lasts almost the whole year.

The Côte d'Azur is one of the most inviting names in the world! Properly speaking, the name Riviera applies to the French coast between Nice and Menton and to the Italian coast between Ventimiglia and Genoa. English visitors, at first for health reasons but later more and more in search of pleasure, have been attracted to the Riviera (especially Nice) since the 18C. The Côte d'Azur (Bandol to Menton) has now become widely known as the French Riviera.

Winter

The proverbial mildness of the French Riviera is due to a number of factors: a low latitude, the presence of the sea, which moderates temperature variations, a wholly southern aspect, and the screen of hills and mountains, which protects it from cold winds. The average temperature for January in Nice is 46°F/8°C. Icy winds blow from the east and from the southeast bringing rain. Fog and sea-mists appear only on the coast in the height of summer and harsh winters with ice and snow are rare.

The thermometer may rise to 72°F/22°C, but at sunset and during the night the temperature drops suddenly and considerably. There is little rainfall; it is the dew that keeps the vegetation fresh. The hinterland is cold and often snow-covered but the air is limpid and the sun brilliant – an ideal climate for winter sports.

Spring

Short but violent showers are characteristic of springtime on the Riviera. This is when the flowers are at their best and a joy to look at. The only drawback is the *mistral*, which blows most frequently at this season, especially west of Toulon. The mountains, however, act as a buffer and the wind is never so intense as it can be in western Provence and the Rhône Valley.

The Romans made a dreaded god of this fearsome wind. It comes from the northwest in cold gusts; after several days this powerful blast of clean air has purified everything and the windswept sky is bluer than ever.

Summer

The coast offers an average temperature of 79°F/26°C throughout July and August. The heat, however, is bearable because it is tempered by the fresh breeze that blows during the daytime. This is not the season for flowers: overwhelmed by drought, the vegetation seems to fall into slumber.

The hinterland offers a wide variety of places to stay at varying altitudes up to 5,905ft/1,800m; the higher one climbs the more invigorating the air.

Autumn

There are plenty of perfect days during the Mediterranean autumn, punctuated by violent storms after which the sun reappears, brilliant and warm. In the whole year, there is an average of only 86 days of rain in Nice (150 in London), but the quantity of water which falls is higher (34in/863mm in Nice against under 24in/609mm in London).

FLORA AND FAUNA

Plants and trees do not grow in the same way on the Riviera as they do further north. New shoots appear, as they do elsewhere, in the spring but a second growth begins in the autumn and continues throughout most of the winter. The dormant period is during the summer when the hot, dry climate favours only those plants that are especially adapted to resist drought. These have long tap roots, glossy leaves which reduce transpiration, bulbs acting as reservoirs of moisture and perfumes which they release to form a kind of protective vapour.

TREES

Olive Trees

2,500 years ago, the Greeks brought olive trees to Provence, where they grow equally well in limestone or sandy soils. The olive has been called the immortal tree for, grafted or wild, it will always grow from the same stock. Those grown from cuttings die relatively young, at about 300 years old. Along the coast, the trees reach gigantic dimensions, attaining 65.6ft/20m in height, their

Umbrella pines of Porquerolles

S. Sauvignier/ MICHELIN

domes of silver foliage 65.6ft/20m in circumference and trunks 13ft/4m round the base. The olive tree, which has more than 60 varieties, is found up to an altitude of 1,968.5ft/600m and marks the limit of the Mediterranean climate. It grows mainly on valley floors and on hillsides. The trees begin to bear fruit between their sixth and twelfth year and are in full yield at 20 or 25; the olives are harvested every two years. Olive groves are numerous in the areas around Draguignan, Sospel and at Breil, in the Roya Valley.

Oak Trees

The oaks native to the Mediterranean region are evergreen. Durmast and holm oaks grow in chalky soil at altitudes below 2,624.5ft/800m. As scrub-oaks, they are a characteristic feature of the *garrigue* (rocky, limestone moors). In its fully developed state the holm oak is a tree with a short, thick-set trunk covered in grey-black bark and with a dense, rounded crown. The cork oak is distinguished by its large dark-coloured acorns and its rough bark. Every eight to twelve years the thick cork bark is stripped off to expose a reddish brown trunk.

Pine Trees

The three types of pine to be found in the Mediterranean region have unmistakable silhouettes.

The maritime pine, which grows only on limestone soil, has dark, blue-tinged green needles and deep red bark.

The **umbrella pine** is typically Mediterranean and owes its name to the easily recognisable outline. It is often found growing alone.

The **Aleppo pine** is a Mediterranean species that thrives on chalky soil along the coast; it has a twisted, grey trunk and lighter, less dense, foliage.

Other Provençal Trees – The smooth-trunked **plane tree** and the **lotus tree** shade the courtyards, streets and squares and also line the roads.

The dark silhouette of the coniferous, evergreen **cypress** is a common feature of the countryside; planted in rows, the pyramidal cypress forms an effective windbreak.

The common **almond tree**, a member of the Rosaceae, is widespread in Provence and blossoms early. The robust **chestnut** flourishes in the Maures Massif. Certain mountain species of **fir** and **larch** are to be found in the Alps; the forest of Turini is a fine fir-growing region.

Exotic Trees

In parks and gardens and along the roads stand magnificent **eucalyptus trees**. This hardy specimen is particularly suited to the climate. In winter another Australian import, **mimosa**, covers the slopes of the Tanneron Massif with a yellow mantle.

The greatest concentration of **palm trees** is to be found in the Hyères district. Two types most common to the Riviera are the date palm, with its smooth, tall trunk sweeping upwards, and the Canary palm, which is much shorter and has a rough, scaly trunk.

Orange and **lemon groves** flourish on the coastal stretches between Cannes and Antibes, and Monaco and Menton.

BUSHES AND SHRUBS

The **kermes oak** is a bushy evergreen shrub, which rarely grows more than 3.3ft/1m in height. Its name comes from the kermes, an insect halfway between a cochineal fly and a flea, which lives throughout its existence attached to stems of the oak.

The **lentisk** is an evergreen shrub with paired leaves on either side of the main stem and no terminal leaf. The fruit is a small globular berry, which turns from red to black when mature.

The **pistachio** is a deciduous shrub which can grow to a height of 13–16.4ft/ 4–5m. Leaves grow in groups of five to eleven, one of which is terminal. The fruit is a very small berry, red at first, ripening to brown.

The **Mediterranean thistle** is a perennial, which attains a height of 3.3ft/1m. Its irregular pointed leaves are bright green on top and covered with white down on the underside.

The Garrigue

Some of the limestone areas are so stony (Vence pass road and D 955 from Draguignan to Montferrat) that even thorns (kermes oak, gorse and thistle) and aromatic plants (thyme, lavender and rosemary) can survive only here and there in between the bare rocks; this is the *garrigue*.

Lavandin

Lavandin is a hybrid plant resulting from the cross of true lavender with spike lavender. Its flowers may be blue, like true lavender or grey, like aspic. The plants are used for landscaping but they also produce oil of an excellent quality. In France, lavandin has been grown in Provence on a large scale for many years. Thanks to its camphoraceous smell with strong eucalyptus overtones, it is often used to scent soaps and detergents.

The Maquis

Scrub *(maquis)* thrives on sandy soil and forms a thick carpet of greenery, which is often impenetrable. In May and June when the cistus is in flower it is a marvellous spectacle, especially in the coverts of the Esterel.

SUCCULENTS

Some varieties of succulent are African in character: Barbary figs, agaves, cacti and aloes grow in open ground. Ficoids, with large pink and white flowers, cling to ancient walls. The **aloe** has thick and fleshy leaves, from which a bitter juice is extracted for medicinal use.

The **Barbary fig** is an unusual plant from Central America, which grows in arid soil in hot climates; its broad, thick, fleshy leaves bristle with spines. The Moroccans call it the Christian fig; it is also known as the "prickly pear".

For a wider knowledge of exotic flora, take a stroll in:

♦ *Jardin Exotique in Monaco*
♦ *Jardin de la Villa Thuret in Cap d'Antibes (⊂see ANTIBES p270)*
♦ *Several botanic gardens in Menton*
♦ *Domaine du Rayol (including Val Rameh ⊂see p352)*
♦ *Jardin Olbius Riquier in Hyères.*

FOREST FIRES

From time immemorial the scourge of the Provençal woodland, especially in the Maures and the Esterel, has been the

The Three Musketeers of the "Silent World"

In August 1937, two young divers with homemade equipment based on recycled tubes attempted to beat a harpooning record. In the absence of any substantial booty, J.Y. Cousteau and P. Taillez found that their dive in the midst of shoals of grouper and bass revealed the potential of underwater exploration.

A third leading harpoonist, J. Dumas, soon joined them and the hunt for pictures superseded the hunt for sea-bass. In the autumn of 1943, Dumas, experimenting with an aqualung, dived to a depth of 203ft/62m and was affected by nitrogen narcosis (rapture of the deep). After the Second World War the underwater explorers' odyssey was immortalised on film and their craft, *Calypso*, was seen all around the world.

forest fire, which causes more damage by man than deforestation, now carefully monitored, and destruction by goats, which live on the tender young shoots. During the summer the dried-up plants of the underbrush, pine needles, resins exuded by leaves and twigs are all highly combustible and sometimes catch fire spontaneously. Once started, a fire may spread to the pines with disastrous results in a strong wind. Great walls of flame, sometimes 6mi/10km in length and 100ft/30m high, spread at speeds of 2–3mi/5–6km per hour. When the fire has passed, nothing remains standing except the blackened skeletons of trees, while a thick layer of white ash covers the ground.

The Riviera still bears the scars of the particularly severe forest fires that raged during the summer of 2003, fuelled by the worst drought and heatwave in 15 years, and it will be many years before regeneration of its natural habitat is complete.

Preventive measures include the removal of undergrowth near residential areas, the creation of fire-breaks and the appointment of fire-watchers and patrols. Active intervention is provided by the fire brigade and the airborne water carriers based in Marignane. In the event of a major fire risk, the ALARME plan enables access roads to private homes to be cleared for firefighters and limits the movements of walkers.

🛈 For information on the closures in forests, there is a recorded message service (📞*04 94 47 35 45*) for the use of hikers.

MEDITERRANEAN MARINE LIFE

Life in the Mediterranean Sea resembles a house full of animal tenants with astonishing characteristics, living

Cacti in the Jardin Exotique, Eze

© Sergio Pitamitz/age fotostock

one above the other. During an under water dive, the following species may be observed.

Brown Grouper

Depending on its age and size, the grouper is first female, then male. It changes sex at about nine years old when it weighs 22lb/10kg. Since the fish can live for about 50 years, it spends most of its life as a male.

The young female grouper lives on rocky seabeds in shallow water (less than 33ft/10m deep), which makes it an easy prey for underwater hunters and other predators. As it reaches adulthood, it makes its home in holes in the rocks at a depth of at least 164ft/50m, where it lives as a formidable carnivore at the extremity of the marine food chain. It may eventually reach a length of 4ft/1.2m and weigh 66–88lb/30–40kg. This fish, which had become very rare in the Mediterranean, has benefited from a 5-year moratorium prohibiting the catching of groupers.

The Parc Naturel de Port-Cros is now designated to protect the grouper within an area around the island.

Jellyfish

Jellyfish, which appear seasonally in coastal waters, sometimes cause problems for holidaymakers. The most common species, **pelagia**, can sting with its mouth, tentacles and umbrella. Its poison, which is intended to immobilise prey, is powerful enough to cause redness and burning of the skin. The population of pelagia follows a 12-year cycle, depending on climatic conditions, and their arrival is usually preceded by a very dry spring. Another species of jellyfish, the Portuguese Man-of-War, has long tentacles (up to 33ft/10m), which are invisible to swimmers and have a very powerful sting. They are fortunately rare in the Mediterranean.

Posidonia

This flowering plant, which has bunches of long, dark-green leaves, plays an essential role in the Mediterranean environment. Its rhizomes grow slowly,

Pelagia noctiluca

©Planctonvideo/Dreamstime.com

thus allowing it to fix the sediments from the coast and create a habitat rich in oxygen and favourable to many animal species. When the posidonia dies, these animal species either die out or migrate.

A dive into the colourful world of the posidonia provides the possibility of seeing many amazing species. The **sea cucumber**, also known as holothurian, is the dustbin of the sandy seabed and lives only in the posidonia. The **sea-slug**, found all over the Mediterranean, is a white mollusc with brown spots, which contrasts with the red sponges. The **striped weever fish** lives on the seabed near the posidonia, buried in the sand with just its head visible. It has an extremely poisonous dorsal fin, the sting of which can be serious. The **sea-horse** likes to hide near its relative, the **pipe-fish**, whose amazing threadlike form, with trumpet-shaped mouth, mimics the leaves of the posidonia, among which it lives.

In the last few decades harbour works and construction along the coast have caused much sedimentation and the resultant pollution is endangering the fragile habitat. Since 1989, a genetically altered strain of algae, the non-toxic **taxifolia**, has spread rapidly along the French Riviera. It is feared the spread of this alga, originally created to decorate aquariums, may be harmful to the posidonia, as well as other marine life in the Mediterranean.

DISCOVERING
THE FRENCH RIVIERA

TOULON AND AROUND

The city of Toulon and its surrounding villages on the western fringes of the French Riviera are often overlooked by travellers passing through on their way to Provence. But this dynamic region has done much to restore its image over the past decade, offering pleasant surprises throughout the year to curious visitors who take the time to explore its mountain views, charming seaside resorts and historic naval harbour.

Highlights

1 Try your hand at wine-tasting in the prestigious **Bandol Vineyards** (p99)

2 Visit the famous harbour of **Toulon**, home of the French Navy since the 16C (p109)

3 Take in the spectacular views from the top of **Mont Faron** (p111)

4 Explore the Gallo-Roman villa at the **Musée de Tauroentum** (p118)

5 Snorkel in the blue waters off the **Îles des Embiez** (p122)

The Largest Naval Base in France

As the third largest city in the Provence-Alpes-Côte-d'Azur region (after Nice to the east and Marseilles to the west), Toulon and its immense harbour have sustained the local economy since the Middle Ages.

Aside from being one of the leading commercial shipping ports in the Mediterranean, Toulon once served as a defensive port for Provence, a departure point for maritime exploration, a renowned centre for ship-building and fishing, and today houses France's largest naval base. While traditionally not considered a tourist destination, the city has restored much of its old town and the public areas of the port used for local sightseeing cruises.

Resort Towns

Although the arrival of the railway in the mid-1800s ended much of the maritime passenger traffic, it ushered in a new era of seasonal tourism that would rejuvenate sleepy fishing villages such as Bandol, Six-Fours-les-Plages and Île des Embiez. Not just popular with French tourists seeking vacation homes, it was also a magnet for writers, filmmakers and artists such as Thomas Mann, Katherine Mansfield, Aldous Huxley and Marcel Pagnol.

Marine explorers Philippe Tailliez, Jacques-Yves Cousteau and Frédéric Dumas perfected their scuba-diving equipment in the waters off Bandol, Sanary and Embiez.

Today these resorts are carefully monitored to protect the local flora and fauna, botanical coastal trails and thriving marine preserves.

Toulon naval harbour

Bandol vineyards in Le Castellet with a view to the perched village

©David Noble/Pictures Colour Library

The Mountains

Toulon and its neighbouring coastal towns are dominated by the towering Mont Faron, Le Gros Cerveau and Mont Caume. A network of steep, winding roads allow you to explore these rocky peaks where you can enjoy panoramic **views** over Toulon and the entire Mediterranean. If you prefer to avoid the verginous drive, take the cable car from Toulon to the top of Mont Faron, where you'll find a monument commemorating the 1944 Allied landings in Provence. One of the more charming perched villages in this area is Le Castellet, which offers **views** over the Bandol vineyards from its historic ramparts.

The Climate

Toulon has the warmest temperatures in metropolitan France, averaging 8.8°C/48°F in winter, although the *mistral* winds make it seem cooler when they blow with their legendary ferocity. Sunny days predominate, with short but heavy rainfall in early spring and late autumn. Its relatively mild climate and sheltered resorts make it a popular destination year round. This climate is also the secret behind one of the most prestigious Côte de Provence appellations, the strong red wines of Bandol, which can be tasted in many of the region's cellars and wine shops.

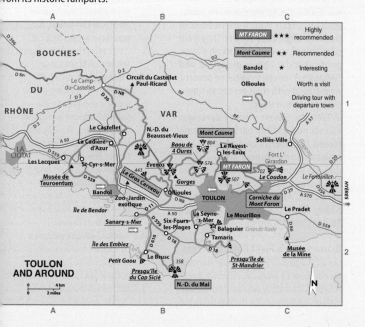

Toulon★

Var

Dominated by the majestic peak of Mont Faron, France's largest naval port sits in one of the Mediterranean's most beautiful natural harbours. Although cruise ships and military freighters have long since replaced the galleys of yesteryear, it is still possible to explore Toulon's nautical heritage in the narrow alleyways of the old town and the bustling quaysides of its historic port.

A BIT OF HISTORY

Mediterranean stronghold

Settled by Ligurian and Celtic tribes, Toulon came under Roman authority in 120BC. Annexed by France in 1481, it grew rapidly after Henri IV ordered the building of its first arsenal in 1595. The port was fortified and expanded by Louis XIV in the late 17C.

The Age of the Galleys

One of the attractions for travellers of the 17C and 18C was to visit the galleys moored in the old port. The triangular sails and masts of these vessels were decorated by craftsmen from the arsenal. Galley slaves were used to power the ships. Four men were needed to pull each of the 25 or 26 oars. They were criminals of various ilk, Turkish slaves, political and religious prisoners, and "volunteers" driven by extreme poverty, who stayed with their oars at all times, even to eat and sleep.

In 1748, the system of galley slaves was abandoned and the oarsmen became forced labourers, building ships and maintaining the harbour. This penal colony, the Bagne de Toulon, is described in detail by Victor Hugo in his novel *Les Misérables*. At its peak the colony held nearly 4,000 convicts. The Bagne de Toulon closed in 1874.

Bonaparte's First Feat of Arms

On 27 August 1793, Royalists handed Toulon over to an Anglo-Spanish fleet. A Republican army was sent to Toulon, with its artillery under the command of

▶ **Population:** 167,816.

◉ **Michelin Map:** 340 K7; local map pp104–105.

ℹ **Info:** Pl. Raimu. ℘04 94 18 53 00. www.toulontourisme.com.

▶ **Location:** The Old Town is located on the Old Port, or Vieille Darse, bounded to the east by Cours Lafayette, to the west by rue Anatole-France and to the north by rue Landrin. The greater Toulon area includes the towns surrounding the harbours as well as the Bay of Lazaret formed by the peninsula of the Presqu'île de St-Mandrier. The Old Town is accessible to pedestrians only.

🅿 **Parking:** The largest parking areas are located on Place d'Armes, Place de la Liberté/Palais Liberté, and at the Centre Mayol.

◉ **Don't Miss:** The most appealing areas of Toulon are the winding streets of the Old Town and the old port around the Arsenal and Quai Cronstadt. If you have access to a car, don't miss the **views** from the top of Mont Faron.

🕐 **Timing:** Plan on a half day for the walking tours, more if you plan to do some shopping along the Rues d'Alger, Jean-Jaurès, Hoche and Place Victor-Hugo. The afternoon can include a boat tour of the harbour and Presqu'île de St-Mandrier, then driving excursions up to Mont Faron.

👪 **Kids:** Children fascinated by model-making will find plenty to keep them occupied in Toulon's arsenal and naval museums.

Toulon and Mont Faron

© Helen Shorey/iStockphoto.com

an obscure junior captain called Bona-parte. A battery was installed facing the British fort, called "little Gibraltar", but was subjected to such terrible fire that the gunners faltered. The young Corsi-an set the example; he laid the guns and manned the sponge-rod, and soon had enough fearless volunteers. "Little Gibraltar" fell on 17 December. The for-eign fleet withdrew after burning the French ships, the arsenal and the provi-sion depots.

Second World War

In November 1942, in response to the Allied Landings in North Africa, Hitler decided to invade the French free zone. To prevent French ships falling into the hands of the enemy, the French admi-alty decided to scupper the entire fleet on 27 November. On 19 August 1944, four days after the Allied Landing on the Maures beaches, French troops attacked the Toulon defences, a plan of which had been smuggled out in 1942 by sailors in the Resistance. The city was liberated on 26 August.

Post-war

Up to 1939 Toulon had been too depend-ent on the naval dockyard and isolated geographically. After the war, efforts were made to diversify its economy: the Arsenal's production was broadened and the port's commercial trade was developed alongside a number of new industries. The construction of holiday homes in the region sustained the build-ing trade after the post-war reconstruc-tion boom, while road improvements made the town more accessible.

WALKING TOUR

As you stroll through the town, keep an eye out for the distinctive painted walls (rue du Noyer, rue Micholet, ave. Franklin Roosevelt) that illustrate the life and times of the town.

Toulon Purple

In Roman times Toulon was famed as a producer of imperial purple dye. The dye was obtained by steeping the colour glands of pointed conches (genus *Murex*), which proliferate along the coast, in salt solution brought to boiling point in lead vats ten days prior to the dyeing process. The purple obtained was used to dye silk and woollen materials. This sumptuous colour was initially reserved for emperors but later its use spread, although the imperial treasury maintained a monopoly over its manufacture. The foundations of the old Toulon dye-works were uncovered during reconstruction work on the arsenal.

PRACTICAL INFORMATION

Aéroport International de Toulon-Hyères – *Bd de la Marine – 83400 Hyères* – ℘*08 25 01 83 87 (0.15 €/min) – www.toulon-hyeres.aeroport.fr.*
Located 14mi/23km from Toulon, this airport is served by a regular 40-min bus service (Réseau Mistral 102) from Toulon coach station. Allow 20 min by car. Air France operates six daily flights to Paris-Orly; Ryanair flies to Liverpool twice a week (Mon and Fri) and London Stansted on Wed, Fri and Sun; CityJet flies twice-weekly to London City.

GUIDED TOURS OF THE CITY
Themed guided tours in English *(2hr)* starting from the tourist office are a great opportunity to discover the old town of Toulon. *Reservations required:* ℘*04 94 18 53 00.*

Train Touristique: Departs (Mar–Oct) from the Carré du Port for a tour with commentary in English *(50min)* of the Old Town, the beaches at Mourillon and the Tour Royale. ℘*06 20 77 44 43. www.traintoulon.com.* ⬭*5€ (child 3€).*

TRANSPORT
Pedestrian area: The historic centre of Toulon bordered by rue Anatole-France, avenue de la République, avenue de Besagne and boulevard de Strasbourg is closed to traffic.

Buses: The RMTT (℘*04 94 03 87 03, www. reseaumistral.com*) provides an efficient bus service covering Toulon and its outskirts. Maps, timetables and tickets can be obtained from "bar tabacs" and newsstands across the city.

Boat shuttle service: *SITCAT/RMTT on Quai Cronstadt or 720 ave. du Colonel-Picot.* ℘*04 94 03 87 03.* Part of the local transport system, several daily "navettes" operate to and from La Seyne-sur-Mer, Tamaris and St-Mandrier-sur-Mer.

Pass Téléphérique: This day pass is good for the entire Réseau Mistral bus and boat network and the téléphérique on Mont Faron. ⬭*6.60€ (child 4.60€).*

---

① FROM THE STATION TO THE ARSENAL

Place de la Liberté
Lying at the heart of modern Toulon, with a monumental Fontaine de la Fédération erected in 1889 to celebrate the centenary of the Republic, this square is home to the superb Grand Hôtel (1870), the city's last remaining Belle Epoque building.
On either side of the square, boulevard Strasbourg and avenue du Général-Leclerc form the city's main thoroughfare. The Opéra Municipal (1862) was a gathering point for Toulon's high society before the Second World War. Today, this neighbourhood's cafés and cabarets give it a festive atmosphere.

Place Victor-Hugo
Further along the boulevard, take a moment to admire the Théâtre de Toulon. Designed by the architect of the Paris Opéra, Charles Garnier, it is one of France's finest regional theatres. Walk around the theatre to best appreciate it restored façade overlooking Place Victor Hugo and its lively pavement cafés.

▷ *Take rue Jean-Jaurès and turn left on rue Anatole France.*

Place d'Armes
Originally called the Champ de Bataille this square was commissioned by Louis XIV's Finance Minister Jean-Baptiste Colbert for the king to take the salute. Formerly sporting a bandstand, café and restaurants, it soon became a popular meeting place for the bourgeoisie and officers leaving on a tour of duty. Today, it is a popular venue for open-air concerts

Corderie
To the south of place d'Armes.
⚠ *Military property, closed to the public.*
Designed by Louis XIV's military architect Vauban to house the naval rope factory *(corderie)*, this 350yd/320m building now houses the navy's administrative offices. The ornately carved **door**

(1689), depicting allegories of Law and Might came from a former Jesuit college and was added in 1976.

Continue on rue Anatole France.

Musée de la Marine★

Pl. Monsenergue. Open daily Jul–Aug 10am–6pm; Sept–Dec and Feb–Jun Wed–Mon 10am–6pm. Free audio guide in English included in entry price. Closed 1 May, 25 Dec. 5.50€ (under 18 free). 04 94 02 02 01. www.musee-marine.fr.

This recently restored and modernised museum (2011) is entered through the 18C **porte de l'Arsenal**. Decorated with trophies and flanked by four columns, it supports a pediment surmounted by representations of Mars (left) and Minerva (right). The collection is divided into two parts, starting on the ground floor with the history of the royal arsenal. The displays include large-scale models of a frigate, *La Sultane*, and an 18C vessel, the *Duquesne*, fine paintings, drawings and other exhibits recalling Toulon's seafaring history and its prison. The second section explores the Mediterranean's maritime history, from 18C galleys to 20C battleships.

Arsenal Maritime

Covering 240ha/595acres and employing around 6,300 civilians, the modern arsenal mainly maintains the Mediterranean fleet: frigates, carriers, sloops, subs and minesweepers. Some of the dry docks are 17C. The Darse Vieille is now a marina and the departure point for passengers heading to the Îles d'Hyères, Corsica and Sardinia.

② A MILITARY PAST

The Port★

The old port (Darse Vieille or Darse Henri-IV) was begun in 1589 and extended by two breakwaters on the south side in 1610.

At that time there was no royal fleet; when the king required ships, he leased them from lords and captains, who had them built, armed and equipped. It was Cardinal Richelieu, chief minister to Louis XIII, who created a military arsenal to build and repair warships from 1631. Under Louis XIV the port proved too small and Vauban had the new port (Darse Neuve) excavated between 1680 and 1700. To accommodate further growth, an annex was built in 1836 at Mourillon, and two harbours added under Napoleon III at Castigneau and Missiessy.

Quai Cronstadt

Lined with shops and cafés, this rather unharmonious wall of tall modern buildings forms a screen between the old port and the old town. The only reminders of the past are the famous **atlantes**★ by Pierre Puget on the old town hall balcony.

Boat Tour of the Rade★

Bateliers de la Côte d'Azur, landing-stage on Quai Cronstadt, beside the Préfecture Maritime. Guided, commentated tours (1hr), hourly departures Feb–Oct. 9.50€. Reservations 04 94 93 07 56. www.bateliersdelacotedazur.com.

Guided tours range from 30-min crossings (Porquerolles) to one-day cruises (La Croisière), although the one-hour "Rade de Toulon" tour is by far the most popular. Kicking off with a tour of the French fleet, including aircraft carriers, minesweepers, anti-submarine and missile-launcher frigates and the slender, dark contours of a nuclear submarine, it continues along the Tamaris coastline with its mussel beds and two forts, Balaguier and Ayguillette, before returning via Lazaret Bay, along the St-Mandrier Peninsula and the long sea wall, affording excellent **views**★ over Toulon.

At the roundabout Gen. Bonaparte, follow the ave. de la Tour-Royale.

Tour Royale

Enquire at the tourist office about visits. Closed Oct–Jun. 04 94 02 02 01.

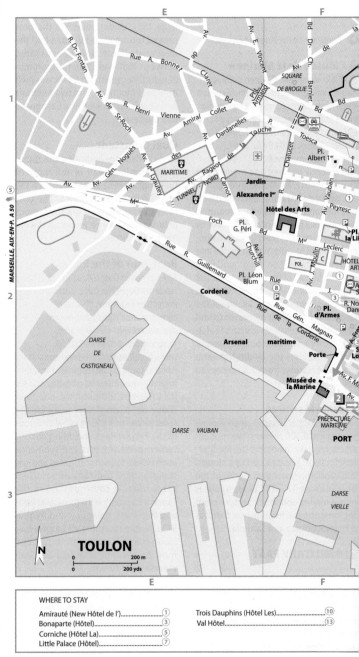

TOULON

WHERE TO STAY

Amirauté (New Hôtel de l')................. ①	Trois Dauphins (Hôtel Les)................. ⑩
Bonaparte (Hôtel)................................ ③	Val Hôtel... ⑬
Corniche (Hôtel La)............................ ⑤	
Little Palace (Hôtel)........................... ⑦	

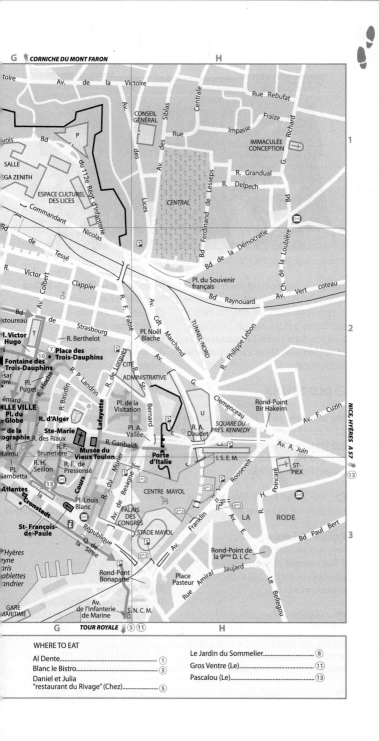

CORNICHE DU MONT FARON

G   H

TOUR ROYALE   ⑤ ⑪

WHERE TO EAT

Atlantes by Puget on the old town hall, Quai Cronstadt

The Grosse Tour or Mitre Tower was built by Louis XII in the early 16C for defensive purposes (its walls are 23ft/7m thick at the base) before mainly serving as a prison. Don't miss the **panorama**★ of Toulon and Mont Faron from the battlements

③ OLD TOWN★

The ancient heart of Toulon is a colourful maze of streets. Many of its charming façades and fountains have been restored as part of a major renovation project begun in 1985.

▶ *Enter pl. de l'Amiral-Senès then turn right onto rue Notre-Dame.*

Église St-Louis
rue Louis-Jourdan.
A fine example of Neoclassical architecture built in the late 18C in the form of a Greek temple.

▶ *Continue on rue Vezzani.*

An 18C reproduction of a ship's prow, which seems to sprout out of a wall, is a tribute to the city's shipbuilders.

▶ *Take rue Pomet on the right.*

The curious fountain on Place du Globe evokes the Bagne of Toulon.

Maison de la Photographie
Pl. du Globe, rue Nicolas-Laugier.
🕐*Open Tue–Sat noon–6pm.*
🎫*No charge.* 𝄞*04 94 93 07 59.*
Housed in a former public bath house, the Musée de la Photographie hosts six temporary exhibitions a year.

▶ *Take rue du Noyer, just off pl. Raimu. On the right is a mural painting on rue Micholet. Return to rue de la Glacière and turn left, then follow rue Andrieux.*

Fontaine des Trois-Dauphins
This shady square lined with café terraces features a curious fountain wrapped in a cloak of moss, ferns, a fig tree, a medlar and an oleander, topped by three intertwined dolphins sculpted in 1780 by two local artists.

▶ *Go down rue Hoche.*

Rue d'Alger
This modernized pedestrian precinct is the main commercial street leading to the old port, Darse Vieille.

▶ *Turn left onto rue Seillon, then follow rue de la Fraternité.*

Église St-François-de-Paule
𝄞*04 94 92 28 91.*
This small church was built in 1744 by the Recollects. Its double-arched façade

and Genoan bell tower identify it with the Nice Baroque style.

▶ *Return to the square and turn right down the first street.*

Rue Méridienne and place à l'Huile (the site of the old olive oil market) lead to place de la Poissonnerie, which for several centuries played host to the fish market, demolished in 1988.

▶ *Go up rue Pressensé, then take rue des Boucheries.*

Cathédrale Ste-Marie

🕐 *Open daily 9am–noon, 2–6pm.*
Constructed in the 11C and restored in the 12C, the cathedral was extended and given a Classical façade in the 17C and a bell tower in 1740. The rather dark interior mixes Romanesque and Gothic, with works by Puget and Van Loo.

▶ *Continue to Cours Lafayette.*

Cours Lafayette

A colourful, bustling vegetable and flower **market** is held here every Tuesday to Sunday.

Musée du Vieux Toulon

🕐 *Open Tue–Sat 2–5.45pm.*
🕐 *Closed public holidays.*
⊜*No charge.* 🖉*04 94 92 29 23.*
This museum, housed in a former 17C episcopal palace, has two galleries displaying maps, engravings and paintings recalling the history of the city since the Middle Ages.
Don't miss the large collection of firebacks salvaged from houses destroyed in bombing raids of 1943-44. The exhibition also features ceramics, statuettes and costumes.

▶ *Leave the Old Town by rue Garibaldi.*

Porte d'Italie

This bastioned gate, built in 1790 on the site of ancient fortifications, is the only remnant of the defences which once surrounded Toulon.

SIGHTS

Musée de Toulon et du Var

113 blvd. du M.-Leclerc. ♿🕐*Open Tue–Sun 9am–6pm.* 🕐*Closed public holidays.* ⊜*No charge.* 🖉*04 94 36 81 10. www.museum-toulon.org.*
Fully-renovated in 2011, this natural history museum housed in the right wing of a Renaissance-style building features exhibitions on the zoology, paleontology and botany of the Toulon and Var region. The left wing is home to the Musée d'Art (👆*see below).*

Musée d'Art

113 blvd. du M.-Leclerc.
🕐*Open Tue–Sun noon–6pm.*
🕐*Closed public holidays.*
⊜*No charge.* 🖉*04 94 36 81 01.*
The Flemish, Dutch, Italian and French Schools (16C–18C) are all represented in the museum's collections, which also feature works by 19C artists, including a large number of Provençal painters such as the Toulon landscapist Vincent Courdouan. The museum also possesses an eclectic contemporary art collection. The adjacent **Jardin Alexandre-I** is home to many attractive trees, including magnolias, palms and cedars. Don't miss the *Fontaine du Buveur* (Drinker's Fountain) by Hercule.

Hotel des Arts – Centre méditerranéen des arts

236 bd du Mar.-Leclerc 🕐*Open Tue–Sun 11am–6pm.* 🕐*Closed public holidays.* ⊜*No charge.* 🖉*04 94 91 69 18. www.var.fr*
This art centre offers five temporary exhibitions exploring the visual arts on two floors, alongside a collection of 160 contemporary artworks (paintings and photos) by over 30 artists.

Plage du Mourillon

▶ *East along the Frédéric-Mistral coast, between the Fort Saint-Louis and the sailing center. Facilities include a restaurant, toilets and a free car park.*
Toulon's large artificial beach has four coves (sand, pebbles and a mix of both) protected by sea walls and a gently sloping shoreline for easy bathing.

Plage des anses Méjean et Magaud

 From Mourillon, follow the signs for La Garde-Le Pradet.

On the outskirts of La Garde, the sea walk explores two natural sandy coves: Magaud (left) and Méjean (right) *90min round trip*. From Fort Saint-Louis via Cap Brun, the **sentier des douaniers** winds its way to Méjean cove, with stunning **views** of the natural harbour along the way.

EXCURSIONS

Mont Faron★★★

The small limestone massif of Mont Faron *(alt 1,916ft /584m)*, bordered by deep valleys, dominates the city of Toulon. It is a pleasant drive in summer over pine-clad slopes, providing good **views**★ of Toulon, the harbours, the St-Mandrier and Cap Sicié Peninsulas.

Téléphérique du Mont Faron★

 Take blvd. Ste-Anne and follow signs (Téléphérique du Mont Faron) to the cable-car station in ave. Perrichi. During peak times, it is possible to park below the station on the left.

 Open Feb–Nov. Check website for details. 6.70€. 04 94 92 68 25. *www.telepherique-faron.com.*

The cable-car ride *(6min)* offers fine **views**★ over the town, the harbour and the limestone cliffs around Toulon. To the left the remains of many small forts can be seen. A pleasant **view** can also be had by walking about 33ft/10m to the left along the road to Mont Faron.

Musée-Mémorial du Débarquement en Provence★

Top of Mont Faron. *Open Jul–mid-Sept daily 10am–1pm, 2–6.30pm; May–Jun and second half of Sep Tue–Sun 10am–1pm, 2–6.30pm; Oct–Apr Tue–Sun 10am–1pm, 2–5.30pm. Last admission one hour before closing* 3.80€. 04 94 88 08 09.

Housed in the Beaumont Tower, to the left of the road, this memorial commemorates the liberation of southeast France by the Allies in August 1944.

An exhibition explores the Liberation with accounts by British, American, Canadian, French and German eye-witnesses, dioramas of the liberation of Toulon and Marseille, and a 15min documentary featuring archive footage. From the terrace *(accessible during tours of the museum)* there is a magnificent **panorama**★★★ *(three viewing panels)* of Toulon, the harbours, and the islands and mountains around Toulon.

Zoo du Faron

Mont Faron. *Open May–Jun and Sep 10am–6pm; Jul–Aug 10am–6.30pm; Oct–Jan 10am–5pm.* *Closed when raining.* 9€ *(child 5.50€).* 04 94 88 09 03. *www.zoo-toulon.com.*

This zoo specialises in breeding endangered animals such as snow panthers and ocelots. There are also lions, tigers, bears and monkeys.

La Garde

 5.5mi/9km via D 29 to the east towards La Valette.

Now part of the industrial suburbs of Toulon, La Garde plays host to the **Musée Jean-Aicard-Paulin-Bertrand**, once home to the author of *Maurin des Maures,* where he was visited by friends including the painter Paulin Bertrand (1852–1940). A reconstruction of Bertrand's studio and some of his works are on display. An exhibition of pottery by **Clément Massier** (late 19C–early 20C) occupies the ground floor *(guided tour (1hr) every 30min Tue–Sat noon–6pm (last entry 30min before closing); no charge).*

Solliès-Ville

 9mi/15km northeast – 1.5hr. From Toulon take A 57 motorway. Follow directions to La Farlède and then D 67 to Solliès-Ville.

Pass through Solliès-Pont, a busy market town in a region famous for its cherry orchards and fig trees, before reaching the old town of Solliès-Ville overlooking the rich Gapeau Plain. On **Esplanade de la Montjoie**, the ruined castle of

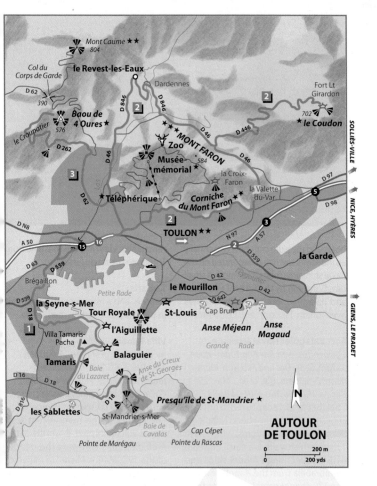

Mont Caume ★★
804
Col du
Corps de Garde
le Revest-les-Eaux
D 62
390
Dardennes
Fort Lt
Girardon
2
le Croupatier
Baou de
4 Oures ★
576
D 62
D 846
2
D 846
D 46
D 446
702
le Coudon
D 262
D 46
D 46
★★★ MONT FARON
Zoo
Musée-
mémorial ★
584
la Croix-
Faron
D 97
3
Téléphérique
D 62
Corniche
du Mont Faron
la Valette
du-Var
D 98
5
D N8
2
TOULON ★★
N 97
3
A 50
15 16
A 57
2 D 559
la Garde
D 63
D 559
Brégaillon
Petite Rade
le Mourillon
D 42
D 42
la Seyne-s-Mer
Tour Royale
St-Louis
Cap Brun
D 18
l'Aiguillette
Anse Méjean
Anse
Magaud
Villa Tamaris-
Pacha
Balaguier
Grande   Rade
Tamaris
Baie
du Lazaret
Anse du Creux
de St-Georges
D 16
D 18
Presqu'île de St-Mandrier ★
D 816
St-Mandrier-s-Mer
les Sablettes
Baie de
Cavalas
Cap Cépet
N
Pointe de Marégau
Pointe du Rascas
**AUTOUR
DE TOULON**
0   200 m
0   200 yds

SOLLIÈS-VILLE
NICE, HYÈRES
GIENS, LE PRADET

the Forbins, lords of Solliès, commands a beautiful **view**★ of the Gapeau Valley and the Maures Massif.

The **church**, a former chapter house, houses a high altar made from a 15C ciborium and a walnut wood organ case from 1499.

Maison Jean-Aicard

🕐 *Open Tue–Sat noon–6pm.*
🚫 *Closed public holidays.*
🎫 *No charge.* 📞 *04 94 33 72 02.*
www.solliesville.fr.

This second house lived in by Jean Aicard (1848–1921) has been converted into a small museum featuring furniture and paintings by Old Masters, with stunning **views** over the massif from the top floor.

🚗 DRIVING TOURS

The roads used in these excursions serve military installations; traffic is permitted up to the entrance of these installations, but the military authorities forbid entrance to certain places indicated by notices.

1 TOUR OF THE HARBOURS★★
10.5mi/17km/south. Allow 1hr.

▶ *Leave Toulon by highway A 50, then D 559 and turn left towards La Seyne.*

La Seyne-sur-Mer

Built beside the bay which bears its name, La Seyne has a port for fishing

Fort Balaguier, Toulon

boats and pleasure craft but is essentially an industrial town that depended on the naval shipyards for its livelihood. A small bay, bordered by the forts of Éguillette and Balaguier, offers excellent **views** over Toulon, Le Faron and Le Coudon.

Fort Balaguier Naval Museum

Open Tue–Sun Jul–Aug 10am–noon, 3–7pm; Sept–Dec and Feb–Jun 10am–noon, 2–5.30pm. Closed 1 May, 25 Dec. 3€ (child 2€). 04 94 94 84 72. The fort was recaptured from the English in 1793 by the young Napoleon. Set up in the fort's rooms, which have 13ft/4m-thick walls, is a naval museum with a collection of model ships and memorabilia from the Napoleonic era. The 17C chapel contains objects from Toulon's galleys and naval prisons: registers, chains and works of art made by the prisoners.
From the terrace overlooking the fort's garden and its aviary, there is a

remarkable **view**★ of the coastline from Toulon to the Île du Levant.

Tamaris

George Sand wrote several of her novels in this shaded resort on the hillside.

Villa Tamaris-Pacha

Av. de la Grande Maison. Open Tue–Sun 2–6.30pm. Guided tours Wed all day, Thu–Fri 4–5.30pm. Closed public holidays. No charge. 04 94 06 84 00. www.villatamaris.fr. The history of this magnificent residence, still unfinished, is worthy of the *Arabian Nights*. Towards the middle of the 19C, Marius Michel, a native of Sanary-sur-Mer, became the concessionaire of the lighthouses, quays and warehouses of Constantinople and created the modern port of Istanbul under the Ottoman administration. He built his wife a palace inspired by Florentine villas in Tamaris, but after three years of

The Unusual Military Career of the St-Mandrier Peninsula

From September 1943 to August 1944, La Croix aux Signaux hill was a secret German naval base where midget submarines were assembled before being transported through a tunnel to Cavalas beach. On the same site in 1929, the Marine Nationale Française buried two enormous gun turrets (14m/46ft deep) each holding two 340 guns, 17m/56ft long, covering a sector from Le Lavandou to La Ciotat. Shelling preparations for the landing in Provence in 1944 brought an end to development of this base. It was from the rifle range at St-Mandrier that the first French liquid-powered rocket was launched in March 1945, inaugurating the European space race.

hard work, she was killed by a mentally ill person in 1893 and all work ceased. The palace remained unoccupied for a century. Now redeveloped, it houses a cultural institution. Beside the bay, a luxurious house (private property), also the work of Michel Pacha, as he was known, displays the ornate Mauresque style.

Les Sablettes

This long, wide beach of fine sand looks out to the open sea. Take the road along the narrow sandy isthmus, which links the peninsula to the land mass, for fine **views** of Toulon and the mountains.

Presqu'île de St-Mandrier★

The road round the peninsula offers a **view**★ of the whole harbour and Toulon before skirting Le Creux St-Georges, home to an aeronaval base and training centre for marine engineers as well as the fishing and leisure port of **St-Mandrier-sur-Mer**. A right-hand turning at the entrance to the town climbs steeply to a small cemetery with a **panorama**★★ of Toulon and the Îles d'Hyères.

2 CORNICHE DU MONT FARON★★
25mi/40km. Allow 2hr.

The Corniche du Mont Faron, a panoramic road, provides the best **views** over the whole of Toulon harbour. Visit in the late afternoon for the best light.

▷ *To reach the Corniche du Mont Faron, take Pont de Ste-Anne, ave. de la Victoire and blvd. Ste-Anne (left).*

The drive along the **Corniche Marius-Escartefigue** and the slopes of Mont Faron offers views of Toulon and its surroundings.
The **view**★ of the harbours includes the Petite Rade between *(west)* Le Mourillon and La Seyne backed by the cliffs of Cap Sicie, and the Grande Rade, partially enclosed *(south)* by the St-Mandrier Peninsula and its low narrow isthmus and *(east)* by Cap Carqueiranne, Giens Bay and Giens Peninsula.

▷ *At the end of the corniche turn left down ave. Canaillette, which leads to D 46, then right down the narrow, steeply-sloping D 446*

Le Coudon★
Alt 2,303ft/702m.
At the start of the climb you can see Mont Coudon in its entirety, La Crau and the surrounding plain. The road crosses a pine forest and several olive groves before opening onto scrubland dotted with evergreen oaks. The **view**★ widens until you reach the Fort Lieutenant-Girardon, from where the entire coast from the Giens Peninsula to the former island of Gaou near Le Brusc is visible.

▷ *Return to D 46 and turn right. After 1.5mi/2.5km, the D 846 crosses a dam to Le Revest-les-Eaux.*

Le Revest-les-Eaux
This delightful village with a 17C church at the foot of Mont Caume is overlooked by a "Saracen tower". Its late-16C château, with two pepperpot turrets, now houses a café-bar. The church dates from the same period.

▷ *Return to Toulon through the Las Valley (D 846) between the mountains of Faron and Croupatier.*

3 BAOU DE QUATRE OURES★
7mi/11km northwest. Allow 1hr.

▷ *From Toulon take ave. St-Roch, rue Dr-Fontan, ave. Général-Gouraud and then left on ave. des Routes; on pl. Macé turn right onto D 62 (ave. Clovis), then left onto D 262.*

Continue 2mi /3km to a platform offering a magnificent **view**★★ of Toulon.

▷ *The narrow road to the top (2.5mi /4km) crosses a firing range (open to traffic).*

At the top there is a fine **panorama**★★ of the coast from Cap Bénat to La Ciotat and inland from Ste-Baume to the Maures.

ADDRESSES

🛏 STAY

Hôtel Little Palace – *6-8 r. Berthelot.* *℘04 94 92 26 62. www.hotel-littlepalace. com. 23 rooms.* ⊒*8€.* A charming and simple hotel, decorated in warm earth tones. Known for its copious breakfast buffet.

Hôtel Bonaparte – *16 r. Anatole-France.* *℘04 94 93 07 51. www.hotel bonaparte.com. 19 rooms.* ⊒*8€.* Provençal-style hotel in the centre of town, with small but well-appointed rooms. Air conditioned on top floor.

Les 3 Dauphins – *9 Pl. des 3 Dauphins.* *℘04 94 92 65 79. 14 rooms.* ⊒*8€.* The windows of this hotel look onto a tiny square. The smallish rooms have been tastefully appointed and decorated in cheerful shades.

Val'Hôtel – *Av. René-Cassin, ZA Paul Madon, La Valette, take exit 5 off the A 57, follow signs to ZI de Toulon-la-Valette.* *℘04 94 08 38 08. www.monalisahotels. com. 42 rooms.* ⊒*7€. Restaurant* ⊜. This hotel offers several advantages: a lush garden setting; large, colourful rooms with balcony or terrace and inexpensive weekend rates. A bit close to the motorway exit.

New Hôtel de l'Amirauté – *4 rue Adolphe-Guiol.* *℘04 94 22 19 67. www.new-hotel.com. 58 rooms.* ⊒*9€.* In the centre of town, the decor is reminiscent of the large luxury liners of bygone times. Functional, efficiently soundproofed rooms.

La Corniche Best Western – *17 littoral Frédéric-Mistral across from the Port St-Louis and near the Mourillon beaches.* *℘04 94 41 35 12. www.hotel-toulon-mer.com. 25 rooms.* ⊒*14€. Restaurant* ⊜. This hotel just two steps from the beaches at Mourillon has **views** over the sea, perfect for those looking for a seaside holiday atmosphere.

🍴 EAT

Al Dente – *30 rue Gimelli.* *℘04 94 93 02 50. Closed Sat, Sun lunch.* The main reason for coming here is the remarkable choice of pasta dishes and Italian specialities, with additional menus at highly affordable prices.

Chez Mimi – *Square Léon Vérane.* *℘04 94 62 87 02. Closed Sun lunch, Sat.* This warm and friendly family restaurant serves couscous and other North African dishes in a simple dining room decorated with traditional Tunisian paintings.

Blanc le Bistro – *290 r. Jean-Jaurès.* *℘04 94 10 20 40. Closed 25 Jul–10 Aug, Sat lunch, Sun, Mon eve.* A contemporary restaurant serving generous French dishes with a modern touch.

Le Gros Ventre – *279 Littoral Frédéric Mistral.* *℘04 94 42 15 42. www.legrosventre.net. Closed Wed–Thu, Fri lunch).* A family-run establishment serving the day's catch and grilled meats, as well as fine wines from their cellar, in an elegant setting just off Le Mourillon beach.

Le Pascalou – *3 Pl. à l'Huile.* *℘04 94 62 87 02. Closed Mon.* The lunchtime restaurant of the fish market of the same name, serving the catch of the day in a tiny square.

Le St-Pierre – Chez Marcel – *47 r. de la Citadelle, Six-Fours-les-Plages.* *℘04 94 34 02 52. www.lesaintpierre.fr. Closed Jan, Wed eve. from Sept to Jun, and Mon.* ♿ Located close to the port, this former fisherman's house offers a choice of fish dishes bursting with regional flavours to savour in a dining room washed with light.

Chez Daniel "Restaurant du Rivage" – *La Seyne-sur-Mer, 2.5mi /4km south of La Seyne by rte. de St-Mandrier and country lane.* *℘04 94 94 85 13. Closed Nov, Sun eve, Mon Sept–Jun.* A small rocky inlet is the choice setting for this seafood restaurant that knows the true meaning of Provençal life. The freshly caught fish offered to diners comes straight from the sea or the big fish tank set up on the premises.

Le Jardin du Sommelier – *20 Allées Courbet.* *℘04 94 62 03 27. www.le-jardin-du-sommelier.com. Closed Sat lunch, Sun.* Gourmet cuisine served in an elegant setting. Try the lobster with any wine from their first-rate *cave*.

🎭 ON THE TOWN

Café-Théâtre de la Porte d'Italie – *Pl. Armand-Vallée.* *℘04 94 92 99 75. Check the programme of events. Closed Jun–Sept.* This café-théâtre presents clarinet and jazz concerts, stand-up comedy and pantomime shows.

Opéra de Toulon – *7 rue Racine.* *℘04 94 92 58 59. Closed Aug. www. operadetoulon.fr.* Built in 1862, the Opéra de Toulon is ranked second in France on account of its seating capacity and remarkable acoustics.

♈/ CAFÉS

La Cade à Dédé – *17 r. Charles-Poncy.* *℘04 94 89 32 32. 8.30am–12.30pm Closed Mon and 3 wks in Jan.* You need to be an early bird to see Dédé at his stove preparing his daily *cade*, Toulon's traditional chickpea flour pancake.

Chichi Fregi – *8 r. Vincent-Courdouan, next to the cours Lafayette. ℘06 09 18 83 27. Jul–Aug Tue–Sat 9am–12.30pm; Sep–Jun Tue–Sat 9am–6pm.* Friendly snack bar selling traditional Toulon fare, including *chichi fregi*, doughnuts fried in olive oil and flavoured with orange-flower water, and *fougasse* – olive flat bread.

♈/ CULINARY SPECIALITIES

The natives of Toulon particularly enjoy *l'escabèche de sardine, la cade* (a flat cake made from chickpeas, similar to *socca* in Nice), *la pompe à l'huile* (a hard cake, oiled and flavoured with orange water) and the famous sweet doughnut (*chichifregi*), which can be bought from the stalls in the Lafayette market.

🛒 SHOPPING

The best place to go shopping is the area around rue Jean-Jaurès, rue Hoche, place Victor-Hugo and rue d'Alger. Rue Lamalgue (near the Port St-Louis) has a good range of gourmet stores.

Provençal Market – *Tue–Sun mornings.* Cour Lafayette (city centre), the Marché du Pont du Las (west) and the Marché du Mourillon (east, close to the beaches).

Les Navires de la Royale – *30 rue des Riaux. ℘06 11 18 55 61. Closed Mon. 9am–noon, 2–6pm.* Amateur sailors should make a point of visiting this shop, owned by an enthusiastic lover of all things maritime. His days are spent making and restoring all sorts of boats, ranging from yachts to schooners and catamarans.

Moulin à huile du Partegal – *159 chemin des Laures, La Farlède. ℘04 94 48 48 85. www.moulindupartegal.com. Open Tue, Thu–Sat. 10am–noon, 3–5pm. Jul–Aug 10am–noon, 3–6pm. Closed mid-Jan–early Feb.* Reservation and payment required for group visits. Located amid an 800-tree olive grove on a site dating from the 14C, this olive oil mill uses traditional production methods. Tours by expert millers.

🎭 EVENTS

Bacchus, Fête des Vins et de la Gastronomie – *℘04 94 91 56 87. www.bacchus-fete.com.* Wine and gastronomy festival, first weekend in April on Place d'Armes. Wine tasting, courses and musical entertainment.

Toulon Music Festival – *℘04 94 93 55 45.* This classical music festival is divided into two seasons: a "summer festival" from mid-June to mid-July and a "festival classics" season from mid-Oct to mid-May. Venues across the region.

Toulon Jazz Festival – *℘04 94 09 71 00.* Ten-day jazz festival in July. Free evening concerts across Toulon.

Festival de Noël – Christmas festivities throughout the month of December, including a nativity scene, crafts market and ice skating.

Festival de Cirque contemporain – Street performances, courses and introductions to circus acts under the big top in La Seyne-sur-Mer in Jan.

Fête de la Mer et des Pêcheurs – A sea and fishing festival in the port of La Seyne-sur-Mer the last weekend in June/first weekend in July.

Summer aïoli festivals – Solliès-Toucas celebrates this traditional Mediterranean dish of fish, garlic mayonnaise and vegetables with a giant aïoli in mid-Jul, followed by an aïoli festival in Solliès-Ville – the last weekend in Aug.

Bandol★

Var

Bandol is a pleasant resort nestling in an attractive bay, sheltered from the north winds by high wooded slopes. Home to one of the most famous vineyards in the south, it is also a paradise for watersports enthusiasts.

RESORT LIFE
The Marina
Enjoy the bracing sea air with a walk along the **Allée Jean-Moulin**★ and Allée Alfred-Vivien, both bordered by pines, palms and flower beds.

The Beaches
This seaside resort has four sandy beaches: the east-facing Lido, the well-sheltered Rènecros facing west and the Centrale and Casino beaches facing due south.
The rest of the coast (⚓towards ST-CYR-SUR-MER) offers smaller beaches alternating with rocky areas.
🚶**Chemin de la Corniche** skirts the little peninsula with Bendor Island lying off shore, affording a fine **view** of the coast from Cap de l'Aigle to Cap Sicié.

SIGHTS
Église St-François-de-Sales
Opposite the port de Bandol.
Built in several stages (the main nave between 1746 and 1748, and the two side chapels in 1773), this church is decorated with 19C **Neoclassical frescoes** by Siro Orsi, the decorator of the Milan opera house. The west nave houses a **statue of Notre-Dame de Grâce** in

---

- ▶ **Population:** 8,647.
- 🜨 **Michelin Map:** 340 J7.
- ▤ **Info:** Allée Alfre-Vivien. ℘04 94 29 41 35. www.bandol.fr.
- ◐ **Location:** Accessible by the A50, the resort town of Bandol lies 18km/11mi west of Toulon.
- 🕐 **Timing:** Allow a full day for a stroll around the port, visits to the exotic gardens and zoo, and a drive through the perched villages. An excursion to Bendor Island takes about 45 minutes, or a half day for a swim at the beach.
- 👪 **Kids:** The zoo and exotic gardens are particularly child-friendly.

---

olive wood by students of Pierre Puget. A statue of Saint Vincent de Saragosse, patron saint of wine-growers, watches over the east nave.

👪Jardin Exotique and Zoo de Sanary-Bandol
2mi/3km north-east towards A 50. At the roundabout leading to the motorway, go down the access road on the right. After 550yd/500m, turn right (sign "Zoo-Jardin Exotique").
♿🕐*Open May–Oct 9.30am–7pm (from 10am Sun and holidays); Nov and Mar–Apr 9.30am–5.30pm. Dec–early Feb Sat, Sun and holidays 9.30am–5.30pm. ≋8.50€ (child 6€). ℘04 94 29 40 38. www.zoosanary.com.*
In these shaded gardens cacti and tropical plants are grown to remarkable sizes. Among hundreds of rare plants, animals from all over the world can be seen – monkeys, coatis, lemurs, peccaries, deer, ponies, miniature goats and llamas. You can also observe colourful parrots, peacocks, pink flamingoes and cranes.

Île de Bendor
The **boat trip** (🕐*departures every 30min leaving from Bandol in season,*

Bandol AOC

Beyond the villas scattered in groves of pine and mimosa behind the seafront are fields of flowers and vineyards which produce Bandol, the best-known of the Côtes-de-Provence wines. Ask at the tourist office for the brochure detailing Bandol vineyard tours

---

7min; ⊙9€ round trip 𝒫04 94 05 90 90 www.bendor.com) to the island makes a pleasant summer excursion. The island is an attractive tourist centre offering fine beaches, a harbour, as well as a Provençal village with craft shops. Named after the famous *pastis* maker, the **Espace Culturel Paul-Ricard** features a curious **Exposition Universelle des Vins et Spiritueux** (⊙open Jul–Aug; ⊷guided tours 1pm and 6pm; ⊙no charge; 𝒫04 94 29 44 34; www.euvs.org). Set up in a large hall decorated with frescoes, it covers the production of wine, aperitifs and liqueurs in 51 different countries, with 8 000 bottles on display.

🚗 DRIVING TOUR

Perched Villages★
Round trip of 29mi/55km.
Allow a half day.

▷ *From Bandol take D 559 northeast; go left on D 559B towards Le Beausset. Pass under the railway bridge.*

Just after Le Beausset (where you should stop on market days), turn right on N8 towards Toulon. The narrow road winds its way through olive groves, orchards and vineyards.

Chapelle Notre-Dame-du-Beausset-Vieux
Leave the car below the chapel.

⊙*Guided tour on request Jul–Aug 3–7pm; Apr–Jun and Sep: 2–6pm; Oct–Mar 2–5pm. 𝒫04 94 98 61 53.*
This stark Provençal Romanesque chapel, with barrel vaulting in the nave and cul-de-four vaulting in the apse, has been restored by volunteers.
The Virgin and Child in the choir comes from Pierre Puget's studio. In the left niche a group of 400-year-old **santons** (⊙see p30) illustrates the Flight to Egypt. Some of the votive offerings (side aisle) date back to the 18C. From the terrace above the chapel a sweeping **panorama★** takes in Le Castellet, Ste-Baume, Gros Cerveau and the coast from Bandol westwards to La Ciotat.

▷ *Return to N 8 and continue north towards Aubagne.*

Circuit du Castellet Paul-Ricard
This track (3.7mi/6km long) was officially opened in 1970 for the first Grand Prix de France, won by Jacky Stewart.
Since then, many international F1 and F3 drivers, such as Alain Prost in 1976, have competed on the circuit.
Although the racing season peaks in April and May, the track offers a full calendar of events.

▷ *On leaving the circuit, turn right down the D N8 towards Aubagne. At Camp-du-Castellet crossroads, turn left on D 26, then left again on D 226.*

Jardin Exotique and Zoo de Sanary-Bandol
© Christelle /Fotolia.com

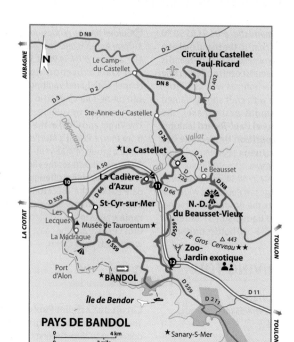

PAYS DE BANDOL

Le Castellet★

Nestled on a wooded hill dominating the vineyards, this remarkable strong-hold has well-preserved ramparts, a carefully restored 12C church and a castle, parts of which date back to the 11C. From beyond the gate on Place de la Mairie there is an attractive **view** inland towards Ste-Baume. Many houses were originally built in the 17C and 18C. There are art and craft workshops.

> *Leave Le Castellet going downhill towards D 66.*

La Cadière-d'Azur

This very old hill town produces Bandol wine. Some of its former defences are still standing. The 13C **Peï gate**, in front of the town hall, leads to a maze of pic-turesque old streets. From the eastern end of the village there is a fine **view**★ inland over Le Castellet to Ste-Baume.

> *Follow D66 to St-Cyr-sur-Mer (see p115) and then the D 559 back to Bandol.*

ADDRESSES

🏠 STAY

🛌 **Golf Hôtel** – *10 Corniche Bonaparte, on Rénecros Beach by bd. Louis-Lumière. ☏04 94 29 45 83. www.golfhotel.fr. Closed Nov–Feb. 24 rooms.* 👫🅿️. ☕8.50€. *Restaurant* 🍴🍴. A seaside hotel, complete with deckchairs and beach restaurant in summer. Most of the cosy rooms give onto the sea; some are fronted by a small balcony. Dinner served only in July and August.

🛌🍴 **Auberge La Cauquière** – *Puits d'Isnard, Le Beausset. ☏04 94 98 42 75. www.lacauquiere.com. 10 rooms.* 🅿️ ☕6€. *Restaurant* 🍴🍴. A charming inn with garden and swimming pool in the centre of Le Bausset. Just ten minutes by car from the beaches and Route des Vins de Bandol. Rooms are arranged around a cosy courtyard.

🛌🍴 **Chambre d'Hôte Les Cancades** – *1195 Chemin de la Fontaine de Cinq-Sous, Le Beausset. 2mi/3km E of Le Castellet, take Chemin de la Fontaine de Cinq-Sous (across from Casino supermarket). ☏04 94 98 76 93. www.les-cancades.com.*

4 rooms. 🍴 🖥. A steep, narrow path leads to the wooded, residential area and this charming Provençal mas. The fine, handsomely furnished rooms, park, swimming pool and summer kitchen are all blissfully quiet and relaxing.

⬤ EAT

⬤ **Snack Bar Le Souco** – *1 rue de la Poste, Le Castellet.* 📞*04 94 32 67 94.* 🍴. This café-restaurant frequented by the locals is open year-round. Terraces at the front and back.

⬤ **L'Oasis** – *15 rue des Écoles.* 📞*04 94 29 41 69. www.oasisbandol. com. Closed Dec, Sun eve off-season.* Delightful dining room painted in warm Mediterranean tones. In summer, enjoy the charming terrace looking out onto the garden. Smallish but impeccably-kept rooms are available for overnight stays.

⬤ **Le Clocher** – *1 rue Paroisse.* 📞*04 94 32 47 65. Closed Wed.* In an ancient stone house at the foot of the church belltower in Vieux Bandol, this tiny restaurant serves typical regional dishes of the Midi. Small terrace on the street.

⬤ ON THE TOWN

Tchin Tchin – *11 Allée Jean-Moulin.* 📞*04 94 29 41 04. www.tchintchin.fr.* This prestigious bar saw its golden age in the 1970s, when it attracted many celebrities from the entertainment world, namely Jacques Brel and Richard Antony, who coined the name of the club. A good selection of cocktails and regular jazz concerts.

Casino de Bandol – *2 Pl. Lucien-Artaud.* 📞*04 94 29 31 31. www.partouche.com.* Not only does this casino have 120 slot machines, a traditional gaming room and a piano bar, it's also a popular place in the region for its nightclub and special events.

⬤ SHOPPING

Beausset Market – Friday and Sunday, 8.30am–noon in the centre of town: fresh produce, gourmet specialities, flowers, local crafts and clothing.

Le Tonneau de Bacchus – *296 avenue du 11-Novembre.* 📞*04 94 29 01 01. 9.30am–12.30pm, 4–8pm. Closed Sun afternoon.* This cellar offers a wide selection of wines from France and especially the Bandol area. The cellarman is extremely knowledgeable about wine and he will be delighted to introduce you to the vintage bottles. Regular oenology courses and themed evenings. Fine gastronomic specialities from Provence are also on sale.

Domaine de Souviou – *RN 8, Le Beausset.* 📞*04 94 90 57 63. www.souviou.com. Closed Sun from Oct–Easter.* Producer and seller of both wine and olive oil. Tastings and tours of the ancient farm available.

Miellerie de l'Oratoire – *rte. des Oratoires, 987 Quartier de l'Estagnol, Ste-Annedu-Castelet.* 📞*04 94 32 65 78. www.miel2lor.com.* Virginie and Olivier love to share all they know about beekeeping and honey. Their boutique offers fresh honey and pollen products, soaps, candles, candies and spice bread.

Moulin de St-Côme – *D266 between St-Cyr and Bandol, Quartier St-Côme, La Cadière-d'Azur.* 📞*04 94 90 11 51. www.moulindestcome.com. Mon–Sat, 9am–noon, 2–6pm.* Free visit to the mill and olive oil tastings. The boutique has olive oils from France and elsewhere, soaps, perfumes, pottery, fabrics and Provençal specialities.

OUTDOOR ACTIVITIES

Bandol offers a wide range of watersports and a renowned diving centre on the Ile de Bandol.

⬤ **Aquascope** – *Quai Charles de Gaulle (opposite the town hall)* 📞*04 94 32 51 41. Closed Oct–Apr, Mon.* 🎟15€ *(child 8€).* Thirty-minute tours on a boat with a transparent hull for underwater observation of marine flora and fauna.

⬤ EVENTS

Fête du Millésime – 📞*04 94 90 29 59. www.vinsdebandol.com.* A wine and gourmet food festival in the port on the first Sunday in December.

Printemps des Potiers – 📞*04 94 63 04 64. www.leprintempsdespotiers.com.* Pottery displays and markets. Mid-April.

Circuit du Castellet Paul-Ricard – historic car races, every April.

Saint-Cyr-sur-Mer

Var

Between Marseille and Toulon, Saint-Cyr-sur-Mer marks the starting point of the French Riviera with its long, fine sandy beaches bordering fertile plains of grapevines and olive trees. Popular for its mild climate, it is home to the only surviving Roman villa on the Mediterranean coast.

> ▶ **Population:** 11,797.
> ⚲ **Michelin Map:** 340 J6.
> ▯ **Info:** Pl. de l'Appel-du-18-Juin. ℘04 94 26 73 73. www.saintcyrsurmer.com.
> ◗ **Location:** Located 3.7mi/6km northwest of Bandol. A long avenue of residential buildings leads to the coastline, with the Port de Lecques to the west, and Port de Madrague to the east.

SIGHTS
Beaches
Follow blvd. de la Plage south to the Chemin du Littoral.
The semicircular bay boasts 1mi/2km of sandy beaches, from the narrow shoreline at Les Lecque to the wide beaches of La Madrague of the south. To the west (10min by car), the Calanque du Port-d'Alon, surrounded by a pine forest, is more secluded.

Musée de Tauroentum★
131 Rte de La Madrague, towards Port de Lecques. ◷*Open Wed–Mon Jun–Sept 3–7pm; Oct–Mar Sat–Sun and school holidays 2–5pm.* ◉3€. ℘04 94 26 30 46.
The museum is built around the foundations of the only **coastal Roman villa** in the region, featuring wreathed columns with Corinthian capitals from the villa's peristyle and a granite column from a pergola that adorned the seafront. The museum contains three 1C black and white **mosaics**, along with fragments of frescoes and amphorae, tools and jewellery. A 1C **dolium**, which could hold 400 gallons/1,500 l of wine or olive oil, a monolithic **sarcophagus**, and France's only **house tomb** stand in front of the museum.

Centre d'Art Sébastien
12 blvd. Jean-Jaurès. ◷*Open Wed–Mon Jun–Sept 9am–noon, 3–7pm; Oct–May 9am–noon, 2–6pm.* ◉*Closed public holidays.* ◉1€. ℘04 94 26 19 20.
Set up in a former factory in 1993, this arts centre hosts temporary exhibitions and a permanent collection of works by the artist Sébastien (1909–90), a friend of Picasso, Matisse and Jean Cocteau.

EXCURSION
Coastal path
◗ *Take D 87 from St-Cyr along the coast to La Madrague. The path starts at Pointe Grenier.*
▯ *3mi/4.5km to port d'Alon (yellow trail markers) or 3.7mi/6km to Bandol. The walk is not difficult, but wear sturdy shoes and bring drinking water.*
☺ *Keep a close eye on children: dangerous cliff drops and a railway line.*
This coastal path from La Madrague to Bandol offers hikers an opportunity to enjoy a commanding **view** of the sea. At the peak of Pointe Grenier is a **Napoleon III military battery** and chapel. On the inland side, admire the vineyards or, if you're a fan of flora, spot local species of violet and mushrooms.

Vineyard path
Leave your car at the car park next to the Aigues Marines residences and the hamlet of La Madrague. Return down rue Abbé-Dol to the bus stop (the walk starts from the path opposite). Ask for more details from the tourist office.
◔ *1.2mi/2km – around 1hr.*
From La Madrague to Port-d'Alon (information panels).
Walk down the steps into the undergrowth at the foot of the Bastide and Nartette vineyards. Continue to the orchid meadow. Pass along an **area of dunes** surrounded by sparse woodland

Diving at Saint-Cyr-sur-Mer

©Mirko Zanni/WaterFr/age Fotostock

to the gateway of the Nartette estate before rejoining the road. The path continues on the other side through an olive grove and leads to the "**immortal tree**". Follow the fencing on the right and enter the undergrowth. When you reach a chain, turn right along the path leading to the **Table des Cultures Traditionnelles**. Walk back along the path in the opposite direction.

Underwater Discovery Tour
Around 2hr. Diving suit, flippers, masks and snorkel supplied. Reservation required. Jun–Sep 9.30am and 2pm. 18€ (child 15€). 04 94 88 06 15. *Discover the marine world, its fauna and flora around Port-d'Alon.*

ADDRESSES

STAY

○ **Le Petit Nice** – *Les Lecques.* 04 94 32 00 64. www.hotelpetitnice.com. *Closed 15 Nov–15 Mar. 31 rooms.* 8.50€. Calm and beautiful garden. Small rooms with contemporary decor; the annexe rooms are simpler

but more roomy. The bay windows of the restaurant open out onto the swimming pool and greenery.

○○○ **Grand Hôtel Les Lecques** – *Les Lecques.* 04 94 26 23 01. www.grand-hotel-les-lecques.com. *58 rooms. Restaurant* ○○○. The paths cutting across the luxuriant park surrounding this hotel are bordered with palms, pine trees and morning glory. A most appealing setting for the stunning 19C mansion. Cheerful rooms appointed in Provençal tradition. Outdoor pool.

○○○○ **Hôtel Dolce Frégate** – *rte. de Bandol.* 04 94 29 39 39. www.dolce-fregate-hotel.fr 133 rooms. 22€. This hotel, leisure complex, conference centre and 27-hole golf course is set amid lush vineyards. The Provençal interior is soothing and simple. Decorated in sunny colours, the Mas des Vignes restaurant enjoys a **panoramic** terrace. The Restanque brasserie is ideal for less formal dining.

SHOPPING

Markets – Traditional market on Sunday mornings; regional specialities at La Madrague Port (Mon and Thu mornings), Place Gabriel-Péri (Tue and Fri mornings) and Les Lecques (Wed and Sat mornings).

SPORT AND LEISURE

Beaches – 1mi/2km of sandy beach lines the semicircular bay running from Les Lecques to La Madrague. Further west *(10min by car)* the **Calanque de Port-d'Alon** affords greater privacy.

Port de la Madrague – *Port authority.* 04 94 26 39 81. 400 moorings, including 37 set aside for tourist traffic.

Golf de Frégate – *D 559, route de Bandol.* 04 94 29 38 00. www.dolce-fregate-hotel.fr/golf/golf. 18-hole, world-class court and 9-hole model court offering **views** of the sea.

Aqualand – *ZAC des Pradeaux.* 08 92 68 66 13. www.aqualand.fr. *Closed Oct–May.* 25€ (child 18.50€). Waterpark with slides, wave pool and swimming pools.

Lecques Aquanaut Centre – *Nouveau Port des Lecques.* 04 94 26 35 35. www.lecques-aquanaut.fr. Diving club.

Sanary-sur-Mer★

Var

This charming resort, all pink and white, is lively year-round. It has a little fishing port bordered by palm trees and a bay with fine beaches well-protected from the Mistral winds by the wooded hills. Exiled German intellectuals and writers, including Berthold Brecht and Thomas Mann, made their home here in the 1930s.

▶ **Population:** 18,023.
Michelin Map: 340 J7; local map p121.
Info: 2 quai du Général-de-Gaulle. ℘04 94 74 01 04. www.sanarysurmer.com.
Location: Located 3mi/5km from Bandol; 8mi/13km from Toulon.

SIGHTS

Chapelle Notre-Dame-de-Pitié

Access via blvd. Courbet.

The 16C chapel on a hillock west of the town is decorated with votive offerings, mostly naive paintings. Outside is a **view**★ of Sanary Bay.

Tour Romane

Port. ○Open 10am–12.30pm, 3–6.30pm. ◎No charge. ℘04 94 74 01 04. www.scuba-museum.com

This 13C watchtower (70.5ft/21.5m tall), enclosed by a hotel, houses a museum dedicated to F. Dumas, a pioneer of deep-sea diving. The collection includes antique tools for underwater hunting and diving, and objects from ancient ship wrecks in Sanary Bay.

🚗 DRIVING TOURS

1 GROS CERVEAU★★

8mi /13km. Allow about 1.5hr.

▷ *From Sanary take ave. Europe-Unie, at Ollioules turn left onto D 20.*

The drive begins through terraced gardens and vineyards, with **views** over the inner harbour of Toulon, gradually extending southeast over Toulon and Cap Sicié Peninsula.

Farther on, the **view**★ is stunning, starting with the Grès de Ste-Anne (enormous rocks honeycombed with caves), on the right, Beausset Plain, the Ste-Baume Massif, the Évenos hills, the Ollioules Gorges and the sweeping coastline.

▷ *5mi/8km after Ollioules pull into the layby (where you can also do a U-turn, if necessary).*

Walk through scrubland along a winding path to the top of Gros Cerveau. At the foot of the small fort (alt. 1,453ft/443m), take in the **view**★★ of the coast from the Giens Peninsula to Île Verte, south of La Ciotat.

2 MONT CAUME★★

14.3mi/23km northeast. Allow 2hr.

▷ *Leave Sanary on ave. de l'Europe-Unie going east on D 11 to Ollioules.*

Ollioules

This flower-growing town is dominated by a 13C castle skirted by historic arcaded houses and a Provençal Romanesque church.

▷ *Beyond Ollioules turn left onto D N8 and through the gorges.*

Gorges d'Ollioules★

Admired by Victor Hugo, these arid and sinuous gorges were formed by the Reppe which flows into Sanary Bay. Higher up on the left are the Grès de Ste-Anne, a curious mass of eroded sandstone rocks.

▷ *In Ste-Anne-d'Évenos, turn right onto D 462. Turn right towards Évenos and park near a cross set in a rock.*

Sanary-sur-Mer harbour

© Wadey James/Apa Publications

Évenos★

🥾 *15min round trip.*

The village is a jumble of grey basalt stone houses, now restored, clinging to the steep rocky slopes beneath the ruins of a 16C castle. Its keep stands on the edge of a volcano of which the lava slag is still visible. A platform affords **views** of Destel, Ollioules Gorges, Gros Cerveau and Sainte Baume on the horizon.

▶ *Continue east along D 62 turning left at Col du Corps-de-Garde onto D 662.*

Mont Caume

Mont Caume rises to 2,628ft/801m, and its steep approach road offers fine viewpoints. From the top there is a magnificent **panorama**★★ of the coast.

3 PRESQU'ÎLE DU CAP SICIÉ★

Round trip of the peninsula 15.5mi /25km. Allow 2hr.

▶ *From Sanary take ave.d'Estienne-d'Orves towards Six-Fours. The road skirts Bonnegrâce beach. Turn right at the foot of Cap Nègre.*

Parc de la Méditerranée

👥 Exotic species for plant lovers and play areas for kids.

The top of **Cap Nègre** affords a **view** over Sanary Bay. The 19C **battery** houses a military history centre.

Le Brusc

Fishing village and resort; ferries to **Île des Embiez** (▶ *see below*) leave from the port.

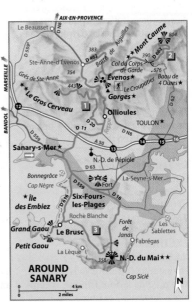

AROUND SANARY

Petit Gaou

The rocky promontory pounded by the sea, once an island, resembles a Breton seascape. Good **views** of the coast.

Grand Gaou

Accessed via a pedestrian bridge, this island was designated a nature preserve in 2000 and enjoys a wild aspect. It is crossed by a botanical path and has designated areas for picnics.

▷ *Return to Le Brusc and take D 16 on the right; turn off to the left at Roche-Blanche.*

The road runs parallel to the coast about 0.6mi/1km inland but gives glimpses of La Ciotat, Bandol and Sanary. At the crossroads there is a **view**★★ of the Toulon harbour, Cap Cépet, the Giens Peninsula and the Îles d'Hyères.

▷ *Turn right; park at the radio station. No access to cars mid-June to mid-September.*

Chapelle Notre-Dame-du-Mai★★

Behind radio station. ⏰*Call for hours.* ☎*04 94 25 50 39.*
The chapel sits at the highest point of Cap Sicié (1,043ft/318m). Perched over a dizzying drop, it affords a **panorama**★★ of the coast from the Îles d'Hyères to the calanques east of Marseilles.

▷ *Make a u-turn; at the crossroads continue straight ahead.*

The narrow road cuts through the **forêt de Janas,** planted with conifers, before rejoining D 16 on the left.

Six-Fours-les-Plages

⏰*see SIX-FOURS-LES-PLAGES.*

▷ *Return to Sanary on D 559.*

EXCURSION
ÎLES DES EMBIEZ★

The biggest of the five islands (95ha/235 acres), Île de la Tour Fondue, is commonly known as Les Embiez.

The second largest island, Grand Gaou, is linked to the mainland by a footbridge. The Île du Grand Rouveau has an automatically manned lighthouse and Petit Rouveau is a bird sanctuary. The smallest island, Petit Gaou, serves as a 🅿 car park on the road from Le Brusc.

Access to the Island – *Société Paul Ricard.* ☎*04 94 10 65 20. www.les-embiez. com.* ⊛*9€ winter/11€ summer round trip (child 7€/9€).* 13 to 24 crossings per day *(8min)* from Le Brusc at Six-Fours.

👤👤 **Aquascope** – *Île des Embiez, Brusc, Six-Fours-les-Plages.* ⏰*Open Jul–Aug 9am–6pm; Apr–Jun and Sept 2.30–5pm.* ⏰*Closed public holidays.* 🔍*Guided tours (30min).* ⊛*16€ (child 9€).* ☎*04 94 34 17 85.* Observe underwater life through the transparent hull of a boat.

👤👤 **Aquavision** – *Île des Embiez, Quai St-Pierre, Six-Fours-les-Plages.* ⏰*Open Apr–Jun and Sept Wed–Sun 2.15pm. Jul–Aug 10.30am, 11.45am, 2.15pm, 3.30pm, 4.45pm.* ⊛*16€ (child 9€).* ☎*06 62 11 72 89. www.littoral-bleu.com.* A 40-minute tour of the port and sealife in a glass-bottomed boat.

VISIT
Île des Embiez★

Separated from the Port du Brusc by a lagoon and surrounded by rich fishing banks, the Île des Embiez is highly popular with anglers and divers. Boasting statues, kitsch houses, an oceanographic museum, creeks and beaches, this island, which belongs to the Fondation Paul-Ricard (⏰ *see BANDOL)* is ideal for a day-long excursion.

👤👤 Institut Océanographique Paul-Ricard★

Aquarium Museum: ⏰*Open daily 10am –noon, 1.30–5.30pm.* ⏰*Closed Sat afternoon Sept–Jun, Wed and Sun mornings Nov–Mar, 24 Dec–1 Jan.* ⊛*4.50€ (child 2€).* ☎*04 94 34 02 49. www.institut-paul-ricard.org.*
An old naval gun site on the St-Pierre promontory houses an oceanographic institute that performs research on marine biology, fish farming and sea pollution. The **museum** has 30 sea-water **aquariums** and 100 species of aquatic animal.

Beaches

The coast is lined with a succession of sandy coves and rocky headlands. Dorée and Gorguette beaches lie between Sanary and Bandol; Cousse Bay is home to Beaucours pebble beach; Portissol beach is nestled in the bay of the same name and Bonnegrâce beach lies between Sanary and Six-Fours.

TOUR OF ÎLE DES EMBIEZ

The island is reserved for walkers and cyclists. A small tourist train also runs regular services.

The Coastal Path★

4.3mi/7km. Maps of the island are available from the Six-Fours tourist office or the island's information point (peak season).

Allow 90min on foot to tour the island's fine gravel beaches, rugged coastline with coves, salt marshes, scrubland, umbrella pine woods, flower gardens and vineyards.

♙♙ Little Train

Timetables available from the info point; approximately 10 departures a day depending on boat service. ⊜6€ (6–18 yrs 3€). ℘ 06 88 69 76 78. 40min discovery tour of the former salt marshes, the Japanese garden and vineyards. Paul Ricard's former chauffeur drives the "micheline".

Les Terres

Start at the **chapelle Ste-Cécile**, with its stained-glass windows celebrating Paul Ricard's passions (a rose, an anchor and a guitar). Statues, low-reliefs and colonnades in the style of ancient Greece scattered among the island's gardens pay tribute to Ricard's interest in Mediterranean culture. To the south, don't miss Ricard's last resting place at the foot of the **Tour du Coucoussan**.

The Marina

Dominated by the ruins of the Château de Sabran, this busy, high-tech marina plays host to some 700 boats a year, mostly sailboats.

ADDRESSES

🏠STAY

⊜⊜ **Chambre d'Hôte Villa Lou Gardian** – *646 rte. de Bandol.* ℘04 94 88 05 73. www.lou-gardian.com. 4 rooms. ⌷.⚐. Despite its location near a main road, the colourful, minimalistically decorated rooms of this recently renovated hotel are comparatively quiet. Choose one nearer the pool. A large garden, a tennis court and a table d'hôte set up in the summer patio await your arrival.

♟/EAT

⊜ **Chez Mico** – *18 rue Barthélémy-de-Don.* ℘04 94 74 16 73. www.chezmico.fr. *Closed Mon–Tue; Jul-Aug Tue and Fri noon; Feb–early Mar.* A local institution for over 35 years, this restaurant serves Mediterranean cuisine in an eclectic dining room decorated with old cooking utensils, travel souvenirs and carnival masks.

⊜ **Restaurant du Théâtre** – *Impasse de l'Enclos, near the theater.* ℘04 94 88 04 16. *Closed Sun eve., Mon.* Take a few steps down and enter this U-shaped restaurant appointed with rustic furnishings. Your attention will soon be caught by the mouthwatering sight of salmon, meats, prawns and skewered game roasting in the open fireplace!

♙ENTERTAINMENT

Centre National de Création et de Diffusion Culturelles – *Chateauvallon.* www.chateauvallon.com. Closed Sun. Indoor and open-air amphitheatre with a diverse programme of theatre, music, dance, circus and arts shows throughout the year.

CALENDAR

St-Pierre et de la Lavande – Festival of the sea, every June.

Fête de la St-Nazaire – Every August, with Provençal games.

Six-Fours-les-Plages

Var

Sandy beaches, a wild coastline and an ancient abandoned village make Six-Fours ideal to explore on foot.

OLD SIX-FOURS

▶ *Access via ave. du Maréchal-Juin; turn left onto a narrow road.*

Fort de Six-Fours★

From the platform (alt. 689ft/210m) at the entrance to the 19C fort (⚊ *closed to the public*), a **panorama**★ extends from east to west over Toulon harbour and coastline.

Collégiale St-Pierre

🕐*Open Wed–Mon 9am–12pm, 2–6pm.* 📞04 94 34 24 75.

At the foot of the fortress stands the church of the now-abandoned village of old Six-Fours. The monks of Montmajour and St-Victor established the priory and chapel in the 11C. Don't miss the polyptych by **Louis Bréa**.

Coastal Trails

To follow this by road, *see Driving Tour* ③*Cap Siciéa in SANARY-SUR-MER.* The first of the two hikes here is easy (3.7mi/6km), the second more difficult (6mi/10km).

🚶 *1.5hr. Start at Bonnegrâce beach.* The path runs along the beaches through low, thorny vegetation and over the **Cap Négre** to the fishing port of **Le Brusc**.

🚶 *4hr. Start from Le Brusc.* From the roundabout, climb the Chemin de Gardiole and, via the Chemin de Lèque, the Haute Lecques The tarred path ends after the chemin des Gargadoux. This part of the coastal trail is called the *Corniche Merveilleuse.* Climb to the **Chapel Notre-Dame-de-Mai** (👞*see p 115*) The trail continues to Cap Sicié's Fabrégas beach.

▶ **Population:** 34,325.
🚲 **Michelin Map:** 340 K7; region map p99.
🏠 **Info:** Promenade Charles-de-Gaulle. 📞04 94 07 02 21. www.six-fours-les-plages.com.
▶ **Location:** The *commune* of Six-Fours-les-Plages encompasses 125 hamlets and districts around the central town of Reynier.

ADDRESSES

🛏STAY

🛏🛏 **Hôtel du Parc** – *112 rue Marius-Bondil, Le Brusc.* 📞04 94 34 00 15. www.locanna.com. 17 rooms. 🍽8€. Just 650ft/200m from the port of Le Brusc and its beaches. The hotel is situated in a large house, its dining room overlooking the back garden.

🍴/EAT

🍽 **Le Ligure** – *60 ave. John-Kennedy, Route de Playes.* 📞04 94 25 63 87. *Closed mid-Nov–mid-Dec, Sun eve, Mon off-season.* Outstanding views can be had of Sanary Bay from the **panoramic** terrace. Fish, seafood and freshly-cooked pizzas.

🚶SPORT AND LEISURE

HIKING & CYCLING

The massif du Cap Sicié has five hiking trails *(about 2hr each)* and five circular bike trails (6mi/10km to 15mi/25km).

WATERSPORTS

Six-Fours/Les Embiez has been awarded the "station nautique" label for its range of watersports facilities.

🎉 EVENTS

Fête de la Bouillabaisse – Held in June, this festival celebrates the local dish *bouillabaisse* (tastings and live shows).

Le Pradet

Var

This charming resort nestled beneath the Massif de la Colle Noire has a good selection of small, easily accessible beaches tucked between rocky outcrops. Its minerology museum and botanical trail make this a pleasant excursion from Toulon.

RESORT LIFE
Beaches
La Garonne Bay is punctuated by remarkable **creeks**. Some are accessible by car, but the best way to explore them is to take the coastal walking path.

Parks and gardens
Bordering the tourist office, the **Cravéro park** is renowned for its palm groves and shady, wooded pet village with parrots, goats and other animals. Also in the park, the Cravéro Le Camus gallery, housed in a former rose pergola, holds regular contemporary art exhibitions (*open Sat–Thu 3–6pm; Fri 10am–noon, 2–6pm; 04 94 08 69 79*). The centrally-located **Bois de Courbebaisse** is home to a 12acre/5ha botanical garden. Don't miss the charming Moorish pavilion.

Coastal Footpath★
4.2mi/7km. Allow 3 to 4hr.
04 94 05 35 26. The winding path is very steep in places. Sheer steps cut from the rock give access to the beaches.
Following a fire that swept through the Colle-Noire massif in 2005, some changes have been made to the path network. To the west, the steep slope above **Pin de Galle** beach offers magnificent **views** over Toulon harbour. The numerous cabins in the pine wood add to the bucolic charm of the setting. The shaded path joins the road through the park before descending steeply to **Monaco Beach**. At the end of this beach, part of which is used by naturists, the path begins beyond a low wall and climbs a cliff covered by superb *maquis* vegetation.
A little further on there is a lovely **view**★ of the inlets along the coast.

- **Population:** 10,603.
- **Michelin Map:** 340 L7; region map p90.
- **Info:** Pl. Général-de-Gaulle. 04 94 21 71 69. www.ot-lepradet.fr.
- **Location:** Pradet sits on the eastern edge of Toulon, at the foot of the Colline de Paradis and Mont des Oiseaux, on route D559.

A well-marked path leads down to **Les Bonnettes beach** at the foot of a remarkable rocky inlet. A former path linking this beach to La Garonne beach is closed due to fire damage, as is the path between the Pas des Gardéens and La Mine. In season there is a lifeguards' post and an open-air café here. Walk to Oursinières along the road. Beyond the port a footpath to the right leaves the road to Le Pradet. It leads past **panoramic** viewpoints on the cliffs to **Bau Rouge**.

SIGHTS
Musée de la Mine de Cap-Garonne★
In Le Pradet take D86 south towards Plage de la Garonne. After the beach, take the road which climbs to the left, signposted "La Mine".
Guided tours (1hr) 2–5pm.
Closed 1 Jan, 24–25, 31 Dec.
6.50€ (child 4€). 04 94 08 32 46. www.mine-capgaronne.fr.
Wearing a hardhat, visitors get to explore the old copper ore mines worked here since the 16C. The mines closed in 1917, when a reduction in the ore's copper content made it unprofitable.
The tour focuses on the redeveloped part of the galleries and, through several reconstructions and presentations, illustrates the long-standing evolution of working methods and the daily lives of miners at Cap Garonne.
At the end of the tour, in the **great hall**★, discover the various colours of copper ore at tables with magnifying glasses.

HYÈRES, THE GOLDEN ISLANDS

When most people think of the French Riviera, they imagine sunbathing on secluded beaches, discovering local crafts in the cobblestone streets of historic villages and partying in glitzy clubs surrounded by celebrities. And that's exactly what visitors to the Golden Islands of Hyères and the Maures Massif will find. This part of the Mediterranean coastline is an Eden-like paradise of unspoilt islands and sandy beaches framed by forested mountains.

Chic resorts full of luxury yachts share a decidedly Provençal spirit with tiny perched villages that haven't changed in centuries. And while humans have made their mark with their lush gardens, Belle Époque mansions, imported palm trees and ancient forts, the natural beauty of the region has been carefully protected from the unchecked development plaguing less fortunate corners of the Côte d'Azur.

Highlights

1 Hire a boat for the day to visit **The Golden Islands**, a world away from the glitz of the French Riviera (p130)

2 Snorkel along the underwater nature trail at the **Île de Port-Cros** (p142)

3 Drive through the scenic forested hills along the **Corniche des Maures** (p147)

4 Escape the crowds of St-Tropez with a coastal hike around the **St-Tropez Peninsula** (p162)

5 Enjoy panoramic views from the 11C ramparts of the perched village of **Grimaud** (p166)

The Green *Département*

The residents of the Golden Islands and Maures Massif take the protection and preservation of their environment very seriously. Situated at the heart of the Var *département*, where 62 percent of land remains undeveloped, this is the second-greenest place in France.

Maritime pines, cork oaks, chestnut trees and maquis scrub make up most of the Maures Massif flora, thriving on the ancient geological formations that form its rocky peaks.

Forest fires are a constant threat and after the partial devastation of the Maures Massif during the heatwave of 2003, the authorities have cracked down on barbecuing and smoking along forest trails.

Aerial view of Petit Langoustier, Île de Porquerolles

126

Environmental Preservation

By far the greatest threat to the local environment is property development. Much of the land, coastline and even the waters around the Golden Islands, named for the glow given off by mica and quartz rock when it catches the sun, has now been placed under the protection of the French National Park of Port Cros. Île de Port-Cros is the only 100 percent car-free island along this stretch of coastline and its clear waters and underwater nature trail are popular with divers. The Golden Islands are also a haven for endangered fauna, with sanctuaries for tropical birds, fish and even the threatened Hermann tortoise.

Clean and Accessible Coastline

Coastal hiking trails, known as the *"sentier littoral"*, have their own special protection agency, the Conservatoire du Littoral. Not only do they keep the coastline clean, they also make sure it stays open to the public. Since 1976, any new properties built on the beach have to leave a 9.8ft/3m path closest to the water for hikers to use. This law covers over 125mi/200km of the Var coastline, including the scenic St-Tropez peninsula. While there are many sandy, family-friendly beaches such as Le Lavandou, Ste-Maxime and Pampelonne, much of the coastline is made up of rocky inlets perfect for fishing or finding a bit of privacy away from the crowds.

From Pirates to Artists

Like most of the French Riviera, the Golden Islands of Hyères were a haven for pirates until they were hounded out of the region in the 17C by Louis XIV, who replaced their lairs with military forts, many of which still dot the coastline today. The early perched villages and monasteries were often given their lands and allowed to cultivate them tax-free in return for keeping an eye out for invaders.

The arrival of the railroad in the mid-1800s attracted the likes of Queen Victoria and other wealthy Anglophone travellers hoping for a little winter sun. The chic crowds eventually moved

Cap Lardier, St-Tropez Peninsula

J. Malburet/MICHELIN

eastward to Cannes and Nice, leaving this area to the writers, artists and filmmakers such as Colette, Anaïs Nin, Matisse, Jean Cocteau, Paul Signac and Roger Vadim, whose 1956 film, *"And God Created Woman"* starring then wife, Brigitte Bardot, launched St-Tropez into the limelight it still enjoys today.

Local Industry

Tourism is the principal industry in this region, with more than 25 percent of properties used as second homes for holidaymakers. Flowers, fruit, and grapes for Côte de Provence wines are also produced here, along with natural cork from cork oak trees. Before becoming part of the nature reserve in 1995, the marshland ponds of the Giens Peninsula were used to harvest over 30,000 tons of sea salt each year.

Although the Var department is named after the river which runs through the Côte d'Azur region, administrative juggling after the French Revolution redrew the boundaries and the river no longer flows through the department that bears its name.

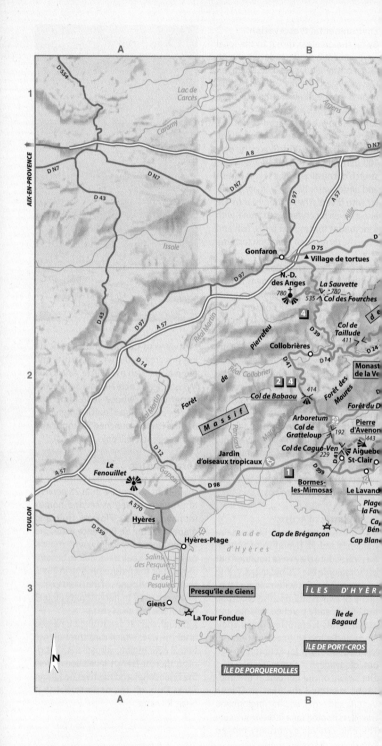

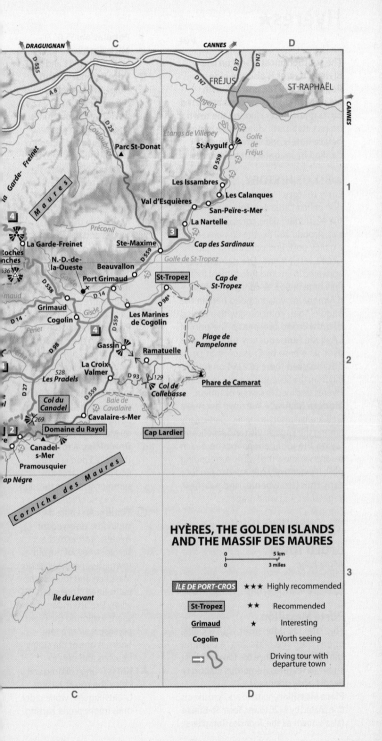

DRAGUIGNAN

CANNES

C

D

D 555

A 8

CANNES

D 37

D N7

FRÉJUS

ST-RAPHAËL

Argens

D 25

Coulaubrier

Étangs de Villepey

Golfe de Fréjus

Parc St-Donat

St-Aygulf

D 559

la Garde-Freinet

Maures

1

Les Issambres

Les Calanques

Val d'Esquières

San-Peïre-s-Mer

La Nartelle

Préconil

4

Roches blanches

La Garde-Freinet

336

N.-D.-de-la-Oueste

Ste-Maxime

3

Cap des Sardinaux

D 559

Golfe de St-Tropez

Beauvallon

Port Grimaud

St-Tropez

Cap de St-Tropez

D 558

D 14

maud

Grimaud

Gisele

D 98¹

Les Marines de Cogolin

Cogolin

D 559

4

D 14

Périer

Gassin

D 98

Ramatuelle

Plage de Pampelonne

2

528

Les Pradels

La Croix Valmer

D 93

129

D 27

D 559

Col de Collebasse

Phare de Camarat

Col du Canadel

Baie de Cavalaire

2

269

Cavalaire-s-Mer

Domaine du Rayol

Cap Lardier

Canadel-s-Mer

Pramousquier

Cap Négre

Corniche des Maures

Île du Levant

**HYÈRES, THE GOLDEN ISLANDS
AND THE MASSIF DES MAURES**

0   5 km

0   3 miles

ÎLE DE PORT-CROS   ★★★ Highly recommended

St-Tropez   ★★ Recommended

Grimaud   ★ Interesting

Cogolin   Worth seeing

⇨   Driving tour with
departure town

3

C

D

Hyères ★

Var

The southernmost resort on the Riviera, Hyères is also the oldest. Popular in the 18C and 19C with wealthy English aristocrats attracted by its mild winter climate, the town boasts elaborate villas, Belle Époque palace hotels and wide avenues flanked by magnificent palm trees.

A BIT OF HISTORY

Early History – A Hellenic trading station called Olbia was founded here in the 4C, trading skins, coral, oil, wine and salt. Around 200 BC, the Romans set up a galley port, Pomponiana, next to the Greek settlement. The name Hyères appeared in an official document for the first time in 963. A nunnery, St-Pierre-d'Almanarre, was founded here in the Middle Ages, coinciding with a period of growth and prosperity. The port of L'Aygade (subsequently silted up) was used as a base by Crusaders; St Louis disembarked there in 1254 on returning from the Seventh Crusade. In the 17C Hyères declined in favour of Toulon.

Modern Revival – The town became a well-known resort in the 19C, particularly among the English, Irish and Americans, laying the foundations for the beach resorts we know today. The surrounding plain is extensively cultivated to produce early fruit (strawberries and peaches), vegetables and wine grapes.

⚓ WALKING TOUR

① OLD TOWN
Allow 1.5hr.

▶ *Leave from pl. Georges-Clemenceau.*

Porte Massillon
This late-13C gate, inset with a clock, opens onto rue Massillon, a bustling shopping street. Once the town's richest street, it features numerous elaborate Renaissance doorways.

Place Massillon, home to a daily market, is dominated by a 12C tower, **Tour St-Blaise** (also known as the Tour des Templiers),

▶ **Population:** 55,007.

⚙ **Michelin Map:** 340 L7; local maps p131 and p132.

ℹ **Info:** Rotonde du Park Hôtel, ave. de Belgique, Hyères. ℘04 94 01 84 50. www.hyeres-tourisme.com.

▶ **Location:** The greater Hyères area is divided in two by the Voie Rapide (Olbia, or N 98), with the old quarters on the slope to the north, and the airport, beaches and harbour to the south. Hyères and the Giens Peninsula operate several bus lines (bus station on pl. Joffre, ℘08 25 00 06 50), mostly serving the beaches (Almanarre and Ayguade). Links to Îles d'Or by boat.

🅿 **Parking:** No charge for parking in the harbour or on place Louis-Versin. Underground car parks *(fee)* can be found outside the Casino, in the Olbia shopping mall and in the Denis gardens on place du Maréchel-Joffre.

👁 **Don't Miss:** A tour of the Belle Époque villas and hotel palaces in summer, available through the tourist office.

🕐 **Timing:** An entire day should be reserved for Hyères. Start with the scenic streets of the old town, shopping on the rue Massillon and tours of the palm-lined streets and 19C villas. The afternoon can be spent exploring the Giens peninsula, with a few hours at one of the sunny beaches and ports.

👪 **Kids:** Young children will enjoy the zoo at Jarsins Olbius-Riquier, while older ones might prefer karting.

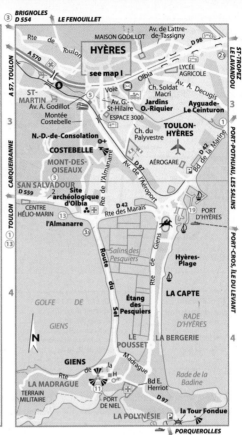

the last remnant of a Knights Templar commandery, which now houses temporary art exhibitions (⏱ open Apr–Oct Wed–Sun 10am–noon, 4–7pm; Nov–Mar Wed–Sun 10am–noon, 2–5pm; ⇔ no charge; ℘04 94 35 22 36).

▶ From pl. Massillon take the steps to rue Ste-Catherine and pl. St-Paul.

Place St-Paul

From this terraced square, once the site of the cloisters of the Collégiale St-Paul, there is a fine **view**★ (viewing table) over the peninsula.

Ancienne Collégiale St-Paul

Pl. Saint-Paul. ⏱ Open Apr–Sept Wed–Mon 10am–noon, 4–7pm; Oct–Mar Wed–Sun 10am–noon, 2–5.30pm. ⇔ No charge. ℘04 94 00 55 50 (Église St Louis).

The Romanesque bell tower of this former collegiate church dates back to the 12C. A fine Renaissance door and monumental stairway lead to a narthex (formerly the nave of the Romanesque church) covered with votive offerings, some dating from the 17C.

Old Streets

Porte St-Paul (gateway) near the collegiate church is incorporated into a handsome Renaissance house with a turret at one corner. Pass beneath and follow rue St-Paul to rue Ste-Claire, where the **porte des Princes** frames the chevet and bell tower of the Collégiale St-Paul. Retrace your steps to rue de Paradis (to the right of the Renaissance house), where there is a fine Romanesque house (no 6), which has been restored.

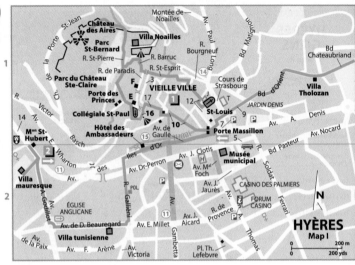

▶ *Continue down rue du Four Cauvin, right into rue Saint Bernard and down rue Barruc. Enter parc St-Bernard.*

Villa de Noailles

Montée de Noailles. ▰Guided tours on request. ⏱Open Jul–mid-Jun Wed–Mon 4–7pm, Fri 4–10pm. ▰No charge. ☎04 98 08 01 98. www.villanoailles-hyeres.com.

In 1923 the Vicomte de Noailles and his wife Marie-Laure, wealthy patrons of the arts, commissioned this winter villa from the Belgian architect Mallet-Stevens. With its covered swimming pool and 60 or so rooms, it was one of the first modern homes on the Riviera and quickly became a favourite rendez-vous for avant-garde artists in the 1920s (Picasso, Giacometti, Man Ray and Dalí). The city restored the villa in 1986 and temporary exhibitions are held on the first floor. The Cubist garden was designed by Gabriel Guévrékian.

Parc St-Bernard(Jardin de Noailles)
Next to the Villa Noailles.

The park encloses the castle ruins and enjoys a remarkable variety of Mediterranean flora. The terraces command a picturesque **view**★ from the old town to the peninsula and the islands.

▶ *Exit the villa to the west and walk north along the rue St-Pierre.*

Château des Aires
*The castle ruins can also be reached by car along Montée de Noailles (car park). The ruins are quite extensive, with sections of wall, square and round towers (13C–15C), and a crenallated keep. The panoramic **views**★ from the northern side are particularly stunning.*

▶ *Return to rue St-Pierre, taking a left down the small rue du Puit St-Pierre onto rue Barbuc. Continue down rue Saint-Esprit and rue Bourgneuf. Before the bottom of the street take a right to pl. Bourgneuf, then left onto rue St-Louis.*

Église St-Louis
Pl. de la République. ℘04 94 00 55 50.
This is the former church of the Cord-eliers convent. The façade with three doors surmounted by a rose window brings to mind the Italian Romanesque style. A fine example of the transition from Romanesque to Provençal Gothic.

2 THE 19C TOWN
By car or on foot.

Between 1850 and 1880, dozens of luxurious hotels and villas were built to accommodate the town's rich win-ter tourists. Its famous visitors include Queen Victoria, the novelist RL Steven-son, Victor Hugo and Maupassant.

The "Godillot" District
This is the name of the western part of the town centre developed by **Alexis Godillot**, arms supplier to the Second Empire, who commissioned the **maison St-Hubert** (70 ave. des Iles-dOr).

▷ Go down ave. Godillot and turn left on ave. de Beauregard.

Across from the Anglican St Paul's Church is the **Villa Tunisienne** in Moorish style, once home to Godillot's architect, Chapoulart. Turn left down rue Gallieni, where you'll find the ex-**Hôtel des Palmiers** (1884). On the avenue des Îles-d'Or, don't miss the **Hôtel des Ambassadeurs** with its entrance flanked by four caryatids mounted on plinths.

▷ At pl. Georges Clemenceau, follow the rue Dr-de-Seignoret, then blvd d'Orient.

Quartier Chateaubriand
The beautiful Classical-style villas in the Quartier d'Orient, developed from 1850, have a touch of fantasy. On boulevard Chateaubriand and boulevard d'Orient, admire the villas Léon-Antoinette, **Tholozan**, La Favorite and Villa Ker-André.

OTHER SIGHTS
Walks and tours
The **tourist office** offers free guides to the medieval town and the region's forests, forts, coastal paths, gardens and parks. Fee-based **guided tours** led by qualified guides are also available by reservation.

Parc du Château Ste-Claire
Ave. Edith-Warton. ⊙ Open summer 8am–7pm; rest of the year 8am–5pm. No charge.
A fine villa built in 1850 by Colonel Voutier, the man who discovered the Venus de Milo sits in the middle of this park filled with exotic plants.

▲▲ Jardins Olbius-Riquier
Ave. Ambroise-Thomas. ⊙Open daily 7.30am–5pm; summer until 8pm. No charge.
These extensive gardens (16 acres/6.5ha) are filled with a rich variety of tropical plants, palms and cacti. In the **green-house** the more fragile species can be seen together with a few rare animals. The gardens include a small **zoo**.

Chapelle Notre-Dame-de-Consolation
Access from Hyères on the D 559, direction Carqueiranne, to the top of Colline de Costebelle. ℘04 94 57 75 93.

A Touch of Exoticism

Hyères is famous for its palm trees. The cultivation of palms began around 1867 and reached its peak in the 1930s. There are no fewer than 10 varieties of Hyères palms, many of which have been exported as far as Saudi Arabia. In Hyères itself, strollers can enjoy the exotic charm of the palms in avenue Godillot, one of the most attractive streets in France, and in three public gardens: the Casino gardens, Roy gardens and Denis gardens. Discover a complete range of existing species in the fine Olbius-Risquier gardens.

Tour Fondue, Gien peninsula

S. Sauvignier/ MICHELIN

There has been a sanctuary on the top of Costebelle hill since the 11C. The present chapel was built in 1955. A huge coloured sculpture of Our Lady against the cross by Lambert-Rucki forms the bell tower's vertical axis. The stark architecture of the interior is enhanced by the monumental blue and gold **stained-glass windows**★. The neighbouring promenade gives a **view**★ of the Hyères and Toulon ports.

☺ Restricted Access ☺

The western tombolo at Giens, under the protection of the Conservatoire du Littoral, is subject to strict regulations:

- ☺ Road traffic is permitted from Easter to All Saints' Day on the tombolo road, with no parking en route; the road is closed the rest of the year.

- ☺ Parking allowed only in the two car parks at each end of the western tombolo.

- ☺ To reach the beaches, use only the marked paths, without walking on the dunes or vegetation, and avoiding the marked protected zones.

- ☺ Drying sails or any canvas on the vegetation is not allowed.

Olbia Archaeological Site

Access from Hyères on the D 559, direction Carqueiranne, located at the northernmost point of L'Almanarre.
🕐*Open Apr–Sep Tue–Sat 9.30am–noon, 2–5.30pm. Closed Oct–Mar.*
📞*04 94 65 51 49. Guided tours in English by reservation.*

A fortified village and maritime market port in the 4C BC, Olbia was a stopping point on the Greek trading routes. It is one of the few sites of its kind still existing on the Mediterranean coast. A museum is scheduled to open in 2014.

BEACHES

Hyères has 12.4mi/20km of beaches under lifeguard supervision in the summer, except those on the Giens Peninsula.

L'Almanarre

This long sandy beach near the ancient site of the Greek town of Olbia is popular with windsurfers. The salt road (Route du Sel; accessible only in summer) leads along the peninsula, passing a vast salt-marsh (988 acres/400ha) and the Étang des Pesquiers.

Hyères-Plage

Fringed by a small forest of umbrella pines, the Hippodrome, La Capte and La Bergerie beaches, which run up to Giens, are lapped by shallow waters (waist-height up to 200ft/60m). Boats leave from the **port** for the Îles d'Hyères.

Ayguade-le Ceinturon

This is the old port of Hyères, where St Louis disembarked on his return from the Seventh Crusade. It is now a pleasant resort area with two sandy beaches, one on the boulevard du Front-de-Mer and the other on avenue des Girelles.

Les salins

The salt marshes were replaced by a beach many years ago. This site is sometimes called Port-Pothuaud after the fishing village.

▷ *Continue via Berriau-Plage to Port-Pothuau, a picturesque little fishing port.*

DRIVING TOUR

TOURING THE COAST
Giens Peninsula★★

The Giens Peninsula was produced by an extremely rare natural phenomenon called **tombolo**. Favourable maritime currents and the mouths of two rivers straddling the former island of Giens created a double isthmus of sand and pebbles on the rocky seabed.

The parallel bars enclose a lagoon, the **Étang des Pesquiers** (🕐 open Apr–Sep for supervised ornithological visits; ☏04 94 12 79 92) that provides an ideal habitat for water fowl. Up to 1,500 flamingos migrate here in mid-September.

The castle ruins in the small seaside resort village of **Giens** form a mound from which there is a magnificent **panorama**★★. To the south lies the port of Niel surrounded by a pine wood.

▶ *Drive east to La Tour Fondue.*

Tour Fondue

Built around 1634 then remodelled, the tower crowns a rocky promontory and once controlled the Petite Passe narrows, along with two other forts (closed to the public) on the isles of Grand and Petit Ribaud. Boats sail to the Île de Porquerolles from here. Beautiful **view** of the islands and peninsula.

Tour of the peninsula on foot

🚶 *11mi/18km. Allow 5hr.*

The partly signed route links the port of La Madrague to Badine beach through a mountainous and pine-forested coastline of hidden beaches and inlets.

EXCURSIONS
Sommet du Fenouillet

4km/2.5mi. From Hyères take ave. de Toulon, turn right onto the road signed "Fenouillet". 🚶 *30min round trip.*

From the neo-Gothic **chapel** follow the path to Le Fenouillet, the highest point of the Maurettes (955ft/291m) with a very good **panorama**★ of the Hyères and Toulon harbours and surrounding mountains.

ADDRESSES

🛏 STAY

🛌 **Hôtel l'Europe** – *45 ave. Édith-Cavell.* ☏04 94 00 67 77. www.hotel-europe-hyeres.com. *25 rooms.* 🍽8€. A restored 19C mansion close to the train station with bright rooms.

🛌 **Hôtel Port Hélène** – *D 559, at L'Almanarre.* ☏04 94 57 72 01. www.hotel-port-helene.fr. *12 rooms.* 🍽9.50€. A cute hotel fronted by a pink façade, lost among umbrella pines and palms. The rooms are well-kept, with balconies offering **views** of the sea. Very reasonable prices.

🛌–🛌 **Hôtel Les Orangers** – *64 ave. Îles d'Or.* ☏04 94 00 55 11. www.orangers-hotel.com. *16 rooms.* 🍽7€. Charming, comfortable and cosy hotel set in the medieval part of Hyères.

🛌 **Chambre d'Hôte L'Aumônerie** – *620 ave. de Fontbrun, Carqueiranne.* ☏04 94 58 53 56. www.laumonerie.com. *4 rooms.* 🍽 🍽 Reservations recommended. This blissfully quiet pink house among the maritime pines has simply appointed rooms. A private path leads directly to the beach.

🛌 **Chambre d'hôte La Buanderie** – *36 ave. des Colibris, le Mont des Oiseaux, Hyères, 2.5mi/4km south of Almanarre.* ☏04 94 38 30 98. www.la-buanderie.com. *Closed 24 Dec–2 Jan. 3 rooms.* 🍽 🍽. On a hillside overlooking the sea, this bed and breakfast is tastefully decorated with minimal fuss. The pool has a teak deck for sunbathing.

🛌 **Hôtel Les Voiliers** – *ave. du Dr-Robin, port St-Pierre.* ☏04 94 38 39 24. www.yachtclubhyeres.fr. *36 rooms.* 🍽7.50€. Decorated with a nautical theme, this hotel on the port has reasonably priced doubles and more expensive rooms with harbour **views**.

🛌🛌–🛌🛌 **Hôtel Le Soleil** – *4 rue du Rempart.* ☏04 94 65 16 26. www.hotel-du-soleil.fr. *20 rooms.* 🍽. Old house with lots of character in the upper part of the old town, near the Nouailles villa. Small, but clean rooms.

🍽/EAT

🍽 **L'Abri-Côtier** – *pl. Daviddi, Plage de l'Ayguade.* ☏04 94 66 42 58. 🍽. *Closed Oct–Mar.* Set in a beach cabana, this cheerful eatery serves Mediterranean dishes such as marinated sardines and octopus stew.

🍽 **Le Poisson Rouge** – *Port du Niel, Giens Peninsula. ✆04 94 58 92 33. www.restaurantlepoissonrouge.com. Closed Mon, Mar Tue–Thu eve., early Oct.* A seafood restaurant in an enchanting stone building. Shaded by olive trees, the terrace overlooks Port Niel.

🍽🍽 **La Colombe** – *663 route de Toulon, 1.5mi/2.5km, in La Bayorre. ✆04 94 35 35 16. www.restaurantlacolombe.com Closed Sat lunch, Mon, Sun off-season, Mon, Tue and Sat lunch Jul–Aug.* Carefully prepared local cuisine served in a traditional Provençal house. A spacious, sunny terrace and friendly service.

🍽🍽 **La Maison des Saveurs** – *18 ave. Jean-Jaurès, Carqueiranne (town centre). ✆04 94 58 62 33. www. maisondessaveurs.com. Closed Mon off-season.* This cosy, central restaurant decorated in Provençal tradition has a lovely terrace shaded by a plane tree and a very affordable menu.

🍽🍷🍽–🍽🍷🍽🍽 **Les Jardins de Bacchus** – *32 ave. Gambetta. ✆04 94 65 77 63. www.bacchushyeres.com. Closed Sun eve.* Town centre eatery serving regional wines and local meals in a renovated and modern-style dining area or on the summer terrace.

🍽🍷🍽–🍽🍷🍽🍽 **Joy** – *24 rue de Limans. ✆04 94 20 84 98. Closed 5–20 Nov, Sun–Mon off-season.* A quiet location in a pedestrianised street, an elegant setting, and contemporary cuisine make this restaurant, run by a Dutch couple, a popular choice.

🛒 SHOPPING

Pastor – *86 ave. Gambetta. ✆04 94 01 46 46. Closed Mon.* One of the most popular bakeries in Hyères, with olive fougasses, lavender bread in summer and sorbet in amazing flavours.

MARKETS

Provençal – Tue mornings on pl. de la République and Sat mornings along ave. Gambetta.

Organic – Tue, Thu and Sat mornings on pl. Vicomtesse de Noailles.

Antiques – Every first Sun of the month on pl. Clémenceau and République.

🏃 SPORTS AND LEISURE

Hyères has been awarded the *station nautique* label for its watersports facilities. Info from the tourist office or *www.france-nautisme.com.*

Diving – The area's many diving clubs include: La Londe in Hyères; Porquerolles Plongée in Porquerolles; Sun Plongée at Port-Cros and Levant-Plongée in Levant.

Funboarding – *Funboard Center, rte. de l'Almanarre. ✆04 94 57 95 33* Almanarre beach (3.7mi/6km) along the Étang des Pesquiers, facing the Golfe de Giens, is a mecca for funboarders when the *mistral* blows.

Hyères-Port Saint-Pierre – *✆04 94 12 54 40 (Hyères). ✆04 94 58 02 30 (La Capte, 125 moorings), ✆04 94 66 33 98 (l'Ayguade, 500 moorings). www.ville-hyeres.fr.* Marinas with 1,350 moorings, 120 of which are for temporary stays.

Casino – *Casino des Palmiers, ave. Ambroise-Thomas. ✆04 94 12 80 80. www.casinohyeres.fr.* Slot machines, roulette, blackjack and nightclub.

CALENDAR

Hyères Fashion and Arts Festival – Last weekend in April. Exhibitions and fashion shows by young designers and artists.

Îles d'Hyères★★★

Var

These popular islands off Hyères harbour are just a short boat trip from the coast. Le Levant, Port-Cros and the Porquerolles – also known as the Îles d'Or (Golden Islands) because of the golden reflections cast by their mica shale rocks in certain lights – offer many beautiful scenic walking trails, sandy beaches and inland hills.

A BIT OF HISTORY

A Land of Asylum

A haven of peace and prosperity for its Greek and Roman settlers, from the Middle Ages the islands came under repeated attack by pirates until François I placed Port-Cros and Levant under the protection (and rule) of the Marquis des Îles d'Or, provided that he kept them under cultivation.

Despite exemption from taxes, the islands lacked manpower until a right of asylum was established, granting criminals immunity if they remained there. Jailbirds swarmed ashore, where they turned to piracy, even attempting the capture of one of the king's ships from Toulon. Only under Louis XIV did the last of these dubious characters leave the area.

A British Coup

In 1793, after the capture of Toulon by French Revolutionaries (*see TOULON p100*), British and Spanish squadrons anchored off the Îles d'Hyères. The

- ⚭ **Michelin Map:** 340 M/N7/8; local maps p139 and p140.
- ⊞ **Info:** Bureau d'Information, Porquerolles. ✆04 94 58 33 76. www.porquerolles. com. Maison du Parc National de Port-Cros, exit village towards the lighthouse. ✆04 94 58 07 24. www.portcros parcnational.fr.
- ▷ **Location:** The three islands of the Îles d'Hyères are accessible by ferry boat. Île de Porquerolles, the largest, is close to the Giens peninsula. The best way to get around is by bike. The Île de Port-Cros, smaller and more mountainous, is a nature reserve; bicycles are not allowed. To the east is the Île du Levant, occupied primarily by a military base and private nudist beaches. No matter which island you visit, be sure to take along plenty of drinking water.
- **Kids:** A bike ride on Île de Porquerolles and, for children who swim, a snorkelling trip to the underwater trail at Port-Cros. A glass-bottomed boat makes trips from Giens to Porquerolles (*see Addresses*).

Mexico-sur-Mer

For 60 years this island was the private property of a single family. In 1911, a Belgian engineer, F. Joseph Fournier, having made his fortune in Mexico, decided to give Porquerolles as a wedding gift to his young bride. Once settled on the island with his family and an army of gardeners, he attempted to recreate the atmosphere of a Latin American hacienda by importing exotic plants. He began with the cultivation of several exotic fruits, then unknown in France – pineapples and kumquats – before adding species such as the bellombra, with its massive roots. The 445 acres/180ha of vines originally planted have been reduced by half but continue to produce a reputable rosé. This was the first vineyard to gain the AOC Côtes de Provence *appellation*.

GETTING THERE

The islands are accessible from several ports, with many companies offering half- or full-day excursions or links. Be sure not to miss the last boat back to the mainland!

From La Tour Fondue (Giens Peninsula) – *TLV (Transports Littoral Varois), Port de La Tour Fondue.* ℘*04 94 58 21 81. www.tlv-tvm.com.* Regular daily service to the Porquerolles. Circuits of the Porquerolles and Port-Cros available weekdays Jul–Aug.

From Hyères – *TLV, Port Saint-Pierre.* ℘*04 94 57 44 07. www.tlv-tvm.com. 1 to 4 departures per day depending on the season.* Trips to Port-Cros (1hr), Le Levant (1.5hrs); circuit of Port-Cros and Levant available Jul–Aug.

From Le Lavandou, Cavalaire – *Vedettes des Îles d'Or.* ℘*04 94 71 01 02. Operates mid-Apr–Sept.* Departures for Port Cros, Le Levant, Porquerolles, and St-Tropez.

A FEW GUIDELINES

Fire – During periods of major fire risk, the ALARME plan comes into force (announced before embarkation); it means that access is limited to the beaches, the coastal path and the villages. A recorded message is available by phone from 7pm the evening before: ℘*04 98 10 55 41.*

Rules – At Porquerolles and Port-Cros, it is forbidden to smoke, make fires, camp, pick the plants or flowers, leave the marked paths, litter or walk pets (outside the village); at Port-Cros it is forbidden to use bicycles, collect seashells, or fish.

Water – There are few or no places to find water on the island (but it can be purchased in the village shops), so bring plenty of your own and be sure to fill up before going on long hikes.

commander of Fort Ste-Agathe at Porquerolles, forgotten on his island by the French authorities, had only the vaguest idea of what was happening on the mainland. The British admiral invited him on board his flagship and the commander went unsuspectingly. While the whisky was circulating, British sailors landed, surprised the garrison and destroyed the fort (it was rebuilt in 1810). The ships then raised anchor taking with them, as their prisoner, the crestfallen commander.

Allied Landing (August 1944)

During the night of 14 to 15 August 1944, American troops landed on the islands of Port-Cros and Levant to eradicate the German batteries threatening the Allied Landing.

 **DRIVING TOUR**

TOURING THE ISLANDS

Île de Porquerolles★★★

Porquerolles measures 4.3mi/7km long by 2mi/3km, and was called Protè (First) by the Greek settlers who came to live along its shores. The best way to discover the island is by bicycle (hired in the village). The north coast has sandy beaches bordered by pine trees, heather and scented myrtle; the south coast is steep and rugged with one or two inlets that are easily accessible. There are few inhabitants inland, where you'll find vineyards, pine and eucalyptus woods and thick Mediterranean vegetation.

The Village

The small village of Porquerolles, which lies at the end of a minute port now used as a harbour for pleasure boats, has given its name to the whole island. The village was built by the military in the mid-19C and consists of a main square, a humble church containing an unusual

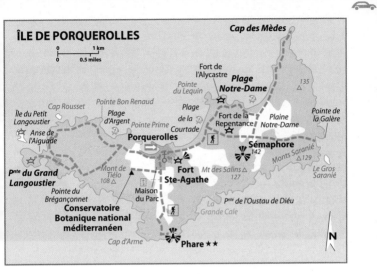

ÎLE DE PORQUEROLLES

Stations of the Cross carved by a soldier with his penknife and a few fishermen's cottages, as well as more recently constructed hotels and private houses.

Fort Ste-Agathe

🕐 *Open May–Sept 10am–noon, 2–6pm.* ⊙*4€.* 📞*04 94 00 65 41.*

This fort occupies a strategic position on a mound overlooking the port. Its walls in the shape of a trapezium are surmounted by a massive corner tower, all that remains of the original structure built by François I in 1532. It was rebuilt in 1810 (after being burnt down by the English in 1793) to meet new military requirements. The round tower is constructed on a massive scale, with walls 13ft /4m thick, 66ft/20m in diameter and 49ft/15m high, where the Parc de Port-Cros organises exhibitions on the history and maritime archaeology of the islands and the Hyères harbour.

The large circular room has a 20ft/6m high ceiling with a magnificent timber frame. From the terrace on top of the tower, with its five embrasures for large-bore cannon, there is a magnificent **view**★ of the beaches of Courtade and Notre Dame to the east, and the wooded massifs to the west.

⊙ *On exiting the village of Porquerolles, follow the route du Phare,* *then turn right at the carrefour des Oliviers to the Hameau Agricole.*

Conservatoire Botanique National Méditerranéen

🕐 *Open Apr–Jun and Sep–Oct 9.30am–12.30pm, 1.30–5pm; Jul 9.30am–12.30pm, 1.30–6pm.* ⊙*No charge.* 📞*04 94 12 30 32.*

Since 1985 most of the island has been managed by the National Park of Port-Cros, which owns the land. Created in 1979, the Conservatoire was set up to preserve the area and to protect the Mediterranean fauna and flora thriving in the basin. Educational displays.

Walks on the Porquerolles
Lighthouse Walk★★

🚶 *1.5hr round trip.*

This walk to the lighthouse *(phare)* is a "must" even for tourists with only a few hours to spend on the island. The **lighthouse** (🚶 *guided tours 10am–noon, 2–4pm;* ⊙*no charge)* stands on the most southerly point of the island and has a beam which carries 34mi /54km. From the top a **panorama**★★ extends over most of the island.

Beach Walk★★

🚶 *2hr round trip.*

This pleasant walk along sandy paths, in the shade of the pine trees, starts from

Plage Notre Dame, Îles de Porquerolles

Fort Ste-Agathe *(bear left)* and skirts the Plage de la Courtade. After Pointe du Lequin the path dips towards the sea, revealing the **Plage Notre-Dame**, a beautiful sandy beach bordered by pine trees. The **signal station** *(sémaphore)*, Plage d'Argent, **Pointe du Grand Langoustier** and **Cap des Mèdes** all make excellent destinations.

Île-de Port-Cros★★★

Port-Cros Island is hillier, more rugged and higher above the sea than its neighbours, and its lush vegetation is unrivalled on the coast. The island is 2.5mi/4km long by 1.5mi/2.5km wide and its highest point, Mont Vinaigre, reaches 679ft/194m. A few fishermen's cottages, a huddle of shops and a small church adorn the bay area, which is commanded by Fort du Moulin (aka the "Château"). Port-Cros, together with Île de Bagaud and neighbouring islets, has been designated a **Parc National**, covering 2.7sq mi/700ha on land and 7sq mi/1 800ha at sea.

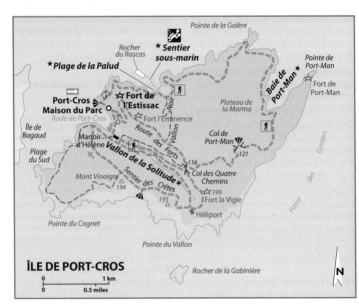

ÎLE DE PORT-CROS

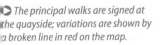 *The principal walks are signed at the quayside; variations are shown by a broken line in red on the map.*

Plage de la Palud★

🚶 *1.5hr round trip.*

Climb up to the castle for a **view** of the neighbouring Île de Bagaud. A **botanical path** with Mediterranean specimens winds its way along La Palud Bay before reaching the beach. It passes by **Fort de l'Estissac** (🕐 *open Jun–Sept;* 🚫 *no charge;* 📞*04 94 01 40 72*), which houses marine environment displays.

🏊 Underwater Trail★

🕐*Open mid-Jun–Sept. Guided tours by one of the park attendants (except in bad weather).* 🚫*No charge.*

This underwater observation point, no deeper than 33ft/10m, is located between the little island of Rascas and La Palud beach, marked by yellow buoys. Here, anyone who can swim – diving is not necessary – can observe a great variety of typical Mediterranean species that live at this depth. Numbered buoys mark the best viewpoints. A preliminary visit to the **Maison du Parc National**, which sells plastified aquaguides, is recommended. If you're diving alone, bring a mask, breathing apparatus and flippers.

▶ *Return to the village, passing between the forts of L'Éminence and L'Estissac.*

Vallon de la Solitude★

🚶 *2hr round trip (marked path).*

This is the ideal walk for visitors spending half a day on the island. At the beginning of the valley stands the Manoir d'Hélène – a manor house converted into a hotel – named after the heroine in Melchior de Vogüé's novel *Jean d'Agrève*, which is set on Port-Cros. The path is in deep shade for almost all its length. Once within sight of Fort de la Vigie start back along the cliff walk (Route des Crêtes), with **views** of the sea.

▶ *At Mont Vinaigre bear right into the Vallon de la Fausse Monnaie (Valley of False Currency).*

Biodiversity on the Islands

Scientists and marine enthusiasts identified 410 groupers in 2002, along with numerous other species, including barracudas, leerfish, sargo breams and large sea breams. The harbour is carpeted with one of the most beautiful Posidonia seagrass beds in the region. This flowering plant is a home to over 70 species of fish. Protected land fauna includes the little-known Mediterranean puffin.

Port-Man★ – *6mi/10km.* 🚶 *4hr round trip (marked paths).* This pleasant excursion along a shaded and nearly-level path affords a **view** of the Île du Levant at the end of the Col de Port-Man, then winds its way to the **Baie de Port-Man**, a sheltered green bay.

▶ *Return via Pointe de la Galère, Plateau de la Marma and Plage de la Palud.*

Other Walks

Indicated by the dotted orange line on the map, these include the Plage du Sud (sand), the Route des Forts, the Vallon Noir and the Col des Quatre Chemins.

Île du Levant

The island consists of a rocky spine 5mi/8km long but only 1,300yd/1,200m wide skirted by vertical cliffs inaccessible except at two points: the Avis and Estable *calanques*. Disembark at the Aiguade landing and follow the path to Héliopolis. The Lérins monks used the island as their garden and granary. Today 90 percent of the island is occupied by the Marine Nationale (🚫*access is forbidden*).

Héliopolis

In the western part of the island, the village of Héliopolis and the Grottes area (🔒 *private property*) have one of the oldest nudist camps in Europe, opened in 1931. In season local clubs organise diving activities, which are open to the general public.

ADDRESSES

🛏 STAY

🛏🛏🛏 **Hôtel Manoir** – *Port-Cros.*
𝄢04 94 05 90 52. Closed early Oct–early
Apr. 22 rooms. ⊑12€. Restaurant🛏🛏🛏.
Charming 1830s hotel in an exceptional
garden setting near the port. Minimalist
rooms, swimming pool. Half-board only.

🛏🛏🛏 **L'Auberge des Glycines** – *22 Pl.
d'Armes, Porquerolles.* 𝄢04 94 58 30 36.
www.auberge-glycines.com. Closed at
lunch. 11 rooms, half-board. ⊑8€.
Restaurant🛏🛏. This adorable
cottage with lavender-blue shutters has
rooms overlooking a shaded patio or
the village square. The restaurant serves
Provençal cooking.

🍴 EAT

ÎLE DE PORQUEROLLES
Bakery – *pl. d'Armes.*
Convenience Store – *pl. d'Armes.
Closed afternoons off season.*

🍴🍴 **Villa Sainte Anne** – *pl. d'Armes.*
𝄢04 94 64 63 00. www.sainteanne.com.
🍴. Closed Nov–25 Dec, Jan–Feb.
This restaurant near the church has a
shady terrace and cuisine based around
the catch of the day. Real Provençal
atmosphere and great people-
watching. 22 rooms available🛏🛏🛏.

🛏🛏🛏–🛏🛏🛏🛏 **Mas du Langoustier**
– *West of the port, Porquerolles.* 𝄢04 94
58 30 09. www.langoustier.com. Closed
Oct–mid-Apr. 45 rooms, half-board. ⊑.
Restaurant🛏🛏🛏. The prices are
usually high on the Porquerolles, but
in this chic hôtel-restaurant the quality
and service are worth it. The dining
room overlooks the sea and the Fort
du Langoustier. The cuisine is gourmet
Mediterranean and French classics.
50 rooms available 🛏🛏🛏🛏.

ÎLE DE PORT-CROS
Deli – *Off the main quay (look for
signs for épicerie). Closed Dec–Mar.*

🍴 **Sun Bistrot** – *At the port.*
𝄢04 94 05 90 16. Closed Nov–Dec.
Brasserie and snack bar frequented
by students from the diving school,
selling pizzas, salads, fish and patés.

ÎLE DE LEVANT
Héliopolis – Apart from the floating
snack boats on the port, this is the
only place to eat.

🏃 SPORTS AND LEISURE

Diving – The great depths and the
lack of strong currents around the
islands and in the Baie de Carqueiranne
provide ideal conditions for diving and
for underwater photography of the
many shipwrecks. There are several
diving clubs in Hyères and La Londe;
Sun Plongée (𝄢04 94 05 90 16. www.
sun-plongee.com) in Port-Cros and
Porquerolles Plongée (𝄢04 98 04 62 22.
www.porquerolles-plongee.com) in
Porquerolles.

👥 **Marabel Aquascope** – *Île de Port-
Cros.* 𝄢06 08 26 91 99. ☞15€ (4–12 years,
10€). Closed Nov–Mar. Guided tours
(30min) in a boat specially designed to
observe underwater life. Departures
every 40min. 10 seats (rest standing).

👥 **TMV** – *Port de la Tour-Fondue, Giens.*
𝄢04 94 58 95 14. www.tlv-tvm.com. Jun
5 departures per day – ☞13.10€ (children
4–10 10€). Glass-bottomed boat tours
of the underwater flora and fauna
(35min).

Île de Levant – www.iledulevant.com.fr.
The accessible areas of the island are
in the west and north; in the north a
channel is reserved for watersports
and an area set aside for windsurfing.
🏖*The main beaches, reached by the coast
path on each side of the landing-stages, are
for naturists only.*

🍷 LOCAL WINES

Domaine de la Courtade – *Porquerolles.*
𝄢04 94 58 31 44. www.lacourtade.com.
Closed Sat–Sun. This reputable vineyard
can be reached after a pleasant 15min
walk. Call ahead if you would like to
purchase wine at the domaine.

Domaine Perzinsky – *Porquerolles.*
𝄢04 94 58 34 32. Created in 1989, this
vineyard is the closest to the village.
Tastings and tours available.

Bormes-les-Mimosas★

Var

Bormes-les-Mimosas stands in an enchanting **setting**★ near the sea at the foot of the Forêt du Dom. Scented by colourful oleander, camomile, eucalyptus and mimosa, the winding, sloping streets of the old village lead down to a modern marina and beaches.

🐾 WALKING TOUR

HISTORIC STREETS★
The streets below the church have retained their traditional Provençal character. Many steep alleyways tumble down from the castle, the steepest known as "neck-breaker" *(Rompi-Cuo)*!

Place St-François
The terrace fronting the 16C **Chapelle St-François** affords a **view** of Bormes port and Cap Bénat. The round tower seen in the distance is an old mill.

Église St-Trophyme
218 yd/200m from the Hôtel de Ville.
The sundial on the façade of this 18C Romanesque-style church bears a Latin inscription: *Ab Hora Diei ad Horam Dei* (from daily time to divine time).

Château
Follow the *Parcours Fleuri*, a flower-lined walk round the partially restored castle

- ▶ **Population:** 7,051.
- 🖥 **Michelin Map:** 340 N7.
- 🚩 **Info:** Pl. Gambetta. ✆04 94 01 38 38. www.bormesles mimosas.com.
- 🔵 **Location:** The beaches of this Var village stretch 10.5mi/17km from Le Lavandou to the bay of Brégançon: La Favière, Gaou Bay, Cabasson and Léoube. The Massif des Maures flank the village.

(13–14C). The terrace provides a fine **view**★ over Bormes, the port, Cap Bénat and the islands of Port-Cros.

SIGHTS
Musée Arts et Histoire
65 rue Carnot. 🕐*Open Tue–Sun Jun–Sept 10am–noon, 3–6.30pm; Oct–May 10am–noon, 2.30–5.30pm.* 🕐*Closed 1 Jan, 1 May, 25 Dec.* 🚫*No charge.* ✆*04 94 71 56 60.*
This local history museum also features several regional paintings, including landscapes by **Jean-Charles Cazin** (1841–1901).

EXCURSION
Cap de Brégançon
East of Hyères harbour the 16C **Fort de Brégançon** (⚠ *closed to the public*) sits on a small island linked to Cap Bénat by a footbridge.

View of Bormes-les-Mimosas © Gerth Roland/age fotostock

Latin American Ties

Two inhabitants of Bormes-les-Mimosas played an important part in the Wars of Independence in Latin America in the 19C: **Hippolyte Mourdeille** (1758–1807) lost his life chasing the Spaniards out of Montevideo; **Hippolyte Bouchard** (1780–1837) organised the Argentinian navy. Today Bormes honours their achievements by celebrating Argentina's National Independence Day (9 July).

Abandoned in the early 18C, then restored under the young General Bonaparte, in 1968 it became the summer retreat of French Presidents.

The coast from Lavandou to Brégançon cove is lined with 11mi/17km of **beaches**. From Lavendou, take the wooden walkway to the marina and beach at **La Favière**, just beyond the Gouron headland. Continue on the **coastal trail**, then west to the beaches of Cap Bénat, Cabasson, Pellegrin and Estagnol (⮾charge for admission).

ADDRESSES

🛏 STAY

🍴🍴 **Le Grand Hôtel** – *167 rte du Baguier, exit north of Bormes, towards Collobrières. ℘04 94 71 23 72. www.augrandhotel.com. Closed Oct–Mar.* 🅿 *45 rooms.* 🍽*8.50€. Restaurant* 🍴. For a whiff of Victoriana, check in at this hillside grand hotel built in 1903. Large, soundproofed rooms, most with a balcony overlooking the sea.

🍴🍴🍺 **Hôtel Les Palmiers** – *chemin du Petit-Fort, 5mi/8km south of Bormes. ℘04 94 64 81 94. www.hotel-palmiers.com. Closed 15 Nov – 31 Jan.* 🅿 *17 rooms.* 🍽*14€. Restaurant* 🍴. Lying in a residential district halfway between the beach and Brégançon Fort, this hotel is a haven of peace. Most of the rooms have large balconies. The dining room opens out onto a flowered terrace. Half-board only in summer.

🍽 EAT

🍴🍴 **La Ferme des Janets** – *378 chemin des Janets, route d'Hyères. ℘04 94 71 4511. www.fermedesjanets.fr. Closed 2 Jan –15 Feb.* A footpath wending its way past vineyards and cyprusses leads to a charming mas, where poultry are raised. After a hearty meal of traditional country food, relax on the leafy terrace or play a game of boules.

🍴🍴🍺 **La Tonnelle** – *23 pl. Gambetta. ℘04 94 71 34 84. www.la-tonnelle-bormes.com. Closed Wed and Thu May, Jun, Sept Wed and Thu lunch, Jul and Aug daily lunch. Reservations recommended.* An intimate Provençal inn with parquet flooring and an eclectic home-from-home décor. Classic Mediterranean dishes with an international twist made from market-fresh produce. Shady summer terrace.

🛍 SHOPPING

Markets – Wednesday mornings in the old village, Saturdays at La Favière (in summer) and Marché Provençal on Tuesday mornings at Pin-de-Bormes.

TOURS

Guided Tour – *Apr–Sept Thu 5pm.* ⮾*Tickets 5€.* A 90min walking tour of the old town architecture and flora. Sign up at the tourist office.

Brochures – Pick up a map of the old village at the tourist office, along with a "Route du Mimosa" brochure of walking and car tours. A guide to local flora, "Guide des Fleurs", is available for *5€.*

Wine – Ask at the tourist office for the brochure "Route des Vins de Bormes-les-Mimosas" for information on the 10 local Côtes-de-Provence vineyards.

CALENDAR

Mimosalia – *Last weekend in January.* Open market for show plants.

Corso – *End of February.* Bormes celebrates Mardi Gras with a Corso parade and floats through the village.

Foire aux Santons – *First weekend in December.* Display and sale of the Provençal dolls called *Santons.*

Le Lavandou★

Var

This genteel resort sheltered by the Cap Bénat was once the biggest fishing port in the Var. Its marina and beaches are now very popular with families.

THE TOWN

The main square, **place Ernest-Reyer**, has **views** of the islands of Levant and Port-Cros. **Boulevard de-Lattre-de-Tassigny** is a pleasant promenade along the beach, with **views** of the port and the coast eastwards to Cap Lardier. There are lively **markets** on place du Marché and avenue du Président-Vincent-Auriol on Thursdays and in Cavalière on Mondays (June to September).

The village

Park in the village (parking voucher from the town hall or tourist office).
Arrive early to admire the "pescadous" returning to port with their daily trawl of sea bass and John Dory. Next, explore the covered market close to the quayside before strolling through this typical Provençal village.

Thirteen fountains walk

Map available from the tourist office.
This walk explores the historic fountains of Le Lavandou, including the **Fontaine des Trois-Dauphins,** which bears the town's arms (three dolphins and a lion), a **drinking fountain** near the boule court on quai Gabriel Péri, the **public laundry fountains** on place de Mado and place du Lou-Lavandou, and the historic tiled St-Louis **wall fountain**.

Gardens

There are three small gardens in the town centre: the **Jardin du Cadran** on rue des Pierres-Précieuses with its giant palm tree and lavender plants, the aromatic **Jardin du Grand Bleu** which boasts a huge jacaranda from the American tropics and honeysuckle from China, and the more secluded **Grand Jardin**, avenue de la Grande-Bastide, which blooms with bright yellow mimosa in late winter.

▶ **Population:** 5,780.
◔ **Michelin Map:** 340 N7.
ℹ **Info:** Quai Gabriel-Péri. 𝄞04 94 00 40 50. Cavalière: La Rotonde, ave. du Golf. 𝄞04 94 05 80 50. www.ot-lelavandou.fr.
▷ **Location:** Le Lavandou sits on the Corniche des Maures (◔*see Massif des MAURES pp147*), east of Bormes-les-Mimosas. The centre of town overlooks the port, while most hotels are situated near the beaches to the southwest.

🥾 *1.5mi/2.5km, 1hr walk or 90min guided tour. Contact the tourist office.*
This walk follows in the footsteps of Neo-Impressionist painters and writers **Henri-Edmond Cross**, **Théo van Rysselberghe** and **Paul Signac**, who

The Song of Summer

The image of the Mediterranean is invariably associated with the song of the cicada, together with the game of boules (*pétanque*) and a siesta under the pine trees.
The song of the cicada is stimulated by a combination of particular conditions – the temperature must be at least 77°F/25°C in the shade and there should not be too much noise. A tiny change – such as a cloud passing in front of the sun or the wind rustling in the trees – is enough to upset the insect. Only the male cicada sings, since the noise is a mating call to females. The dawn serenade is produced when the insect contracts two rigid plates – cymbals – on its abdomen, which vibrate at 500 times a second. The sound is amplified by a ventral cavity full of air which acts as a resonance chamber. When the female has located the sound using ears on her abdomen, she joins her suitor in the tree.

lived in St-Clair between 1892 and 1926. Panels depicting works by the artists are featured along the route.

BEACHES

All beaches are sand. Supervised by lifeguards, they are equipped with warning flags and information panels. Standards of comfort, hygiene and sporting facilities vary from beach to beach. More adventurous types will head to St-Clair for windsurfing and La Fossette for canoeing. There is nude sunbathing on Plage du Rossignol and a nudist beach in Le Layet.

BOAT TRIPS

Îles d'Hyères★★★
Allow one day.
(For maps and description ⬅ see ÎLES d'HYÈRES p137).

ADDRESSES

🏠 STAY

🛏🛏 **Hôtel Les Alcyons** – *In Aiguebelle, 3mi/ 4.5km from Le Lavandou. ☎04 94 05 84 18. www.beausoleil-alcyons.com. Closed mid-Oct-Apr. 24 rooms.* 🅿 🚭.
At the foot of the Maures Massif, barely 20min from the beach, this friendly hotel is perfect for swimming and hiking. Each room has a balcony and air-conditioning.

🛏🛏🛏 **Roc Hôtel** – *In St-Clair, 1mi/2km from Le Lavandou. ☎04 94 01 33 66. www.roc-hotel.com. Closed Nov–Feb. 29 rooms.* 🅿 🚭. This beach-front hotel is housed in a modern ochre building. Most rooms have sea views.

🍴 EAT

🍽🍽 **Chez Zète** – *41 ave. du Général-de-Gaulle. ☎04 94 71 09 11. Closed Dec, Mon, and Sun evening (except Jul–Aug).* In Le Lavandou's main shopping street, this family business draws large crowds year round with succulent Provençal cooking and a shaded terrace.

🍽🍽 **Hélios Plage** – *In Aiguebelle, ave. du Général-Bouvet, then take the footbridge. ☎04 94 71 49 79. Closed mid-Nov–Apr and eves.* 🚭. If you want to lounge around on the sand and

enjoy views of Levant Island, try this charming cabin with white wainscoting and choose between a salad, the chef's special or a tasty dish of pasta.

🛒 SHOPPING

Domaine de l'Anglade – *ave. Vincent-Auriol. ☎04 94 71 10 89. www.domaine delanglade.fr. Call for hours or check website.* This attractive and central vineyard produces red, white and rosé wine, wine for apéritifs and vinegar. Tasting sessions and shop.

Markets – Thursday morning *(all year)* at ave. Vincent-Auriol and Monday morning *(Jun–Sept)* in Cavalière.

🎭 OUTDOOR THEATRE

Théâtre de Verdure – *Cinéma Plein Air, Av. du Grand-Jardin. ☎04 94 00 41 71. Closed Sept–Jun. See the programme for events.* This outdoor theatre puts on summer plays and concerts.

🤸 SPORT AND LEISURE

École de Voile de Cavalière – *ave. du Cap-Nègre. ☎04 94 05 86 78. www.ecole voilelavandou.com. Closed Nov–Mar.* This club gives sailing lessons and rents various sailing boats (catamaran, dinghy, optimist) and windsurfing boards.

🧑‍🤝‍🧑 **Seascope** – *Gare Maritime. ☎04 94 71 01 02. www.vedettesilesdor.fr.* 🚢*13€ (children 9.50€).* The Seascope's transparent hull affords wonderful **views** of the sea depths, marine flora and many Mediterranean fish species.

CIP Lavandou – *Le Lavandou Port, Quai Gabriel-Péri. ☎04 94 15 13 09. www.cip-lavandou.fr.* Local diving club with a friendly atmosphere.

Lavandou Scuba Diving School – *New Port, underneath the restaurant Le Barracuda. ☎04 94 71 83 65. www.lavandou-plongee.com.* Lessons for beginners and experienced divers and various other services (equipment hire, shipwreck tours, exploring sites around Port-Cros, etc.). *Call to reserve.*

Massif des Maures★★

Var

The emerald forests of the Massif des Maures stretch along the coastline from Hyères to St-Raphaël and up into the Gapeau and Argens river valleys. A drive along the **Corniche des Maures** reveals glimpses of the cobalt blue sea against rocky inlets, contrasting with the wilder landscape of the inland hills.

A BIT OF HISTORY

Les Maures, from the Provençal "Leï Mauro", meaning "black mountain" (a reference to its dark rocks and dense forests), is the most heavily wooded area in the Var, with 371,000 acres/150,000ha of forest. Its schist rock provides ideal growing conditions for cork oaks, which supplied the region with its main source of revenue from the 17C to 19C centuries. The vogue for sea-bathing brought this magnificent coast back to life in the 20C and provided it with a new source of income. On 15 August 1944 the Allied armies landed on the Maures beaches before liberating the south of France.

 DRIVING TOUR

Corniches des Maures★★
From Le Lavandou to St-Tropez on D 559

Le Lavandou★
see Le LAVANDOU pp 145.

St-Clair
This small resort is a short distance from the main road with a large, beautiful beach.

Aiguebelle
A peaceful seaside resort nestled in a small pine-fringed cove.

Cavalière
Cavalière has a fine **view** over Cap Nègre and a beach sheltered from the *mistral*. Excellent watersports facilities.

- **Michelin Map:** 340 M/P5/7 or 528 folds 47 to 49.
- **Info:** Several tourist offices cover this region: contact Var Tourisme to locate the nearest one. ✆04 94 18 59 60. www.visitvar.fr.
- **Location:** The Maures is made up of four parallel chains of geographical relief, two along the coast (including the Îles d'Hyères) and two inland (La Verne and La Sauvette), separated by the River Grimaud and the River Collobrières.
- **Kids:** The tropical bird garden in La Londe.
- **Don't Miss:** Guided nature hikes through the Massif des Maures.
- **Timing:** Set aside 1–2hr for a guided nature hike. Allow one day for a drive along the Maures corniche. Other tours require half a day.

Pramousquier
A modest resort with a sheltered beach of fine sand and attractive villas. The road leaves the shore to wind through pines and gardens.

Canadel-sur-Mer
Lying at the base of the last foothills of the Pradels range and flanked by superb pine woods, Canadel has one of the most sheltered beaches on the Maures coast. The **Allied Landings** in Provence were launched here at midnight on 14 August 1944.

Cavalaire-sur-Mer
A perfect holiday destination, with a fine sand beach, scuba diving and a port with 1,200 moorings. Just beyond are the beaches of Le Rayol (*see Domaine du RAYOL pp155*).

La Croix-Valmer
Surrounded by 741 acres/300ha of protected countryside, this village boasts

147

GENERAL ADVICE ABOUT VISITING THE MASSIF

Cars – Roads belonging to the DFCI (Défense Forestière Contre l'Incendie – forest fire-fighters) are closed to public traffic. They count as private roads; an open barrier does not indicate that access is permitted. Parking in front of these barriers is prohibited and cars should be parked well to the side of narrow roads to allow the passage of emergency vehicles. Pedestrian access is always possible.

Fire Risk – Fires are prohibited at all times and smoking is not permitted Mar–Oct. During periods of high fire risk, the ALARME plan is put into action and certain public roads (classed as major fire risks) may be closed to vehicles. Offenders are liable for heavy fines. Walkers are strongly advised to avoid such areas for reasons of safety. To check for closures, call ℘04 98 10 55 41.

Camping – Camping is prohibited in the massif and within 656ft/200m of any of the forests.

Animals – Pets must be kept on a leash; do not disturb wild animals.

Plants and chestnuts – Do not stray from marked paths or pick plants or fruit in particular – chestnuts – as you may be requested to pay a fine.

Litter – Use the rubbish bins provided or take any rubbish with you.

4mi/6km of beaches and has been a winter retreat and spa since the early 1900s. Today it is known for its reputable Côtes de Provence wines. According to legend, Constantine saw a cross in the sky here with the words, *In hoc signo vinces* "in this sign you will conquer", a prediction of his forthcoming victory and succession as Roman Emperor. A stone cross erected on the pass commemorates the story and gives the village its name.

St-Tropez to Fréjus★★
On the opposite side of the peninsula, the Massif des Maures slopes gently towards the sea. On the sunny coast along the D 559, these seaside resorts have fine beaches (♿ *see Driving Tour* 3).

Beauvallon
Beauvallon is on the north shore of St-Tropez Bay, well shaded by pines and cork oaks.

Ste-Maxime★ ♿*see STE-MAXIME.* Circling the Cap Sardinaux, the rugged coastline between **La Nartelle** and **St-Aygulf** is broken up by rocky inlets *(calanques)* with small beaches.

Massif des Maures

© DANO/Var Tourisme

Les Issambres

Along with Val d'Esquières, San Peïre and Les Calanques, this pretty resort is part of an extensive tourist development. Popular with bathers for its 5mi/8km of sand beaches and creeks, it boasts a small port offering local boat trips.

St-Aygulf

Shaded by forests of pine, eucalyptus, holm oak and cork oak, this resort has one of the biggest fine sand beaches on the Riviera, with **views** over Les Issambres and Fréjus Bay. The dunes are currently being restored and walkers are asked to tread carefully. Follow the chemin des Douaniers to access four **calanques** (rocky inlets). St-Aygulf also has a small sheltered marina.

🚗 DRIVING TOURS

1 IN MAURES COUNTRY
*44mi /70km leaving from Hyères.
Allow one day. See map pp128–9.*

◯ *Leave Hyères northeast on N 98.*

After crossing the Gapeau, the road hugs the salt-marshes as it passes through the Hyères plain, with good **views** of Cap Bénat and Port-Cros.

🚶 Jardin d'Oiseaux Tropicaux

*Open Jun–Sept 9.30am–7pm; Oct and Feb–May 2–6pm, Nov–Jan Wed, Sat, Sun, public holidays 2–5pm.
9€ (child 5€). 04 94 35 02 15.
www.jotropico.org*
Filled with palms and exotic plants from Australia, Mexico and Asia, this nature park in La Londe is home to tropical birds of all sizes and colours from every continent, many of them in danger of extinction.

◯ *D 98 to La Môle, then D 27 towards Le Rayol and right into Col Canadel.*

Col du Canadel★

Alt 876ft/267m.
A superb **panorama**★★ of Canadel, Pramousquier beach, Cap Nègre, the Bormes harbour and Cap Bénat.

🚶 *Park your car on the col and follow the forest track on the right to the Col de Caguo-Ven.*

This is a picturesque route with magnificent **views**★ of the Maures Massif and to the south, the coast and the Îles d'Hyères. Vieux-Sauvaire is reached after one hour's walk *(restaurant open in season)*, after which the path goes back down to Col de Barral (1,220ft/372m). If you're feeling fit, walk another two hours to reach Col de Caguo-Ven.

◯ *Continue along D 27 then turn left onto N 98, towards La Môle, then straight to Dom Forest.*

Forêt Domaniale du Dom★

This state forest, composed mainly of pines, cork oaks and chestnuts, spreads over the Les Pradels and La Verne ranges. **Jean Aicard** (1848–1921), poet and novelist, set his work *Maurin des Maures* in this area.

Arboretum de Gratteloup

P *Car park beside the D 98, by the Maison Forestière. Open daily.
No charge. 04 97 71 06 07.*
This arboretum (7.4 acres/3ha), created in 1935, contains mostly Mediterranean species (cypress, pines, juniper, yoke elms and hop hornbeams) and an area specifically devoted to chestnut trees.

◯ *At Col de Gratteloup, take D 41 and head for Bormes-les-Mimosas.*

Col de Caguo-Ven

Alt 778ft/239m.
From the pass, there is a **view** of the Hyères and Bormes ports and the Île de Porquerolles.
🚶 *At the peak, take the forest trail towards Col de Barral and Col du Canadel.*
After 45 minutes, you will arrive at the giant boulders of **Pierre d'Avenon** *(alt 1,450ft/443m)*, where the circular **view**★ encompasses the whole Maures coastline from Cap Lardier to Hyères, the port of Le Lavandou and Bormes.

Guided Nature Hikes

The 10 communes of the Massif des Maures organise hikes of 1–2.5hr with different themes (flora & fauna, forest life, cultural heritage, evening walks, etc.). The calendar of walks is available from the Comité Départemental du Tourisme du Var *(www.visitvar.fr)*. Information and registration at the following tourist offices: Bormes-les-Mimosas ℘04 94 01 38 38; Hyères ℘04 94 01 84 50; La Londe-les-Maures ℘04 94 01 53 10; Le Muy ℘04 94 45 12 79; Le Pradet ℘04 94 21 71 69; Pierrefeu-du-Var ℘04 94 28 27 30; Ramatuelle ℘04 98 12 64 00; Roquebrune-sur-Argens ℘04 94 19 89 89.

▷ *Return to Hyères via Le Pin then D 559.*

2 PASS ROAD★★
67mi/109km leaving from Le Lavandou. Allow one day. See map pp128–9.

This beautiful, circular tour along very hilly, but quiet roads, goes over at least seven passes *(cols)* and penetrates deep into the heart of the massif.

▷ *From Le Lavandou take D 559 west to Le Pin and turn right onto D 41.*

The road winds uphill, with a fine **view** ahead of Bormes and its castle.

Bormes-les-Mimosas★
see BORMES-LES-MIMOSAS p143.

▷ *Continue on D 41 to Col de Caguo-Ven. Continue downhill to Col de Gratteloup (alt 656ft/199m).*

The road passes over wooded slopes of cork oak and chestnut, cuts through deep valleys *(east)* and offers glimpses of the sea and the mountains around Toulon *(west)*.

▷ *Continue along D 41.*

Col de Babaou★
Alt 1,362ft/414m.
A stunning **panorama**★ of the Hyères salt marshes, the Giens peninsula and the Îles d'Hyères. Beyond the pass rise the tallest of the Maures summits, wooded by magnificent chestnuts and cork oaks.

▷ *Turn right onto D 14.*

Collobrières
The picturesque houses of this shaded town overlook the river swirling beneath an old humpback bridge. The local specialities are *marrons glacés* (sugared chestnuts) and other delicacies made with chestnuts.

▷ *Continue east on D 14.*
After 3.7mi/6km turn right at La Croix d'Anselme.

After 2mi/4km a narrow road leads to the ruins of the former Carthusian monastery of La Verne in its majestic forest setting.

Monastère de la Verne★★
Open Wed–Mon Sep–Dec, Feb–May 11am–5pm; Jun, Jul, Aug until 6pm.
Closed religious holidays. 6€.
℘04 94 43 48 28.
The monastery was founded in 1170 on an isolated wooded slope in the Maures. Rebuilt several times, it survived until being abandoned by the monks during the Revolution. Since 1983 it has been occupied by the Order of Bethlehem.
The central **porch** is built from blue-green serpentine stone. Two annulated columns flank the doorway, surmounted by a triangular pediment resting on two pilasters.
Enter through the **gatehouse** (*to the left of the building*), now a display area for products made by the monks, before exploring the buildings where **guests** were once received. A window at the end of the barn, where the grain was stored, overlooks the monks' cells and the Romanesque church. A stair-

case leads down to the bakery and a vast oven, where bread was baked for 45 people. Take the spiral staircase to the **chapelle d'adoration**, the ramparts, and the remains of the small **17C cloister** before entering the restored Romanesque church. From the window of the side chapel, admire the **great cloisters** complete with 100yds/90m of galleries covered by surbased groin vaulting. On the ground floor, don't miss the **oil mill** and **vaulted cellars** where the monks kept their wine.

▷ *Return to D 14 and proceed east.*

After **Col de Taillude** the road looks across La Verne Valley to the ruins of the charter house crowning the opposite slope and then, after passing high above the hamlet of Capelude, makes its way into the upper valley of the Le Périer stream. From the centre of the valley there is a **view** of the Grimaud Plain and St-Tropez Bay.
The road turns sharply into the valley of the Giscle (or the Grimaud rivulet) from where Grimaud can be spotted in the distance.

Grimaud★ ◉*see GRIMAUD pp166.*
▷ *From Grimaud take D 558 south, crossing the Grimaud Plain.*

Cogolin ◉*see COGOLIN pp157.*
▷ *N 98 follows the Môle Valley upstream. 5.1mi/8km from Cogolin, just before La Môle, the winding D 27 strays from the valley to cut across the coastal range. Go back to Le Lavandou by the coast road.*

③ FROM ST-TROPEZ TO ST-AYGULF
20mi/30km. Allow half a day not including tours of St-Tropez and St-Raphaël. ◉See map pp128–9.

St-Tropez ★★ ◉*see ST-TROPEZ p159.*

▷ *Leave St-Tropez to the southwest on D 98A. After 4km/2.5mi turn right.*

Port-Grimaud ★ ◉*see GRIMAUD p166.*

▷ *Return to D 559, which skirts the north shore of the bay overlooking St-Tropez. Follow D 559 to St-Aygulf.*

St-Aygulf ◉*see above.*
Beyond St-Aygulf the **view** sweeps over the lower Argens Plain. The splendid rocks of the Montagnes de Roquebrune stand out from the Maures Massif. Turning towards the Esterel range, you can see the Dramont Signal with the peak of Cap Roux looming in the background.

④ THE SUMMITS ROUTE★
74.5mi/120km. Allow one day. ◉See map pp128–9.

Round trip starting from St-Tropez
This excursion passes through wooded countryside to the lower slopes of the twin peaks of Notre-Dame-des-Anges and La Sauvette.

▷ *Leave St-Tropez to the southwest on D 98A along the bay of St-Tropez. At La Foux turn left onto D 98 to Cogolin.*

Cogolin ◉*see COGOLIN p157.*

▷ *Stay on N 98 towards Môle Valley.*

Shortly before the village of La Môle stands a château *(right)* with two pepperpot turrets where **Antoine de Saint-Exupéry** (1900–44), aviator and writer, lived as a child (◉*see Massif de l'Esterel*). Vineyards give way to the forest-covered slopes of **Dom Forest★**.

▷ *Continue along D 98. At Col de Gratteloup turn right onto D 41, up to Collobrières, then after La Rivière turn right onto D 14. After 2mi/3km to the east of Collobrières, turn left onto D 39.*

The road winds through wooded countryside overlooking a steep-sided stream and affords the occasional glimpse of La Sauvette peak to the right. Shortly before Col des Fourches the road to the left leads to the Notre-Dame-des-Anges Hermitage, pinpointed by the television relay mast.

Notre-Dame-des-Anges★

Restored in the 19C, the priory near the summit (2,559ft/780m) stands in an attractive **setting**★ amid schist rocks and chestnut trees.

Beyond the screen of trees surrounding the chapel there is a remarkable **view**★ *(north)* of the Argens depression backed by the Alps, *(west)* Ste-Baume, *(south)* over the Maures to the sea, the Iles d'Hyères, the Giens Peninsula and Toulon.

▷ *Return to Col des Fourches and turn left towards Gonfaron.*

The road passes by **La Sauvette** (2,556ft/779m), the highest point in the Massif des Maures, before descending to Le Luc Plain.

Gonfaron

This village set within the Massif des Maures is still an active centre for cork production. At the north edge rises an isolated hill, crowned by a chapel dedicated to St Quinis.

Village de Tortues de Gonfaron

In Gonfaron turn right onto D 75 for 2km/1mi. The best times to visit are 11am or 4pm. ⏱Open Mar–Nov 9am –7pm. 9€ (children 6€). ℘04 94 78 26 41. www.villagetortues.com.

The village is a breeding centre for the Hermann tortoise species *(Testudo hermanni hermanni),* a one-million-year-old herbivorous species threatened with extinction. This tortoise can live up to one hundred years. Mating takes place in April, May and September, egg-laying in mid-May and hatching in early September. The village is also home to France's freshwater turtle and the common or European tortoise *(Testudo graeca).* Don't miss the hot house and museum.

▷ *Continue east on D 75 then onto D 558 towards La Garde-Freinet.*

Hermann Tortoise, Gonfaron

© sofiattitude/Fotolia.com

Hermann's Tortoise

This tortoise, the only species native to France, appeared in Mediterranean Europe about one million years ago. It lives in the scrub *(maquis),* which provides its food – oak leaves, fruit and molluscs. After hibernating in a tree stump until about June, the female lays her eggs in a nest which she immediately abandons. If they survive the first two months of life, as well as predatory badgers, the baby tortoises can look forward to a life of 60 to 100 years.

Falling victim to man-made alterations in its habitat and unregulated collecting, the tortoises now survive only in Corsica and in the Massif des Maures, where a tortoise village has been established to protect the species.

Cork Oak

The cork oak is an evergreen that requires heat and humidity. It grows near the sea up to a height of 1,640ft /500m and has proved particularly resistent to fire. It is easy to spot on account of its large blackish acorns and scored bark.

Bark is gathered (*démasclage*) for the first time when the tree is 25 years old; this is known as the male bark. Subsequent harvests, which take place in July and August when the sap is rising, occur every nine or 10 years, which is the time it takes for a new layer of cork to form; this is known as the female bark, which is highly prized by industry (manufacture of chipboard at Le Muy) and craftsmen (boards, ornamental objects and materials for ceramicists).

By the mid-1960s the Maures area was producing 5,000t of cork yearly, supplying 100 or so local firms. In 1994 the foresters of the Var department produced 500t of cork. Nowadays, the cork is mostly exported to Sardinia.

La Garde-Freinet

1 pl. Neuve. ✆04 94 43 67 41.
www.lagardefreinet-tourisme.com.
Strategically placed between the Argens Valley and St-Tropez Bay, the quiet village of La Garde-Freinet is a flourishing crafts centre surrounded by scenic cork oak and chestnut forests, perfect for a day of hiking, biking or horseback riding.

The tourist office has marked out a route through the steep, winding streets of this perched village *(1hr)* with arrows and an accompanying map.

A Provençal market is held on place Neuve Sunday and Wednesday mornings.

A Bit of History

Owing to its strategic location **La Garde-Freinet** suffered over a century of occupation by the Saracens. In local tradition the name Saracen is applied collectively to the Moors, Arabs, Turks and Berbers, who harassed the country from the 8C to the 18C. After being defeated by Charles Martel at Poitiers in 732, the Arabs drifted down into Provence.

Although driven back several times, they managed to hold on to the region around La Garde-Freinet. On the height which dominates the present village they built a fortress from where they pillaged inland Provence. It was only in 973 that Count William, the Liberator, managed to expel them.

In contrast to the damage they caused, the Saracens taught the Provençal people about medicine, how to use the bark of the cork oak and how to extract resin from pine trees. They also introduced the flat house tile and the tambourine.

Ruins of Fort Freinet
0.6mi /1km.

▷ *Take the road south towards Grimaud. Just before leaving the village after the boule court, turn right up a steep road towards La Croix. Park on the side of the road and follow the arrow painted on a rock: this path is not suitable for the elderly or children. Map available from the tourist office.*

🚶 *1hr round trip.*
There is a good **view** of Le Luc Plain and the first Alpine foothills. A path leads to a mission cross (Croix des Maures), then climbs steeply to the ruins of a fortress and the foundations of a fortified village (12C–16C), with a chapel, cistern, oven and seigniorial lodgings.

▶ *Return to your car and follow the forest track on foot for 3mi/5km until you reach the sign for Roches Blanches.*

Panorama des Roches Blanches★

Alt. 2,093ft/638m. At this spot *(for access, walk round the barrier),* there is a **view** of *(left)* Garde-Freinet Forest and the River Argens valley *(right)* across to the north Maures and *(east)* St-Tropez Bay.

▶ *Take D 558 south.*

The road passes cork oak and chestnut-covered slopes with glimpses of the bay and peninsula of St-Tropez.

Grimaud★
see GRIMAUD p166.

▶ *Return to St-Tropez by D 14, D 98 and D 98A at La Foux.*

ADDRESSES

🏠 STAY

🛏 **Chambre d'Hôte Le Mas des Oliviers** – *chemin les Ferrières, Puget-Ville, 2.5km/1.5mi by N 97 Route de Cuers. ℘04 94 48 30 89. www.masdesoliviers. com. 3 rooms. ⊟ Meal ⊜⊜.* This charming Provençal *mas* seems lost among vineyards and olive groves. Large, carefully kept rooms are decorated in Mediterranean style. Sauna and fitness room. Horse riding and cycling nearby.

🛏 **Golfe Bleu** – *rte. de La Croix-Valmer, Cavalaire-sur-Mer, 1km/0.6mi from the wayside cross on D 559. ℘04 94 64 07 56. Closed Nov–Jan. 15 rooms. 🅿 ⊑7€. Restaurant ⊜.* Neat, homely establishment away from the town center. The rooms are soundproofed and air-conditioned. The simply decorated restaurant opens out onto a small terrace.

🍷 EAT

🍴 **Alizés** – *Promenade de la Mer, Cavalaire-sur-Mer. ℘04 94 64 09 32. www.alizescavalaire.com. ⊑12€.* A lively atmosphere and the undeniable charisma of the owners are the main assets of this modern hotel and restaurant offering sea views. Family cooking with an emphasis on fish and homemade desserts. 18 guest rooms.

🍴⊜ **Maures** – *19 blvd. Lazare-Carnot, Collobrières. ℘04 94 48 07 10.* This village inn enjoys a well-deserved reputation among its regular clientele on account of its excellent value for money and warm welcome. In summer meals are served on the terrace beneath the plane trees.

🛒 SHOPPING

Confiserie Azuréenne – *Bd. Koenig, Collobrières. ℘04 94 48 07 20. www.confiserieazureenne.com.* This confectioner's is entirely devoted to chestnuts. It makes and sells marrons glacés, chestnut jam, sugared chestnut purée, etc. Visitors can also be shown around the factory museum.

MARKET
Marché de la Croix Valmer every Sunday morning.

🏃 SPORT AND RECREATION CENTRE

Smash Club – *ave. du Golf, Cavalière. ℘04 95 05 84 31. Closed mornings Nov–Mar.* A sports centre with six tennis courts, golf links, a weight room, an archery gallery, a sauna and mountain bikes for rental. Tennis tournaments and badminton, beach-volley, football and boules competitions are organised during the summer season.

Domaine du Rayol★★

Var

The Domaine du Rayol is one of the most beautiful spots on the Var coastline. Forming an amphitheatre of wooded slopes carpeted with cork oaks, mimosas and pines, it started life as an exclusive seaside resort in the early 20C, when European industrialist and bankers built holiday seaside resorts amid the lush virgin landscape. The beach at Rayol-Canadel-sur-Mer *(2km/1mi west via D 599)*, a sheltered cove bordered by pines, is one of the most breathtaking in the region.

SIGHTS

The Domaine★★

Ave. des Belges. ◔*Open Jul–Aug 9.30am–7.30pm; Apr–Jun and Sept–Oct 9.30am–6.30pm; Nov–Mar 9.30am –5.30pm.* ◉*8€.* ☎*04 98 04 44 00. www.domainedurayol.org.*

The first exotic gardens on the site were commissioned by a Parisian banker named Courmes, who had a house built on the estate in 1910. After the stock market crash of 1929, the estate fell into disrepair and it wasn't until the aeronautics engineer Potez, who took refuge on the coast in 1940, renovated the property, that the garden returned to its former glory. He had a belvedere built by Patek, with a circular pergola, linked to the coast by a magnificent flight of steps.

After several more decades of neglect, in 1989 the Conservatoire du Littoral acquired the entire estate (49.5 acres/20ha) to preserve some of the last wild shores of the Corniche des Maures. The landscape gardener Gilles Clément was then brought in to create a patchwork of gardens planted with rare and exceptional species found growing in Mediterranean climates around the world, including dragon trees from the Canary Islands, agaves from Central America and rare honey palms from Chile.

☷ **Michelin Map:** 340 N7.

▫ **Info:** Jardin des Méditerranées, Ave. des Belges, Rayol-Canadel-sur-Mer. ☎04 98 04 44 00. www.domainedurayol.org.

▷ **Location:** Coming from St-Tropez, the road into the domaine branches left at the entrance of the village Rayol-Canadel-sur-Mer.

Domaine du Rayol

D. Pazery/ MICHELIN

Posidonia – the Lungs of the Mediterranean

This flowering plant, which looks like bunches of long green leaves, is an essential element of marine life in the Mediterranean, where it grows in sandy seabeds on narrow coastal fringes.

Posidonia plays the same role as a forest: it provides a habitat for animal and plant species, produces oxygen and stabilises the seabed.

It is now threatened with damage and extinction from unpurified sewage discharge, uprooting by boat mooring, building along the coast and by the invasion of another species (*Caulerpa taxifolia*).

The estate's many winding paths offer glimpses of the turquoise sea and the pine-carpeted headland. Both farm and beach feature educational displays.

Sentier Marin★

Open Jul–Aug. Guided underwater tours of Mediterranean flora and fauna. Allow 2hr (45min in the water). Daily Jun–Sept, reservation required. 18€ (children 14€). All equipment supplied.

A trip from the little beach at Rayol offers an unusual view of underwater life in the Mediterranean. This tour, accompanied by wardens from the Conservatoire, is preceded by an introduction to the species most likely to be seen, their description and the best place to look for them among the posidonia.

ADDRESSES

⏲ CAFÉS

Le Café des Jardiniers – *Open noon-6.30pm - 𝒫 04 98 04 44 00.* This café serves seasonal dishes and homemade desserts with a selection of hot and cold drinks. The grocery sells fair trade products and regional items such as vinegar, preserves and cordials.

CALENDAR

Concerts – During the summer season, evening classical music concerts are held in the Domaine du Rayol, with an opportunity to stroll through the illuminated gardens during the interval. Reservation required 𝒫 04 94 05 63 07.

Themed visits and workshops – Discover everything from the secrets of aromatherapy to edible plants and waterless gardens.

Ramatuelle★

Var

Set on a slope among vineyards and scrubland, this pink-roofed village is a typical Provençal mix of narrow winding streets, vaulted arches and historic houses huddled against an ancient town wall.

VISIT

The Village

Despite its isolated location, in the 10C, the village fell to the Saracens who had otherwise made their lair in La Garde-Freinet *(Rahmatu'llah means "divine providence" in Arabic)*. During the Wars of Religion in 1592, having opted to side with the Catholic League, Ramatuelle was once again placed under siege and almost entirely destroyed. Many door lintels mention the year in which the village was rebuilt (1620), including that on the entrance to the Romanesque **church**. Entered through a 17C serpentine door on its flat east end, the church contains two 17C Baroque altarpieces of magnificent gilded wood.

At the bottom of the village, on rue du Moulin Roux, you'll find the prison built

▶ **Population:** 2,271.
🚗 **Michelin Map:** 340 O6.
🛈 **Info:** Pl. de l'Ormeau. 𝒫04 94 12 64 00. www.ramatuelle-tourisme.
▶ **Location:** Ramatuelle lies 7mi/11km east of La Croix-Valmer (*see Massif des MAURES p147*) and south of St-Tropez on the D 93.
🅿 **Parking:** There are parking areas around the church, the cemetery and the Town Hall *(Mairie)*.

under Napoleon III (late 1800s) often wrongly attributed to the Saracens because of its Arabic style.

The central square - place de l'Ormeau – plays host to restaurants, cafés and a Provençal market twice a week on Thursdays and Sundays.

Monument to the Resistance

Opposite the cemetery stands a memorial to the members of the Special Services who died during the Second World War. The submarines that stayed in contact with the members of the Resistance during the Occupation used to wait offshore by the Roche-Escudelier.

EXCURSIONS
Moulins de Paillas★★
▶ *2mi/3km to the north of Ramatuelle.*
At an altitude of 1,066ft/325m, these three ruined olive mills *(one restored,* 🕐 *open Mar–mid-Oct, ask at tourist office;* ⊘ *no charge;* ☎*04 98 12 64 00),* were active until the 19C. Don't miss the **panoramic view★★** over the Esterel, the coast of the Massif des Maures, the Pradels range *(southwest)* and the Sauvette chain *(northwest).*

Gassin *Alt 659ft/201m.*
This village, which lies at an altitude of 201m, has retained its Provençal char-

acter and is especially lively on market day (Sunday). The **Terrasse des Barri,** planted with lotus trees, provides a **view★** of St-Tropez Bay, the Îles d'Hyères and the Alps on clear days.

ADDRESSES

🛏 STAY
⊖⊜🍴 **Chambre d'hôte Leï Souco** – *Plaine de Camarat.* ☎*04 94 79 80 22. www.leisouco.com. Closed mid-Oct.–Mar.* 🅿.⊟. ☁ Nestled amid vineyards and olive trees, this peaceful mas offers charming rooms decorated with Salernes earthenware. The family rooms sleep four, each with a private terrace. Tennis court.

Cogolin
Var

This typical Provençal village in the St-Tropez Bay lies at the foot of an ancient tower. A wine-growing centre, Cogolin is also known for its artisan crafts and hand-made pipes.

🐾 WALKING TOUR
The top of the village, with its alleyways and small squares joined by vaulted passageways, has kept its medieval character. Local craft workers produce briar pipes made from heather roots, reeds for musical instruments and even carpets.

▶ *From the tourist office, pass the Hôtel de Ville, and turn left onto rue du 11-Novembre 1918.*

Église St-Sauveur
Dating back to the 11C, the church is entered through a Renaissance serpentine gateway.
A side chapel contains an altarpiece by Hurlupin (1540) depicting St-Antony. On exiting the church, don't miss the fountain on Place Abbé-Toti.

▶ **Population:** 11,066.
◉ **Michelin Map:** 340 O6; local map: *see Massif des MAURES p147.*
🛈 **Info:** Pl. de la République. ☎04 94 55 01 10. www.cogolin-provence.com.
▶ **Location:** Located south of Grimaud on the D 558 and west of St-Tropez on the N 98 (beware seasonal traffic jams).
👪 **Kids:** The rooster museum is filled with cute animal models.
🕐 **Timing:** Allow 2hr to soak up the charm of Cogolin.

Rue Nationale
This street is lined with Renaissance doorways, some dating from the 12C; the bourgeois building at no 46 is the 17C Château Sellier (🔍*see Sights*). Continue to place Bellevue and the **Chapelle St-Roch**, decorated with contemporary artworks. Further up the hill, via Montée Aloes, is the **clock tower** (14C), the only remaining trace of the fortified castle.

Nuts about them!

Pine nuts, also called *pignons*, are delicately flavoured seeds taken from the cones of the stone pine. Their presence in Provençal cooking is by no means recent as the Romans are believed to have used them to make wine and mustard. Today, pine nuts are a common feature of Mediterranean cuisine. In savoury dishes, they add texture to green vegetables and lend a crunchy consistency to stuffings. They are also used in pastries, preferably toasted, notably in delicious almond tarts known as *amandines*.

SIGHTS

Musée Sellier

46 rue Nationale ⏰*Open Tue–Sat Jun–Sept 10am–1pm, 3–6.30pm; Oct–May 10am–12.30pm, 2.30–5.30pm.* 👓*No charge.* 𝒞*04 94 54 63 28.*
This château houses arts exhibitions, the "Rooster Museum" (the town's symbol), and the **Knights Templar Museum**, with documents and uniforms illustrating the history of the religious order.

Musée Raimu

18 ave. G. Clémenceau ⏰*Open Mon–Sat Jun–Sept 10am–12.30pm, 4–7pm, Sun 4–7pm; Oct–May 10am–noon, 3–6pm, Sun 3–6pm.* 👓*4€.* 𝒞*04 94 54 18 00.*
Housed in the ground floor of a cinema, this exhibition explores the life of film actor **Jules Muraire**, aka Raimu, through his letters, posters and costumes.

Coastal Cogolin

▶*3mi /5km northeast by N 98 and D 98A.*
Near Cogolin lies a fine sand beach and a marina with 1,500 moorings offering regular boat shuttle services to nearby ports. The more secluded **Port-Cogolin** has 150 moorings.

ADDRESSES

🛏 STAY

👓 **Le Coq'Hôtel** – *pl. de la Mairie.* 𝒞*04 94 54 13 71. www.coqhotel. com. Closed Jan. 24 rooms.* 🅿 ☕*9€. Restaurant* 👓👓. The hotel's mascot is the rooster, whose emblem can be found on the façade and perched inside the lounge. Lively colours adorn the eclectically furnished rooms. Double-glazed windows overlook the square; other rooms face the inner courtyard.

🍴/EAT

👓 **Côté Jardin** – *rue Pasteur, facing pl. du Marché, aka pl. des Boules; also by the passage at 1 rue Gambetta.* 𝒞*04 94 54 10 36. Closed Nov–Mar.* This open-air restaurant in the heart of Cogolin serves grilled meats, sandwiches, snacks and ice cream in a leafy garden.

🛒 SHOPPING

Provençal Market – There is a lively market every Wednesday and Saturday, and on Friday nights in July–August.

Fabrique de M. Rigotti – *Zone Industrielle, 5 rue François-Arago.* 𝒞*04 94 54 62 05. www.rigotti-reeds. com. Closed Aug.* Rigotti *(guided tours)* produces and sells locally-made reeds and parts for musical instruments.

Cogolin Pipes – *Maison Courrieu, 42/58 ave. G.-Clémenceau.* ♿ 𝒞*04 94 54 63 82. www.courrieupipes.fr.* Briar roots from the nearby Maures Forest have been providing the raw material for pipes in Cogolin for over 200 years. Discover manufacturing techniques and finished products.

Manufacture de Tapis de Cogolin – *10 blvd. Louis-Blanc (off ave. G.-Clemenceau). Exhibition open weekdays 8.30am–noon, 2–5.30pm (Fri 5pm).* 𝒞*04 94 55 70 65. www.tapis-cogolin.com.* Armenian refugee weavers established the Cogolin carpet factory in 1928. A special tour explores hand-weaving using low-warp looms and hand-tufting.

St-Tropez★★

Var

A magnet for celebrities, artists, musicians and their admirers, St-Tropez enjoys an enviable location on the southern shore of arguably the most beautiful bay on the Riviera. The little port's mix of modern luxury yachts and scruffy but colourful Provençal facades clustered around an ancient citadel never seems to go out of fashion.

▶ **Population:** 5,612.

🕙 **Michelin Map:** 340 O6; local maps p160 and p163.

▯ **Info:** Quai Jean-Jaurès. ℰ0892 68 48 28. www.ot-saint-tropez.com.

◖ **Location:** Unless you arrive by yacht, access is slow and frustrating, with infamous summer traffic jams on the only road to the town (D 98a) in July and August; try to get there early in the morning, or stay on the less crowded southeastern coasts of the St-Tropez Peninsula.

🅿 **Parking:** Parking in the village, even in parking garages, is difficult. The map designates free covered and paying parking areas on the peninsula.

A BIT OF HISTORY

The Legend of St Tropez – The town is named after the Christian centurion **Torpetius** (Torpès), whose body, beheaded by Nero, was cast adrift in a boat with a cockerel and a dog, who were meant to devour his remains. Instead it arrived ashore intact, where St-Tropez stands.

Republic of St-Tropez (15C–17C) – In 1470 the Grand Seneschal of Provence accepted the offer of a Genoese gentleman, Raffaele de Garezzio, to settle with 60 Genoese families in St-Tropez, which had been destroyed by war at the end of the 14C. De Garezzio rebuilt the town and its defences, and St-Tropez grew into a sort of small, prosperous republic administered by the heads of these families and later, by elected consuls.

Judge Suffren (18C) – Among the St-Tropézian navigators who contributed to the rise of the town and the defence of France in the 17C the most famous is Pierre-Andre de Suffren (1729–88), a judge under the Knights of Malta who became a captain in the Royal Navy *(his statue can be seen on the quayside)*. He was sent to the Indies, where he won several victories against the British.

The "bravades" – Two *bravades* or "acts of defiance" take place every year. The first, a simple religious procession in honour of St Tropez, has been held in the town since the end of the 15C. On 16 and 17 May a gilded wooden statue of St Tropez is carried through the festive town decked out in red and white (the colours of the corsairs). The second "bravade" celebrates the victory of the St-Tropez militia who, on 15 June 1637, fended off 22 Spanish galleys attempting to take the town by surprise.

Intellectual haven – When the writer **Maupassant** sailed into St-Tropez on his yacht in 1887, it was a charming little village unknown to tourists. A decade later, the painter **Paul Signac** was blown into the port during a storm. He was so impressed, he invited his artist friends to join him, including **Matisse**, who spent several months here, immortalising the town in a number of major works. A campaign to rebuild the war-damaged port led by the writer **Collette** in the 1950s revived its fortunes, attracting a new generation of visitors, including Errol Flynn, Anaïs Nin and **Jean Cocteau**. The arrival of Brigitte Bardot in 1956 finally sealed St-Tropez's reputation as a playground for the rich and famous.

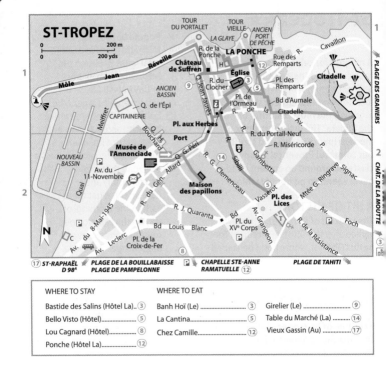

RESORT LIFE

The Port★★

Lined with luxury yachts, the bustling centre of life in cosmopolitan St-Tropez is a star-spotter's paradise. The old pink and yellow houses of the waterfront and neighbouring streets have been converted into cafés and pastry shops, cabarets and restaurants, luxury boutiques, galleries and antique shops.

The Beaches

The 6mi/10km of beaches around St-Tropez are truly heavenly, with their fine sand and charming rocky coves. The nearest is Bouillabaisse Beach (perfect for windsailing when the *mistral* is blowing). To the east of the town lies **Graniers Beach** (*access from rue Cavaillon*). Further east round the headland stretches **Les Salins Beach** (*on ave. Foch*). But by far the most appealing and the most fashionable are the **Pampelonne Beaches**, well sheltered from the *mistral* winds.

Reached by a **coastal path** that skirts the entire peninsula, Cannebiers Bay affords glimpses of the superb villas of the rich and famous.

WALKING TOUR

Môle Jean-Réveille

The attractive **panorama**★ from the top of the jetty includes all of St-Tropez, Ste-Maxime, the Esterel and in fine weather, the Alps.

La Ponche Quarter

Tucked between the port and the citadel, this is the oldest and most charming district of St-Tropez, where fishermen and artists used to live.

▷ *Turn right at the seaward end of quai Jean-Jaurès onto pl. Hôtel-de-Ville.*

On the left stands a massive tower, all that remains of the 16C **Château de Suffren**, the residence of the lords of St-Tropez.

▷ *Turn left beyond the Hôtel de Ville to reach La Glayel cove.*

Rue de la Ponche leads through the old gateway to a beach overlooked by the Vieille Tour (*old tower*), where fishing boats ride at anchor.

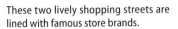 *Follow the street to the adorable pl.des Remparts, then to blvd. d'Aumale.*

Citadelle★

The citadel stands on a hillock at the east end of town. The hexagonal keep with three round towers was built in the 16C. A fortified wall was added in the 17C (*open Apr–Sept 10am–6.30pm, Oct–Mar 10am–12.30pm, 1.30–5.30pm; 2.50€ (5.50€ Jun–Sept); 04 94 97 59 43).* The ramparts command a fine **panorama**★ of St-Tropez to the Maures.

Retrace your steps to rue d'Aumale, then to pl. de l'Ormeau.

Notre-Dame-de-l'Assomption

Rue du Cdt Guichard.
Open 9.30am–noon.
Built in the Italian Baroque style in the early 19C, this church has a finely carved woodwork interior. To the left of the high altar, a bust of St Tropez is surrounded by several old blunderbusses, which are set off during the May bravade.

From rue du Clocher, turn left on rue Commerçants and right on rue Marché.

The charming **Place aux Herbes** is the backdrop to a small morning market. Walk past the lively fish stalls underneath Porte de la Poissonnerie and proceed to Quai Jean-Jaurès.

Leaving the port, take rue Laugier, then rue Gambetta.

These two lively shopping streets are lined with famous store brands.

Place des Lices
A popular meeting place with cafés, a Provençal market and leafy plane trees.

SIGHTS

L'Annonciade, Musée de St-Tropez★★

Pl. Grammont. Open Dec–Oct 10am–noon, 2–6pm, Wed–Mon. Closed 1 Jan, 1 May, Ascension, 25 Dec. 5€. 04 94 17 84 10.
The chapel of Our Lady of Annonciade, built in 1510 and deconsecrated during the Revolution, was split into two levels and opened as a museum in 1937, with artworks dating from 1890 onwards. The collection includes works by **Pointillists** Paul Signac, H-E Cross, Théo van Rysselberghe, Maximilien Luce and Picabia, **Fauvists** Matisse, Braque, Manguin, Vlaminck, Kees Van Dongen and Dufy, and painters from the **Nabis** school, including Bonnard, Vuillard and Félix Vallotton. **Expressionist** painters are represented by Rouault, Chabaud, Utrillo and Valadon.

Maison des Papillons (Musée Dany-Lartigue)

9 rue Étienne-Berny. Open Mon–Sat 2.30–6pm (and Apr–Oct and Christmas holidays Mon, Wed, Fri 10am–12.30pm). 3€ (children under 10 free). 04 94 97 63 45.

La Nioulargue Sailing Festival

First held in 1981, this major European meeting of vintage boats, which takes place every year in October, now attracts more than 250 competitors.

The race starts at the Tour du Portalet, skirts the shallows marked by the Nioulargue (sea nest, in Provençal) buoy and returns to the harbour. The skilful dances performed by ketches (recognisable by the small mast at the stern) and schooners (with the small mast in the bows) call on the sailors to anticipate each manœuvre. The stress at the foot of the main mast can be as much as 500t, so the entrants need braun as well as brains. Watch the race from a boat shuttle service in the bay (*see Addresses p164*), or share the rental of a small boat. A more peaceful view of the scene is possible from the citadel. Binoculars are a must.

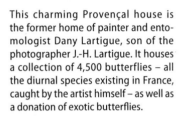

History of the Cap Lardier Estate

In Edwardian times a vineyard occupied the site of the present development and the Mas de Gigaro. In the early 1970s, a banking institution purchased the estate, together with a few plots of land around Brouis beach, with a view to building a marina. The residents rallied against this plan and the Conservatoire du Littoral bought the estate in 1976, guaranteeing the preservation of this stretch of coastline.

The Customs Officers' Footpath – This footpath, which follows 124mi/200km of the Var coastline, dates from the First Empire (early 19C). It was commissioned by Fouché when he was Minister of Police and was intended to help armed customs officers protect the coast against smugglers. Since 1976 the path has been restored and all private properties adjoining the shore are obliged to allow a pathway (at least 10ft/3m wide) across their land.

This charming Provençal house is the former home of painter and entomologist Dany Lartigue, son of the photographer J.-H. Lartigue. It houses a collection of 4,500 butterflies – all the diurnal species existing in France, caught by the artist himself – as well as a donation of exotic butterflies.

EXCURSIONS
Chapelle Ste-Anne
0.7mi/1km. Exit St-Tropez to the south and take ave. Paul Roussel, then route de Ste-Anne. Open 26 July.

Standing on a volcanic peak in the towering shadow of a cypress tree, this attractive Provençal chapel (1620) is a place of pilgrimage for seafarers and *bravadeurs* with a **view**★ of St-Tropez Bay, the Maures and the start of the southern Alps in the distance.

Ramatuelle★
See RAMATUELLE pp156.

HIKING TOURS
Presqu'île St-Tropez★★
Wear a good pair of walking shoes and avoid the hottest times of the day.

Although in high season tourism takes over St-Tropez, the surrounding country presents a traditional landscape of vineyards, cypress trees and immaculate farmhouses *(mas)* shaded by umbrella pines. The **St-Tropez Peninsula**★★ consists of the rocky headlands of Cap Camarat, Cap Taillat and Cap Lardier, the long ribbon of fine sand at Pampel-onne Bay, the beaches of Gigaro, Briande and Escalet, and countless creeks for secluded bathing.

St-Tropez to Tahiti Beach
Allow 3hr.

The path, with superb **views** of the foothills of the Maures and red rocks of the Esterel, leaves from Graniers Beach at the west end of the harbour. After running along the Rabiou Point and Cap de St-Tropez, the path wends its way to Les Salins beach, where refreshments are available in open-air cafés *(guingettes)* in summer. The path then rounds Cap Pinet and ends at Tahiti beach in Pampelonne Bay.

Tahiti Beach to Cap Camarat
Allow 2hr.

The path runs parallel to the long sandy stretch of Pampelonne Beach *(3mi/5km)* to Bonne-Terrasse Point. At Bonne-Terrasse Bay the path climbs the rocks through thicker vegetation. Near Rocher des Portes there is a footpath *(right)* to Camarat lighthouse.

From Ramatuelle take D 93 east to the "Route du Phare" and beyond the Tournels camp site.

Phare de Camarat★
This **lighthouse**, commissioned in 1831, was converted to electricity after the Second World War and automated in 1977. At 425.8ft/129.8m above sea level, it is one of the tallest in France,

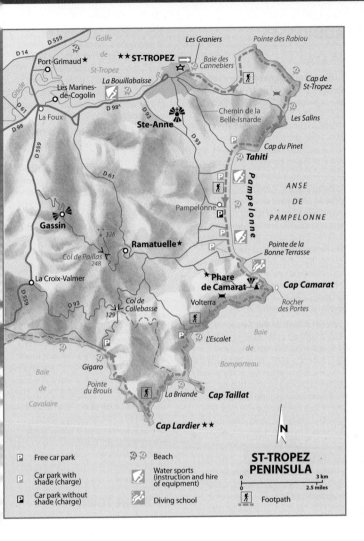

P	Free car park
P	Car park with shade (charge)
P	Car park without shade (charge)

	Beach
	Water sports (instruction and hire of equipment)
	Diving school

ST-TROPEZ PENINSULA

0 — 3 km
0 — 2.5 miles

| Footpath |

with a 37mi/60km range. From the summit there are **views**★★ over the whole peninsula.

Cap Camarat to Cap Taillat
No refreshments, except in L'Escalet.
Allow 2hr. After skirting Rocher des Portes, the path leads to L'Escalet beach over isolated, accessible coves that are ideal for sunbathing **Views** of the **Château de Volterra** (*closed to the public*). The path ends at Cap Taillat.

> You can rejoin the road from the customs shed at the L'Escalet car park.

The path cuts across the base of the headland through scrubland and oak forests. **Cap Taillat** is a tombolo sand bar connecting the reef to the coast, turning it into a peninsula.

Cap Taillat to Gigaro via Cap Lardier★★
Allow 2hr.
Most of the path runs through the **protected**★★ Cap Lardier with **views** of Briande Bay from the cliffs. Return to Gigaro from Briande Beach by the inland path *(route DFCI)*.

ADDRESSES

🛏 STAY

Hôtel Lou Cagnard – *ave. Paul-Roussel.* ☎*04 94 97 04 24. www.hotel-lou-cagnard.com. Closed Nov–Dec.* 🅿*19 rooms.* ⊐*11€.* Enjoy breakfast seated in the shade of a mulberry tree in the tiny garden of this Provençal house, just off Place des Lices. At night you'll be lulled to sleep by the chirping of cicadas. Very reasonable prices.

Bello Visto – *pl. deï Barri, Gassin.* ☎*04 94 56 17 30 or 04 94 56 47 33. www.bello-visto.fr. 9 rooms.* ⊐*8€. Restaurant*⊜⊜. A small family-run hotel and restaurant posted on Place des Remparts *(barri)*, at the top of Gassin. The majority of the rooms, such as the terrace, profit from **views** over the Massif des Maures and the gulf of St-Tropez. Dining room with fireplace and Provençal cuisine.

Bastide des Salins – *2.5mi /4km southeast of St-Tropez.* ☎*04 94 97 24 57. www.bastidedessalins.com.* 🅿*13 rooms.* ⊐*17€.* You will be greeted like friends of the family at this old Provençal house surrounded by extensive leafy grounds. Barely 5min from Place des Lices and yet totally isolated, this hotel offers large rooms decorated in the Provençal spirit, appointed with great simplicity.

Hôtel Ponche – *pl. Révelin.* ☎*04 94 97 02 53. www.laponche.com. Closed Nov– Mar.* 🅿*18 rooms.* ⊐*20€. Restaurant*⊜⊜⊜. The rooms of this cosy hotel occupy four village houses formerly belonging to fishermen; the blue one was a favourite of Romy Schneider's. Warm, bright hues and considerate service make the Hôtel Ponche an absolute must.

🍴 EAT

La Cantina – *16 rue des Remparts.* ☎*04 94 97 40 96. Closed Nov–Mar.* After sipping your tequila, savour generous helpings of Mexican cuisine in this typical setting featuring religious statues and painted wood furnishings. Youngish clientele, relaxed ambience.

La Table du Marché – *38 rue Georges-Clémenceau.* ☎*04 94 97 85 20. www.christophe-leroy.com.* A temple of gastronomy located near Place des Lices, open all hours of the day. In addition to the restaurant offering traditional French cuisine, La Table du Marché also sells homemade pastries: croissants, cakes and the legendary "gendarme de St-Tropez" – mouthwatering chocolate mousse filled with vanilla crème brûlée.

Au Vieux Gassin – *pl. deï Barri, Gassin.* ☎*04 94 56 14 26. Closed mid-Oct– mid-Mar.* A ravishing little hilltop village serves as the backdrop for this popular restaurant. A terrace with **panoramic views** is partially enclosed and heated in cooler weather, taking over a large section of the charming place deï Barri. The regional menu has a few "exotic" specialities.

Le Banh Hoï – *12 r. Petit St-Jean.* ☎*04 94 97 36 29. Closed 12 Oct–3 Apr.* Low lighting, black lacquer walls and Asian artworks decorate this restaurant specialising in Thai and Vietnamese cuisine.

Chez Camille – *quai de Bonne Terrasse.* ☎*04 98 12 68 98. Closed early Oct–early Apr.* A family-run restaurant on the waterfront serving *bouillabaisse* (spicy fish stew) and grilled fish since 1913. Ask about the boat shuttle service.

Le Girelier – *quai Jean-Jaurès.* ☎*04 94 97 03 87. www.legirelier.fr. Closed Nov–mid-Mar.* A harbourside fishermen's hut converted into a stylish, contemporary dining room with simply-cooked shellfish platters and bouillabaisse.

🍸 ON THE TOWN

In summer, St-Tropez is the place for the rich and wealthy and is given over to sailing, bathing, entertainment and nightlife. However, in winter it looks more like a ghost town. Most businesses close down between November and April, when the swinging bars, restaurants and hotels become completely deserted.

Bar du Château de la Messardière – *route de Tahiti.* ☎*04 94 56 76 00. www.messardiere.com. Closed mid-Oct– mid-Mar.* This bar belongs to one of the Riviera's most prestigious hotels. Hushed, cosy ambience in the piano bar of this former 18C private residence. The terrace commands **views** of St-Tropez Bay.

Bar Sube – *15 quai de Suffren.* *04 94 97 30 04. www.hotel-sube.com. Closed mid- to late Jan.* This is one of the most beautiful bars of the city. Model boats decorate the interior, where the leather armchairs and fireplace make for a cordial and comfortable atmosphere. Small tables are installed on the balcony, with prime **views** of the old port.

SHOPPING

Markets – Tuesdays and Saturdays on Place des Lices.

Foire de la Ste-Anne – Fair on Place des Lices, every 26 July.

Shopping streets – The most lively shopping streets are rue Clémenceau, rue Gambetta and rue Allard, offering an impressive selection of local arts and crafts: pottery, glassware, etc.

Les Sandales Tropéziennes – *16 rue Georges Clémenceau.* *04 94 97 19 55. www.rondini.fr. Closed Nov–Feb.* The Rondini house has been crafting natural leather St-Tropez sandals since 1927.

Le Petit Village – *La Foux, near the shopping centre just outside Gassin.* *04 94 56 32 04. www.mavigne.com. Closed Sun.* This showroom brings together wines from eight prestigious vineyards on the St-Tropez peninsula just off the busy La Foux intersection. Includes the famous Château de Pampelonne vineyard. Free tastings and many regional products for sale.

FOR YOUR SWEET TOOTH
La Tarte Tropézienne – *pl. des Lices.* *04 94 97 71 42. www.tarte-tropezienne. com.* It was in this pâtisserie that the famous *tarte tropézienne* saw the light of day, invented in 1955 by Polish baker Alexandre Micka: a round delightfully moist, brioche cake flavoured with orange blossom, filled with custard and sprinkled with crystallised sugar.

Sénéquier – *quai Jean-Jaurès.* *04 94 97 00 90. www.senequier.com. Closed early Jan–late Feb.* The pavement terrace and crimson chairs of this tea room are famous throughout the world, or so say the locals! Renowned personalities such as Jean Marais, Errol Flynn and Colette would come here for a cup of delicately fragrant tea, an iced coffee, a delicious ice cream or a few squares of homemade nougat.

Tarte Tropézienne

S. Sauvignier/ MICHELIN

SPORTS & LEISURE

Octopussy Plongée – *Capitainerie du port.* *04 94 56 68 71 or 06 83 25 34 83. www.octopussy-plongee.fr. Closed Dec–Mar.* Scuba diving lessons and excursions for all levels in the blue waters around St-Tropez.

Maison du Tourisme du Golfe de St-Tropez – *Carrefour de la Foux, Gassin.* *04 94 55 22 00. www.st-tropez-lesmaures.com.* This tourist office issues a list of all the companies based in St-Tropez Bay who specialise in deep-sea diving. Or see the website.

TRANSPORT

Les Bateaux Verts – *14 quai Léon Condroyer, Ste-Maxime.* *04 94 49 29 39. www.bateauxverts.com.*

Return trip from St-Tropez to Ste Maxime (20min) 12.50€ (children 7€)

Return Trip from Ste Maxime to Baie des Canoubiers (45min) 14€ (children 7.40€)

Return Trip from St Tropez to Baie des Canoubiers 9€ (children 5€).

Grimaud★

Var

A warren of narrow cobbled streets, shady squares and flights of stone steps running up to the ruins of a medieval castle, the perched village of Grimaud has retained its traditional Provençal character. In contrast, the modern Port-Grimaud, built in the 1960s, although not to everyone's taste, is a lively and bustling summer destination.

▶ **Population:** 4,181.
 Michelin Map: 340 O6.
 Info: Bd. des Aliziers.
 $\wp$04 94 55 43 83. www.
 grimaud-provence.com
 Location: The old town is 6mi/10km west of St-Tropez on the N 98A, then D 61.
 Parking: In high season it's best to leave your car near the cemetery *(Parking du Château)*, on the north side of town near the Pont des Fées.

WALKING TOUR

OLD TOWN★
Allow 1hr.

Tour marked by arrows. A map with commentary is available from the tourist office.

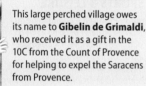

The Ancient Grimaldi Feifdom

This large perched village owes its name to **Gibelin de Grimaldi**, who received it as a gift in the 10C from the Count of Provence for helping to expel the Saracens from Provence.

Start at the **Eglise St-Michel**, a small Romanesque church (12–13C) with a 16C bell tower, 18C sacristy and restored 19C frescoes *(time switch to the left on entering)*, before exploring the imposing ruins of the nearby 11C **castle**. Home to the powerful comtes de Provence and the Cossa and Castellane families, it was originally surrounded by a triple-walled enclosure protected by four three-storey corner towers. The towers were demolished in 1655, but the castle still boasts a stretch of 23ft/7m-high crenellated ramparts. One medieval tower survives to the north. The two southern towers date from the 17C, when the fortifications were rebuilt. From the upper ramparts

Castle at Grimaud

there are fine **views**★ of the Maures, St-Tropez Bay and, in the foreground, the restored olive mill of Grimaud.

Head east to the 15–18C **Chapelle des Pénitents**, which houses the relics of St. Theodore, then join the Route Départementale *(county road)*, where you'll find the **Musée d'Art et Traditions Populaires** (⚲*open Mon–Sat May–Sept (Tue–Sat Jul–Aug) 2.30–6pm, Oct–Apr 2–5.30pm,* ⚲ *closed public holidays;* ⚲*no charge;* ✆*04 94 55 43 83)*. Housed in a 17C olive mill, this folk museum explores the history of the village in the 19C through a series of archive photographs. A collection of tools illustrate the village's traditional activities, such as cork-making, silkworm breeding and wine-growing. A farmer's residence filled with household objects, garments and headdresses offers a glimpse of pre-industrial agricultural life.

▷ *Pass by the tourist office and walk towards pl. Neuve.*

A fountain here commemorates the installation of running water in Grimaud in 1886. Head towards the church along the rue des Templiers, where a 15C Maison des Templiers still stands. Once home to a garrison of Knights Templars, it has an impressive façade of basalt arcades and a serpentine doorway.

EXCURSION
Port-Grimaud★

▷ *Follow signs for Port-Grimaud (north) 3mi/5km to the car park outside the port complex.*

Designed in 1966 by the architect **François Spoerry** (1912–99), Port-Grimaud is a luxury housing complex designed to look like a fortified Mediterranean fishing village, complete with a fully-equipped marina and a fine sand beach. Public transport is available in passenger barges *(coches d'eau)*.

The ecumenical church of **St-François-d'Assise** is resolutely modern, although inspired by the Provençal Romanesque style. The tower affords a pretty **view**★ of Port-Grimaud, St-Tropez Bay and the Maures Massif.

ADDRESSES

⚲STAY

⚲⚲**Chambre d'Hôte La Toscane** – *route départementale, Villa la Toscane, 2.5mi/4km from Grimaud Village.* ✆*04 94 43 24 11. www.la-toscane.com. 4 rooms.* 🍴. ⚲. The rooms of this Tuscan-style villa are cheerfully decorated with Provençal furnishings and tiled floors. Nice garden; swimming pool.

⚲⚲**La Bastide de l'Avelan** – *Quartier Robert, 1mi/2km from Grimaud Village by the D 94.* ✆*04 94 43 25 79. www.bastideavelan.com. 4 rooms.* 🍴. ⚲. Simple but charming rooms in a typical Provençal house, all facing the gardens and swimming pool.

⚲/EAT

⚲⚲**L'Écurie de la Marquise** – *3 rue Gacharel.* ✆*04 94 43 27 26. Closed lunch Jul–Aug. Reservations recommended.* Located on a small pedestrian street in the old town, this unpretentious restaurant has a rustic decor and tasty Provençal cuisine.

⚲⚲**Auberge La Cousteline** – *1.5mi/2.5km southeast on D 14.* ✆*04 94 43 29 47. www.aubergelacousteline.fr. Closed Jan, Tue, Wed lunch Oct–May, lunch Jul–Aug.* This converted farm-house set in lush vegetation has a cosy country atmosphere and a market-fresh menu that changes with the seasons.

GUIDED TOURS
⚲⚲**Coches d'Eau de Port-Grimaud** – *12 pl. du Marché.* ✆*04 94 56 21 13.* ⚲*mid-Jun– mid-Sept 9.30am–12.30, 2.30–7.30pm; mid-Sept–mid-Jun (call for hours).* Boat tours on Port-Grimaud and electric boat rental.

⚲⚲**Petit Train Touristique** – *Apr–Oct.* ✆*04 94 97 22 85.* ⚲*6€ (children 3€).* This train circles between Grimaud *(place Neuve)* and Port-Grimaud *(main entry to Port-Grimaud Nord, near the car park).*

CALENDAR
Markets – Thursdays on Place Vieille. Thursdays, Sundays in Port-Grimaud.
Fête du Moulin – June.
Les Grimaldines – Festival of World Music, mid-July to mid-August (Tuesday eves).

Sainte-Maxime★

Var

Less glamorous than its neighbour St-Tropez, this small family resort has a tastefully-restored old town, fishing harbour, well-appointed marina and fine sand beaches.

▶ **Population:** 13,739.

⏲ **Michelin Map:** 340 O6.

ℹ **Info:** 1 promenade Simon-Loriere. ℘04 94 55 75 55. www.sainte-maxime.com.

▶ **Location:** Ste-Maxime sits on the edge of the Massif des Maures and 8.7mi/14km across the bay from St-Tropez on the N 98.

VISIT

Seafront and beaches

Running from the beach to the port, the **Promenade Simon-Lorière**, shaded by umbrella pines and palm trees, commands **views** of St-Tropez. Not far from place du 15-Août-1944, a **stele** commemorates the Allied landings in 1944. Running below the promenade, **Casino beach**, one of the 6.5mi/10km of fine sand beaches in Ste-Maxime, is flanked by La Croisette *(east)* and La Madrague *(west)* beaches. For more secluded sunbathing, try La Nartelle, Eléphants and La Garonnette beyond Sardinaux Point.

Tour Carrée des Dames

This square defensive tower built in the 16C is now the **Musée des Traditions Locales** (Ⓞopen Wed–Sun 10am–noon, 3–6pm (Jul 7pm); ⚬⚬2.30€; ℘04 94 96 70 30) devoted to local folklore and traditions.

Church

This church features a Baroque interior (1672) decorated with a green and ochre marble altar. Note the 15C choir stalls.

EXCURSION

Parc St-Donat

6mi/10km. Allow 1hr.

▶ *From Ste-Maxime take blvd. Georges-Clemenceau, D 25 north.*

A leisure park has been laid out in the woods between Col de Gratteloup and St-Donat Chapel. The main attraction is the **Musée du Phonographe et de la Musique Mécanique** (♿Ⓞopen Apr–Jun and Sept Wed–Sun 10am–noon, 4–6pm, Jul–Aug 10am–noon, 4–6.30pm; ⚬⚬3€; ℘04 94 96 50 52) housing an astonishing collection of 350 musical instruments and sound recording machines.

Port at Sainte Maxime

ADDRESSES

🏨 STAY

L'Auberge Provençale – *19 blvd. Aristide-Briand.* ☎ *04 94 55 76 90. Closed late Dec–early Jan. 15 rooms.* ☐ *6€. Restaurant* 🍽️. Despite its unprepossessing façade, this inn close to the beach offers charming accommodation in keeping with Provençal tradition. The bedrooms have been given warm, earthy hues and the southern cuisine uses fresh market produce.

Le Chardon Bleu – *29 rue de Verdun.* ☎ *04 94 55 52 22. www.aubergedu chardonbleu.fr. 25 rooms.* ☐ *8€.* Conveniently situated at the heart of the resort, barely 150 yards from the sea, this hotel offers air-conditioned rooms with small balconies. Two rooms have a big terrace.

🍽️ EAT

Chez Sophie – *4 pl. des Sarrasins.* ☎ *04 94 96 71 00. Closed Nov–Dec.* Charming restaurant that epitomises the Provençal spirit: colourful decoration, wooden furnishings, terrace shaded by a plane tree, menu inspired by regional cuisine. The dishes and tasty homemade desserts are served by charming locals.

La Maison Bleue – *48 r. Paul Bert.* ☎ *04 94 96 51 92. Closed Nov–Dec.* A Provençal house entirely dedicated to pasta and its history: early advertising posters and enamelled plaques adorn the ochre walls of this restaurant, whose terrace is pleasantly shaded by plane trees.

🍷 ON THE TOWN

Café de France – *pl. Victor-Hugo.* ☎ *04 94 96 18 16. www.lecafedefrance. fr.* A whiff of the past permeates this brasserie, opened in 1852 when Ste-Maxime was a fishing village. Old-time photographs and an ancient mirror evoke this bygone era. The big terrace sheltered by plane trees faces the marina. Fresh oysters in season.

Bar de l'Amarante Golf Plaza – *ave. Célestin.* ☎ *04 94 56 66 66. www. golf-plaza.fr.* Prestigious hotel bar set against a backdrop of cork oaks and Mediterranean scrubland, overlooking Ste-Maxime and St-Tropez Bay. Golf course, fitness club and large-scale game of chess.

🛒 SHOPPING

MARKETS

Artisan Market – Daily 5am–11pm on the pedestrian streets mid-June to mid-July.

Food Market – A covered market near place du Marché every morning (except Monday in winter); open market Thursday morning on Place des Sarrasins.

Fair – Lively fair every Friday at Place Jean Mermoz.

🎭 OUTDOOR PERFORMANCES

Théâtre de la Mer – *promenade Simon Lorière.* ☎ *04 94 55 75 55/04 94 49 20 01. www.ste-maxime.com. Closed Oct–May.* Every summer this open-air theatre stages concerts of classical music and contemporary pop, folk dance and firework displays.

🏃 SPORTS AND LEISURE

Héli Sécurité – *Quartier Perrat, Z.A. Grimaud.* ☎ *04 94 43 39 30. www.helicopter-saint-tropez.com.* Recreational flights in helicopters and shuttle services between airports or resorts.

Club Nautique de Sainte Maxime – *blvd. Jean-Moulin.* ☎ *04 94 96 07 80. www.club-nautique-sainte-maxime.fr Open school holidays.* This watersports club organises sailing courses during the school holidays.

Golf de Sainte-Maxime – *rte. du Débarquement.* ☎ *04 94 55 02 02. www.bluegreen.com. Closed winter.* Superb, undulating golf course laid out over the heights of Ste-Maxime, dominating St-Tropez Bay. Bar with terrace facing the sea.

Les Bateaux Verts – *14 quai Léon-Condroyer.* ☎ *04 94 49 29 39. www.bateauxverts.com.* Coastal excursions from Easter to October: tours of the St-Tropez Bay, the inlets of the Esterel, Îles d'Hyères.

INLAND PROVENCE

Despite its historic towns and villages, lush green vineyards, dense pine forests and plunging cliffs, the *arrière pays* or "hinterland" of Provence manages to keep well below the tourist radar. Ideally explored at a leisurely pace, this region is filled with historic gems, from prehistoric funeral monuments and cave villages to towering ramparts and clock towers. Renowned for its olives, truffles and world-famous organic wines, it is also the ideal place to embark on a culinary adventure or two. Tucked away in millennial forests, perched on rocky peaks, hidden in deep valleys or simply located on fertile plains, these towns and villages offer a welcome respite from the crowded coastal cities of the French Riviera.

Villages of Character
Since 1999, an exclusive group of villages in eight French regions, including the Var, have been awarded the "Villages de Caractère" label. To qualify for this label, a village must have a harmonious blend of historic architecture, fewer than 3,500 residents and at least one registered monument or sight. In the Var *département*, Aups and Cotignac are two of the eight villages which have been awarded this prestigious designation and are well worth a detour.

Historic Riches
There are more than 70 megaliths in this region, making it one of the richest sites for prehistoric treasures in the country. One of the most famous is in Lorgues, where visitors can see the Peyrcervier Dolmen, a type of megalithic tomb resembling a stone table.

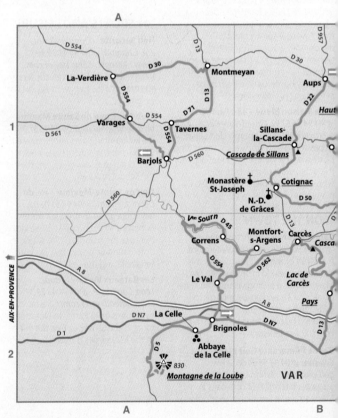

Gallo-Roman ruins can be found in many villages, including vestiges of the Roman road from Spain to Italy in Draguignan, the Gayole Tombstone in Brignoles and artefacts from the Bouverie caves, now on display in the Musée du Patrimoine in Roquebrune-sur-Argens. The towns and villages of Inland Provence have been marked by history at every turn, from the Middle Ages and the Ancien Régime to the Third Republic and the Second World War.

Local Economy

Dotted with ancient stone mills, Inland Provence has been producing wine and olive oil since Roman times. Today Brignoles lies at the heart of its rapidly growing organic wine-growing industry. A stop-off at one of the region's dozens of vineyards is now a must for wine lovers. Pottery, faïence and terracotta Santon dolls are produced in the region,

while Aups is famous as the Black Truffle capital of Provence. Tourism, however, is not so prevalent in this part of the French Riviera, despite its ideal location between the sea and the Gorges de Verdon.

Highlights

1 Taste the local wines in and around **Brignoles** (p172)

2 Take part in the colourful *Fête de St-Marcel* in **Barjols** (p176)

3 Take a tour of the cave dwellings in **Villecroze** (p178)

4 Listen to medieval music at **Abbaye du Thoronet** (p183)

5 Visit the perched village of **Châteaudouble** (p192)

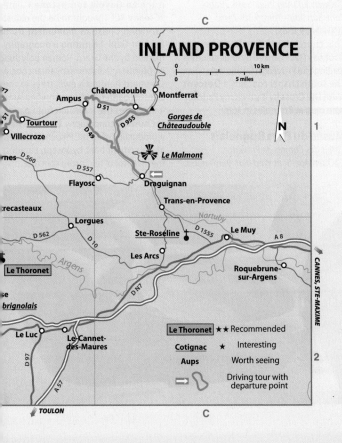

INLAND PROVENCE

0 ——— 10 km
0 ——— 5 miles

N

Châteaudouble · Montferrat
Ampus · D 51
Tourtour · D 49
Villecroze · D 955
···nes · D 560 · *Gorges de Châteaudouble*
D 557 · ☀ *Le Malmont*
Flayosc · Draguignan
Trans-en-Provence
···recasteaux · *Nartuby*
Lorgues · Ste-Roséline · D 1555 · Le Muy
D 562 · D 10 · A 8
Argens
Le Thoronet · Les Arcs
···se · Roquebrune-sur-Argens
brignolais · D N7

Le Luc · Le Cannet-des-Maures
D 97 · A 57
▲ TOULON

Le Thoronet	★★	Recommended
Cotignac	★	Interesting
Aups		Worth seeing
⇨		Driving tour with departure point

CANNES, STE-MAXIME

171

Brignoles

Var

The narrow, winding streets of old Brignoles sit on the northern side of a low hill crowned by a venerable crenulated castle that once belonged to the counts of Provence. Lying on a rich, fertile plain, this market town is renowned for its peaches, honey, olives, oil and wine.

▶ **Population:** 14,963.
⊙ **Michelin Map:** 340 L5.
🔲 **Info:** Office de Tourisme. La Provence Verte, carrefour de l'Europe. ℘04 94 72 04 21. www.la-provence-verte.net.
🅿 **Parking:** Large parking area in town and at place des Augustins.

VISIT

Head south of place Carami and stroll through the medieval streets to the church of St-Sauveur and the 12C castle, the birthplace of several counts of Provence. Walk along the covered rue du Grand-Escalier, rue du St-Esprit and rue des Lanciers with its twin-windowed **Romanesque house**.

Église St-Sauveur

🕙Open Jul–Aug Wed–Sat 8.30am–7pm, Sun 9am–1pm, 5.30–7pm. ℘04 94 69 10 69.
This church has a fine Romanesque doorway (12C) flanked by ionic columns leading to a Provençal Gothic style nave. The south chapel contains a **Descent from the Cross** by Barthélemy Parrocel, who died at Brignoles in 1660.

Musée du Pays Brignolais

Palais des Comtes de Provence.
🕙Open Apr–Sept Wed–Sat 9am–noon, 2.30–6pm, Sun 9am–noon, 3–6pm; Oct–Mar Wed–Sat 10am–noon, 2.30–5pm, Sun 10am–noon, 3–5pm. 🕙Closed public holidays. ◎4€. ℘04 94 69 45 18. www.museebrignolais.com. Dominated by a large tower, this regional museum is housed in the former castle of the Counts of Provence (partly 12C). The highlight of the exhibition is the **La Gayole tombstone**★ (late 2C–early 3C), thought to be the oldest surviving Christian monument from Ancient Gaul. Featuring iconography marked by the Greco-Roman polytheist tradition (a fisherman, an anchor, a shepherd herding a ewe, trees in the celestial garden and a personified sun), it illustrates the transition from pagan to Christian iconography. Don't miss the reproduction of an 18C Provençal kitchen and a cement boat by Joseph Lambot, the inventor of reinforced concrete.

Musée du Pays Brignolais

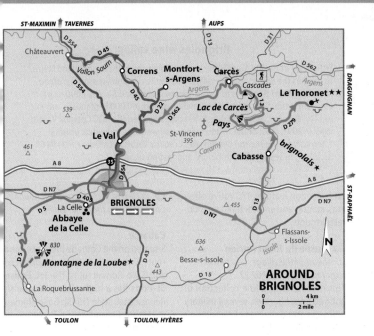

ST-MAXIMIN ↑ TAVERNES   ↑ AUPS

Châteauvert

Vallon Sourn

Correns   Montfort-s-Argens   Carcès

Cascades

Le Thoronet ★★

DRAGUIGNAN

Lac de Carcès

Pays

St-Vincent

Le Val

Cararmy

Cabasse

brignolais ★

ST-RAPHAËL

La Celle

Abbaye de la Celle

BRIGNOLES

Montagne de la Loube ★

La Roquebrussanne

Besse-s-Issole

Flassans-s-Issole

Issole

AROUND BRIGNOLES

N

0   4 km
0   2 mile

TOULON   TOULON, HYÈRES

EXCURSION
Abbaye de la Celle

◗ *Leave Brignoles by the D 554 going south and turn right on the D 405.*

☞ *Guided tours (45min) Apr–Sept Mon–Fri 9am–12.30pm, 2–6.30pm, Sat–Sun 9am–1pm, 2.30–6.30pm; Oct–Mar Mon–Fri 9am–noon, 2–5pm, Sat 9am–noon, 2–5pm (from 10am Sun).* ◷ *Closed 1 Jan, 1 May, 11 Nov, 25 Dec.* ☞ *2.30€.*
℘ *04 94 59 19 05.*

This Benedictine convent was home to one hundred cloistered nuns in 1268. From the 14C, a decline in morals (many of the nuns lived openly with their lovers) led to the transfer of the order to Aix en Provence in 1658. Sold after the Revolution, the abbey was used as a farm, then turned into a luxury hotel. The minster, cloisters, chapter house and refectory are all open to visitors. The Romanesque abbey church featuring a cul-de-four nave contains an astonishingly realistic early-14C Christ.

▲▲Little Train

◗ *Gare de Carnoules, 19mi/31km SE of Brignoles by D 43, D 15 and D 13.*
◷ *Operates Apr–Oct and Dec, phone for details.* ☞*15/9€ (4–10 years 9/5€).*
℘ *06 07 98 03 09. www.attcv.fr.*

Hop onboard the *Picasso* (1955) railcar and admire the countryside between Carnoules and Brignoles via St-Anastasie-sur-Issole, Besse-sur-Issole, Forcalquier and La Celle.

🚗 DRIVING TOURS

① BRIGNOLES COUNTRY★
35mi/56km Allow 3hr. ◖ *See local map above; route marked in green.*

◗ *Leave Brignoles north on the D 554.*

Le Val
Lying beside the Roman Via Aurelia, Le Val's narrow houses are clustered around the 18C wrought-iron campanile of the **Tour de l'Horloge**. The Romanesque church is decorated with 18C **frescoes**. Near the entrance to Le Val, the **Hôtel des Vins** sports a fresco by **Le Couëdic**, one of Dalí's pupils.
Musée d'Art Sacré
North of the village. ♿ *Reservation required.* ℘*04 94 37 02 22.* Located in a 16C Pénitents Noirs chapel, this religious

Brignoles wine valley

Either side of the Via Aurelia, the ancient Roman road that once linked Fréjus to Aix, lies the Brignoles wine valley. This fertile clay and limestone plateau stretching from Brignoles to Sainte-Baume boasts 3,953 acres/1,600 ha of vineyard producing an annual 1.5 million gallons/60,000 hl of mostly organic red (40%), rosé (55%) and white (5%) wine. Awarded the AOC Coteaux Varois label in 1993, most of the region's vineyards welcome individual visitors. Alternatively, the Maison des Vins des Coteaux Varois in La Celle (&04 94 69 33 18) organises regular exhibitions and tasting sessions.

art collection features 17C votive offerings, statues and embroidered sacerdotal garments.

👥 Musée du Jouet Ancien
Southeast of the village. Reservation required. &04 94 37 02 22.
This museum has a fine collection of antique toys, figurines, several military uniforms and dioramas of Napoleon's most famous battles.

▷ *Take the D 562 northeast to Carcès.*

Carcès
The town produces oil and honey and has extensive wine cellars. The colourful glazed roof tiles of Carcès afford protection against the strong *mistral* winds.

▷ *Head towards Cabasse on the D 13 along the banks of the Carami.*

Carami Falls
🥾 *2.5hr.* Park at the bridge and follow the signed trail 5mi/8km to a tiered waterfall (22ft/7m per tier).

▷ *Continue along the D 13.*

Lac de Carcès
The pine-clad shores of this lake, created in 1936, are a favourite haunt of fishermen (🚫*swimming not allowed*).

▷ *Continue on D 13 and turn left onto D 79 for the Abbaye du Thoronet.*

Abbaye du Thoronet★★ –
🕐*see Abbaye du THORONET p183.*

▷ *Return to D 13 and turn left towards Cabasse along the Issole Valley.*

Cabasse
Situated on the Côtes de Provence wine route, Cabasse is dotted with dolmens and Gallo-Roman ruins. The 16C **Église St-Pons** has a **high altar**★ in Spanish Renaissance style (1543). Gallo-Roman milestones stand near a 2C funerary inscription set in the outside wall.

▷ *Proceed along D 13, then turn right onto D N7 back to Brignoles.*

② VALLON SOURN
Round trip 25mi/39km.
Allow about 1hr. 🕐See local map; route marked in purple.

▷ *Take D 554 north to Le Val. Turn right onto D 562, then left onto D 22.*

Montfort-sur-Argens
A former Templar commandery, this walled village is dominated by the ruins of a forboding **feudal castle** featuring two square towers, mullioned windows and a 15C spiral staircase. Grapes and peaches fill the surrounding fields.

▷ *Return to the crossroads and turn right onto D 45, following the Argens.*

Correns
Straddling the River Argens, this village has a castle and keep with interesting gargoyles. Renowned for its organic **white wine**, Correns plays host to an annual wine festival (third weekend in August, contact the tourist office for more details, &04 94 37 02 22).

Vallon Sourn

The steep cliffs of this valley (*sourn* means sombre in Provençal) are honey-combed with caves which served as a refuge during the Wars of Religion. It is now an ideal spot to walk, swim or hire a canoe. The hillsides are also popular with rock-climbers.

○ *In Châteauvert turn left onto D 554 to return to Brignoles.*

3 **MONTAGNE DE LA LOUBE★**
8.7mi/14km southwest. Allow about 3hr, including hike. ⓒ*See local map; route marked in blue.*

○ *Take D 554 south. Turn right onto D 405; turn left onto D 5. Park on a road 0.6mi/1km before La Roquebrussanne.*

Montagne de la Loube★
2hr on foot round trip.
🚶 The narrow road skirts a formation of eroded dolomitic rocks, some of which resemble animals and human beings.

○ *Climb the final steps to the telecommunications mast.*

From the summit (2,723ft/830m) is an interesting **panorama★**. The farmland is hemmed by barren ridges and the bauxite mines tear red gashes in the green quilt of pine and holm oak.

○ *Return to Brignoles by D 5 and N 7.*

ADDRESSES

🛏 STAY

⊜⊜⊜**Chambre d'Hôte Château de Vins** – *Vins-sur-Caramy, 6mi/9.5km from Brignoles on D 24, rte du Thoronet.* ℘*04 94 72 50 40. www.chateaudevins. com. Closed Nov–Apr.* 🍴. *5 rooms.* Listed 16C castle with four turrets and austere, imposing rooms. The grounds include a small, family-sized gîte.

⊜⊜⊜**La Cordeline** – *14 rue des Cordeliers.* ℘*04 94 59 18 66. www. lacordeline.com. Reservation required. 4 rooms. Restaurant*⊜⊜. Handsome 17C

mansion providing accommodation in tastefully furnished rooms with fully equipped bathrooms and small salon. A haven of tranquillity at the heart of the town.

⊜⊜⊜**Hôtel La Cabro d'Or** – *5 ave. Giraud-Florentin.* ℘*04 94 04 50 26. www.lacabrod-or.com. 5 rooms. Restaurant*⊜⊜ Close to the town centre, this small, unpretentious hotel housed in a renovated 19C hospice boasts a Provençal restaurant.

🍴 EAT

⊜**La Remise** – *4 ave. de la Libération, Besse-sur-Issole, 9mi/15km southeast of Brignoles on N 7 towards Le Luc and right on D 13.* ℘*04 94 59 66 93. Closed Mon Jul–Aug.* Small, unpretentious establishment discreetly located at the entrance to the village. The white walled decor has a simple, minimalist feel. Outside is a shaded courtyard. Simple fare with a Mediterranean touch.

⊜**Le Val Bohème** – *3 pl. du 4-Septembre, Le Val.* ℘*04 94 86 46 20.*🍴. The special of the day at this small restaurant depends on the seasonal produce found at the local market. A charming terrace overlooks the church.

🛍 SHOPPING

Open-Air Markets – Every Wednesday on pl. Carami and Saturday on pl. Général du Gaulle and pl. du 8 Mai.

Maison des Vins Coteaux Varois – *Abbaye de la Celle, La Celle.* ℘*04 94 69 33 18. Closed Sun in winter.* Housed in a 12C abbey, this store stocks wines from 80 different regional producers.

🎉 EVENTS

Agricultural Fair – Dedicated to wines from Provence and the Var region, as well as honey, olives and olive oil. Held for 10 days in April.

Foires à la Saucisse au Val – Sausage festival the first weekend in September.

Barjols

Var

The village of 30 fountains, Barjols is surrounded by a natural amphitheatre of lush green hills irrigated by dozens of waterfalls. Once a major centre for earthenware and leather tanning, the village is still home to dozens of workshops.

▶ **Population:** 2,963.
Michelin Map: 340 L4.
Info: Office de Tourisme de Barjols, boulevard Grisolle. ℰ04 94 77 20 01. www. ot-barjols.provenceverte.fr.
Location: Barjols is located in the Var, 13.6mi/22km north of Brignoles, off the D 554.
Parking: West of the village near the tourist office.

WALKING TOUR

THE OLD TOWN

Maps of the 30-fountain tour are available from the tourist office.

Old Barjols contains 12 wash-houses and 30 **fountains**. Start with the limestone-encrusted mushroom-shaped fountain near the town hall, known locally as the *Champignon*. A magnificent **plane tree** (circumference 39ft/12m), said to be the largest in Provence, dominates the town hall square. In the lower town, the **Pontevès House**, named after an old Provençal family, sports a Renaissance doorway.

Collegiate church

Av. de la République.

The original 11C Romanesque structure was rebuilt in the 16C with a Gothic nave. The organ loft, choir panelling and carved misericords are 17C. A 12C font stands to the right of the entrance.

Réal★

Clinging to the hillside, north of the church, Réal has been inhabited since the 12C by tanners, who used three levels of partially troglodyte (16C–17C) basins for tanning their hides.

Maison Régionale de l'Eau

Blvd. Grisolle. ◷*Open Mon–Fri 9am–noon, 1–5pm.* ◉*No charge.* ℰ04 94 77 15 83. www.maisonregionaledeleau. com.

A former 18C hospice, this regional water institute features displays on water management.

EXCURSIONS

Source d'Argens

◐ *9mi/15km to the southwest. From Barjols take D 560.*

Vallon de Font-Taillade

The road plunges into a green valley of forests and vineyards, following a winding stream.

◐ *547yd/500m after Brue-Auriac a path to the left leads to a chapel.*

Chapelle Notre-Dame

Next to a graveyard stands an abandoned Romanesque chapel built from local red stone. Its pleasant façade topped by a wall-belfry with twin windows is obscured by undergrowth.

◐ *Return to D 560 and turn left. Stop in front of the bridge after 2mi/3km.*

Source d'Argens

On the right of the road a path leads through the bushes to a spring which feeds the River Argens.

DRIVING TOUR

Plateaux du Haut-Var

32mi/52km – half a day.

◐ *Leave Barjols just before the public pool, following a small road northwest towards Varages.*

Festival of St Marcel

On 17 January 1350, a group of pious citizens were removing the relics of St Marcel (a 5C bishop) from the abandoned abbey of Montmeyan when they came across a group of villagers. These villagers were washing tripe to commemorate a siege they had survived, thanks to the presence of an ox within their village walls. Every year since then, on the Sunday nearest to 17 January, St Marcel's bust is carried in procession throughout the town. Every three years, an ox is decorated before the patron saint of Barjols, blessed and led round the town on its way to the abattoir. After High Mass on the following day, the procession winds its way to the place de la Rougière, where the ox is roasted on a spit. At the end of a Provençal-style celebration with flutes, tambourines, music and dancing, the roasted ox is distributed to the crowd (*see Calendar of Events*).

Varages

This village has been producing faience since 1695. Many of the workshops organise regular visits. Contact the tourist office for times and dates.

Musée des Faïences

12 pl. de la Libération. Open Jul–Aug Wed–Sun 10am–noon, 3–7pm, Mon–Tue 3–7pm; Sept–Jun Wed–Sun 2–5pm (6pm Jun and Sep). Closed 23 Dec–Jan. 2.50€. ℘04 94 77 60 39. *www.musee-faience-varages.fr*
Once the residence of a Napoleonic general, this museum explores the history of faience in Varages from the late 17C.

Church

Built in the 17C in Provençal Gothic style, the church has a bell tower covered in glazed multicoloured tiles. Inside, the altar of St Claude, patron saint of faïence-makers, is decorated with medallions.

▷ *Take D 554 north from Varages.*

La Verdière

This hillside village is dominated by a church and an abandoned 10C **castle**.

▷ *East of La Verdière take D 30 towards Montmeyan.*

Montmeyan

This medieval perched village dominates the mouth of Verdon Gorge. There is a fine **view**★ from the southern entrance to the village. The belvedere beyond the Tour Charlemagne, once part of the 14C castle, affords more views.

▷ *D13, then D 71 to Tavernes.*

Tavernes

Set amid olive groves and vineyards, this typical Provençal village boasts a square belfry with an 18C wrought-iron campanile and ruined medieval walls.
⌛ 2hr. At the top of the village sits Notre-Dame-de-Bellevue (1642).

▷ *The D 554 back to Barjols crosses then runs along a charming brook called the Ruisseau des Écrevisses.*

ADDRESSES

STAY

⊜⊜ **Logis Hôtel du Pont d'Or** – *rue Eugène, Payan, rte. St-Maximin.* ℘04 94 77 05 23. Closed early Dec–mid-Jan. 🅿. 15 rooms. ⊊8.50€. Restaurant ⊜⊜. Each cosy room in this fomer coach house is decorated differently. Provençal cuisine.

EAT

⊜⊜ **Le Resto** – *pl. Capit.-Vincens* – ℘04 94 77 29 87. Closed Nov–mid-Jan, Wed low season. Typical, homemade dishes with a regional twist served in a modern dining room or on the shady terrace.

SHOPPING

Market – Sat and Thu (flower market), Leather market every weekend in Aug.
Local arts – Traditional artisans can be found in the old tannery district to the east of the town.

Aups

Var

Shaded by magnificent plane trees, the squares and historic alleyways of Aups burst into a riot of colour on market days when stalls of olives, truffles, thyme, honey and wine line the streets.

▶ **Population:** 2,029.
◉ **Michelin Map:** 340 M4.
🛈 **Info:** Pl. F.-Mistral. 📞04 94 84 00 69. www.aups-tourisme.com.
▷ **Location:** Aups sits at the foot of the Espiguières hills, bordered to the northwest by the highlands of Haute-Provence with the Massif des Maures dominating the horizon to the south.
🅿 **Parking:** Parking can be found just off avenue Verdun, near the tourist office.

⟿ WALKING TOUR

THE OLD TOWN

A detailed walking tour map is available at the tourist office.

Heading north from the tourist office, take a moment to explore the **Collégiale St-Pancrace** on place du Gén.- de-Gaulle. Originally built between 1489 and 1503, this Provençal Gothic collegiate church was severely damaged during the Wars of Religion. Entered through a Renaissance doorway, the church houses some interesting 15C–18C gold- and silver-plate tableware. Continue north along rue G.-Péri to place L. Gauthier, with its 82ft/25m-high **clock tower**, originally built in the 16C as a lookout before serving as a prison. Walk down rue des Aires past an ornate rock balcony (crowned by a Latin motto, "I aspire to heaven") to the **Porte des Aires**, flanked by 12C and 16C ramparts. Skirt along the ave. Victor Maria and left into place Mar. Joffre, where the **Saracen Tower** rises in the south. Formerly protected by a drawbridge, this was

once the town's main gate. Next, head north onto ave. Albert I to the Musée Simon-Ségal (*○ open Jun–mid-Sep Wed–Mon 10am–noon, 4–7pm; ⌗no charge; 📞04 94 70 01 95*). This modern art museum contains 280 paintings, including 175 from the Paris School.

🚗 DRIVING TOUR

Le Haut Var★

33mi/53km. Allow about 5hr.

▷ *From Aups take D 77 east.*

After Château de la Beaume bear left on D 51 through **Tourtour**★ (*⌖ see TOUR-TOUR pp180*) , passing olive trees, pines and vineyards on the way to Villecroze.

Villecroze

Surrounded by vineyards, orchards and olive groves, Villecroze lies in the wooded foothills of the Provençal plateau. Once squeezed into a ring of ramparts, the medieval village lingers on in the 15C clock tower and the surprising rue des Arcades. The 18C Romanesque church and wall belfry are worth a detour.

The **Parc Municipal** (*○ open 8.30am–8.30pm; entrance via route d'Aups, then a right-hand turn leading to a car park*) sports a waterfall that cascades 130ft/40m

---

Black Gold of the Haut-Var

The truffle (called *rabasse* in Provence) is a fungus which grows on the secretions seeping out of diseased oak trees. There are two categories of truffle: the white and the black, which are recognisable by their distinctive smell. They are harvested from November to February by dogs or by sows that take two years to train. The largest truffle market in the Var takes place in Aups every Thursday during the gathering season.

down the cliff face to form a stream in an oasis of greenery beside a rose garden. A marked path leads to the **caves** (grottes; *guided tours (30min) Jul–Aug Tue–Sun 10am–noon, 2.30–6.30pm; Feb–Mar Sat–Sun during school holidays 2–5pm; May–Jun Wed–Sun 2–6pm; Jul–Aug daily 10.30am–12.30pm, 2.30–7pm; Sept Wed–Sun 2–7.30pm; Oct Sat–Sun 2–5pm school holidays; ⌨2.50€; ☏04 94 70 63 06)*. The lords of Villecroze turned these caves into dwellings in the 16C. The tour includes several small chambers pierced by mullioned windows. The **Belvédère de Villecroze** affords a circular **panorama**★ of Tourtour, Villecroze, Salernes and the Maures.

◐ *From Villecroze continue along the D 51, then turn right at the D 560.*

Salernes
Salernes is known for the manufacture of pottery and hexagonal russet-coloured Provençal tiles known as *tomettes*. The **church**, set among 17C houses, boasts a belfry at both ends. The open-air market takes place every Wednesday and Sunday.

🛈 A fold-out map of walking and mountain biking trails is available from the tourist office in Salernes. (*Pl. G.-Péri; ☏04 94 70 69 02; www.ville-salernes.fr).*
Terra Rossa, Maison de la céramique architecturale – ⌚*Open Jun–Jul, Aug–Sep Mon, Wed–Sat 10am–1pm, 3–7pm, Sun 10am–7pm; Apr–May, Oct–Nov: Mon 3–6pm, Wed–Sat 10am–1pm, 3–6pm, Sun 10am–6pm. ⌨€3 (under-12 no charge). ☏ 04 98 10 43 90. terrarossasalernes. over-blog.fr.* Housed in a former factory, this museum explores the production of *tomettes* in the early 20C.

◐ *Take D 31 south by Bresque Valley.*

Entrecasteaux
See ENTRECASTEAUX p181.

◐ *Take D 31 south. Turn right on D 50.*

Cotignac
See COTIGNAC p182.

◐ *Take D 22 north.*

Cascade de Sillans★
Before the village turn right onto a signed path.
🚶 *30min round trip.*
The Bresque cascades over a 138ft/42m drop into an emerald pool.

Sillans-la-Cascade
Perched on La Bresque, this village surrounded by woodland boasts ancient ramparts and picturesque streets. The 18C château hosts regular art and artisan exhibitions (⌚*open Apr–Dec Wed–Sun; ⌨no charge*).

◐ *Continue on D 22 to return to Aups.*

ADDRESSES

⑂/ EAT
⊜⊜ **Des Gourmets** – *5 r. Voltaire. ☏04 94 70 14 97. ⌚Closed late Jun–early Jul, Dec, Mon, Sun eve except Jul–Aug.* Located next to the biggest truffle market in the Var, this family eatery serves traditional Provençal cuisine in cheerful rustic surroundings.

🛒 SHOPPING
Specialities – Here, the famous truffle reigns supreme and can be found in many dishes. The area is also known for its production of honey and goat's cheese made in the Upper Var Valley.

Moulin à Huile Gervasoni – *montée des Moulins. ☏04 94 70 04 66. Closed Oct–Mar.* This 18C olive mill still manufactures and sells olive oil alongside other regional specialities such as tapenade, Provençal fabrics and olive wood.

Markets – Aups: Wed and Sat on place Frédéric-Mistral. Truffle market on Thu *(Nov–mid-Mar)*. Artisan market eves. *(Jul–Aug).* Villecroze: Thu mornings on pl. du Gén.-de-Gaulle.

🏃 SPORT AND LEISURE
Office du tourisme de Salernes – *☏04 94 70 69 02. www.ville-salernes.fr.* Salernes is surrounded by hiking and mountain bike trails. Hunting (boar) and fishing are also extremely popular.

Tourtour★

Var

Set in a cool, wooded region, this village flanked on either side by ancient castles occupies a dominant position on a ridge affording views over the Varois Plain.

▶ **Population:** 533.
🖒 **Michelin Map:** 340 M4.
🅸 **Info:** Av. des Ormeaux, 𝒫04 94 70 59 47. www.tourtour.org.
◗ **Location:** Located east of Aups at the foothills of the Pre-Alps, facing the Varois plain.

🚶 WALKING TOUR

OLD VILLAGE★

Linked by vaulted passageways, the sloping streets of this village converge on a central square lined with restaurants and cafés shaded by two venerable olive trees.

Head out of the square to the **clock tower** *(tour de l'horloge)* and the old mill, which now houses the Fossil Museum. *(🖒 see Sights below)*

To the left of the museum is a restored 12C castle that now plays host to an art and antiques gallery. Continue up the street, past a charming wash house on the right, to a two-storey medieval tower, the **Tour Grimaldi**.

On the other side of the central square, the town hall occupies the former **Château des Raphelis**, a solid 16C building with pepperpot towers.

Église St-Denis

This 11C church, standing on the southeastern edge of the ridge, was extensively modified in the 20C.

Viewpoint★

From the church esplanade there is a wide **panorama★★** *(viewing table)* over the Argens and Nartuby valleys, extending *(east)* to the Maures and *(west)* to Ste-Baume, Mont Ste-Victoire and the Lubéron.

SIGHTS

👥 Musée des Fossiles

rue des Moulins. 🖒🚶*Guided tours (15min) mid-Jun–mid-Sept Wed–Mon 11am–12.30pm, 3.30–7pm.* 🚶*Guided tours by request.* ☜*No charge.* 𝒫04 94 70 59 47. www.tourtour.org.

This museum contains local fossils, including dinosaur eggs, reptilian teeth and ammonites. Ammonites are fossilised molluscs in spiral shells that abounded in the region 130 million years ago.

Moulin à Huile

rue des Moulins. 🖒🚶*Guided tours (1hr) mid-Jun–mid-Sept 11–12.30pm, 3.30–7pm; mid-Dec–mid-Jan or mid-Feb depending on harvest.* ☜*No charge.* 𝒫04 94 70 59 47. www.tourtour.org.

This communal oil mill has been in service since the 17C and has three presses producing 1,100 gallons/5,000 l of oil every autumn. During the summer, the mill houses exhibitions of paintings. *ⓘThe tourist office organises guided tours (1.5hr) in English of the village, museums and church.*☜*2.50 € (children 1 €).* 𝒫04 94 70 59 47.

ADDRESSES

🛏 STAY

☜☜**Auberge St-Pierre** – *2mi/3km east of Tourtour on the D 51 and secondary road.* 𝒫04 94 70 57 17. www.guideprovence.com/hotel/saint-pierre. *Closed mid-Oct–Apr.* 🅿*16 rooms.* ☜*12– €. Restaurant*☜☜. Nature lovers will enjoy this hotel hidden within the vast grounds of a Provençal estate. The rooms are calm, bright and handsomely furnished. Pool, tennis, fitness room and mountain biking trails.

🛒 SHOPPING

MARKETS
Wednesday and Saturday on place des Ormeaux.

Entrecasteaux

Var

Built on the slopes of a hill overlooking the banks of the River Bresque, this village prides itself on its public gardens designed by Le Nôtre. The streets are shaded by 100-year-old plane trees.

VISIT

The town's narrow streets wind around an old fortified church with a buttress spanning the road. From the church esplanade, head down to the Pont St-Pierre and the wash house (*lavoir*), where you'll see the château's round ice house. Go around the back through the ancient entance gate, cross the gardens and exit by the pretty horseshoe- shaped staircase to the **Chapelle des Pénitents** (now home to the Town Hall). Finally, follow the pleasant path up to the **Chapelle Ste-Anne**, where you'll discover a fine **view**.

Château

Guided tours (1.5hr) Easter–Oct Sun–Fri 4pm (and 11.30am in Aug). 8€. 04 94 04 43 95.

This austere 17C building dominating the valley of the Bresque has a high façade topped by a double row of tiles and wrought-iron balustrades. The château was the stronghold of the Castellane clan, followed by the Grignans

- ▶ **Population:** 1,016.
- **Michelin Map:** 340 M4.
- **Info:** Cours Gabriel-Péri. 04 94 59 95 64. http://tourisme.entrecasteaux.fr
- **Location:** The town sits 15mi/24km south of Aups on D 31. There is a tourist map on the square next to the garden.

before passing to the Bruni family. After a long period of neglect, the château was restored by the British painter Ian McGarvie-Munn, who turned part of it into a museum before his death in 1981. The tour includes the castle kitchen, outbuildings, guard-rooms and salons.

ADDRESSES

STAY

Chambre d'hôte Bastide Notre-Dame – *L'Adrech de Ste-Anne. 04 94 04 45 63. http://bastidenotredame.free.fr. 4 rooms. Closed one month in winter.* This hillside B&B estate has four simple rooms, a pool and veranda.

EAT

La Fourchette – *Le Courtil, near the château. 04 94 04 42 78. Closed mid-Dec–mid-Feb, Sun eve–Tue.* Light and refined cuisine made from fresh market produce. The tiny, tiled dining room with a fresco of the village provides an intimate place for winter meals.

SPORT AND LEISURE

Provence Canoë – *New Évasion, on the D 562 between Lorgues and Carcès. 04 94 29 52 48. www.new-evasion.fr. Closed Dec–Mar.* Discover the Argens River by canoe or kayak. Half-day excursions.

CALENDAR

Local patron saints – Ste-Anne is celebrated on 26 July and St-Sauveur during the first weekend in August.
Pesto soup banquet – Last Sun in July.
Floralies – Plant and flower fair, third weekend in April.

Château, Entrecasteaux

© Var Tourisme

Cotignac★

Var

This peaceful Provençal village clings to the side of an imposing cliff (262ft/80m) shaped over the millennia by the course of the Cassole River.

VISIT

The Old Village

A detailed walking tour map is available at the tourist office.

Shaded by plane trees, the **cours centrale** (main square) is lined with 16C–18C houses clustered around a **fountain** depicting the four seasons. Admire the three caryatids at 7 Grande Rue before heading to the 18C **hôtel de ville** and 15C belfry on place de la Mairie. The **Théâtre de Verdure** (*opposite*) hosts summer arts events.

Follow the path to the clifftop dominated by two 14C towers, vestiges of a castle once belonging to the lords of Castellane, then up to a two-storey **grotto** (*guided tours Tue–Sat Jul–Aug 10am–noon, 3–7pm; 15 Apr–Sept 2–5pm; Mon morning only; 2€*), where the villagers once hid their goods from pillagers. Return to place de la Mairie via the ancient **olive oil mill**. *30min round trip. South of the village.*

A walk through the Vallon Gué follows a pathway along the Cassole to a **waterfall**.

Chapelle Notre-Dame-des-Grâces

0.6mi/1km south on D 13 via a road to the right. Open daily 8am–7pm. 04 94 69 64 92.

The esplanade of this chapel, visited in 1660 by the young Louis XIV and his mother Anne of Austria, affords a pleasant **panorama** of the Argens Valley and Brignoles region.

50min round trip. A wooded path from the chapel leads to the **St-Joseph Monastery**. Church open to the public.

- **Population:** 2,146
- **Michelin Map:** 340 L4.
- **Info:** 475 route de Carcès, 04 94 04 61 87.
- **Location:** Cotignac is 9mi/15km south of Aups on the D 22.
- **Parking:** Parking is available near the main square and the outskirts of the village.

ADDRESSES

STAY

Chambre d'Hôte Domaine de Nestuby – *3mi/5km south of Cotignac towards Brignoles. 04 94 04 60 02. www.nestuby-provence.com. Closed 15 Nov –1 Mar. 5 rooms. Restaurant.* At the heart of a vineyard, this cottage contains comfortable rooms furnished with antiques. Wine tasting sessions are organised in the table d'hôte.

EAT

Restaurant Le Clos des Vignes – *route de Montfort, 3mi/5km south of Cotignac towards Brignoles. 04 94 04 72 19. www.restaurant-le-clos-des-vignes.fr. Closed Mon. Reservations recommended.* This former sheep barn surrounded by vineyards has been restored with a dining room–verandah and a summer terrace. Cuisine made with fresh regional produce.

SHOPPING

Local Specialities – The village is famed for its wine, oil, honey and pine nuts (*pignons*). In the bakeries you'll find the delicious *croissants aux pignons*.

Markets – *cours Gambetta and pl. Joseph-Sigaud*– Provençal market on Tuesday and agricultural market on Fridays (*mid-Jun–mid-Sept*).

Les Ruchers du Bessillon – *5 rue de la Victoire. 04 94 04 60 39. www.les ruchersdubessillon.com.* This boutique sells a large selection of organic honey.

Abbaye du Thoronet ★★

Var

Le Thoronet, the oldest of Provence's three Cistercian abbeys (along with Sénanque and Silvacane) is surrounded by wooded hills in an isolated spot, in keeping with the strict rules of the Cistercian Order.

A BIT OF HISTORY

Granted a parcel of land by Raymond Bérenger, Marquis of Provence, a group of monks from the abbey of Mazan (Ardéche) moved to Le Thoronet in 1136 and built the church, cloisters and monastic buildings between 1160 and 1190. Weakened by internal wrangling, like many other Cistercian abbeys, Le Thoronet declined in the 14C. Abandoned during the Revolution, it was bought by the French State in 1854.

ABBEY TOUR *Allow 1hr*

Open Apr–Sep Mon–Sat 10am–6.30pm, Sun 10am–noon, 2–6.30pm; Oct–Mar Mon–Sat 10am–1pm, 2–5pm, Sun 10am–noon, 2–5pm. 7€. 04 94 60 43 90.

Church ★

Squat, austere and geometric with stonework blocks accurately cut and assembled without mortar, the church

Michelin Map: 340 M5; (*see BRIGNOLES p173*)

Info: 04 94 60 43 90. http://thoronet.monuments-nationaux.fr/

Location: The abbey is situated between Lorgues and the Lac de Carcès (*see Driving Tour in BRIGNOLES pp173*). From the A 8, exit Le Cannet.

The Poet Abbot

The abbey's most famous resident was **Folquet de Marseille**. His family came from Genoa but he gave up a career in trade to devote himself to poetry. He became a famous troubadour, quoted by Dante, and then in 1196 decided to become a Cistercian monk. In 1201 he was appointed Abbot of Le Thoronet and then Bishop of Toulouse in 1205.

is an example of the Provençal-Romanesque style. Built to withstand violent winds and the risk of fire, the square stone bell tower is an exception to the Order's preference for simple wooden structures. The **nave** is covered with barrel vaulting, slightly pointed,

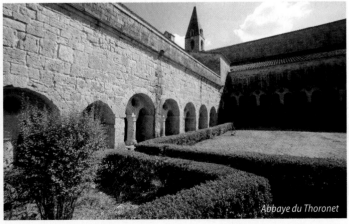
Abbaye du Thoronet
© Wadey James/Apa Publications

supported on transverse arches. It consists of three bays, prolonged by a fourth of the same height at right angles to the transept: only the raised arches indicate the presence of two arms of the transept which are vaulted like the nave. The **chancel** ends in a cul-de-four vaulted apse and is lit through three windows. It is preceded by a shallow bay, featuring a triumphal arch surmounted by an oculus. The aisles are lower than the nave and covered with rampant pointed vaulting.

Cloisters★

The cloisters on the north side of the church are austere and solidly built in the form of a trapezium. The south gallery is at the same level as the church, but the west (exhibition of manuscripts and illuminated texts) and the north and east (which once supported another storey beneath a pitched roof) are lower because of the uneven ground. The galleries have transverse arches and barrel vaulting. The solid, round-headed arches which open onto the cloisters' garth (now a garden) are each divided in two by a stout column. Opposite the refectory door, projecting into the garth, is the **lavabo**, where the monks washed their hands before meals.

Conventual buildings

These stand on the north side of the church near the cloisters. The door of the **library** (*armarium*), which is on the ground floor, is surmounted by a triangular lintel. The **chapter house**★ dates

from the early Gothic period. The ogival vaulting, in which the ribs fan out like palm trees, is supported by two columns with roughly sculpted capitals, ornamented with leaves, pine cones, palm fronds and a hand gripping a staff. These are the only carvings in the abbey. Next to the chapter house is the **parlour** which also serves as a passage between the cloisters and the outer garden. The **dormitory** over the chapter house is reached by a vaulted stairway and roofed with pointed vaulting supported on transverse arches. At the southern end, jutting out above the cloisters, is the Abbot's chamber. The doors in the north gallery opened into the monks' room, the warming room, the refectory and the kitchen, which have all disappeared. The **store room**, on the west side of the cloisters, has pointed vaulting and contains 18C vats for wine and olive oil, as well as the remains of a press. The **lay-brother building**, at the northwest corner of the store room, provided separate housing for the lay-brothers, who carried out manual labour for the monks and lived a less restrained life.

Outbuildings

Beside the stream, the foundations of the **guesthouse** have been excavated. The tithe barn on the south side of the church was later converted into an oil mill and contains some mill stones.

ADDRESSES

⚑/EAT

🍴 **Le Tournesol** – *9 rue des Trois-Ormetox, Le Thoronet, 2.5mi/4km from the Abbey.* 📞*04 94 73 89 81. Closed Jan.* 🍴. This tiny 17C house in a village alley with colourful walls and furniture serves homely food. Its charming terrace gives onto the street.

CALENDAR

Rencontres de Musique Médiévale – A medieval music festival takes place in and around the abbey and church the last two weeks of July. *www.musique-medievale.fr.*

Monastic Austerity

There is hardly any sculpture or carved decoration in the church to detract from its majestic proportions and purity of line. There is, however, a gentle curve on the imposts on the pillars and the half-columns supporting the transverse arches rise to only 9.5ft/2.9m above the ground according to Cistercian tradition.

Le Luc

Var

Dotted with mossy fountains, impossibly narrow streets, uneven cobblestones and lazy cats in flowered courtyards, Le Luc oozes the romantic scruffiness of a typical Provençal village. Despite its sleepy atmosphere, it is also an important farming centre, serving as the collection point for regional harvests of grapes and olives in the Var plain.

▶ **Population:** 8 711.
Michelin Map: 340 M5; region map: pp170–171.
Info: Château des Vintimille, Pl. de la Liberté. ℘04 94 60 74 51. www.mairie-leluc.com.
Location: Le Luc lies at the crossroads between the A 8 (viaduct high above the village), RN 7, Brignoles and Draguignan.

THE OLD VILLAGE
An Imposing Belfry

Le Luc lies in the shade of a 16C hexagonal bell tower (89ft/27m high) built in the style of Italian campaniles. Information panels on the main buildings provide a handy way of exploring the village.

View from the Oppidum de Fouirette

1.5hr round trip. Walk towards Vergeiras, then follow the signposted path (information available from the tourist office).

From the top of the hill (984ft/300m high) is a wonderful **view**★ over the Maures plain, from Gonfaron to Rocher de Roquebrune.

SIGHTS
Musée Historique du Centre-Var

24 rue Victor-Hugo. Open mid-Jun–mid-Sept Mon–Sat 3–6pm. Closed public holidays. No charge. ℘04 94 60 70 12. www.coeurduvar.com.

This local history museum housed in the 17C Chapelle Ste-Anne features collections of historical artefacts uncovered during local excavations, including fossils (dinosaur eggs), a carved Roman sarcophagus, medieval sculptures, minerals from the Maures Massif and ancient weapons. There is also a historical display on Le Luc and the life of the local marine engineer Jean-Baptiste Lebas (1797–1873), who transported the famous obelisk from Luxor to Place de la Concorde in Paris.

Musée régional du Timbre et de la Philatélie

Pl. de la Convention. Open Wed–Thu 2.30–5.30pm, Fri–Sun 10am–noon, 2.30–5.30pm. Closed 1 Jan, 1 May, 25 Dec. 2€. ℘04 94 47 96 16. www.lemuseedutimbre.com.

This regional museum devoted to the history of postage stamps and philately is housed in the Château de Vintimille, a striking 18C building. The display follows the different stages in the traditional manufacture of postage stamps and philatelic counterfeiting.

16C hexagonal bell tower

© Var Tourisme

185

Campaniles in the Var

Les Arcs	Clock Tower (18C)
Aups	Clock Tower
Carcès	Campanile atop a fortified gate (18C)
Carnoules	Belfry (17C)
Cotignac	Campanile (16C)
Draguignan	Tower (17C)
Flassans	Atop the belfry (18C)
Le Luc	Tower (16C)
St-Tropez	Campanile (19C)
Salernes	Belfry (18C)
Tavernes	Campanile (18C)
Toulon	Arsenal tower (18C)

ADDRESSES

🛏 STAY

🍴🍴 **La Haute Verrerie** – *rte. de St-Tropez, Le Cannet-des-Maures, 3.7mi/6km east of Le Luc by D 558.* ☎04 94 47 95 51. *4 rooms.* 🍴 🛏. A lively brook flows at the foot of this charming 1839 Provençal house, once used as a glass-making workshop. The rooms, housed in several outbuildings, are each decorated in their own style. The prettiest has a solarium.

Lorgues

Var

Lorgues is a small medieval town with a beautiful market square shaded by plane trees. Beyond the village are wooded hilltops, cultivated with vines and olive trees.

THE OLD QUARTER
A Touch of Medieval Charm

The tourist office provides maps of the village walking tour.

The streets of Lorgues radiate from a central square. Dotted with fountains and fortified 12C gateways, these narrow alleyways are lined with attractive houses decorated with lintels and wrought-iron work.

Start your tour at the 18C **Collégiale St-Martin** (*rue de l'église.* Open 9am–

🍴🍴 **Chambre d'hôte Le Hameau de Charles-Auguste** – *rte. de Baraouque.* ☎04 94 60 79 45. *4 rooms.* 🍴 🛏10€. Set within a group of outbuildings constructed around the original 18C farmhouse, this B&B has been lovingly decorated with flea-market finds and antiques.

🍽 EAT

🍴🍴🍴 **Le Gourmandin** – *pl. L.-Brunet.* ☎04 94 60 85 92. www.legourmandin.com. *Closed late-Aug–late-Sept, late-Feb–early-Mar, Sun and Thu eves, Mon.* This *auberge* in the heart of the village has a convivial atmosphere and a rustic dining room. Traditional cuisine.

🛍 SHOPPING

Provençal Market – Friday mornings.
Domaine de la Lauzade – *rte. de la Lauzade.* ☎04 94 60 72 51. www.lauzade.com. *Closed Sun.* Guided tours, tastings and direct sales of Côtes-de-Provence at this small vineyard. There are also regular art exhibitions.
Domaine de la Pardiguière – *rte. des Mayons, Fontaines aux Grives.* ☎04 94 60 75 37. *Open by request.* There are excellent **views** over the countryside from this family-run organic vineyard and olive orchard. Olives, olive oil and wine sold on-site.

- **Population:** 8,550.
- **Michelin Map:** 340 N5.
- **Info:** Pl. d'Antrechaux. ☎04 94 73 92 37. http://lorgues-tourisme.fr.
- **Location:** Lorgues is 8mi/13km southwest of Draguignan on the D 557 and D 562. The medieval city stretches along the main shopping street. The more modern, 20C buildings lie to the west.
- **Timing:** Allow half a day to discover Lorgues, 1hr for the old town, and 2–3hrs for the chapels in the vicinity.

6pm. ℰ*04 94 73 92 37).* This collegiate church was built by Bishop Fleury of Fréjus, who served as Louis XV's chief minister. It is unusually large, with a dressed stone façade and a **Virgin and Child** attributed to Pierre Puget. Don't miss the organ and carved pulpit. Continue along rue de la Bourgade to the 13C **Font-Couverte**, one of only two covered fountains in Europe.

EXCURSIONS
Ermitage de St-Ferréol
◑*0.6mi/1km. Follow the signs to the northeast of the town.*
This chapel stands on a low wooded hill surrounded by traces of a Roman settlement.

Chapelle Notre-Dame-de-Benva
◑*2mi/3km northwest, rte de St-Antonin.* ◷*Open Jul–Sept Thu 10am– noon, 3.30–5pm.* ℰ*04 94 73 92 37.*
Designed to attract passing pilgrims, the chapel of Our Lady of Benva (a corruption of the Provençal *ben vai* "good journey") stands on a hillside with its porch astride the old Entrecasteaux road. It is decorated inside and outside with 15C frescoes in the Naïve tradition.

Monastère Orthodoxe St-Michel
◑*8km/5mi north by D 10 or 6mi/10km by D 77.* ⬥*Guided tours (40min) 10am, 2pm, 3pm, 4pm.* ℰ*04 94 73 75 75.*
These stone buildings were once home to an Orthodox community. The crypt, refectory and church are adorned with Romanesque and Byzantine frescoes.

Taradeau
◑*5.6mi/9km – southeast on D 10. On arriving in the village, take the D 73 towards Flayosc.*
A Saracen tower and a ruined Romanesque chapel crown the bluff dominating the village of Tardeau, which produces reputable wines.

◑ *Take D 73 north. After 0.5 mi/1km, turn right onto a stony path marked "Table d'Orientation 800m".*

⚐ From the top there is a vast **panorama**★ over Lorgues, Les Arcs, the Provençal plain and the Grasse Pre-Alps, the Esterel and the Maures.

Abbaye du Thoronet ★★
8mi/13km southwest. From Lorgues take D 562 towards Carcès. Bear left onto D 17 and turn right onto D 79.
◔*See Abbaye du THORONET p183.*

ADDRESSES

🛏 STAY
🍽 **Les Pins** – *3630 rte. de St-Antonin.* ℰ*04 94 73 91 97. www.le-clos-de-tiffanie. com. Closed mid-Nov–mid-Mar. 5 rooms.* 🍴 *(at dinner).* 🍽 *. Restaurant* 🍽🍽*.* This grand villa under the pines is surrounded by vineyards. Three suites with a terrace next to the pool are located in an annex building. Two other rooms, in the main building, are decorated in the same Provençal style.

🍽🍽🍽 **Chambre d'hôte La Bergerie du Moulin** – *55 rte de la Passerelle.* ℰ*04 94 99 91 51. www.bergeriedumoulin. com. 5 rooms.* 🍴🍽*. A rustic stone residence offering air-conditioned rooms with a Provençal feel. Pool and spa-jacuzzi.

🍴 EAT
🍽🍽 **Le Chrissandier** – *18 cours de la République.* ℰ*04 94 67 67 15. http://lechrissandier.com. Closed Tue and Wed out of season.* Nestled in the old medieval quarter, this rustic-style restaurant attracts a regular clientele at lunchtime and caters for tourists in the evening. The market-fresh menu changes every day.

🛒 SHOPPING
Marché – Tuesdays – and small producers on Friday.
Wine – A dozen vineyards can be found around Lorgues, many offering tastings and sales of their Côtes-de-Provence and Vins de Pays du Var and d'Argens. Ask for a list at the tourist office.

Les Arcs

Var

A major staging post on the Provence Wine Route, Les Arcs sits amid leafy vineyards under the shadow of a medieval keep.

OLD TOWN
▶ *From pl. de l'Église take rue de la Paix up to the dungeon keep.*

Explore the historic quarter of **Le Parage** (an Occitan word for the upper reaches of a village next to a keep), before admiring the side aisles of the **church** with its frescoes of *(left)* the miracle of St Roseline's roses *(right)* and a **polyptych**★ in 16 sections by Louis Bréa (1501).

EXCURSION
Chapelle Ste-Roseline★
▶ *2.5mi/4km east of Les Arcs by the D 91.*
🕑*Open Wed–Sun Jun–Sept 2.30–6.30pm; Mar–May 2–6pm; Oct–Feb 2–5pm.* No charge. ℘*04 94 73 30 13.*
This rural Provençal-style Romanesque chapel outside Les Arcs was once part of the 11C Abbaye de la Celle-Roubaud. The **interior**★ features a Baroque high altar (1635) framed by a wooden altarpiece (1514). A rare Provençal rood screen surmounted by a statue of St Catherine of Alexandria closes the choir, which is

- **Population:** 6,108.
- **Michelin Map:** 340 N5.
- **Info:** Pl. du Général-de-Gaulle. ℘04 94 73 37 30. www.mairie-les-arcs-sur-agens.fr
- **Location:** The town is located in the Var, 15.5mi/25km west of Fréjus on the R N 7 and D 57. The modern town sits below the historic quarter, separated by a clock tower.

furnished with finely carved stalls (17C). **Marguerite Maeght** commissioned many contemporary works of art for the church, including a large mosaic by **Chagall** *(right side aisle)* and a bronze low relief and lectern by **Giacometti**.

ADDRESSES

🏠 STAY 🍴 EAT
🍽 **Aurélia** – *rte nationale 7, Le Pont-d'Argens.* ℘*04 94 47 49 69. www.hotel-aurelia-83.com. Closed Jan. Restaurant closed off season Sun eve, Mon, holidays.* 20 rooms. 🅿 ⊇9€. Restaurant 🍽🍽.
On the outskirts of the village, this hotel is sheltered from the noise of the RN7. Many rooms have their own balcony. The restaurant has a fireplace and terrace overlooking the Argens River.

🛒 SHOPPING
Maison des Vins Côtes-de-Provence – *rte nationale 7.* ℘*04 94 99 50 20. www.caveaucp.fr.* This country estate along the Argens River is the headquarters of Côtes-de-Provence appellation wines, with 700 different winemakers, a modern tasting area *(free)* and a gourmet restaurant.

CALENDAR
Juillet – ℘*06 10 45 83 64 – www.les-medievales.asso.fr.* Held every odd year, the four-day Médiévales festival features medieval costume parades, banquets and weaponry demonstrations *(10am–10pm pl. du Gén.-de-Gaulle).*

The Legend of Sainte Roseline

The young Ste Roseline (1263–1329) of Château de Villeneuve, daughter of Lord Arnaud de Villeneuve, would hide food in her apron to distribute to the poor. One day a palace guard stopped her and asked what she was carrying. "Roses," she replied, and when she opened her apron the roses miraculously appeared. Her body is buried in a shrine in the church. Pilgrimages take place five times a year, including Trinity Sunday and the first Sunday in August.

Draguignan

Var

Situated between the Haut-Var and the Haute Provence plateau, Draguignan's wealth was built on the production of honey, olive oil, cork and silk. This prosperous market town is still the hub of agricultural life in the region today.

A BIT OF HISTORY

From the Middle Ages

Draguignan grew rapidly throughout the Middle Ages and by the 15C it was the fourth-largest town in Provence. Only two of the original gates that once pierced its 13C walls, now remain (porte des Portaiguières and porte Romaine). Louis XIV ordered the keep to be razed in retribution for a conflict between local factions in 1649.

The town became the administrative centre *(préfecture)* of the Var by order of Napoleon in 1797, a position it only lost to Toulon in 1974. Azémar and Haussmann, both prefects of the Var, laid out its shady tree-lined walks and straight boulevards in the 19C.

An American Cemetery to the east of the town and a memorial to the Liberation on the corner of avenue Lazare-Carnot and avenue Patrick-Rosso recall the fighting that took place here in August 1944.

The town has been home to an artillery school since 1976.

St Hermentaire and the dragon

The name Draguignan is derived from the Latin root *draco,* meaning dragon. Legend has it that, in the 5C, pilgrims on their way from Ampus to the renowned Lérins Abbey via Lentier encountered a dragon roaming the surrounding marshes.

The terrified pilgrims appealed for help from the hermit Hermentaire, who lived in the area. He slayed the dragon and built a chapel dedicated to St Michael the Archangel. The existing church of **St-Michel**, north of place du Marché, contains an 18C statue of St Hermentaire in gilded wood.

▶ **Population:** 37,088.
⌚ **Michelin Map:** 340 N 4.
ℹ **Info:** Av. Carnot. ℘04 98 10 51 05. www.dracenie.com. Guided tours of the town available through the tourist office. Call for more information.
◉ **Location:** The town is in the Var off the N 555, 18.6mi/30km northwest of Fréjus.
🅿 **Parking:** Allées d'Azémar car park *(first hour free),* between the tourist office and the old town.

 WALKING TOUR

THE OLD TOWN

▶ *Begin at pl. du Marché.*

The rue des Marchands opens onto Old Draguignan (pedestrian district), where the 14C gates, **Porte Romaine** and **Porte des Portaiguières,** frame an intricate maze of streets lined with ornate doorways and lop-sided houses. Continue along rue de l'Observance, one of the town's oldest streets and home to the nobility and bourgeoisie in the 15C and 16C.

▶ *Turn left up montée de l'Horloge.*

The **clock tower** replaced the keep demolished in 1660. It has four flanking turrets and an ornate wrought-iron campanile. The **view** from the top encompasses the town and the Nartuby Valley. The tower of the **théâtre de verdure** affords a closer view over the roofs of the old town (⊙*open mid-Jul–late-Sep, 9.30am–12.30pm, 3–7pm;* ⊛*no charge).*

▶ *Double back to the rue des Tanneurs, to the porte de Portaiguières, which pierces a 15C square tower.*

Don't miss the vast façade of an old 13C **synagogue** in rue de la Juiverie and the old mansion at no 42.

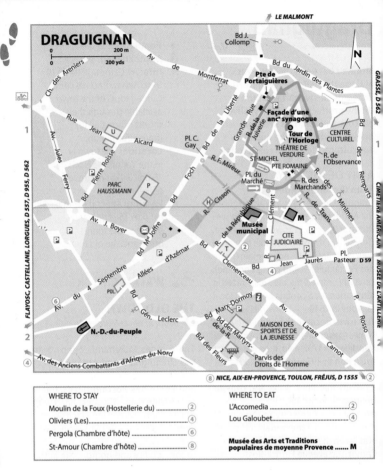

WHERE TO STAY	
Moulin de la Foux (Hostellerie du)	②
Oliviers (Les)	④
Pergola (Chambre d'hôte)	⑥
St-Amour (Chambre d'hôte)	⑧

WHERE TO EAT	
L'Accomedia	②
Lou Galoubet	④

Musée des Arts et Traditions populaires de moyenne Provence .... M

▶ *At the end of the street turn right to the church and the pl. du Marché.*

SIGHTS

Cimetière Américain et Mémorial du Rhône

553 blvd. J.F.-Kennedy.

♿⏰*Open daily 9am–5pm.*

💬*No charge.* ✆*04 94 68 03 62.*

The Draguignan area was the scene of fierce fighting in 1944, particularly around the village of Muy. Laid out over 12 acres/5ha of landscaped lawns are the graves of 861 American soldiers from General Patch's 7th Army.

A bronze map at the foot of the memorial retraces the campaign launched on 15 August 1944 in support of the Normandy landings.

The inside of the chapel is decorated with mosaics by the American Austin Purves.

Chapelle Notre-Dame du Peuple

Southwest of the old town; see map.

This chapel was originally built in the 16C in Flamboyant Gothic style and enlarged in the 19C. It contains votive offerings to the Virgin who, according to local legend, saved the town from the plague *(pilgrimage 8 September)*. On the north wall is the central panel of a 16C altarpiece from the Brea school.

Musée Municipal

9 rue de la République.

♿⏰*Open Tue–Sat 9am–noon, 2–6pm.*

💬*No charge.* ✆*04 98 10 26 85.*

www.dracenie.com.

A former 17C Ursuline convent remodelled as the summer residence of the Bishop of Fréjus in the 18C, this museum, one of the oldest in France, boasts a collection of antique furniture, sculpture, ceramics from France (Vallauris, Moustiers, Sèvres) and the Far East, and Dutch and French paintings by Rembrandt, Rubens and Van Loo. Don't miss *Rêve au coin du feu*, a sculpture by Camille Claudel (1903), the *Enfant au béguin* by Renoir and Gallo-Roman items discovered during local digs.

♟♟Musée des Arts et Traditions Populaires★

15 rue Joseph-Roumanille. ○*Open Tue–Sat 9am–noon, 2–6pm.* ○*Closed Sun morning, public holidays.* ⊛*3.50€.* ℘*04 94 47 05 72. www.dracenie.com.*
Exhibitions, workshops and events are organised for children throughout the year. This museum contains everyday objects from the region's farming, wine growing, olive and cork, bee-keeping, sheep-rearing, hunting, arts and crafts and silkworm industries.

Musée de l'Artillerie

Av. de la Grande-Armée, 2mi/3km east of Draguignan by blvd. J.F.-Kennedy and D 59; at the artillery school's main entrance. ○*Open mid-Jan–mid-Dec*
Sun–Wed 9am–noon, 1.30–5.30pm. ○*Closed public holidays.* ⊛*No charge.* ℘*04 83 08 13 85. http://musee-artillerie.chez-alice.fr.*
The artillery school (founded in 1791) was transferred to Draguignan in 1976 and merged with the Nîmes anti-aircraft school in 1983. The museum presents the evolution of weaponry and military strategy from ancient times to the contemporary period. The ground floor holds displays of heavy arms and modern artillery, including field weapons and trench equipment.

EXCURSIONS
Pays Dracénois
Malmont Viewpoint★

▶ *3.7mi/6km – about 45min. From Draguignan take blvd. Joseph-Collomp north 4mi/6km to a pass. Turn left onto a narrow road for 330yd/300m.*
The **view**★ takes in large swathes of Provence, including Mont Vinaigre in the Esterels, Agay port, the Argens Valley, the Maures hills and Toulon.

Trans-en-Provence

▶ *3mi/5km south of Draguignan by N 1555.*
Up to the Second World War, this lively village was renowned for its silk spinning. The town hall, built in 1779, with

Musée de l'Artillerie

© DANO/Var Tourisme

its **façade**★ decorated in *trompe-l'œil*, is a rare example of 18C civic architecture. There is a fine reredos in the 14C **St-Victor** church. A path leads from place de la Mairie in front of the town hall to the **waterfalls and gorges of the Nartuby**. This outstanding **site**★ is best viewed from between Pont Vieux and Pont Bertrand.

On the Chemin du Cassivet is a Puit Aérien *(look for the signs on the left when entering the village; the path passes under the D 555)*. This "aerial well" was designed by the Belgian engineer Knapen in 1930. The well works by recovering moisture in the night to water crops during the day. Designed for use in Africa, it was never put into operation in Trans.

Flayosc –
4.3mi/7km. About 45min. From Draguignan take D 557 southwest.

This charming Var village overlooking vineyards, meadows and orchards has retained its 14C fortified gates. The typically Provençal **place de la Reinesse** has plane trees, a mossy fountain and a small wash-house; the Romanesque **church** has a massive square bell tower.

Chapelle Ste-Roseline★
6mi/10km. South of Draguignan on N 555 and turn right onto D 91.
See Les ARCS p188.

🚗 DRIVING TOUR

Gorges de Châteaudouble★
25.4mi/41km. Allow about 1hr.

Leave Draguignan on ave. de Montferrat and follow D 955.

Pierre de la Fée
This 'fairy's stone' is a fine dolmen, with a table 19.7ft/6m long, 14.7ft/4.5m wide and weighing 40t resting on three raised stones more than 6.5ft/2m high.

Gorges de Châteaudouble★
This serpentine gorge was carved by the Nartuby, a tributary of the Argens.

View of Châteaudouble

Return to Le Plan and turn right onto D 51 to the village of Châteaudouble.

Châteaudouble village occupies a cliff overhanging the gorges of the Nartuby by 330ft/100m. Its medieval passages are interspersed with little squares and fountains.

The Saracen Tower offers a superb **view**★ over the whole village. Steep paths lead from the gorges to the prehistoric caves of Mouret, Chèvres and Chauves-Souris.

From Châteaudouble drive north towards Ampus. D 51 crosses a plateau through the Bois des Prannes.

Ampus
The village church is a well-restored Romanesque building. Just behind it, a path marked by modern Stations of the Cross (1968) leads to a rocky outcrop.

*Return to Draguignan on D 49 for a good **view** of the town.*

ADDRESSES

🛏 STAY

Chambre d'hôte La Pergola – *192 ave. du 4-Septembre. ℘04 94 99 18 54. 4 rooms. ▭7.50€. Restaurant ☺.* A B&B in the centre of town, with a pretty terrace and fountain at the entrance. The comfortable rooms have en suite bathrooms and air conditioning.

Hostellerie du Moulin de la Foux – *941 chemin St-Jean-de-la-Foux. 2mi/3km south on D 1555, rte de Fréjus. ℘04 98 10 14 14. www.hotel-du-moulin-de-la-foux.com. ▣. 27 rooms. ▭7€. Restaurant☺.* This charming inn inside an ancient olive mill has a large leafy terrace overlooking the river. Rooms are comfortable, the renovated ones have better facilities.

Hôtel Les Oliviers – *2.5mi/4km West of Draguignan by D 557 (route de Flayosc). ℘04 94 68 25 74. www.hotel-les-oliviers.com. Closed early to late Jan. 12 rooms. ▣. ▭8€.* Roadside hotel conveniently situated on the way to Flayosc. The rooms, all on the ground floor, are light and neatly arranged.

Chambre d'Hôte St-Amour – *986 rte. de la Motte, Trans-en-Provence, 3mi/5km S of Draguignan. ℘04 94 70 88 92. www.domainedesaintamour.com. 3 rooms. ▭. ☺.* A large, rambling park and a curious swimming pool are the backdrop to this 18C stone house offering a self-contained flat and several rooms, each of them decorated in a distinctive style.

🍴 EAT

L'Accomedia – *13 rue des Endronnes. ℘04 94 50 72 72. Closed last 3 wks in Aug.* An Italian restaurant opposite the local theatre embellished with a fresco evoking the Carnival. Typical Mediterranean specialities served in a light, modern setting.

Lou Galoubet – *23 blvd. Jean Jaurès. ℘04 94 68 08 50. www.lou galoubet.com. Closed mid-Jul– mid-Aug, Sun and Tue eves, Mon.* Classic French dining with fine, contemporary decor in a sunny dining room.

Oil mill

E. Baret/ MICHELIN

🛒 SHOPPING

Markets – Place du Marché hosts a lively, colourful market on Wednesday and Saturday mornings.

Moulin Traditionnel "Lou Calen" – *1 r. de l'Observance. ℘04 94 47 21 87. Open Wed and Sat, 9am–noon or by reservation.* This 20C mill located in the hills above Draguignan presses olives from local producers using traditional stone blades. Oil can be bought directly from the owners.

Moulin du Flayosquet – *rte. d'Ampus, Le Bastidon, Flayosc. ℘04 94 70 41 45. Closed Sun–Mon Sept–Jun, Sun Jul–Aug, two weeks in Mar and Nov.* This superb 13C mill has preserved its original equipment and still uses traditional blades for pressing. The boutique sells a selection of regional products in addition to olive oils.

Domaine Rabiega – *route de Lorgues. ℘04 94 68 44 22. www.rabiega.com. Closed Sun.* A beautiful property situated among the olive trees and vineyards, the domain produces 20,000 bottles of organic wines (mostly reds) per year.

GETTING AROUND

Buses – *℘04 94 50 94 05.* Buses serve Draguignan and the surrounding districts. Single tickets available from bus drivers, books of tickets from the bus station on Rue des Martyrs-de-la-Résistance *(closed Sun)*. **Coaches** will take you to St-Raphaël *(60min)*, Toulon *(120min)* and to the SNCF train station Les Arcs-Draguignan *(25min)*. *℘04 94 68 15 34.*

Roquebrune-sur-Argens

Var

A labyrinth of arches and alleyways, Roquebrune-sur-Argens is perched on a rocky peak at the foot of the Rocher de Roquebrune, a popular spot for hiking and canoeing.

SIGHTS
The Village

Originally a stronghold, this *castrum* was once surrounded by a curtain wall. Mostly destroyed in 1592, during the Wars of Religion, traces of the wall are still visible, particularly in boulevard de la Liberté. Across from the **clock tower** is the picturesque rue des Portiques, lined with mostly 16C arcaded houses. The fortifications and narrow, winding streets recall Roquebrune's medieval legacy.

Église St-Pierre-St-Paul

The 16C Gothic church features an unusual 18C façade and 12C remnants *(left)* of two chapels with thick quadripartite vaulting of rectangular-shaped diagonal and transverse arches. The first chapel contains a wooden altarpiece (1557) of John the Baptist, while the second houses an altarpiece from the same period depicting the Last Judgement. In

Chapelle St-Pierre
© Olivier Simon/Var Tourisme

- ▶ **Population:** 11,405.
- ⚅ **Michelin Map:** 340 O5.
- ⧈ **Information:** 12 avenue Gabriel Péri. ✆04 94 19 89 89. www.paysmesterel.com.
- ⊙ **Location:** The town lies 7.5mi/12km west of Fréjus on the D 8, then the D 7. From the A 8, exit Puget-sur-Argens and take the N 7 west, then left on D 7.
- 🅿 **Parking:** At the foot of the village.

the nave is a 16C altarpiece composed of carved panels depicting the Passion.

Musée du Patrimoine

Impasse Barbacane, off rue des Portiques. ♿⊙*Open Jul–Aug daily 9am–noon, 2.30–6.30pm; Oct–May Tue–Sat 8am–noon, 1.30–5pm; May–Jun; Sep Tue–Sat 9am–noon, 1.30–6pm.* ⬤*No charge.* ✆*04 98 11 36 85.*

The museum houses prehistoric and Roman finds excavated in the Bouverie caves *(nearby)*, which were inhabited from 30,000 to 8,000 BC by the **Bouverian** culture unique to southeastern France. Also displayed are fine objects from the Neolithic Era and a remarkable reconstruction of a roofed Roman tomb.

Chapelle St-Pierre

From Roquebrune take D 7 southeast. ⊙*Open during exhibitions.*

The chapel has a Carolingian apse but was rebuilt in the Romanesque style in the 11C, with a recessed Renaissance tomb on the façade. A rock tomb cemetery lies to the east.

Le Muy

▶ *5mi/8km west of Roquebrune by D 7, then D N7.*

Muy's popular Sunday morning market *(smaller on Thursdays)* offers a wide selection of regional products. The market is held around the **church** (16C) surmounted by an elegant wrought-iron campanile. Next to the **Charles-Quint tower** *(entrance to the village from D N7),* which hosts temporary exhibitions, is the **Musée de la Libération** (⏱*open Jul–Aug Tue–Sun 9.30am–noon, 3–7pm, Sun 9.30am–12.30pm, Apr–Jun Sun 10am–noon;* ⊜*no charge).* Housed in a cramped room charged with emotion, this collection of artefacts and documents explores the airborne operation mounted on the night of 14 to 15 August around Le Muy in support of the Allied landings in Provence.

🚗 DRIVING TOUR

Rocher de Roquebrune

8.5mi/14km round trip. Allow 1hr. Privately owned, the Rocher is accessible only on tours organised by Le Muy tourist office. 📞*04 94 45 12 79.* ⊜*6€.*
The proud silhouette of Roquebrune's rock (red sandstone) forms a small, solitary massif between the Maures and Esterel. Its jagged silhouette dominates the lower Argens Valley.

▷ *From Roquebrune-sur-Argens, take the small road to the south opposite the cemetery.*

Chapelle Notre-Dame-de-Pitié

The chapel stands on rising ground amid pine and eucalyptus trees. Next to the chapel, there is a **view** ★ of the Argens Plain, Fréjus, St-Raphaël and the Esterel heights.

▷ *Return to Roquebrune and turn left onto D 7. After 547yd/500m bear left; 0.6mi/1km further on turn left again onto a forest road. After 1mi/2km park, where a path veers right.*

Roquebrune Summit★

🚶 *2hr on foot round trip; a difficult walk; keep to the path.*
From the summit (alt. 1,073ft/372m), there is an extended **view**★ of the Maures, Fréjus Bay, the Esterel and the Alps on the horizon.
At the rock's summit stand three crosses by Vernet in memory of three Crucifix-

ions painted by Giotto, Grünewald and El Greco. The summit symbolises Golgotha.

▷ *Drive down the southern face of Roquebrune rock and turn right onto D 25. After 0.6mi/1km, turn right along the northern face. Drive through the hamlet of La Roquette.*

Chapelle Notre-Dame-de-la-Roquette

🚶 *30min on foot round trip. Park in the car park by the road and take the path on the right.*
The ruined chapel, a meeting point for local hikers, is located in an attractive **setting**★ of lotus, chestnut and holly trees beside a rocky outcrop of red sandstone. From the terrace (alt. 470ft/143m) the **view** includes the lower Argens Valley and the Provençal tableland.

ADDRESSES

🛏 STAY

⊜⊜⊜ **Chambre d'hôte Au Bois Fleuri** – *rte de Marchandise, La Commande quarter, 5mi/8.3km north of Roquebrune-sur-Argens, dir. La Bouverie.* 📞*04 94 45 42 28. www.auboisfleuri. com. 3 rooms, 2 studios.* Surrounded by dense woodland, this new house decorated with larchwood furniture has two ground floor studios with private terraces and three upper rooms.

🛒 SHOPPING

L'Amie Ailée – *36 rue St-Éloi.* 📞*04 94 45 30 20. www.lamieailee. fr. Closed Sun.* Sale of honey, pollen, nougat and Royal Jelly.

LOCAL TREATS

Local markets Monday morning on place San Peïre; Friday morning on place Alfred-Perrin. The delicious Honey Fair takes place in late October.

🏃 SPORT AND LEISURE

Activities – Quad-bikes, canoeing, kayaking, diving, fishing, guided nature walks, leisure parks, Zen Océane, a health outfit/spa and much more.

Tucked away in the farthest corner of Provence, on the eastern edge of the Var, Fréjus and the Esterel Massif may not have the "flash and cash" of Cannes to the east or St-Tropez to the west, but nevertheless impress visitors with their perched villages, natural beauty, unspoilt forests and red rock mountains framing the cobalt-blue sea. Many come to this part of the Riviera to escape the summer crowds, while lively towns like Fréjus and St-Raphäel, as well as the convenient proximity to Nice, keep it from feeling overly secluded. For those who enjoy sweeping panoramic views, coastal hikes, Provençal meals overlooking deep gorges, ancient history and sandy beaches, this is an ideal area to explore.

Highlights

1 Attend a musical concert in Fréjus' **2C Roman arena** (p200)

2 Take a guided tour of the ancient cloisters and baptistery of Fréjus' **Groupe Episcopal** (p202)

3 Explore underwater wrecks with the diving club at the **Port-Fréjus** (p208)

4 Drive along the Corniche d'Or to the **Pic de l'Ours** (p217)

5 See the works of Dada artist Max Ernst in **Seillans** (p222)

History

Like much of the French Riviera, Fréjus and the Esterel Massif were inhabited by the Romans, invaded by Saracen pirates, cultivated by monks, discovered by 19C travellers and liberated in the Second World War when the Allies landed on its beaches. What makes this area remarkable is how many historic sites still survive.

As one of the most important settlements of the Gallo-Roman era, Fréjus is home to some of the oldest buildings in France, including the 2C Roman amphitheatre and the 5C baptistery at the Groupe Episcopal. France's colonial troops from Africa and Asia acclimatised to French weather in Fréjus in the early 20C, leaving behind colourful examples of their religious devotion, including a Buddhist pagoda and a Sudanese mosque.

Other historic treasures dating back to pre-historic times can be found at the archaeological museum in St-Raphäel.

View of the Massif de l'Esterel from the coast

View from the Pic du Cap-Roux

The Fréjus–St-Raphäel Hub

The dynamic centre of this area is found in the twinned cities of Fréjus, known for its prestigious history dating back to the Romans, and St-Raphäel, a modern resort town which became popular during the Belle Époque. Here, approximately 85,000 residents (and visitors) benefit from the cities' combined municipal services, coordinated environmental preservation policies and complementary cultural development.

Natural Beauty

The red porphyry rocks that define the Massif de l'Esterel make this one of the most aesthetically outstanding sites on the French Riviera. It remained relatively unspoilt throughout the 19C due to the late construction of a scenic road, the Corniche d'Or, in 1903, connecting the coastline to the peaks that afford panoramic **views** over the region.

The rocky inlets, interspersed with natural sand beaches, are framed by the gently sloping mountains covered in pine, holm oak, heather and arbousiers (wild strawberry trees). The inland areas are crossed by rivers and lakes such as Lac de St-Cassien in Fayence and the Villepey marshes outside Fréjus. Nature-lovers will find a range of outdoor activities in the region, from snorkelling and windsurfing to hiking and mountain biking.

Resort Living

Sun-seekers have a variety of sandy beaches, secluded inlets and picturesque pleasure ports to explore, particularly around Fréjus Plage and St-Raphäel's historic riverfront walk. Watersports, underwater sightseeing and boat rentals can all be arranged through the local tourist offices.

For more peace and quiet, several high-end resorts such as the Four Seasons have opened inland around Fayence.

Local Economy

The main economic activity of the Fréjus and Massif de l'Esterel area is tourism, like most of the French Riviera.

Fishing and the production of wine, honey, olive oil, and fruits and vegetables has continued throughout the centuries, although agriculture in general is not very significant. Visitors will also find many local artisan crafts such as the clay *santon* figurines.

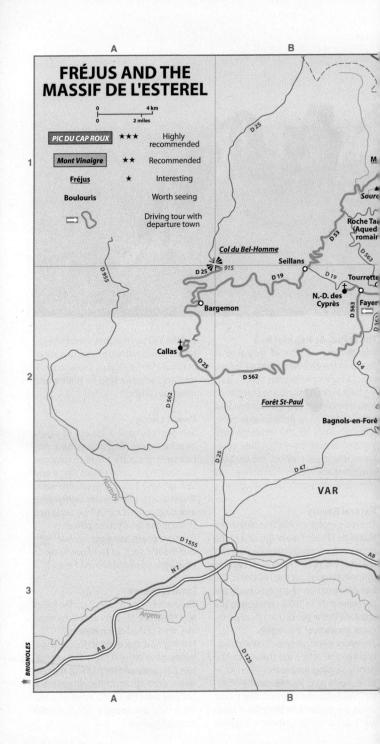

FRÉJUS AND THE MASSIF DE L'ESTEREL

0		4 km
0		
	2 miles	

PIC DU CAP ROUX ★★★ Highly recommended

Mont Vinaigre ★★ Recommended

<u>Fréjus</u> ★ Interesting

Boulouris Worth seeing

Driving tour with departure town

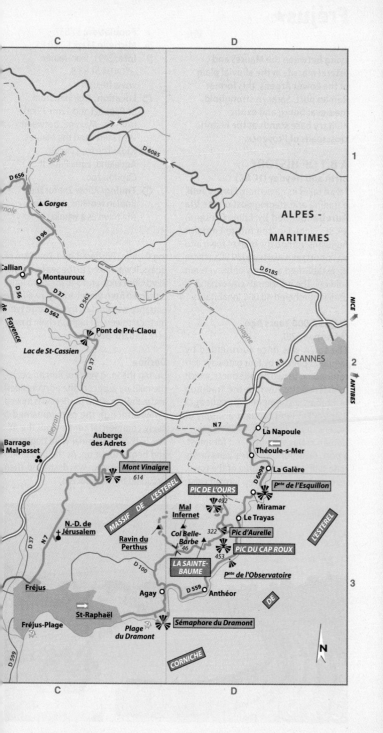

C   D

D 6085

D 656

Siagne

▲ *Gorges*

ALPES -
MARITIMES

Callian

D 96

Montauroux

D 562

D 37

D 562

D 6185

NICE

Siagne

Pont de Pré-Claou

D 37

Lac de St-Cassien

Reyran

A 8

CANNES

ANTIBES

Barrage
Malpasset

Auberge
des Adrets

N 7

La Napoule

Théoule-s-Mer

D 6098

La Galère

Mont Vinaigre
614

MASSIF DE L'ESTÉREL

PIC DE L'OURS

Pᵗᵉ de l'Esquillon

Miramar

N.-D. de
Jérusalem

D 37

N 7

Mal
Infernet

492

Le Trayas

L'ESTÉREL

Ravin du
Perthus

Col Belle-
Barbe
46

322

Pic d'Aurelle

PIC DU CAP ROUX

453

D 100

LA SAINTE-
BAUME

Pᵗᵉ de l'Observatoire

3

Fréjus

Agay

D 559

Anthéor

DE

Fréjus-Plage

St-Raphaël

Plage
du Dramont

Sémaphore du Dramont

D 599

CORNICHE

N

Fréjus★

Var

Lying between the Maures and Esterel massifs in the alluvial plain of the Lower Argens, this former Roman port, Saracen stronghold, medieval bourg and exotic military base stands at the historic crossroads of Provence.

▶ **Population:** 51,537.
Michelin Map: S 340 P5.
Info: 249 r. Jean-Jaurès.
𝒫04 94 51 83 8.
www.frejus.fr
Location: 3mi/5km from St-Raphaël and 12mi/19km from Ste-Maxime, between the Esterel and the Maures.
Kids: The frog circuit, Aqualand, Luna Park, the Capitou zoo.
Timing: Allow 2hr for the Roman remains, 1 day for the town as a whole.

A BIT OF HISTORY

Birth and Heyday (1C BC)

Fréjus takes its name from **Forum Julii**, a trading and staging post on the **Via Aurelia** founded by Julius Caesar in 49 BC. Octavian, the future Emperor Augustus, turned the market town into an important naval base (39 BC), where he established a colony of his veteran soldiers. The prosperous city expanded until it numbered 40,000 inhabitants.

Fréjus 2,000 Years Ago

See map p201.

The town was once surrounded by ramparts pierced by four gateways corresponding to two broad streets, which quartered the town in the tradition of Roman settlements. An aqueduct 25mi/40km long brought a supply of fresh water.

Roman Fréjus was, first and foremost, a port. Measuring 54 acres/22ha (more than half the surface area of the town, its bassin was sunk deep into an exist-ing lagoon. Bordered by 1.2mi/2km of quays, it was linked to the sea by a canal 32yd/30m wide and 546yd/500m long, protected from the mistral by a wall. The entrance was marked by two large symmetrical towers. At night, a chain barred access to the port.

Decline

During the long years of Roman peace, the military aspect of the port declined and in the late 2C AD the fleet was moved away, although the port remained a lively commercial centre until the 4C. The harbour and canal were neglected and began to silt up. At the beginning of the 10C the town was destroyed, then occupied by the Saracens.

Amphithéâtre

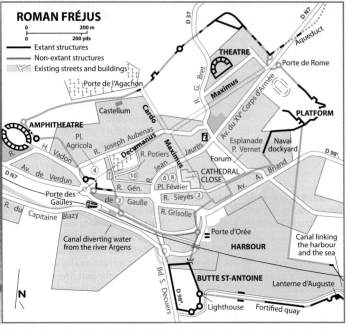

ROMAN FRÉJUS

0 — 200 m
0 — 200 yds

- Extant structures
- Non-extant structures
- Existing streets and buildings

THEATRE
Porte de Rome
Porte de l'Agachon
Castellum
AMPHITHEATRE
PLATFORM
Pl. Agricola
Joseph Aubenas
Esplanade P. Vernet
Naval dockyard
R. H. Vadon
R. Joseph
Decumanus
R. Potiers
Jaurès
Forum
Av. de Verdun
R. Jean
CATHEDRAL CLOSE
Briand
Porte des Gaules
R. Gén.
Pl. Février
de Gaulle
R. Sieyès
R. du Capitaine Blazy
R. Grisolle
Porte d'Orée
Canal diverting water from the river Argens
HARBOUR
Canal linking the harbour and the sea
N
Bd S. Decuers
BUTTE ST-ANTOINE
Lanterne d'Auguste
Lighthouse
Fortified quay
D 37
D N7
Aqueduct
Cardo
Maximus
Av. du XVᵉ Corps d'Armée
R. G. Bret
Maximus
D 98ᵉ
D N7
Av. A.

WHERE TO STAY

Aréna (L') .... ②

WHERE TO EAT

Amandier (L') .... ②
Grand Café de l'Estérel (L') .... ④

Micocouliers (Les) .... ⑥
Poivrier (Le) .... ⑧
Potiers (Les) .... ⑩

In 990, under Bishop Riculphe, the city rose again on a much smaller scale. The medieval town walls followed the line of rue Jean-Jaurès and rue Grisolle. Henri II turned Fréjus into a large naval base and during the French Revolution the port was sold as a national estate.

✺ WALKING TOURS

AN EARLY ROMAN SETTLEMENT★

▷ The Roman ruins are scattered over a large area. Allow 1.5–2hr.
🅿 Park at pl. Agricola.

From place Agricola you can see one of the two remaining towers of the **Porte des Gaules**, the old gateway through the Roman ramparts.

▷ Go down rue H. Vadon.

Amphithéâtre (Arènes)★

Rue Henri-Vadon 🕐*Open Tue–Sun 9.30am–12.30pm, 2–6pm (until 5pm Oct–Mar).* 🚫*Closed public holidays.* 💶*2€.* 📞*04 94 51 34 31.*
www.ville-frejus.fr.

Built outside the city in the 2C, the amphitheatre could accommodate approximately 10,000 spectators. Destined primarily for the pleasure of soldiers and veterans, it was clearly built with an eye to austerity and economy. In this respect it differs from the larger amphitheatres erected in Arles and Nîmes. On the esplanade stands *Le Gisant*, a sculpture commemorating the Malpasset disaster, which claimed more than 420 lives (🕐 *see Excursions*).

▷ *Take rue Joseph-Aubenas, then ave. du Théâtre Romain. A detour via rue Gustave-Bret leads to the medieval ramparts.*

PRACTICAL INFORMATION

Guided tours – The Fréjus tourist office and Ministry of Culture organise **8 itineraries** *(2hr ⌘5€)* covering the old city and the Roman ruins, as well as a **special tour** of a different site or monument each month *(1hr ⌘3€)*. In partnership with the ONF (National Office of Forestry), the tourist office also organises **forest hikes** in the Esterel.

Fréjus'Pass – *On sale at each site.* ⌘*4.60€ (12–18 years 3.10€)*. This pass allows access to the Amphithéâtre, Archaeology Museum, Notre-Dame-de-Jérusalem, Jean Cocteau Chapel and Roman Théâtre with one ticket.
Buses – *Information and tickets on Pl. Paul-Vernet.* ✆*04 94 53 78 46.* The 11 Esterel Bus lines serve Fréjus, St-Raphaël, Draguignan, and Roquebrune.

"Philippe Léotard" Roman theatre
Ave. du Théâtre-Romain.
🕒*Same conditions as the Arènes.*
This theatre is far smaller than the amphitheatre; it consists of only the radial walls on which the arches supporting the tiers of seats once rested. It measures 92yd/84m by 66yd/60m.
Inside, the orchestra pit is clearly visible, together with the stage foundations and the slot into which the curtain was lowered.

▶ *Return to the top of the street, taking a right and then a left to the Aqueduct on ave. Quinzième-Corps-d'Armée.*

Aqueduct
Only the pillars and ruined arcades remain of the aqueduct that channelled water 25mi/40km from Mons to Fréjus. Rising level with the ramparts, the aqueduct ran beneath the northern parapet as far as the water tower *(castellum)*, from where it was channelled into distribution conduits. Nearby are traces of a Roman **platform**, which served as the military headquarters *(praetorium)*: offices, storerooms, lodgings and baths. To the south lay the naval dockyard.

▶ *Go down ave. du Quinzième-Corps-d'Armée to pl. Paul-Vernet and take a right on rue Raynaude, then a left to pl. Castelli. Across the square take the vaulted rue du Portalet to reach the porte d'Orée, down rue des Moulins.*

The Old Port
The porte d'Orée consists of a fine archway, most likely the remains of a chamber formerly attached to the harbour baths. Follow the path skirting the **Butte St-Antoine** to the southern quay, where a tower known as **Augustus' Lantern** was built in the Middle Ages atop Roman ruins as a landmark for sailors entering the port. The wall marking the line of the sea canal stretches away to the southeast.

THE OLD CITY
45min from place Formigé.
Walk down the rue du Beausset to the former **Episcopal Palace** (now the town hall), with its original 14C façade in pink Esterel sandstone.

▶ *Return to pl. Formigé and head north along rue de Fleury.*

At no 58, the Maison du Prévôt (also called Capitou) has an interesting façade and doorway pierced into a fortified tower, now the entrance to the Groupe Episcopal (🕯*see Sights below*). At the end of the street *(no 92, right)* there is a doorway in green serpentine from the Maures.

▶ *Turn left onto rue Jean-Jaurès, following the medieval rampart ruins.*

The former 18C **town hall** *(no 112)* features an unusual façade embellished with a curved balcony and a loggia.

▶ *Take a right on rue Sleyès.*

At no 53, the doorway framed by two 17C stone atlantes is all that remains of the former mansion of Abbé Sieyès.

▶ *Continue past pl. Liberté to rue Grisolle on the right.*

This street follows the line of the **medieval ramparts**, with a handsome round tower *(no 71)* and a medieval façade *(no 84, right)*. The picturesque **passage du Portalet** connects a string of little squares leading to place Formigé.

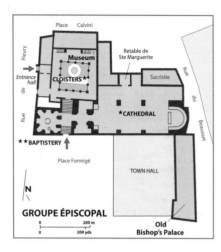

GROUPE ÉPISCOPAL

SIGHTS
Groupe Épiscopal★★
Allow 1hr.
Pl. Formigé. At the bottom of the steps, the Baptistery is to the left, the cathedral to the right and the cloisters straight ahead. ☉*Open Jun–Sept daily 9am–6.30pm; Oct–May Tue–Sun 9am–noon, 2–5pm.* ☉*Closed public holidays.* ☞5€. ☎04 94 51 26 30. www.Fréjus.fr.

Portal `
☜*Guided tours only.*
Under an ogee arch are two **panels**★ carved in the 16C to illustrate scenes from the life of the Virgin, St Peter and St Paul, portraits and military motifs.

Baptistery★★
☜*Guided tours only.*

This baptistery, one of the oldest buildings in France, is thought to date back to the 5C. Separated from the cathedral by the porch, it has an octagonal-shaped interior featuring alternate curved and rectangular niches separated by black granite columns. These are topped by marble capitals taken from the ancient forum.

Cathedral★
The cathedral, an early example of Provençal Gothic art, is dedicated to Our Lady and St Stephen. Some parts of the building may date back to an earlier basilica. The porch supporting the 16C belfry was erected some 200 years later.

Cloisters of the cathedral

© Var Tourisme

203

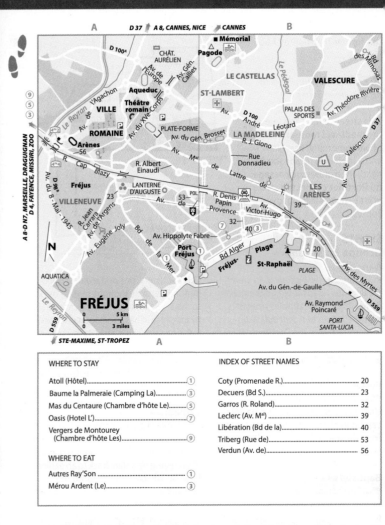

Over the apse rises the crenulated tower, which once protected the Episcopal Palace. The **choir stalls** date from the 15C and the white marble high altar from the 18C. There are also two 14C tombs; at the end of the aisle, near the tombs of the bishops of Camelin (17C), is a remarkable Renaissance crucifix in wood.

Cloisters★

The 12C–13C cloisters were intended for the chapter canons and comprised two storeys; only one upper gallery remains. The groined vaults once covering the galleries were replaced by a pinewood ceiling with exposed beams, decorated in the 14C with curious little **painted panels**★ of animals, chimerae, grotesques and characters from the Apocalypse. Of the original 1,200, 400 are still visible (8min film).

Archaeological Museum

Pl. Calvini (first floor of the Cloisters).
Open Tue–Sun 9.30am–12.30pm, 2–6pm (until 5pm Nov–Apr). ⌾2€.
℘04 94 52 15 78.

This museum presents a fine collection of Gallo-Roman antiquities recovered from local excavations. Finds include a rare Roman floor mosaic (one of the few to have survived whole), a two-headed marble bust of a faun and Hermès or Bacchus (now the town's symbol),

Aerial view of the port

© Olivier Simon/Var Tourisme

uncovered in 1970, a head of Jupiter (1C BC) and several bronze statuettes.

ON THE WATER
Port-Fréjus

In 1989, after 10 years' work, Fréjus paid tribute to its long-standing maritime traditions by opening a yachting marina whose style recalls the town's Roman origins. The different areas are joined by gangways, which in summer are the scene of much colourful and lively activity.

Fréjus-Plage

This magnificent beach of fine sand runs several miles from Port-Fréjus to the Pont du Pédégal. Another fine sand beach, Plage d'Aviation, lies slightly further west. Beside the sea (at blvd. de la Libération) stands a memorial recalling the sacrifice of Senegalese infantrymen (L'Armée Noire).

MILITARY HISTORY

In 1910 Fréjus resumed an active military role with the creation of the first air and sea base in France.
At the beginning of the First World War this became a centre for colonial troops from Africa and Asia, who established a rest and recreation base here as a gentle acclimation to the European climate.

Their different cultures left a legacy of exotic buildings.

Mosquée de Missiri

◗ *Leave Fréjus by ave. de Verdun, then proceed towards Fayence on D 4. After 2mi/3km turn left (⊶ closed to the public).*

In a pine wood stands a large, ochre Sudanese mosque, a concrete replica of the celebrated Missiri de Djenné mosque in Mali, built in the 1920s by **Senegalese soldiers**.

◗ *Continue in the same direction. 0.6mi/1km after the bridge over the A 8 motorway. Rte de Bagnols-en-Forêt.*

Musée des Troupes de Marine

21 rue de Bagnols. ◷*Open Wed–Fri and Sun–Mon mid-Jun–mid-Sept 10am–noon, 3–7pm; mid-Feb–mid-Jun and mid-Sept–mid-Nov 2–6pm; Dec–Jan 2–5pm.* ◷*Closed 24 Dec–2 Jan.* ⊛*No charge.* ℘*04 94 17 86 55. www.aamtdm.net.*
This museum retraces the history of the Marine Corps since 1622. The expeditions during the great colonial period from the Second Empire (1852–70) to 1914 (Africa, Indochina, Madagascar) are recreated with arms, uniforms, pen-

nants, dioramas, drawings and photographs. In the crypt are buried unknown marines from the Infantry Division, who fell when fighting the Bavarians at Bazeilles (Ardennes) in 1870.

> *Take ave. du Quinzième-Corps and then ave. du Général-Callies towards Nice. Turn right after the roundabout. Park in the car park between the two monuments and continue on foot.*

Mémorial des Guerres en Indochine

862 ave. du Gén.-d'Armée-Jean-Calliès, via the ave. du Quinzième-Corps-d'Armée, ⊙*Open Wed–Mon 10am–5.30pm.* ⊙*Closed 1 Jan, 1 May, 25 Dec.* ⊙*No charge.* ℰ*04 94 44 42 90. www.memorial-indochine.org.*

At the foot of a hill this imposing circular necropolis symbolically faces the sea. Since 1987, the remains of 24,000 soldiers and civilians who died in active service in former Indochina have been repatriated here. Illuminated maps and models are used to describe the historic events and battles.

Pagode Bouddhique Hông Hiên

Near the Memorial. ⊙*Open daily 10am–noon 2–5pm; Apr–Oct 10am–7pm.* ⊙*2€.* ℰ*04 94 53 25 29.*

Traditional Vietnamese architecture was the inspiration for this Buddhist Pagoda, built in 1917 by Vietnamese soldiers who had come to fight for France. The grounds surrounding the pagoda are planted with exotic flowers.

EXCURSIONS

Chapelle Notre-Dame de Jérusalem★

Ave. Nicolaï, 3mi/5km north of Fréjus by the R N 7. Park, then 5min on foot. ⊙*Open Wed–Mon 9.30am–12.30pm, 2–5pm.* ⊙*Closed public holidays.* ℰ*04 94 53 27 06.*

This tiny chapel, situated in the Tour de Mare district, was the last building to be designed by **Jean Cocteau**. He had finalised the layout and the interior decor as early as 1961 but the chapel

remained unfinished until two years after the poet's death, in 1965. The exterior mosaics were added in 1992.

Parc Zoologique

In Capitou, 3mi/5km north of Fréjus on Ave. de Verdun (N 7), then right onto D 4 towards Fayence. ⊙⊙*Open daily Mar–May Sep–Oct 10am–5pm (until 6pm Jun–Aug); Nov–Feb 10.30am–4.30pm.* ⊙*14.50€ (child 3–9 years 10€).* ℰ*04 94 40 70 65. www.zoo-frejus.com.*

The Zoological Park covers about 49 acres/20ha in the foothills of the Esterel Massif. Walk or drive beneath the pines, oaks and olive trees and observe a variety of birds (pink flamingos, vultures and parrots) and wild animals (African elephants, zebras and lemurs). Regular animal shows.

Étangs de Villepey

> *3mi/5km. South from Fréjus take D 559 towards St-Tropez. Parking on the premises (fee charged at the entrance).*

Fed by both seawater and by freshwater streams, these 360 acres/255ha of protected wetland, one of the rare lagoons between Marseille and Nice, include reed-beds, umbrella pine groves and brackish stretches along the N 98. More than 200 species of bird thrive here. Spring is the best time to see pink flamingos, herons and egrets.

Remains of Malpasset Dam

> *From Fréjus follow signs to "Nice par l'autoroute A 8". At the last roundabout before the motorway sliproad, take D 7 signposted "Barrage de Malpasset" for 3mi/5km.* ⚑ *1hr round trip.*

The arch dam, built in 1954 with a capacity of 1,730 million cu ft/49 million cu m, was intended to relieve the scarce water supplies in the Var coastal region. On the evening of 2 December 1959, torrential rains of previous weeks caused the abutments of the arch to collapse. Within 20 minutes, a 180ft/55m high wave surged through Fréjus, claiming 400 victims. A footpath goes up the Reyran Valley through sparse *garrigue* vegetation scattered with vast blocks of concrete torn off the dam.

ADDRESSES

🛏 STAY

🔵**Camping La Baume la Palmeraie** – r. des Combattants-d'Afrique du Nord. 2mi/4.5km north on D 4, rte. de Bagnols-en-Forêt. ℘04 94 19 88 88. www.la baume-lapalmeraie.com. Closed Oct–Mar. Campsite set in lush surroundings with swimming pool and 👫👫play equipment. Bungalow rentals possible.

🔵🔵**Chambre d'hôte les Vergers de Montourey** – Vallée du Reyran. ℘04 94 40 85 76. vergers. montourey.pagesperso-orange.fr. 4 rooms, 2 suites. 🍽. Beautiful 18C farmhouse with six good-sized rooms, each named after a fruit.

🔵🔵**Hôtel Atoll** – 923 blvd. de la Mer. ℘04 94 51 53 77. www.atollhotel.fr. 30 rooms. 🍽6€. Just 109yd/100m from the beach and near a theme park stands this renovated hotel. Simply decorated rooms.

🔵🔵**Hôtel L'Oasis** – impasse Charcot. ℘04 94 53 01 04. www.hotel-oasis.net. Closed mid-Nov–Jan. 27 rooms. 🍽6.90€. Built in the 1950s, this hotel stands back from the promenade nestling in a quiet street in a wealthy neighbourhood. Family atmosphere. Pergola in the middle of the pine trees.

🔵🔵🔵**Hôtel L'Aréna** – 145 blvd. du Général-de-Gaulle. ℘04 94 17 09 40. www.arena-hotel.com. Closed Nov. 36 rooms. 🅿14€. Restaurant 🔵🔵. This former staging post with a colourful front provides pleasant accommodation in carefully-kept rooms arranged in the Provençal style. Relax sipping your cocktail on the terrace or reclining by the pool.

🔵🔵🔵**Chambre d'hôte Mas du Centaure** – 1821 impasse du Gabron, Puget Sur Argens, 4.3mi/7km northwest of Fréjus. ℘04 94 81 58 25. www. lemasducentaure.com. 1 room, 2 suites (reduced fees for children). 🍽. Set in stunning natural surroundings, rooms are beautifully decorated and well equipped. Separate room for children. Swimming pool and private terrace.

🍴 EAT

🔵🔵**Grand Café de l'Estérel** – 14 pl. Agricola. ℘04 94 51 50 50. www.grand.cafe-esterel.com. Closed Sun. A convivial and popular brasserie with a single menu offered at rock-bottom prices, renewed every day for lunchtime diners.

🔵**Les Micocouliers** – 34 pl. Paul-Albert Février. ℘04 94 52 16 52. This restaurant set up on the square opposite the Groupe Episcopal has a summer terrace. Inside, the brightly coloured tablecloths and rustic-style decoration blend in well with the owner's Provençal cooking.

🔵**Le Mérou Ardent** – 157 blvd. de la Libération. ℘04 94 17 30 58. Closed early Jun, mid-Nov–mid-Dec, Sat–Sun, Thu lunches in season, Wed–Thu off season. Restaurant 🔵🔵–🔵🔵🔵. A small restaurant with a nautical decor located on the beachfront Boulevard. Good service, fish specialities.

🔵**Le Poivrier** – 52 pl. Paul-Albert Février. ℘04 94 52 28 50. Closed Nov, Mon Sept–May, Sun. The tasty homemade cuisine is a mix of Mediterranean tradition and a pinch of exotica, served in a small, vaulted cellar going back to Roman times. Summer terrace.

🔵🔵🔵**L'Amandier** – 19 r. Marc-Antoine Desaugiers. ℘04 94 53 48 77. Closed late-Oct–early Nov, 1–14 Jan, Mon lunch, Wed lunch, Sun. Restaurant located along a pedestrianised street, close to the town hall. Charming welcome, trendy, tasty and carefully prepared cuisine at very reasonable prices.

🔵**Autres Ray'Son** – quai Marc Antoine. ℘04 94 17 11 21. www. autresrayson.com. Closed Mon. Reservations required. Traditional yet creative French cuisine is served at this restaurant situated right on the quay.

🔵🔵🔵**Les Potiers** – 135 rue des Potiers. ℘04 94 51 33 74. Closed 1–20 Dec, lunch Jul–Aug, Wed lunch, Tue Sept–Jun. Reservations required. In a tiny street near the Église St-François and Place Agricola, this friendly, family-run restaurant serves French classics and seafood dishes with a Mediterranean touch. The décor is rustic and cosy.

🛍 SHOPPING

Fréjus Markets – Wed and Sat in the old quarter; Sun on blvd. d'Alger and blvd. de la Libération; Tue and Fri on pl. de la République (Fréjus-Plage), pl. de la Poste (St-Aygulf); Thu on Tour de Marre.

🏃 LEISURE ACTIVITIES

CIP Port Fréjus – *Aire de Carénage, Port Fréjus Est.* ℰ*04 94 52 34 99. www.cip-frejus.com.* A deep-sea diving centre for both beginners and experienced swimmers will take you round the shipwrecks of the Var coastline.

Aqualand – *RN 98, Le Capou.* ℰ*04 94 51 82 51. www.aqualand.fr. Closed Sept–May.* ⊙*25€ (child 3–12, 18.50€).* Watersports enthusiasts will love this theme park, with its amazing waterslides, *Rapid Rafting* and *White Hole*, and its swimming pool with waves (the biggest in Europe). Miniature golf course.

Marina – *Capitainerie/Harbour Authority.* ℰ*04 94 82 63 00. www.port-frejus.fr.* The 722ft/220m pier can accommodate more than 750 boats.

Base Nature – *blvd. de la Mer.* ℰ*04 94 51 91 10. www.base.nature.free.fr. Closed mornings off season.* This nature park welcomes hikers, cyclists (198 acres/80ha) as well as swimmers and sun-bathers over a 1mi/2km stretch of beach. Additional activities include sand-yachting, flying kites, playing boules and roller-skating.

CALENDAR

Bravade Saint-François – Third Sunday after Easter, a traditional religious procession through the historic centre of town.

Fête du Raisin – Celebration of the first wine grapes, harvested the first week in August. Wine tasting from the local producers on Pl. Formigé.

St-Raphaël★

Var

Situated on one of the last slopes of the Esterel, St-Raphaël lies on the eastern fringes of Fréjus Bay. Its sheltered beach and lively seafront make it a popular choice for sun-seekers. A former Roman trading post, its collection of ancient artefacts is also among the finest on the Riviera.

- ▶ **Population:** 33,084.
- **Michelin Map:** 340 P5; region map: pp198–199.
- **Info:** quai Albert 1er. ℰ04 94 19 52 52. www.saint-raphael.com
- **Location:** St-Raphaël stretches along the Esterel coast for 21mi/35km.
- **Kids:** Zoo; Luna Parc and Parc Aquatica in Fréjus.
- **Timing:** One day for the town and coastline.

A BIT OF HISTORY

Origins – St-Raphaël, like Fréjus, is a daughter of Rome. A Gallo-Roman holiday resort stood on the site now occupied by the large Casino, built on terraces with mosaics, thermal baths and a *vivarium* (fish reserve), where rich Romans came to enjoy the sea air.

In the Middle Ages the villas were plundered by Saracen pirates. After their expulsion by the Count of Provence at end of the 10C, the land was given to the monks of Lérins. The village that grew up around their monastery was subsequently handed to the Knights Templar in the 12C. During the 18C, the old town was occupied by fishermen and peasants. A spate of lead poison-ing earned the town's inhabitants the nickname *visages pâles* or "pale faces". After Corsica became part of France in 1768, the port became the terminus for a short-lived sealink with the island.

Bonaparte in St-Raphaël – On 9 October 1799 the small village was suddenly thrust into the limelight when Bonaparte, returning from Egypt, landed there after a voyage of 48 days (a pyramid standing in Avenue Commandant-Guilbaud commemorates this event). In 1814 St-Raphaël received Napoleon once again, this time as a defeated man leaving for exile in Elba.

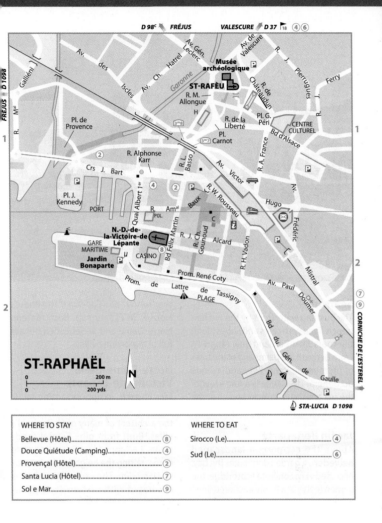

ST-RAPHAËL

0   200 m
0   200 yds

N

WHERE TO STAY		WHERE TO EAT	
Bellevue (Hôtel)	⑧	Sirocco (Le)	④
Douce Quiétude (Camping)	④	Sud (Le)	⑥
Provençal (Hôtel)	②		
Santa Lucia (Hôtel)	⑦		
Sol e Mar	⑨		

Popular resort – Alphonse Karr (1808–90) was an extravagant personality, who used his talents as a journalist and pamphleteer to oppose Napoleon III from Nice, where he was in exile. He settled in St-Raphaël in 1864, in a villa named "Maison Close". Writing to a Parisian friend, he said: "Leave Paris and plant your stick in my garden: the next morning, when you awake, you will see that it has grown roses." Writers and artists responded to his invitation, including Alexandre Dumas, Maupassant, Berlioz and Gounod.

Félix Martin, local mayor and civil engineer, followed Karr's lead and transformed the village into a smart resort, encouraging building, and linking St-Raphaël with Hyères by means of a small railway along the coast. Illustrious guests marked their stay in St-Raphaël with works of art: Gounod composed *Roméo et Juliette* in 1869, Scott Fitzgerald wrote *Tender is the Night* and Félix Ziem painted here.

THE TOWN CENTRE

The original town centre consists of an important and somewhat rare collection of seaside architecture dating from the beginning of the Third Republic (in the late 19C).

209

St-Raphaël harbour

© Wadey James/Apa Publications

Seafront

The bustling waterfront by the old harbour is lined with cafés and shops along the cours Jean-Bart and quai Albert-Ier. From beneath the palms and plane trees of promenade René-Coty and avenue du Général-de-Gaulle is a fine **view** of the sea and the twin rocks known as the "Land Lion" and the "Sea Lion".

Jardin Bonaparte

Above the car park, a landscaped **belvedere★** garden dominates the bay. Accessed via a concrete footbridge, the garden feels like a firmly anchored liner. It is also accessible via steps from the car park. Admire the azur blue of the Mediterranean and the fishing port below.

Villas

The rehabilitation of the residential district between the promenade René-Coty and the rue Alphonse Karr led to the demolition of a number of villas and Normandy-style homes.

Among the exotically decorated historic villa façades to survive, are the **Villa Roquerousse** (1900) on the promenade René-Coty with its lavish ornamentation. Along Boulevard Félix-Martin is the charming oriental **Villa Sémiramis**, **Villa Paquerettes** decorated with ceramic, and a little farther on, the shadow of Gounod still haunts

the *Oustelet dou Capelan* ("The Priest's House" in Provençal). Both Plateau Notre-Dame and St-Sébastien hill are full of remarkable villas.

Notre-Dame-de-la-Victoire-de-Lépante

This **church**, in neo-Byzantine style, was designed in 1883 by **Pierre Aublé**, the architect of many of St-Raphaël's villas. Built from pink Esterel sandstone, it is topped by a Byzantine-style dome, raising the height of the interior to 115ft/35m. The vault of the choir is decorated with Eastern-style paintings recalling the frescoes of St Sophia basilica in Istanbul.

QUARTIER DE VALESCURE

This district was once much patronised by foreign visitors. Carvalho – director of the Paris Opera in 1880, laid out, with advice from Charles Garnier – a park decorated with vestiges from the Palais des Tuileries in Paris, including a fountain at the crossroads of rue Allongue and rue Maréchal-Leclerc.

Musée archéologique-Église St-Rafèu

◷ Open Dec–Oct Tue–Sat 9am–12pm, 2–6pm. ✎ No charge. ☎ 04 94 19 25 75. www.saint-raphael.com.

Situated at the crossroads between several major land routes (Via Aurelia) and shipping lanes between Massalia (modern–day Marseille) and the trading posts of the Western Mediterranean, St-Raphaël understandably enjoys an incredibly rich archaeological history. This museum houses an extensive collection of **amphorae**★ uncovered from Roman ships wrecked in the bay from the 5C BC to the 5C AD, completed by a display on the evolution of scuba diving equipment, maritime archaeology and underwater photography.

The collection also includes finds from local Prehistoric sites, from the Palaeolithic Era to the Bronze Age, and an introduction to the Var's many dolmens and menhirs. The museum garden (and stretches of rue Allongue) feature vestiges of the town's former ramparts.

Standing within the museum grounds, the **medieval church**★ is built on a site occupied for over 2000 years. A visit to its crypts reveal, to spectacular effect, how archaeologists have uncovered each progressive layer of this occupation. Many of the funereal and architectural artefacts found during **excavations** on this site are on display in the sacristy, including religious objects and low-reliefs.

Built in the 12C in the Romanesque-Provençal style, the church, which has a single nave, served as a fortress and a refuge for the population during pirate attacks. In one of the side chapels, a red sandstone pagan monolith supports the altar table.

The gilded wooden bust of St Peter is carried by the fishermen in procession to the Sea Lion in August. From the 14C fortified tower, there is a wonderful **view**★ over the sea, the Fréjus St-Raphaël bay, the Esterel massif and its rocky red rhyolite spurs.

The resort is dominated by the marvellous red porphyry slopes of the **Rastel d'Agay**, bordering by far the finest natural harbour of the Esterel.

The main **beach** with its seasports centre stretches out to the left to a small jetty, beyond which lies the town's most popular beach, appreciated for its shade.

Trips and Tours

Guided Tours – Discover St-Raphaël's heritage, every Thursday 10am. 2.30€. For information contact the tourist office, 04 94 19 52 52.

Nature Walks – The tourist office can also organise nature walks along the coastal footpaths or in the Esterel hills, in partnership with the Office National des Forêts.

Boat Trips – 04 94 95 17 46. www.tmr-saintraphael.com. Departures from the old port (gare maritime) to St-Tropez Jul–Aug 9.30am, 11.30am, 2.30pm, 5pm (and 7pm mid-Jul–late Aug); mid-Apr–late-May 9.30am (except Sun), 2.30pm; Jun and Sep 9.30am, 2.30pm. 23€ Round trip (2–9 yrs 13€). Excursions also available in the Esterel or Îles de Lérins. The Agay boat offers underwater views.

Anthéor

This smart little resort is dominated by the peaks of Cap Roux. Anthéor-Plage lies along the western approaches to the town, while rocky inlets dominate the eastern coastline.

Le Trayas

The coastline that runs along the foot of the Esterel massif is fringed with creeks and rocky inlets at the foot of which lie the occasional sand beach. Le Trayas was a major tuna fishing port in the 17C, when nets were cast into the open sea and left in place for four months. A tower was built on the shoreline to watch over them.

20min round trip. Part of the village sits on a steep slope. Walk along the street bordered with villas and follow the signs for "Gare SNCF" to access the belvedere with a stunning **panorama**★.

ADDRESSES

🛏 STAY

◎ **Camping Douce Quiétude** – *3435 Bd J.-Baudino. 2mi/3km via north-east exit towards Valescure. ℘04 94 44 30 00. www.douce-quietude.com. Closed Nov–late Mar. Reservations recommended. 400 pitches.* Take a siesta under the shady pine trees before heading to the beach just minutes from this campsite reserved for caravans. Joint activities for children and parents; mini-club for young children. Bungalow and mobile home rental.

◎ ⊜ **Hôtel Provençal** – *197 Rue Garonne. ℘04 98 11 80 00. www.hotel-provencal.com. Apartments with 3 beds. ⊆8€.* Slightly away from the busy port, an entirely renovated building containing modern, functional rooms with good soundproofing.

◎ ⊜ ⬚ **Hôtel Bellevue** – *22 blvd Félix-Martin. ℘04 94 19 90 10. ⊆8€ 🅿.* This modest hotel enjoys a central location close to the casino and beach. Simply decorated rooms with air-conditioning and double-glazing. Affordable rates for the station district.

◎ ⊜ ⬚ **Hôtel Santa Lucia** – *418 Route de la Corniche. ℘04 94 95 23 00. www.hotelsantalucia.fr. Closed 20 Dec–mid-Feb. 12 rooms. ⊆. 🅿.* Beautiful, recently renovated hotel. Each room recreates the atmosphere of a different country (England, Morocco, Italy, Japan…). Choose one at the back, overlooking the sea.

◎ ⊜ ⬚ **Hôtel Sol e Mar** – *Rte de la Corniche d'Or, 83530 Agay, 3.7mi/6km east along D 559. ℘04 94 95 25 60. www.monalisahotels.com. 🅿. 45 rooms. Restaurant ⊜ ⬚.* Authentic seaside hotel: most rooms look out towards the Îles d'Or; swimming pool open to the sky, beach-solarium and seawater pool with overflow dug out of the rocks on the shore. Panoramic restaurant with opening roof and fine terrace.

🍴 EAT

◎ ⊜ **Le Sud** – *16 Bd. Darby. ℘04 94 44 67 86. Closed 1–10 Jun, Tue–Wed except Jul–Aug, Sat–Mon lunches.* Located in an open-air shopping centre, this sunny restaurant is decorated with paintings and old photographs. Terrace surrounded by a garden. Appetising, trendy provençal menu.

◎ ⊜ **Le Sirocco** – *35 quai Albert-1er. ℘04 94 95 39 99. www.lesirocco.fr. Closed mid-Dec–mid-Jan. Reservations recommended.* The hot dry Sahara wind may guide you towards this restaurant. Located for the past 20 years opposite the old harbour, it has consistently served tasty cuisine with a seaside flavour. Carefully laid tables, small summer terrace in front. Seaside atmosphere.

🎭 ON THE TOWN

Casino de St-Raphaël – *Sq. Gand. ℘04 98 11 17 77. www.luciensbarriere.com. Open Summer daily 10am–4am (Sat 5am); rest of year daily 10am–3am (Sat 4am).* This casino was built in 1881 on the site of a Roman villa. It contains more than 150 slot machines and traditional games.

🤸 SPORT AND LEISURE

Golf de Valesscure – *Ave. des Golfs. ℘04 94 82 40 46. www.golfvalescure.fr. Open Jul–Aug 8am–8pm; May–Jun, Sept–Oct 8am–7pm; Nov–Apr 8am–6pm.* This beautiful 18-hole golf course also boasts a restaurant located in a charming house, a hotel and a bar.

Écol de Cirque – *Cap Esterel. ℘04 94 82 58 11. www.capesterel.com. Open Mon–Fri 9am–noon, 4–6pm. Closed early Jan–early Feb and early Nov–mid-Dec.* Circus training (trapeze, juggling, large or small trampoline, acrobatics, etc.) for children aged 6-12. Flying trapeze for adults and teenagers aged over 13.

🎭 EVENTS

Les fêtes de la Lumière – The town bursts into light in Dec with street theatre and a Christmas market.

La fête du Mimosa – Second week in Feb. Procession of floral floats Sun afternoon.

Compétition du Jazz – Three days in July.

Massif de l'Esterel★★★

Var

Carpeted with pines and holm oaks, the slopes of the Esterel between St-Raphaël and La Napoule plunge steeply down to the sea. The contrast between the hustle and bustle of coastline and the seclusion of the inland roads will come as a welcome respite for nature lovers.

A BIT OF HISTORY

The Massif – The Esterel, separated from its neighbour the Maures by the Argens Valley, has been worn down by erosion. Its highest point, Mont Vinaigre, stands at an altitude of just 2,027ft/618m. However, the deep ravines and broken skyline of this mountain range dispel any impression of a mere succession of hills.

The Esterel is made up of volcanic rocks (porphyry), which give the range its characteristic profile, harsh relief and vivid red tints. Agay is where the Romans found the blue porphyry particular to their Provençal monuments.

Via Aurelia – The Esterel was bordered to the north by the Via Aurelia (Aurelian Way), one of the most important routes of the Roman empire, connecting Rome and Arles via Genoa, Cimiez, Antibes, Fréjus and Aix. Paved, cambered and more than 8ft/2.5m wide, the road made use of many bridges and other civil engineering works to create the shortest route possible.

RESORTS

Stretching more than 18.6mi/30km between St-Raphaël and La Napoule, the striking landscape of the Corniche de l'Esterel is punctuated by several pleasant seaside resorts.

Boulouris

This small resort, where villas are dotted among pines in beautiful gardens, has several modest beaches and a harbour.

Michelin Map: 340 P/Q5.

Info: The tourist offices of St-Raphaël-Agay, Fréjus, Mandelieu and Le Muy work with the National Office of Forestry to organise tours of the forests in the Massif de l'Esterel. 04 94 19 52 52 (St-Raphaël tourist office). www.saint-raphael.com, www.agay.fr, www.ville-frejus.fr, www.ville-lemuy.fr, www.onf.fr.

Location: The Esterel stretches along the coastline of the Var between Cannes and Fréjus, and encompasses several small villages and resorts such as St-Raphaël.

Parking: Except in high season around the major towns, free parking is relatively easy to find near hiking trailheads. It is advisable to remove all valuables from your car when hiking.

Don't Miss: The panoramic view from the Pointe de l'Esquillon, the scenic port in Agay, and for the robust hikers, the views from the Pic de l'Ours.

Timing: You could easily drive through the Esterel along N 98 coastal road from Cannes to Fréjus in less than an hour, with a pause for a short hike at Dramont or the Point d'Esquillon. For the longer hikes, plan for at least a half day and be prepared by taking enough drinking water, food and appropriate footwear.

Agay

This resort borders a deep port, the finest in the Esterel, which was once used by the Ligurians, the Greeks and the Romans. The scenic bay of the

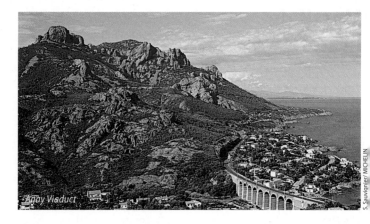

Agay Viaduct

S. Sauvignier/ MICHELIN

Rastel d'Agay is lined by a large, sunny beach.

Anthéor
see St-Raphaël p208.

Le Trayas
see St-Raphaël p208.

Miramar
This elegant resort, with its private harbour, lies in Figueirette Bay. In January 1942, the British Special Operations Executive landed its first officer, Peter Churchill, at Miramar to make contact with the *Carte* Maquis network and the French Resistance.

La Galère
Built on the wooded slopes of the Esterel, this resort forms the western limit of La Napoule Bay. Below the road, the seaside development of **Port-la-Galère** *(private port)*, an astonishing design by the architect Jacques Couelle, seems to merge with its rocky environment.

Théoule-sur-Mer
This resort, sheltered by the Théoule promontory, has three small public beaches accessible from the pedestrianised **promenade André-Pradeyrol**, popular with line fishermen. The town's villas blend perfectly with their surroundings, which include a crenulated building flanked by two turrets. A soap factory in the 18C, it has now been transformed into a private château.

The **pointe de l'Aiguille** departmental park offers 17 acres/7ha of creeks and rocky inlets, with stunning **views** for hikers from its highest reaches.

Antoine de St-Exupéry

Born in Lyon in 1900, Antoine de St-Exupéry attended the Jesuits College and completed his education in Fribourg, Switzerland. Interested in flying from an early age, he joined the French Army Air Force in 1921 but resigned five years later to become a civilian pilot. He began writing in 1928. His second novel, *Vol de Nuit*, was awarded a prize by the French Academy in 1931. However, the book for which he will always be fondly remembered is *Le Petit Prince* (1943), a charming fable for children. In the Second World War, he served as an instructor and carried out reconnaissance flights. On 31 July 1944, he set out for the Alps on one of these assignments but never returned.

A few days later, he was officially reported missing. His body was never recovered from the ocean waters, but the remains of his Lockheed Lightning P-38 were discovered off the coast of Marseille in 2004.

The Kingdom of Auguste I

The **Île d'Or** is a small red porphyry island off Dramont beach marked by a strange tower, which appears to grow out of the rock. This Medieval-style tower was built in 1897 by an eccentric Parisian doctor, Auguste Lutaud, who transformed the island into his own private kingdom, proclaiming himself King Auguste I of the Île d'Or. He became the darling of fashionable Riviera society and organised lavish receptions during the Belle Époque. The monarch died in 1925. His island remains private property.

🚗 DRIVING TOURS

1 CORNICHE DE L'ESTEREL★★★
25mi/40km. Allow about 4hr.

▷ *From St-Raphaël (●see ST-RAPHAËL pp208), take D 559 south.*

The road skirts the St-Raphaël marina. On the seafront is a memorial to the French Army campaigns in Africa.

▷ *Drive through Boulouris to the D 559.*

Plage du Dramont
●*See ST-RAPHAËL p208.*
A **stele** erected to the right of the road commemorates the landing of the US Army, 36th Division, on 15 August 1944. Running alongside the Camp-Long beach and Dramont Forest, the road leads to the resorts of Agay and Anthéor. Shortly before reaching the Pointe de l'Observatoire, admire the **view** to the left, encompassing the red rocks of St-Barthélemy and Cap Roux.

Pointe de l'Observatoire★
The ruins of a blockhouse command a stunning **view**★ of the blood-red porphyry rocks against the cobalt blue of the sea, and **views** of the Anthéor, Cap Roux, Esquillon Points and La Napoule Bay.

▷ *Drive through Le Trayas. On a bend near the Hôtel Tour de L'Esquillon, pull off the road into the car park. A path (sign) leads up to Pointe de l'Esquillon.*

Pointe de l'Esquillon★★
🚶 *15min round trip.*

A beautiful **panorama**★★ *(viewing table)* of the Esterel heights, the coast, Cap Roux, the Îles de Lérins and Cap d'Antibes. After La Galère, the road skirts Pointe de l'Aiguille, opening up a **view**★ of La Napoule Bay, Cannes, the Îles de Lérins and Cap d'Antibes.
Théoule-sur-mer (●*see RESORTS above*).

2 VIA AURELIA★
20.5mi/33km from Théoule-sur-Mer to St-Raphaël. Allow about 5hr. Most of this route runs through woodland.

The ancient Via Aurelia *(camin aurélian in Provençal)*, one of the most important roads in the Roman Empire, skirted the Esterel to the north. At the end of each Roman mile (1,617yd/1,478m) distances would be indicated by a tall milestone, one of which is on display in St-Raphaël (Musée Archéologique). Riders used the milestones as steps to mount their horses. Imperial messengers benefited from a string of posthouses along the road to catch up on their sleep, change horses and make repairs.

Théoule-sur-mer (●*see RESORTS above*). *Leave Théoule-sur-mer by the D 6098 then turn left at the Balcon d'Azur roundabout, left again at the San Peyre roundabout, then left on entering the D 6007 (called D N7 in the Var).*

Auberge des Adrets
Dating from 1653, this inn was the favourite haunt of the notorious 18C highwayman **Gaspard de Besse**. He also spent time in a cave on Mont Vinaigre, the highest peak in the Esterel (2,027ft/618m), which hugs the road after the Logis-de-Paris crossroads. This

smart highwayman, dressed in red with silver buttons, robbed stagecoaches and postriders, helped by his loyal band of accomplices. He ended his career by being broken on the wheel on place d'Aix in 1781, at the age of 24. His head was nailed to a tree on the Via Aurelia, the scene of many of his exploits.

▶ *At carrefour du Testannier, turn left onto a road marked "Forêt Domaniale de l'Esterel". At Maison Forestière du Malpey, follow signs to Mont Vinaigre.*

Mont Vinaigre★★
🚶 *30min round trip.*
A path leads to the top of the mountain (2,027ft/618m) which offers a splendid **panorama**★★ on all sides: along the coast to Cap d'Antibes, Pointe de la Croisette, Cannes and La Napoule Bay, Pic de l'Ours with its tower and TV mast, Pic du Cap Roux and Fréjus Bay, and inland across to the Massif des Maures, the Argens Valley, the limestone hills of Provence and the extreme south of the Ste-Baume lake. The Italian Alps and on the other side, Ste-Baume, are visible on a clear day.

This imposing setting would have been even more awe-inspiring in previous centuries when it was teeming with highwaymen such as **Gaspard de Besse**, who haunted the route de l'Esterel towards Italy. For many years, the phrase "to pass the Esterel pass" was used to describe any action involving a high degree of risk. The most dangerous spot was near Mont Vinaigre. Starting out from the D N7 to the Logis-de-Paris crossroads, the road passes in front of the Maison Forestière du Malpey (Provençal for "bad mountain"). Taking this route on foot, as the naturalist de Saussure did in 1787, took a lot of courage. Until the end of the 19C, the Esterel was still a perfect hideout for galley slaves escaping from the *bagne de Toulon*.

▶ *Return to the N 7.*

At the bend, there is a **view** on the right towards the limestone plateau of Inland Provence as it passes into the Fayence region; the road then follows the Moure Valley. The original Via Aurelia followed the line of the forest road on the opposite bank.

Fréjus★ ◔*See FRÉJUS p200.*

▶ *Return to St-Raphaël by blvd. S.-Decuers.*

③ PIC DE L'OURS★★
35.4mi/57km along steep, narrow roads that are not always surfaced. Allow one day.

▶ *From St-Raphaël take D 559 southeast. Leaving Agay, take the Valescure road and bear right towards Pic de l'Ours. Pass over the ford after the Maison Forestière du Gratadis, leave the*

Visiting the Massif

- Roads marked as "RF" on the map are open to traffic under certain conditions: speed limited to 25mph/40kph, no vehicles weighing over 3.5t and no traffic between 9pm and 6am. The roads marked with a red dotted line are closed to public traffic, but pedestrian access is possible.
- During periods of high fire risk, the ALARME plan is put into action and some roads may be closed to vehicles. Hikers are advised to avoid such areas.
- Camping is prohibited throughout the massif.
- When walking in the massif, respect plants and wild animals, do not litter the grounds, stay on the paths and keep dogs under control. Mountain bikers must not stray from the signposted paths and tracks laid out in the forests.
- For up-to-date information concerning the massif, call ℘04 98 10 55 41.

Pic de l'Ours

© Sylvain Sonnet/hemis.fr

Anthéor plateau on the right and take the route du Pic de l'Ours (Moutrefrey crossroads).

The road climbs to the summit past oaks, barren land and red rocks, with the Mal Infernet ravine in the distance. It winds around the northern peaks of St-Pilon and Cap-Roux to reach the Col de l'Évêque and then Col des Lentisques *(one-way traffic between the two passes: take the road to the east of the peak on the outward journey, and the interior road on the way back)*, with frequent glimpses of the sea to the right.

Pic d'Aurelle★★

🥾 *1hr round trip by a marked path starting from Col des Lentisques.*

The Aurelle is one of the major peaks in the Esterel coastal chain. From the top (1,060ft/323m) a fine **panorama**★★ takes in the area running from Cap d'Antibes to the Pointe de l'Observatoire. The stretch between Col des Lentisques and Col Notre-Dame is one of the most beautiful drives in the Esterel, with **bird's-eye views**★ of the Corniche de l'Esterel. From Col Notre-Dame (1,060ft/323m), a remarkable **panorama** extends over Cannes and La Napoule Bay.

Pic de l'Ours★★★

🥾 *1.5hr round trip.*
🅿 *Car park at Col Notre-Dame.*

The series of hairpin bends *(forbidden to private vehicles)* by which the path reaches the summit affords constantly changing **views** of the wooded ranges of the Esterel and coastline.
The remarkable **panorama**★★★ from the summit (1,627ft/496m), where there is a television transmitting station, includes the coast and the Var countryside.
Beyond Col Notre-Dame, the road to the Col des Trois-Termes is forbidden to vehicles, but it is possible to continue to the Col de la Cadière on foot, where the **view**★ opens to the north towards La Napoule and the Massif du Tanneron.

◗ *Return to St-Raphaël on D 559.*

④ ROUTE DU PERTHUS★

12.4mi/20km. Allow 3hr.
See map below.

◗ *Leave St-Raphaël by D 559 south, as far as the Maison Forestière de Gratadis, then turn left towards the Col de Belle-Barbe. Parking at the pass. Vehicles are forbidden beyond this point.*

Ravin du Mal Infernet★

🥾 *2hr round trip.*

Follow the footpath which leads into the wooded ravine of Mal Infernet, a majestic setting overlooked by many jagged rocks. The path goes as far as the Lac de l'Écureuil. It is possible to continue on

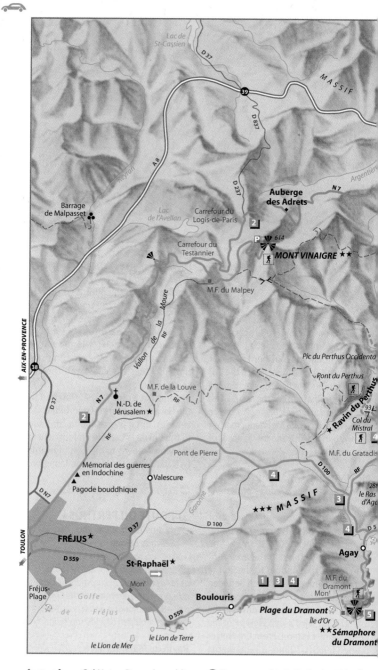

foot as far as Col Notre-Dame (an additional 1.8mi/3km) by skirting around the Pic and Dent de l'Ours to the north.

▶ *Return to col de Belle-Barbe. Take the road heading northwest. Leave the car in the col du Mistral car park and take the left-hand path.*

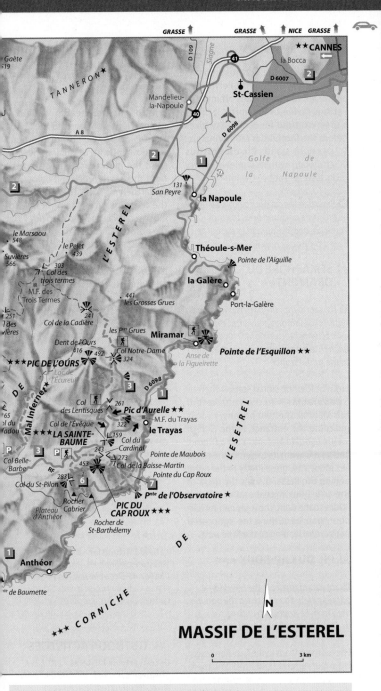

MASSIF DE L'ESTEREL

0   3 km

N

Hiking Map
The ONF (National Office of Forestry) has a trail guide and hiking map
available for sale at local tourist offices. *www.onf.fr*.

Ravin du Perthus ★

🚶 *1.5hr.*

The road skirts the Perthus summits to the south. At Pont du Perthus an unmarked footpath leads off into the Perthus ravine to the north. It offers a pretty setting for some easy hikes before the foothills of Mont Vinaigre. To the right stands **Pic du Perthus** (887ft/266m), with its scarlet porphyry rocks towering above the forest.

▶ *Return to the car park at Col du Mistral by the same path and head towards Valescure and St-Raphaël by the Col de Belle-Barbe on D 100 and D 37.*

⑤ SÉMAPHORE DU DRAMONT★★

🚶 *1hr round trip; the path is paved and signposted. Immediately after the Dramont campsite, turn right. 110yd/100m further, leave the car and take the path to the signal station.*

From below the signal station there is a **panorama**★★ to the southwest of the Maures, the two porphyry rocks guarding the entrance to the Gulf of Fréjus (*Lion de Mer* and *Lion de Terre*), and Île d'Or with its tower. To the north lies Mont Vinaigre; slightly to the right, behind the Rastel d'Agay, the rocks of the Cap-Roux massif and the Pic de l'Ours; to the right, the Agay natural harbour. Walk back along the signposted path (*right*) leading to the little port.

⑥ PIC DU CAP-ROUX ★★★

🚶 *2hr round trip from the Ste-Baume parking area. You can reach the parking area from St-Raphaël by taking tour ③ by D 559 and the forest road.*

The footpath leads to the Cap-Roux pass. From the summit (1,483ft/452m), there is a superb sweeping **panorama**★★★. If you continue straight on to the Col de l'Evêque, you can see as far as the Lérins Islands before continuing on to the refreshing **Sainte-Baume spring**.

⑦ LA SAINTE-BAUME★★★

🚶 *5.5hr round trip from the Ste-Baume parking area.*

This longer and steeper version of the previous walk leads to the Col du Saint-Pilon. As you progress through meadows of wild rosemary, the view from the high road unfolds: on the right the Cabrier rock and below, the St-Barthélemy rock. The path follows the coastline on a sloping trail leading to a railway line and road (*RN 98*) at the **pointe Maubois**. After the railway tunnel, continue to the Col de la Baisse-Martin and Col du Cardinal. Then it's all downhill. At the bottom is a delightful spring.

ADDRESSES

🏠 STAY

⊖⊜🛏 **France-Soleil** – *206 ave. Pléiades, Agay. ℘04 94 82 01 93. Closed Nov–Easter. 18 rooms.* 🅿. ⊑*10€.* This modest, family-run hotel has basic rooms spread out over three buildings, most overlooking the sea.

⊖⊜⊜🛏 **Miramar beach** – *47 ave. Miramar. ℘04 93 75 05 05. www.tiara-hotels.com. 55 rooms.* This charming hotel is nestled in a red rock cove. Refined Provençal-style rooms and Oriental spa. **Panoramic** restaurant with terrace service in summer.

🍴 EAT

⊖⊜🛏 **L'Arbousier** – *6 ave. de Valescure, St-Raphaël. ℘04 94 95 25 00. Closed mid-Dec–mid-Jan, Mon–Tue.* This restaurant in a house in the old town centre serves Mediterranean cuisine in a bright dining room or on the shaded terrace with wrought-iron furniture.

🏃 OUTDOOR ACTIVITIES

Découverte de l'Esterel – *281 r. du 11-Novembre-1943. ℘06 09 09 73 90. www.decouvertedelesterel.com.* Joseph works with the French forestry office to offer original tours of the Esterel forest in an open-top vehicle. Visits end with a tasting session of regional products. Advance reservation by phone advised.

Fayence

Var

Surrounded by perched villages, Fayence enjoys a privileged setting between the mountains and the sea. Potters, stone and wood carvers, weavers, painters and coppersmiths still ply their trade in its warren of sloping cobbled streets.

 **WALKING TOUR**

OLD TOWN

The town's steep streets play host to a 17C gateway, fountains and wash-houses, and the Porte Sarrasine, still crowned with machicolations. The **18C church** has a Classical interior and a Baroque high altar, the work of the Provençal marble mason Dominique Fossatti (1757). From the terrace to the right of the church, the **view** ★ extends beyond the hang-gliding field to the Maures and Esterel heights.

From the top of the hill, where the ancient château used to be, is a **view** of the Pre-Alps of Castellane and Grasse. On the upper reaches of town, **the Four du Mitan** (*r. du Four-du-Mitan;* ⊙*open high season 10.30am–7.30pm; low season: 10.30am–7pm;* ⊚*2€ with slide show, 15min*) is a 16C communal bakery that has been turned into a small **bread museum**. The nearby **Musée d'Histoire de Fayence** (*r. de la Ferrage;* ⊙*open Jul–Aug: 10am–noon, 4–7pm; Sep–Jun enquire for details;* ⊚*no*

- ▶ **Population:** 4,790.
- ⌖ **Michelin Map:** 340 P4.
- ▣ **Info:** Pl. Léon-Roux, Fayence. ℘04 94 76 20 08. www.ville-fayence.fr. Rue du Valat, Seillans. ℘04 94 76 85 91. www.seillans.fr
- ▷ **Location:** Fayence lies on the edge of the Provençal tableland in the Var, opposite its twin village, Tourrettes (⌖*see p224*), on the road from Draguignan to Grasse. Seillans is in the foothills of the Canjuers plain (⌖*see FAYENCE Driving Tours*).
- ▟ **Kids:** St-Cassien lake.
- ⊙ **Timing:** Allow half a day for each driving tour through the Fayence countryside.

charge; ℘ 06 73 87 01 70; http://une semaineenaout.blogspot.com) has a collection of military equipment dating from the Napoleonic Empire to the wars in Algeria and Indochina.

EXCURSION
Bagnols-en-Forêt

▷ *14km/8.7mi south by D 563 then D 4.*
Beyond the Pic de la Gardette, this charming hilltop village of sloping streets shaded by plane trees was abandoned in the 14C and repopulated in 1447, when a group of Italian immigrants from

View from Fayence

© webpicture/Fotolia.com

Liguria settled here and manufactured millstones for making oil *(examples are on display in the* **Musée Archéologique** *in the tourist office on place de la Mairie,* ℘ *04 94 40 64 68).* The town is a departure point for walks through the **forêt domaniale de Saint-Paul**★.

🚗 DRIVING TOURS

Col du Bel-Homme
56mi/91km. Allow about 4hr.
▷ *From Fayence take D 563 south. Immediately on the right, then on the left, the road plunges deep into the vineyards (signposted tour).*

Notre-Dame-des-Cyprès
1.8mi/3km from the village – chemin Notre-Dame-des-Cyprès. In a setting of tall cypress trees, this Romanesque chapel (12C) looks out over Fayence, Tourrettes and Montauroux.

▷ *At 4-Chemins head towards Callas.*

0.9mi/1.5km from Callas, take a small trail to the St-Auxile (7–12C) Romanesque church, which crowns a rocky promontory on a Gallo-Roman site. Fully restored in 1988..

Callas
Grouped round the castle ruins against a hillside, Callas is still a typical village of the Haut-Var with its 17C belfry, porches and dovecote. The Romanesque **church** displays a 17C altarpiece above nine hooded penitents.

▷ *Continue along D 25 over Col de Boussague.*

Bargemon
The narrow alleyways, ramparts and 12C gateways of this former stronghold nestled amid olive and orange trees are guarded by a stately seigniorial castle. The 15C **church** near the town gateway was incorporated into the town's fortifications, with a 17C square bell tower and a flamboyant **doorway**. The angel heads on the high alter are by Pierre

Puget. Note the 16C triptych portraying St Antoine, St Raphaël and St Honorat. The village is dominated by the spire of the **Chapelle Notre-Dame-de-Montaigu** containing a miraculous statue of the Virgin Mary.

Housed in the Chapelle St-Etienne, the **Musée-Galerie Honoré Camos** (🕐 *open Jun–Oct Wed–Sun 10am–12.30pm, 3.30–7pm, Mon 2–5pm; Dec–Apr Wed–Sun 10am–12.30pm, 2.30–6pm, Mon 2–5pm;* 🎟 *no charge;* ℘ *04 94 76 72 88)* explores the town's history, traditional activities and the work of the painter **Honoré Camos** (1906–91). At 8 rue de la Résistance the **Musée des fossiles et minéraux** *(8 r. de la Résistance;* 🕐 *open Jul–Aug Wed, Fri–Sat 3–6.30pm, Thu–Sun 10am–noon, 3–6.30pm; Sept–Jun Wed–Sun 2–5.30pm;* 🎟 *no charge;* ℘ *04 94 67 61 44)* features a collection of 3,000 artefacts from across the region. One of the three rooms is dedicated to ammonites.

▷ *Leave Bargemon and take D 25 west.*

The road rises sharply, offering **views** over Bargemon and its surroundings. This road was once used to transfer livestock to the fertile pastureland above the village.

Col du Bel-Homme★
A path on the left leads to the top *(alt. 3,210ft/951m).* From the viewing table a **panorama**★ extends south to the coast, northeast to Grasse, and north to the Canjuers plateau and the Castellane mountains. Canjuers is the largest military camp in Europe (87,000 acres/35,000 ha).

▷ *Return to Bargemon and take D 19 towards Fayence.*

After skirting the heights of Bargemon the road winds through forests of pine and holm oaks with the Maures and Esterel on the horizon.

Seillans
In the foothills of the Canjuers plain, the ivory and pink houses of Seillans cas-

cade down the slope of the Canjuers Plateau at an even steeper angle than the average perched village. Dadaist illustrator **Max Ernst** (1891–1976) chose to live here towards the end of his life. Quaint cobbled lanes lead up to the **church**, which was rebuilt in 1477 and incorporates 11C elements. The Romanesque **Chapelle Notre-Dame de l'Ormeau** *(1.2mi/2km southeast on the Fayence road – ℘ 04 94 76 85 91).* *Guided tours with commentary year round. Visit by reservation at Seillans tourist office)* is flanked by a bell tower of dressed stone. The interior contains a remarkable 16C **altarpiece**★★. In the centre, a crowd of people climb the tree of Jesse. To the left of the altarpiece is a fine low-relief sculpture of the Assumption (17C). To the left of the entrance is a Roman tombstone.

▶ *On leaving the village, turn left on D 53, then left again on D 563.*

Mons★
At an altitude of 2,625ft/800m.
🏠 *Pl. St-Sébastien.* ℘*04 94 76 39 54.*
This old village is perched between earth and sky on a wild and sunny mountain plateau flourishing with every single type of sub-Alpine Provençal plant. Mons was repopulated after several plagues in the Middle Ages by Genoan families, who rebuilt the village and cultivated the land with olives and wheat.

The Dada Master
Max Ernst settled in Seillans with his wife, the painter Dorothea Tanning, in 1964. A small **museum** *(Collection Max Ernst – Dorothea Tanning; open Jul–Aug Mon–Sat 2.30–6pm; Jun and Sept Tue–Sat 3–5.30pm; closed public holidays; ⊙2€; ℘04 94 50 45 54)* displays over 70 of his lithographs and engravings, remarkable for their sense of humour.

Place St-Sébastien
Offset by an 18C fountain, the square has a terrace (505ft/814m) that looks out over the Siagne and Siagnole Valleys and provides an exceptional **view**★★, which on a clear day extends from Le Coudon (north of Toulon) via the Lérins islands and to the Italian Alps *(viewing table).*

Church
Guided tours 2–6pm by request. Apply at the tourist office.
℘*04 94 76 39 54.*
The building, which was started in the Upper Provençal Romanesque style, was greatly altered in the 15C and 17C. It is fitted with unusually uniform furnishings: five Baroque altarpieces, including a huge triptych dating from 1680 on the high altar. To the right stands a beautiful

Terraced café in Mons

S. Sauvignier/ MICHELIN

15C silver processional cross. The bell in the belfry was cast in 1438.

Dolmens

There are 11 dolmens around Mons, three of which are listed historic monuments dating from the late Neolithic period. Only the **dolmen de Riens** with its ogival pillars is open to the public.

Walk to the dolmen by following rue Jean-Vadon across Mons. Take the D 56 for 98ft/30m on your right, then take the first road on the left to the chapelle St-Pierre. Continue for 230ft/70m and take the pathway on the left *(signposted)*. Return to the chapel road and climb towards Louquiers for views of the dolmen de la Colle (1.8mi/3km), then head for Escragnolles and the dolmen de la Brainée (4.3mi/7km).

◗ *Take D 56 towards St-Cézaire-sur-Siagne, then continue right along D 56*

Aqueduc de la Roche Taillée
Park on the embankment 218yd/200m beyond the site.

To supply Fréjus with drinking water, the Romans tapped into the Neissou source at the foot of the Mons headland and channelled it through a canal 8ft/2.5m wide, 164ft/50m long and 32ft/10m deep. A section of the canal is still in service today.

◗ *Return along D 56, then straight ahead on D 656 towards St-Cézaire-sur-Siagne, then right on D 96 towards Montauroux.*

The road overlooks the wooded **Siagne gorge** and the village of St-Cézaire-sur-Siagne, scattered along its deep green ridges.

◗ *Turn left onto D 37, then right onto D 56.*

Callian

The ancient streets of this village spiral towards a castle. **Views** from the main square look southwest over the Lac de St-Cassien beneath the Tanneron heights. French designer Christian Dior and Nadia, wife of Fernand Léger, are buried in the local cemetery.

◗ *Continue along D 56, then turn right on D 256, right at the D 562 roundabout, then right on D19 to Fayence.*

Around the Lac de St-Cassien
18mi/29km. Allow about 2hr.
Leave Fayence on the Tourettes road heading SE.

Tourrettes
0.8mi/1.3km east by D 563.

This quiet village affords **views** of the Maures and Esterel massifs from **place de l'Horloge**. The **castle** (*closed to the public*), modelled on the St Petersburg Cadet School, was built in 1830.

◗ *Continue on D 19, then take D 562 and D 56 towards Callian.*

Callian
See Caillan.

◗ *To the east of the village, take D 37 to Montauroux.*

Montauroux
13mi/21km east by D 19.

This pretty village, known for its 13 fountains and 16C and 17C houses *(r. Eugène-Segond)*, was once home to the French designer **Christian Dior**. He paid for the restoration of the **Chapelle St-Barthélemy**, built in the 17C by the Pénitents Blancs.

Les Bambous du Mandarin
Pont de Siagne – 04 93 66 12 94 - *Open Easter–Nov Sat and first Sun of month 8am–6pm. Guided tour (1hr) 10.30am, 3pm, 4.30pm. 5€ (+7yrs 2.50€).* Explore more than 80 varieties of bamboo in lush green surroundings.

◗ *Take D 37, and cross D 562 towards Lac de St-Cassien.*

Lac de St-Cassien

The Montauroux tourist office orga-
nises walks led by nature guides.
This scenic lake nestled at the foot of the
Tanneron (*see Massif du TANNERON*
p243) was filled with water in 1965
following the destruction of the Malpasset dam (*see Fréjus*). It is fringed
by wooded shores and a network
of walking trails. The **pont de Pré-
Claou** affords **views** of the entire lake
(2.1 billion cu ft/60 million cubic m)
and is used for various sporting activities (swimming, canoeing and pedal
boats). It is the largest stretch of water
(430 ha/1,062 acres) on the Esterel. To
the west, a reedy marsh is home to
150 species of migratory waterfowl in
the Fondurane nature reserve.

ADDRESSES

STAY

Auberge des Pins – *Domaine*
Le Chevalier, Tourrettes. 1mi/2km
south on D 19. ℘*04 94 76 06 36.*
www.aubergedespins.com. Surrounded
by an estate offering a range of leisure
facilities, this inn's modern rooms and
studios are housed in three pavilions.
Local cuisine and grilled meats
(evenings only).

Combes Longues – *Les Hautes*
Combes Longues. 2.4mi/4km north by
D 53, rte de Mons and road on right.
℘*04 94 47 65 27. www.combeslongues.*
com. 3 rooms. Restaurant (   ).
A peaceful 18C stone farm hidden
amid woodland. Ask for a room in the
converted stables with valley **views**.
The restaurant serves homely fare made
with organic produce.

Les Deux Rocs – *pl. Font-*
d'Amont, Seillans. ℘*04 94 76 87 32.*
www.hoteldeuxrocs.com. Closed Jan–Feb.
14 rooms. � *13€. Restaurant   .*
Imposing inn housed in an old village
building. The original staircase leads
to rooms appointed with antique
furniture. Enjoy your meal by the
fireplace or on the summer terrace.

Moulin de la Camandoule –
1mi/2km west of Fayence by D 19
route de Seillans and a country lane.
℘*04 94 76 00 84. www.camandoule.*
com. Closed Thu (except eve. in high
season), Wed. 12 rooms. P ⊡*12€.*
Restaurant   . An old olive mill at
the foot of the village converted into
a quaint Provençal hotel decorated in
warm, southern colours. The grounds
are home to a pool, a Gallo-Roman
aqueduct and a terrace.

EAT

Au Bec Fin Chez Alain – *Pl. de*
l'Église, St-Paul-en-Forêt. ℘*04 94 76*
30 71. Closed Mon and Wed. Both the
décor and menu are heavily influenced
by the colours of Provence. Rabbit
stew, fresh vegetables and homemade
desserts top the list.

La Farigoulette – *pl. du*
Château, Fayence. ℘*04 94 84 10 49.*
www.la-farigoulette.com. Closed Tue and
Wed. This former sheepfold offers the
perfect rustic setting (exposed beams
and stone walls, farmhouse furniture)
to enjoy traditional cuisine with a
modern twist.

Le Temp des Cerises –
Pl. République. ℘*04 94 76 01 19. Closed*
Tue, lunch Mon–Sat, 1–27 Dec. A typical
Fayence restaurant serving regional
specialities in an ochre-and-red dining
room or on the shady terrace.

SHOPPING

LOCAL MARKETS

Fayence – Pl. de l'Église, Tue,
Thu and Sat.

Bargemon – Pl. St-Étienne, Thu.

Callas – Sat mornings.

Mons – Pottery market the first
weekend in August.

SPORT AND LEISURE

**Aviron St-Cassien-Club
Intercommunal du Pays de Fayence** –
In Biançon, by D 37. Montauroux.
℘*04 94 39 88 64. www.avironstcassien.*
com. Closed Sat–Sun, Aug. Introductory
rowing courses on the lake.

CANNES & THE GRASSE REGION

For centuries, Cannes and the Grasse region have been enchanting visitors from around the world. Encompassing the legendary perfume-making town of Grasse and its surrounding perched villages, Grasse includes three of the most dynamic resort towns in France. Travellers can enjoy the quiet Provençal atmosphere of the Îles de Lérins and inland villages like Biot and Gordon, or take advantage of the lively nightlife and window shopping in Cannes, Juan-les-Pins or Antibes. This is where prestigious museums and chic art galleries easily coexist with ancient fortified ramparts and centuries-old ruins. The proximity to Nice International Airport, easy access to major coastal and inland routes, and regional train services also make this an ideal base from which to explore the rest of the French Riviera.

Highlights

1 Visit the newly restored Musée Picasso in **Antibes** (p273)

2 See **panoramic views** from the **Baou de St-Jeannet** (p291)

3 Rent a *chaise-longue* on one of the private beaches in **Cagnes-sur-Mer** (p292)

4 Watch the sunset from the fortified ramparts in **St Paul de Vence** (p284)

5 Dine in the monks seaside restaurant on **Île St-Honorat** (p240)

Lively Year Round

While many people think of the French Riviera first and foremost as a summer vacation destination, Cannes and the Grasse region are bustling throughout the year. A large population of "locals" work in its various technology parks, in the greenhouses producing the region's flowers and fruits, on the superyachts requiring constant upkeep, and in the conferences centres that attract international visitors. Cannes, Antibes, Villeneuve-Loubet and Grasse are the liveliest towns, with most hotels and restaurants remaining open year-round.

Illustrious Cultural History

Almost every town in this part of the French Riviera has attracted a loyal following of artists, writers and musicians. Antibes was home to the writer Nikos Kazantzakis, the cartoonist Peynet and Picasso during one of his more prolific periods. Renoir lived in Cagnes-sur-Mer until his death, Fernand Léger left his mark forever on the tiny village of Biot, while Modigliani and Soutine made St-Paul-de-Vence a trendy place for artists. Many of these towns have

Boulevard de la Croisette, Cannes

Musée Picasso, Antibes

©Nicolas Thibaut/Photononstop/Tips Images

museums dedicated to their artists. Juan-les-Pins, on the other hand, holds an event – the Jazz Festival – to commemorate the great jazz artists who once lived there, such as Cole Porter and Sydney Bechet. Today the stars of the silver screen continue to visit the region during the Cannes Film Festival, making their temporary homes in the luxury hotels on the Croisette and the Cap d'Antibes.

Military Reminders

The forts in Antibes and on the Île Ste-Marguerite are no longer active military sites, although the greatest French general of them all, Napoleon Bonaparte, has left an indelible mark on the region with the Route Napoléon, which traces his triumphant journey from Juan-les-Pins to Grenoble following his escape from the island of Elba. Museums throughout the region attest to the military importance of this coastline throughout the centuries, from Greek and Roman times through to the Middle Ages and the 17C, when Antibes still protected the eastern border of France. The only invasion today comes in the form of summer sun-seekers.

Nautical Fans

Visitors with a nautical interest will find their heart's delight in the ports of Cannes and Antibes, where sleek private superyachts as big as cruise ships line up at the quays alongside more humble fishing boats and stunning sailing yachts. Water sport enthusiasts can pay homage to the man who invented water-skiing in Juan-les-Pins, while divers can head to Antibes to discover more about France's greatest marine explorer, Jacques Cousteau.

Sailing events take place throughout the year; the local museums provide a detailed history of every aspect of shipping, sailing and boating on the Mediterranean back to Roman times.

Natural Wonders

This part of the Riviera has no shortage of natural beauty and sights of interest to nature lovers, including the stalactites of the Baume Obscure and the observatory in Saint-Vallier-de-Thiey, where you can spend an evening gazing at the stars.

Alternatively, hop along to Marineland to admire the sharks and performing dolphins, discover rare plants in the botanical gardens of Antibes or cool off in the waterfalls at the Gorges du Loup. Hiking trails offer stunning cliff **views** around Gourdon and an opportunity for peaceful contemplation on the Îles des Lérins.

Tourist offices in the region can provide special maps for those interested in the local flora and fauna.

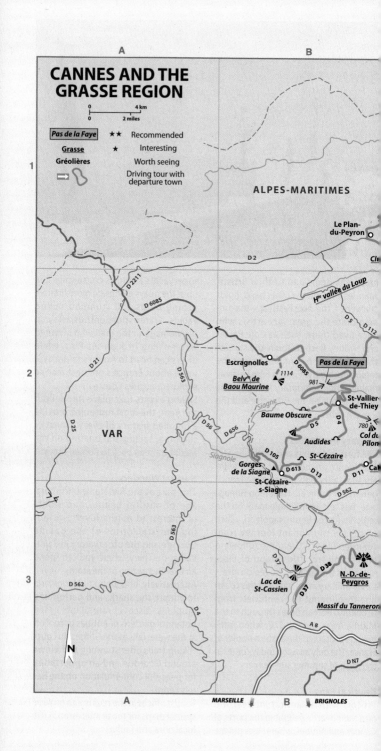

CANNES AND THE GRASSE REGION

0   4 km
0   2 miles

Pas de la Faye   ★★   Recommended

Grasse   ★   Interesting

Gréolières   Worth seeing

⟶   Driving tour with departure town

ALPES-MARITIMES

Le Plan-du-Peyron

Cle

D 2

Hᵗᵉ vallée du Loup

D 2211

D 6085

D 5

D 112

Escragnolles

Belvᵉ de Baou Maurine   1114

Pas de la Faye

981

St-Vallier-de-Thiey

Siagne

Baume Obscure

D 5

D 4

780

Col du Pilon

Audides

Ca

D 21

D 563

D 56

D 656

D 105

St-Cézaire

D 13

D 11

VAR

D 25

Siagnole

Gorges de la Siagne

D 613

St-Cézaire-s-Siagne

D 562

D 563

D 37

D 38

N.-D.-de-Peygros

Lac de St-Cassien

D 37

Massif du Tanneron

D 562

D 4

A 8

N

D N7

MARSEILLE   B   BRIGNOLES

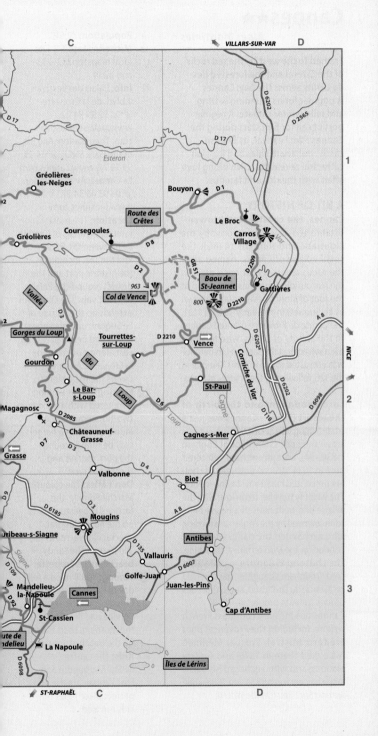

D 17

D 6202   D 2565

Esteron   D 17

1

Gréolières-
les-Neiges

Bouyon   D 1

Le Broc   Route des
Crêtes

Coursegoules   †   Carros
Village

Gréolières   D 8

Vallée   D 2   Baou de
St-Jeannet   GR 51

Gorges du Loup   963   Col de Vence   Gattières   †

800   D 2210

Gourdon   du   Tourrettes-
sur-Loup   D 2210   Vence   Corniche du Var

2

Le Bar-
s-Loup   Loup   St-Paul

Magagnosc   †   D 6   Cagnes-s-Mer   D 6098

D 2085

Châteauneuf-
Grasse   D 7   D 3

Grasse   D 9   Valbonne   D 4   Biot

D 6185   D 3   A 8

Mougins

uribeau-s-Siagne   D 135   Antibes

Siagne   Vallauris   D 6007

D 109   Golfe-Juan   Juan-les-Pins

Mandelieu-
la-Napoule   D 92   Cannes   3

St-Cassien   Cap d'Antibes

ute de
ndelieu   La Napoule

D 6098   Îles de Lérins

Cannes★★
Alpes Maritimes

Framed to the west by the red rocks of the Esterel and the forested Îles de Lérins across the bay, Cannes is popular for its stunning setting and mild winter climate. A regular port of call for film stars during the Cannes Film Festival, its English castle, Italianate villas and Russian cathedral reveal the town's long love affair with the rich and famous.

A BIT OF HISTORY

Cannes, the coastal watchtower – Established as a trading post by the Ligurians and Romans (42BC), the small village of Canoïs, named after the reeds (cannes) that once grew in the surrounding marshes, sprang up at the foot of Mont Chevalier (also known as Le Suquet) in the early 10C. In 1131, the Comte de Provence granted Cannes to the abbots of Lérins, who fortified the town against the Saracens. Its defence was entrusted to the Knights Templar in the 12C, followed by the Knights of Malta.

Lord Brougham and the birth of the resort (1834) – Cannes was just a small fishing village of 4,000 inhabitants when the Lord Chancellor of England (1830–34), Lord Brougham, wintered here in 1834 after an outbreak of cholera prevented him from staying in Nice. The wealthy traveller fell in love with the village and built himself a house here, soon followed by the English aristocracy, who exchanged the damp winters of London for the Mediterranean sunshine. The **château Eléonore**, named after Lord Brougham's daughter, has survived on avenue du Dr-Picaud, at the Croix des Gardes (private property).

Cannes has inspired countless French writers, including the Provençal poet **Frédéric Mistral**, Prosper Mérimée (who died there in 1870) and Guy de Maupassant, who anchored his yacht in the bay between 1884 and 1888 while writing Sur l'Eau (On the Water).

▶ **Population:** 70,610.

Michelin Map: 341 D6; local maps: pp232–233 and p234

Info: Palais des Festivals, 1 blvd. de la Croisette. ℰ04 92 99 84 22. www.palaisdesfestivals. com. Train station: Ailé Est of the Gare SNCF: ℰ04 93 99 19 77. www.cannes.com. Le Cannet: Av. du Campon. ℰ04 93 45 34 27. www.lecannet.com.

Location: The most interesting areas of Cannes lie between the RN 7 and the sea, including the historic port and the district around the Palais des Festivals. The Old Town extends up the hillside of Le Suquet; upscale shops, hotels and beaches extend east along boulevard de la Croisette. A tourist train covers the main sights.

Parking: Street parking is metered with a maximum two-hour limit. Large indoor car parks (charge) may be found around the port, market and the train station.

Don't Miss: The colourful Marché Forville, the fortified monastery ruins on the Île St-Honorat, spectacular yachts in the Old Port, or the sandy beaches of La Croisette.

Timing: You'll need a full day to enjoy the sights of Cannes. Visit the Marché Forville and Îles de Lérins in the morning, then shop or hit the beach afterwards.

Kids: The car-free Île Ste-Marguerite and Fort Vauban are the perfect place to let the kids run free.

Cannes Festivals – Cannes hosts several world famous festivals. **The International Film Festival** (*see p237*) is one of the highlights of the Riviera's artistic calendar. Other popular events include prestigious regattas, the International Record and Music Market (MIDEM) and the World Entertainment Content Market (MIPCOM).

WALKING TOUR

1 EXPLORING CANNES: SEAFRONT★

Follow the route marked on map pp232–233. Allow 2hr.

Boulevard de la Croisette★

This elegant seaside promenade bordered by palms and gardens is popular with winter strollers. Luxury hotels and chic boutiques line the sea front and side streets as far as rue d'Antibes. At the top end of La Croisette, east of the port, stands the ultramodern **Palais des Festivals et des Congrès** and casino. Known as "The Bunker", the building comprises a 2,300-seater auditorium, theatre, broadcasting studios and the tourist office.

Between the conference centre and the gardens lies the **Allée des Stars**, an avenue of 200 slabs bearing handprints of movie stars who have attended the Film Festival. Further east on the opposite side of the road, beyond the Majestic Hotel, stands a private 19C mansion, **La Malmaison** (*open Jul–Sept Tue–Sun 11am–8pm (until 10pm Fri); Oct–Mar 10am–1pm, 2–6pm, closed public holidays; 3.40€; 04 97 06 44 90; www.cannes.com*). Once part of the Grand Hotel, it now houses the municipal culture department and art exhibitions. Nearby the Noga-Hilton hotel incorporates the façade of the former Palais des Festivals, pulled down in 1988 after serving as the venue for the Cannes Film Festival for 40 years. Further on is the Belle Epoch Carlton Hotel, the Art Deco Martinez Hotel and the modern Port-Canto.

▷ *Proceed east along blvd. de la Croisette to pointe de la Croisette.*

PRACTICAL INFORMATION
TOURS AND TRANSPORT
Bus – *Gare routière, pl. de l'Hôtel-de-Ville. 04 93 39 11 39. www.rca.tm.fr.*
TAM buses operate between Cannes and Nice, with direct airport service.
Train Station – *SNCF Gare de Cannes. 0 892 35 35 35. www.ter-sncf.com/paca.* This train station is served by SNCF trains, the TGV and the local TER trains (service between Mandelieu-La-Napoule and Vintimille).
Trans Côte d'Azur – *3 quai des Îles 04 92 98 71 30. Closed Nov–Jan. 11€ (5.50€ children). www.trans-cote-azur.com.* Regular service to the Île Ste-Marguerite (15min), plus seasonal tours to l'Île de Porquerolles, Monaco, St-Tropez, etc.

Pointe de la Croisette★

This point owes its name to a small cross, which used to stand here. It offers splendid **views** of Cannes, the Îles de Lérins and the Esterel. Modern tourist developments include artificial beaches and the Palm Beach Casino complex, built in 1929. Beyond Palm Beach is a splendid **view**★ of Golfe-Juan and Cap d'Antibes.

▷ *Follow the avenue Maréchal-Juin and rue d'Antibes back into town.*

2 OLD CANNES AND THE PORT

Follow the route marked on map pp232–233. Allow 1.5hr.

The Harbour

Between the Palais des Festivals and Le Suquet lies the Old Port, teeming with fishing boats and luxury yachts.
The west side of the harbour is lined with shops and restaurants. The embarkation point for trips to the Îles de Lérins (*see pp238–40*) lies to the southwest.

Allées de la Liberté

Beneath the plane trees, overlooking the port, is a large square featuring a statue of Lord Brougham, where an early morning flower market gives way to *pétanque* matches in the afternoon.

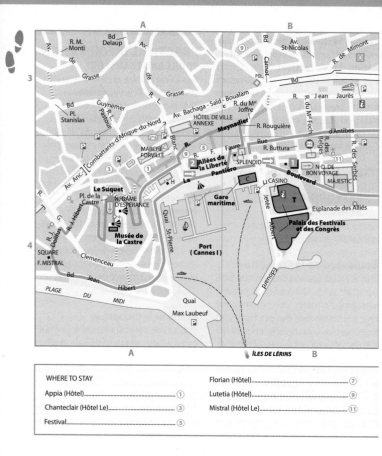

◐ *Take rue Félix-Faure and rue Rouguière to rue Meynadier.*

Rue Meynadier

Formerly the main street linking the new town to Le Suquet, rue Meynadier is bordered by a variety of local specialty shops and some fine 18C doorways.

◐ *Head for Le Suquet via rue Louis-Blanc, rue Félix-Faure and rue Mont-Chevalier.*

Le Suquet

The old town is built on the site of the former Canoïs *castrum* or "citadel" on the slopes of Mont Chevalier. Rue Perrissol leads to Place de la Castre surrounded by a defensive wall and dominated by **Notre-Dame-d'Espérance**, built in the 16–17C in Provençal Gothic style. The old bell tower leads to a long tree-lined terrace, offering a fine **view** of the town, port and Île Ste-Marguerite.

BELLE ÉPOQUE CANNES★

Discover 19C Cannes and its aristocratic past on this tour of the town's luxurious villas and gardens.

Quartier de la Croix des Gardes

To the west of Cannes, this hill offers a wonderful **panorama** over the bay, both day and night. Begin your tour at the early 20C **château de la Croix des Gardes**, which has an interesting Florentine façade. Continue towards Lord Brougham's villa (**Château Eleonore**) and its neighbour, the **villa Marie-Thérèse**, at no 2 av. J.-de-Noailles. Once the residence of the dowager baroness de Rothschild and now home to the town's media library, it is set in pleas-

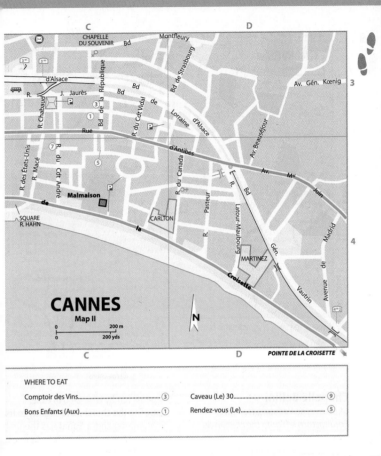

CANNES
Map II

0 ——— 200 m
0 ——— 200 yds

N

POINTE DE LA CROISETTE

WHERE TO EAT

Comptoir des Vins............③	Caveau (Le) 30............⑨
Bons Enfants (Aux)............①	Rendez-vous (Le)............⑤

ant parkland. The **palais Vallombrosa** and its park and the **villa Victoria**, once belonging to Victorian property developer and botany enthusiast Sir Thomas Robinson Woolfield, continue this prestigious promenade.

Quartier de la Californie

To the east of the town lie several residences that have marked the history of Cannes: on avenue du Roi-Albert-Iᵉʳ, the **villa Kazbeck** was the scene of sumptuous parties given by the Russian Grand Duke Mikhail Mikhaïlovitch; the **villa Champfleuri** remains famous for its exotic gardens (which form the backdrop for the film *Gambling Hell* by J. Delannoy). *The Mystery of the Yellow Room* (1930) by Marcel L'Herbier was shot in the **château Scott**, a Flamboyant Neo-Gothic pile on avenue du Mar.-Juin.

SIGHTS
Musée de la Castre★★

Le Suquet. ⏱*Open Tue–Sun Apr–Jun and Sept 10am–1pm, 2–6pm; Jul–Aug 10am–7pm; Oct–Mar 10am–1pm, 2–5pm.* ⛔*Closed public holidays.* 🎟*6€, free the first Sun of the month Nov–Mar.* ☎*04 93 38 55 26. www.cannes.com.*
This 11C castle, built by the Lérins monks to watch over the harbour, houses substantial archaeological and ethnographic collections, mainly from the Mediterranean Basin. The small Cistercian Chapelle Ste-Anne at the entrance has a collection of musical instruments from around the world. Room 4 looks out onto the 12C square watchtower (72ft/22m), **Tour du Suquet**. There's a panoramic **view**★ of La Croisette, Îles de Lérins and the Esterel hills from the top floor.

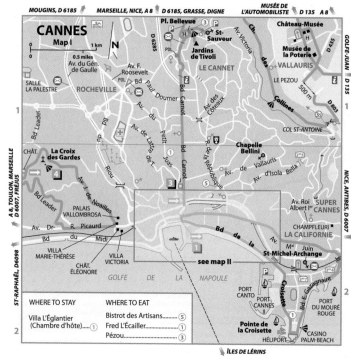

CANNES
Map I

WHERE TO STAY	WHERE TO EAT
Villa L'Églantier (Chambre d'hôte).....①	Bistrot des Artisans............⑤
	Fred L'Écailler..................①
	Pézou............................③

Chapelle Bellini

61 bis ave. de Vallauris; from ave. Poralto, turn left onto the chemin du Parc-Fiorentina. ♿ ⊙*Open Mon–Fri 2–5pm, Sat–Sun by request.* ⊙*No charge.* ☎*04 93 38 61 80.*

Once part of a sumptuous Tuscan palace, the "Villa Fiorentina", this chapel was built in elaborate Baroque style in the late 19C for a Balkan noble family. The interior is decorated with works by Cannes painter Bellini (1904–89).

Église Orthodoxe St-Michel-Archange

40 blvd. Alexandre-III.

Since Empress Maria Alexandrovna, wife of Tsar Alexander III, had taken to spending the winter months in Cannes, it was necessary to build a church large enough to accommodate her court. Inaugurated in 1894, its richly ornamented interior contains remarkable icons and banners from the Russian imperial family.

The crypt (⊶*closed to the public*) contains the bodies of members of the imperial family who died in exile. Opposite the church, and slightly to its right, in Alexandra Square, is the first Russian Orthodox church in Cannes, **Chapelle Tripet-Skryptine**.

Villa Domergue

Impasse Fiesole, 15 ave. Fiesole. ⊙*Open Jul–Sep Tue–Sat 3–7pm.* ⊙6€. ☎*04 97 06 44 90. 40min walk from town centre.* Designed and decorated by the painter Jean-Gabriel Domergue in 1934, this sumptuous Italian-style villa is surrounded by gardens laid out by the sculptor Odette Domergue.

③ LE CANNET

♿*See map of Cannes above.*
▶*Leave Cannes by blvd. Carnot.*

Sheltered from the wind by a circle of wooded hills, Le Cannet, at an altitude of 361ft/110m, offers breathtaking **views**. The artist **Pierre Bonnard** (1867–1947) spent the last years of his life painting views of Le Cannet from the Villa Le Bosquet (avenue Victoria).

Le Vieux Cannet

The old town is reached by rue St-Sauveur, lined with 18C houses and pleasant shady squares. At no 19 is a mural by the artist Peynet representing *Les Amoureux (The Lovers)*. Further on the left is the little 15C **Chapelle St-Sauveur** *(108 rue St-Sauveur)* housing mosaics and stained-glass windows by the artist **Théo Tobiasse** (b. 1927).

Place Bellevue offers a superb **view** of Cannes and the Îles de Lérins. The old **Calvys Tower** (12C) still stands nearby, as well as the taller **Danys Tower** (14C). Both have fine façades topped with machicolations. The Jardins de Tivoli can be reached from the Hôtel de Ville via the pedestrian rue Cavasse, passing luxurious 1900 villas.

Chemin des Collines★

This road along the flanks of the hills above Cannes offers fine **views** over La Napoule bay and the Îles de Lérins.

▶ *Continue east to Col St-Antoine.*

On the left in avenue Victoria sits the **Villa Yakimour** *(⊶ private property)*, an Oriental residence given by the Aga Khan to his wife Yvette Labrousse.

▶ *Continue to Vallauris over Col de St-Antoine, then left onto D 803.*

Vallauris *See VALLAURIS p265.*

Golfe-Juan★ *1mi/2km southeast of Vallauris by D 135 (see GOLFE-JUAN p266).*

On returning towards Cannes on D 6007, the road skirts the hills of Super-Cannes revealing the Îles de Lérins and the red Massif de l'Esterel on the horizon; the **view**★ is at its best at sunset.

▶ *Return to Cannes along the seafront.*

③ LA CROIX DES GARDES★

15min round trip, 5mi/8km (steep climb).

▶ *Leave Cannes on ave. du Dr Picaud. Turn right on blvd. Leader. 110yd/100m beyond the entrance to the Pavillon de la Croix des Gardes, turn right onto ave. J-de-Noailles and continue 110yd/100m.*

🚶 Take the footpath to the top of the hill (alt 538ft/164m) and a strategically-placed 39ft/12m-high cross, which gave the area its name in the 16C. From the foot of the cross there is a marvellous **panorama**★ over Cannes, the Îles de Lérins and the Esterel.

▶ *Continue along avenue J.-de-Noailles to return to Cannes.*

Îles de Lérins★★

See Îles de LÉRINS p238.
Allow half a day's walk.

Lunch at Le Cannet

© Sylvaine Poitau/Apa Publications

ADDRESSES

🛏 STAY

🍴 **Le Chanteclair** – *12 rue Forville.* 📞*04 93 39 68 88. Closed mid-Nov–late Jan. 15 rooms.* 🚭 ⌑*6€.* This friendly hotel offers a selection of variously priced rooms depending on the level of comfort. Breakfast is served in a pleasant inner courtyard.

🍴 **Hôtel Lutetia** – *6 rue Michel-Ange.* 📞*04 93 39 35 74. www.hotel-lutetia-cannes.com. 8 rooms.* ⌑*6€.* A simple and comfortable hotel on a quiet side street, with air-conditioning and Provençal decor close to the train station.

🍴 **Hôtel Florian** – *8 rue du Cdt André.* 📞*04 93 39 24 82. www.hotel-leflorian.com. 20 rooms.* ⌑*6€.* A family-run hotel between the train station and the Palais des Festivals, on a semi-pedestrian street in the old town.

🍴 **Hôtel National** – *9 rue du Maréchal-Joffre.* 📞*04 93 39 91 92. 17 rooms.* ⌑*8€.* The main advantage of this hotel is its location near the Palais des Festivals and the sea. The white-and-grey air-conditioned rooms with tiled bathrooms are on the small side, but clean and carefully maintained.

🍴 **Hôtel Appia** – *6 rue Marceau.* 📞*04 93 06 59 59. www.appia-hotel.com. Closed mid-Nov–late Dec. 31 rooms.* ⌑*7.50€.* Practicality takes precedence over comfort in this downtown hotel, where the well-kept, small rooms are air-conditioned and double-glazed.

🍴 **Chambre d'hôte Villa L'Églantier** – *14 rue Campestra.* 📞*04 93 68 22 43. www.maison-eglantier.com. 3 rooms.* 🚭 ⌑. Impressive white villa dating from 1920, surrounded by palm trees and other exotic species. The large, peaceful rooms are extended by a terrace or a balcony.

🍴 **Hôtel Festival** – *3 rue Molière.* 📞*04 97 06 64 40. www.hotel-festival.com. 14 rooms.* ⌑*8.50€.* Recently renovated family-run hotel within walking distance of the Croisette and the rue d'Antibes shopping area. Rooms have air-con, soundproofing and WiFi, marble bathrooms and minibar. Jacuzzi and sauna available for guests.

🍴 **Hôtel Le Mistral** – *13 rue des Belges.* 📞*04 93 39 91 46. www.mistral-hotel.com. Closed mid-Nov–late Dec. 10 rooms.* ⌑*8€.* A new boutique hotel with modern decor, just behind the Palais des Festivals. Rooms have air-conditioning, WiFi and a safe.

🍽 EAT

🍴 **Aux Bons Enfants** – *80 rue Meynadier.* 📞*No phone.* 🚭 *Closed Aug, Sat eve off-season, Sun.* An old-fashioned cantina near the Forville market serving ratatouille, grilled anchovies, aïoli, stuffed sardines, etc. Wine by the pitcher and a friendly family atmosphere.

🍴 **Le Caveau 30** – *45 rue F.-Faure.* 📞*04 93 39 06 33. www.lecaveau30.com.* Large restaurant comprising two dining rooms decorated in the style of a 1930s brasserie. The terrace overlooks a shaded square. Fish and seafood are house specialities.

🍴 **Le Comptoir des Vins** – *13 blvd. de la République.* 📞*04 93 68 13 26. Closed Tue eves, Sat lunch, Sun–Mon.* This handsomely stocked wine boutique leads to a colourful dining area, where light snacks can be served with a glass of wine.

🍴 **Le Rendez-Vous** – *35 rue F.-Faure.* 📞*04 93 68 55 10.* A chic bistro with an Art Deco-style ceiling, serving fish, seafood and other Mediterranean-flavoured dishes.

🍴 **Fred L'Écailler** – *7 pl. de l'Étang.* 📞*04 93 43 15 85. www.fredlecailler.com.* A large neon sign marks the entrance to this rustic-style restaurant, the walls of which are draped with fishing nets. Fine selection of freshly-caught fish and seafood.

🍴 **Pézou** – *346 r. St-Sauveur* 📞*04 93 69 32 50. www.lepezou.fr. Closed late Jun, Nov, Mon lunch in Jul–Aug, Sun eve Sept–Jun.* Far from the hustle and bustle of the Croisette, this pleasant restaurant situated on a small square has a summer terrace. Provençal cuisine.

🍴 **Bistrot des Artisans** – *67 blvd. de la République.* 📞*04 93 68 33 88.* Enjoying a surprising decor of vintage craft tools, helmets, naïve-style mural frescoes and basic furniture, this restaurant serves generous portions of lovingly prepared Mediterranean food.

🛒 SHOPPING

Marché de Forville – *closed Mon in low season*. Stalls displaying fresh regional produce.

Shopping streets – *rue Meynadier*: tempting window displays of food and craftwork in a lively pedestrian area. Rue d'Antibes: luxury clothes and luggage.

Cannolive – *16 rue Vénizelos*. ℘*04 93 39 08 19. Closed Sun, two weeks in Dec.* This shop boasts an incredible choice of Provençal products to take back home: household linen, tapenade, crockery, santons, soap and even Lérina liqueur from the nearby islands.

La Boutique du Festival – *blvd. de la Croisette*. ℘*09 61 56 56 82. www.festival-cannes.fr.* 🕒*Open daily 9am–7pm (Jul–Aug 8pm).* Located on the ground floor of the tourist office in the Palais des Festivals, this store is a paradise for movie buffs.

🍸 NIGHTLIFE

Palais des Festivals et des Congrès – *Espl. Georges-Pompidou, blvd. de la Croisette*. ℘*04 93 39 01 01. www.palaisdesfestivals.com.* Opened in 1982, the palais includes the Grand Auditorium (seating 2,300) and the Théâtre Debussy (seating 1,000).

L'Amiral – *73 blvd. de la Croisette.* ℘*04 92 98 73 00. www.hotel-martinez. com.* Attached to the Martinez Hotel, this bar is by far the most popular meeting place along the coast. It owes its reputation to the head barman and Jimmy, the American pianist (every evening from 8pm).

Le Bâoli – *Port Pierre Canto, blvd. de la Croisette.* ℘*04 93 43 03 43. www.lebaoli.com. Closed Sun–Tue, Mon–Fri off-season.* The hottest night spot in Cannes with beachfront **views** over the bay, this bar-restaurant-nightclub with an exotic decor can host up to 1,500 jetsetting partygoers in high season.

Pavillon Croisette – Havana Room – *42 blvd. de la Croisette.* ℘*04 92 59 06 90.* 🕒*Open daily noon–3pm, 7–10.30pm (summer 11pm). Closed Nov–Feb.* Worthy of the best London private members clubs, this bar offers a seemingly infinite drinks list.

🚴 LEISURE ACTIVITIES

For sailing, deep-sea diving or water-skiing, contact the tourist office or visit www.station-nautique.com.

Beaches – Not all the beaches on La Croisette charge a fee (details of prices are listed at the top of the steps), or belong to a hotel (located opposite). There are also three free beaches, one of which is located behind the Palais des Festivals. The other public beaches lie west of the old port, on boulevard Jean-Hibert and boulevard du Midi, at Port Canto and on boulevard Gazagnaire beyond La Pointe.

Ponton Majestic Ski Nautique – *blvd. de la Croisette.* ℘*04 92 98 77 47. Closed Nov–Mar.* Water-skiing or parascending for the adventurous.

Air Odyssey – *Aéroport de Cannes-Mandelieu. Reservations:* ℘*06 09 56 06 54. www.air-odyssey.com. Departures hourly from 9am. 155 €/person. 45min.* The company organises flights with a commentary offering **panoramic views** above the Riviera over 80mi/130km at 1,300ft/400m altitude. The "Sea and volcanoes" tour takes you over Cannes Bay and the Massif de l'Esterel in a tourist aircraft.

CALENDAR OF EVENTS

Cannes Film Festival – 🔖*see p231.* Ten days in May; free open-air cinema retrospectives on the beach (official screenings open to accredited professionals only). *www.festival-cannes.org.*

Nuits Musicales du Suquet – End of July; classical concerts on the esplanade in front of the Église du Suquet. ℘*04 92 99 33 83.*

Îles de Lérins★★
Alpes Maritimes

Surprisingly peaceful despite their proximity to the hustle and bustle of Cannes, the wooded Îles de Lérins afford a fine panorama of the coast from Cap Roux to Cap d'Antibes. Famous as the island prison of the Man in the Iron Mask, St-Marguerite and its fortified monastic neighbour, St-Honorat, were not always havens of peace and tranquillity.

- **Michelin Map:** 341 D6.
- **Info:** Palais des Festivals, 1 Bd. de la Croisette, Cannes. *℘*04 93 39 24 53. www.cannes-on-line.com.
- **Location:** The islands can be reached by Cannes (*see Practical Information opposite*), or on your own boat (just drop anchor in one of the coves).
- **Timing:** Allow at least half a day to visit both islands.

A BIT OF HISTORY
The Island in Antiquity
In ancient times the Île Ste-Marguerite was a Roman port called **Lero** after a Ligurian hero. Excavations near Fort Royal have uncovered houses, wall paintings, mosaics and ceramics dating from 3C BC to 1C AD, while various shipwrecks and port substructures have been found off the coast.

VISITING THE ISLANDS
Île Ste-Marguerite★★
The closest and largest of the two islands, Ste-Marguerite is 2mi/3km long and 1,000yd/900m wide, separated from the mainland by a shallow channel. The island belongs to the State except for the Domaine du Grand Jardin in the south.

Botanical Nature Trail
Many broad paths flanked by explanatory panels on Mediterranean flora cut through the **forest**. Starting from the landing pier, follow the marked trail around the side of the fort, then join the Eucalyptus Walk, which leads to the Domaine du Grand Jardin, crossing the length of the island from north to south. Views of the bell tower and abbey on Île St-Honorat. The Allée Ste-Marguerite leads back to the landing pier.
The cliffs are fairly steep, making it difficult to reach the shore, but there is a path that skirts the edge of the entire island (*2hr walk*).

Coastline of Île Ste-Marguerite

PRACTICAL INFORMATION

REACHING THE ISLANDS (FROM CANNES)

To the Île Ste-Marguerite – *Cie Trans Côte d'Azur, Quai Laubeuf, Cannes.* ℘*04 92 98 71 30. www.trans-cote-azur. com.* Regular shuttle service, 4–8 departures daily depending on the season. Excursions to Monaco, St-Tropez, etc.

To the Île St-Honorat – *Société Planaria, Quai Laubeuf, Cannes.* ℘*04 92 98 71 38. www.cannes-ilesdelerins.com.* ◎*11€ round trip (5.50€ children).*

Regular shuttle service throughout the year.

ON THE ISLANDS

On the Île Ste-Marguerite – No hotels, only restaurants and cafés. Visitors are advised to bring food and water supplies for the day.

On the Île St-Honorat – The whole island is occupied by the monastery. A restaurant and boutique are run by the monks. Bicycles are forbidden and tourists are expected to dress appropriately.

Fort Royal

◷*Open Tue–Sun Apr–May 10.30am– 1.15pm, 2.15–5.45pm; Jun–Sept 10am– 5.45pm; Oct–Mar 10.30am–1.15pm, 2.15–4.45pm.* ◷*Closed public holidays.* ◎*3.30€.* ℘*04 93 38 55 26. www.cannes.com.*

This fortress was built by Richelieu and overhauled by Vauban in 1712, with a monumental entrance on the west side. The disgraced Maréchal Bazaine, blamed for France's humiliating defeat at the hands of the Prussian army in 1871, was imprisoned here (1873–74) until his escape to Spain. From the terrace there is an extensive **view**★ of the coast.

Prisons

The entrance hall gives access to the museum (*right*) and the prisons (*left*). On the right is the cell of the **Man in the Iron Mask** (◐*see box*). The adjacent cells were occupied by six Protestant pastors, imprisoned after the Revocation of the Edict of Nantes (1685).

Musée de la Mer

The Marine Museum houses a display of archaeological finds excavated in the fort and offshore from a 1C BC Roman galley and a 10C Saracen ship. The collection of amphorae and Roman glass and pottery are surprisingly well preserved and includes a bowl of 2,000-year old hazelnuts.

The Riddle of the "Iron Mask"

In 1687 the fortress of Ste-Marguerite, then a state prison, received the famous "Man in the Iron Mask", who, according to Voltaire, wore a leather mask with steel springs. Theories as to the identity of this prisoner abound. He is said to have been an illegitimate brother of Louis XIV, a secretary who had tricked the "Sun King", an accomplice of Madame Brinvilliers the poisoner, and even the son-in-law of a doctor whose autopsy of Louis XIII revealed the King's inability to father a child. An even wilder theory maintains that a lady companion to the Man in the Iron Mask gave birth to a son, who was taken away to Corsica. Entrusted (*remis de bonne part*) to foster parents, this child is said to have been "Buonaparte", the great-grandfather of Napoleon. The most likely explanation is, however, a little less romantic. Since prison governors were paid more for keeping high-ranking prisoners, the new governor of Ste-Marguerite, running low on condemned aristocrats, appears to have masked one of his prisoners and paraded him through Provence on his way to the island. This generated a buzz of excitement in far-off Paris, where rumours of an important prisoner whose identity was so sensitive it could bring down the kingdom spread like wildfire.

Brotherly Love

According to local legend, St Honoratus settled on Lérina, the smaller of the two islands, in the 4C and founded a monastery which was to become one of the most famous in all Christendom. Women were banned from the island, so his sister Marguerite set up a convent on the neighbouring island, where Honorat could come to see her regularly.

St Aigulf founded the Benedictine Order in this monastery in 660. Raids by pirates and the arrival of military garrisons were not favourable to monastic life, so by 1788 the monastery was closed. In 1859 the monastery once more became a place of worship and in 1869 it was taken over by Cistercians from Sénanque Abbey.

Île St-Honorat★★

St-Honorat (1mi/1.5km long, 437yd/400m wide) is the private property of the monastery, but walking and bathing are permitted. Some of the land is used by the monks, who make a liqueur called Lérina, along with a small selection of wines, but the rest is covered by a fine forest of umbrella and sea pines, eucalyptus and cypress trees.

Island Tour★★

🚶2hr.

Starting from the landing pier, an attractive shaded path skirts the coastline. Occasionally veering inland, it offers **views** of the island, its cultivated fields and forest paths, as well as Île Ste-Marguerite and the mainland.

Ancien Monastère Fortifié★

⏰Open daily May–Sept 9.30am–6pm; Oct–Apr 9.30am–5pm. www.abbaye delerins.com.

The remarkably high "keep" of this old fortified monastery on the southern coastline was built in 1073 by the Abbot of Lérins to protect the monks from Saracen pirates.

The **cloisters** with pointed arches and the 14C and 17C vaulting (one of the columns is a Roman milestone) enclose a square courtyard covering a rainwater tank paved with marble.

The upper gallery houses the chapel of the Ste-Croix. From the platform with its 15C battlements and crenulations is a **view**★★ extending over the coastline.

Monastère Moderne

Only the church is open to the public.
⏰*Open daily 8.30am–6pm.*
🎫*No charge. ℘04 92 99 54 00.*
www.abbayedelerins.com.

The early buildings (11C–12C) occupied by the monks have been incorporated into the "new" 19C monastery.

Two of the original seven ancient **chapels** scattered about the island have retained their former appearance: **La Trinité** (5–11C) to the east and the 17C **St-Sauveur** to the northwest.

ADDRESSES

⏹/ EAT

🍽️🍽️**L'Escale** – *Ste-Marguerite (Island).* ℘*04 93 43 49 25. Closed Oct–mid-Mar, eves.* Views of Cannes and the Cap d'Antibes from this enchanting restaurant and its long beachfront terrace. Buffet and seafood platters.

🍽️🍽️**La Tonnelle** – *St-Honorat (Island).* ℘*04 92 99 18 07. www.tonnelle-abbaye delerins.com.* Views of Île Ste-Marguerite from the large terrace of this restaurant (heated in winter). Gourmet French cuisine and snacks.

🛒 SHOPPING

CISTERCIAN SOUVENIRS
Boutique de l'Abbaye de Lérins – *Île St-Honorat. ℘04 92 99 54 00. www.abbayedelerins.com. Closed early Nov–Dec.* This shop attached to the Cistercian abbey sells wine, honey and *Lérina* liqueur.

Mandelieu-la-Napoule

Alpes Maritimes

Refreshed by the River Siagne and bordered by lush plains, this small town begins inland at the foot of the Tanneron in Mandelieu and stretches down to a pretty bay at La Napoule, popular for its small, family beaches.

THE SEASIDE

Three scenic beaches (of which two are private) run along the bay, offering impressive **views** of the area.
The Port de la Napoule can accommodate 1,140 pleasure craft, while the smaller Port de la Rague has 688 moorings. A coastal path *(0.6mi/1km)* connects the two.

Panoramic Tour★

🚶 *Leave from the post office by rue des Hautes-Roches. 45min round trip.*
This pleasant walk wends its way up the **Colline de San Peyré** and affords fantastic views★ over the Tanneron, La Napoule Bay, Cannes and Cap d'Antibes.

Along the Siagne

🚶 A trail follows the River Siagne from the centre of Mandelieu *(behind the Salle Olympie)* all the way to the sea.

▶ **Population:** 20,200.
⚙ **Michelin Map:** 341 C6; region map: pp228–229.
🛈 **Info:** 806, avenue de Cannes. ℰ 04 93 93 64 64. www.ot-mandelieu.fr.
▶ **Location:** Lying at the foot of the Esterel and Tanneron Massifs, Mandelieu sits on the coast 5mi/8km west of Cannes on the N 98.
🅿 **Parking:** There are several free parking areas near the casino and along the coastline in La Napoule.

PRACTICAL INFORMATION

Guided Tours – The **Mandelieu** tourist office runs guided mimosa tours of the Esterel and Tanneron massifs (Jan–early Mar). Guided tours of **La Napoule**, the castle and coastline are available from the La Napoule tourist office *(reserve 48 hours in advance)*.

SIGHT

Château-Musée

Ave. Henry Clews, La Napoule.
🕐 *Open daily Feb–Nov 10am–6pm; Nov–Jan 2–5pm, Sat–Sun and public*

Château-Musée garden

D. Pazery/MICHELIN

holidays 10am–5pm. ◉⛟*Guided tours (45min)* ◉*6€.* ☏*04 93 49 95 05.* *www.chateau-lanapoule.com.*

Only two towers remain of the original 14C stronghold converted by the American sculptor **Henry Clews** and his architect wife, Marie. Located in an outstanding **site**★ at the foot of the Esterel corniche, the château is a curious blend of Romanesque and Gothic styles with an Oriental twist. The salon, Gothic dining room, painting studio and crypt are open to the public. The architecture is embellished with fantastical animals and human figures sculpted by the artist. The tearoom terrace (Apr–Dec) has an impressive **panorama** of the sea (arrive early to secure a table).

ADDRESSES

🛏 STAY

◎ **Corniche d'Or** – *pl. de la Fontaine, La Napoule.* ☏*04 93 49 92 51.* *www.cornichedor.com. Closed 29 Nov – 16 Dec. 12 rooms.* ◻*8€.* On a tiny square near the station, this modest hotel has simple rooms. Many have a small balcony, and two have a large terrace.

◎ **Hôtel Villa Parisiana** – *rue Argentière.* ☏*04 93 49 93 02.* *www.villaparisiana.com. 13 rooms.* ◻*6.50€.* This Edwardian villa located in a residential area houses a congenial, family-style hotel with a trellised terrace for a pleasant stay, despite the proximity of the noisy railway.

🍽 EAT

◎◙🍲 **Le Marco Polo** – *ave. de Lérins, Théoule-sur-Mer.* ☏*04 93 49 96 59. Closed mid-Nov to mid-Dec, Mon off-season.* Casual restaurant ideally situated on the beach, with rattan furniture and a terrace overlooking the Bay of Cannes. Salads at lunch, hearty dinner menus.

◎◙🍲 **La Pomme d'Amour** – *209 ave. du 23 août.* ☏*04 93 49 95 19. Mid-Nov–early Dec, Tue lunch, Mon.* A small restaurant with a big reputation in La Napoule, close to the station. Pleasantly cosy, artfully furnished dining room. Traditional and regional cuisine.

🛍 SHOPPING

MARKETS
Mandelieu – Place du Mail, Wednesday and Friday mornings.

La Napoule – Place St-Fainéant Thursday morning, and Place Jeanne-d'Arc on Saturday morning.

🤼 SPORT AND LEISURE
👪 **Domaine de Barbossi** – *3300 ave. Paul-Ricard, San Estello.* ☏*04 93 49 64 74.* A perfect outing for the whole family. Besides the tennis club, there are facilities for mountain biking, trampolining, miniature golf, pony rides and several playing areas for children. Red and rosé wines, produced and bottled on the estate, are available for sale.

Golf de Cannes-Mandelieu Riviera – *ave. des Amazones.* ☏*04 92 97 49 49.* An 18-hole golf course at the foot of the Esterel, with putting green and driving range. Club house restaurant.

👪 **Guy-Durante Organisation** – *ave. du Gén.-de-Gaulle at plage de Robinson.* ☏*04 93 49 44 19. http://mandelieufunspot.over-blog.com.* ⏰*Jul–Aug 7.30am–7pm, May–mid-Oct 8am–6pm.* A popular spot with surfers and wake-boarders.

CASINO

Pullman Cannes Mandelieu Royal Casino – *605 ave. du Général de Gaulle.* ☏*04 92 97 70 00. www.pullmanhotels.com. Bar Royal Baie: 9am–2am.* This luxury establishment with two tennis courts, terrace, pool overlooking Cannes Bay and a private beach features a casino, two restaurants, a nightclub and a piano bar with live music.

CALENDAR

La Fête du Mimosa – Beginning of February. Ten-day festival and parade celebrating the mimosa blossoms.

Les Nuits du Château – In July and August the Cour d'Honneur hosts a summer festival of dance, concerts and theatre.

Massif du Tanneron★

Alpes Maritimes

Far from the beaten path and yet easily accessible from Cannes, the rounded contours and rock formations of the Massif du Tanneron lie to the north of the Esterel. From mid-January to March, the countryside is covered in brilliant displays of yellow mimosa.

- **Michelin Map:** 341 C6.
- **Info:** 806, avenue de Cannes. ℰ04 93 93 64 64. www.ot-mandelieu.fr
- **Location:** Situated halfway between the Lac de St-Cassien and La Siagne, the Massif du Tanneron is separated from the Esterel to the north by a valley, through which the N 7 and Provençal motorway run.
- **Timing:** Time your visit to coincide with the blossoming of the area's mimosa trees between January and March.

🚗 DRIVING TOUR

From Cannes to Mandelieu
40mi/65km. Allow half a day.

▶ *From Cannes take D 6007 west towards Fréjus. For a description of the route as far as the Logis-de-Paris crossroads 🕭see ② Massif de l'ESTEREL p213.*

Then turn right onto D 237, which offers **views** of La Napoule Bay and Mont Vinaigre. Beyond Les Adrets de l'Esterel the view extends to the Pre-Alps of Grasse. The road crosses the Provençal motorway before skirting St-Cassien lake.

▶ *Turn right onto D 38.*

Lac de St-Cassien
🕭 *See Fayence p221.*

The road rises through a pine wood with glimpses of the lake, the dam and the mountain peaks on the horizon. Near the hamlet of Les Marjoris, it winds over mimosa-clad slopes down to the River Verrerie.

▶ *Before reaching Tanneron village, turn right onto a steep narrow road.*

Chapelle Notre-Dame-de-Peygros★
Alt. 1,352ft/412m.
From the terrace of the small Romanesque chapel, there is a fine **panorama**★ of the Lac de St-Cassien, the Vallée de la Siagne and Grasse; to the east, Mont Agel and the Franco-Italian Alps; to the south, the Esterel and Maures.

▶ *Turn left after passing through Tanneron.*

Mellow Yellow

The Mimosa tree was introduced into the Mediterranean region from Australia in 1839. Sweeping down the slopes of the Tanneron Massif, it has brought financial success to the region. There are three main varieties. Silver wattle *(Mimosa argenté)* has bluish-green bushes that blossom in winter and thrive on the terraces west of Cannes; blue-leaved wattle *(Mimosa glauque)* is characterised by its greyish pendant twigs and used for decorative purposes; the third and most common variety in Provence is four-seasons wattle *(Mimosa des quatre saisons)*, which grows in huge swathes and flowers all year round. The leaves are light green and its delicately fragrant pale yellow balls are a familiar sight in many parks and gardens on the Riviera.

Massif du Tanneron at Mandelieu-la-Napoule

The descent affords **views** of Auribeau and its surroundings, Grasse and the vast hollow of the Siagne valley.

Auribeau-sur-Siagne★

4.3mi/7km – leaving from the Val-Cros crossroads (alt. 971ft/296m).

A twisting road between banks of mimosa leads up to the charming 12C village. Pass under the 16C Porte Soubran gateway and stroll through the stepped, narrow streets. The old houses huddle around the **church**, which contains a 15C silver-gilt and enamelled reliquary, and a 16C chalice. From the church square the **view** encompasses the Siagne Valley, Grasse and its ring of mountains. Take the stepped streets (Degrés de l'Église and Degrés Soubran) leading to Porte Soutran, the fortified gateway.

Walk along the left bank of the Siagne to the north of Auribeau, along the D 38, and head for the gorges.

Return to the D 9 (towards Pegomas), then the D 109 towards Mandelieu-la-Napoule. Take the D 309 towards Tanneron, and turn left onto the D 138.

Road to Mandelieu★★

The drive through the mimosa down the steep hill to Mandelieu-la-Napoule affords **views**★★ of the Esterel, La Napoule Bay, Cannes and the Îles de Lérins, the Siagne Valley, Grasse and the Pre-Alps.

Return to Cannes by D 92 and D 6098 along the seafront.

ADDRESSES

See also addresses for Cannes p236 and Mandelieu p242.

⤒ SHOPPING

Vial Bernard – *Les Carreiros, Tanneron.* ☎*04 93 60 66 32.* This honey producer's domain, surrounded by 25 acres/10ha of mimosa, eucalyptus and citrus trees, has hives on site, in the Mercantour and in the Alps. Honey can be tasted and purchased on the premises. Other honey/wax products also for sale.

HIKING

The Grand Duc forest has three hiking trails beginning at the picnic area. *Information available from the tourist office in Mandelieu.*

Grasse and the Grasse region ★
Alpes Maritimes

The perfume capital of France sits at the foot of a high plateau overlooking fragrant plains. The modern town affords views of the cobalt-blue sea off the coast of Cannes, while boutiques and perfumeries line the narrow alleyways of the old town below.

A BIT OF HISTORY

In the Middle Ages, Grasse was a tiny republic, administered by a council whose members called themselves "Consuls by the Grace of God". Raymond Bérenger, comte de Provence, put an end to this independent existence in 1227. Thanks to its mild climate, the town later became a popular winter resort, hosting the estranged Princess Pauline Bonaparte in 1807–08 (her brother, the Emperor, would pass through the town on 2 March 1815 on the way to Paris following his escape from Elba Island). Queen Victoria spent several winters in Grasse at the Grand Hotel.

A KALEIDOSCOPE OF FRAGRANCES

The Perfume Industry

Grasse had long specialised in leather work when perfumed gloves came into fashion in the 16C, marking the beginning of the perfume industry. The town's great *parfumeries* emerged in the 18C and 19C. The essences produced in Grasse, which are the base material of the perfume industry, are used locally or sent to Paris, where the great perfume houses blend them according to secret formula. The Grasse perfume industry has now diversified into the production of food flavourings.

Musée International de la Parfumerie ★★

2 blvd. du Jeu-de-Ballon. ○*Open Jun–Sept daily 10am–7pm (Thu 9pm), Oct–May Wed–Mon 11am–6pm.* ◎*3€.* ℘*04*

▶ **Population:** 48,801.
Ġ **Michelin Map:** 341 C6.
🗊 **Info:** Palais des Congrès, 22 Cours H.-Cresp. ℘04 93 36 66 66. www.grasse.fr.
◖ **Location:** Grasse is located 10.5mi/17km northwest of Cannes on the N 85, leading past industrial and residential zones into the heart of the old town *(vieille ville)*. The most interesting part of Grasse is in the pedestrian streets between cours Honoré-Cresp, boulevard du Jeu-de-Ballon and place du 24 Août.
🅿 **Parking:** There are five indoor car parks in the centre, including place du Cours Honoré Cresp, place de la Foux and at the Hôtel de Ville. ℘04 92 60 91 17.
◉ **Don't Miss:** The Musée International de la Parfumerie brings to light the town's main industry.
🕐 **Timing:** Plan on half a day for the old town, starting off with a visit to the perfume museum before taking a free tour of one of the perfume-makers. Then explore the streets of the old town, or a hike around the surrounding countryside for some excellent **panoramic views**.
👫 **Kids:** The Grottes de St-Cézaire are popular with children.

97 05 58 00. www.museesdegrasse.com. Fresh from a four-year renovation, this modern museum, topped by a glass atrium, covers more than 3,000 years of perfume-making history. Among the 50,000 artefacts on show are items from Guerlain, Patou, Lanvin and Chanel, including perfume flasks, vessels, scent bottles, boxes, chests

PRACTICAL INFORMATION

Guided Tours – There are several themed guided tours of the town, its history, perfumeries and artists in English from July to September.
Enquire at the tourist office or visit www.vpah.culture.fr.

TRANSPORT

Buses – *Bus station at the Notre-Dame-des-Fleurs car park, pl. de la Buanderie.* 04 93 36 37 37. The city is served by 17 lines, which also go to Nice and Cannes.

Petit Train Touristique – *Runs Apr–Sept Mon–Sat 10am–6pm.* 06 07 75 63 60. 6€ *(3€ children 3–12).* Guided tours with a commentary *(45min)* from Cours Honoré-Cresp to the heights of Grasse and the Parc de la Princesse-Pauline on a small tourist train.

SNCF Train – There is newly reopened train service between Grasse and Nice via Cannes. *www.regionpaca.fr or www.grasse-riviera.com.*

---

and even travel accessories belonging to Marie-Antoinette.

Parfumeries

Visitor parking. See Addresses for addresses and admission times.
There are several perfume manufacturers in Grasse (also known as *parfumeries* or *usines*), which give free guided tours of their perfume-making process, such as Fragonard, Molinard and Galimard. Try to visit on weekdays when workers can be seen making the *eau de toilette* and scented soaps on sale in the boutiques.

Flower Fields

Information from the tourist office and parfumeries.
In spring and summer, Fragonard and Molinard organise tours of their flower fields. The **Domaine de Manon** *(Chemin de Servin, 4.3mi/7km from Grasse;* 04 93 60 12 76) allows access to its rose garden (May–Sept, afternoons) and jasmine fields (Aug–Oct, mornings).

WALKING TOUR

THE OLD TOWN★

Allow 1hr.
The houses of old Grasse are the colour of the sunset: red ochre, orange, yellow, pink... and sometimes grey, since many of the villagers have abandoned the historic centre for more modern housing in the valley.

Leave the car in the car park on cours Honoré Cresp and take rue Jean-Ossola, then rue Marcel-Journet. Turn right on rue Gazan and walk to pl. du Puy.

Cathedral Notre-Dame-du-Puy

Pl. du Petit-Puy. Open Mon–Fri 9.30am–11.30am, 3–6pm.
This 10C cathedral was restored in the 17C. The double staircase at the entrance and two crypts were added in the 18C. The high narrow nave with heavy pointed rib-vaulting marks the beginning of the Gothic style in Provence. In the south aisle there are three **paintings★** by **Rubens** (*The Crown of Thorns, Crucifixion* and *St Helen in Exaltation of the Holy Cross*). The cathedral also sports a fine **triptych** attributed to Louis Bréa depicting St Honoratus and a rare religious painting by Fragonard, *The Washing of the Feet.*

Place du 24-Août

From the far side of the square admire the chevet and bell tower of the cathedral. There is a fine **view** eastwards over the Grasse countryside. Close at hand is the Clock Tower (Tour de l'Horloge).

Turn left onto rue de l'Évêché.

Place de l'Évêché

In the centre of place de l'Evêché stands an elegant three-tiered **fountain**. At the tiny place de la Poissonnerie, follow the

View of Grasse

J. Malburet/MICHELIN

street of the same name to place aux
Herbes and the town's market.

◗ *Walk along rue Courte, turn left on
rue Droite, then right onto rue Amiral-
de-Grasse to pl. aux Aires.*

Place aux Aires
This square was once used by local
tanners. At no 33 is the **Hôtel Isnard**,
an attractive town house built in 1781.

◗ *Leave the square on your left and
exit the old town via blvd. du Jeu-de-
Ballon down to pl. du Cours.*

Place du Cours★
This fine terraced promenade offers a
charming **view**★ over the countryside.

Gardens of Grasse
Jardin de la Princesse Pauline
*Access via ave. Thiers, blvd. Alice-de-
Rothschild and blvd. de la Reine-Jeanne.
Keep to the left and look for the signs.*
This grove of oaks that Napoleon's sister adored during her winter stay here
is now a large ornamental garden with
panoramic views★ of Grasse, the Massif
du Tanneron, the Esterel and the coast.

Parc Communal de la Corniche
*Access as above, then turn a sharp left
on blvd. Bellevue and then right on blvd.
du Président-Kennedy.*

🚶*30min round trip.* At the bend, a path
to the right *(sign)* leads to the edge of
the steep Pre-Alps of Grasse. From the
lookout point, the **view**★★ extends
from the Baou of St-Jeannet to the coast
and from the Tanneron mountains to
the peaks of the Esterel.

SIGHTS
Musée d'Art et d'Histoire
de Provence
2 rue Mirabeau. ◑*Open May–Sept
daily 10am–7pm (Sat 9pm); Oct–Mar
Wed–Mon 11am–6pm; Apr daily
11am-6pm.* ◑*Closed public holidays.*
No charge. ✆*04 97 05 58 00.*
www.museesdegrasse.com.
This museum, set in an 18C mansion
called "Petit Trianon", explores the art
and history of eastern Provence. The
ground floor displays pottery (18C–19C)
from Apt and Le Castellet and paintings
by 19C Provençal artists (Chabaud, Camoin). In the basement are the mansion's
reconstructed kitchens and an archaeological display evoking the daily life of
local people, from Prehistoric times to
the late Middle Ages.

Villa-Musée Fragonard
◑*Same times and charges as the Musée
d'Art et d'Histoire de Provence, p247.*
The famous 18C painter Jean-Honoré
Fragonard, who was born in Grasse,
offered the Comtesse du Barry, the

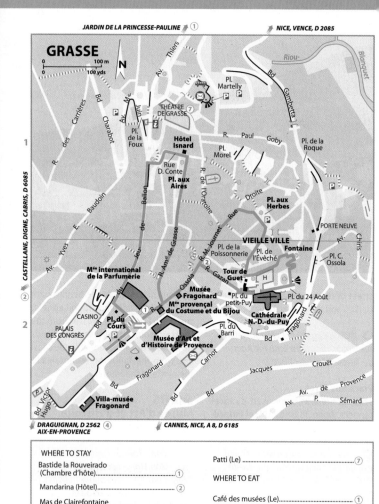

WHERE TO STAY	
Bastide la Rouveirado (Chambre d'hôte)	①
Mandarina (Hôtel)	②
Mas de Clairefontaine (Chambre d'hôte)	④
Patti (Le)	⑦

WHERE TO EAT	
Café des musées (Le)	①
Gazan (Le)	②

favourite of Louis XV, four paintings depicting each stage of a love affair: *The Meeting*, *The Pursuit*, *The Letters* and *The Lover Crowned*. During the Revolution, he took refuge in this elegant country house, which now displays a selection of his original drawings and etchings, sketches and paintings.

Musée Provençal du Costume et du Bijou

2 rue Jean-Ossola. ⏰*Open daily 10am–1pm, 2–6pm (Sun in summer).* 🎫*No charge.* ✆*04 93 36 44 65. www.fragonard.com.*
These private collections housed in an annexe of the Fragonard perfumery focus on women's clothing during the 18C. Peasants' robes, weavers' skirts and middle-class finery are on show alongside curious ornaments made out of sea fossils *(étoiles de Digne)*. All the exhibits are genuine, except for the aprons.

🚗 DRIVING TOURS

Préalpes de Grasse★★
Round trip of 56mi/90km. Allow 5hr.

▶ *From Grasse take blvd. Georges Clemenceau and turn left onto D 11.*

Following a winding mountain road with **views** of the countryside between Grasse and St-Cézaire, the tour leads through the majestic route Napoléon and down to Grasse.

Cabris★

🛈 *9 rue Frédéric Mistral.* 🖉*04 93 60 55 63. http://cabris.chez-alice.fr.*
This charming village occupies a magnificent site on the edge of the Provençal plateau, looking out over the Grasse countryside to Lac de St-Cassien and the sea *(12mi/20km)*. The village has long been a favourite haunt of writers and artists. **Saint-Exupéry** wrote part of *Wind, Sand and Stars* there.
The village has several small **chapels**, including the 16C chapelle St-Sébastien (10am–6pm) and the primitive chapelle St-Jean-Baptiste (5C), restored in the 16C. From the defensive wall and terrace of the château there is a superb **view**★★ southeast to Mougins and the hills running down to Le Cannet, out to sea over La Napoule Bay to the Îles de Lérins, south beyond Peymeinade to the Esterel and west to the Lac de St-Cassien *(orientation table)*.

◐ *Towards St-Cézaire, a small twisting route (on the right) passes close to the "9 Puits de la Vierge", nine wells of Roman origin.*

🏊🚶 Grottes de St-Cézaire★

Outside the village de Saint-Cézaire.
🕐*Guided tours (40min) Jun–Aug 10.30am–6.30pm; Feb–May and Sept–Nov 10.30–noon, 2–5.30pm.* ⊛*7.50€ (5€ children 6–12).* 🖉*04 93 60 22 35. www.lesgrottesdesaintcezaire.com.*
Discovered accidentally in 1888, the caves emerged from the sea 6 million years ago and descend 131ft/40m underground. They remain at a constant temperature of 57°F/14°C. Both the stalactites and the stalagmites are remarkable for the variety of their shapes – toadstools, flowers, animals – and their reddish colour, ascribed to the presence of iron oxide in the rock.

St-Cézaire-sur-Siagne

From its site dominating the steep Siagne Valley, the walls and towers of this interesting village testify to its feudal past. A marked path from the church leads to a **viewpoint** *(viewing table)*.

◐ *Leaving St-Cézaire, take a left onto the narrow D 105, direction Mons.*

Gorges de la Siagne

The road runs up through rich vegetation in the deep gorge cut into the limestone by the waters of the Siagne.
After crossing the river (from the bridge, **view** up and down the gorge), turn right onto the D 656, which is a very steep and narrow road. After meandering steeply above the gorge, the road broadens out into an area of dry stone walls, fig and olive trees and holm oaks.

◐ *At the crossroads turn left onto D 56.*

Sources de la Siagnole

🚶 *30min round trip.*
On the right beyond the bridge a path leads to a very pleasant spot, where several Vauclusian springs rise to form the River Siagnole. Further on, a sign indicates the remains of a Roman aqueduct at **Roche Taillée**, still in use. There is a **view**★ eastwards towards Grasse.

◐ *At the pont de la Siagne, turn around and return to the D 105, then left towards St-Vallier-de-Thiey.*

St-Vallier-de-Thiey
🏛 *10 pl. de la Tour. ☎04 93 42 78 00.*
🅿 *Park at place du Grand-Pré (except on market day on Fri in summer) or pl. St-Roch (Fri market autumn–spring).*
Dominated by a seigniorial château with loopholes, this medieval village (once a Roman stronghold) is situated in the middle of a plateau of grassy "lunar" scrubland at the foot of the Pre-Alps. The 12C Romanesque **church**, restored in the 17C, has a 13C nave with pointed barrel vaulting and two Baroque altarpieces.

○ *Exit the village south and head towards St-Cézaire, then down the road to the cemetery and the "Grotte Baume Obscure". Continue beyond the cemetery for 1mi/2km to a large car park opposite a shelter over the ticket office.*

‍ Souterroscope de la Baume Obscure
🕐*Open early-Mar–early-Apr Wed, Sat–Sun 10am–4pm, early-Apr–Jun Tue–Sun 10am–5pm, Jul–Aug daily 10am–6pm, Sep–early-Nov Tue–Sun 10am–5pm.*
◉*8€ (4€ children). ☎06 80 90 70 59. www.baumeobscure.com.*
✎*A warm sweater and shoes with non-slip soles advised. Narrow passages.*
The cave consists of an underground network of galleries. The tour covers 547yd/500m and takes visitors down 164ft/50m to the **Galerie du Pas de Course** and its stalactites.

Pas de la Faye★★
At an altitude of 3,228ft/984m, there is a **view★★** west towards Grasse, the Lac de St-Cassien, south towards the Esterel and Maures massifs, La Napoule bay and the Îles de Lérins.

Belvédère de Baou Mourine★
Park at La Colette car park. Signed pathway (red arrows).
🚶*30min round trip.* The path leads to a terrace with a **viewing point★** over the Vallée de la Siagne, La Napoule golf course, the Esterel and Maures.

○ *Return to D 6085. Turn around and head back to St-Vallier-de-Thiey, cross the village and turn right on D 4.*

‍ Grottes des Audides
2mi/3.5km to the south of St-Vallier-de-Thiey on D 6085, then D 4. Take rainproof clothing. 🕐*Open Jul–Aug daily 11am–6pm (closed Mon morn), Sept–Jun. Call for details (from 2 pers.)*
◉*5€. ☎ 04 93 42 64 15.*
http://grottesdesaudides.free.fr.
These six swallow-holes were discovered in 1988. A tour takes visitors 197ft/60m underground to explore a geological landscape of concretions and stalagmites, cracked limestone pavements and a subterranean river. The tools, fossils and bones found in the caves, inhabited since the dawn of humanity, are on display in a nearby park *(audio-guide tour 30min).*

○ *Return on D 6085 and turn right.*

Col du Pilon
View★★ over Grasse and the sea.

Le Plateau de Grasse
24mi/38km. Allow 2.5hrs.

○ *Leave Grasse on the D 2085, heading northeast.*

Magagnosc
On avenue Auguste Renoir, heading towards Nice, turn right on the road leading to St-Laurent's church.
This church and St-Michel's chapel both feature works by contemporary painter **R. Savary**. From the cemetery behind St-Laurent church, don't miss the **view★** over the sea towards Cannes and the Esterel.

○ *At the D 3 crossroads, turn left to Pré-du-Lа, then continue on D 2210 to Le Bar-sur-Loup.*

Le Bar-sur-Loup
🔖*See Le Bar-sur-Loup*

○ *At the crossroads with D 2085, turn left and take D 3 right towards Châteauneuf-Grasse.*

Châteauneuf-Grasse
Built on a hill planted with centuries-old olive trees overlooking the Opio plain, this is a typical perched Provençal village with ancient houses clustered along narrow alleyways leading to a church topped by a campanile. Don't miss the **view** from the cemetery.

○ *Drive towards Valbonne south on D 3. After the village of Opio, head towards the golf course, drive round it and turn left before the entrance.*

Notre-Dame-du-Brusc – This charming restored chapel is all that remains of a basilica (11C), once the size of the Abbaye de Lérins (☞ *guided tours by reservation at the tourist office; ℘04 92 60 36 03).*

○ *Return via Opio and the Moulin de la Brague, then by D 7 to Grasse.*

From St-Vallier-de-Thiey to Gourdon
19mi/30km. Allow 2hr.

○ *Leave St-Valliers-de-Thiey and head north on D 6085 towards Pas de la Faye, then D 5 to the right. After going through a pass, Col de Ferrier, the road overlooks the valley of Nans. Leave the main road, taking D 12 leading off to the right (sign "Caussols").*

The **Plateau de Caussols**★, sitting at an average altitude of 3,281ft/1,000m, is itself enclosed by higher land. It is one of the rare examples of karst relief in France. The plateau features dolines, swallow-holes and chasms, where the limestone has been eroded by rainwater. ⊛ *Walkers should take care when near these pits and chasms, especially in rainy weather.* Leave the centre of the sprawling village of **Caussols** to the east. The narrow road crosses the plateau diagonally to reach **Les Claps**★ (Provençal for "rocks"), a remarkably rugged rock formation. Some stone dwellings *(bories)* indicate human habitation. Face the plateau for a view of the domes of the CERGA Observatory.

○ *Return to D 12 for 1mi/2km towards Gourdon. 1mi/2km after Caussols on D 12, a road leads off to the left signposted "St-Maurice – Observatoire du CERGA". After passing the houses, continue past the sign "Route Privée", which indicates the entrance to the CERGA property.*

Observatoire de Calern
2130 rte. de l'Observatoire. Call for information on guided tours. ℘04 93 40 54 54. www.oca.eu.
The **Plateau de Calern** (4,265ft/1,300m) is home to the various installations and equipment of the CERGA Observatory, specialising in geodynamic and astronomical research. Teams work with interferometers (for measuring diameters of stars), the Schmidt telescope and astrolabes.

○ *Return to D 12 towards Gourdon.*

The road continues to the eastern edge of the plateau and then descends into Gourdon.

Gourdon★
⬑ *See GOURDON p258.*
The first major bend in the road on the way to Gourdon reveals a magnificent **view**★ of the Vallée du Loup (⬑ *see Vallée du LOUP p254).*

ADDRESSES

🏠 STAY

GRASSE
⊜⊜ **Chambre d'hôte Le Mas des Anges** – *1377 chemin des Moulins, Le Tignet. ℘04 93 77 78 49. www. lemasdesanges.info.* ⬜ *Reservation required Nov–Easter. 5 rooms.* Located at the end of a winding path on the edge of a forest, this B&B dominates the San Peyre valley, with **views** on the Tanneron massif. Simple, well-maintained rooms. Swimming pool with woodland **views**.

🍷🍷🏠 **Bastide La Rouveirado** – *22 chemin des Colles, Chateauneuf.* 📞*04 93 77 78 49. www.larouveirado.com. 5 rooms.* 🛏. This modern B&B is hidden among evergreen oaks near Opio. Rooms have direct access outside to the pool and gardens through French doors. Simple décor, yet comfortably appointed.

🍷🍷🏠 **Hôtel Le Patti** – *p. Patti.* 📞*04 93 36 01 00. www.hotelpatti.com. 73 rooms.* 🍽*9€. Restaurant*🍷🏠. This 18C hotel in the old town is decorated in charming Provençal style with wrought-iron beds and patina'd walls. Rooms have air-conditioning, WiFi and a stereo. Provençal products for sale in the boutique. Mediterranean cuisine is served in the restaurant.

🍷🍷🏠 **Mandarina Hôtel** – *39 ave. Y.-E.-Baudoin.* 📞*04 93 36 10 29. www.mandarinahotel.com. 31 rooms.* 🅿. 🍽*8€. Restaurant*🏠. Overlooking the city of Grasse, peace and quiet are guaranteed in this hotel with brightly decorated rooms and pretty **views** of the coastline. Provençal fabric adds a lively touch to the dining room.

🍷🍷🏠🏠 **Chambre d'Hôte Mas de Clairefontaine** – *3196 route de Draguignan, Val du Tignet, 6mi/10km southeast of Grasse on Route de Draguignan/RD 562.* 📞*04 93 66 39 69. www.masdeclairefontaine.fr. 3 rooms.* 🛏. 🛏. A stone cottage surrounded by a terraced garden dotted with umbrella pines and reeds is the charming backdrop to your stay at this bed and breakfast. The rooms are tastefully appointed. Excellent service. Grounds include a terrace shaded by a century-old oak tree and swimming pool.

CABRIS

🍷 **Chambre d'Hôte Mme Faraut** – *14 rue de l'Agachon.* 📞*04 93 60 52 36. Closed mid-Oct–early-Apr.* 🛏. *5 rooms.* Nestled in the old quarter, this hotel fronted by a yellow façade offers simply decorated rooms painted in white. Pretty views of St-Cassien Lake and the Esterel Massif from the lounge and some of the bedrooms.

ST-VALLIER-DE-THIEY

🍷 **Villa Quercus** – *2 chemin Blaqueirette, at the edge of the village, across from the pharmacist's shop.* 📞*04 92 60 03 84.* 🛏. *4 rooms.* The main advantages of

this villa are its large, shaded garden with swimming pool, and its pleasing covered terrace for summer breakfasts. The rooms display an interesting medley of decorative styles. Fully equipped kitchen at residents' disposal.

🍷🏠 **Chambre d'hôte L'Ousteau de l'Agachon** – *14 r. de l'Agachon, 8km/5mi east of Grasse on D 11.* 📞 *04 93 60 52 36 or 06 03 44 16 84. www.cabris-chambres-hotes.com. Closed mid-Oct–end of Mar. 5 rooms.* Stroll through the alleyways of this village and stop at this yellow-fronted building. White, simple, quiet rooms. Some have pleasant **views** of the Esterel massif and the Lac de St-Cassien.

🍴 EAT

CABRIS

🍷🏠 **Le Petit Prince** – *15 r. Frédéric Mistral.* 📞 *04 93 60 63 14. www.lepetitprince-cabris.com. Closed Wed except Jul–Aug, Tue.* Hidden behind plane trees opposite a large meadow, this restaurant has a pleasant rustic dining room. A high standard of Provençal cuisine. Large shady summer terrace.

GRASSE

🍷🏠 **Le Gazan** – *3 rue Gazan. Closed Dec–Jan, Mon–Thu eves off-season, Sun.* 📞*04 93 36 22 88.* Two delightful dining rooms with rustic furniture, linked by a spiral staircase, provide the setting for a succulent meal seasoned with local olive oil and aromatic herbs. Located in the old quarter of Grasse.

🍷🏠 **Café des Musées** – *1 rue Jean Ossola. Closed Sun Oct–Mar.* 📞*04 92 60 99 00.* A chic tearoom and café across from the Musée Provençal, serving light dishes for lunch, such as beef carpaccio, smoked salmon, goats' cheese salad and homemade tarts. There's also a fine selection of local wines.

🛒 SHOPPING

Palais des Olives – *1 blvd. du Jeu-de-Ballon.* 📞*04 93 36 57 73. Closed two weeks in Jan and Nov, Sun–Mon.* Traditional Provençal-style boutique featuring high-quality olive oils from Grasse and around the world, local olives and organic products.

Le Moulin de la Brague – *2 rue de Châteauneuf, Opio.* 📞*04 93 77 23 03. www.moulin-opio.com. Closed Mon*

Parfumerie Fragonard, Grasse

© Christopher Rennieage/age fotostock

morning Oct–Mar, Sun. This rare working olive mill (part of which dates back to the 15C) has been run by the Michel family for six generations. The pretty boutique sells olive oil, tapenade, honey, jams, pottery, soaps and fabrics.

PARFUMERIES

Usine Fragonard – *20 blvd. Fragonard.* *04 93 36 44 65. www.fragonard.com.* Perfume has been made here since 1782. Introductory course on "The Essence of Aromas" (*Absolus Aromatiques*) by request.

Fragonard-La Fabrique des Fleurs – *carrefour des Quatre-Chemins, route de Cannes.* *04 93 77 94 30.* A modern perfume factory on the edge of Grasse, with tours and an aromatic flower and herb garden.

Parfumerie Molinard – *60 blvd. Victor-Hugo.* *04 92 42 33 28. www.molinard. com. Closed Oct–Mar.* No charge. Traditional Provençal perfume house founded in 1849. Visitors are guided through each stage of the perfume-making process. There are also courses on how to create perfumes (*fee*).

Usine Galimard – *73 route de Cannes (going towards Mouans-Sartoux).* *04 93 09 20 00. www.galimard.com.* Guided tours year round. No charge. Created in 1747, Galimard organises free tours of the perfume museum, labs, workshops and boutique.

Galimard-Studio des Fragrances – *5 route de Pégomas, rond point des 4 Chemins.* *04 93 09 20 00. www. galimard.com. Course (2hr) on perfume-making. Open by appointment Mon–Sat.*

Make your own fragrance with the help of a real "nose" from Grasse (they keep the "formula" you create on file in case you want to order more).

ENTERTAINMENT

Casino – *blvd. du Jeu-de-Ballon.* *04 93 36 91 00. www.casino-grasse. com.* Come here to indulge in a spot of gambling (roulette, blackjack). The café is open from 8.30pm to 2am. Musical evenings and package formulas are available (casino, dinner, transport).

CALENDAR

GRASSE

Rallye de Grasse – April.

Exposition Internationale de la Rose – Over 30,000 cut roses on display in bouquets mid-May, along with exhibitions on the use of roses in perfume.

Fête du Jasmin – First weekend in August. Don't miss the famous "flower battle".

Women's Festival on Ste-Agathe Day during the first weekend in February.

St-Pierre Festival towards the end of June (children's events, dance shows, barbecues).

Local festivities in honour of **Our Lady** on 15 August.

Vallée du Loup★★

Alpes Maritimes

Emerging from Mount Audibergue and running down to the sea, the Loup is one of the best preserved gorges in Haute-Provence, framed by orchards, pine forests, high solitary plateaux and picturesque perched villages.

🚗DRIVING TOURS

Gorges du Loup★★

56km/35mi. Allow one day.
From Vence take D 2210 northwest.
After 1.2mi/2km turn right 👐See map pp228–229.

Tourrettes-sur-Loup★

🅿 *Park outside the village and follow the pavement to the central square.*
The road offers surprising **views** of Tourrettes on its rocky plateau above a sheer drop, then follows the cliff road that clings to the split limestone face of the Vallée du Loup. Views of the perched village of Bar-sur-Loup (👐see opposite) and the hamlet of Gourdon (👐see GOURDON p258).

Old Village★

Enter this medieval village through the belfry gate in the south corner of the main square. Restored and inhabited by craftsmen and women, artists and restaurant owners, this village is crossed by cobbled streets, vaulted alleys and narrow stairways.
The Grande Rue, lined with artisans' shops, curves through the village to the other side of the square. Follow the line of the ramparts, fringed with Barbary fig trees, where the 16C fortifications are still visible, and admire the **panorama**★. The **church** on place de la Libération has a 15C nave and a Gallo-Roman altar.
Cross the route de Grasse, the village's main road, for a refreshing stop at the wash-house, fed by a spring since 1900.

♿ **Michelin Map:** 341 C/D5/6.
🛈 **Info:** Office de tourisme de Tourrettes-sur-Loup, 2 pl. de la Libération. ℘04 93 24 28 93. www.tourrettessurloup. com. Office de tourisme de Bar-sur-Loup, pl. F.-Paulet. ℘04 93 42 72 21. www. lebarsurloup.fr.
▶ **Location:** Countryside with olive orchards and snow-capped peaks. These driving tours, starting from Vence (👐see VENCE p280), lead you through both the high and low valleys of the scenic river.
👁 **Don't Miss:** The road through the gorges with **views** over the Loup.
👪 **Kids:** The Florian sweet shop at Pont-du-Loup.
🕐 **Timing:** One day for the gorges or 2hr for the upper Loup valley.

Chapelle St-Jean

Route de St-Jean 🕐*Open Apr–Sept.* ℘04 93 24 28 93.
This chapel was decorated in 1959 with naïve frescoes depicting the inhabitants of Tourrettes going about their daily business.

Pont-du-Loup

The Draguignan–Nice railway line, which crossed the entrance to the Gorges du Loup, was blown up by the Germans in 1944; the viaduct ruins are still visible.

▶ *At the entrance to the village, turn right onto D 6.*

The road runs through the splendid **Gorges du Loup**★★, which cut vertically through the Grasse mountains, with huge, gaping holes, smooth and round, hollowed out of its sides. Just before the second tunnel, in a semicircular hollow, the **Cascade de Courmes**★ spills down onto a mossy bed (130ft/40m).

Tourrettes-sur-Loup

© Christian Goupi/age fotostock

▶ *Park your car after the third tunnel.*

Saut du Loup
🕐 *Open Jul–Oct daily 10am–7pm.*
💶 *1€. ✆04 93 09 68 88. www.cascade-sautduloup.com. Restaurant, snack bar.*
Amid lush vegetation, a huge megalith marks the entrance to the Saut du Loup, an enormous cauldron shaped by prehistoric marine and glacial erosion. The **Cascades des Demoiselles** waterfall gushes down through a strange setting of petrified vegetation.

▶ *Just before the bridge, Pont de Bramafan, take a sharp left onto D 3.*

As the road rises to Caussols Plateau, there are **views**★ down into the gorges and the village of Courmes. An overhang has been built out from a sharp right-hand turn *(signposted)* with a fine **view**★★ of the gorges to the sea.

Gourdon★
🔎 *See GOURDON p258.*
Drive down the slopes of the Caussols plateau on the D 3 towards **Le Pré-du-Lac**, with **views** of the Mediterranean in the background. The road (D 2210) winds sharply, offering stunning **views** at each turn of the Gorges du Loup and the steep flanks of the mountains.

Le Bar-sur-Loup★
🅿 *Park at place des Carteyrades, near the tourist office.*
Nestled between the River Loup and its tributaries, Le Bar enjoys a privileged **hillside site**★ surrounded by terraced orange trees, jasmine and violets. The medieval village features a well-preserved castle dungeon. The narrow streets of the old town wind around the imposing 16C **castle** of the comtes de Grasse, with its four-corner towers and ruined keep. The **Amiral de Grasse** was born here in 1722. He went on to become a leading figure in the American War of Independence, winning the famous naval battle of Chesapeake Bay in 1781.

Église St-Jacques le Majeur
🔒 *Closed indefinitely for restoration.*
A Roman tombstone is embedded in the stonework at the foot of the bell tower.

Take the D 6 on the right. Clinging to the hillside at an altitude of 217ft/350m overlooking the middle Vallée du Loup, the road follows the lower banks of the river. From the Vallon de la Siagne, there are **views** of the Loup and the Pre-Alps of Grasse in the distance. The road then descends along the valley floor.

The Land of Violets

Violets have been grown in the fertile soil of Tourrettes-sur-Loup since 1880, although the "Parme" variety has long since given way to "Victoria", the only species grown here today. For an unforgettable walk along these colourful, fragrant fields, time your visit between October and March. Violets are grown in the open fields or under greenhouses on a dozen farms, covering a total area of 15 acres/6ha. From 15 October to 15 March, the flowers are picked in bouquets of 25 stems. At the end of the season, when the violets are in full bloom, the flower is picked without the stem for the region's confectioners (7,600 flowers per kilo-gramme). In early May and late July, the leaves of the violet are cut and the same day sent to the factories in Grasse to be processed and turned into perfume.

La Colle-sur-Loup

A picturesque village in the plain where fruit and flowers are cultivated at the foot of the St-Paul hills. The name of the village comes from the Latin *collis* or "hill". It was populated by villagers from St-Paul, whose houses were stranded outside the walls erected by François I in 1537. Don't miss the **view** over St-Paul from avenue de l'ancienne gare.

1.5hr round trip. Map from tourist office. This hike along the banks of the Loup through the Berges du Loup nature park offers a **panorama** over the steep, dramatic Canyon de St-Donat gorges.

▶ *Return to Vence by D 2 and D 236.*

St-Paul-de-Vence★★

See ST-PAUL-DE-VENCE p284.
Beyond St-Paul the **view** extends to the foothills of the Pre-Alps of Grasse.

Haute Vallée du Loup★

22mi/35km. Allow about 2hr. This tour carries on from the gorges described above.
From the pont de Bramafan, the D 3 emerges into the **upper Loup Valley**★, a stretch of country with **views** both before and after Gréolières (*D 2 on the left*).

Gréolières

This is a perched village at the south-ern foot of the Cheiron ridges; to the north are the extensive ruins of Haut-Gréolières. To the south are the remains of an important stronghold.

The alleys are extremely narrow especially "L'Androne", which is no more than 27in/70cm wide.

The **church**, which has only one aisle, has a Romanesque façade and a square bell tower. It contains (high on the right) a **retable of St Stephen**★ by an unknown artist (15C).

West of Gréolières the road climbs 1,312ft/400m above the River Loup and snakes westward along the side of the gorge passing through brief tunnels and beneath huge rock spurs of fantastic shapes and sizes. The **Clue de Gréolières**★, popular with canyoners, was formed by a tributary of the Loup, its bare slopes pitted with giant holes and spiked with curious dolomitic rocks. The road emerges from the rift onto a broad plateau, Plan-du-Peyron.

▶ *In Plan-du-Peyron turn right onto D 802, a road flanking Mont Cheiron.*

Gréolières-les-Neiges

Alt. 4,757ft/1,450m. ⧉ Ski-lift, ☎04 93 59 70 02.
The resort, which lies on the north face of Mont Cheiron, is the most southerly of the Alpine ski stations. It is well equipped (14 lifts, 25 runs, 18.6mi/30km of cross-country trails), easily-accessible and attracts crowds of local skiers.

▶ *Drive back via Col de Vence (see VENCE: Excursions p281) or via the Gorges du Loup.*

ADDRESSES

🏠 STAY

Auberge de Courmes – *3 rue des Platanes, Courmes.* ℘*04 93 77 64 70. www. aubergedecourmes.com. 5 rooms. 6€. Restaurant.* This recently renovated local inn on the square of a tiny hamlet dominating the Loup Gorges offers five small rooms and a welcoming dining area. Outstanding **views** of the mountains, facilities for hiking and rambling and a peaceful atmosphere.

Chambre d'Hôte La Cascade – *635 Chemin de la Cascade, Courmes.* ℘*04 93 09 65 85. www.gitedelacascade.com. 6 rooms. Meal.* Guest house with swimming pool near the waterfall of Courmes. The original building, now enlarged and restored, has six tidy rooms particularly suitable for nature lovers plus WiFi.

Chambre d'hôte Le Clos de St Paul – *71 chemin de la Rouguière, La Colle-sur-Loup.* ℘ *04 93 32 56 81. www.stpaulweb.com/closstpaul. 3 rooms and 1 apartment.* Situated in a residential area at the foot of the village of St-Paul, this villa has classic ground-floor rooms. Generous breakfasts to enjoy under the veranda, opposite the swimming pool.

Chambre d'Hôte Mas des Cigales – *1673 rte. des Quenières, 1mi/2km from Tourrettes, rte. de St-Jean.* ℘*04 93 59 25 73. www.lemasdescigales. com. 5 rooms.* Handsome villa surrounded by a leafy garden. From the terrace running alongside the pool, you can look down onto a small waterfall, a tennis court and in the far distance, the sea. Air-conditioned rooms are charmingly decorated.

🍴 EAT

Crêperie l'Hirondelle – *14 ave. Georges-Clemenceau, La Colle-sur-Loup.* ℘ *04 92 11 05 27. Closed Sun eve except Jul–Aug and Mon.* Ideally located at the centre of the village. Ask for a seat in the brighter, more lively dining room. A relaxed, young restaurant that stays open all afternoon.

Le Médiéval – *6 Grand Rue, Tourettes.* ℘*04 93 59 31 63. Closed 15 Dec–15 Jan, Wed–Thu, eves Nov–Mar.* While strolling the charming village streets stop off at this family-run restaurant with a rustic dining room. Traditional, hearty French cooking without surprises or big prices.

Auberge des Gorges du Loup – *Le Pont du Loup.* ℘*04 93 59 38 01. www. auberge-gorgesduloup.com. Closed mid-Nov–mid-Dec, mid-Jan–mid-Feb, Sun eve and Mon.* Flanked by palms and lemon trees, this inn boasts a traditional dining room serving local cuisine around a large fireplace. Simple, affordable food. Pleasant summer terrace.

La Jarrerie – *8 ave. Amiral-de-Grasse, Le Bar-sur-Loup.* ℘*04 93 42 92 92. www.restaurant-la-jarrerie.com. Closed Jan, Wed lunch, Tue.* Housed in a wing of a former 17C monastery, this restaurant provides first-rate cuisine in a majestic setting: exposed beams, huge fireplace and stonework. Large reception hall and a pleasantly shaded summer terrace.

🛍 SHOPPING

Confiserie des Gorges du Loup (Florian) – *Pont-du-Loup. www.confi-serieflorian.com. Guided visit of the sweet manufacturing 9am–noon, 2–6.30pm. Store noon–2pm.* Candied fruits, citrus jams, sugared flowers and preserves made with rose, jasmine, violet and chocolate, all made on site.

CALENDAR

Fête de l'Oranger – Every Easter Monday the villagers celebrate the annual orange blossom harvest, with plenty of *vin d'orange*.

Fête des Violettes, Tourettes – Every first or second week in March (according to the flowering season), a two-day festival is held with a Provençal market, tours of the flower fields and a huge parade of violets through the village.

Gourdon★

Alpes Maritimes

Nicknamed "the eagle's nest", Gourdon is perched on a rocky spur more than 1,640ft/500m above the River Loup. Lined with craft workshops and art galleries, its medieval streets spring to life in summer.

A BIT OF HISTORY

Settled by the Romans, who built a double enclosure around the site, Gourdon was a feudal dependency of the comtes de Provence during the Middle Ages. Protected by a long rampart on the northern side of the village, the only vulnerable point in the fortifications, it was entered through a single gateway (on the site of the current place du Portail). Due to its isolated situation, the village was largely spared the ravages of war and revolution and remained in the hands of the Lombard family from 1598 to 1905.

🐾 WALKING TOUR

GOURDON VILLAGE

Allow 1hr. Park at the "Parking de la Rougière" at the entrance to the village and walk to the end of the car park. Situated on the edge of the village, the modest 12C **Chapelle Saint-Pons** stands in a **medieval garden.**

▶ **Population:** 437.
🕐 **Michelin Map:** 341 C5.
ℹ **Info:** 1 place Victoria. ✆04 93 09 68 25. www.tourisme-gourdon.com.
▶ **Location:** The secluded Alpes-Maritimes village is found 8.7mi/14km northeast of Grasse on D 2085, then D 3. Gourdon can also be reached by a scenic route through the Gorges du Loup, leaving from Vence.
🅿 **Parking:** All roads lead to a parking area just below the village. The village is accessible by foot only.

Formerly used for threshing wheat, it now contains several species of Mediterranean plant.

▶ *Continue east towards the village. At place du Portail, turn right onto pl. de la Fontaine.*

The Classical **fontaine de Gourdon** was erected in 1859. Surmounted by a tall column and supported by a pedestal, it was installed upon the request of a local benefactor, who bequeathed 20,000 francs for the purpose, a very large sum at the time.

View of Gourdon

Forming a backdrop to the fountain is a restored **washing place** (1871). It has the singularity of being located on the ground floor of a house and is accessible through a dressed stone arcade of semi-circular arches.

▶ *Continue to pl. du Château.*

Château★

🔓 *Closed to the public.*

Built in the 12C on the foundations of an old Saracen fortress, the castle was remodelled in the 17C. The trapezium-shaped courtyard forms an impluvium sporting rivulets to channel rainwater into a well. It is skirted by an arcade similar (though on a much smaller scale) to place des Vosges in Paris.

Château Gardens

Guided tours Apr–Sept on request for groups of over 10 people only. Inquire about charges. 04 93 09 68 02. www.chateau-gourdon.com.

The terraced gardens were designed by Le Nôtre in the 17C and laid out on three levels. They are now part of a botanical garden centre, preserving typical Pre-Alpine flora.

▶ *Continue along rue du Verger, pl. de la Citerne and into rue de l'Ecole.*

Stop to admire the Chapelle Sainte-Catherine and the **oldest house** in Gourdon (*la maison du Chevalier*), whose wooden door carved with foliage is surmounted by a beautiful sundial.

▶ *Retrace your steps and enter place de l'Eglise.*

Built directly onto its rock base, the 12C **Eglise Saint-Vincent** contains the tombs of several lords of Gourdon, along with the relics of St Vincent, St Luce and St Just. Don't miss the small Romanesque font.

▶ *Exit the church and turn right onto place Victoria.*

Local Specialities

From the surrounding forests of cork oaks and chestnut trees comes the raw material for the manufacture of bottle corks and the production of sweet chestnuts, known locally as *Marrons de Luc*. In the autumn, **Chestnut Festivals** are organised to celebrate the harvest. Local markets are held on Wednesdays and Sundays. The chestnut festival runs from late October to late November. Other towns also celebrate the chestnut at this time: Cagnes-sur-Mer, Valdeblore, Guillaumes, Fontan and Roquebrune-Cap-Martin.

Named after Queen Victoria, who visited Gourdon in April 1891, this small square offers a magnificent **panorama** over the Loup River, which emerges from the upper gorge and wends its way to the distant coast.

ADDRESSES

♥/ EAT

Au Vieux Four – *rue Basse (in the village). 04 93 09 68 60. Closed Sat, weekday eves off-season. Reservations recommended.* The perfect place to round off your visit to the village. The young owners prepare delicious Provençal food and grilled meat in an open fireplace before your eyes. Simple, refreshing decoration and reasonable prices.

🛒 SHOPPING

Sainte-Catherine – *rue de l'École. 04 93 09 68 89.* Gourmet food lovers will be at home in this delicious-smelling boutique stocked full of herbs and spices, jams, jellied fruits and plenty of regional mustards, vinegars, honey and olive oils.

La Source Parfumée – *rue Principale. 04 93 09 20 00. www.galimard.com.* A boutique of scented candles and perfumes blended on request in the old distillery, sold at wholesale prices. Also tours of the flower fields (*3€*).

Mougins★

Alpes Maritimes

The old village of Mougins dominates the summit of a hilltop crowned by ancient ramparts and a 12C fortified gateway (known as the "Saracen Gate"). Restored houses and cobblestone streets corkscrew up the hill amid lush greenery.

SIGHTS

Begin at **Place du Commandant-Lamy** *(map with commentary available at the tourist office)*, a lively square with restaurants and an ancient fountain shaded by a giant elm.

Wander northwest and turn left towards **place des Patriotes**, which has a beautiful **panoramic view**★ over the coast *(orientation table)*.

Espace Culturel

Pl. du Commandant-Lamy.
Open Oct–Mar Mon–Fri 10am–1pm, 2–6pm, Sat–Sun 11am–6pm; Apr–Sep Mon–Fri 10am–1pm, 2–7pm, Sat–Sun 11am–6pm. Closed public holidays. No charge. 04 92 92 50 42.

The former St-Bernardin chapel now houses the town hall, the Salle des Mariages and the **Musée Maurice Gottlob** (1885–1970), an artist who lived in Mougins from 1924–60. There is also an interesting retrospective of the history of Mougins, including a section on the African explorer **Commandant Lamy**, born here in 1858.

- **Population:** 19,361.
- **Michelin Map:** 341 C6.
- **Info:** 15 Av. Ch-Malet. 04 93 75 87 67. www.mougins.fr.
- **Location:** Mougins lies between Cannes (3.7mi/6km) and Grasse (7mi/11km) on the N 85. The vestiges of the old ramparts, which date back to the town's fiefdom under the Lérins Abbots, mark the limits of the pedestrian-only Old Town.
- **Parking:** Several parking areas can be found at the foot of the Old Town.

Musée de la Photographie

Porte Sarrazine.
Open Feb–Dec Mon–Fri 10am–12.30pm, 2–6pm; Sat–Sun 11am–6pm. No charge. 04 93 75 85 67.

Located behind the church bell tower, adjoining the 12C Saracen gateway this photography museum, on three floors, includes a collection of old cameras, such as the **cidoscope**, numerous photographs of Picasso by his friend André Villers, and works by famous photographers such as Clergue, Doisneau, Duncan, Lartigue, Roth, Otero, Denise Colomb and Ralph Gatti.

Village of Mougins

Gallery in Mougins

© Damian Davies/age fotostock

Musée d'Art Classique

32 rue Commandeur. ⏰*Open Apr–Oct 9.30am–8.30pm; Nov–Mar Tue–Sun 9.30am–7pm.* 15€. ☎*04 93 75 18 65. www.mouginsmusee.com*

Displayed over four floors, this collection of over 600 artefacts harmoniously combines objects from a diverse range of cultures, including Roman, Greek and Egyptian sculptures in marble and bronze, sarcophagi, vases, coins, jewellery and glassware.

From the Egyptian crypt on the lower ground floor to the collection of antique weapons on the fourth floor, the collection is dotted with paintings, drawings and sculptures by artists inspired by the south, including Chagall, Matisse, Dufy, Cé-zanne, Yves Klein and Jean Cocteau, along with two Mougins residents, Picasso and Picabia. A display worthy of a national museum.

EXCURSIONS
Ermitage Notre-Dame-de-Vie

▶ *3.7mi/6km. Leave Mougins to the north west by D 235, then right onto D 35; after 1mi/2km turn right.* ⏰*Open during Mass Sun mornings, 9am.*

The **site**★ is strikingly beautiful: the **hermitage** of Notre-Dame-de-Vie stands at the top of a long meadow bordered by two rows of giant cypresses (on the right beneath the trees stands a 15C stone cross). The **view**★ towards Mougins is reminiscent of a Tuscan landscape. Picasso chose to spend his last years here (1961–73), in the house just opposite, with his wife Jacqueline. The 17C **chapel**, roofed in colourful tiles, has three Gallo-Roman funeral inscriptions and a collection of votive offerings.

▶ *A track suitable for motor vehicles leads to the D 3, which takes you back to Mougins.*

The Minotaur's Lair

As early as 1935 **Pablo Picasso** discovered Mougins in the company of painter and photographer Dora Maar and the American-born avant-garde photographer Man Ray. He and his wife Jacqueline Roque settled in Mougins in 1961 and remained there until his death in 1973. They lived in the Notre-Dame-de-Vie district in the *mas* called L'Antre du Minotaure (The Minotaur's Lair), which became a creative workshop for artists – Picasso painted Jacqueline an astonishing 160 times in 1963 alone. In 1986, Jacqueline killed herself here with a gun.

Étang de Fontmerle

▶ *2mi/3km by the D 35 towards the golf course. At the roundabout take avenue de Grasse and then turn right on promenade de l'Étang.*

This 15acre/5ha pond was neglected for many years until it became a protected site for the cultivation of lotus flowers (*Nelumbo nucifera*). It is now the largest in Europe. Visit July to mid-September to see the flowers in full bloom. The pond is also popular with migratory birds (egrets, grey herons and ducks).

Mouans-Sartoux

2mi/3km northwest on the D 6185.
This town is made up of the medieval village of Sartoux, ruined by the Saracens, and the ancient fortress of Mouans that once protected the route de Grasse. In 1588, Suzanne de Villeneuve, widow of a Huguenot, defended her village against the troops of the duc de Savoie. After he razed the château despite a pact signed between them, Suzanne had him chased all the way to Cagnes, where he was forced to pay heavy compensation.

Espace de l'Art Concret★★

Château de Mouans. ⏱*Open daily Jul–Aug 11am–7pm, Sept–Jun Tue–Sun noon–6pm.* 🎫*5€ (no charge for temporary exhibitions).* 📞*04 93 75 71 50. www.espacedelartconcret.fr.*
This lush green park is home to the 19C Château de Mouans. A delightful setting for temporary contemporary art exhibitions, it also plays host to the **Albers-Honegger Collection**, which is housed in a green-yellow concrete cube building on the site. This exceptional collection of over 500 works by Abstract, Cubist and Minimalist artists and designers includes pieces by Swiss designers and artists Max Bill, Richard Paul Lohse and Camille Graeser, as well as Gottfried Honegger, Antonio Calderara and François Morelle. Contemporary artists, such as Daniel Buren, Olivier Mosset and Niele Toroni are also featured in the collection.

ADDRESSES

🛏 STAY

🛏 **Hôtel du Val de Mougins** – *95 ave. du Maréchal-Juin.* 📞*04 92 28 37 77. www.val-de-mougins.com. 23 rooms.* 🍴*7.50€.* This family-run establishment on the route Napoléon, at the foot of Old Mougins, has air-conditioned rooms decorated with pretty linens, many with balconies. The quietest rooms face the mountain behind the hotel.

🍴 EAT

🍴 **La Broche de Fer** – *427 ave. St-Basile, Rte. de Valbonne.* 📞*04 92 92 08 08. Closed mid–end Feb, end-Oct–early Nov and Wed.* On the route towards Valbonne, this restaurant on four levels has been charmingly decorated in the true Provençal spirit. The main specialities are grilled and roasted meats.

🍴 **L'Amandier de Mougins** – *pl. du Vieux Village.* 📞*04 93 90 00 91. www.amandier.fr. Closed mid–end Feb.* A 14C press has been converted into a ravishing inn with a vaulted dining area and a tiny terrace that is invariably booked for both lunch and dinner. It has earned a well-deserved reputation, thanks to its attractive setting, homely cooking and warm, congenial welcome.

🍴🍴 **Brasserie de la Méditerranée** – *32 pl. du Commandant Lamy.* 📞*04 93 90 03 47. www.restaurant lamediterranee.com. Closed early–mid Jan, Tue Nov–Mar.* This bistro on the village square has a fine terrace overlooking the main street. The menu presents Provençal specialities made with fresh local produce.

🍴🍴 **La Ferme de Mougins** – *10 ave. St-Basile.* 📞*04 97 21 95 76. Closed Sun eve. and Mon.* This restaurant offers several terraces, including one bordering a small stream, and an artfully decorated dining room. All-you-can-eat buffet with 50 starters, several hot main courses and 20 desserts.

Valbonne
Alpes Maritimes

Valbonne's tidy grid of picturesque, lovingly restored streets lined with art galleries and chic boutiques stands in stark contrast to its high-tech neighbour Sophia-Antipolis, Europe's answer to Silicon Valley.

SIGHTS
Old Village
Map available from the tourist office.
A haven of calm, light years from the technology park next door, this village was rebuilt by the monks of Lérins on a grid pattern in the 16C, with the houses doubling as ramparts. The **place des Arcades**, with its 15C–17C arcading and old elm trees, provides an attractive backdrop to its lively cafés and restaurants. The 19C drinking troughs and fountains, rings for tethering horses and donkeys, and *chasses-roues* wheel-blockers placed at the corner of buildings to slow down speeding carriages hint at the village's car-free past.

Church
South of the village on the Brague River.
An abbey founded in 1199 by the Chalais Order now serves as the parish church.

▶ **Population:** 12,114.

Michelin Map: 341 D6.

Info: 1 pl. de l'Hôtel-de-Ville. 𝒫04 93 12 34 50. www.tourisme-valbonne.com.

Location: Valbonne is situated between Grasse (7mi/11.5km) and Biot (5.6mi/9km) on the D 4.

Parking: The village itself is a pedestrian zone, with several large free-parking areas to the west and south of the town.

Don't Miss: The parc de Valmasque for a short hike.

Timing: Allow 2hr to visit the historic village and the musée du Patrimoine.

Kids: Nature discovery walks and play areas in the parc de Valmasque.

Its Latin cross layout with a square chevet is typical of austere Chalais buildings. The abbey houses an interesting **Musée du Patrimoine** (*open Tue–Sat Jun–Sept 3–7pm; Oct–May 2–6pm; 2€; 𝒫04 93 12 96 54; www.abbyvalb.*

Place des Arcades

© ARCO/Lenz, G/age fotostock

org) that explores the area's heritage through 2 000 items of furniture, tools, utensils and costumes displayed in authentic settings. The highlight of the museum, a vast room on the upper floor, presents the ancient crafts of Valbonne, traditional domestic life in the village and the leisure pursuits of yesteryear.
Guided tour of the village – *𝄐 04 93 12 96 54*. *8€*. The "Amis de l'Abbaye" organises tours of the Romanesque Chalais abbey church, the heritage museum and the town's glass-blowing and pottery workshops (1.5hr).

FOREST HIKES
Parc de Valmasque
Stretching between the districts of Valbonne Sophia-Antipolis and Mougins, this 1,386 acre/561ha park offers 12.4mi/20km of paths shaded by pines and oak trees, 300 picnic tables, bird-spotting platforms and play areas. Nature walks, workshops, introductions to ecosystems and climbing for adults and children are regularly organised by local organisations (visit www.cg06.fr for more details).
5.6mi/9km. A scenic, wooded path runs along the Brague River between Valbonne and Biot village, accessible from the bridge by the church.

Sophia-Antipolis
Covering an area of 5,930 acres/2,400ha and dotted with buildings that blend perfectly into its vast green spaces, this site has been designed on the model of an American campus. Sophia-Antipolis was founded by an association of the same name in 1969, under the auspices of the director of the École des Mines, Pierre Laffitte. Its proximity to the motorway and Nice-Côte d'Azur international airport make Sophia-Antipolis an ideal location for 1,200 French and international businesses specialising in four main sectors: information technology, electronics and telecommunications; health sciences and biotechnology; teaching and research; and environmental sciences. A total of 26,000 people work on the site. Europe's leading technology park, Sophia-Antipolis

marks the end of the **high-tech route** that links a number of hubs between Aix-en-Provence and Valbonne. Exhibitions are held at the Fondation Sophia Antipolis on site.

ADDRESSES

🏠 STAY

Chambre d'hôte Le Cheneau – *205 rte d'Antibes*. *𝄐 04 93 12 13 94*. *http://riviera-bandb.vadif.com*. *3 rooms*. Located between Valbonne and Mougins, this spacious Provençal villa set in parkland has comfortable, well-appointed rooms with large bathrooms. A fully-equipped kitchen is available for the use of guests. Shady terrace.

Château de la Bégude – *Opio, 2km/1mi northeast of Valbonne by rte de Biot*. *𝄐 04 93 12 37 00*. *www.opengolfclub.com/begude*. *Closed mid-Nov–mid-Dec. 35 rooms*. *19€*. *Restaurant*. This luxurious 17C manor with a pool on the site of the Opio-Valbonne golf course combines the sensuality of old stone with modern conveniences. The restaurant is also used as a club-house and bar for golfers.

🍴 EAT

Auberge Fleurie – *rte. de Cannes, 0.6mi/1.5km by the D 3*. *𝄐 04 93 12 02 80*. *Closed early Dec–mid-Jan, Mon–Tue*. Choose between the dining room or the outdoor veranda to enjoy the generous helpings of imaginative and carefully prepared cuisine, with dishes such as duck pâté with aubergines (eggplant).

CALENDAR OF EVENTS
Village market – Every Friday.

Antiques fair – First Sunday of every month in Valbonne village.

La Fête du servan – On the feast of St-Blaise (3 February), discover local wines, honey, olives and olive oil and herbs during the "servan" festival.

Christmas market – 22–24 December in Valbonne.

Vallauris
Alpes Maritimes

Pablo Picasso chose to spend his final years in this small village on a gently sloping hill, where he indulged his passion for ceramics and revived the village's ancient pottery-making traditions.

SIGHTS
Château-Museum★
Pl. de la Libération. ⏰Open Wed–Mon 10am–noon, 2–6pm (winter until 5pm). ⸙3.25€. ☎04 93 64 71 83. www.vallauris-golfe-juan.fr.
A rare example of Renaissance architecture in Provence, this former Lérins priory with pepperpot towers houses three museums.

Musée national "War and Peace" – Produced by Picasso in 1952 and gifted to the French state in 1956, this huge narrative painting housed in the vestibule of a former 12C Romanesque chapel consists of two panels: the first, dominated by black, depicts invaders attacking the symbols of civilisation, justice and peace; the second is an explosion of bright colours representing the innocent joys of peace and prosperity.

Musée Magnelli – A major collection of works donated by **Alberto Magnelli** (born in Florence 1888, died 1971), retraces the development of his style from pure colours to abstraction (*Explosion lyrique*), which he abandoned in 1920 and returned to in 1931 (*Attention naissante, Rien d'autre, Volontaire no 3*).

Musée de la Céramique – One of the rare French museums dedicated to contemporary ceramics, this collection features award-winning pieces donated by renowned ceramists (vaulted rooms). On the first floor, centred around a major display of works by Declein, the collection explores traditional designs from Vallauris, including superb pieces by Massier featuring naturalist and symbolist forms. The surprising collection of **pre-Colombian ceramics** reveals the ingenuity of their creators.
A beautiful balustraded staircase then leads to a collection of ceramics by

▶ **Population:** 30,561.
🎗 **Michelin Map:** 341 D6.
🖺 **Info:** Sq. 8-Mai-1945. ☎04 93 63 82 58. Golfe-Juan annexe: Vieux-Port, ☎04 93 63 73 12. www.vallauris-golf-juan.fr.
◗ **Location:** Attached to the same municipality as the seaside resort of Golfe-Juan *(0.9mi/2km on the D 135)*, the modern town of Vallauris stretches eastward of the Old Town and its château.
🅿 **Parking:** Park above the château or next to the tourist office.
🕓 **Timing:** Allow half a day to visit the village, museum and workshops.

Picasso, who developed a passion for this artform while living in Golfe Juan in 1946. Among the 4,000 works he created over the next 20 years, some are on display here. Superb and fantastical, they combine the genius of his painting and sculpture in human and animal forms.

Musée de la Céramique Kitsch
r. de la Fontaine. ⏰Open Wed–Mon 10am–noon, 2–6pm (winter until 5pm). ⸙No charge on presentation of entry ticket to Musée Magnelli or Musée de la Céramique. ☎04 93 64 71 83. www.vallauris-golfe-juan.fr
This new museum houses the collection of Gil Camatte who spent years collecting items sold to tourists in Vallauris from the 1960s to the 1980s.

Musée de la Poterie et de la Céramique
21 rue Sicard. ♿⏰Open Feb–Oct 9am–noon, 2–6pm (Sun 2–6pm). ⸙2€. ☎04 93 64 66 51.
Located in a working pottery studio, this museum shows how clay was worked in the first half of the 20C. The neighbouring streets are lined with pottery shops and workshops.

La Route Napoléon

After landing at Golfe-Juan on 1 March 1815, Napoleon and 700 loyal troops, preceded by an advance guard, made a brief overnight stop at Cannes. Wishing to avoid the Rhône area, which he knew to be hostile, Napoleon headed towards Grasse in order to reach the Durance Valley by way of the Alps. Beyond Grasse the small column had a difficult time proceeding along the mule tracks. They halted at St-Vallier, Escragnolles and Séranon, from whence, after a night's rest, they reached Castellane on 3 March. The next day, the party lunched at Digne and halted that evening at Château de Malijai.

Napoleon lunched in Sisteron on 5 March and left the town in an atmosphere of growing support for his cause. Once more on a coach road he arrived that night at Gap, where he was given an enthusiastic welcome. On 7 March he reached La Mure, only to find royalist troops from Grenoble facing him at Laffrey. They ended up joining the Emperor en masse and that same evening he entered Grenoble with thousands at his side to shouts of: "Long live the Emperor!"

Espace Jean-Marais

3 ave. des Martyrs-de-la-Résistance.
&Open Jul–Aug Tue–Sat 10am–1pm, 3–7pm; Sept–Jun Tue–Sat l0am–12.30pm, 2–6pm. No charge. ℘04 93 63 46 11. www.vallauris-golfe-juan.fr.
Housed in the former gallery of the artist-actor Jean Marais are sculptures, paintings and ceramics inspired by the Jean Cocteau films in which he acted (*Beauty and the Beast, Orphée*).

🚗 DRIVING TOUR

35mi/57km. Allow one day.

Route Napoléon

The Route Napoléon – Napoleon's Road – follows the route taken by the Emperor on his return from exile in Elba, from the point where he landed in Golfe-Juan to his arrival in Grenoble. The new road was opened in 1932.

▷ *Leave from Golfe-Juan*

Golfe-Juan

It was on the beach of Golfe-Juan that Napoleon and his army of 1 100 men landed from the island of Elba on 1 March 1815 (*see Route NAPOLÉON above*). This fishing port developed in the second half of the 19C by exporting local ceramics. With its 1.8mi/3km of fine sand and large choice of watersports,

Golfe-Juan is now a popular summer resort. The natural harbour is sheltered by the hills of Vallauris, the Cap d'Antibes (*see ANTIBES p270*) and the Îles de Lérins (*see ILES DE LERINS p238*).

The road winds round the west face of Super-Cannes hill, facing the Îles de Lérins and the Esterel Massif.

Cannes★★

See CANNES p230.

▷ *From Cannes take N 85 to Mougins.*

The road rises above the town and the sea past the perched village of **Mougins**★ (*see MOUGINS p260*).

Mouans-Sartoux

See MOUGINS p260.
On leaving Mouans-Sartoux, the road reveals Grasse spread out across the mountain slope ahead.

Grasse★ See GRASSE p245.
▷ *From Grasse take N 85 northwest.*

The road skirts "Napoleon's Plateau" where he halted on 2 March outside the town. Pass through the Provence Plateau and then the Pre-Alps of Grasse. The route crosses three passes in succession: **Col du Pilon** (2,566ft/782m), **Pas de la Faye** (3,218ft/981m) and

Col de Valferrière (3,805ft/1,169m), where the **view south** is magnificent.

Col du Pilon
From the southern slope there is a **view**★★ of La Napoule Bay.

St-Vallier-de-Thiey
♨ *See ST-VALLIER-DE-THIEY p250.*
As the road climbs to Pas de la Faye there are some very fine **views**★.

Pas de la Faye★★
Similar **view** to that seen from Col du Pilon. Those travelling south over the pass suddenly discover the Mediterranean and the Riviera coastline below.

◗ *0.6mi/1km before Escragnolles, near a petrol station, a road to the Belvédère de Baou Mourine branches off left.*

Belvédère de Baou Mourine★
0.6mi/1km, plus 30min on foot round trip. 🥾 *Path marked with red arrows.*
Walk to the terrace **viewpoint**★ over the Siagne Valley. After Escragnolles, where Napoleon made a brief halt, there are fine **views** to the south.

◗ *For an alternative route to Cannes via Grasse described in reverse order* ♨ *see GRASSE: Driving Tours p249.*

ADDRESSES

🛏 STAY

🍽🍽 **Hôtel Val d'Aurea** – *11 bis blvd. Maurice-Rouvier.* ✆*04 93 64 64 29. Closed mid-Sept–early Apr.* Although the hotel is fairly unimpressive from the outside, once you pass through the door, a warm, family welcome awaits you. The rooms are standard and functional. Request one at the back of the house. The bathrooms are decorated with colourful tiles.

🍽🍽 **De la Mer** – *226 ave. Liberté.* ✆*04 93 63 80 83.www.hotelmer.com. 33 rooms. Closed early Nov–early Dec.* 🏊. Although this hotel is close to the road, all of its simple rooms are double-glazed and located to the rear, some with balconies. Swimming pool.

🍴 EAT

🍽🍽 **Le Clos Cosette** – *1 ave. du Tapis-Vert.* ✆*04 93 64 30 64. www.lecloscosette.com.* Ordinary from the outside, this city centre restaurant has a spacious reception room and a dining room with a dry stone wall decorated with drawings and paintings. Traditional, market-fresh cuisine of a consistently high standard.

🍽🍽🍽🍽 **Nounou** – *On the beach at Golfe-Juan.* ✆*04 93 63 71 73. www.nounou.fr. Closed Nov–Mar.* Regional cuisine and seafood specialities are on the menu at this landmark seaside restaurant open since 1928.

CERAMICS

Tour of traditional pottery workshops – *Closed Sat–Sun.* 🎫*No charge. Information at the tourist office:* ✆*04 93 63 82 58.*
Pottery classes – *Espace Grandjean, blvd. des Deux-Vallons. Closed winter, Sat–Sun in summer.* ✆*04 93 63 07 61.* Pottery classes for kids and adults at the fine arts school (10, 20 or 30hr).
Galerie Madoura – *rue Suzanne et Georges-Ramié.* ✆*04 93 64 66 39. www.madoura.com. Open Dec–Oct Mon–Fri 10am–12.30pm, 3–6pm.* Exhibition and sales of ceramics produced by Picasso.

CALENDAR

Fête de la Poterie – This pottery festival takes place on the second Sun in Aug.

Biennial International Festival of Ceramic Art – ✆*04 93 64 34 67, http://biennale.vallauris.free.fr.* Even years, July to mid-October.

Festival Jean Marais – Theatre and variety festival every summer, Jul– Aug.

Reenactment of Napoleon's landing – First weekend of every Mar on Golfe-Juan beach.

Juan-les-Pins★
Alpes Maritimes

Renowned for its jazz festival, trendy nightclubs and endless stretch of sandy beaches, Juan-les-Pins is one of the Riviera's most lively summer resorts. Protected by the Cap d'Antibes and Pointe de la Croisette, the bay enjoys a mild climate and easy access to Cannes and Antibes.

A BIT OF HISTORY

The "Swing" Era

The thriving musical nightlife of Juan-les-Pins began during the 1920s with the arrival of the first American tourists, who revolutionised the atmosphere of the resort: they sunbathed on the beaches, water-skied and listened to an unfamiliar music called jazz. **Frank Gould** founded the first summer casino, frequented by the likes of Douglas Fairbanks, Mary Pickford and actress Mistinguett. After the Liberation, Sydney Bechet restored music to the town and the first jazz festival took place in 1959, a year after his death, attracting legends such as Louis Armstrong, Count Basie, Duke Ellington, Dizzy Gillespie and Miles Davis.

- **Michelin Map:** 341 D6.
- **Info:** 51, boulevard Charles Guillaumont – Juan-les-Pins ℘04 97 23 11 10. www.antibesjuanlespins.com.
- **Location:** Technically part of the same municipality, Juan-les-Pins is connected to Antibes on the east by the Cap d'Antibes (see ANTIBES p270) and to the west by Golfe-Juan, along the RN 7 or the coastal N 98. The train station is only a few blocks from the beaches.
- **Parking:** Parking spots are difficult to locate in summer, but typically can be found by the station (gare) or along the beach (fee).

RESORT LIFE

Down by the shore, the Promenade au Soleil, running between the landing-stage and the casino, is teeming with restaurants, open-air cafés and nightclubs. The **port Gallice**, to the east, is home to dozens of luxury yachts. During the day, admire the architecture of many hotels and private homes built in the 1920s and 1930s (request a map at the tourist office).

Beach at Juan-les-Pins

Beaches

The pines grow right down to the gently sloping beach of Juan-les-Pins, a superb stretch of fine sand some 1.8mi/3km long and sheltered from the winds. There are several private and public beaches all around, dotted between the ports of Golfe-Juan and La Gallice.

Parc Exflora

Off the D 6007 towards Golfe-Juan.
🕐*Open daily Sept and Mar–May 9.30am–7pm; Jun–Aug 9.30am–9.30pm; Oct–Feb 9.30am–5pm.*
📞*04 97 23 11 10 (tourist office).*
Set within this vast orchard of olive tree are many different incarnations of Mediterranean garden from antiquity to the 19C. The settings include a Roman garden, a palm tree garden, a labyrinth, a winter garden and an oasis overlooking the sea.

ADDRESSES

🛏 STAY

🍽🛌 **Hôtel Cécil** – *rue Jonnard.* 📞*04 93 61 05 12. www.hotelcecil-france. com. Closed 3 Nov–Jan. 21 rooms, half-board.* 🍴*6.50€* A traditional residence converted into a hotel in 1920. The impeccably-kept rooms are laid out over three floors. Dinner is served on the terrace in summer. Situated in the town centre, not far from the beach.

🍽🛌 **Éden Hôtel**– *16 ave. L. Gallet.* 📞*04 93 61 05 20. www.edenhoteljuan. com. Closed Nov–Feb. 17 rooms.* 🍴*€7.* Built in 1930, this hotel offers guests breakfast on the terrace and a welcoming atmosphere, just minutes from the beach. Simple rooms, some with **sea views**.

🍽🛌🛌 **Hôtel Ste-Valérie** – *rue de l'Oratoire.* 📞*04 93 61 07 15. www.hotel-sainte-valerie.fr. Closed mid-Oct–early Mar. 26 rooms.* 🅿. 🍴*20€*. Just off a quiet street, this hotel has carefully-kept, air-conditioned rooms with terraces or balconies overlooking pretty gardens, where breakfast is served on warm days. Outdoor pool.

🍴 EAT

🍽 **Le Capitole** – *26 ave. Amiral-Courbet.* 📞*04 93 61 22 44. Closed Dec.* Only the shelves remain in this former grocery shop, converted to a smart restaurant serving traditional fare.

🍽 **L'Amiral** – *7 ave. Amiral-Courbet.* 📞*04 93 67 34 61. www.lamiral-restaurant06.com. Closed early to mid-Mar, 1st 2 wks Jul, late Nov–early Dec, Mon.* Small, family-run business providing tasty local cuisine on prettily decorated tables in a modern, friendly setting. If you like couscous, go on Thursday, but book first!

🍽 **Bijou Plage** – *blvd. Guillaumont.* 📞*04 93 61 39 07. www.bijouplage.com.* Locals and tourists alike flock to this beach restaurant on the road to Golfe-Juan. The menu pays tribute to *bouillabaisse* and other fish dishes. Private beach and watersports facilities also available.

🌙 NIGHTLIFE

Eden Casino – *blvd. Édouard-Baudoin.* 📞*04 92 93 71 71. www.partouche-casino-juan-les-pins.fr.* Seaside casino with traditional table games and 180 slot machines, restaurant and themed bars.

Le Crystal – *ave. Gallice.* 📞*04 93 61 02 51. Closed mid-Nov–late Dec, Mon off-season.* First opened in 1936, this was a family brasserie housed in a small hut surrounded by grazing sheep. Today the popular club is hemmed in between the Casino and a host of other bars.

🚵 LEISURE ACTIVITIES

Watersports – Ask at the tourist office about beaches offering water skiing, wind surfing, scuba diving and paragliding.

Visiobulle – Leaves from the Embarcadère Courbet, opposite the Maison du Tourisme. 📞*04 93 67 02 11. www.visiobulle.com. Closed Oct–Mar. Booking recommended in Jul and Aug.* 🎫*13€ (6.50€ children).* This glass-bottomed boat offers **views** of the sea depths right up to the tip of Cap d'Antibes, which cannot be reached by land.

Antibes★★

Alpes-Maritimes

Situated on the western shores of the Baie des Anges, Antibes hugs the coastline between two coves, Salis and St-Roch. The marina, the old town with its covered market and the Cap d'Antibes deserve a place on everyone's Riviera must-do list.

A BIT OF HISTORY

Greek Antipolis – From the 4C BC the Greeks of Massalia, modern day Marseille, set up a chain of coastal trading posts with the Ligurian tribes. Antipolis, the new Greek city that grew opposite Nice, was contained between the Cours Masséna and the sea. The Greeks were succeeded by the Romans and then by pirates and Barbarians, whose invasions gradually undermined the city's prosperity.

Antibes, frontier outpost – The kings of France realised the key military role that Antibes could play from the 14C, when the town stood on the Franco-Savoyard frontier. It became the property of the Grimaldis in 1386 and was later purchased by King Henri IV. Each reign improved or enlarged the fortifications until the work was completed by Vauban with the Fort Carré in the 17C.

Bonaparte at Antibes – In 1794, Napoleon Bonaparte, charged with defending the coast, settled his family in Antibes.
Although a general, his pay seldom arrived on the appointed day, so his mother did the household laundry herself in a nearby stream. Bonaparte was imprisoned for a time in Fort Carré after the fall of Robespierre during the French Revolution.

Notable inhabitants – **Nikos Kazantzakis** (1885–1957) wrote *Zorba the Greek* and the *Last Temptation of Christ* while living in Antibes. **Nicolas de Staël** (1914–55) painted his last canvasses in Antibes, before taking his own life. A young, glamorous American couple,

▶ **Population:** 75,820.
◔ **Michelin Map:** 341 D6
▯ **Info:** 11 Pl. du Général-de-Gaulle. ℘04 97 23 11 11. www.antibesjuanlespins.com.
▶ **Location:** Antibes has four major areas: the Port Vauban and Fort Carré to the north, the Old Town *(vieil Antibes)*, La Salis beaches and Cap d'Antibes to the south. The narrow streets of the Old Town should be explored on foot, but there is also a sightseeing train *(◔see Le Petit Train d'Antibes; Mar–Oct daily; ℘06 03 35 61 35)*.
🅿 **Parking:** There are a few underground car parks in the Old Town, but it's easier to park in one of the vast car parks along the Port Vauban *(fee in high season)*.
◎ **Don't Miss:** The Picasso Museum in the Château Grimaldi, the Provençal market at the Cours Masséna, the immense yachts on the Quai de la Grande Plaisance, the **panoramic views** of the coastline from La Garoupe lighthouse, and the scenic beach and walking trail at the Plage de la Garoupe.
🕐 **Timing:** Antibes deserves a full day. The sights of the Old Town and port should be visited first, then any museums or the Fort Carré. Then drive around the Cap d'Antibes and hike along the coastal path *(sentier)* or the sandy beaches.
👪 **Kids:** At the northeast end of Antibes is the popular Marineland waterpark, La Petite Ferme du Far West and Aventure Golf.

Port Vauban and the Fort Carré

J. Malburet/MICHELIN

Sara and Gerald Murphy, fell in love with Antibes in the mid-1920s and their villa became a favourite holiday haunt for their many American friends, including the Fitzgeralds and the Hemingways.

☞ WALKING TOUR

OLD ANTIBES★
Allow 3hr (⚫ see map I overleaf).
To reach the old town follow the signs for "Palais-vielle-ville" and park in the "Chemin des pêcheurs" car park.
▶ *Begin at avenue de Verdun.*

Port Vauban
Avenue de Verdun commands a good **view** of the marina and the 16C **Fort Carré** (⚫ see Sights p274), with the

heights of Nice in the background. The **Port Vauban**, one of the largest in the Mediterranean, is lined with luxury cruise yachts, the largest of which can be found along the Quai de la Grande Plaisance (also known as *Quai des Millionaires*).

▶ *Enter the old town by the sea gate and follow the montée des Saleurs around the ramparts to the promenade Amiral-de-Grasse.*

Promenade Amiral-de-Grasse
This former seafront promenade runs along the vestiges of the 17C ramparts below the old cathedral and the **Château Grimaldi** (Musée Picasso, ⚫ see overleaf). The original 12C castle overlooking the sea was built on the

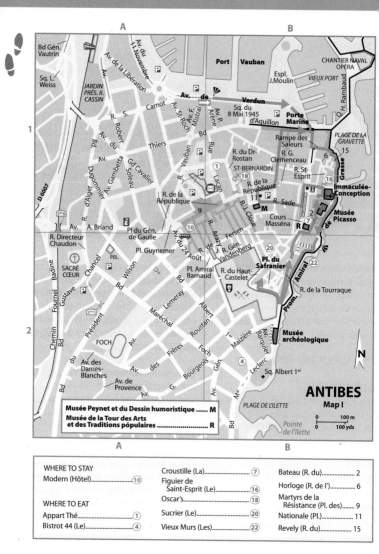

ANTIBES
Map I

0   100 m
0   100 yds

Musée Peynet et du Dessin humoristique ...... M
Musée de la Tour des Arts
et des Traditions pópulaires .... R

foundations of a Roman camp situated on the Antipolis acropolis. It was reconstructed in the 16C but the square Roman tower, battlement walk and pairs of windows remain from the original structure. The castle was home to the Grimaldi family until the 17C.
It gives a fine **view**★ of the coastline stretching towards Nice and the Alps.

▶ *Return along the promenade to the Musée archéologique.*

Musée Archéologique

1 ave. Maizière (Bastion Saint-André). &·⏲*Open Tue–Sun mid-Sep–mid-Jun 10am–1pm, 2–5pm; mid-Jun–mid-Sep 10am–noon, 2–6pm (until 8pm Wed and Fri in Jul–Aug).* ⏲*Closed 1 Jan, 1 May, 1 Nov, 25 Dec.* ⊚3€. ℘*04 92 90 53 36. www.antibesjuanlespins.com.*
The 17C Bastion St-André contains an **archaeological collection** illustrating 4,000 years of local history, including the reconstruction of a Roman ship used for transporting amphorae and an ornamented lead sarcophagus. The back of

a large vaulted room, built on a reservoir, houses a bread oven and objects salvaged from shipwrecks from the Middle Ages to the 18C. New acquisitions include a marble statuette of Dionysus (1–2C).

▶ *Retrace your steps to the promenade and take the first street on the left.*

Place du Safranier
This square is at the heart of the free commune known as "Le Safranier", set up in the wake of the Second World War. The writer Nikos Kazantzakis lived at 8 rue du Bas-Castellet. The plaque on the façade encapsulates his philosophy: "I fear nothing. I expect nothing. I am a free man".

▶ *Return to rue de la Tourraque and take rue de l'Orme on the right.*

Musée de la Tour des Arts et Traditions populaires
1 rue de l'Orme. Reservation required (minimum 8 people). ℘04 92 90 54 28. www.antibesjuanlespins.com.
Housed in the Tour de l'Orme, this museum displays everyday folk objects from the 18C and 19C, along with a pair of water skis belonging to **Léo Roman**, who invented the sport in 1921 in Juan-les-Pins.

▶ *Turn left down rue du Bateau.*

Musée Picasso★★
Pl. Mariejol. ♿🕐Open Tue–Sun mid-Sept–mid-Jun 10am–noon, 2–6pm; mid-Jun–mid-Sept 10am–6pm (Jul–Aug Wed and Fri 8pm). 🕐Closed 1 Jan, 1 May, 1 Nov, 25 Dec. 🎫6€ (3€ students). ℘04 92 90 54 28. www.antibesjuanlespins.com.
Recently renovated, the museum's new wood-and-concrete design provides a more spacious setting for the works on display and easier circulation for visitors. The vaulted groundfloor rooms play host to the **Donation Hartung-Bergamn**. A large staircase leads to the first floor, devoted to temporary exhibitions and the works of **Nicolas de Staël**, who

spent his last winter in Antibes. Note in particular *Still Life with Chandelier, Fort Carré* and the gigantic canvas entitled *Grand Concert*.
The **Picasso collection** is displayed on the second floor, which was once the artist's studio.
Donation Picasso★ Soon after his arrival on the Riviera in the autumn of 1946, **Pablo Picasso** (1881–1973), who had part of the castle at his disposal, began work on some large-scale paintings. Over the course of one season he produced the majority of the 23 paintings, lithographs and 44 drawings in the collection. Due to post-war canvas shortages, he painted on fibro-cement and plywood.
His **paintings** are joyful works bursting with imagination, inspired by the marine and mythological life of the Mediterranean: *Ulysses and the Sirens, Fish, La Joie de Vivre, Watermelon, The Oak Tree* and an imposing triptych, *Satyr, Faun* and *Centaur with Trident*.
An impressive collection of Picasso's **ceramics**, created at Vallauris between 1948 and 1949, are displayed in showcases scattered around the museum.
In the **courtyard** there is a composition by the sculptor Arman depicting guitars inspired by Picasso's *À ma Jolie*. In the **terrace garden** are statues by Germaine Richier and works by Miró, Pagès, Amado Spoerri and Poirier.

▶ *Take the steps leading to the church.*

Cathédrale de l'Immaculée-Conception
Only the east end of the original Romanesque church, which served as a cathedral in the Middle Ages, remains. The belfry is a converted 12C watchtower. Art treasures include a wooden Crucifix (1447) in the choir, a former pagan stone altar in the south apsidal chapel, a 16C **Recumbent Christ** carved in limewood and a 1515 **altarpiece** by Louis Bréa in the south transept.

▶ *Return to the cours Masséna (morning market) and take rue Sade to place Nationale.*

EDEN-ROC, an Edwardian Paradise

This majestic palace surrounded by an estate (8ha/20 acres) is set on a promontory of Cap d'Antibes. Famous for its quaint huts *(cabanes)* and its private beach, it has become an essential port of call for film stars visiting the Riviera. A party given by Russian princes in spring 1870 launched the Grand Hôtel du Cap. After a slack period the Grand Hôtel was resuscitated on the instigation of the American Gordon Bennett. In 1914, an annexe – the Eden Roc – together with its private beach was built. Since then it has known unflagging success, with a varied and cosmopolitain clientele featuring such eminent figures as General Eisenhower (who used it as his winter quarters), the painters Picasso and Chagall who worked here, and a number of rich eccentrics like the oil magnate Gulbenkian *(Mister 5%)*.

Musée Peynet et du Dessin humoristique★

Pl. Nationale. &. ○*Open Tue–Sun 10am–noon, 2–6pm; Jul–Aug open late Wed and Fri until 8pm.* ○*Closed public holidays.* ⊙*3€ (under-18s free).* ℘*04 92 90 54 29.*

Housed in a 19C school, the museum has a collection of lithographs, ink drawings, watercolours, sculptures and greeting cards by the cartoonist **Raymond Peynet** (1908–99), who moved to Antibes in 1950. He is best known for his two young lovers, "Les Amoureux", whose adventures were published in *Paris Match, Marie-Claire* and *Elle*.

ADDITIONAL SIGHTS
Fort Carré

Ave. du 11 Novembre. ○*Open Tue–Sun Oct–May noon–4.30pm; Jun–Sept 10am–6pm.* ☞*Guided tours (30min).* ○*Closed 1 Jan, 1 May, 1 Nov, 25 Dec.* ⊙*3€.* ℘*04 92 90 52 13. www.antibesjuanlespins.com.*

Built atop an isolated outcrop in 1550, the central St-Laurent tower was consolidated by four surrounding citadels 15 years later. Thanks to the fortification work carried out by Vauban, this stronghold braved many an assault during its existence, yielding only to the duc d'Epernay and Napoleon's enemies.

EXCURSIONS
⛟ Marineland★

▶ *2.5mi/4km north towards Nice.*
&. ○*Open Jul–Aug daily 10am–11pm; rest of year: enquire for details.* ⊙*36€*

(28€ children 3–12), Marineland only. Combined one- and two-day tickets available. ℗ ℘*04 93 33 49 49. www.marineland.fr.*

The largest marine zoo in Europe (4,000 animals), Marineland has many large pools with **killer whales**, dolphins, elephant seals and sea lions. There are regular acrobatic shows. A spectacular **"Sharks"** exhibit takes visitors down a 98ft/30m tunnel with a **view** of a dozen grey sharks and tiger sharks. Marineland also houses a small museum of models and marine instruments.

⛟ Parc Aqua-Splash

Entrance via Marineland. ○*Open mid-Jun–early Sept daily 10am–7pm.* ⊙*25€ (20€ children 3–12), combined entrance for Marineland available.* ℘*04 93 33 49 49. www.marineland.fr.*

The largest water leisure park on the French Riviera features a swimming pool with waves, water slides (2,187yd/2,000m), a giant pool, space boat, kiddie pool and a pirate island.

⛟ La Petite Ferme du Far West

Entrance via the Marineland car park. &. ○*Open Feb–Dec daily 10am–dusk. Opening days change every month, check for details.* ⊙*13€ (10€ children 3–12).* ℘*04 93 33 49 49. www.marineland.fr.*

This Wild West town recreates the spirit of the frontier with a fort, Mississippi riverboats, train raids, friendly horses and a farmyard for younger children.

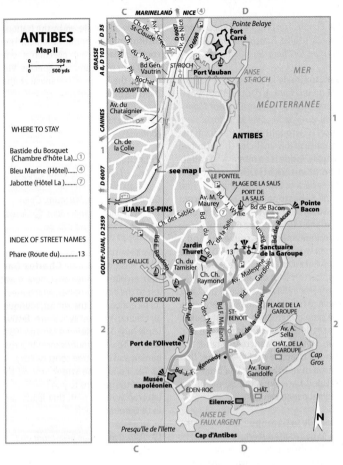

👫 Adventure Golf

Entrance via the Marineland car park.
♿🕐*Open May–Sept daily noon–midnight. Rest of year: enquire for details.*
📧*11€ (9€ children 3–12).* 📞*04 93 33
49 49. www.marineland.fr.*
Miniature golf featuring three
different 18-hole courses with a
Jules Verne theme.

🚗 DRIVING TOURS

Cap d'Antibes★
6mi/10km. Allow 2hr (🕐see map II).

The garden-like peninsula, which
stretches from the south of Antibes to
Juan-les-Pins, is dotted with sumptuous
hotels and villas catering to both summer and winter visitors. They include
the **Hôtel Eden-Roc**, a Belle Epoque
paradise popular with stars in town for
the Cannes Film Festival.

🚶 1hr. The coastal path, which
extends from the plage de la Garoupe
to villa Eilenroc, passing Pointe Bacon
(🕐*see below*).

▶ *Begin at the Pointe Bacon, just past
La Salis beach on blvd. de Bacon.*

Pointe Bacon
This point gives a **view**★ of Antibes and
Fort Carré, sweeping across the Baie des
Anges opposite Nice and the surround-
ing countryside to Cap Ferrat.

▷ *Continue on blvd. de La Garoupe and right on to blvd. Francis Meilland. Follow the signs for Phare de La Garoupe.*

Sanctuaire de la Garoupe

635 rte. du Phare. ᯡᰙ Open May–Sept 10am–noon, 2.30–7pm (Oct–Apr 10am–noon, 2.30–5pm). ℘04 93 67 36 01.

Two 17C wrought-iron gates form the entrance to this small church and its two chapels. Inside is an interesting **collection of votive offerings**; the oldest dates back to 1779. Over the high altar is the **Sebastopol icon**, a magnificent Russo-Byzantine work believed to date from the 14C. There are 60 naval votive offerings, maritime souvenirs and a gilded wood statue of **Notre-Dame de Bon-Port** (Our Lady of Safe Homecoming), patron saint of sailors.

Every year in July the statue of Our Lady, taken to the old cathedral in Antibes on the previous week, is brought back in procession to La Garoupe by the seamen. Beside the sanctuary stands the curious Oratoire de Ste-Hélène, first patron of Antibes, who has been worshipped here since the 5C AD in the original pagan shrine.

Phare de la Garoupe

☞ Closed to the public.

This **lighthouse**, one of the most powerful on the Mediterranean coast, has a beam that carries 32mi/52km out to sea and 62mi/100km for aircraft.

▷ *Double back and turn right on blvd. Meilland. Follow blvd. du Cap to the INRA - VIlla Thuret.*

Jardin Thuret★

90 chemin Raymond. ᰙ Open Mon–Fri Apr–Oct 8am–6pm; Nov–Mar 8am–5.30pm. ᰙ Closed public holidays. No charge. ℘04 93 67 88 66. http://jardin-thuret.antibes.inra.fr.

These **botanical gardens**, covering 10 acres/4ha, were created in 1857 by the scientist Gustave Thuret, who used them to acclimatise plants and trees from hot countries, including the first eucalyptuses from Australia.

Bequeathed to the state, the gardens are currently administered by the National Institute of Agronomic Research. They contain a magnificent collection of some 3,000 rare plant and tree species. Villa Thuret, the gardens' botanical centre, contains offices and research labs.

▷ *Return to blvd. Meilland and continue along ave. L.H. Beaumont.*

Villa Eilenroc

*ᯡ Av. L.-H.-Beaumont. **Villa:** ᰙ Open Sept–Jun Wed 9am–noon, 1.30–5pm; **Gardens and Eco-Museum:** Open Tue–Wed and Sat 9am–5pm. ᰙ Closed public holidays. No charge. ℘04 93 67 74 33.*

This beautiful seaside estate built in 1867 was designed by **Charles Garnier**, architect of the Paris Opera. It was left to the city of Antibes, which uses it for receptions and the annual "Musiques au Cœur d'Antibes" lyrical arts festival (early July). The interior retains its 1930s decor. The villa grounds include a rose garden and olive tree conservatory.

🚶 *1hr.* Follow the street around the back of the gardens to join the "Sentier Littoral" walking path that leads back to La Garoupe beach.

▷ *Return to avenue Beaumont and turn left onto blvd. J F. Kennedy.*

Espace du Littoral et du Milieu Marin

Bd J.-F.-Kennedy, Juan-les-Pins. ᰙ Open Tue–Sat mid-Sept–mid-Jun 10am–6pm; mid-Sept–mid-Jun 10am–4.30pm). ᰙ Closed public holidays. 3€. ℘04 93 61 45 32.

Part of the Musée Naval, the former Le Grillon battery has been converted into a coastal and marine museum. The displays include a number of ingenious inventions, such as the shark cage in which the great French marine explorer Jacques Cousteau was lowered into the sea, surrounded by swirls of deadly sharks, an underwater jet ski used to travel along the ocean currents, and one of the first ever deep-sea cameras. From the roof, there is a fine **view**★ over the wooded headland to the Îles de Lérins and to the distant Alps.

ADDRESSES

🛏 STAY

🍴🍴 **Modern Hôtel** – *1 rue Fourmilière. 𝒞04 92 90 59 05. www.modernhotel06. com. 17 rooms.* ⚏*7€.* At the entrance of a pedestrian zone, this small hotel has simple, minimalist decor.

🍴🍴 **Hôtel Bleu Marine** – *chemin des 4-Chemins (north Antibes, near hospital). 𝒞04 93 74 84 84. www.bleumarine antibes.com. 18 rooms.* 🅿. ⚏*7€.* A contemporary hotel near Marineland and the pebble beaches, with easy access to the A 8 and N 7. Top-floor rooms have **sea views**.

🍴🍴 **Hotel La Jabotte** – *13 avenue Max-Maurey, Cap d'Antibes. 𝒞04 93 61 45 89. www.jabotte.com. 10 rooms.* 🅿. ⚏. *Restaurant*🍴🍴🍴. On a street perpendicular to La Salis beach, this hotel features individually decorated rooms overlooking a sunny patio.

🍴🍴🍴 **Chambre d'Hôte La Bastide du Bosquet** – *14 chemin des Sables, (Domaine des Mûriers), Cap-Antibes. 𝒞04 93 67 32 29. www.lebosquet06.com. Closed mid-Nov–late Dec. 4 rooms.* ⚏. Attractive 18C country house at the heart of a residential area. Provençal furnishings. Leafy garden and terrace.

🍽 EAT

🍴 **Appart Thé** – *24 rue Lacan. 𝒞04 93 34 08 24. Closed Sun.* This small and stylish tearoom just off the pedestrian square serves salads, quiches and ice cream, in addition to 15 types of tea. Small summer terrace.

🍴 **La Croustille** – *4 cours Masséna. 𝒞04 93 34 84 83.* Settle on the charming terrace of this creperie-salad bar in old Antibes and soak up the lively, colourful atmosphere of the local market. The cosy interior is decorated with family photographs. Reasonable prices.

🍴🍴 **La Bonne Table – Bistro 44** – *44 blvd. Albert-1er. 𝒞04 93 34 43 08. Closed Nov, eves in winter.* A family restaurant, just off the seafront, serving traditional French dishes.

🍴🍴 **Le Figuier de St-Esprit** – *14 rue St-Esprit. 𝒞04 93 34 50 12. www.restaurant-figuier-saint-esprit.com. Closed Tue, Wed lunch, late Nov–late Dec.* A modern, stylish restaurant on the ramparts recently taken over by chef Christian Morriset. Contemporary French cuisine. Shady terrace.

🍴🍴 **Oscar's** – *8 r. Rostan. 𝒞04 93 34 90 14. www.oscars-antibes.com. Closed Sun–Mon. Reservations required.* Italian-inspired Provençal cuisine is served in an elegant dining room.

🍴 **Le Sucrier** – *6 rue des Bains. 𝒞04 93 34 85 40. Closed Tue.* Tucked down a side street, this cosy restaurant serves contemporary French dishes made using market-fresh, seasonal produce.

🍴🍴🍴 **Les Vieux Murs** – *25 promenade Amiral-de-Grasse. 𝒞04 93 34 06 73. www.lesvieuxmurs.com.* Red stone walls, Murano chandeliers and silk fabrics give the dining room of this seafront restaurant a refined atmosphere. The cuisine is Mediterranean with an emphasis on fish and fresh market produce.

🛍 SHOPPING

Marché Provençal – *Cours Masséna. Closed afternoons, Mon in low season.* This colourful, covered market features typical regional produce.

Rue Sade – The picturesque street stretching from the Cours Masséna to Place Nationale is full of charming boutiques and gourmet food shops.

🏃 SPORT AND LEISURE

Beaches – The long pebble beach of Antibes extends way beyond Fort Carré. Four other public beaches are covered in fine sand: La Gravette (south of the old port), the Îlette, La Salis and La Garoupe.

Watersports – Antibes is a *station nautique* with a wide variety of watersports on offer, from water-skiing and scuba diving to sailing and windsurfing. *Contact the tourist office for more details or visit www.station-nautique.com.*

AMC Croisères – *1228 blvd de la Garoup, Cap-d'Antibes. 𝒞04 92 93 16 39. www.am-catamaran.com. From 40€.* Catamaran cruises leave from Antibes, St-Raphael or St-Tropez, with diving and sea-kayaking equipment on board.

Biot★

Biot is a picturesque hillside village famous for its pottery, blown glass and museum dedicated to the artist Fernand Léger.

SIGHTS
Old Village
To appreciate the authentic charm of the picturesque streets, start from the tourist office and head for porte des Migraniers (Grenadiers) and porte des Tines (both 16C), leading to the beautiful **place des Arcades** with its rounded and pointed arches.

Church
Set back from place des Arcades with a mosaic stone pavement, the church is actually below street level with stairs leading down from the entrance. Rebuilt in the 15C, it was decorated with murals, which the bishop of Grasse considered crude and had painted over in 1699. On the west wall is an **altarpiece**★ of the Virgin of the Rosary attributed to **Louis Bréa**. At the far end of the church is another altarpiece, attributed

2,500 Years of History

Built on a bed of clay, sand, manganese and tuff deposit (oven stone), Biot was already known for its earthenware jars under the Phocaeans, Celto-Ligurians, Greeks and Romans. The tradition was continued during the Middle Ages under the Templars, who took possession of the village in 1209, and survived war and the Black Death in the 14C. Famous until 18C for its varnished jars, which were used for storing oil shipped from the ports of Antibes and Marseille, Biot is still home to a number of potters specialising in decorative ware. Since 1956, the town's reputation has been built on its glass-blowing workshops, which produce brightly-coloured bubble-flecked glass.

▶ **Population:** 8,791.
⟳ **Michelin Map:** 341 D6.
Info: 46 rue St-Sébastien. ℰ04 93 65 78 00. www.biot.fr.
▶ **Location:** Biot lies 2.5mi/4km inland, about 4.6mi/7.5km from Antibes on the N 7, then the D 4.
P **Parking:** Only residents can drive into the village, but there are several free parking areas around the town, with regular shuttles to the village centre.
⏱ **Timing:** Allow half a day for the town and museums.
Kids: Glass-blowing demonstrations at the Verrerie de Biot.

to **Canavesio**, in the form of an **Ecce Homo** with two cherubs and the instruments of the Passion. The panel above shows the Flagellation, Christ Reviled and the Resurrection.

Musée National Fernand-Léger★★
Southeast of the village, just off D 4 (signposted). &⏱*Open Wed–Mon May–Oct 10am–6pm; Nov–Apr 10am–5pm.* ⏱*Closed 1 Jan, 1 May, and 25 Dec.* ⬮*7.50€.* **P** ℰ*04 92 91 50 20. www.musees-nationaux-alpesmaritimes.fr/f.leger.*
Built in 1960 by local architect **Andreï Svetchine**, this museum houses 348 works by **Fernand Léger** (1881–1955). The gardens were donated to the State by Nadia Léger and Georges Bauquier. The **façade** is decorated by a vast **mosaic** (5,382sq ft/500sq m) celebrating sports, designed for the Hanover Stadium. The **interior** was redesigned in 2008 by the architect Marc Barani. On the ground floor, the large stained-glass windows are inspired by one of Léger's drawings.
The **permanent collection** on the first floor features 450 works displayed chronologically in two large areas sepa-

Success Story

The architect Andreï Svetchine was the son of a Russian general. Born and raised in Nice, he attended the Academy of Decorative Arts there. He soon demonstrated remarkable skills as an architect and was to design some of the most prestigious private residences and museums on the Riviera, notably the Fernand Léger Museum in Biot (👁 see Sights opposite). In the early 1960s, the artist Marc Chagall asked him to build a house and adjoining studio. The result, "La Colline", was a splendid construction in white Provençal stone arranged in rectangular shapes. Svetchine also refurbished La Colombe d'Or, the famous hotel in St-Paul-de-Vence catering to an exclusive international clientele. In 1984, towards the end of his life, he supervised the challenging task of restoring St-Nicolas, the superb Russian Orthodox Cathedral in Nice.

rated by a biographical room. After his early Impressionist works, such as *Portrait of the Uncle* (1903) and *My Mother's Garden*, Cézanne's influence becomes increasingly evident in *Study of a Woman in Blue* (1912–13) and *14 July*.

After 1945 the artist painted large canvases praising the virtues of hard work, industrial civilisation (*Builders*, 1950, marks a significant achievement in style and inspiration), relaxation and *joie de vivre* (*Campers*). *The Great Parade* (1954) pays homage to the circus.

Musée d'Histoire Locale et des Céramiques Biotoises

9 rue Saint-Sébastien. 🕐 *Open summer Wed–Sun 11am–7pm; winter Wed, Sat–Sun 2–6pm, Thu–Fri 10am–6pm.* 💶*4€.* 📞*04 93 65 54 54.*

Opened in 1981, this museum of local history and ceramics is situated in the restored **Chapelle des Pénitents-Blancs**, topped by a three-sided pinnacle. The displays feature ancient ceramics, a reconstruction of a local kitchen, photographs and artefacts exploring life in Biot.

👥 Bonsai Arboretum

Chemin du Val de Pôme, 100m/110yd south of Musée Fernand Léger. 🕐 *Open Wed–Mon 10am–noon, 2–6pm.* 💶*4€ (2€ children).* 📞*04 93 65 63 99.*

This sloping garden (1 000sq m/10 763sq ft) displays a large collection of bonsai trees against the backdrop of a reconstructed Japanese garden.

Group and individual bonsai courses are available. A small store sells trees, pots and tools.

ADDRESSES

🍴 EAT

🍽🍽 **Le Café de la Poste** – *24 rue St-Sébastien.* 📞*04 93 65 19 32. Closed 11 Nov–11 Dec.* One of the oldest cafés on the Riviera, the decor of this bistro-type restaurant features a pretty wooden counter and a huge fresco on painted ceramics. Traditional cuisine.

🛍 SHOPPING

Verrerie de Biot – *chemin des Combes, at the foot of the village, along D 4.* 📞*04 93 65 03 00. www.verreriebiot.com.* ♿. This small factory, founded in Biot in 1956, features several workshops that demonstrate the successive stages of the art of glass blowing, characterised by a bubbly texture peculiar to the Biot production. The different shops sell all kinds of glassware: vases, glasses, etc. Discover the history of glass-blowing in the **ecomuseum**.

TOURS

Several themed self-guide maps to the village are available at the tourist office. For exploring the area, purchase a copy of their Vallée de la Brague hiking map with 11 trails along the Brague River (👁 *see VALBONNE p263*).

Vence★

Alpes Maritimes

Perched on a rock at the foot of the Baous mountain range, Vence is surrounded by rivers, ravines and pine forests. Famous for its modern and contemporary art galleries, the old town also plays host to a regular Provençal market.

A BIT OF HISTORY

An Episcopal Town – A major Roman town, Vence became a powerful episcopal seat under bishops St Veranus (5C) and St Lambert (12C), and the Italian prince Alessandro Farnese, the future Pope Paul II (16C). During the Wars of Religion, Vence survived a siege by the Huguenot Lesdiguières in 1592. The victory is celebrated each year at Easter.

Bishop Godeau (17C) – The memory of Antoine Godeau has remained vivid throughout the region. He began as the oracle of the House of Rambouillet, in great demand among cultured society ladies *(les précieuses)* because of his wit, fluency and rich-and-ready poetical vein. Richelieu made him the first member of the French Academy. At the age of 30, Godeau took holy orders and became Bishop of Vence. He took the new role seriously, repairing his cathedral and introducing various industries (perfumery, tanning and pottery).

▶ **Population:** 18,931.
◔ **Michelin Map:** 341 D5.
🏛 **Info:** Pl. du Grand-Jardin.
     ℘04 93 58 06 38.
     www.vence.fr.
◖ **Location:** Vence sits on a hillside 6mi/10km inland, between Nice and Antibes.
🅿 **Parking:** Three indoor car parks are located to the west of the village.
◕ **Timing:** Allow 2hr to explore the medieval town centre.
👫 **Kids:** Contact the tourist office for children's events.

🐾 WALKING TOUR

◖ *Start from pl. du Grand-Jardin.*

Before entering the old town, admire the large ash tree at **place du Frêne**, supposedly planted for the visit of François I and Pope Paul III in 1538.

Old Town

The old town was enclosed within elliptical walls pierced by five gateways. Skirt the 15C square tower adjoining the château to reach the Peyra Gateway (1441), one of five that enclosed the old town. Today the village bustles with artists, craftsmen and boutiques.

Fountain at the Place du Peyra, Vence

S. Sauvignier/MICHELIN

▶ *Walk through the gate and onto pl. du Peyra.*

Château de Villeneuve – Fondation Émile Hugues

2 pl. du Frêne. 🕐*Open Tue–Sun 10am–12.30pm, 2–6pm.* ⬛*5€.* 🖉*04 93 58 15 78. www.museedevence.com.*

The 17C castle of the barons de Villeneuve incorporates a 13C watchtower. The castle organises regular themed exhibitions of contemporary and 20C works inspired by Vence, including paintings by Matisse, Dubuffet, Dufy and Chagall.

▶ *Exit the château and return to pl. du Peyra.*

Place du Peyra★

The striking square with its gushing fountain in the form of an urn (1822) was the forum of the Roman town.

▶ *From the south side of the square take rue du Marché and turn left onto pl. Clemenceau, site of the cathedral.*

Cathédrale Notre-Dame-de-la-Nativité

Pl. Clémenceau.

The Roman temple of Mars and a 5C Merovingian church originally occupied this site. The present church was begun in the Romanesque style, with Roman inscriptions on the Baroque façade dedicated to the emperors Elagabalus and Gordian.

The tomb of St Lambert is in the second chapel *(right)*. A 5C Roman sarcophagus of Veranus is in the third chapel *(right)*. The north aisle contains a handsome carved doorway with Flamboyant Gothic rose windows and a 16C retable of angels. The baptistery features a mosaic by Chagall.

The **gallery** has a lectern and **stalls★** from the choir with risers, elbow rests and misericords by Jacques Bellot, a sculptor from Grasse (15C).

Chapelle du Rosaire (Chapelle Matisse)★

466 ave. Henri-Matisse. 🕐*Open mid-Dec–mid-Nov Mon, Wed & Sat 2pm–5.30pm; Tue & Thu 10–11.30am, 2pm–5.30pm.* ⬛*3€.* 🖉*04 93 58 03 26.*

"Despite its imperfections I think it is my masterpiece... the result of a life-time devoted to the quest for truth." This was Henri Matisse's opinion of the chapel, which he designed and decorated between 1947 and 1951. From the outside it resembles an ordinary Provençal house. Inside, everything is white except for the stained-glass windows and the mural compositions, a play of black lines on a white background. The gallery contains studies made by Matisse for his finished designs.

Ramparts

Leave the cathedral through the east door onto **place Godeau**, overlooked by the square tower with its parapet. At the centre stands a Roman column erected to the god Mars.

▶ *Take rue St-Lambert and rue de l'Hôtel-de-Ville to the 13C Signadour Gateway. Turn left.*

The **porte de l'Orient** was opened in the 18C (the date 1592 carved on a stone refers to the siege during the Wars of Religion). Boulevard Paul-André follows the line of the ramparts, where several narrow stepped streets branch off to fine **views** of the foothills of the Alps. Re-enter the old town through the Gothic Lévis Gateway (13C) and walk up rue du Portail-Lévis between handsome old houses to place du Peyra.

🚗 DRIVING TOUR

Routes des Crêtes★★
Round trip 37mi/59km. Allow half a day.

▶ *Leave Vence by D 2210, going northeast towards St-Jeannet.*

The road skirts three peaks – Baou des Blancs, Baou des Noirs and Baou de

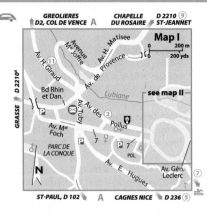

WHERE TO STAY	WHERE TO EAT	INDEX OF STREET NAMES
Diana .... ②	Armoise (L') .... ①	Alsace-Lorraine (R.) 2
Mas de Vence (Hôtel) .... ⑤	Pêcheur de Soleil (Le) .... ④	Hôtel-de-ville (R. de) 4
Miramar (Hôtel) .... ⑦	Seigneurs (Auberge des) .... ⑦	Place-Vieille (R.) 6
Tour de Vence (Chambre d'hôte La) .... ⑨	Vieux Couvent (Le) .... ⑨	Résistance (Av. de la) 7
Villa Roseraie (Hôtel) .... ⑪		

St-Jeannet – and provides a long, leisurely **view**★ of St-Jeannet (&see Driving Tour, Cagnes-sur-Mer).

Gattières

This perched village looks out over vineyards and olive groves to the Var Valley. The charming Romanesque-Gothic **church** contains a naïve painted sculpture of St Nicholas and the three children he revived (right of chancel).

▷ Leave Gattières by D 2209.

Carros

The old village occupies a remarkable position huddled around the **castle**★ (13C–16C). Just below the village a rock bearing traces of an old mill has been made into a terrace: **panorama**★★. The road from Carros to Le Broc provides magnificent **views**★ of numerous hill villages and of the Var.

▷ Follow the D 1.

Le Broc

This hill village has a fountain (1812) in the arcaded square and a 16C **church**

decorated by the modern painter Guillonet. From the village there is a fine **view** of the Var Valley. The road overlooks the confluence of the Esteron and the Var before turning west into the Bouyon ravine.

Bouyon

Every part of the village offers a **view**★ of Mont Cheiron (alt. 5,833ft/1,778m), the Var and Esteron valleys and the Alps.

▷ South of Bouyon the road (D 8) skirts Mount Chiers.

Coursegoules

Perched on a rocky spit at the foot of Mont Cheiron, the tall houses rise above the ravine of the nascent River Cagne. The Jaboulet workshops established in this tiny village are famous for their santons.

▷ Take D 2 southeast to Vence.

The road runs through barren countryside above the River Cagne.

Col de Vence★★

Alt. 3,182ft/970m. Just south of the pass, a fine **panorama**★★ opens up to the peaks east of the Var as far as Mont Agel, along the coast from Cap Ferrat, past the Baie des Anges, Cap d'Antibes and the Iles de Lérins to the Esterel. To the north, the white slopes of Mont Cheiron stand out dramatically.

Hike *From the pass to St-Jeannet. 4hr.* After the Col de Vence, a trail to the left leads to St-Jeannet via the GR 51 footpath, stretching alongside the Cagne.

ADDRESSES

🏠 STAY

Hôtel Mas de Vence – *539 Ave. E.-Hugues. ℘04 93 58 06 16. www. azurline.com/mas.* 🅿. ⌖10€. A modern Provençal-style hotel with ochre walls overlooking the main route into town, a covered terrace and wimming pool. Air-conditioned rooms have free WiFi.

Hôtel Miramar – *167 Av. Bougearel. ℘04 93 58 01 32. www.hotel-miramar-vence.com. Closed 17 Nov–12 Dec. 18 rooms.* 🅿. ⌖12€. In a pretty, 1920s house with a pink façade overlooking the valley, this hotel has charming, flower-themed rooms.

Le Vieux Couvent – *37 Ave. Alphonse-Toreille. ℘04 93 58 78 58. www.restaurant-levieuxcouvent.com. Closed 15 Jan–15 Mar, Thu night off-season and Wed.* The stone-vaulted ceilings of this former 17C chapel provide a unique setting for this restaurant serving regional specialities.

Villa Roseraie – *Rte. de Coursegoules. ℘04 93 58 02 20. www.villaroseraie.com. Closed Dec–Jan. 14 rooms.* 🅿. ⌖13€. A 1900 villa is the setting for this tastefully appointed hotel, in which the small rooms are cool and attractive. Tempting outdoor pool; pretty terrace adorned with sculptures.

Hôtel Diana – *79 Ave. des Poilus. ℘04 93 58 28 56. www.hotel-diana.fr. 28 rooms.* 🅿. ⌖13. In the heart of Vence, with an open-air Jacuzzi, solarium and fitness room, this stylish hotel has **panoramic views**. Some rooms equipped with kitchenette.

La Tour de Vence – *310 Chemin du Baou-des-Noirs, on the road to St-Jeannet. ℘04 93 24 59 00. www.la tourdevence.com. Closed Nov–Dec. 5 rooms.* 🅿. Restaurant. Constructed entirely of stones from a Burgundian monastary, this luxurious B&B overlooking the valley is equipped with a swimming pool, pétanque court, tennis and spacious guest suites, all tastefully decorated.

🍴 EAT

Le Pêcheur de Soleil – *1 Pl. Godeau. ℘04 93 58 32 56. www.pecheurdesoleil.com. Closed mid-Dec –mid-Feb.* This restaurant in the medieval quarter of Vence has an astounding choice of homemade pizzas, freshly baked in an open oven and served in the rustic dining room.

L'Armoise – *9 Pl. du Peyra. ℘04 93 58 19 29. www.larmoise.com. Closed Sun eve, Mon, Tue lunch off-season.* A tiny seafood restaurant overlooking the pretty square. Try the house bouillabaisse.

Auberge des Seigneurs – *1 r. du Dr Binet. ℘04 93 58 04 24. Closed Jan.* Handsome 17C mansion at the entrance to the medieval district. Here, the rustic setting, with its thick wooden tables, is alleviated by the refined silverware.

🛒 SHOPPING

MARKETS
Flowers and regional produce – This market takes place from Tuesday to Sunday on Place du Grand-Jardin and Place Surian.

CALENDAR

Fête de Pâques – Coinciding with Easter celebrations, this festival commemorates the village victory over the Hugenot siege during the Wars of Religion, 1592, with parades, music and dancing.

"Les Nuits du Sud" – Music Festival, mid-July to early August.

Fête Ste-Elizabeth – Village patron saint festival, first weekend in August.

Moyen Pays Fête – Traditional Folk Festival, beginning of October.

St-Paul-de-Vence★★

Alpes Maritimes

St-Paul's slender silhouette rises up from the peaceful hills and fertile valleys of the Pays de Vence. Part of a chain of fortified towns guarding the Var frontier until 1860, St-Paul has been a leading centre for modern art since the arrival of the Fondation Maeght in 1964.

WALKING TOUR

Place des Jeux de boules

Officially known as place du Général de Gaulle, this small square at the entrance to the village plays host to a modest market after daybreak before reverting to its primary role as the village boule court. Yves Montand and Lino Ventura were both regular *tireurs* here, as many of the older players will confirm.

Rue Grande

Rue Grande is the main street *(closed to traffic)* running the full length of the village. Many of the arcaded 16C and 17C houses bearing coats of arms are now artists' studios, antique shops and art galleries. Don't miss the urn-shaped **fountain**(1850), supplied with water from the Malvan and Font Renaude springs, and the vaulted washing place.

Narrow street of St-Paul-de-Vence.

© Sergio Pitamitz/age fotostock

- ▶ **Population:** 3,336.
- **Michelin Map:** 341 D5.
- **Info:** Maison de la Tour, 2 rue Grande. ℘04 93 32 86 95. www.saint-paul devence.com.
- **Location:** The village is 2.5mi/4km south of Vence on the D 2. Enter through the north gate. A square machicolated tower houses the tourist office *(Syndicat d'Initiative),* together with a permanent exhibition of modern paintings. In high season the narrow streets of the village are packed with tourists.
- **Parking:** Park your car in one of the car parks provided at the entrance to the village, before passing through the north gate.
- **Timing:** Allow one day for the town and the Fondation Maeght.

▷ *Climb up the stepped street above the fountain. Take the first right and then the first left to the church.*

Church

Perched at the highest point of the village, this 14C Gothic building with 17C vaulting and an 18C bell tower has three naves and four chapels, 17C choir stalls in carved walnut, and a chapel adorned with a Madonna of the Rosary (1588), with Catherine de' Medici in the crowd. The **treasury** is rich in 12C to 15C pieces: statuettes, a processional cross, reliquaries, a 13C enamel Virgin and Child, and a parchment signed by King Henri III.

Musée d'Histoire Locale

Pl. de l'Eglise. ◐*Open Apr–Sept 11am– 1pm, 3–6pm; Oct–Mar 2–5pm.* ▭*3€.* ℘*04 93 32 41 13.*

Eight illustrated scenes with life-size figures depict stages in the village's history, which often mirror those of Provence

Illustrious Visitors

After a period of prosperity in the Middle Ages, the village declined in the 19C to the benefit of Vence and Cagnes. It was "rediscovered" in the 1920s by painters such as Signac, Modigliani, Bonnard and Soutine, who used to meet in a café that has since become the sumptuous Auberge de la Colombe d'Or, whose walls are covered in paintings by famous artists. Other artists were to follow suit – sculptors, illustrators, writers and entertainers – making St-Paul a famous Riviera landmark. The village was once a great favourite among celebrities from the silver screen, such as Simone Signoret and Yves Montand.

itself, starting with the arrival of the comte de Provence, Raimond Bérenger V, in St-Paul in 1224. An exhibition of photographs of famous people who have stayed in St-Paul adds a contemporary note to this historical display.

Chapelle des Pénitents Blancs

Pl. de l'Eglise. ○*Open Apr–Oct 10am–noon, 3–6pm; Nov–Mar 2–5pm.* ∞*3€.* ℘*04 93 32 41 13.*
Surmounted by a three-sided clock tower, this 17C chapel was converted into an artistic site in 2008. Decorated by the artist Jean-Michel Folon, it features stained-glass windows, a mosaic, eight canvases and two sculptures.

Donjon

The only surviving element of the former castle of St-Paul, the **keep** opposite the church currently houses the town hall and a bell founded in 1443.

▷ *Return to rue Grande and continue down to the south gate.*

Ramparts★

From the bastion of the south gate, overlooking the cemetery, there is a superb **view** of the Alps and the coastline. The ramparts remain much as they were when built (1537–47) by François I to rival the citadelle in Nice. Follow them round anti-clockwise using the parapet walk, where possible.

SIGHTS
Fondation Maeght★

Chemin des Fumerates. Reduced permanent collection during temporary exhibitions. ○*Open daily Oct–Mar 10am–1pm, 2–6pm; Apr–Jun 10am–6pm; Jul–Sept 10am–7pm.* ∞*14€.* ℘*04 93 32 81 63. www.fondation-maeght.com.*
This modern art museum located northwest of St-Paul on the colline

View of St-Paul-de-Vence

© yanc/Bigstockphoto.com

des Gardettes was designed by **Josep Lluís Sert** in true Mediterranean style using white concrete and rose-coloured bricks. Surrounded by a sculpture park, its two buildings, divided by a courtyard adorned with sculptures by Giacometti, house a collection of modern art exhibited in rotation, including works by Braque, Chagall, Léger, Kandinsky, Miró, Giacometti, Bonnard, Hartung, and Alechinsky, as well as artists of a younger generation (Adami, Garache, Messagier, Viallat).

ADDRESSES

🛏 STAY

⊜⊜🍽 **Les Bastides de St-Paul** – *880 chemin Blanquières, D 336.* ℘*04 92 02 08 07. www.hotelbastides.fr.* 🅿. *20 rooms.* ⊑*10€.* Set just off a main road, this colourful farmhouse inn has spacious, soundproofed rooms. In the garden is a shamrock-shaped swimming pool.

⊜⊜🍽 **Hostellerie des Messugues** – *Quartier des Gardettes, by route de la Fondation Maeght 1mi/2km.* ℘*04 93 32 53 32. www.hotel-messugues-saintpaul. com. Closed Nov–Easter.* 🅿. *15 rooms.* ⊑*14€.* Just below the Fondation Maeght, in a lush and peaceful garden, lies this big Provençal villa surrounded by vines. The upstairs rooms are larger and slightly more comfortable. Don't miss the heated pool and its small island.

🍴 EAT

⊜⊜ **Chez Andréas** – *Western ramparts.* ℘*04 93 32 98 32.* Settle on the delightful terrace of this restaurant and sip a *pastis* as you admire the setting rays of the sun. A tastefully decorated dining room, with salads, the day's special and a choice of local wines.

⊜⊜ **La Cocarde de Saint Paul** – *23 rue Grande.* ℘*04 93 32 86 17.* In the main street at the heart of St-Paul, this restaurant-tea shop offers an artful blend of Mediterranean dishes. Excellent cuisine and homemade pastries.

⊜⊜ **La Ferme de St-Paul** – *1334 route de la Colle.* ℘*04 93 32 82 48. Closed Nov–late-Dec.* Tastefully restored old farmhouse boasting a superb decor: Provençal overtones, wooden beams, mahogany furniture, wrought-iron accessories and fine crockery. Quality cooking and interesting menu, where fish takes pride of place. Charming terrace and antique shop.

⊜⊜ **Café de la Place** – *pl. du Général-de-Gaulle.* ℘*04 93 32 80 03. Closed Nov–Dec.* This café, set up on the main square where villagers like to congregate and play pétanque, is at the heart of life in St-Paul. It belongs to the legendary Colombe d'Or Hotel *(located opposite)*, once the property of the actor Yves Montand.

🛍 SHOPPING

MARKETS
Marché d'Yvette – Fruit and vegetable market every Tuesday, Thursday, Saturday and Sunday beneath the wash-house at the village entrance.

Flower Market – Fresh flowers beneath the wash-house at the village entrance, every Saturday morning.

Regional Products – Provençal market on place de Gaulle every Wednesday morning.

🏃 LEISURE

Walking itineraries – The tourist office has a map of four self-guided walking and hiking itineraries of the old town and nearby historical sites.

CALENDAR OF EVENTS

Les Nuits de la Courtine – ℘*04 93 32 86 95. www.saintpauldevence. com.* Place de la Courtine is transformed into a giant stage for concerts and theatre plays in July and August.
La Fête de la Ste-Claire – This three-day festival honouring the town's patron saint includes a procession on Friday evening and fireworks on Sunday, followed by a dance.

Cagnes-sur-Mer★

Alpes Maritimes

Surrounded by rolling hills carpeted with olive, cypress and citrus trees, Cagnes-sur-Mer has always been a magnet for artists. Its long stretch of pebble beach is popular with fans of windsurfing, water skiing, diving and fishing.

A BIT OF HISTORY

The Grimaldis of Cagnes – Originally a fortress built by Rainier Grimaldi in 1309, Cagnes castle was converted by Henri Grimaldi in 1620 into a sumptuous palace. Loyal to the King of France, he persuaded his cousin, Honoré II of Monaco (*see MONACO p334*), to place himself under French protection (Treaty of Péronne, 1641). The Grimaldi family was finally driven out during the Revolution.

THE VILLAGE
Haut-de-Cagnes★

▶ *Take the free daily shuttle from the central bus station or walk up to Haut-de-Cagnes along montée de la Bourgade (steep climb).*

This quaint **bourg**, circled by ramparts and dominated by a medieval castle, has steep, cobbled streets and vaulted

- ▶ **Population:** 48,313.
- **Michelin Map:** 341 D6.
- **Info:** 6 Bd. Maréchal-Juin. ℘04 93 20 61 64. www.cagnes-tourisme.com.
- **Location:** Cagnes is on the coast between Nice and Antibes. It comprises Haut-de-Cagnes, crowned by a medieval castle; Cagnes-Ville, the modern quarter and Cros-de-Cagnes, a fishing village and beach.
- **Parking:** The largest car park *(fee)* is at Place St-Luce (*see map p289*) in Cagnes-Ville near the bus station. There are also some spaces in Haut-de-Cagnes at the *Boule de Château* car park.
- **Don't Miss:** The ancient streets of Haut-de-Cagnes, the **views** from the Château Museum, and jet-skiing at the beach.

passageways lined with 15C and 17C houses. The **Porte de Nice** near the church tower dates back to the 13C.

Église St-Pierre

The entrance to the church is through the gallery. The early-Gothic nave contains the Grimaldi tombs, while a larger

Haut-de-Cagnes

© mirko albini/Fotolia.com

287

PRACTICAL INFORMATION

Guided Tours of the City – The tourist office organises tours of the small fishing village in Cros-de-Cagnes *(Tue 10am in front of the Cros-de-Cagnes tourist office)* and the picturesque cobbled district of Haut-de-Cagnes *(Tue 2pm at the Haut-de-Cagnes tourist office). Contact the tourist office for rates.*

Museum Pass – Available at the tourist office. ⊚6€ double ticket for the Renoir Museum and Château Museum.

nave added in the 18C houses a statue of the Virgin and Child and an altarpiece of the 18C Spanish School.

SIGHTS

Château-Musée★

Pl. Grimaldi. ◷*Open Nov–Apr 10am–noon, 2–5pm (May–Oct until 6pm).* ◷*Closed public holidays.* ⊚4€. ℘04 92 02 47 30.

A double staircase and a Louis XIII doorway give access to this imposing castle crowned with machicolations. The elegant Renaissance **patio**★★ contrasts with the feudal castle's austere façades. Eight low-vaulted medieval rooms open onto the patio galleries, featuring exhibits of medieval artefacts, 2C Roman sculptures discovered in Cagnes, and an **Olive Museum**. The former boudoir of the marquise de Grimaldi on the first floor houses 40 paintings donated by the famous singer **Suzy Solidor**. The ceiling of the banqueting hall features

the **Fall of Phaeton**★, a 17C *trompe-l'œil* painted by the Genoese artist, Carlone. The **Musée d'Art Moderne Méditerranéen** on the second floor explores contemporary Mediterranean art, with a rich collection of works by 20C painters, such as Dufy and Vasarely. From the top of the tower there is a fine **view**★ over the roofs of Old Cagnes from the Ailps to the sea.

Musée Renoir

Chemin de Collettes. ◷*Open Wed–Mon Nov–Apr 10am–noon, 2–5pm (May–Oct until 6pm).* ⊚4€. ℗*Free.* ℘04 92 20 61 07. www.cagnessurmer.fr.

Pierre-Auguste Renoir (1841–1919) spent the last 12 years of his life at Les Collettes amid a peaceful olive grove. Ten of the **canvasses** belonging to his last, particularly sensual period (**Bathers, 1901–02**) are exhibited on the ground floor. The museum garden planted with olive, orange and lemon trees is dotted with sculptures by the artist, including his large bronze **Venus Victrix**★.

Chapelle Notre-Dame-de-Protection

🚶 *Access via montée du Château.* ◷*Open for group tours. Reservation required* ⊚*Enquire for details.* ℘04 93 20 61 64. www.cagnes-tourisme.com.

The Italianate porch and bell tower of this chapel inspired Renoir. The apse is decorated with 16C frescoes attributed to Andrea de Cella. A 17C altarpiece of the Virgin of the Rosary is displayed in the north chapel.

Renoir at Les Collettes

Pierre-Auguste Renoir was born in Limoges and moved to Paris as a young man, where his talents blossomed under the Impressionists. From 1882, he made several visits to Provence with Cézanne and in 1900, with his wife and son Jean, who later became a film director. In 1907, his reputation universally established, Renoir settled permanently at Les Collettes in Cagnes-sur-Mer. His last years were saddened by the death of his wife, the wounding of his sons in the First World War and the inexorable progress of his illness, which confined him to a wheelchair and paralysed his right hand. In August 1919, having received many honours and exhibitions in the major museums of the world, his work was officially accepted by the Louvre in Paris. On 2 December 1919, just before his death, Renoir was still at work painting a bouquet of anemones.

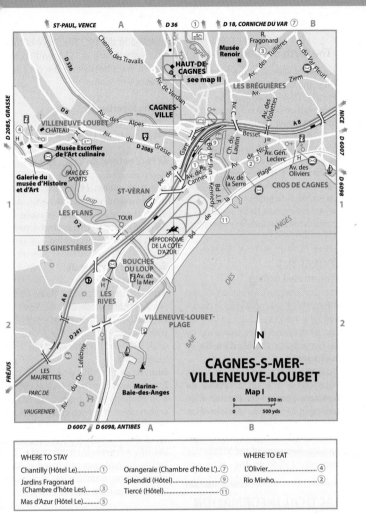

D 2085, GRASSE

Chemin des Travaux

R. Fragonard

Musée Renoir

Ch. du Val Fleuri

D 336

D 6

HAUT-DE-CAGNES
see map II

R. du Tullières ③

Av. de Verdun

Ziem

LES BRÉGUIÈRES
Av.

CAGNES-VILLE

Av. des Violettes

A 8

NICE   D 6007

VILLENEUVE-LOUBET

■ CHÂTEAU

④ ■ ■ ❑ H

D 2085

Av. des Alpes

Av. de Grasse

Besset

Ch. du Lautin

Av. Gén. Leclerc

H ⚓

Av. des Oliviers

D 6098

Musée Escoffier de l'Art culinaire

Galerie du musée d'Histoire et d'Art

PARC DES SPORTS

Av. de la Gare

Av. de Cannes

Bd. Mar. Juin

Bd J.F. Kennedy

Plage

Av. de la Serre

② ⑤

CROS DE CAGNES

ST-VÉRAN

Loup

LES PLANS

D 2

TOUR

Av. de la Plage

DES ANGES

① 1

LES GINESTIÈRES

HIPPODROME DE LA CÔTE-D'AZUR

⑪

FRÉJUS

A 8

D 241

BOUCHES DU LOUP

Av. de la Mer

H
LES RIVES

⑰

VILLENEUVE-LOUBET-PLAGE

BAIE

N

CAGNES-S-MER-VILLENEUVE-LOUBET

Map I

| 0 | 500 m |
| 0 | 500 yds |

LES MAURETTES

Av. du Dr. Lefebvre

⑯

PARC DE

Marina-Baie-des-Anges

VAUGRENIER

WHERE TO STAY		WHERE TO EAT	
Chantilly (Hôtel Le)	①	L'Olivier	④
Jardins Fragonard (Chambre d'hôte Les)	③	Rio Minho	②
Mas d'Azur (Hôtel Le)	⑤	Orangeraie (Chambre d'hôte L')	⑦
		Splendid (Hôtel)	⑨
		Tiercé (Hôtel)	⑪

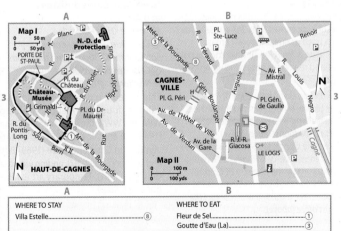

Map I

| 0 | 50 m |
| 0 | 50 yds |

Blanc

PORTE DE ST-PAUL

R. Guis

N.-D. de Protection

Pl. du Château

R. du Prolet

R. Hippolyte

Château-Musée

Pl. Grimaldi

Pl. du Dr-Maurel

R. du Pontis-Long

R. Sous-Barri

M. de la Bourgade

① Rue

N

HAUT-DE-CAGNES

Mtée de la Bourgade ③

Pl. Ste-Luce

R. J. Féraud

Renoir

⑧

CAGNES-VILLE

Pl. G. Péri

H

R. Gén.-Boulanger

Av. Auguste

Av. F. Mistral

Pl. Gén. de Gaulle

R. Negro

riv Cagne

N

Av. de l'Hôtel de Ville

Av. de Verdun

Av. de la Gare

R. J.-R. Giacosa

❑ LE LOGIS

Map II

| 0 | 100 m |
| 0 | 100 yds |

WHERE TO STAY		WHERE TO EAT	
Villa Estelle	⑧	Fleur de Sel	①
		Goutte d'Eau (La)	③

The Birth of Peach Melba

A native of Villeneuve, the "chef of kings and king of chefs" Auguste Escoffier (1846–1935) made his name in Nice before moving to the Petit Moulin-Rouge in Paris. In 1898, César Ritz persuaded him to set up the kitchens of his new luxury hotel, where Escoffier delighted guests by creating dishes tailored to their tastes. Peach Melba, made in honour of the Australian soprano Nellie Melba, is perhaps the most famous example.

EXCURSIONS
Villeneuve-Loubet

Located on the coast between Nice and Antibes, this Provençal village dominated by a medieval castle sits on the banks of the Loup River, bordered by a vast beach and the **Marina-Baie-des-Anges**.

Follow the charming sloping alleys to the foot of the 13C **château de Villeneuve** (⏰*open May–Oct Wed–Mon 10am–noon, 2–6pm, Nov–Apr Wed–Mon 10am–noon, 2–5pm;* ⏰ *closed 1 Jan, 25 Dec;* ⊚4€; *www.villeneuve-tourisme.com*). Property of the Villeneuve family with a 9C keep, the castle was

PRACTICAL INFORMATION
Nature Walk

🚶 The Vaugrenier Natural Park *(access by the RN 7)* stretches over 247 acres/100ha with both prairie and forest areas. There are 3.7mi/6km of trails and a small wetland marsh for observing waterfowl.

Tours

The Balade Gourmande combines a tour of the village, a visit to the Musée Escoffier and a special surprise tasting. *Contact the tourist office (above).*

Called the Concrete Mountains by some, the Marina-Baie-des-Anges has been recognised by the Ministry of Culture as a 20C heritage site. It's up to you to decide. Take a guided tour. *Contact the tourist office (above).*

restored in the 19C. The Truce of Nice was signed here in 1538, ending the Italian Wars between François I and Charles V of Spain.

🚶 The Riverbanks *1mi/2km*

This hike leads from the village along the banks of the Loup River.

🚶 Parc naturel de Vaugrenier
Access via RN 7.

The park covers 247 acres/100ha of meadow and woodland (pines and several species of oak) crossed by 3.7mi/6km of pathway and a pond that's ideal for birdwatching.

👥 Musée Escoffier de l'Art Culinaire★

3 rue Escoffier. ⏰*Open Jul–Aug 2–7pm (Wed, Fri 10am–noon, 2–7pm); Sept–Oct and Dec–Jun 2–6pm.* ⏰*Closed public holidays.* ⊚5€ *(child 2.50€).* 📞*04 93 20 80 51. www.fondation-escoffier.org.*

Housed in the villa where Auguste Escoffier was born in 1846, this collection of items once belonging to the ambassador of French cuisine reveals his unique approach to the culinary arts. Includes a display of contemporary utensils, a Provençal kitchen and a collection of miniature cars (used as part of the dining room service), alongside 1,500 menus from 1820 to today.

Galerie du Musée d'Histoire et d'Art

137 rue de l'Hôtel-de-Ville.
⏰*Open 9am–noon, 3–6pm, Sat 9.30am–12.30pm, Sun 11am–1pm.*
⏰*Closed public holidays.*
⊚*No charge.* 📞*04 92 02 60 39.*

This museum is devoted to major 20C conflicts fought by France, including WWI and WWII, the wars of Indo-China (1945–54) and Algeria (1954–62), interventions in Chad and Zaire (1969–84), and Lebanon (1982–87), ending with the Gulf War (1991). Temporary art exhibitions *(first floor).*

🚗 DRIVING TOURS

The Baous and the Corniche du Var★

Round trip of 20mi/32km. Allow about 1hr15min (excluding the ascent of the Baou of St-Jeannet).

▷ *From Cagnes take avenue Auguste-Renoir and D 18 north to La Gaude.*

La Gaude

From the ridge above the River Cagne, La Gaude – which owes its prosperity to vineyards and flower cultivation – now houses research centres in the fields of data processing and horticulture. The 14C castle in the St-Jeannet district is attributed to the Templars.

▷ *At Peyron take the D 18 north through orchards and vineyards.*

St-Jeannet

This charming village occupies a remarkable **position**★ on a terrace at the foot of the Baou of St-Jeannet. Behind the church on the left a "Panorama" sign points to a terrace offering a **view**★ of the peaks (*baous*) and the coastline.

Baou de St-Jeannet

The signposted path starts from pl. Ste-Barbe by Auberge St-Jeannet.
🚶 *2hr round trip.*

This sheer cliff 2,657ft/810m high, dominates the village. From the top (*orientation table*) a huge **panorama**★★ extends from the Esterel to the Alps.

▷ *Return to D 18 towards La Gaude. Turn left onto D 118.*

Centre d'Études et de Recherches IBM

The huge buildings on the left of this Research Centre, consisting of two opposing Y-shapes raised on concrete pillars, provide a good example of architecture harmonising with its natural surroundings.

Corniche du Var★

This scenic road clings to the hillside on the west bank of the Var, with a clear **view** of the river valley and Nice's hinterland. The steep slopes of the valley are covered in flowers and olive groves.

St-Laurent-du-Var

Until the County of Nice passed to France in 1860, the Var formed the frontier with the Kingdom of Sardinia. Locals usually forded the river, often on a man's back. The first permanent bridge was built downstream in 1864. Near the mouth of the River Var, a vast lake protected by a dyke has been developed into a yachting harbour.

▷ *Return to Cagnes by D 6007.*

Castle and village, Villeneuve Loubet

© AGE/Photononstop

ADDRESSES

🛏 STAY

Hôtel Le Mas d'Azur – *42 avenue de Nice.* ℰ*04 93 20 19 19.* 🅿 *15 rooms.* 🍴*7€.* Just off a main road, in an 18C building, this hotel has small, tidy rooms. Lush, flowery setting and breakfast terrace.

Hôtel Chantilly – *31 rue Minoterie.* ℰ*04 93 20 25 50. www.hotel-lechantilly.fr. 20 rooms.* 🅿. 🍴*8€.* This hotel, housed in a villa behind the racecourse, offers modest comfort at reasonable prices. Clean rooms in a verdant setting and a relaxed, family atmosphere.

Chambre d'hôte L'Orangeraie de la Baronne – *66 chemin du Maoupas, La Gaude.* ℰ*04 92 12 13 69. www.orange raie.fr.* 🅿 *4 rooms.* 🍴. *Restaurant*🍴. Located in the heart of a fruit and citrus orchard, this bed & breakfast has four spacious, simply decorated rooms with air-conditioning. There is also an organic restaurant serving dinner nightly, a swimming pool and bike rental.

Les Jardins Fragonard – *12 rue Fragonard.* ℰ*04 93 20 97 12. www.babazur.com. 3 rooms.* 🍴. *Restaurant*🍴. A peaceful park planted out with Mediterranean species forms the heavenly backdrop to this 1925 bed and breakfast. The large rooms are decorated in the Provençal spirit with rattan furniture; modern bathrooms.

Hôtel Splendid – *41 blvd. du Maréchal Juin.* ℰ*04 93 22 02 00. www.hotel-splendid-riviera.com.* 🅿. *26 rooms.* 🍴*9€.* A quiet, modern hotel in the centre of town. Although somewhat dated, the rooms are comfortable and most face the inner courtyard.

Hôtel Tiercé – *33 blvd. Kennedy.* ℰ*04 93 20 13 89. 23 rooms.* 🅿 🍴*10€. Closed 25 Oct–29 Nov.* The bright and tidy rooms in this modern hotel face the sea or the hippodrome next door. Air-con, WiFi.

Villa Estelle – *5 montée de la Bourgade.* ℰ*04 92 02 89 83. www.villa-estelle.com.* 🍴. *5 rooms.* 🍴. This tastefully renovated inn offers individually decorated rooms (some with **sea views**), a cosy lounge, a pleasant courtyard terrace and a charming garden.

🍴 EAT

Rio minho – *34 ave. de Nice.* ℰ*04 92 02 86 05. Closed Aug, Sun eve. and Mon.* Once the haunt of General de Gaulle, this charmingly decorated inn is known for its couscous dishes and Oriental tearoom.

L'Olivier – *4 pl. Verdun, Villeneuve-Loubet.* ℰ*04 93 20 85 11.* Pleasant restaurant serving traditional cuisine.

La Goutte d'Eau – *108 montée de la Bourgade, Le Haut-de-Cagnes.* ℰ*04 93 20 81 23.* After climbing the steep, cobbled alleys, you reach this small restaurant serving simple fare. The sun-blessed terrace welcomes you in fine weather.

Fleur de Sel – *85 montée de la Bourgade.* ℰ*04 93 20 33 33. www.restaurant-fleurdesel.com. Closed Thu eve, Wed.* A rustic little restaurant next to the church, with Provençal decor and an open kitchen, where you can watch the chef whip up seasonal specialities.

🏃 SPORT AND LEISURE

Watersports – Cagnes-sur-Mer has 2.2mi/3.5km of pebble beaches, including several private beaches, where you can dine or rent *chaise longues*. It's possible to water-ski, wakeboard, jet-ski and parasail in season at Tampa Beach *(between the Madrague and Neptune restaurants;* ℰ*04 93 20 17 46).*

Hippodrome de la Côte d'Azur – ℰ*04 92 02 44 44. www.hippodrome-cotedazur.com.* 🎟*4.50€.* This famous racecourse is the backdrop to many equestrian events between December and March, as well as in July and August.

🎭 EVENT

Fête Médiévale Haut-de-Cagnes – A medieval festival takes place in the village the 1st weekend in August.

Fête de la Châtaigne – Craft market, events and a countryside picnic celebrating the chestnut in all its forms. Mid-November.

NICE, THE RIVIERA AND MONACO

Nice and Monaco are the uncontested stars of the French Riviera, the headliners who never fail to impress or draw a crowd. Nice's seaside Promenade des Anglais and Monte-Carlo's majestic casino have been the stuff of legend since the late 19C, when the arrival of the railway brought throngs of tourists eager to see this millionaires' playground of sumptuous villas, private yachts and palace hotels. Of course, one doesn't have to break the bank to enjoy this part of the French Riviera, where the roads winding between coastal resorts and precariously perched villages offer panoramic views and scenes of stunning natural beauty. Important vestiges of Roman, Greek and medieval structures enrich this architectural heritage and a vibrant arts and music scene continue to enhance the cultural character of this dynamic region for the millions of visitors who still flock to its sunny shores.

Almost Not French

This part of the French Riviera is, historically speaking, hardly French at all. Although much of the southeast of France was controlled by the comtes de Provence, Nice and its surrounding villages were mainly governed by the ducs de Savoie and the kings of Sardinia, from their secession from Provence in 1388 until their purchase by Napoleon III in 1860. Monaco's Grimaldi lords purchased their own principality from the Genoese in 1308 and, although ruled independently, have been under French "protection" since 1861, when they sold Menton and Rocquebrune to France. Not only has the architecture, cuisine and even language of the Niçois, Monégasques and their neighbours been strongly influenced by their colourful and diverse Italian roots, they have also contributed to the fiercely independent and highly distinctive character of the region's inhabitants.

Highlights

1 Taste traditional Niçoise socca at the **Cours Saleya market** (p300)

2 Enjoy the scenic drive along the famous **Grande Corniche** (p317)

3 Tour the villa and gardens of the **Villa Ephrussi de Rothschild** (p327)

4 Hike the breathtaking coastal path around the **Cap Ferrat** (p328)

5 Place your bets at the Belle Époque **casino in Monte Carlo** (p339)

View of Monaco Port

© Sylvaine Poitau/Apa Publications

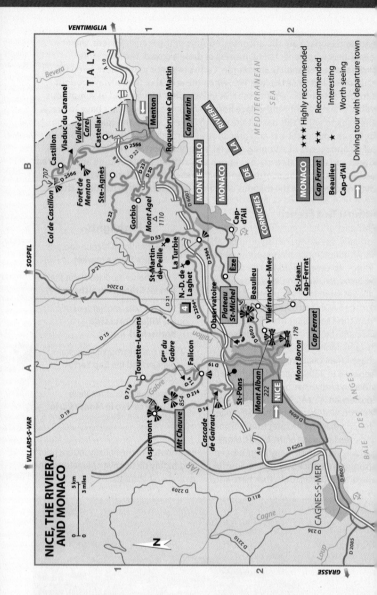

NICE, THE RIVIERA AND MONACO

VENTIMIGLIA

ITALY

MEDITERRANEAN SEA

Bevera

Viaduc du Caramel

Vallée du Carei

Menton

Castillon

Roquebrune Cap Martin

Cap Martin

Castellar

D 2566

MONTE-CARLO

Col de Castillon

707

Forêt de Menton

Ste-Agnès

MONACO

Cap-d'Ail

CORNICHES

LA RIVIERA

DE MONACO

Gorbio

Mont Agel 1110

St-Martin-de-Peille

La Turbie

N.-D. de Laghet

Éze

Beaulieu

Villefranche-s-Mer

St-Jean-Cap-Ferrat

Observatoire

Plateau St-Michel

Cap Ferrat

Tourette-Levens

G.ges du Gabre

Falicon

Gabre

Mont Boron 178

854

D 214

St-Pons

Mont Alban 222

NICE

Aspremont

Mt Chauve

Cascade de Gairaut

BAIE DES ANGES

CAGNES-S-MER

Cagne

Loup

VILLARS-S-VAR

SOSPEL

GRASSE

N

5 km
3 miles
0

★★★ Highly recommended
★★ Recommended
★ Interesting
Worth seeing
Driving tour with departure town

MONACO
Cap Ferrat
Beaulieu
Cap-d'Ail

A Haven for Artists

"When I realised that every morning I would wake up to this light, I couldn't believe my luck..." When Matisse moved to Nice in 1917, at the age of 48, it was a revelation. He found the quality of the light so intense, the colours so vivid, that he spent the next 27 years on the Riviera, channelling this new landscape into the airy flowing lines of his paintings and the vivid blues of his later gouache cut-outs, many of which are on display at the Musée Matisse in Nice. Matisse often drew inspiration from the coast, travelling everywhere "from the hills of Éze to Cagnes-sur-Mer". It was here, in 1917, that he met one of the founders of impressionism, Pierre-Auguste Renoir, at the Villa des Collettes, now the Musée Renoir, where the artist spent the last twelve years of his life. Matisse himself received regular visits from another

Street in the Old Nice

J.L. Gallo/ MICHELIN

artist, Raoul Dufy, who fell in love with the Riviera's *joie de vivre* on the first of his many visits to the region in 1919. His paintings of the Baie des Anges and its palm trees have come to define his work, much of which is now on display in the Musée des Beaux Art in Nice.

As well as its light and landscape, the Riviera's artistic traditions have also worked their charm on many other artists. Arriving in Vence in 1950, Marc Chagall swapped his paintbrush for the potter's wheel when the Ramié family, owners of the Madoura ceramics factory in Vallauris, lent him a studio. The result was a series of haunting and colourful pieces reflecting the biblical themes now explored in the Chagall Museum in Nice. The Madoura studio was also the regular haunt of another major artist. After moving to the Riviera in 1947, Picasso transformed the manufacturer's everyday jugs into sinuous women and its plates into bullrings, marking the start of a new chapter in his career, which you can now explore at the Musée Picasso in Antibes.

Picasso's presence in the south inevitably attracted a host of other artists, including his friend, Jean Cocteau. Influenced by the mythology of the Mediterranean, Cocteau has left his mark along the coast, from the Villa Santo Sospir in Cap Ferrat to Le Bastide in Menton, where a major new museum was recently opened in his memory. Unsurprisingly, Nice continued to attract artists throughout the 20th century, becoming a hotbed for France's abstract, Fluxus, figurative and conceptual movements, which can all be explored at the MAMAC.

Not Just for Tourists

Nice and Monaco may owe their international prominence to the lucrative tourism industry, but today the region is also an important centre for scientific research and high-tech development. With the encouragement of local governments, an enviable setting and a pool of qualified graduates from local universities, many international companies have opened offices here. The region's hotels, international airport, and top-notch restaurants make it the ideal place for business conferences, which take place throughout the year. While some corners of the French Riviera are virtually closed down in winter, Nice and Monaco never stop moving.

Time to Celebrate

The month of February is the best time to join in the festivities on the Riviera, when the 16-day carnival takes over the streets of Nice, and mountains of lemons and oranges decorate the processions for Menton's Fête du Citron. In May, Monaco's Grand Prix attracts the biggest crowds, who come from around the world to watch the Formula 1 cars race through the centre of Monte-Carlo.

Nice★★★

Alpes Maritimes

Overlooking the vast sweep of the Baie des Anges, the capital of the French Riviera is a city of contrasts. A medley of medieval red and ochre façades, Belle Epoque villas, Art-Deco apartments, fishermen's cottages and luxury hotels, the architectural diversity is only rivalled by its cuisine, which fuses French, Italian and Provençal flavours. A muse for generations of artists, Nice boasts the richest modern and contemporary art collections outside Paris.

A BIT OF HISTORY

From the Greeks to the House of Savoie – Excavations along the eastern reaches of Nice, at a site called Terra Amata (*see Musée Terra Amata p311*), have revealed evidence of a human presence in Nice 400,000 years ago. The first Greek settlement in the Ligurian trading-post of Nikaia (from the Greek niké, "victory"), founded in 4C BC on the rock that currently dominates the port to the east of the quai des Etats Unis, was eclipsed three centuries later by the Romans, who shifted the settlement north to Cimiez (Cemenelum), where they built a thriving town, complete with baths, an amphitheatre and a temple complex.

Following the Barbarian and Saracen invasions, which left Cimiez in ruins, ancient Nikaia returned to prominence under the comtes de Provence in the 10C. At the end of a long civil war, in 1388 Nice switched its allegiance from Louis d'Anjou, comte de Provence, to Amédée VII,comte de Savoie. Nice now formed part of a vast transalpine territory with its capital in Turin and stretching as far as Sicily and Sardinia to the south.

Catherine Ségurane – In 1543, the King of France, François I and his Turkish allies besieged Nice, an ally of the Holy Roman Emperor, Charles V. According to local tradition, Catherine Ségurane was bringing food to a soldier on the ramparts when the Turkish assault began. Knife in hand, she flung herself at the Turks,

▶ **Population:** 347,060.
◔ **Michelin Map:** 341 E5.
▯ **Info:** 5 promenade des Anglais. ✆0 892 707 707 (0.34€/min). Train Station Annex: Av. Thiers. www.nicetourisme.com.
◖ **Location:** The Old Town is wedged between the Château Hill (east), the seaside Promenade des Anglais and the Promenade du Paillon. West of this promenade is Place Masséna, surrounded by shopping streets. To the east of the Château Hill is the old port and Cap de Nice. On the hills to the north are the museums and gardens of Cimiez district. **Getting around** on foot is not difficult, but for Cimiez or the port consider using the city bus or take a double-decker bus sightseeing tour (*see Practical Information p297*).
▣ **Parking:** Car parks can be found all over town, at the market and near the port. There are no free spots, even on the streets.
◉ **Don't Miss:** The winding streets and market of the Old Town; sunset **views** from Château Hill; Cimiez's Gallo-Roman ruins.
◷ **Timing:** You could easily spend a week in Nice, but if you have just one full day, start on the seafront and the Old Town, then visit Cimiez and one or two of the major museums.
👪 **Kids:** Children will enjoy the merry-go-round at the Jardin Albert I or the playground in the park at the top of the Château Hill.

who appeared at the top of the wall, and hurled several attackers into the moat

PRACTICAL INFORMATION

SIGHTSEEING AND TOURS

Since 1 July 2008, entrance to Nice's municipal museums and galleries is free.

Guided tours – *Centre du Patrimoine, 75 quai des Etats-Unis.* 📞*04 92 00 41 90.* Tours of the Old Town *(2hr).* 🚶*3€.*

Nice Riviera Pass – A 1-, 2- or 3-day sightseeing pass with free entry to many sights, tours and shopping and dining advantages, from 24€–54€. Available at the tourist office or online at www.frenchrivierapass.com.

🚶 Petits Trains Touristiques – 🚶♿🚋*Tours (40min) Apr–Sept 10am–6pm (Jun–Aug until 7pm); Oct–Mar 10am–5pm. Closed mid-Nov–mid-Dec, 1–15 Jan.* 🚶*7€ (3€ child under 9).* 📞*06 16 39 53 51. www.petittrainnice.com.* Departures from the seafront at the Jardin Albert I. Tours of the Old Town, port and château.

Nice le Grand Tour – *Departures every 30 minutes.* 🚶*20€ (children 5€).* 📞*04 92 29 17 00.* Double-decker, open-top bus tours with commentary in English (90min), departing from the Jardins Albert I. Hop-on, hop-off the 14 different stops from the Promenade des Anglais, Cimiez and the Port.

Trans Côte d'Azur – *quai Lunel.* 📞*04 92 00 42 30. Operates Mar–Apr Tue–Wed, Fri and Sun 11am, 3pm; May–Oct Tue–Sun noon, 4pm; www.trans-cote-azur.com.*

🚶*15€ (children 4–10 years, 9€).* Guided tours *(1hr)* of the coast of Nice, the Bay of Villefranche and Baie des Anges. Reservations a must.

PUBLIC TRANSPORT

Bus/Tram – The Ligne d'Azur network *(10 ave. Félix-Faure;* 📞*0 810 061 006; www.lignedazur.com)* includes buses for the city of Nice and its suburbs, and a new tram line in central Nice. Tickets 1€ each or 4€ for an unlimited 1-day pass *(includes airport buses 23, 98 and 99).* The TAM coach network *(various departure points across the city;* 📞*04 93 85 61 81; www.rca.tm.fr)* has services to towns such as Antibes, Cannes and Grasse.

TER Train – *SNCF Gare, Avenue Thiers.* 📞*0 891 70 30 00. www.ter-sncf.com/paca.* Local train services to Draguignan, Fréjus, St-Raphaël, Cannes, Antibes, Menton, Vintimille (Vintimiglia in Italy), Monaco. The Nice-Cuneo line crosses the Bévéra and Roya valleys.

Vélos bleues – Since 2009, Nice has set up dozens of self-service bicycle rental docking stations across the city. Guidelines and rates (per hour, day, week or month) are available at www.velobleu.org. A similar scheme for electric cars, **Auto Bleue**, was launched in 2011 with a slightly more complicated registration process. Visit www.auto-bleu.org for more details.

Promenade des Anglais, Nice

Nice Carnival★★

King of the Carnival!

The **Nice Carnival**★★★ is one of the biggest celebrations in the region, with two weeks of parades, confetti battles, fireworks and masked balls *(veglioni)*. The **floral parades**, or *batailles de fleurs,* offer a picturesque spectacle and attract huge and excited crowds, drawn by the colourful fruit and flowers.

The tradition dates back a long way in Nice, with references as long ago as 1294, on the occasion of the visit of the comte de Provence, Charles II. Nice Carnival has always been a welcome diversion from social tensions and conflicts, which were constantly breaking out as a result of Nice's geographical location and disputed ownership. Until the end of the 18C, the carnival took place after the Lenten fast in the form of local festivities in the old part of the city.

After a break of several years, caused by the Revolutionary and Napoleonic wars, the first parade of carnival floats took place in 1830 in honour of the royal visit of King Charles Félix to Nice and the return to Sardinian sovereignty. The modern form of carnival dates back to 1873, with the establishment of the various stages of the festivities and the setting of a different official theme every year.

Carnival-going families from Nice belong to long lines of tradition verging on outright dynasties. Each "stable" of carnival floats has its own characteristics. Before the advent of synthetic materials, about one tonne of papier-mâché was used in the making of each float. Famous painters from this area have also played their part in enriching the carnival decorations.

The festivities begin with the triumphal entry of "Sa Majesté Carnaval" about three weeks before Shrove Tuesday, or Mardi Gras. An effigy of the King of the Carnival is later ceremoniously burned to mark the end of the carnival season. During the intervening period celebrations are in full swing, with parades of carnival floats accompanied by people in costumes sporting huge comical heads made of papier-mâché.

below. As a final insult to the enemy, she gathered her skirts and bared her behind. Their morale boosted, the men of Nice contained the attack and a statue was erected to Catherine by her fellow citizens.

Bonaparte in Nice – Overrun by French revolutionary troops in 1792, the comté de Nice became the Département des-Alpes-Maritimes the following year. In 1794 Bonaparte, then General of Artillery in the army, lived at no 6 in the street which now bears his name, where he was arrested after the fall of Robespierre. In 1796 he stayed in Nice again, on rue St-François-de-Paule, as commander-in-chief of the French armies in Italy. He had married Josephine only a few days earlier and it was from Nice that he wrote his famous letter: "My darling, anguish at our parting runs through my veins as swiftly as the waters flow down the Rhône..." At the fall of the Empire in 1814, Nice was handed back to the Kingdom of Piedmont-Sardinia under the Treaty of Paris.

Two local heroes: André Masséna (born in Nice, 1758; died in Paris 1817), son of a wine merchant, became one of Napoleon's most successful generals, beating the Austrians and Russians at the Battle of Zurich, and helping Napoleon to clinch the Battle of Marengo over the Italians. He conquered the Kingdom of Naples in 1806.

Giuseppe Garibaldi (born in Nice, 1807; died in Caprera, 1882) fought alongside Mazzini to unify Italy during the 1848 and 1859 revolutions. Exiled to South America, he rallied to the cause of republicans in Uruguay and Brazil. The "Che Guevara" of Nice earned himself the nickname "hero of the Two Worlds".

Plebiscite – As a result of the 1858 alliance between France and the King of Sar-dinia, Napoleon III helped the Sardinians drive the Austrians out of the provinces of northern Italy. As his reward, the 1860 Treaty of Turin between France and Sardinia stipulated that Nice be returned to France

"without any constraint on the will of the people". The plebiscite was an overwhelming victory for France: 25,743 in favour, 260 against. The regions of Tende and La Brigue were to remain Italian territory for 87 years until the treaty of 10 February 1947 allowed France to extend its natural frontiers to the Alps.

Nice Today – Now the fifth largest city in France, Nice is home to the Sophia-Antipolis technology park. A major administrative centre, it boasts dozens of prestigious museums, a music conservatoire, a national contemporary art centre and a world-class university.

✎ WALKING TOURS

THE SEAFRONT★★
Allow 2hr.

▶ *Begin from the intersection of Blvd. Gambetta and Promenade des Anglais.*

Promenade des Anglais★★
Closed to traffic one Sunday per month.
This wide promenade, facing south and flanking the sea along its entire length, provides wonderful **views** of the Baie des Anges. Until 1820 access to the shore was difficult so the town's rich English residents, present in large numbers since the 18C, paid for the construction of a coastal promenade. Although taken over by six lanes of traffic, it has retained its mythical aura and many legendary buildings still overlook the sea. Start with the recently restored **Palais de l'Agriculture** (1900) and continue to the **Hôtel Negresco** (c. 1900), both striking Belle Époque structures. Pass the imposing Classical façade of the **Musée Masséna** to reach the **Palais de la Méditerranée**, designed in 1928 by Frank Jay Gould. Narrowly escaping demolition in the 1980s, it has now been turned into a luxury casino and hotel. Pass in front of the rather incongruous glass-and-steel **Ruhl Casino** and Hotel Méridien (1973), then take avenue de Verdun around the **Jardin Albert I**, an oasis of greenery surrounding a fountain, The Three Graces by Volti.

Cours Saleya

Place Masséna

Stradling the **promenade du Paillon**, which follows the course of the covered mountain torrent of the same name, this harmonious square built in Turin style is lined with restored, red ochre buildings with arcades at street level. The north side of the square opens into **avenue Jean-Médecin**, the main shopping street. To the west is the area the English called "Newborough" in the 18C, running along **rue Masséna** and **rue de France**, a pedestrian area filled with smart shops, cinemas, cafés and restaurants.

Continue along the promenade, which is currently being transformed into a "green corridor" (set for completion in 2014) to the marble cubes of the national theatre and modern art gallery,

and down to the corner of the **jardin Maréchal-Juin** and the **Tête Carrée** (Square Head) by Sacha Sosno, housing the Louis-Nucéra Library.

The Port

For 2,000 years ships were simply moored at the foot of the Château Hill. The deep-water port was only created as recently as 1750 under the duc de Savoie, who ordered the excavation of an area of marshland called the Lympia. It was further extended in the 19C. **Place Île de Beauté**, a square facing the port, is lined with porticoed houses with pleasing 19C façades.

Today, Nice harbour is a busy maritime centre frequented by fishing boats, yachts, Corsican ferries, luxury liners and merchant ships. Stroll through the flea markets at quai Lunel, then return along the **quai Rauba Capeu**, which links the port to the Promenade des Anglais.

OLD NICE★

After soaking up the dazzling Riviera sunshine, head for the Baroque district of Nice, tucked between the Château Hill and rue des Ponchettes.

Cours Saleya

Lined with shops and restaurants, this elegant Baroque square is home to the famous **flower and vegetable market** (antiques on Monday). Note the yellow façade of the **Caïs de Pierla Palace**,

Midday Cannon

Each day at noon a short cannon shot can be heard. This custom was introduced by a visiting Englishman, Sir Thomas Coventry, who grew tired of irregular meal times. He offered to buy and maintain a cannon for the town so that each day a shot could be fired at noon from the castle hill. The tradition continues, but the cannon has been replaced by a harmless explosive charge.

where Matisse lived between 1921 and 1938, first on the third floor, then on the fourth floor facing the sea.

Chapelle de la Miséricorde★

2 Pl. Pierre-Gautier. ○*Open mid-Sept–Jun Tue 2.30–5pm.*

Halfway along the market, this fine example of Niçois Baroque belongs to the brotherhood of the Black Penitents. Recently restored, it was built in 1740 by Vittone according to the plans of the famous 17C Italian priest-architect Guarini. Inside, angels circle the gilded beams and faux-marble columns. Two primitive Niçois **retables**★ in the sacristy represent the Virgin of Mercy: one painted in hieratic Byzantine style by Jean Miralhet (1429) and the other by Louis Bréa (1515), whose graceful work, typical of the Italian Renaissance, features probably the earliest depiction of Nice.

▷ *Move back towards the east end of the square and turn left onto rue de la Poissonnerie.*

Chapelle de l'Annonciation

○*Open 8am–noon, 2.30–6pm.* ✆*04 93 62 13 62.*

Built in the 13C and remodelled in the 17C, this chapel, known locally as the **Chapelle Ste-Rita**, has a stern exterior typical of Nice Baroque and a lavish Baroque **interior**★ with altars and rails inlaid with marble, sumptuous altarpieces, painted and coffered vaults and fine panelling. Ordered according to a typical Baroque hierarchy, it is plain and austere at eye-level and rises in an increasingly complex swirl of decoration as it mounts towards the sky.

▷ *Continue straight ahead then take a right on rue de la Place-Vieille, then take a left.*

Église St-Jacques or Gésu★

○*Open by request* ✆*04 93 92 01 35.*

Built as a chapel in the 17C (the façade dates from 1825), this church is typical of the Counter Reformation style with its single, wide, fairly low nave and strict, straight lines mitigated by its highly ornate, gilded decorations, including 164 painted and 48 carved cherubs. The ceiling is painted with scenes from the life of St James. The **sacristy**, formerly the chapter house, contains 14 huge, walnut cupboards (1696), displaying the church treasures.

▷ *Rue du Jésus (across from the church) leads to rue Ste-Réparate and the cathedral on the right.*

Cathédrale Ste-Réparate

Pl. Rossetti. ✆*04 93 92 01 35.*

○*Open Mon–Sat 9am–noon, 2–6pm.*

Designed in 1650 by local architect J.-A. Guiberto in honour of Nice's patron saint, the cathedral is topped by an 18C bell tower and a magnificent dome of 14 000 glazed tiles that stands out on the Nice skyline. The **interior**★ is a riot of Baroque plasterwork and marble. Note above the high altar, to the right of the painting *La Gloire de Sainte-Réparate*, a view of Nice and its castle in the 17C. The frieze, emblazoned with the arms of the ducs de Savoie, is particularly vivid.

▷ *Proceed along rue Rossetti opposite and take the third left turning into Rue Droite.*

Palais Lascaris – Musée de la Musique

15 rue Droite. ○*Open Wed–Mon 10am–6pm.* ✎*Guided tours Fri 3pm.* ○*Museum no charge; tour 5€.* ✆*04 93 62 72 40.*

This Genoese-style palace, influenced by local tradition, was built in 1648 by J.B. Lascaris, a descendant of the counts of Ventimiglia. On the ground floor a pharmacy from Besançon (1738) has been reconstructed to display a fine collection of flasks and tripods.

A grandiose balustraded and vaulted **staircase**★ decorated with 17C paintings and 18C statues of Mars and Venus in rockwork niches leads to the "noble floor" (second floor). These rooms reveal how a noble family would have lived in Nice before the Revolution. Flemish tapestries based on sketches by Rubens hang in the antichamber to

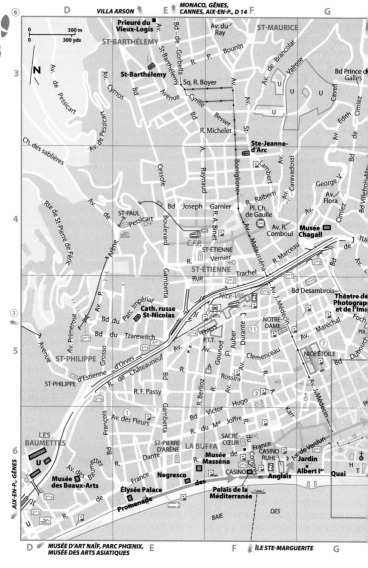

the grand salon decorated with 18C trompe-l'oeil ceiling frescoes attributed to the Genoese painter Carlone. Superb atlantes and caryatides hold up the stucco partition leading through to the ceremonial room. On the other side of the staircase is a private apartment with 18C ceilings and painted medallions framed in stuccowork and Louis XV woodwork inlaid with silver-plated copper. Don't miss the bed in its glazed alcove, where the head of the household would receive visitors to discuss local administrative affairs. A collection of 18C instruments acquired in 2009 are housed in the **Musée de la Musique**.

▶ *Turn left along rue Droite and rue St François. Note the cannon ball on the corner of rue Droite and rue de la Loge, which dates from the siege of Nice by the Turks in 1543.*

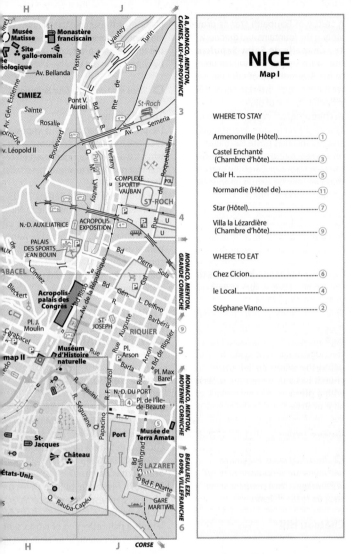

NICE
Map I

Place St-François

This square, home to the morning fish market, is overlooked by a fine 18C building, the former labour exchange, behind which is the **St-François clock tower**, once part of the Franciscan monastery transferred to Cimiez. Continue along lively rue Pairolière, where several eateries serve socca, a local speciality (&see p306).

Place Garibaldi

One of the most attractive squares in Nice, place Garibaldi was laid out in the 18C in typical Piedmont style. Lined with Sardinian-red and yellow ochre arcaded buildings decorated with recently restored trompe l'oeil pediments and balustrades, it marks the northern limit of the Old Town and the beginning of the new, and was the start of the royal route to Turin in the 1700s (which is where the Café de Turin got its name).

A statue of Garibaldi stands proudly among the fountains and greenery. The 18C **Chapelle de Saint-Sépulcre** on the south side of the square belongs to the Brotherhood of Blue Penitents, with a Baroque interior decorated in different shades of blue.

Archaeological crypt – The remains of a medieval bridge over the Paillon and the fortified porte Pairolière were uncovered during construction work on the new tramway. Carefully preserved, they can now be visited upon reservation at the tourist office.

From Pl. Garibaldi, take rue Neuve past the Café de Turin to the church of St-Martin-St-Augustin.

Église St-Martin-St-Augustin

1 Pl. Sincaire. ○*Open Tue–Fri 9am–noon, 2–5pm.* ℘*04 93 92 60 45.*

This is the oldest parish in Nice, dating back to 1510. It is the site of Garibaldi's baptism as well as a mass performed by the Augustinian monk, Martin Luther, before the Protestant Reformation. The church has a fine Baroque **interior**★ with a **pietà** at the centrepiece of an altar by **Brea**. Outside the entrance is a low-relief sculpture that pays tribute to the local heroine, Catherine Ségurane.

Turn right out of the church and along rue St-Augustin to rue de la Providence, then climb the steep steps up to the château.

Château Hill

Château lift. ○*Open Jun–Aug 9am–8pm; Apr–May and Sept 9am–7pm; Oct–Mar 10am–6pm.* ℘*04 93 85 62 33.* ◉*1€.*

This 302ft/92m high hill, arranged as a garden walk, was where Nice's fortress stood until it was destroyed in 1706 on the orders of Louis XIV. Walk around the cemetery boundary for a bird's-eye **view** of the roofs of Nice and the Baie des Anges. On the southeastern side admire the exposed **foundations of an 11C cathedral** (apse and apsidal chapels), built on top of Roman and Greek buildings. From the wide platform on the summit there is a sweeping **panorama**★★ (viewing table). Below the terrace is an artificial waterfall fed by waters from the Vésubie river.

Steps lead down to Tour Bellanda.

Tour Bellanda

Despite its appearance, this imposing circular bastion only dates from the 19C, when it was built as an identical replacement for one of the towers of the citadel destroyed in 1706.

The composer Hector Berlioz (1803–69) lived here during his time in Nice, of which he enthusiastically wrote of: "Here I am in Nice, breathing the warm, balmy air... Here life and happiness come running swiftly to greet me, music folds me into her arms, and the future smiles on me..."

THEMED VISITS
MODERN AND CONTEMPORARY ART

See the map opposite for locations.

Musée des Beaux-Arts Jules-Chéret★★

33 Ave. des Baumettes. Bus 38 (stop at Chéret). ○*Open Tue–Sun 10am–6pm.* ◉*Guided tours (1hr) Thu 2.30pm.* ○*Closed public holidays.* ◉*No charge.* ℘*04 92 15 28 28. www.musee-beaux-arts-nice.org.*

This 1878 residence, built in the style of a 17C Genoese Renaissance palace for the Russian princess Kotschoubey, houses a rich collection of works sent to Nice by Napoleon III in 1860, along with a number of donations.

Ground Floor

European masterpieces of the 17C, 18C and 19C are displayed on the ground floor, including a rare work by A. Tassi, *Paysage avec Jésus guérissant l'aveugle.* One room is devoted to the **Van Loo** dynasty, including works by **Carle Van Loo** (born in Nice, 1705). The main gallery is lined with female portraits and Thamar by Cabanel. The patio is home to *Bronze Age* by Rodin and *Triumph of Flora* by Carpeaux.

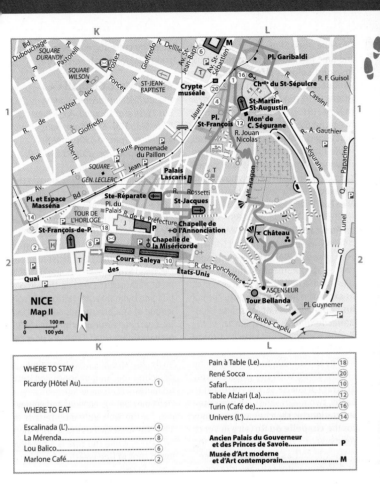

NICE
Map II

First Floor

The main staircase, once used for concerts, leads to displays of late 19C and early 20C artists, starting with **Jules Chéret**, the inventor of the modern poster, who died in Nice in 1932. Works by Orientalists and Romantics include several sculptures by Carpeaux. A room devoted to **Raoul Dufy**, which features his work *Bois de Bologne*, leads onto a series of paintings by the pre-Impressionist Félix Ziem, ceramics by Picasso, and a **Van Dongen** gallery housing the Fauvist's major works.

Musée Matisse★★

164 Avenue des Arènes. Bus 15, 17, 20, 22, 25 (stop Les Arènes/musée).
🚻 🕐 *Open Wed–Mon 10am–6pm.*

🎧 *Guided tours available.* 🕐 *Closed public holidays.* 🎟 *No charge.* 📞 *04 93 81 08 08. www.musee-matisse-nice.org.*
Built on the site of a cabin *(cabanoun)* surrounded by the ancient remains of Cimiez, this 17C Genoese villa with a pebble-dash façade and trompe-l'oeil decora-tion extended by balustraded terraces was once owned by the Consul of Nice. After it fell into ruin, the city of Nice bought it in 1950. Since its rede-velopment in 1993, it has housed the Musée Matisse.
This collection includes over 30 paint-ings and provides an overview of Henri Matisse's career (1869–1954), exploring the transition from his sober, northern palette to the dazzling hues of the Mediterranean. Taking his cue from

Cézanne, then Signac in St-Tropez, by the time he reaches Collioure in 1905, his solid colours propel him to the vanguard of the Fauvist movement. After a short stay in Morocco, on arrival in Nice (1916), he makes increasingly masterful use of simple, evocative colours edged in black (*Portrait of Laurette*), while his gouaches, oil paintings and drawings begin to reveal a heightened sensuality, nourished by his travels and the **view** over the sea from his studio in Nice (1921–38): *Odalisque with a Red Box* (1926), *Window in Tahiti* (1935), *Nude in an Armchair* (1937), *Woman Reading at a Yellow Table* (1944) and *Still Life with Pomegranate* (1947). His favourite subjects – light, women and the sea – are now approached with a joyful abandon, as expressed through the pure lines of his paper cut-outs of "absolute blue" gouache (*Blue Nude IV, Bather in the Reeds*). A number of Matisse's bronze sculptures are also on display, including *The Serf* (c.1900), and the *Serpentine* (1909), along with the progressively abstract *Jeanette* series (1910-1913). Lastly, two major series are presented in rotation: his sketches and drawings for the **chapelle du Rosaire** in Vence (⊙ *see* VENCE p280), regarded by the artist himself as his "master-piece", and 41 preparatory studies (drawings, gouache cut-outs, engravings and oil paintings) for the Merion Dance.

Musée Marc-Chagall★★

Ave. du Docteur-Ménard, Cimiez. Bus 15 (stop at Chagall). ♿ ⊙ *Open Wed–Mon May–Oct 10am–6pm; Nov–Apr 10am–5pm.* ⊜ *7.50€ (free first Sun and under-26).* ☏ *04 93 53 87 20. www.musee-chagall.fr.*

This museum, built in 1972, houses the most important permanent collection of the painter's works, including all **17 canvasses** which make up the "Biblical Message", an uninterrupted endeavour lasting 13 years (1954–67) and donated to the mu-seum by the artist himself. Designed to resemble a "house" in fulfilment of the artist's wishes, this simple building by architect A. Hermant (a colleague of Le Corbusier) is surrounded by a garden featuring a mosaic (1970) of the prophet Elijah. Chagall's poetical lyricism is visible in 12 paintings based on the Jewish Bible, while five paintings depicting the Song of Songs illustrate his fantastical imagination.

Don't miss the 105 etchings and engravings for the Bible edited by Tériade in 1956. The museum has a new bookshop and store, while the café is a popular lunch spot in fine weather (*no admission required*).

Socca

The day started early in those days in the Nice bar where my uncle and I enjoyed our *socca*. The ingredients include chick-pea flour, olive oil and salt beaten into a smooth mixture in a large copper pan. It is baked in a wood fire oven, a cooking time based on exact calculation or long experience and a speedy hand in cutting the cake into pieces when it is served. Socca will not wait; it must be eaten piping hot and seasoned with pepper.

The recipe has never changed. This is the same *socca* that used to be delivered all over the town. It was put in a box with a zinc lid and the trays in the delivery vans were kept warm with charcoal heaters. Nothing was more satisfying to labourers, office workers, women shopping or anyone else overcome by the desire for a little something in the morning. It is the same socca which the dockers, who had knocked back a laced coffee at 5 o'clock, used to consume in the bars of Nice at half past six. It was their breakfast.

Louis Nucera
Chemin de la Lanterne (1981)
Published by Éditions Grasset

Ruins of the baths, Site Archéologique Gallo-Romain and Musée Matisse in the background

J. Malburet/MICHELIN

Musée d'Art Moderne et d'Art Contemporain★★

Promenade des Arts. ◷*Open Wed–Mon 10am–6pm.* ◷*Closed public holidays.* ✆*No charge.* ✆*04 93 62 61 62.* *www.mamac-nice.org.*

Designed by Yves Bayard and Henri Vidal, the Museum of Modern and Contemporary Art is made up of four square towers with roof-top terraces linked by glass passageways.

The collections present works by the **Nice School** and the French and American avant-garde art movements from the 1960s to the present day. The permanent collection is displayed on the two upper floors, with temporary exhibitions housed on the first floor. In the early 1960s Nice became a hothouse for the **French Nouveau Réalisme** (✆*see Klein below*) movement, which attempted to express the reality of daily life in a modern society of consumerism and popular culture. While Pop artists Andy Warhol, Roy Lichtenstein and others appropriated objects belonging to mass culture, the New Realists more derisively sought inspiration from those same objects as symbols of modern life, by collecting or breaking them (Arman), compressing them (César), capturing them under glass (Spoerri), or wrapping them (Christo).

A section of the museum is devoted to the French painter **Yves Klein** (1928–62), the movement's founding father, whose happenings reflected the idea of total art, while his monochrome works explore the concept of pure abstract art. Total art was also the inspiration of the neo-Dada **Fluxus** movement, whose principle representative, Ben, enjoys a strong presence in the museum.

The development of abstract ideas in France is illustrated by the **Supports/Surfaces** galleries, which extend the work of American abstract expressionists such as Morris Louis and Frank Stella by reducing painting to its material reality. Influenced by American Minimalism (Sol Le Witt, Richard Serra), the BMPT (Buren, Mosset, Parmentier and Toroni) reduced art to its simpler expression – medium, colour and material.

The 1980s saw the return of figurative works by artists such as Niki de Saint Phalle and the classical beauty of Ernest Pignon-Ernest's murals in Naples.

Villa Arson

20 Ave. Stephen Liégeard. Bus 4, 7 (Deux Avenues), 36 (Villa Arson). ◷*Open Wed–Mon 2–6pm (Jul–Aug until 7pm).* ◷*Closed between exhibitions.* ✆*No charge.* ✆*04 92 07 73 73.* *www.villa-arson.org.*

The Villa Arson is situated to the north of the city in a Mediterranean garden on St-Barthélemy hill affording a **panoramic view** of the Baie des Anges. The 18C villa, influenced by the Bauhaus architectural movement, houses the

École Nationale Supérieure d'Art, an artists' residence and a national centre of contemporary art showcasing international artists.

CIMIEZ

Allow 3.5hr. See the city map p305. Served by bus 15 (stop at Arènes).

Long before Cimiez was occupied by the French and visited by Queen Victoria (who is commemorated by a statue at the top of Boulevard de Cimiez), this was the site of the Roman city Cemelenum. In 2C there were at least 20,000 Romans living here. Many vestiges of their city remain.

▶ *Starting from pl. Jean-Moulin, behind the Acropolis, drive W along blvd. Carabacel and follow the map.*

Arènes

The ellipse-shaped amphitheatre, which is only 220ft/67m by 184ft/56m, could hold 4,000 spectators. Traces remain of the gangways and of the sockets on the external façade, which held the posts supporting a huge adjustable awning *(velum)*. The amphitheatre was designed for spear contests and gladiatorial bouts, but not for animal fights. Traditional festivals take place here all year round *(see Calendar of Events p316).*

Musée Archéologique

160 Ave. des Arènes.
Open Wed–Mon 10am–6pm (last entrance 1hr before closure).
No charge. 04 93 81 59 57.
www.musee-archeologique-nice.org.

The collections include finds excavated at Cimiez and around Nice, along with a number of donations. There are ceramics and bronzes from the great Mediterranean civilisations (Greece, Etruria and Roman Africa) and artefacts such as the superb **mask of Silenus**★, many salvaged from shipwrecks. Ligurian and Roman items include the Bronze Age statue of a warrior from Mont Bégo, Iron-Age finds from perched strongholds or oppida) and mile-stones (1C) from the Via Julia Augusta. Roman civilisation is represented through examples of every-day artefacts, a display of imperial coins, as well as representations of Cimiez.

Site Archéologique Gallo-Romain★

Same as the Musée Archéologique.

Steps lead down into the *decumanus maximus* (the main east–west street of a Roman town) with its central drain and shops. To the left are the **northern baths** for high-ranking Romans containing a **frigidarium** (cold room), the dimensions of which (33ft/10m high by 30ft/9m wide) give an idea of their huge scale. The warm room and the hot rooms are built above a **hypocaust** (a system of channels through which hot air passed). Still visible today, it is one of the best-preserved examples anywhere in the former Roman Empire. On the eastern side are the latrines. On the other side of the main street are the less elaborate but fully-equipped **eastern baths** for the general public, which can be viewed from a walkway.

The western end opens into the cardo maximus (main street running north–south). To the left of this street are the remains of the more recent **western baths**. Turned into a Paleo-Christian bapistry in the 5C, some parts of an early cathedral are still visible and the choir, in the former frigidarium, contains traces of an altar.

▶ *Cross the public olive tree gardens to pl. du Monastère.*

Place du Monastère

A twisted column of white marble, rising in the square in front of the church, bears a Calvary dating from 1477. The Fauvist painters Raoul Dufy and Henri Matisse are buried in the nearby **Notre Dame cemetery**. Matisse's tomb lies in an olive grove to the north of the wall.

Monastère Franciscain★

The Franciscans, who in the 16C took over the buildings of a former Benedictine monastery founded in the 9C, have restored and considerably enlarged the abbey church.

Studios de la Victorine: the Story of Film-Making in Nice

With the dawn of cinema, Nice provided film-makers with the ideal ingredients for their future success: almost constant light and sunshine, the sea and the presence of magnificent hotels as natural backdrops.

Louis Feuillade, who made *Fantômas*, was one of the first to spot the potential of the area; the roofs of the Hôtel Négresco passed into cinematic posterity in the Fantômas-Judex chase.

"Azure cinema" really took off in 1920, when a large unoccupied estate west of the town centre, La Victorine, was acquired by the fabulously rich Hollywood producer Rex Ingram, who had launched Rudolf Valentino and Roman Navarro. He produced the epic *Mare Nostrum* to promote his new studios. For the following 10 years the Victorine studios were an essential part of the prosperous French and European film industry before changes in public tastes brought about a decade of inactivity. The Armistice of 1940 caused French cinema to seek refuge in Nice (Abel Gance, Prévert, Carné) and in 1943 the filming of *Les Visiteurs du Soir* revived the production of large-scale films. In 1944 came *Les Enfants du Paradis,* the greatest production at La Victorine, co-produced by Marcel Carné and Jacques Prévert, with Arletty and Jean-Louis Barrault. The reconstruction of *Boulevard du Crime* in the middle of the Second World War required more than 30t of scaffolding and nearly 4,186sq yd/3,500sq m of fencing for the sets, as well as 2,000 extras, who were recruited in Nice. A worsening economic situation temporarily brought a halt to Nice's creativity. The post-war years were good, but were followed by a lull. A revival now seems to be underway.

Église Sainte-Marie-des-Anges

Pl. du Monastère. 🕐*Open Sept–Jun.* 📞*04 93 81 00 04.*

The church possesses three **master-pieces**★★ by the local artist Louis Bréa, illustrating the Nice School. To the right of the entrance stands a **Pietà** (1475), one of his best works. The arms of the cross and the stiff body of Christ emphasise the horizontal perspective. The **Crucifixion** to the left of the choirs remarkable for the total absence of a Gothic aesthetic. The **Deposition** in the third chapel complements the Crucifixion and adheres to Renaissance principles: the figures aligned obliquely on the body of Christ are counterbalanced by the vertical lines of the landscape.

Musée Franciscain

🕐*Open Mon–Sat 10am–noon, 3–6pm.* 🕐*Closed public holidays.* 🎫*No charge.* 📞*04 93 81 00 04.*

The museum recalls the work of the Franciscans in Nice from the 13C to the present day.

Monastery Gardens★

On the south side of the monastery there are terraced gardens with flower beds and a **viewpoint** looking down on the Paillon Valley, the castle hill and the sea, Mont Boron and the observatory. A copse of cypress and holm oak marks the site of the former Ligurian *oppidum*.

NICE'S RUSSIAN HERITAGE

Around the middle of the 19C, after Empress Alexandra Fedorovna, widow of Tsar Nicolas I, settled in Nice, many wealthy Russian aristocrats chose the city as their winter residence. These "eccentrics", as the locals called them, recreated the atmosphere of their native land on the Riviera. Baron Von Dewies, who designed the Russian railway system, commissioned the Gothic **Château de Valrose** (Nice University) and set up an izba, shipped especially from Kiev. To the west of Nice, the **Château des Ollières** features an impressive keep flanked by four turrets. The nearby **Palais Kotschoubey** houses the Musée des Beaux-Arts.

Two other notable examples of Russian architecture are the **Palais Impérial** and the **Résidence Palladium** on blvd. Tsarévitch.

Cathédrale Orthodoxe Russe St-Nicolas★

⏰*Open daily Mar–Apr and Oct 9.15am–noon, 2.30–5.30pm; May–Sept 9am–noon, 2.30–6pm; Nov–15 Feb 9.30am–noon, 2.30–5pm;* ⏰*Closed Sun morning.* ⬗*3€.* ℘*04 93 96 88 02. www.acor-nice.com.*

With its six gilded onion domes and its ochre brick façade, the **Russian Orthodox cathedral** is the largest Russian religious building outside Russia. Inaugurated in December 1912, the cathedral's domes are coated with gold leaf. The choir is decorated with an **iconostasis**★ featuring religious artworks from Moscow. At the end of the park on the left is a **Byzantine chapel** dedicated to Tsarevich Nicolas, the son of Tsar Alexander II, who died here in 1866.

SIGHTS
Musée des Arts Asiatiques★★

405 promenade des Anglais. From the promenade, head to Nice airport, then right towards "parc Phoenix".
♿⏰*Open Wed–Mon mid-Oct–Apr 10am–5pm; May–mid-Oct 10am–6pm.* ⬗*No charge.* 🅿*(fee).* ℘*04 92 29 37 00. www.arts-asiatiques.com.*

Delicately poised on the lake in Phœnix Park, this white marble construction (1998) by the Japanese architect **Kenzo Tange** presents sacred and traditional objects from Asia. The ground-floor galleries are devoted to China, Japan, India and South-East Asia, while the rotunda explores the history of Buddhism. Tempo-rary exhibitions are held on the lower ground floor. Tea ceremonies are organised in the Japanese tea room *(Sun 3pm by reservation;* ℘*04 92 29 37 02).*

Parc Phœnix★

405 Promenade des Anglais.
♿⏰*Open daily Apr–Sept 9.30am–7.30pm; Oct–Mar 9.30am–6pm.* ⬗*No charge.* ℘*04 93 18 03 33. www.nice.fr.*
This vast botanical garden (over 17 acres/

7ha) inaugurated in 1991 is organised by theme and contains over 1,500 plant species from all over the world. The "Île des Temps Révolus" (Island of Bygone Times) features a display of living plant fossils: cycads, ginkgo biloba, tree ferns, etc. An aviary houses a colourful collection of parrots and other tropical birds, while the **giant greenhouse**★, a tropical hot-house covering 75,300sq ft/7,000sq m beneath a 82ft/25m high roof, contains seven different climates. Next door are the carnivorous plants and the butterfly house.

Musée d'Art Naïf Jakovsky★

Château Sainte-Hélène, ave. de Fabron. Leave the town centre by promenade des Anglais. ⏰*Open Wed–Mon 10am–noon, 2–6pm.* ⬗*No charge.* ℘*04 93 71 78 33.*

Housed in an elegant château, the Anatole Jakovsky Bequest comprises 600 canvasses by naïve artists from around the world, including Croatian artists Generalic and Rabuzin, French artists Bauchant and Vieillard, and works from Italy, Belgium and the Americas.

Musée Masséna★

65 rue de France. Museum: ⏰*open Wed–Mon 10am–6pm; Gardens: open Jun–Sept 9am–8pm; Oct–May 9am–6pm.* ⬗*No charge.* ℘*04 93 91 19 10.*
Recently reopened after a major renovation, this museum explores the history of Nice from the 19C to the 1930s. Built in 1898 for Victor Masséna, great-grandson of Napoléon's famous general, his son André gave it to the town in 1919. Presented on two floors, the exhibits retrace the life of André Masséna and explore the history of Nice during the Revolution and Empire, the Sardinian restoration, and its rise as a fashionable seaside resort. A restored library on the top floor houses over 30,000 photos and 3,000 maps (reservation required).

Acropolis-Palais des Congrès★

1 Esplanade Kennedy. ℘*04 93 92 82 35. www.nice-acropolis.com.*
This enormous convention centre resembles a majestic vessel anchored

Cathédrale Orthodoxe Russe St-Nicolas

© Sylvaine Poitau/Apa Publications

to five robust vaults spanning the River Paillon. Designed by a group of local architects it features works by contemporary artists including Volti *(Nikaia)*, Vasarely, Arman *(Music Power)*, César *(Thumb)*, Paul Belmondo and Cyril de la Patellière *(Mediterranean Tribute)*.

Théâtre de la Photographie et de l'Image

27 Blvd. Dubouchage. ⏰*Open Wed–Mon 10am–6pm.* ⊶*No charge.* ☎*04 97 13 42 20. www.tpi-nice.org.*
This exhibition space dedicated to photographic images benefits from an original architectural setting.

👥 Muséum d'Histoire Naturelle

60 Blvd. Risso. ⏰*Open Tue–Sun 10am–6pm.* ⊙*Guided tour Wed 3pm.* ⏰*Closed public holidays.* ⊶*No charge.* ☎*04 97 13 46 80. www.mhnnice.org.*
Nice's first museum has a large collection of zoological, geological and botanical specimens.

👥 Musée de Terra Amata

25 Blvd. Carnot. ⏰*Open Tue–Sun 10am–6pm.* ⊶*No charge.* ☎*04 93 55 59 93. www.musee-terra-amata.org.*
Situated on the site of one of the earliest human settlements known in Europe, dating back 400 000 years, this museum features tools, animal bones and traces of a hunter's hearth.

Prieuré du Vieux-Logis

59 Ave. St-Barthélémy. ⊶*Guided tours (1hr 45min, 3€) by reservation Sat Oct–May 3pm; Jun–Sept 5pm.* ☎*04 93 88 11 34.*
A medieval home has been reconstructed within a 16C farm and richly decorated with works of art, 14C to 17C furniture and items from everyday life (note the outstanding kitchen). There are numerous statues, including a 15C Pietà from Franche-Comté.

Église St-Barthélémy

13 montée Claire-Virenque.
This church houses a triptych *(right side aisle)* by François Bréa of the *Virgin in Majesty* flanked by *Saint Jean the Baptist* and *Saint Sebastian*.

Église Ste-Jeanne-d'Arc

11 rue Gramond.
This is a modern concrete church designed by Jacques Droz with an ellipsoidal porch as its main doorway. The belfry wreathed in flames rises to 215ft/65m. Inside, the soaring vaulting is striking. *The Stations of the Cross* frescoes are by Klementief (1934).

🚗 DRIVING TOURS

L'Arrière Pays Niçois

The hinterlands of Nice are dotted with cliff-top villages and **panoramic** peaks accessible by narrow winding roads.
🛈 Tourist offices at Gilette Val d'Esteron, *𝒞 04 92 08 98 08, www.esteron.fr*; at l'Escarène, *𝒞 04 93 7962 93, www.escarene.fr*; or at Contes, *𝒞 04 93 79 19 99, www.ville-contes.fr.*

1 LES DEUX MONTS★★
Round trip of 7mi/11km.
Allow 1hr15min.

▷ *Leave Nice from pl. Max-Barel on D 6007, Moyenne Corniche, going east. After 1.5mi/2.5km, turn a sharp right onto a forest road. After 0.6mi/1km turn left onto a signposted path to the fort.*

Mont Alban★★
Alt. 728ft/222m. A footpath circles up to a splendid **view**★★ of the coastline: to the east lie Cap Ferrat, Cap d'Ail, the Bordighera Point and the Tête de Chien. To the west lies the Baie des Anges. A small pathway leads to the massive 16C fort bastions and watchtowers (**private**).

16C fort of Mont Alban

©Guy Thouvenin/Robert Harding

▷ *Return to the fork and proceed straight ahead to Mont Boron.*

Mont Boron★
Alt. 584ft/178m.
Views★ extending over Villefranche harbour, along the coast to Cap d'Antibes and the mountains around Grasse. Bones, stone tools and a hearth used by Acheulian hunters were found on the western slope of this mountain (ⓒ *see Musée Terra Amata p311*)
🚶 Walk along the 710yd/650m botanic woodland trail featuring dozens of species of aromatic and medicinal plants with a **view**★ over the Baie des Anges.

▷ *Return to Nice along the Corniche Inférieure (N 98).*

2 PLATEAU ST-MICHEL★★
Round trip of 12mi/19km. Allow 1hr.

▷ *Leave Nice going E along ave. des Diables-Bleus and the Grande Corniche (D 2564).*

Nice, Cap d'Antibes, the Esterel and Bassin du Paillon lie to the rear. Ahead are La Drète fort, with Mont Agel beyond.

Observatoire du Mont-Gros
Turn right off the Grande Corniche onto a private road. 👁‍🗨 *Guided tours (1.5hr) Wed and Sat 2.45pm.* ✏6€. *𝒞 04 93 85 85 58. www.astrorama.net.* This international centre for astronomical research was founded in 1881. The shell was designed by Charles Garnier, while the metal frame for the great dome (85ft/26m in diameter) housing the astronomical telescope was built by Gustave Eiffel. At 59ft/18m long, with an optical diameter of 30in/76cm. it was once the largest instrument of its kind.

▷ *Take the D 2524 towards Eze for 1mi/1.5km, then E 34 right; after 547yd/500m, park in the car park.*

Plateau St-Michel Viewpoint★★
Views along the coast to Cap de St-Hospice in Nice and Cap Ferrat.

▶ *Continue along D 34 and then bear left onto the Moyenne Corniche (D 6007).*

After a tunnel there is a **view**★ of Beaulieu, Cap Ferrat, Villefranche-sur-Mer, Nice and Cap d'Antibes. The road winds round above Villefranche harbour.

▶ *Return to Nice via Pl. Max-Barel.*

③ **TOUR OF MONT CHAUVE**★
Round trip of 33mi/53km.
Allow half a day.

▶ *From Nice take blvd. Cessole, ave. St-Sylvestre and ave. du Ray north; turn sharp left on ave. de Gairaut (D 14). Pass under the motorway (0.6mi/1km), bear right on D 14 and then left (follow signs).*

Cascade de Gairaut
The waters of the Vésubie Canal tumble down into a basin over two great rock shelves. From the chapel terrace there is a beautiful **view** of the town.

▶ *Return to D 14.*

Views to the left of Nice, Mont Boron, Cap d'Antibes. The road then rises towards Aspremont, the *baous* and the Var valley.

Aspremont
The village, built to a concentric plan, is perched on a hilltop site (1,800ft/550m). The **church** has a Gothic nave decorated with frescoes. From the terrace above the town is a **panorama**★ of several hill villages, Cap d'Antibes, the hills beyond Nice and Mont Chauve. On leaving the village a small road on the left signposted "Mona Cima" leads to a sheepfold (*park at pl. des Selettes and continue on foot*) with **views** of Aspremont and the Var.

▶ *On leaving the village, take D 719 over Col d'Aspremont between Mont Chauve and Mont Cima.*

Tourrette-Levens
Circled by mountains, this village on the Salt Route clings to a knife-edged rock.

The **18C church** has a carved wooden altarpiece. Walk through the village to the partially restored château and the **Musée des Métiers Traditionnels** (☉*open Tue–Sun Apr–Oct 2–6pm; Nov–Mar 2–5.30pm;* ☞*no charge;* ✆*04 97 20 54 60*) exhibiting over 6,000 tools. The walk ends at the **Musée d'Histoire Naturelle**, a view of which boasts a collection of exotic butterflies (☉*open Tue–Sun May–Oct 2–6.30pm; Nov–Apr 2–5.30pm;* ☞*no charge;* ✆*04 93 91 03 20*).

▶ *Return to D 19, turning left into the Gabre Valley, then right on D 114.*

Falicon
This typical Niçois village huddles on a rocky outcrop among olive groves. Illustrious guests include Queen Victoria. The **church**, founded by the Benedictines of St-Pons, has a square belfry and *trompe-l'oeil* façade. Climb the stairway (left of the church), then turn right to the terrace **views**★ of Nice and Mont Angel.

▶ *Return to D 114 on the left. At the chapel of St-Sébastien turn right onto D 214, a narrow road, to Mont Chauve. Leave the car at the end of the road.*

Mont Chauve d'Aspremont
Alt. 2,802ft/854m.
🚶 *30min on foot round trip.*
"Chauve" means bald and the mountain lives up to its name. A disused fort stands on the naked summit offering a magnificent **panorama**★★of the snow-clad Alps and the coast from Menton to Cap Ferrat.

▶ *Return to D 114 left; then right on D 19 after 1mi/2km. After 0.6mi/1km turn right to St-Pons.*

Église St-Pons★
The Benedictine abbey of St Pontius was founded during the reign of Charlemagne. The church, rebuilt in the 18C, stands on a headland above the Paillon Valley, its Genoese campanile visible from all sides.

ADDRESSES

🛏 STAY

🛏 **Au Picardy Hôtel** – *10 blvd. Jean-Jaurès. ℰ04 93 85 75 51. 🍴 11 rooms. 🍽3€.* Between the train station and Old Town, this friendly, family-run hotel has basic rooms: small, yet soundproofed.

🛏 **Clair Hotel** – *23 blvd. Carnot, Impasse Terra Amata. ℰ04 93 89 69 89. 10 rooms. 🍽7.50€.* This converted schoolhouse near the archaeological museum has rooms all on one floor (in the old classrooms) and a Mediterranean garden terrace, where breakfast is served in summer. Quiet neighbourhood; friendly, family-run atmosphere.

🛏 🛏 **Hôtel Armenonville** – *20 ave. des Fleurs. ℰ04 93 96 86 00. www.hotel-armenonville.com. 12 rooms. 🅿. 🍽11€.* At the end of a passage in the old Russian district of Nice, this retro hotel built in 1900 has charming rooms decorated with antiques. WiFi, garden, air-conditioning and free parking.

🛏 🛏 **Hôtel de Normandie** – *18 rue Paganini. ℰ04 93 88 48 83 . www.hotel-normandie.com. 44 rooms. 🍽7€.* Practical location a few steps from the train station with a typical Niçoise decor. Rooms are simple, yet well-equipped, and there's free WiFi and a hot meal distributor in the lobby.

🛏 🛏 **Star Hôtel** – *14 rue Biscarra. ℰ04 93 85 19 03. www.hotel-star.com. 24 rooms. 🍽7€.* Small hotel close to the Nice Étoile shopping centre, offering simple accommodation with air-conditioning and free Internet access.

🛏 🛏 🛏 **Chambre d'hôte Castel Enchanté** – *61 route St-Pierre-de-Féric. ℰ04 93 97 02 08. www.castel-enchante. com. 🍴. 4 rooms. Closed mid-Nov–mid-Mar. 🍽.* A beautiful 19C villa on the hills above Nice, with a huge terrace surrounded by orchards. Rooms are lovingly decorated by Jacques and Martine, who also serve their homemade jams at the breakfast buffet.

🛏 🛏 🛏 **Chambre d'hôte Villa la Lézardière** – *87 blvd. de l'Observatoire. ℰ04 93 56 22 86. www.villa-nice.com. 5 rooms. 🅿. 🍽.* Perched on the Grande Corniche, this Provençal-style villa has great **views** over the Alps. Personalised bedrooms, some with kitchenettes. Also a large pool and enclosed garden.

🍴 EAT

Salade niçoise, socca, pan bagnat, poutine, tourte aux blettes, beignets de fleurs de courgettes... to experience the best in local cuisine, look for the restaurants displaying the "Cuisine Nissarde" label. A guide to these restaurants is available free of charge at the tourist office.

🍴 **Lou Balico** – *22 ave. St-Jean-Baptiste. ℰ04 93 85 93 71. www.loubalico.com.* Three generations of the same family have been serving classic Niçois dishes in this cosy dining room, adorned with a piano and guest book with signatures from around the world.

🍴 **Marlone Café** – *4 rue de l'Opéra. ℰ04 93 85 96 15 . www.marlonecafe.com. Closed Mon.* A gourmet refuge just off Place Masséna, with traditional meals and a comfortable, thoughtfully decorated dining room.

🍴 **Le Pain à Table** – *3 rue St-François-de-Paul (cours Saleya). ℰ04 93 62 94 32.* Sit at one of the communal wooden tables and order fresh breads with spreads, salads, open sandwiches and brunch on the weekend.

🍴 **Réné Socca** – *2 rue Miralhéti. ℰ04 93 92 05 73 . 🍴 Closed Mon.* The most popular "Nissart" restaurant in town. Follow the line, order your food and sit at one of the long tables with your meal. Don't miss the *socca*, cooked fresh in the wood-fired oven, the *pissaladière* and stuffed courgette blossoms.

🍴 **Safari** – *1 cours Saleya. ℰ04 93 80 18 44. http://restaurantsafari.fr.* A trendy address overlooking the market at Cours Saleya, this restaurant has a beautiful terrace and local specialities, including a large selection of fish and seafood. Great for people watching.

🍴 **La Table d'Alziari** – *4 rue François-Zannin. ℰ04 93 80 34 03. Closed mid-Jan, early Jun, early Oct, mid-Dec, Sun–Mon.* Unpretentious family restaurant in a small alley of the old town. Typical dishes from Nice and the Provence area, chalked up on a slate, are served in a homely decor, with wines recommended by the owner.

◉◉ **L'Escalinada** – *22 rue Pairolière.* ☎*04 93 62 11 71. www.escalinada.fr.* 🚭*. Closed mid-Nov–mid-Dec.* Nestled in the old quarter, this charming restaurant offers attractively presented regional cuisine in a spruce dining room with rustic overtones. Friendly service.

◉◉ **Grand Café de Turin** – *5 pl. Garibaldi.* ☎*04 93 62 29 52.* This brasserie, which is over 200 years old, has become an institution in Nice. It serves seafood dishes à la carte at reasonable prices throughout the day. Pleasant, welcoming setting, although a bit noisy on the terrace.

◉◉ **Le Local** – *4 rue Rusca.* ☎*04 93 14 08 29.* Minimalist decor for this deli-restaurant specialising in Neopolitan and Sicilian dishes such as *antipasto del mare.*

◉◉ **La Mérenda** – *4 r. Raoul Bosio F.* ☎*04 93 14 08 29.* 🚭*.* Uncomfortable stools, no telephone and credit cards are not accepted. Despite all of this, crowds flock to La Mérenda every day to sample its authentic Niçois cuisine!

◉◉◉ **L'Univers-Christian Plumail** – *54 blvd. J. Jaurès.* ☎*04 93 62 32 22. www.christian-plumail.com. Closed Sat and Mon, Sun.* Decorated with modern paintings and sculptures, this prestigious Niçois restaurant serves regional cuisine with a twist. Very reasonable set menus.

🎭 NIGHTLIFE

Casino Ruhl – *1 promenade des Anglais.* ☎*04 97 03 12 22. www.lucienbarriere. com.* The casino boasts 300 slot machines and has facilities for French and English roulette, blackjack, stud poker, etc. American bar. Live cabaret performances on Fridays and Saturdays (except July–August). Bring photo ID.

Le Relais – *Hôtel Negresco, 37 promenade des Anglais.* ☎*04 93 16 64 00. www.hotel-negresco.com.* The sumptuous decoration of this bar belonging to the legendary Negresco Hotel has remained the same since 1913: Brussels tapestry (1683), 18C paintings, replicas of the wall lamps adorning the Ballroom in Fontainebleau. Piano bar every evening.

La Trappa – *rue de la Préfecture and rue Gilly.* ☎*04 93 80 33 69. Closed Sun–Mon.* A lively tapas bar with deep, comfortable settees and red walls

awaits you at La Trappa, open since 1886. Sip a Cuban cocktail while you listen to Latin American music (DJ weekends). Friendly atmosphere and local wine list.

🛒 SHOPPING

Many shops in Old Nice are closed on Mondays.

Shopping streets – The streets surrounding the Cathédrale Ste-Réparate are lined with shops selling typical Provençal articles: fabrics *(rue Paradis and rue du Marché)*, arts and crafts *(rue du Pont-Vieux and rue de la Boucherie)*, olive oil and *santons* (clay figures) *(rue St-François-de-Paul).*

Alziari – *14 rue St-François-de-Paule.* ☎*04 93 85 76 92. www.alziari.com.fr. Closed Sun–Mon.* One of the best addresses in town for olive oil and regional specialities.

La Maison de l'Olive – *18 rue Pairolière.* ☎*04 93 80 01 61. Closed Mon.* Marseille soaps made from pure olive oil, lotions and scents for the body and home, and regional products such as dried tomatoes, lemon jam, marinated capers and olives; also Provençal herbs and spices.

À l'Olivier – *7 rue St-François-de-Paule.* ☎*04 93 13 44 97.* Every brand of French olive oil with the AOC label is sold in this boutique, originally opened in 1822, in Nice since 2004. Also, a fine selection of elegant glassware, dishes, tablecloths.

Confiserie Auer – *7 rue St-François-de-Paule.* ☎*04 93 85 77 98. www.maison-auer.com. Closed Sun.* A gorgeous vintage boutique selling sugared fruit and crystallised flowers from the Nice region, as well as chocolates and *calissons* from Aix (iced, candied fruit with almond paste).

Confiserie Florian – *14 quai Papacino, on the Port.* ☎*04 93 55 43 50. www.confiserieflorian.com.* 📷*Guided tours of the factory 9am–noon, 2–6.30pm.* Sugared fruit, lemon, orange and grapefruit preserve, chocolates and sweets, crystallised petals and delicious jams made with rose, violet and jasmine blossom.

Maison Poilpot – Aux Parfums de Grasse – *10 rue St-Gaétan.* ☎*04 93 85 60 77. Closed Mon.* This traditional perfumery produces more than

80 different fragrances, including popular Mediterranean scents such as mimosa, rose, violet and lemon.

L'Art Gourmand – *21 rue du Marché.* ℘*04 93 62 51 79.* This Old Nice boutique has many treats available to go or eat in: nougats, *calisson*, sugared fruit, cookies, pastries, ice cream and northern French specialities. There's a tea room on the mezzanine decorated with murals.

Fenocchio – *2 pl. Rossetti, Old Town.* ℘*04 93 80 72 52. Closed Nov–Jan.* This famous ice cream and sorbet maker has some of the most amazing flavours, from avocado and sun-dried tomato to honey and pine nut. With almost 100 flavours to choose from, you'll have to go back more than once!

Maison Poilpot – *Aux Parfums de Grasse, 10 rue St-Gaëtan.* ℘*04 93 85 60 77. Closed Mon, two weeks in Nov, lunch in holidays.* This artisan perfume-maker proposes 80 different scents (lavender, mimosa, rose, violet and lemon).

MARKETS

Marché aux Poissons – The fish market is on pl. St-François Tue–Sun 6am–1pm.

Marché aux Fleurs – The flower market is on the cours Saleya Tues–Sun 6am–5.30pm.

Marché aux Fruits et Légumes – The colourful food market on the cours Saleya takes place Tue–Sun 6am–1.30pm.

Marché de la Liberation – Locals' food market from the avenue Malausséna to place Charles de Gaulle.

Marché aux Puces – Flea market on place Robilante Tue–Sat 10am–6pm.

Marché de la Brocante –Antique market on cours Saleya Mon 7.30am–6pm.

🏃 LEISURE ACTIVITIES

Beaches – The Baie des Anges covers a 3mi/5km stretch of coastline with smooth pebbles *(galets)*. There are many public beaches placed under close surveillance and 15 private beaches hosting sporting activities.

Hiking – *14 ave. Mirabeau.* ℘*04 93 62 59 99. www.cafnice.org. Office open Mon–Fri 4–8pm.* CAF (Club Alpin Français) organises one-day hiking tours across the Nice hinterland and Mercantour Park leaving from Nice.

Skiing – *www.cotedazur-tourisme.com.* The nearby ski resorts of Auron (℘*04 93 23 02 66*) and Valberg (℘*04 93 02 52 27*), which are only a 2hr drive away, are undoubtedly among the main attractions of the Nice area.

CALENDAR OF EVENTS

There are many traditional festivals throughout the year. Ask at the tourist office for a complete schedule.

Nice Carnival – This colourful, extravagant event invariably attracts large crowds every year. Festivities take place around Shrove Tuesday *(Mardi Gras)* and last for a fortnight. They include processions, floats, firework displays, costume balls and battles where showers of flowers and confetti are thrown!

Cougourdons Festival – Cougourdons are gourds that have been dried and painted. The city of Nice pays homage to these curious vegetables in early April.

Fête de la Mer et de la St-Pierre – A festival celebrating the sea and St-Peter on the port and quai des Etats-Unis the last weekend in June.

Nice Jazz Festival – The jazz festival is held in Nice the last two weeks of July on pl. Massena, attended by leading performers from all over the world. *www.nicejazzfestival.fr.*

Fête de la San Bertoumiéu – A festival of traditional arts and crafts, regional foods and entertainment in the Old Town the first weekend in September.

Crèche Vivante Lou Presèpi – A living nativity scene with people and animals on place Rossetti the week of Christmas.

Corniches de la Riviera★★★

Alpes Maritimes

Between Nice and Menton the mountains plunge sharply down to the sea. Running along these heights are three famous routes: the Grande Corniche, the Moyenne Corniche and the Basse Corniche. The first affords the most stunning views, climbing to 1,476ft/450m, the second offers beautiful vistas along the shore, while the third provides access to the coastal resorts.

- ⚙ **Michelin Map:** 341 F/G5.
- 🚩 **Info:** Cap d'Ail tourist office: 87bis Ave. du 3-Septembre. ✆04 93 78 02 33. www.cap-dail.com
- 🔎 **Don't Miss:** The Grande Corniche has the best **panoramic views**.
- 👪 **Kids:** Check out the stars from Astrorama.
- 🕐 **Timing:** If time is short, take a 3-hr drive along the Grande Corniche.

🚗 DRIVING TOURS

1 GRANDE CORNICHE★★★

MENTON TO NICE

19mi/31km. Allow 3hr.
The Grande Corniche, built by Napoleon along the route of the ancient **Via Julia Augusta**, passes through La Turbie 1,470ft/450m above Monaco.

▶ *From Menton take ave. Carnot and ave. de la Madone (D 6007). Leaving the Moyenne Corniche on the left, the road (D 2564) runs above the town and Cap Martin. 437yd/400m after entering Roquebrune-Cap-Martin, take a sharp right onto a small road leading to the village.*

Roquebrune-Cap-Martin★
⚙*See ROQUEBRUNE-CAP-MARTIN p346.*

▶ *Return to D 2564.*

Le Vistaëro★★
From nearly 1,000ft/300m above the sea is a marvellous **view**★★ extending out over Bordighera Point, Menton and, immediately below, Monte-Carlo Beach. Further inland is the Alpine Trophy.

La Turbie★
The hilltop village of La Turbie *(alt. 1,575ft/480m; population 3,155)*, built in a pass on the Grande Corniche, is most famous for its Alpine Trophy, a masterpiece of Roman art.

When Caesar died, the Alps were occupied by unconquered tribes who posed a constant threat to communications between Rome and its possessions in Gaul and Spain. **Augustus** ended this by extending Roman rule into this region. In 6 BC the Senate and the Roman people commemorated the victory with the erection of the trophy on the Via Julia Augusta. There is only one other Roman trophy still standing (in Romania).

On ave. Générale de Gaulle is a 19C fountain, built at the end of a Roman aqueduct. Below, from the southwest corner of place Neuve, is a fine **view**★ of the coast.

Rue Comte-de-Cessole (once part of the **Via Julia Augusta**). Pass through the West Gate, climbing past medieval houses to the Trophy. A house on the right bears a plaque with verses Dante dedicated to La Turbie.

Église St-Michel-Archange – The 18C church is a fine example of the Nice Baroque style, with paintings attributed to J-B Van Loo and Veronese *(light switch in the chapel on the right)*.

Return to the rue de Cessole and climb to the top of the hill to take a look at the Trophy *(⚙ see overleaf)*, then return towards rue Droite (also once part of the Via Julia), passing under the East Gate. Bring your camera to capture the great **panoramic views**★★★ of Monaco, the Italian Riviera, Èze and the heights of Mont Agel from the terraces here.

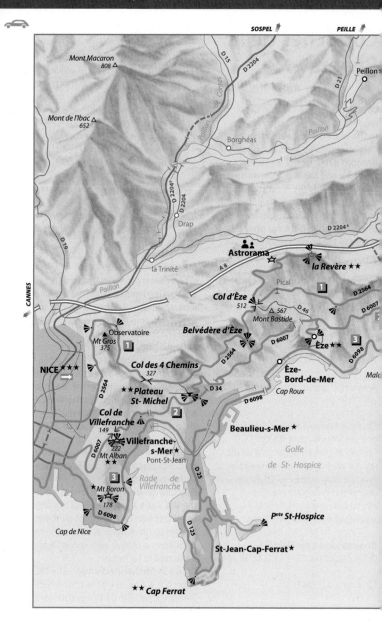

SOSPEL   PEILLE

Mont Macaron
808 △

Peillon

Mont de l'Ibac △
652

Borghéas

Drap

la Trinité

Astrorama

la Revère ★★

Pical

Col d'Èze
512

Mont Bastide
△ 567

Observatoire
Mt Gros
375

Belvédère d'Èze

Èze ★★

NICE ★★★

Col des 4 Chemins
327

Èze-
Bord-de-Mer
Cap Roux

★★Plateau
St-Michel

Col de
Villefranche
149

Beaulieu-s-Mer ★

Villefranche-
s-Mer ★
Pont-St-Jean

Mt Alban
★★

Golfe
de St- Hospice

Rade   de
Villefranche

★ Mt Boron
178

Pⁿᵗᵉ St-Hospice

Cap de Nice

St-Jean-Cap-Ferrat ★

★★ Cap Ferrat

Trophée des Alpes★

&. ⊙Open Tue–Sun mid-May–mid-Sept
9.30am–1pm, 2.30–6.30pm; mid-Sept–
mid-May 10am–1.30pm, 2.30–5pm.
⊚5€. ℘04 93 41 20 84.
www.ville-la-turbie.fr.
The **Alpine Trophy** consisted of a
circular doric colonnade with niches
for statues of the Roman generals who
took part in the campaign to conquer
the Alps. The base featured a long dedi-
cation to Augustus, whose statue probably stood on a small dome over the
monument. In the Middle Ages it was
converted into a fort, then served as a
source of building stone, before being
mined by Louis XIV. It has been partially
restored to a height of 115ft/35m. The

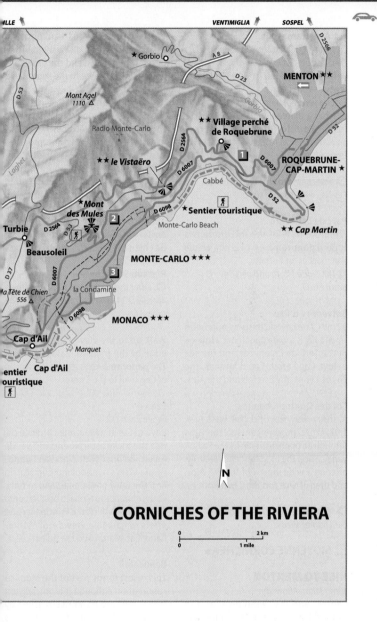

CORNICHES OF THE RIVIERA

```
0              2 km
0        1 mile
```

N

museum recounts the story of the Trophy and its restoration.

The Grande Corniche reveals distant **views** of Cap Ferrat, then of Èze village as the road reaches its highest point at 1,804ft/550m.

Col d'Èze
Alt. 1,680ft/512m. Extended **view** to the north over the mountains and valleys. Mont Bastide, on the left, was a Celto-Ligurian *oppidum* and a Roman camp.

▶ *On leaving Col d'Èze towards Nice, turn right up the road signed "Parc Départemental de la Grande Corniche-Astrorama".*

👥 Astrorama

La Trinité. 🕐*Open Mar–Jun Sept–Oct Fri–Sat (Tue–Sat in Jul–Aug) 7pm–11pm.* 🎟️*10€ (6–25 yr 8€). 📞04 93 85 85 58. www.astrorama.net.*

After a series of hairpin bends, the road reaches a plateau, which is home to a former **Feuillerins** gun battery, now an astronomical research and observation centre.

🔵 *Park at the foot of the Fort de la Revère (🔒 closed to the public).*

Parc de la Revère

From the base of the fort there is a superb **panorama**★★ over the whole Var coast as far as Italy.

🚶 *1hr. Signed flora and geology nature trail.*

Belvédère d'Èze

0.7mi/1.2km beyond the pass, opposite a small café, is a wide panoramic **view**★★ of the Tête de Chien, Èze and the sea below, Cap Ferrat, Cap d'Antibes, the Iles de Lérins, the Esterels and the Alps.

Col des Quatre-Chemins

A short way beyond the pass (alt. 1,037ft/327m) one can see the Alps through an opening made by the Paillon Valley. Soon the road descends steeply, offering a wide **view**★ of the Pre-Alps, and then of Nice and the Cap d'Antibes.

🔵 *Enter Nice from the east by ave. des Diables-Bleus.*

2️⃣ MOYENNE CORNICHE★★

NICE TO MENTON

19mi/31km. Allow 2hr.

Shorter and less winding than the Grande Corniche, the Moyenne Corniche is a modern road built between 1910 and 1928. It tunnels through the larger mountain chains and provides the only access by road to Èze.

🔵 *Leave Nice by pl. Max-Barel on D 6007 heading east. Look for the designated roadside parking areas provided at all the best viewpoints.*

Views of Nice, the château, port and the Baie des Anges give way to **views** of the Esterel chain and the limestone mountains of Grasse to the southwest.

Col de Villefranche

Alt. 489ft/149m. From a bend in the road soon after the pass, Villefranche-sur-Mer harbour and Cap Ferrat come into sight. Just before entering a 200yd/180m-long tunnel, there is an extraordinary **view**★★ of Beaulieu, Cap Ferrat, Villefranche-sur-Mer, Nice and Cap d'Antibes. After the tunnel, the village of Èze comes into view, perched high on its rock against the backdrop of Tête de Chien (alt. 1,880ft/556m).

Plateau St-Michel★★

🔵 *After the tunnel turn right onto the narrow D 34, which climbs back over the tunnel for 1mi/2km to a terrace car park.*

Walk up to the viewing table on the edge of the plateau (2,339ft/731m). The **panorama**★★ extends from the tip of Cap d'Ail to the Esterel.

Èze★★

🍷*See Èze p332.*

Beyond Èze, the Moyenne Corniche circles the rocky escarpments of Tête de Chien and brings into sight new **panoramic views** overlooking Cap Martin and the Bordighera headland in Italy. At the entrance to Monaco bear left onto D 6007, which skirts the Principality and offers remarkable **views**★ of Monte-Carlo, Cap Martin and the Italian coast.

Beausoleil

This resort forms part of the Monaco conurbation although it is officially on French territory. Its houses, reached by stepped streets, project from the slopes of Mont des Mules like balconies.

🔵 *Bear left onto D 53.*

Mont des Mules★

🚶 *0.6mi/1km, plus 30min round trip along a marked path.*

From the top there is a fine **panorama**★ (viewing table).

▷ *Passing below the Vistaëro belvedere, the road joins the Basse Corniche at Cabbé.*

Cap Martin★★ ⚭ *See ROQUEBRUNE-CAP-MARTIN p346.*

③ **CORNICHE INFÉRIEURE★★**

NICE TO MENTON
21mi/33km. Allow about 6hr.
First floated in the 18C by the princes of Monaco, the idea of constructing the Basse Corniche finally took shape in 1857 when it was inaugurated by the Empress of Russia. It was completed in 1881. The road, running at the foot of the mountain slopes and following the contours of the coast, serves all the Riviera resorts.

▷ *From Nice take blvd. Carnot, D 6098, heading southeast.*

The road skirts the base of Mont Boron with **views**★ of the Baie des Anges, Cap Ferrat, Villefranche-sur-Mer port, Èze and Tête de Chien in succession.

Villefranche-sur-Mer★
⚭ *See VILLEFRANCHE-SUR-MER p324.*

Cap Ferrat★★
⚭ *See CAP FERRAT p327.*

Beaulieu★
⚭ *See BEAULIEU p330.*
As the road skirts Cap Roux, there is a view across the water to Cap d'Ail.

Èze-Bord-de-Mer
The resort lies beneath the cliffs on which Èze-Village is perched. **Views** over Cap d'Ail.

Cap d'Ail
Controversial stock market magnate **baron de Pauville**, founder of the "Petit niçois" regional weekly paper, was very attached to this small resort and built his first speculative properties here in 1879. The arrival of the railway and the main road at the end of the 19C further boosted its development. In 1908, the resort was finally opened.

Dominated by the Tête de Chien (1,640ft/500m) escarpment, of which it occupies the last slopes, the resort, which includes over 70 early 20C villas, runs down to the sea, surrounded by palm trees, cypresses and pines. Countless celebrities have made their homes here, including Sacha Guitry (villa Les Funambules), Greta Garbo (villa Le Rock), the Caritta sisters (Villa Le Chien Bleu aka "the bamboo cabin"), and one of the Lumière brothers.

Its six parks and gardens fill the village streets with Mediterranean scents (parc Sacha-Guitry and the jardin des Oliviers) and afford stunning **views** over the sea and the small port (the Balcon des Salines). The **pointe des douaniers**, which resembles a wild volcanic landscape, offers exception flora and sea **views**.

For sun-seekers the **plage Marquet**, close to the port, is open to everyone. The wild **plage Mala**, niched in the rock, and **Les Pissarelles**, fringed by rocks, are difficult to access but offer excellent **views**.

Coastal Path of Cap d'Ail★
🚶 *1hr round trip. On the east side of the station, descend the steps into a tunnel that comes out on a road. Turn left and at Restaurant La Pinède, take another flight of steps on the right down to the sea.*
A coastal footpath running eastwards skirts the rocks at the foot of Cap d'Ail. To the west lie Beaulieu, Cap Ferrat and Monaco Rock. The footpath ends on Marquet beach. You can take the road into Monaco.

Monaco★★★
⚭ *See MONACO p334.*
The road joins the Moyenne Corniche close to Cabbé beach.

Cap Martin★★
⚭ *See ROQUEBRUNE-CAP-MARTIN p346.*

④ **BASSE CORNICHE★★**

AROUND MONT-AGEL
80km/50mi. Allow half a day.
See map p294.

Notre-Dame-de-Laghet

▷ *Leave Nice on the Turin road (D 2204) heading NE. At La Trinité turn right on to the D 2204A towards Laghet.*

Notre-Dame-de-Laghet

Surrounded by woods, this Italianesque village was the setting for a series of miracles said to have been worked by the Virgin Mary in 1652 and it has attracted pilgrims from Nice and Italy ever since. An example of High Baroque, the church is decorated with a carved wooden Madone de Laghet on the high altar. The cloister and church are filled with **ex-votos**. The most beautiful examples are displayed in a **museum** on place du Sanctuaire (⚓ ⏱ *sanctuary open 7am–9.30pm; museum open in summer 3.30–5.30pm; open Wed–Mon May–Oct 3.30–5.30pm; ⚓no charge; ℘04 93 41 50 50; www.sanctuaire-laghet.cef.fr).*

▷ *Continue on D 2204A and D 2564 to La Turbie.*

La Turbie

◐ *See LA TURBIE p317.*

▷ *Turn left out of the village onto the D 53 towards Peille.*

St-Martin-de-Peille

This isolated **church** (℘04 93 91 71 71) rises out of olive groves planted up the mountain slopes. Modern and strikingly simple, it has plastic stained-glass windows and an altar made from a length of olive wood.

▷ *Continue beyond St-Martin-de-Peille on D 53 for several kilometres and turn right onto D 22 towards Ste-Agnès.*

The small road winds around the foot of **Mont Agel** with **views** over the Peille below and Berre-les-Alpes in the distance.

The **Col de la Madone** (3,041ft/927m) lies at a high altitude, just miles from the sea as the crow flies, which can be seen in the distance.

⚑ *3hr round trip.* From Col de la Madone, a trail leads to the **Cîme de Baudon** (4,153ft/1,266m) affording a breathtaking 360° **panorama**.

Ste-Agnès★ *8mi/13km – about 45min.*
The road is uphill all the way with **views** of the Gorbio Valley. Bear right at **Col St-Sébastien** (alt. 1,969ft/600m) which has a particularly picturesque **view★** of Ste-Agnès. Located barely 2mi/3km from the sea, yet at an altitude of 2,559ft/780m, this is the highest coastal village in Europe.

The picturesque cobblestone streets of the village, lined with craft shops, include rue Longue and the vaulted rue des Comtes-Léotardi. A rocky path leads from behind the graveyard to the ruins of the castle and a marvellous **panorama**★★.

Fort Maginot de Ste-Agnès
At the village entrance, turn towards the parking Sud and park the car on the left, near the fort. ☃*The interior is chilly.* ☞*Guided tours (1hr) Jun–Sept Tue–Sun 10.30am–noon, 3–7pm, Oct–May Sat-–Sun 2.30–5.30pm.* ☜5€. ☎04 93 51 62 31. www.sainteagnes.fr.
This imposing building camouflaged by overhanging rocks was built between 1931 and 1938 as part of the Alpine Maginot Line. Its firing slots are equipped with 81mm mortars and 75/135mm guns facing southeast over Menton Bay.
The barracks, deep in the cliff, still house an electric generator, a neutralisation room and kitchens.
The tour gives an insight into life in a fort in WWII. Outside, set slightly downhill, a platform overlooking the intricacies of the Provençal motorway is a **view**★★ of the coast from Bordighera in Italy to Cap Martin.

▷ *Head towards Menton on D 22, right onto C17 towards Gorbio, then right again onto D 23.*

Gorbio★ *5.6mi/9km.*
The Gorbio Valley, with its flowers, olives and pines, and luxury residences, contrasts with the stark appearance of the village, perched on its wild and rocky **site**★. For the feast of Corpus Christi, the villagers organise a parade, known as the **Procession des Limaces**, in which everyone carries a snail-shell filled with olive oil and lit with a small wick. Behind the church is a fine **viewpoint** across to Bordighera Point.

▷ *Take the D 50 to the Grande Corniche (D 2564) and return to Nice.*

ADDRESSES

⬤ STAY

⬤⬤⬤ **La Réserve de la Mala** – *plage de la Mala, down ave. Combattants-Afrique-du-Nord (at the Spar store).* ☎04 93 78 21 56. www.capresort.com. *Closed mid-Oct–late Mar.* A small corner of paradise located right on the beach and accessible on foot from the cap d'Ail tourist trail or the town centre. Mediterranean fish and world flavours.

⬤ EAT

⬤ **Le St-Yves** – *St-Agnes.* ☎04 93 35 91 45. *Closed Fri. 7 rooms.* ⬤€5.50. This restaurant serving regional fare enjoys a warm, rustic atmosphere and breathtaking countryside **views**. Homemade antipasti, rabbit with herbs, boar stew... Vast **panoramic** terrace. Simple rooms with open **views**.

⬤⬤⬤⬤ **Le Relais St-Martin Chez Cotton** – *St-Martin-de-Peille –* *12.5mi/4km from La Turbie, north of Peille.* ☎04 93 41 16 03. www.chezcotton.com. *Closed Nov, Wed.* A refreshing spot to escape the summer heat. Regional dishes and grilled meat served in a bright dining room (fireplace on winter evenings) or on the shady terrace. **View** over the valley and mountains.

CALENDAR OF EVENTS

LA TURBIE

Soupe au pistou and Retraite aux flambeaux – Local pine nut and basil soup festival and evening torch-lit parade, 13 July on pl. Neuve, 8.30pm.

Les Musicales du Trophée – *www.musicalesdutrophee.fr – Second half of July.* Classical music concerts at Saint-Michel church and Le Trophée.

GORBIO

Snail procession – Early to mid-June. Snail shells filled with oil are lit with a wick and paraded through town.

⬤ LEISURE ACTIVITIES

Discovery hikes – Five-day hikes around the perched villages of the Corniches with Destination Merveilles, *www.voyages-randonnees.com.*

Villefranche-sur-Mer★

Alpes Maritimes

Villefranche is a fishing port and holiday resort overlooking one of the most beautiful harbours in the Mediterranean, with a deep bay where cruise liners lie at anchor. The town has preserved its 17C character, with a picturesque port, citadel and streets lined with sherbet-coloured houses.

A BIT OF HISTORY

The Origins of Villefranche – The town was founded in the 14C by the comte de Provence, Charles II of Anjou, nephew of St Louis. Between its cession to Savoie in the late 17C and the excavation of the harbour in Nice in the mid-18C, Villefranche was a major port, popular for its tax privileges and free port rights (Villefranche literally means "Free Port"), granted by its Savoyard and Sardinian rulers.

The Congress of Nice – In 1538, the Congress of Nice was convened by Pope Paul III to bring peace between François I and Charles V. The Queen of

▶ **Population:** 6,610.

⚅ **Michelin Map:** 341 E5; local map: *see Corniches de la RIVIERA pp318–319.*

ℹ **Info:** Jardin François-Binon. ℘04 93 01 73 68. www.ville franche-sur-mer.com.

◑ **Location:** Located 3.7mi/6km east of Nice on the Basse Corniche. Rue du Poilu is the main street in a network of narrow alleys, some of which are stepped or vaulted.

🅿 **Parking:** There is parking (absolutely packed in summer) around the citadel and the old port.

France, sister of Charles V, went to see her brother, whose ship was moored a Villefranche. Charles, giving his hand to the Queen and followed by the duc de Savoie and the lords and ladies of hi. suite, advanced majestically to the jetty from the ship, when the gangway col lapsed. The Emperor, Queen and Duke soaked and dishevelled, were pulled ashore by onlookers. The peace of Nice lasted barely five years.

Villefranche-sur-Mer

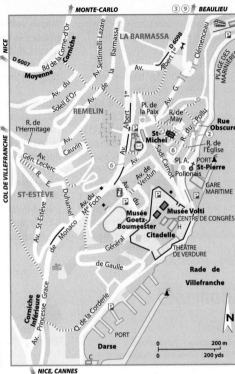

VILLEFRANCHE-SUR-MER

WHERE TO STAY

Patricia (Hôtel)......................③
Riviera (Hôtel Le)...................⑥
St-Michel (Hôtel)...................⑨

WHERE TO EAT

Grignotière (La)....................②
Oursin Bleu (L')....................⑥

From Naval Base to Zoological Station

– After the Crimean War, in 1856, Villefranche harbour was used by the Russian military fleet, deprived of access to the Mediterranean via the Bosphorus. In 1893, the sailors were replaced by a team of Russian scientists from Kiev, who conducted oceanographic research until the 1930s, when the premises were reclaimed by the Université de Paris as the site of a marine zoology station.

SIGHTS

Old Town★

The old town opens onto a charming port whose quaysides are lined with brightly-coloured houses. The **rue du Poilu** is the main thoroughfare through this labyrinth of alleyways, often stepped or vaulted, like the curious **rue Obscure**, whose foundations date back to the 13C, and which once followed the medieval ramparts. Covered to a length of 142yd/130m, it provided the inhabitants with shelter during bombardments.

Église St-Michel

6 rue Baron-de-Brès.

This Italian Baroque church contains 18C altarpieces and, in the north transept, a 17C crucifix carved with impressive realism from the trunk of a fig tree by an unknown convict.

Harbour (Darse)

Once a military port where galleys were built and manned, this is now a marina for yachts and pleasure boats.

➤To admire the harbour from above, climb the wooded Mont Alban and Mont Boron (see p.312).

Chapelle St-Pierre★

Open Tue–Sun mid-Mar–mid-Sept 10am–noon, 3–7pm; mid-Sept–mid-Nov and mid-Dec–Mar 10am–noon, 2–6pm. 2.50€.
04 93 76 90 70.

In 1957, this chapel was decorated with frescoes by **Jean Cocteau** (1889–1963) His theme, the life of St Peter, is illustrated by simple realistic scenes. There are also some secular scenes celebrating the young women of Villefranche.

Citadelle

🕐 *Open daily Oct–May 10am–noon, 2–5.30pm, (Sun 2–5.30pm); Jun–Sept 10am–noon, 3–6.30pm (Sun 3–6.30pm).* 🎫*No charge.* 🕿 *04 93 76 33 27.*

This stronghold was constructed in 1554 by the Duc de Savoie to guard the port. Admired by Vauban, Louis XIV spared it, along with the fort on Mont Alban, when he ordered the destruction of Nice's defences. Restored in 1981, it now comprises the town hall, the former chapel of St Elme used for temporary exhibitions and an open-air theatre. The citadel is also home to three museums (🕐*same hours as the Citadelle*).

Musée Volti★

Housed in the main courtyard of th citadel, this collection features sculp tures by Antoniucci Volti (1915–89), citizen of Villefranche of Italian origin.

Musée Goetz-Boumeester

This museum displays over 100 work by Picasso, Miró, Hartung and Picabi gifted to Villefranche by the painter engraver **Henri Goetz** (1909–89).

Collection Roux

An exhibition of ceramic figurines dis played in small tableaux evokes every day life in the Middle Ages and durin the Renaissance.

ADDRESSES

🏠 STAY

🛏 **Le Riviera** – *2 ave. Albert-1.* 🕿*04 93 76 62 76. www. hotelriviera villefranche.com. Closed Jan. 26 rooms.* 🍽*10€.* Unpretentious, prettily restored hotel on the Basse Corniche. Some rooms afford **views** of the sea. Agreeable rooftop terrace for summer breakfasts.

🛏 **Hôtel Patricia** – *ave. de l'Ange-Gardien via the Corniche Inférieur.* 🕿*04 93 01 06 70. www.hotel-patricia. riviera.fr. Closed Nov–Dec.* 🅿. *13 rooms.* 🍽*7.50€.* Despite the close proximity of the train tracks, this hotel is well-placed just a few steps from the beach. The rooms are tastefully decorated, ones on the upper floors have **views** of the sea.

🛏 **Hôtel St-Michel** – *2000 ave. Olivula.* 🕿*04 93 01 80 42. www.hotel-saint-michel.com. 35 rooms.* 🍽*8.50€.* Located in the peaceful residential hills above the town, this hotel has recently renovated rooms in the main building and larger ones in the annexe, some with kitchenettes. WiFi available.

🍴 EAT

🍽 **La Grignotière** – *3 rue du Poilu.* 🕿*04 93 76 79 83. Closed Mon–Sat lunches, Wed eve off-season.* This restaurant makes a point of serving hearty meals made with fresh ingredients. Follow the locals and tuck into a gargantuan dinner Mediterranean dishes.

🍽🍽 **L'Oursin Bleu** – *11 quai Courbet.* 🕿*04 93 01 90 12. Closed early Jan–early Feb, and Tue off season.* The charming nautical decor and large aquarium complement this popular port-side seafood restaurant.

TOURS

Guided tours – Guided tours of the old town and citadel *(1hr45min)* on Fridays at 10am. 🎫*5€;* morning tour of the citadel on Fridays May–Sept at 9.30am. *8€. Reserve at the tourist office.* 🕿*04 93 01 73 68.*

Tourist Train – *Apr–Oct.* 🎫*6€ (child 3€).* 🕿*04 89 00 47 76. www.train-touristique-de-villefranche-sur-mer.com.* Departures from Wilson car park for round trip tour *(45min)* of the town with commentary.

Cap Ferrat★★
Alpes Maritimes

Tucked between Villefranche and Beaulieu, the prestigious Cap Ferrat peninsula is known for its lush vegetation, rugged cliffs and luxurious villas, including the spectacular Villa Ephrussi. Some of the best views of the coast can be had from the Sentier Littoral and St-Hospice Point.

▶ **Population:** 2,103.
Michelin Map: 341 E5.
Info: 59 Ave. Denis-Semeria. ℘04 93 76 08 90. www.saint-jean-cap-ferrat.fr.
▶ **Location:** Also known as St-Jean-Cap-Ferrat (St-Jean being the name of the actual town), the peninsula is accessible by the narrow Bas Corniche, along the coastline.
Kids: Shell museum.
🕐 **Timing:** At least half a day: 2hr at the Villa Ephrussi and 3hr on the coastal path.

SIGHTS
Villa Ephrussi-de-Rothschild★★
🕐 *Open daily Feb–Oct 10am–6pm (7pm Jul–Aug); Nov–Jan 2–6pm, Sat–Sun 10am–6pm.* ⊛*12€.* ℘*04 93 01 33 09. www.villa-ephrussi.com.*
Built in 1905 by baronne Ephrussi de Rothschild to house her collection of over 5,000 works of art, the villa enjoys a unique **garden setting**★★★ with sea **views** to Villefranche and Beaulieu. The tour begins with a covered patio, surrounded by columns of pink marble from Verona and decorated with furniture and paintings from the Middle Ages to the Renaissance, including a 15C altarpiece and a painting by Carpaccio. The patio gives onto two period rooms: the grand salon lined with panelling from the Hôtel de Crillon in Paris and decorated with Louis XVI furniture displayed on a carpet from a chapel in the Château

de Versailles. The small salon is decorated with late-18C Gobelin tapestries. The fireguard bears the monogram of Marie Antoinette. The private apartments include a bedroom, bathroom, dressing room and boudoir.

Musée Île-de-France★★
👣 *Guided tours only. 11.30am, 2.30pm, 3.30pm and 4.30pm (5.30pm Jul–Aug)* ⊛*3€ supplement.*
Housed in the Villa Ephrussi, the first floor of this museum displays an exceptional collection of Vincennes, Sèvres and Saxe porcelain. The curious "monkey room" features an orchestra of Meissen porcelain monkeys.

Cap Ferrat

©Mgvuvan/Dreamstime.com

ST-JEAN-CAP-FERRAT

WHERE TO STAY

Brise Marine
(Hôtel)........................ ①

Clair Logis (Hôtel)...... ②

WHERE TO EAT

Capitaine Cook.......... ⑤

Plage
de Passable............... ⑦

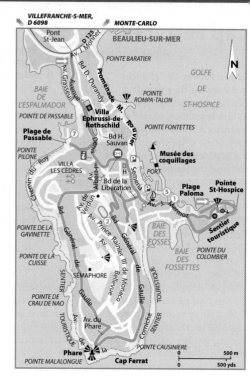

Gardens★★

The villa is surrounded by beautiful grounds (17 acres/7ha). The central French garden, shaped like a ship's deck decorated with waterfalls and a rock garden with the sea on either side, was designed so the baroness could imagine herself on the steamship "Ile de France", on which she had enjoyed an unforgettable voyage. Below the steps is the Spanish garden shaded with arum lilies, pomegranate trees and daturas. Further on, the Florentine garden is graced with an ephebe surrounded by cypress trees. Fountains, capitals, gargoyles and low-reliefs (medieval and Renaissance) decorate the more romantic stone garden. After the delightful Japanese garden, an exotic garden filled with surprising plants leads to the rose garden.

Villa Santo Sospir

Guided tours only. Contact for details: ☎04 93 76 00 16. ☞12€.
In 1950, Jean Cocteau was invited by his friend Francine Weisweller to spend a few days in her villa on Cap Ferrat. The days turned into weeks, then several months. In gratitude, he "tattooed" (as he called it) the villa's white walls with paintings on mythological themes.

Musée des Coquillages★★

Quai Lindbergh Mon–Fri 9am–noon, 2–6pm, Sat–Sun 2–6pm. ☞2€. ☎04 93 76 17 61. www.musee-coquillages.com
Discover over 4,600 shells, including microscopic specimens that can only be seen through binoculars.

Cap-Ferrat Peninsula★★

6mi/10km. Allow about 1hr.
🚶 *3.7mi/6km from the port.*
For those who prefer to walk, this footpath winds along the steep cliffs and creeks of the peninsula, skirted with typical Mediterranean vegetation.

St-Jean-Cap-Ferrat★

Once a fishing village, St-Jean is now an exclusive winter resort. A few historic houses overlook the port and its luxury yachts. The stepped street south of boulevard de la Libération leads to a **viewpoint**★ over the Tête de Chien mountain, Èze, Mont Agel and the Italian Alps in the distance.

🚶 *1hr round trip from the port of St-Jean.*
The Promenade Maurice-Rouvier★ runs along the coast to Beaulieu bay with **views** of Eze and the Tête de Chien.

Pointe St-Hospice

A pleasant stroll between private houses, past an 18C prison tower, leads to a 19C chapel affording a good **view**★ of the coast and inland from Beaulieu to Cap Martin.

🚶 *2mi/3.5km.* A **path**★ winds around the pointe St-Hospice from **plage Paloma** to the baie des Fossettes.

ADDRESSES

🏠 STAY

⊜⊜⊜⊜**Hôtel Brise Marine** – *ave. Jean-Mermoz.* ☎*04 93 76 04 36. www.hotel-brisemarine.com. Closed Nov to Jan. 18 rooms.* ⊡*14.50€.* Located in a quiet street, this charming house is reached through lush grounds. Superb **views** of the bay and Cap Ferrat. Book the rooms in the villa, rather than the annexe.

⊜⊜⊜⊜**Hôtel Clair Logis** – *12 ave. Centrale, 06230 St-Jean-Cap-Ferrat.* ☎*04 93 76 51 81. www.hotel-clair-logis.fr. Closed early Jan–early Feb, early Nov– 22 Dec.* 🅿 *18 rms.* ⊡*€12.* Provençal villa hidden away in pretty grounds. A choice of grand or more modest rooms in an annexe.

🍴 EAT

⊜⊜**Capitaine Cook** – *ave. Jean-Mermoz.* ☎*04 93 76 02 66. Closed early Nov–late Dec, Thu lunch and Wed.* Halfway between Paloma beach and the marina, this family-style restaurant serves classic Mediterranean cuisine.

⊜⊜**Plage de Passable** – *chemin de Passable.* ☎*04 93 76 06 17. www. plage-de-passable.com. Closed mid-Oct–Mar.* Beach restaurant located in Villefranche port on the way to Cap-Ferrat, serves salads, pizza, pasta and seafood. Enchanting spot sheltered by pines and palms.

🏃 LEISURE ACTIVITIES

Beaches – There are several "galet" (smooth stone) beaches in Cap Ferrat. **Plage de Passable** facing Villefranche, **Plage Paloma** facing Beaulieu, **Plage du Cro des Pins** near the port and a beach at the **Pointe St-Hospice**.

Plage de Passable

©David Noble/Pictures Colour Library

Beaulieu-sur-Mer★

Alpes Maritimes

This fashionable resort, sheltered by a belt of wooded hills, has been renowned since Antiquity as one of the warmest spots on the Riviera. This haven of peace is centred around the Baie des Fourmis and the exotic gardens of the *Petite Afrique* neighbourhood along boulevard d'Alsace-Lorraine.

WALKS

Sentier du Plateau St-Michel★★

2hr round trip – stiff climb.
Starting north of Boulevard Édouard-VII, the path leads up the Riviera escarpment to the plateau, affording wonderful **views** from Cap d'Ail to the Esterel.

Promenade Maurice-Rouvier★

1hr on round trip.
This remarkable promenade runs parallel to the Mediterranean shore from Beaulieu to **St-Jean-Cap-Ferrat**, passing fine white villas set in beautiful gardens, including La Fleur du Cap, home to both Charlie Chaplin and David Niven. Amazing **views** of the Riviera coastline to pointe St-Hospice.

▶ **Population:** 3,720.
Michelin Map: 341 F5.
Info: Pl. Georges-Clemenceau. ℘04 93 01 02 21. www.beaulieusurmer.fr
Location: Hugging the coastline between Nice and Monaco, Beaulieu sits right next to Villefranche. The best way to get here is via the Basse Corniche (*see Corniches de la RIVIERA p312*).
Parking: The best places are around the port, behind the Hôtel de Ville. For walking along Promenade Maurice-Rouvier, leave the car on Avenue Blundell-Maple.

SIGHT

Villa Grecque Kérylos★★

Free audio guide. Open Mar–Oct daily 10am–6pm (Jul–Aug 7pm); Nov–Feb Mon–Fri 2–6pm; Sat–Sun 10am–6pm. 9€. Combined ticket with Ephrussi de Rothschild 17€. ℘04 93 01 45 90. www.villa-kerylos.com. On a **site**★ reminiscent of the Aegean, this faithful reconstruction of an ancient Greek villa was the brainchild

Promenade Maurice-Rouvier

Villa Grecque Kérylos, Beaulieu-sur-Mer

© Mauritius/Photononstop

of archeologist **Théodore Reinach** and designed by the architect Pontremoli in 1902. It was bequeathed to the Institut de France in 1928. Built from precious materials (Carrara marble, alabaster and exotic woods, such as Australian plum and Cylon lemon), the villa is furnished with authentic objects from ancient Greece, including mosaics, lamps, amphorae, vases and lamps, alongside replicas of chests, desks and tripod tables incrusted with ivory, bronze and leather inspired by illustrations on antique vases. The windows give directly onto the sea, the Baie des Fourmis, Cap Ferrat, Èze and Cap d'Ail. On the lower ground floor a **gallery** features reproductions of classical statues.

ADDRESSES

STAY

Le Sélect – 1 rue André-Cane and Pl. Général-de-Gaulle. ℘04 93 01 05 42. www.hotelselect-beaulieu.com. Closed Jan. 19 rooms. ⌓7€. Housed in a handsome residence, this hotel with a Provençal decor offers air-conditioned rooms with large beds and well-equipped bathrooms.

EAT

Le Marco Polo – On the marina. ℘04 93 01 06 50. Closed late Nov–mid-Dec, Tue–Wed Oct–May, Wed–Thu

A Love Story

In 1891 this small harbour was discovered by the American press tycoon **Gordon Bennett**, who immediately fell in love with it. He offered to finance the building of a pier but the proud local fishermen declined his offer. However, the winding corniche road linking Beaulieu to Villefranche was his doing and it still bears his name.

morning Jun–Sept. Served on a radiant veranda or terrace facing the marina, the dishes here all pay tribute to the Mediterranean, centring on fish, seafood and pasta. Reasonably priced.

Les Agaves – 4 ave. Mar.-Foch. ℘ 04 93 01 13 12. www.lesagaves.com - Closed late Nov–mid-Dec. Decorated in Provençal tones of blue and yellow, complete with original stucco and panelling, this restaurant serves inventive cuisine. Evenings only.

LEISURE ACTIVITIES

Beaches – The small, sheltered pebble beaches with a southern exposure are located on either side of the marina: Baie des Fourmis beach and Petite Afrique at Nord beach.

Èze★★

Alpes Maritimes

A quaint, isolated hamlet dominating the coast, Èze clings to its rocky outcrop 1,410ft/427m above the sea. This stunning site★★ never fails to impress.

SIGHTS

A 14C double gateway with crenulations and a sentry walk leads into the steep, narrow streets of the **medieval village**★. Stepped and vaulted, these alleyways are lined with boutiques, artists' studios and tastefully restored houses fronted by flower pots. Most streets afford **views** of the mountains or the Mediterranean.

The **church** was rebuilt in the 18C with a Classical façade and a two-storey tower. The Baroque interior contains a fine statue of the Assumption (18C), attributed to Muerto and a 15C font.

Chapelle des Pénitents-Blancs
Carriera Plana.

This simple 14C chapel is decorated with enamelled panels illustrating the life and death of Christ and the Virgin. To the left is a Crucifixion, an early example of the Nice School attributed to Ludovic Bréa; on the high altar is an unusual Catalan crucifix (1258) with a smiling Christ.

- **Population:** 2,932.
- **Michelin Map:** 341 F5.
- **Info:** Pl. du Général-de-Gaulle. ℘04 93 41 26 00. www.eze-riviera.com.
- **Location:** Between Nice and Monaco, Èze is accessible by RN 7 – Moyenne Corniche (*see Corniches de la RIVIERA*).
- **Parking:** There are two parking areas *(next to the tourist office)* where you'll need to leave your car before climbing up to the village. Parking is also available at the two perfume houses, for clients only (*see Addresses opposite*).
- **Timing:** Allow 1hr to stroll through the old village. The gardens merit half a day.

Jardin d'Èze
Rue du Château. Open winter 9am– 5.30pm; summer 9am–7.30pm. 5€ (children under-11 free). ℘04 93 41 26 00. www.eze-riviera.com.

Many varieties of succulents and cacti flourish in these gardens crossed by a maze of pathways and crowned by the remains of a 14C château. The terrace

View from Jardin d'Èze

has a splendid **panorama**★★★ over the sea and coastline.

EXCURSIONS

Astrorama

Take D 46 to the Col d'Èze (see Corniches de la RIVIERA p312, circuit ①).

ADDRESSES

STAY

 Hôtel Hermitage du Col d'Eze – 1.5mi/2.5km by D 46 and Grande Corniche. 04 93 41 00 68. www.ezehermitage.com. 14 rooms. 8€. An elegant and peaceful hotel with splendid terraces, overflow pool and sea **views**. Rooms are elegantly decorated, with air conditioning and free WiFi.

Philosopher's muse

The philospher Friedrich Nietzsche first visited the Riviera between December 1883 and April 1884 to complete his masterpiece, *Thus Spoke Zarathustra*. Although his morale was low when he arrived – his books were selling badly and he had fallen out with his close friend Wagner – the light and landscape of Èze transformed his mood. A keen walker, he notably recalls composing a chapter of the book:

"as I climbed the steepest rocks from the station to the wonderful Moorish village built in the middle of the rocks."

Sentier Frédéric-Nietzsche★

About 2hr round trip.

Nietzsche thought out the third part of his masterpiece *Thus Spoke Zarathustra* on the picturesque mule path, which leads through pines and olive groves to the seaside resort of Èze-Bord-de-Mer.

FRAGRANCES

Parfumerie Fragonard –

Èze *Guided tours (30min) daily Feb–Oct 8.30am–6.30pm; Nov–Jan 8.30am–noon, 2–6.30pm. No charge.* 04 93 41 05 05. www.fragonard.com. This annexe of the Grasse perfumery displays the various stages in the manufacturing of essential oils, perfumes and soaps. Boutique on-site.

Parfumerie Galimard – *pl. du Général-de-Gaulle.* 04 93 41 10 70. www.galimard.com. *No charge.* Founded in 1747, this perfume house gives free tours of its manufacturing and small museum. Products are on sale in the boutique.

Monaco★★★

The Principality of Monaco, a sovereign state overlooking the Mediterranean between Nice and the Italian border, perfectly captures the essence of the Côte d'Azur with its Rococo palaces, lush gardens, world-famous casino and glamorous royal family. Luxury hotels, exclusive shopping boutiques and the annual Formula 1 Grand Prix make this a popular jet-set destination.

A BIT OF HISTORY

The Grimaldi family – Although Monaco was a Greek settlement and a Roman port, its place in history begins with the Grimaldi dynasty. **François Grimaldi**, expelled from Genoa during a family feud, captured Monaco with a small band of armed men in 1297, disguised as a monk. François was soon forced from the town and it was another Grimaldi, **Charles I** (1331–57) who secured Monaco in 1331.

A turbulent history – The history of Monaco has been fraught with family and political dramas. In the 16C Jean II was killed by his brother Lucien, who in turn was assassinated by his nephew; in 1604, Honoré I was thrown into the sea by his subjects. Monaco has also been subjected to foreign occupation on several occasions: by the Spanish from 1524 to 1641; by the French from 1641 to 1814; and by the kingdom of Sardinia from 1815 to 1861. Menton and Roquebrune, which originally belonged to the Principality, were bought in 1861 by Napoleon III, following the annexation of Nice.

Birth of Monte-Carlo – The first casino was an unremarkable establishment in

▶ **Population:** 32,020.

◉ **Michelin Map:** 341 F5; local map: *see Corniches de la RIVIERA pp318–19.*

Info: 2A Bd. des Moulins. ☏00 377 92 16 61 66. www.visitmonaco.com.

◑ **Location:** The 487 acres/ 197ha making up the Principality are divided into five districts: Monaco-Ville, the old town on The Rock (*La Rocher*); Monte-Carlo, with its luxury shops and casino; the busy La Condamine port; the new district of Fontvieille to the east; and the beaches of Larvotto to the west.

P **Parking:** Parking garages (free for the first hour) can be found at Place du Casino and the Parking des Pêcheurs in Monaco-Ville. Access to the Rock (Le Rocher) is permitted only to vehicles with local (06) licence plates.

◉ **Don't Miss:** The interior of the Monte-Carlo Casino and Opéra, the winding streets of old Monaco-Ville leading to the Prince's Palace and the **panoramic views** from the hillside Jardin Exotique.

◔ **Timing:** Count on at least a half day to see the best of Monaco, or a full day if you plan on shopping or going to the beach. Start in Monaco-Ville, which has the most attractions and souvenir shops in one area. The casino tables don't open until 5pm.

♟ **Kids:** Child-friendly museums include the Collection des Voitures Anciennes and the aquariums of the Musée Océanographique.

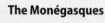

The Monégasques

There are just over 7,000 native Monégasque citizens in the Principality, all exempt from taxes and military service. They are not, however, permitted to gamble in Monaco's casinos.

PRACTICAL INFORMATION

TELEPHONE

To telephone Monaco from France, dial 00 followed by 377 (code for Monaco) and then the 8-digit telephone number.

CURRENCY AND POSTAGE

Monaco uses euros just like France, but it has an independent postal system. All letters mailed from within the Principality must have Monégasque stamps.

PUBLIC LIFTS

Large-capacity lifts are available to make it easier to move around certain neighbourhoods. The main roads and sites served are: pl. Ste-Dévote to blvd. de Belgique (the longest route), plages du Larvotto (and Musée national) to pl. des Moulins, ave. Hector-Otto to blvd. de Belgique, auditorium Rainier-III (blvd. Louis-II) to the casino terraces, the Pêcheurs car park to the Musée océanographique, ave. de Grande-Bretagne to ave. des Citronniers, Centre Commercial de Fontvieille to pl. d'Armes, port de Monaco to ave. de la Costa.

TOURS AND PUBLIC TRANSPORT

BUS: C.A.M. – ✆00 377 97 70 22 22. *www.cam.mc. Service every 10min from 7.30am–8.30pm.* Tickets 1€ *each or 3€ for day pass.* Six regular bus lines loop around the Principality. Maps available at the tourist office.

TAXI: Two main **taxi** stands are located near the casino and at the train station. ✆00 377 93 50 56 28 or 00 377 93 15 01 01.

TOURIST BUS: Le Grand Tour – *Twelve stops around the Principality, including the Palais Princier and the Casino.* ✆00 377 97 70 26 36. *www.visitmonaco.com.* 17€. This small hop-on, hop-off tourist bus makes 1hr round trip journeys around the Principality.

BOAT TRIPS: Aquavision – *Compagnie de Navigation et de Tourisme de Monaco, Quai des Etats-Unis.* ✆00 377 92 16 15 15. *www.aquavision-monaco. com. Daily departures Apr–Oct.* 11€ (child 8€). Glass-bottomed boat trips affording **views** of the sea depths, and marine fauna and flora (55min).

HELICOPTER: Héli Air Monaco – *Héliport de Monaco, Fontvieille.* ✆00 377 92 05 00 50. *www.heliairmonaco. com. Prices start at 107€.* Regular daily service (6min) every 15min between Monaco and the Aéroport de Nice-Côte d'Azur. Also 10min sightseeing tours of Monaco and daily flights between Monaco and Fréjus.

SPORT: Monaco is home to a number of exclusive sporting facilities. For tennis fans, the **Monte-Carlo Country Club** has 23 courts (✆04 93 41 30 15. www.mccc.mc). Golfers will enjoy the prestigious **Monte-Carlo Golf Club**, which boasts an 18-hole course at an altitude of 2,650ft/810m (✆04 92 41 50 70).

Le Rocher

© Alex Treflow/Bigstockphoto.com

Changing of the guards, Monaco

Changing of the Guard

The tightly choreographed Changing of the Guard takes place daily on place du Palais at 11.55am.

Monaco-Ville itself, set up in 1856 by the Prince, who was short of funds. Only in 1862 did the casino move to its own premises in Monte-Carlo, where it remained in humble isolation for several years. The arrival of **François Blanc**, director of the casino and spa in Bad Hamburg, transformed its fortunes. Within a few years the casino became fashionable and the surrounding land was covered with luxurious residences, mostly owned by the Société des Bains de Mer (SBM), directed by Blanc himself. Profiting from the presence of the rich and famous, Monaco organised its first Rallye Monte-Carlo rally in 1911, followed by the Grand Prix de Monaco in 1929, one of the most famous Formula 1 championships in the world.

A thriving economy – To accommodate the influx of visitors attracted by its gambling tables and tax concessions, Monaco began to throw up buildings at a furious pace. Once all the available space had been occupied the shoreline was extended into the sea (the 55acre/22ha Fontvieille district), expanding its territory by 25%.

Tourism remains its main activity, along with its conference facilities (such as the **Grimaldi Forum** on the Larvotto shoreline), which rival those of Cannes and Nice. Home to around 40 international banking institutions, Monaco is also a player in the financial world.

Original and revolutionary town-planning – Following the construction of a dozen high-rise buildings in the late 1970s, the 1980s saw the emergence of a new urban strategy designed to satisfy the growing demand for residential and service facilities: underground buildings. All new access roads are now linked to the French network by deep tunnels, the train station is below ground level, and connections between neighbourhoods are made via groups of lifts or escalators. Behind the façade of some of Monaco's luxury hotels are access ramps to large public car parks hollowed out of the rock.

WALKING TOUR

THE ROCK★★

Tour: allow 3hr. Park in Parking des Pêcheurs and take the elevator.
Crowned by the old town of Monaco-Ville and its ramparts, the Rocher de Monaco juts 875yd/800m out to sea over the bay. Resembling a studio set, its neat little 18C houses with their salmon-pink façades are squeezed along quaint alley-

ways. This is the medieval heart of the Principality, home to some of its most popular sights.

👥 Musée Océanographique★★

Ave. Saint-Martin. ♿🕐*Open Jul–Aug 9.30am–7.30pm; Apr–Jun and Sept 9.30am–7pm; Oct–Mar 10am–6pm.* 🎫*14€ (child 6–18 years 7€).* 📞*00 377 93 15 36 00. www.oceano.mc.*

The Oceanographic Museum and Research Institute overlooks the Mediterranean from an impressive cliff (280ft/85m). Founded in 1910 by marine research enthusiast Prince Albert I to house his scientific collections dating back to 1885, it has one of the most impressive **aquariums**★★ in Europe, with more than 6,000 specimens representing 350 different species of tropical fish, shark, turtle, and live coral reef from the Red Sea. Located on the lower ground floor, the aquarium is divided into a Mediterranean section and a colourful series of 90 tanks teeming with tropical species, including clown fish, moray eels and leopard sharks.

The **Salle d'Océanographie Zoologique**★, also known as Salle de la Baleine, contains the skeletons of large marine mammals, including a 66ft/ 20m-long whale beached on the Italian coast in 1896. It also features the "Marine inspirations" exhibition of objects inspired by the sea from the 4C to the present day, including carved shells and ceramics.

From the second-floor terrace *(lift)* is a magnificent **view**★★ along the coast, including the Tête de Chien and the Mont Agel beyond. The restaurant is also located on this floor.

▶ *Take ave. St-Martin towards the cathedral.*

Jardins St-Martin★

The shaded pathways of this Mediterranean garden afford delightful **views** over the sea. A bronze statue of Albert I by François Cogné (1951) stands in the centre.

Cathédrale

Built between 1875 and 1903 in Romanesque Byzantine style with white stone from La Turbie on the ruins of the church of St-Nicolas, the cathedral houses a series of royal family tombs in the ambulatory, including that of Princess Grace.

The cathedral has a collection of **early paintings from the Nice School**★★ along with two alterpieces by Louis Bréa.

▶ *Follow rue Comte Félix Gastaldi (featuring fine Renaissance doorways) to rue Princesse-Marie-de-Lorraine.*

Chapelle de la Miséricorde

This chapel's classic pink and white Baroque façade was built between 1639 and 1646 by the brotherhood of the Black Penitents. The **Recumbent Christ** by the Monégasque sculptor

Musée Océanographique de Monaco

© Sylvaine Poitau/Apa Publications

Bosio is carried through the old town on Good Friday.

▷ On leaving turn right onto picturesque rue Basse to pl. du Palais.

Place du Palais★

This vast square, ornamented with cannons given to the Prince of Monaco by Louis XIV, is bordered to the northeast by a crenulated parapet from which there is a **view** of the port de la Condamine, Monte-Carlo and the coast as far as the Bordighera headland. To the southwest is the **Promenade Ste-Barbe**, which gives onto Cap d'Ail.

🔁 Don't miss the Changing of the Guard. The soldiers are dressed in black in winter and white in summer.

Palais Princier★

🕐*Open Apr 10.30am–6pm; Apr–Oct 10am–6pm.* 🎫*8€.* 📞*00 377 93 25 18 31. www.palais.mc*

The palatial home of the Grimaldi family was built in the 17C on the site of the original 13C Genoese fortress. The formidable perimeter is built into the vertical rock, with battlemented towers.

A monumental doorway with the Grimaldi arms adorns this robust-looking ensemble. The tour leads visitors through the Hercules Gallery decorated with 16C and 17C frescoes, past the main courtyard paved with 3 million stones, through to the Throne Room with a ceiling attributed to Orazio Ferrari (17C), then onto the state apartments where official receptions are held.

▷ Follow the Rampe Major to the right of the palace through 16C, 17C and 18C gates down to pl. d'Armes. Turn right onto ave. du Port.

LA CONDAMINE

Allow 30min.

In the Middle Ages this term applied to land owned by a lord and cultivated exclusively for him at the foot of a village or castle. Nowadays La Condamine is the commercial district and port stretching between the Rock and Monte-Carlo.

Port Hercule

Prince Albert I commissioned this harbour, with its luxury yachts and terraced promenade. From the northwest corner of the harbour a valley separating La Condamine from Monte-Carlo runs under a viaduct to the church.

▷ Follow the blvd. Albert I to the passage leading to pl. Ste-Dévote.

Église Ste-Dévote

Ste-Dévote was martyred in Corsica in the 3C when, according to tradition, the skiff carrying her body to Africa was guided by a dove to the shores of Monaco. In the Middle Ages relics of the saint were stolen by sailors. But the thieves were caught and their ship razed – a legend commemorated every 26 January when a ship is burned in the church square.

▷ Turn right down rue Grimaldi, a popular shopping street, to rue Princesse Caroline and finish at pl. d'Armes.

MONTE-CARLO★★★

Allow 1.5hr.

Monte-Carlo is a name famous throughout the world, bringing to mind high-

The Grimaldi Family Today

In July 2005, the 47-year-old Prince Albert II of Monaco succeeded his father, Prince Rainier III, who died in April 2005 after ruling the Principality for 56 years. Albert and his sisters (Princesses Caroline and Stéphanie) lost their mother, the Hollywood actress Grace Kelly, in a car accident in 1982. For many years the Prince's single status and his sisters' rocky relationships were closely followed in the European tabloids. At the age of 53, the Prince married former South African Olympic swimmer Charlene Wittstock on 1 July 2011.

stakes gambling as well as the majestic setting of its palaces, casinos, luxurious shops and exotic gardens.

Place du Casino
Pl. du Casino lies at the centre of the action, where the Café de Paris and the Hôtel de Paris flank the **casino**, surrounded by beautiful gardens. Around the back of the casino is a fine **terrace**★★ with **views** towards Italy.

Le Casino de Monte-Carlo
Forbidden to anyone under 18 years of age. ⏱*Slots and European gaming rooms open from 2pm (noon on weekends); blackjack tables open from 8pm.* ⏱*Closed when the last person leaves.* ☺*10€ Public rooms, 20€ private rooms. ID/Passport required.* ☎*00 377 98 06 21 21. www.casinomontecarlo.com.*
The façade facing the sea and the theatre/opera house opposite the vast central hall were built by Charles Garnier in 1878. Once home to Diaghilev's Ballets Russes, it rose to fame under Nijinsky. Before entering the casino, admire the *Olive Gatherers* fresco by Jundt and, in the public gaming rooms on the left, the sumptuous late 19C Renaissance Room. An oasis of palms, the **casino terrace**★★ affords **views** from Monaco to Bordighera.

Avenue Princesse Grâce
Beyond the sleek Grimaldi Forum are the luxurious beaches of **Larvotto Plage**. Here you'll find shops, cafés and restaurants overlooking the beach. Two diving platforms are anchored offshore.

Musée des Souvenirs Napoléoniens et des Archives du Palais★
Pl. du Palais. ⏱*Open Tue–Sun Dec–Apr 10.30am–5pm; Apr–Oct 10am–6pm.* ☺*4€.* ☎*00 377 93 25 18 31. www.palais.mc.*
One wing of the Palace is devoted to a museum dedicated to Napoleon, including geneological charts showing how the Bonapartes are related to the Grimaldi princes. Many of the Emperor's personal souvenirs are on display. The upper floor explores the history of Monaco, including the charter recognising its independence granted by Louis XII.

Nouveau Musée National de Monaco★
Villa Sauber, 17 ave. Princesse Grâce ☎*00 377 98 98 91 26 and Villa Paloma, 56 blvd. du Jardin Exotique* ☎*00 377 98 98 48 60* ⏱*Open daily Jul–Sept 11am–7pm, Oct–Jun 10am–6pm.* ☺*6€ (child 3.50€). www.nmnm.mc.*
Split between two sites, the New National Museum of Monaco (NNMM) is dedicated to the preservation, continuity and communication of Monaco's extensive cultural and natural heritage, including many artworks rarely displayed in public. The **Villa Sauber**, housed in a **Charles Garnier** villa fronted by a rose garden, and the **Villa Paloma**, a stark white residence built for an American millionaire at the beginning of the 20C, will both invite artists, curators and other personalities to explore a contemporary subject, such as fashion, the environment or the ocean using objects as varied as diving equipment from the oceanographic museum, or the Principality's extensive collection of early-19C dolls and automata.

Collection des Voitures Anciennes★
Terrasses de Fontvieille. ⏱*Open daily 10am–6pm.* ⏱*Closed 25 Dec.* ☺*6€ (child 3€).* ☎*00 377 92 05 28 56. www.palais.mc.*
Housed in a sumptuous exhibition hall, some 100 vintage vehicles and carriages from the royal collection are displayed over five levels. On the first level are the barouches used by Prince Charles III. Next is the De Dion Bouton (1903), the first car owned by Prince Albert I, and a 1952 Austin London taxi converted for Princess Grace. The 1929 Bugatti (winner of the 1st Grand Prix) and a 1989 Ferrari F1 (600hp) have pride of place in the Formula 1 hall.

MONACO
MONTE-CARLO

0   200 m
0   200 yds

WHERE TO STAY

WHERE TO EAT

INDEX OF STREET NAMES

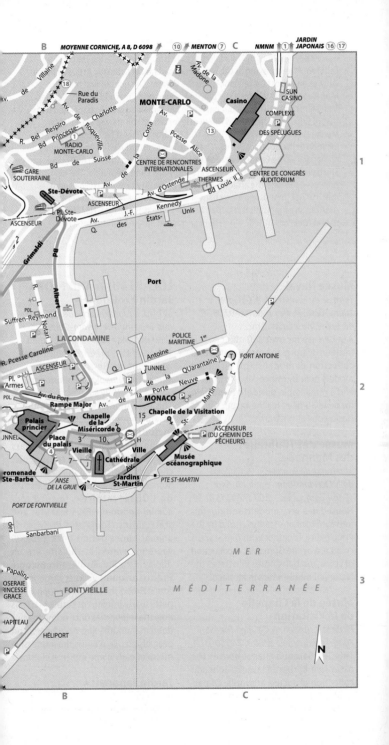

Princess Grace

Grace Kelly was born in Philadelphia on 12 November 1929, the third of four children. After studying at the New York Academy of Dramatic Arts, she began work as an actress for television and the theatre. She got her first break in *High Noon* (1952), in which she played a young bride married to Gary Cooper. Many films were to follow but her name has remained closely associated with that of British director Alfred Hitchcock, for whom she starred in *Dial M for Murder* (1954), *Rear Window* (1954) and *To Catch a Thief* (1955), shot entirely on location in the South of France. Grace Kelly was introduced to Prince Rainier of Monaco at the Cannes Film Festival and they were married in April 1956. She gave birth to three children, Caroline, Albert and Stéphanie. The new princess soon won the affections of the Principality's residents. She spent much of her time supporting charitable causes such as the Red Cross and AMADE, an organisation set up to help developing countries. Her life was to end tragically in 1982 when her car crashed off the Grande Corniche.

Musée Naval

Terrasse de Fontvieille. ♿ ◷*Open 10am–6pm.* ✆*4€.* ✆*00 377 92 05 28 48. www.musee-naval.mc.*

A showcase for over 250 objects, this museum features the cream of the royal collection of model ships, including models built by Prince Albert I in 1874, and a remarkable **gondole impériale** made in 15 days for the inspection of Napoleon I at Antwerps.

Musée des Timbres et des Monnaies

11 terrasse de Fontvieille. ♿ ◷*Open daily Oct–Jun 10am–5pm; Jul–Sept 10am–6pm.* ✆*3€.* ✆*00 377 93 15 41 50.*

Housed in a very modern setting, this museum contains stamps issued by the Principality, together with rare stamps collected by the Grimaldis. A collection of coins and bank notes illustrates the history of numismatics in Monaco.

Musée de la Chapelle de la Visitation

Pl. de la Visitation. ♿ ◷*Open Tue–Sun 10am–4pm.* ✆*3€.* ✆*00 377 93 50 07 00.*

This 17C Baroque chapel houses the extensive Barbara Piasecka-Johnson collection of sacred artworks. Of particular interest are masterpieces by Zurbarán, Rubens and Ribera.

LOCAL FAUNA AND FLORA

Jardin Exotique★★

52 blvd. du Jardin-Exotique. ◷*Open mid-May–mid-Sept 9am–7pm; mid-Sept–mid-May 9am–6pm.* ◷*Closed 19 Nov, 25 Dec.* ✆*7€ (combined ticket with Grotte de l'Observatoire and Musée d'Anthropologie Préhistorique).* ✆*00 377 93 15 29 80.*

This exceptional collection, grouping several thousand species of succulent, including huge candelabra-like euphorbia, giant aloe and Barbary figs, some more than a century old, clings dramatically to the cliffs above Monaco. Down 279 steps is the **Grotte de l'Observatoire**★ *(guided tour 30min)* adorned with stalactites and stalagmites. Tools and Prehistoric animal bones dating back 200,000 years excavated at the site are on display in the **Musée d'Anthropologie Préhistorique**★ *(access through the Jardin Exotique; same times apply).* This particularly intelligent display reveals how the region was once home to reindeer, mammoths and cave bears, and even hippos. Don't miss the impressive group of early *homo sapien* skeletons

Jardin Japonais★

Ave. Princesse Grace. ♿ ◷*Open 9am–dusk.* ✆*No charge. www.visitmonaco.com.*

Jardin Exotique

©Photononstop/Tips Images

Designed by the Japanese landscape artist **Yasuo Beppu**, this garden (17 acres/ 7ha) in the luxurious **Larvotto district** is a green oasis beside the sea. A miniature representation of Shintoist philosophy, it includes symbols of longevity and a **Zen garden** for meditation.

Jardin Animalier

Fontvieille. Open Jun–Sept 9am– noon, 2–7pm; Mar–May 10am–noon, 2–6pm; Oct–Feb 10am–noon, 2–5pm. 4€ *(child 2€).* 00 377 93 50 40 30. The zoo terraces, on the southwest face of the Rock, present 50 species of mammal, reptile, exotic bird and numerous monkeys.

Parc Paysager

Terre-plein de Fontvieille. This park features plant species from across the world clustered around a charming lake. Nearby lies the **Princesse Grace Rose Garden,** with more than 4,000 bushes belonging to 150 different rose varieties.

Coastal Path to Cap Martin★★

3hr round trip leaving from Monte-Carlo, preferably in the afternoon – local maps see MENTON p349 and Corniches de la RIVIERA p312. Tourists wishing to take a shorter route can drive to the train station of Roquebrune-Cap-Martin and join up with the path running below. On the left of the Monte-Carlo Beach Hotel, follow the steps down between two villas.

For a description of the walk in the opposite direction, see ROQUEBRUNE-CAP-MARTIN: COASTAL PATH p348.

Before Laying a Bet

Stroking the knee of the equestrian statue of Louis XV in the entrance of the Hôtel de Paris before heading into the casino is said to bring the gambler good luck. Admission is free to the slot machine rooms in the casino, in the Café de Paris (also on Place du Casino), and at the Sun Casino (in the Fairmont Hotel, 12 avenue des Spélugues). During the summer season (July–mid-Sept) gambling takes place in the Salles des Palmiers of the Sporting-Club de Monte-Carlo. Gaming tables usually require a fee of 10€–20€ to play.

ADDRESSES

🏠 STAY

Hôtel Miramar – *126 ave. du 3–Septembre, Cap d'Ail.* ℘*04 93 78 06 60. www.monte-carlo.mc/hotel-miramar-capdail. 25 rooms. Closed Feb.* 🅿. 🍽*7.50€.* A good-value, family-run hotel in the neighbouring village of Cap d'Ail. Rooms have WiFi; some face the sea.

Hôtel de France – *6 rue de la Turbie. Near the train station.* ℘*00 377 93 30 24 64. www.monte-carlo.mc/france. 26 rooms.* 🍽*10€.* Charming, soundproofed rooms decorated in Provençal hues and a modern breakfast lounge enhanced with metal and wood furniture.

Novotel Monte Carlo – *16 blvd. de la Princesse Charlotte.* ℘*00 377 99 99 83 00. www.novotel.com. 218 rooms.* 🅿. 🍽*16.50€.* A stylish, modern hotel in the heart of Monaco with all the latest amenities, including heated pool, fitness centre, bar and restaurant.

🍴 EAT

Le Bistroquet – *Galerie Charles III, ave. des Spéluges.* ℘*(00 377) 93 50 65 03. www.mcpam.com.* Lively restaurant and bar with a heated terrace facing the casino gardens. Serves a combination of bistro fare and French classics; wines by the glass. Live music Fri–Sat evenings.

Castelroc – *pl. du Palais.* ℘*00 377 93 30 36 68. www.restaurant-castelroc. com. Closed mid-Dec–mid-Jan, Sat.* The terrace under the trees with a **view** of the palace makes a lovely setting for a meal of Mediterranean specialities.

La Maison du Caviar – *1 ave. St-Charles.* ℘*00 377 93 30 80 06. Closed Sat lunch, Sun.* This prestigious house has been serving choice caviar to Monaco's residents for the past 50 years. In an unusual setting made up of bottle racks and wooden panelling, you can also purchase salmon and foie gras.

Polpetta – *2 r. Paradis.* ℘*00 377 93 50 67 84. Closed early–late Jun, first half Nov, Sat lunch and Mar.* This small Italian restaurant offers three different settings: the veranda close to the road; the rustic dining room; and a more intimate cosy space to the rear. Don't miss the family specialities.

Café de Paris – *pl. du Casino.* ℘*(00-377) 98 06 76 23. www.monte carloresort.com.* An elegant and chic brasserie with terraces overlooking the casino square and the sea. Seafood and traditional French dishes, as well as light salads and sandwiches.

Loga – *25 blvd. des Moulins.* ℘*(00-377) 93 30 87 72. www.leloga.com. Closed Sun.* A friendly family-run establishment popular with the locals, serving traditional regional cuisine and daily specials on the slate board.

Petrossian – *11 ave. Princesse Grace.* ℘*(00-377) 97 77 00 24. www.petrossian.fr. Closed Sun–Mon.* The romantic dining room of this caviar house is decorated in luminous shades of white and mother-of-pearl. Specialities focus on fresh seafood to complement the caviar, as well as gourmet foie gras and rare vodkas.

Zébra Square – *10 ave. Princesse-Grace, 98000 Monaco.* ℘*00 377 99 99 25 50. www.zebrasquare.com.* Same trendy feel, zebra theme and modern cuisine as its big Parisian sister, with the added extra of a terrace overlooking the sea.

🌙 NIGHTLIFE

Casino de Monte-Carlo – *pl. du Casino.* ℘*00 377 92 16 20 00. www.casino-monte-carlo.com.* Europe's leading casino. The gambling salons and lavish dining hall Le Train Bleu, decorated in the style of the Orient-Express, are truly impressive.

La Terrasse (Bar du Vistamar) – *square Beaumarchais.* ℘*00 377 92 16 40 00. www.montecarloresort.com.* This famous bar has been patronised by many celebrities, such as Onassis and Maria Callas. Its superb terrace affords beautiful **views** of Monaco harbour. The specialities of the house are American cocktails, particularly those made with champagne!

Sass Café – *11 ave. Princesse-Grace.* ℘*00 377 93 25 52 00. www.sasscafe.com.* Exclusive bar-restaurant with a cosy atmosphere, where members of the local jet set drop in for a fancy vodka or champagne cocktail before meeting up at Jimmy'z.

Le Jimmy'z – *quai Princesse-Grace.* ℘*00 377 92 16 22 77. fr.jimmyzmonte carlocom.* It would be unthinkable to

Le Casino de Monte Carlo

D. Chapuis/MICHELIN

leave Monte-Carlo without having paid a visit to the legendary Jimmy'z. Formal eveningwear is expected in this small, but select club, where the rich and famous love to congregate, whether they come from banking, advertising, fashion or entertainment world.

Stars'N'Bars – *6 quai Antoine-1.* *℘00 377 93 50 95 95. www.starsnbars.com.* This is a popular American bar, where the ambience is slightly more relaxed than in the Principality's other establishments. Stars'N'Bars caters for a younger clientele eager to drink beer, eat a hamburger or two, play billiards, surf on the Internet and dance the night away.

🎭 ENTERTAINMENT

Le Cabaret – *pl. du Casino.* *℘00 377 92 16 36 36. www.montecarloresort.com. Shows mid-Sept–mid-Jun Wed–Sat from 10.30pm; bar/restaurant open from 8.30pm.* This cabaret, run by the Monte-Carlo Casino, presents nightly flamenco, jazz or pop concerts.

🛍 SHOPPING

All the famous fashion brands have boutiques in Monte-Carlo. Shops specialising in traditional goods are to be found in the narrow streets of the Rock *(Le Rocher)* opposite the palace.Hunt out Boutique du Rocher on ave. de la Madonne for traditional Monégasque handicrafts, made in the on-site workshops.

If exclusive brands such as Dior and Chanel on ave. des Beaux Art are beyond your reach, head for the Fontevielle shopping centre, where you'll find dozens of ready-to-wear chain stores, a hypermarket and fast-food outlets. Most of the Principality's high-street stores (music, books, electronic equipment, furniture and cosmetics) are situated in Monte-Carlo along ave. Saint-Charles (which is where you'll also find the Marché de Monte-Carlo, selling fresh fruit and vegetables) and further south around ave. des Spélugues. For traditional open-air markets, hop over to the port d'Hercule in the Espace Commercial de la Condamine, where you'll also find a host of specialist delicatessens and other food stores.

CALENDAR

Monte-Carlo Rally – Held every year since 1911 at the end of January.

Feast of Ste-Dévote – Monaco's Patron Saint feast, 27 January.

Sciaratù Carnival – Monégasque festival during the week of Mardi Gras.

Spring Arts Festival – Art, music, theatre and dance festival throughout April.

International Tennis Masters Series – Held every April.

Monaco Grand Prix – Every May in the streets of the Principality on a winding circuit (2mi/3,145km).

Monte-Carlo Golf Open – Held in the hills of Mont Agel every June.

National Day of Monaco – Picturesque procession around the Rocher, plus a range of other cultural events and shows: 19 November.

Roquebrune-Cap-Martin★

Alpes Maritimes

This pretty resort extends along the coast below the perched medieval village of Roquebrune and its Carolingian-era castle keep.

A BIT OF HISTORY

The castle was built at the end of the 10C by the Conrad I, comte de Ventimiglia, to hold back the Saracen invaders. For several centuries it belonged to the Grimaldis (*see MONACO p334*). The fortress enclosed the keep and the village within its battlements, with six gateways. In the 15C the keep (donjon) became known as the castle (château) and the fortress became the village.

✦ WALKING TOUR

THE PERCHED VILLAGE★

Allow 1hr. This maze of steep covered alleys and stairways has preserved its medieval appearance despite the influx of art galleries and souvenir shops.

▷ *Start on pl. de la République (the former barbican), then cross the pl. des Deux-Frères (two rocks) to rue Grimaldi, then turn left.*

▶ **Population:** 13,067.
⌖ **Michelin Map:** 341 F5; local maps: *see MENTON: DRIVING TOURS p355 and Corniches de la RIVIERA p318–19.*
▤ **Info:** 214 ave. Aristide-Briand. ℘04 93 35 62 87. www.roquebrune-cap-martin.com.
▷ **Location:** Roquebrune village sits on the Grande Corniche above Menton and the resort of Roquebrune-Cap-Martin.
Ⓟ **Parking:** Available at the village entrance.
◉ **Don't Miss:** Nature lovers should hike the coastal path on the Cap Martin.

Rue Moncollet★

This street, long and narrow, has many covered and stepped passageways. Medieval houses with barred windows, where those invited to join the seigneurial court once lived, face the road in front, while at the back they lie against or are cut right into the rockface.

▷ *Rue Moncollet leads into rue du Château. Turn left towards the keep.*

View of Roquebrune-Cap-Martin

Sylvaine Poiteau/Apa Publications

Église Ste-Marguerite
© Sylvaine Poitau/Apa Publications

Donjon★

Pl. William–Ingram. Open daily Apr–Jun and Sept 10am–12.30pm, 2–6.30pm; Jul–Aug 10am–12.30pm, 3–7.30pm; Feb–Mar and Oct 10am–12.30pm, 2–6pm; Nov–Jan 10am–12.30pm, 2–5pm. 3.70€.
04 93 35 07 22.

The keep (80ft/26m) has 6–12ft /2–4m thick walls complete with remarkable defensive features, including cannon embrasures, machicolations, battlements and loopholes. Steps lead up to the Hall of Feudal Ceremonies, a small guard-room, a prison and the archers' dormitory. On the third floor are furnished baronial apartments, a dining room, a primitive kitchen and a bedroom containing ancient weapons. The fourth floor includes the upper artillery platform, with a sweeping, circular **panorama**★★ of the picturesque roofs of the village, the sea, Monaco and Mont Agel.

▶ *Return to rue du Château, turn right then turn left onto rue de la Fontaine.*

Olivier Millénaire

On the Chemin de Menton (219yd/200m) beyond the end of the village) you'll find a 1,000-year-old **olive tree**, said to be one of the oldest trees in the world.

▶ *Return to rue du Château (left).*

Église Ste-Marguerite

The fairly plain Baroque façade masks the original 12C church, which has undergone many alterations over the years. Inside are two paintings by a local painter, **Marc-Antoine Otto** (17C).

Protected Marine Areas

The coastline around Vallauris-Golfe-Juan, Beaulieu-sur-Mer and Roquebrune-Cap-Martin is subject to a number of restrictions (no mooring, diving or fishing of any kind) in order to protect and nurture its biodiversity. Posidonia seagrass and gorgonia are closely monitored in these areas and artificial reefs have been placed along the sea bed.

Marine pollution is taken very seriously by these coastal towns. Checks are performed and protective measures put in place to optimise the quality of bathing water and fishing grounds, including the taking of water samples in high season, improving the quality of the water channelled into the sea via purification plants, aerial surveillance of the coast and the fining of polluters. A *Ports Propres* or Clean Ports scheme has been set up to eliminate land and sea pollution in the region.

▷ *Return to rue de la Fontaine and turn right into the cemetery, where you'll find the tomb (square J, no 3) of Le Corbusier, designed by the architect himself.*

TOURING THE RESORT
Cap Martin★★

With its magnificent estates, Cap Martin is the wealthy residential suburb of Menton. A massive tower of feudal appearance rises at the centre, formerly the old beacon, now converted to a telecommunications relay station. At its foot lie the ruins of the 11C basilica of St-Martin, built by the monks of the Iles de Lérins and destroyed by pirates in 1400. From the road along the eastern shore is a marvellous **view**★★ of Menton in its mountain setting and the Italian coast. There are several beaches below the old village at Cabbé and Carnolès to the east.

Le Cabanon de Le Corbusier

Guided tours Tue and Fri 9.30am on reservation at the tourist office. 8€. 04 93 35 62 87.

Built in 1952, this "cabin", is located below the promenade Le Corbusier, which stretches along the coast between Cap-Martin and Cabbé. The architect lived in this deceptively plain

---

Traditional Processions

For the past 500 years a procession, representing the principal scenes of Christ's Passion in six tableaux, has been held on 5 August for two hours. The **Procession of the Entombment of Christ**★ takes place at 9pm on Good Friday with a train of some 60 people walking through the village streets representing Roman centurions and legionnaires, disciples carrying the statue of Christ and holy women. The town is decorated with lighted motifs recalling the symbols of the Passion and illuminated by countless tiny lights formed by snail- and seashells filled with olive oil.

---

construction every summer until his death in 1965. Measuring 12ft by 12ft/3.6m by 3.6m, it consists of a simple 107sq ft/10sq m room and a corridor decorated with a fresco. This unique design applies Le Corbusier's **modulor** system to a traditional Marseille cabin. Calculated to suit the proportions of the human body, modulor was a measuring tool invented by the architect for use in the design of the "Cité Radieuse" apartment block in Marseille.

Coastal Path★

P *Ave. Winston-Churchill car park at the end of Cap Martin. A sign "Promenade Le Corbusier" marks the start of the footpath.* 4hr round trip. This coastal footpath runs from Cap Martin to Monte-Carlo beach and skirts the grounds of private early-20C villas with **views** of Cap Ferrat, the Tête de Chien and Mont Agel.

▷ *A flight of steps on the right crossing the railway line provides a shortcut back to Carnolès beach via the town hall.*

ADDRESSES

STAY

Hôtel Alexandra – *93 avenue Winston-Churchill.* 04 93 35 65 45. *www.alexandrahotel.fr. 40 rooms.* 10€. A beachside hotel typical of the 1960s/1970s. Make sure to request upper floor rooms facing the sea.

EAT

La Roquebrunoise – *12 ave. Raymond-Poincaré.* 04 93 35 02 19. *www.laroquebrunoise.com. Closed Nov–Dec, Mon except Mon eve Jul–Aug, lunch Tue–Fri.* This pretty pink house on the edge of the village has a country-style dining room. The food is unpretentious and tasty; a terrace overlooks the sea.

L'Hippocampe – *44 ave. W. Churchill* 04 93 35 81 91. *www.hippocampe-restaurant.com. Closed Nov–Dec, evenings Jan–May and Mon.* Family-run place specialising in fillets of sole and, if you order in advance, bouillabaisse and coq au vin.

Menton★★

Alpes Maritimes

Menton is a coastal resort famous for its annual lemon festival and mild climate. The picturesque old town is framed by mountain cliffs and terraced citrus and olive groves.

A BIT OF HISTORY

Although there is evidence of a human settlement on this site in the **Palaeolithic Era**, the name Menton was only mentioned in an official document for the first time in 1261. Purchased by the **Grimaldis of Monaco** in 1346, it occupied a strategic position on the border between France and the Kingdom of Sardinia, and swapped hands several times before being permanently attached to France in 1860. In the late 19C and early 20C Menton was highly popular with the European aristocracy, who flocked here to nurse their health or simply enjoy the mild winters. Today, Menton is a lively, cosmopolitan resort town.

WALKING TOUR

THE OLD TOWN★★

Allow 2hr.

Rue St-Michel

This pedestrian street linking the old and new towns is bordered by boutiques and orange trees. **Place aux Herbes**, with its coloured paving stones, decorative colonnade and a fountain, gives onto the market. Note the splendid Belle Epoch façades of the former Hôtel d'Orient *(1 rue de la République)*, Winter-Palace *(20 ave. Riviera)*, Riviera-Palace *(28 ave. Riviera)* and covered market *(quai de Monléon)*.

At pl. du Cap, walk up rue des Logettes to rue Longue.

Rue Longue

This was once the main street of Menton and formerly part of the Via Julia Augusta.

▶ **Population:** 27,655.
Michelin Map: 341 F5; local maps: *see p294 and Corniches de la RIVIERA pp318–19.*
Info: Palais de l'Europe, 8 Av. Boyer. ℘04 92 41 76 76. www.tourisme-menton.fr.
Location: Menton is the last coastal town before the Italian border, about 18.6mi/30km east of Nice on the Corniches *(see Corniches de la RIVIERA p317).* For those interested in getting there faster on a less scenic route, take the A 8.
Parking: Most of the public parking places are around the port; all require payment, whether parking garages or metered street parking.
Don't Miss: The colourful parades during the annual Lemon Festival *(Fête du Citron)* in February, the picturesque streets of the old town *(vieille ville)* and the scenic **views** from the Cap Martin.
Kids: A visit to the Serre de la Madone gardens (special tour) and the Koaland park.
Timing: Allow at least a half day to walk around the pedestrian streets of the old town and the Promenade du Soleil, and visit one of the sights, such as the Musée Jean Cocteau or the Musée des Beaux-Arts. A full day would include a trip to the beach, a hike along the Cap Martin or a driving excursion inland to Castillon, with a walk in the Forêt de Menton.

Menton with Basilique St-Michel Archange

© Taylor Richard/Sime/Photononstop

Parvis St-Michel★★

Access by the Chanoine-Gouget ramps.
At the top of the steps is a charming square in the Italian style framed by Baroque façades, overlooking the sea. The square is paved with a mosaic depicting the Grimaldi arms.

Façade of the Chapelle de la Conception★

The façade of this chapel of the White Penitents (1685, restored in the 19C) has statues of the theological virtues.

Basilique St-Michel-Archange

⏲ *Open Mon–Fri 10am–noon, 3–5.15pm; Sat–Sun 3–5pm.*
☎ *04 93 35 81 63.*
This is the largest and finest Baroque church in the region. Its two-tier **façade** in yellow and pale green reflects a variety of architectural influences. The tower (15C) on the left, which belonged to an earlier building, was crowned with an octagonal campanile with a glazed tile roof in the 17C, and the great Genoese-

style campanile (174ft/53m) was added in the 18C. Local artists such as Puppo and Vento contributed to the decoration of the side chapels. Above the handsome 18C choir stalls is the **altarpiece of St Michael** (1569) by Manchello. The exuberant Baroque high altar is crowned by St Michael slaying the Devil.

▷ *Climb the steps to the rue du Vieux-Château, leading to the cemetery.*

Cimetière du Vieux-Château

⏲ *Open May–Sept 7am–8pm; Oct–Apr 7am–6pm.* ☎ *04 93 57 95 99*
This international cemetery, laid out in the 19C on the site of the former medieval castle, has terraces with tombs arranged by religion or nationality. The cemetery recalls a time when Menton welcomed rich residents from all over the world, including Russian princes (Volkonsky and Ouroussov), the uncle and aunt (Delano) of Franklin D. Roosevelt, and rugby founder Revd. William Webb Ellis. From the southern corner of the English graveyard there is a beautiful **view**★ of the old town and the sea.

THE SEAFRONT AND BEACHES★★

▷ *Start from the Casino Municipal.*

Promenade du Soleil★★

1.2mi/2km. The wide promenade facing the sea follows the shore beneath the old town.

> ### 😊 A Bit of Advice 😊
> Many pedestrian streets in Menton are decorated with traditional mosaics made with smooth *galets*, or river stones, which are colourful yet a bit uncomfortable to walk on. Be sure to have thick-soled shoes if you plan on doing a lot of walking.

Old Port

The harbour, used by local fishermen and tourists alike, is flanked by the **jetée Impératrice-Eugénie** and **quai Napoléon-III** and its lighthouse. The far end of the port, home to Volti's sculpture of St Michael, commands pleasant **views**★ of old Menton. In the distance you can admire the Italian coastline.

Plage des Sablettes

Windsurfing and jet-skiing forbidden. The gravel beach is dominated by the promenade de la Mer and **quai Bonaparte**. From the top, there is a nice **view** of the old quarter. A huge flight of steps leads up to the church of St-Michel.

Garavan

This luxurious residential suburb, running between promenade de la Mer and boulevard de Garavan, has many examples of the eclectic architecture of the Belle Epoch (like the Fondation

"Artium Civitas"

This inscription on the front of the town hall declares Menton's ambition to be a city of the arts. Art exhibitions are held throughout the year at the Palais de l'Europe. The **Classical Music Festival** enjoys an international reputation and features world-famous guest artists. There are flower carnivals throughout the summer, but the most famous festival is the **Fête du Citron**, held in the Biovès Gardens since 1929. The event calls for more than 100t of citrus fruit – oranges, lemons, grapefruit and kumquats – used to cover decorative metal frames erected in the gardens to illustrate a different theme each year. The festival closes with a procession of floats decorated with citrus fruit.

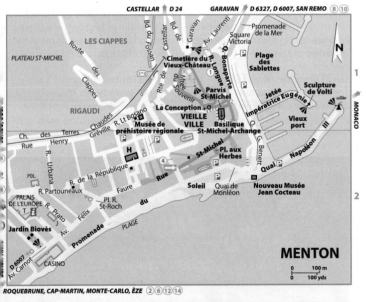

MENTON

Katherine Mansfield (1888–1923)

This writer from New Zealand spent a year in Menton from spring 1920. Her delicate health caused her to choose Garavan and she moved into the Villa Isola-Bella *(now on avenue Katherine-Mansfield)*.
In this peaceful haven she wrote five of her best works, including *The Stranger*, *The Chambermaid* and *The Girl*. Writing in her diary, she said: "The house faces the sea; on the right is the old town with its little port and pepper plants growing on a tiny quay. This old town is the loveliest place I have ever set eyes on."

Barriquand-Alphand, d'Abel Gléna on Boulevard de Garavan). The marina can accommodate boats up to 132ft/40m long.
The pretty 17C Baroque **Chapelle St-Jacques** houses a municipal gallery of contemporary art.

GARDENS OF MENTON★
The choice of tropical species and the unusual layout of these gardens reflects the fertile imagination of the town's foreign residents over the past century.

Serre de la Madone★
74 rte. de Gorbio ⊙*Open Tue–Sun Apr–Oct 10am–6pm; Dec–Mar 10am–5pm.* ⊙*Closed public holidays.* ⊗*8€.* ℘*04 93 57 73 90. Guided tours daily at 3pm. www.serredelamadone.com.*
This private garden, created between 1924 and 1939, survived war and neglect before being purchased by the Conservatoire du Littoral in 1999. Its *palazzo* and restored terraces feature rare plants from around the world, including a Moorish garden, a rock garden, and antique garden statues.

Jardin du Val Rameh★
Chemin de St-Jacques. ⊙*Open Wed–Mon Apr–Sept 10am–12.30pm, 3.30pm–6.30pm; Oct–Mar 10am–12.30, 2–5.50pm.* ⊗*6€. Guided tours Mon 3pm.* ℘*04 92 41 76 76. www.jardins-menton.fr.*
These grounds arranged around the English Val Rameh Villa in the 1930s are now part of the Musée d'Histoire Naturelle de Paris. The terraced garden features 700 species of Mediterranean, tropical and sub-tropical flora, with magnificent views of the town and the sea.

Jardin Fontana Rosa
Avenue Blasco Ibañez. 🔊*Guided tours only with the Maison du Patrimoine, Mon and Fri, 10am (1.5hr).* ⊗*5€.* ℘*04 92 41 76 76. www.jardins-menton.fr.*

Serre de la Madone, Menton

Musée des Beaux-Arts, Menton

D. Chapuis/MICHELIN

This unusual residence, built in 1921 by the Spanish novelist **Blasco Ibañez**, features a porch adorned with ceramics that pay homage to leading names in Spanish literature.

Jardin de Maria-Serena
21 promenade Reine-Astrid. ⟶Guided tours only with the Maison du Patrimoine, Tue 10am (1hr 30min). ⊜5€. ℘04 92 41 76 76. www.jardins-menton. fr. Supposedly built by Charles Garnier (architect of the Paris Opera House), this garden is known for its extensive collection of palm trees and **views** over Menton.

Jardin Biovès
Next to the tourist office.
These beautiful gardens in the town centre are bordered by palms and lemon trees, planted with flowers and ornamented by fountains and statues (*Goddess of the Golden Fruit* by Volti).

Oliveraie du Pian
Blvd. de Garavan. Also accessible from a staircase in the Val Rameh gardens.
This olive grove is planted with more than 530 olive trees, many of them over 100 years old.

SIGHTS
Musée des Beaux-Arts (Palais Carnolès)★

Access by ave. Carnot, 3 ave. de la Madone. ⟡Open Wed–Mon 10am–noon, 2–6pm. ⊜No charge. ℘04 93 35 49 71.
This former summer residence of the princes of Monaco was built in the 17C in the spirit of the Grand Trianon in Versailles. After heavy remodelling in the 19C, it was restored by the Danish architect Georg Tersling and decorated with frescoes on antique themes. The original stuccowork and gilding have survived in the Grand Salon de Musique and the Salon Bleu. The garden features over 50 species of citrus tree. The first floor is dedicated to a collection of **early religious art** by French, Italian and Flemish masters, including Bréa, da Vinci, Luini and Orsi. There are also modern works by Suzanne Valadon, Kisling and Camoin. A collection of **contemporary and modern art work** is housed on the ground floor, including pieces from the Wakefield Mori Collection (Picabia, Forain, Dufy) and contributions from various Biennales de Peinture (up to 1980).

Musée Jean-Cocteau – Collection Séveran Wunderman
2 quai Monléon. ⟡Open Wed–Mon 10am–6pm. ⊜3€. ℘04 89 81 52 50.
Designed by Rudi Ricciotti, this resolutely 21C semi-transparent maze fringed by wave-like structures on the seafront features 1,700 drawings, paint-

ings, books, jewellery, ceramics, stained glass, photographs and tapestries by Jean Cocteau, including a portrait of Picasso (1917), illustrations from his novel and studies for the film *Orphée*.

Musée du Bastion

Bastion du Vieux Port. ○*Open Wed–Sun 10am–noon, 2–6pm.* ⊛*3€.* ℘*04 93 57 72 30.*
This 17C bastion, built by Honoré II of Monaco, was restored and converted into a museum by Cocteau in 1957. Its pebble mosaics in traditional Menton style explore several themes close to his heart. Le Bastion now houses temporary exhibitions of work by artists from around the world.

Hôtel de Ville

17 rue de la République. ○*The hall decorated by Jean Cocteau is open Mon–Fri 8.30am–12.30pm, 2–5pm.* ⊛*2€.* ℘*04 92 10 50 00.* *www.villedementon.com.*
The **salle des mariages**★, where marriages are celebrated, is decorated with paintings by Jean Cocteau depicting the story of Orpheus and Eurydice. The furniture, which includes palm tree-shaped candelabra, was also chosen by Cocteau, who drew Mariannes (the symbol of the French Republic) on the room's two large mirrors.

Musée de Préhistoire Régionale

Rue Lorédan-Larchey. ○*Open Wed–Mon 10am–noon, 2–6pm.* ○*Closed public holidays.* ⊛*No charge.* ℘*04 93 35 84 64.*
This museum was opened in 1909 in a building specially designed by the architect Adrien Rey. The ground floor features items discovered in the Grottes de Grimaldi and other local prehistoric sites, from 1 million years ago to 1,500 BC. Reconstructions of the interiors of Menton houses during the 19C and a poster gallery commemorating the golden age of Menton, from 1870 to 1914, are also on display.

Église Orthodoxe Russe

Rue Morillot, access by ave. Carnot. *Guided tours 4th Sat of each month Sept–Jun at 2.30pm.* ⊛*5€.* ℘*04 92 10 97 10.*
The Russian Orthodox Church (1892) was designed by Georg Tersling, a Danish architect. Although its small size would be more suited to a chapel, the interior is lavishly decorated with murals by Prince Gagarin and many icons.

🚗 DRIVING TOURS

Menton to Roquebrunne-Cap-Martin *Route marked in green.*

L'Annonciade★ *3.7mi/6km.*

▷ *From Menton take ave. de Verdun, then ave. de Sospel, following the signs to the left up a steep, narrow road.*

The 17C **chapel** has been a centre for pilgrimages to the Virgin since the 11C. From the terrace (738ft/225m) there is a **panorama**★ of the coastline.

Castellar – *8mi/13km – about 45min.*
▷ *Take rte. de Castellar north.*

Castellar is an attractive hilltop village and a popular place for hiking (it lies at the crossroads of the GR 51 and 52 trails). Fine **view** from pl. Clémenceau.

▷ *Return to the road. After 2.5km/1.5mi, turn right on the "Chemin du Mont-Gros".*

Roquebrune-Cap-Martin★ – ⓖ*See ROQUEBRUNE-CAP-MARTIN p346.*

Col de Castillon Road
8mi/13km – about 1.5hr; route marked in red.

▷ *Leave Menton by ave. de Verdun and ave. de Sospel.*

The road over Col de Castillon – also called "route de la Garde" – makes its way through a break in the ridge of

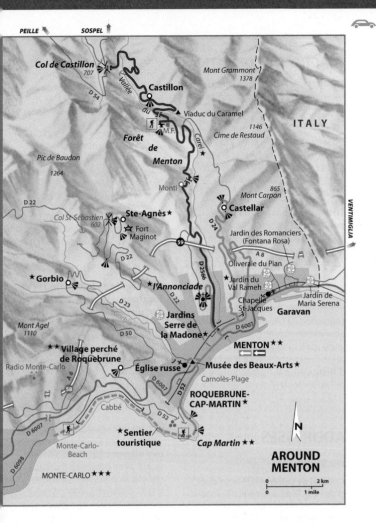

PEILLE   SOSPEL

AROUND MENTON

0   2 km
0   1 mile

N

ITALY

VENTIMIGLIA

hills running parallel to the coast. The D 2566 climbs up the beautiful **Vallée du Careï**★ beneath the ridges of the Franco-Italian border. After leaving the hamlet of Monti, the road skirts Menton Forest, with fine **views**.

Forêt de Menton

🚶 *1hr round trip.* To the left of the forest refuge a marked path leads to a **view**★ *(viewing table)* of the coast. The road passes the **Caramel Viaduct**, part of the former Menton-Sospel tramway.

Castillon

The village was reconstructed twice: after the earthquake of 1887 and after the bombardments of 1944. Its main district overlooking the village is occupied by artisans, painters and sculptors. **Views** of the Careï Valley and the sea.

◐ *After the village, turn left towards the vallée de Sospel following the tracks of the old tramway. The road to the right leads to the pass.*

Col de Castillon

Alt. 2,320ft/707m. The **view** to the north takes in the Bévera Valley with the Peïra-Cava and Aution peaks in the distance. To the left D 54 takes a picturesque route to Col St-Jean.

PRACTICAL INFORMATION

TRAIN: *pl. de la gare – ℘08 92 35 35 35, www.ter-sncf.com/paca.* Regional TER Nice/Vintimille line serving Monaco and Menton.

BUS: *av. de Sospel – ℘ 04 93 35 93 60.* SIngle tickets and carnets of 10 tickets on sale from drivers. Monthly pass from coach station. Ten routes serving Menton and the surrounding area.

TOURS: The mosaics made from **pebbles** turned sideways are a traditional form of decoration in Menton. Make sure you wear a good pair of shoes if you are planning to walk around the old town.

Guided tours – *Contact the Maison du Patrimoine, Palais d'Adhémar de Lantagnac, 24 r. St-Michel. Programme on www.menton.fr. ℘ 04 92 10 97 10. www.vpah.culture.fr.* Menton has been awarded the **Ville d'art et d'histoire** label; guided tours given by professional guides registered with the Ministry for Culture and Communication, are organised regularly by the tourist office - *reservations: ℘ 04 92 41 76 76, www.tourisme-menton.fr.*

Garden tours – The Maison du Patrimoine *(see above)* organises tours of the town's gardens throughout the year. Highlight: Garden Month *(Jun)*, Mediterranean Garden Days and Heritage Days *(Sept)*.

Tourist train – *Departs from the promenade du Soleil (near the Bastion). ℘ 04 93 41 31 09. Guided tour (30min) 10am–noon, 2–5pm. Jul–Aug, evening tours to admire the town's lights.*

Compagnie de Navigation et de Tourisme *–3 bis Traverse du Bastion, quai Napoléon-III, Vieux Port. ℘ 04 93 35 51 72. Contact for times and charges. Closed mid-Oct–mid-Apr.* This company organises sea trips with a commentary in French, leaving from Menton.

ADDRESSES

🛏 STAY

Hôtel de Londres – *15 ave. Carnot. ℘04 93 35 74 62. www.hotel-de-londres. com. Closed Nov–15 Jan. 27 rooms. ⊇10€. Restaurant.* This hotel near the coast features soundproofed rooms of varying sizes, appointed with either rustic or modern furniture and WiFi. Pleasant terrace.

Hôtel Paris Rome – *79 porte de France. ℘04 93 35 70 35. www.paris-rome.com. Closed Nov–Dec. 22 rooms. ⊇. Restaurant.* Run by the same family for a century, this rustic Provençal hotel and restaurant offers themed package stays and a friendly welcome.

Hôtel L'Aiglon – *7 avenue Madone. ℘04 93 57 55 55. www.hotelaiglon.net. 29 rooms. P. ⊇9.50€. Restaurant.* This hotel is in a beautiful villa with a garden terrace and swimming pool. Elegantly appointed rooms with WiFi. Fine dining restaurant.

Hôtel Chambord – *6 ave. Boyer. ℘04 93 35 94 19. www.hotel-chambord. com. 40 rooms. P. ⊇10€.* Modern, sound-proof hotel near the Palais de l'Europe and casino. Breakfast served exclusively in the rooms.

Hôtel Prince de Galles – *4 ave. General de Gaulle. ℘04 93 28 21 21. www.princedegalles.com. 64 rooms. P ⊇11.50€. Restaurant.* Formerly the HQ for the Monaco palace guards, this hotel offers all modern comforts and **views** over the sea. The Petit Prince restaurant has a large garden terrace.

Hôtel Princess et Richmond – *617 promenade du Soleil. ℘04 93 35 80 20. www.princess-richmond.com. 46 rooms. P. ⊇11€. Restaurant.* This seaside hotel features a smooth pebble beach and rooftop solarium and Jacuzzi. Some rooms face the sea, all have air-conditioning, WiFi and classic contemporary decor.

Hôtel Napoléon – *29 porte de France. ℘04 93 35 89 50. www. napoleon-menton.com. 43 rooms. P.*

⊑12€. *Restaurant* ⊜⊜. Elegant, contemporary hotel right on the beach. Air-conditioned rooms; ones facing the sea have pretty teak balconies. The beachside restaurant has grilled fish, barbecue meats and ice-cream desserts.

⫿/EAT

⊜⊜ **Auberge Pierrot-Pierrette** – pl. de l'Église, Monti. Closed Dec–mid Jan, Mon. ℘04 93 35 79 76. www. pierrotpierrette.fr. In a tranquil hamlet perched on the hills above Menton, this family-run restaurant surrounded by gardens serves hearty Provençal meals.

⊜⊜ **A Braijade Méridiounale** – 66 rue Longue. ℘04 93 35 65 65. www.abraijade.fr. Closed early–mid-Jan, mid-Nov – early Dec, Wed, lunch Jul–Aug. Hidden in an alley of the old quarter, this homely restaurant provides Provençal dishes and grilled meats at very reasonable rates. Pretty dining room with visible stonework, beams and a fireplace.

⊜⊜ **La Cantinella** – 8 rue Trenca. ℘04 93 41 34 20. Closed Jan, lunch in Aug, Tue. The Sicilian owner delights in sharing his Mediterranean-influenced cuisine in a friendly, laid-back atmosphere.

⫿⫿ ENTERTAINMENT

Palais de l'Europe de Menton – 8 ave. Boyer. ℘04 92 41 76 50. www.villedementon.com. Exhibition gallery: Wed–Mon 10am–noon, 2–6pm; tourist office ticket office: Mon–Fri 10am–noon, 2–5pm. An attractive 730-seater events centre featuring ballets, opera and operetta, theatre and classical music concerts. It also houses a free contemporary art gallery showcasing current artists.

Casino Barrière de Menton – 2 bis ave. Félix-Faure. ℘04 92 10 16 16. www.lucienbarriere.com. Open from 10am. Traditional games and slot machines, restaurant, disco, amphitheatre and bar-lounge.

⫿ SHOPPING

Lemons – Many shops in Menton pay tribute to this sunny fruit by selling a wide range of produce made or flavoured with lemons: tarts and pies, gingerbread, wine, jam, soaps, etc.

Marchés – Open daily in the morning. Covered market on quai de Monléon. Careï market at the top of the Biovès Gardens, beneath the railway bridge.

Confitures Herbin – 2 rue du Vieux-Collège. ℘04 93 57 20 29. www.confitures-herbin.com. Kitchen tours Mon, Wed, Fri 10.30am. Shop closed Sat–Sun. An impressive range of mouthwatering jams made on the premises of this family business. There are also different types of honey, vinegar, confit and mustard.

⫿⫿ SPORT & LEISURE

Sports – La Promenade de la Mer is where most of the sports and recreation companies are found, including scuba diving, sailing, tennis and windsurfing clubs.

⫿⫿ **Koaland** – ave. de la Madone. ℘04 92 10 00 40. www.parckoaland. fr Closed Oct–May, Tue. Leisure park for children and the younger generation with a miniature golf course.

CALENDAR

Fête du Citron (Lemon Festival) – Two weeks in February–March (around Mardi Gras). Book at least two months in advance for this popular event.

Salon des Orchidées – Held during the lemon festival, this orchid exhibition includes flower parades and fireworks.

Menton Classical Music Festival – In August on the esplanade of the Église St-Michel. This prestigious event is attended by talented soloists and conductors from around the world.

Ma Ville est Tango – Mid-July. Courses, competitions, shows and gastronomic events based around this passionate South American dance.

Christmas Fair – First weekend in Dec to first week in Jan. Ice-skating, Christmas market, concerts and walks.

THE PRE-ALPS OF NICE

Although officially part of the Alpes-Martimes, and therefore grouped with the French Riviera, the mountains and valleys north of Nice have their own distinctive character. There are no fancy casinos or palace hotels, no beaches or yachts and few examples of the conspicuous wealth found along the coast. This is a region of modest inns and humble perched villages, where nature-loving visitors come to admire the flora and fauna, try their hand at forest skiing, discover its religious art treasures and ancient churches, or simply to get away from the crowds and heat of the Riviera. And, while the deep ravines and vertiginous peaks make for impressive panoramic vistas, the narrow, winding roads require attentive driving as they hairpin up and down the mountains, and through the often icy or even snow-covered forest roads.

Highlights

1 Stunning **views** from the **Madone d'Utelle Panorama** (p373)

2 Drive the Authion or Col de Braus Road in the **forest of Turini** (p380)

3 Rafting or canyoning on the **Bévéra River in Sospel** (p382)

4 15C frescoes in the **Chapelle Notre-Dame-des-Fontaines** (p389)

5 Prehistoric engravings in the **Vallée des Merveilles** (p393)

Nature Close-Up

These hinterlands running along the Italian border at the foot of the Alps don't quite meet the sea, but their proximity contributes to the unique mix of Mediterranean and Alpine landscapes. Olive groves and Maritime pines give way at higher altitudes to oaks, firs, spruces, and Swiss pines, as well as flowering plants such as edelweiss and saxifrage. The rivers, notably the Roya and Bévéra, have cut deep into the valleys on their way to the sea, creating fascinating rock formations and waterfalls as the snow melts on the pre-Alpine peaks. Much of this natural beauty is protected as part of the Parc National du Mercantour, which, partnered with the bordering Parco Naturale della Alpi Marittime in Italy, is home to the prehistoric engravings of the Vallée des Merveilles, over 200 rare plant species including wild orchids, and many endangered or rare animals, including grey wolves, golden eagles, ibexes and bearded vultures.

Sporting Activities

The uniquely rugged character of this landscape provides ample opportunity for sports enthusiasts of all abilities. There is a variety of trails for hikers, some of which follow sections of the national GR (Grand Randonnée) trails

Chapelle Notre-Dame-des-Fontaines

Village of Utelle

J. Malburet/MICHELIN

with several refuges providing food and shelter. Rock climbing is also popular, particularly teamed with the *via ferrata* routes, which traverse some of the deeper canyons. For watersports fans, Sospel and Tende host many river rafting and canyoning companies, which provide proper equipment and seasoned guides in the summer months. Of course, the hinterlands of Nice also attract visitors in the winter season to a handful of slopes in La Colmiane-Valdeblore, Camp d'Argent in the forest of Turini, and Peira-Cava near Lucéram. Regardless of the season, anyone setting out into the wild should check the local weather reports and be sure to dress and pack accordingly for inclement weather.

Religious Heritage

There are no large monasteries in this part of the French Riviera, but the mountain passes and perched villages house a surprising number of Gothic chapels, with 14C frescoes, Italian-style churches with their distinctive bell towers, and many rare artworks by Louis Bréa, Giovanni Baleison and altarpieces from the Nice School. Many of these churches and chapels are only open during services or on request, so be sure to call ahead before making a long journey to avoid disappointment.

Unique biodiversity

A succession of lakes, passes, peaks and gorges, the pre-Alpine landscape passes from meadows of Mediterranean orchids to rocky glaciers within the space of just a few miles. Home to 25 species of reptile and amphibian, it's a good place to spot sun-loving green grass snakes sharing the slopes with cold-blooded sand lizards, which are found at altitudes as high as 7,545ft/2,300m. It also numbers over 10,000 species of insect, many endemic to these valleys. Lucky hikers might catch a glimpse of the rare red-and-black spotted Petit Apollon butterfly, for example, which is only found in Boréon and Gordolasque. The Massif de Mercantour alone is crossed by 12 rivers, each flowing into its own basin, giving rise to an extremely original range of indigenous fish species, including the arctic char and the white-clawed crayfish. Of the 101 species of land mammals found in France, at least 60 are present in the pre-Alps region, including chamois, ibexes and wolves, along with both Arctic and Mediterranean bat species. Its 155 species of migratory, occasional and nesting birds include the rare Alpine ptarmigan, a species of grouse with a remarkable talent for mimicry.

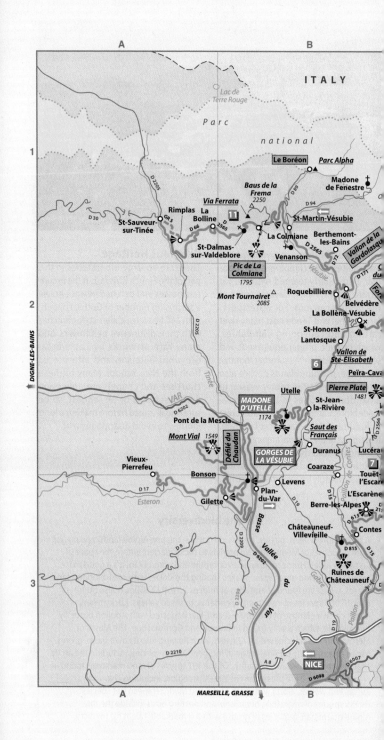

ITALY

Lac de Terre Rouge

Parc

national

1

Le Boréon | *Parc Alpha*

Madone de Fenestre

Baus de la Frema 2250

Rimplas

Via Ferrata

La Bolline

St-Sauveur-sur-Tinée

St-Martin-Vésubie

D 30

D 2205

GR 5

D 66

D 2565

1

La Colmiane

D 94

Berthemont-les-Bains

Vallon de la Gordolasqu

St-Dalmas-sur-Valdeblore

Venanson

D 2565

D 171

Pic de La Colmiane 1795

Roquebillière

Mont Tournairet 2085

Vésubie

Belvédère

La Bollène-Vésubie

St-Honorat

Fort

du

D 2205

Lantosque

Vallon de Ste-Élisabeth

6

Tinée

Peïra-Cava

Pierre Plate 1481

VAR

D 6202

Utelle

St-Jean-la-Rivière

MADONE D'UTELLE 1174

D 2566

Pont de la Mescla

Saut des Français

Mont Vial 1549

Duranus

Lucéra

Défilé du Chaudan

GORGES DE LA VÉSUBIE

Coaraze

7

Touët-l'Escar

Vieux-Pierrefeu

Bonson

Levens

L'Escarène

D 17

Berre-les-Alpes

DIGNE-LES-BAINS

Esteron

Gilette

Plan-du-Var

D 19

Châteauneuf-Villevieille

D 615

D 21

D 15

Contes

D 2209

Basse

D 6202

Vallée

D 815

Ruines de Châteauneuf

D 8

du

Var

Gabre

D 2210

A 8

NICE

D 19

Peillon

D 6007

D 6098

MARSEILLE, GRASSE

A | B

THE PRE-ALPS OF NICE

TORINO

Col de Tende/
Colle di Tenda

ne du Gélas

cade del'Estrech

Fontanalbe

**Vallées des
Merveilles**

Tende

St-Dalmas-
de-Tende

**La
Brigue**

N.-D.-des-Fontaines

Levense

Mercantour

Granile

10

Gorges de Bergue

**Pte des
3-Communes**
2082

L'Authion

Mon' aux morts

Saorge

**Gorges
de Saorge**

La Giandola

ol de Turini

Vallée

Moulinet

de

N.-D.-de-
la-Menour

Breil-s-Roya

879

9

ges du

Col de Brouis

Col du
Perus

654

Piène-Haute

ITALY

Bévéra

St-Roch

847

Sospel

Fort Suchet

642

Col St-Jean
ue de Braus

Col de
Castillon

Col des
Banquettes

S 20

GENOVA

GENOVA

Peille

A 10

Peillon

MENTON

S 1

MONACO

MADONE D'UTELLE	★★★	Highly recommended
Pierre Plate	★★	Recommended
Sospel	★	Interesting
Lantosque		Worth seeing

⇨ Driving tour with departure town

MEDITERRANEAN SEA

N

0 — 5 km
0 — 3 miles

L'Arrière Pays Niçois

The cradle of *nissard* culture and the gateway to the metropolis, the Arrière Pays Niçois is light years away from the hustle and bustle of its urban neighbour. Set in an irresistible mountain landcape of valleys that rise and fall through a myriad of vales, its bare summits rise giddily above steep slopes carpeted with pine forests. As you wind along its hairpin bends, you'll glimpse perched villages nestled among olive trees and copses of cypresses, their ancient churches filled with religious treasures created by the comté de Nice's finest artists and craftsmen, such as the organ-building Grinda brothers, the architect Guibert, and the paint-ers of the Nice *primitif* school.

Info: Tourist offices at: Gilette Val d'Esteron, ℘04 92 08 98 08, www.esteron.fr; l'Escarène, ℘04 93 79 62 93, www.escarene.fr; Contes, ℘04 93 79 13 99, www.ville-contes.fr; Peillon Mairie (Town Hall), ℘04 93 91 71 71, www.peille.fr.

Location: The Arrière Pays lies in the mountains and valleys north of Nice, towards the Alps, along the Italian border.

Don't Miss: Views from the Plateau St Michel or Mont Alban.

Kids: Lou Ferouil museum at Gilette.

Timing: Allow one day for the perched villages of the vallée du Paillon and half a day for the vallée de l'Estéron.

🚗 DRIVING TOURS

1 THE TWO PAILLONS★
Round trip of 56mi/90km. Allow 1 day.

The Paillon de l'Escarène emerges from the northeast of Col St-Roch, whereas the Paillon de Contes springs from the slopes of Rocca Seira to the northwest. They meet at Pont de Peille and flow into the sea at Nice. The suggested route goes up one valley and down the other, with detours at Peille and La Turbie.

▷ *Leave Nice by boulevard J.-B.-Vérany northwards and the route de Turin (D 2204).*

Hugging the left bank of the Paillon, pass along the village of Drap, with its glazed-tile bell tower and trompe-l'oeil façades.

▷ *After crossing the bridge over the Paillon, take D 21 right, then a few miles*

View of Peillon

Rock climbing in Peille

© Kaliste A/Fotolia.com

further, right again onto D 121, which leads to Peillon village.

Peillon★

Set back on a narrow spur overlooking the vallée du Paillon, Peillon is a spectacular village of strict architectural unity, a layout imposed both by its site and defences.

Virtually untouched since the Middle Ages, the **village** has a few, narrow streets linked by steep steps and covered alleyways lined with flower-decked houses. The 18C **Eglise St-Sauveur**, with its octagonal lantern, crowns the village. Inside are 17C and 18C paintings and an 18C wooden statue of Christ. There's a magnificent panoramic **view**★ from the Plaça dei Gleia (place de l'Église), the Esterel and St-Martin valley (orientation table).

Chapelle des Pénitents-Blancs

⏱ *Open by request Apr–Oct 10am–noon, 3–6pm, Nov–Mar 2–5pm. A timed lightswitch on the outside allows you to see the frescoes through the bars.* 📞*04 24 97 42 25.*

The chapel's most interesting feature are the **frescoes**★ by Giovanni Canavesio. At the far end is the Crucifixion with St Antony and Ste Petronella. On the walls and ceiling are scenes from the Passion, in particular the *Flagellation* and *Judas' Kiss*, vividly portrayed. On the altar stands a Pietà in painted wood.

🚶 You can still walk along the old Roman road from Peillon to Peille *(2hr)*.
Oil and flour mill – Standing at the confluence of the Launa and Paillon rivers, the aptly named hamlet of Moulins ("mills" in French) is home to two 19C mills, both perfectly preserved and in good working order. The oil mill and flour mill (the only grain mill in the vallée du Paillon) operate using the same original cannon wheel.

▷ *Take D 21 on the right and up the vallée du Paillon. After passing the cement works, turn right after the bridge onto D 53 to Peille village.*

Peille★

Peille's Ligurian name, Pilia, which means "on the naked and grassy heights", is a perfect fit for this medieval village, perched dramatically above olive groves and rocky ravines.

From the 13C **Tower**, at the edge of the D 53, follow the steps going down the rocky rue de la Sauterie, with its intersecting staircases and arched passages, until you arrive at place A. Laugier.

On the right, the rue Centrale leads to the Town Hall, housed under the dome of the 13C **Chapelle Saint-Sébastien**. You can also admire the former **Hôtel des Consuls** with its coupled windows and archways.

Pelhasque: a Local Dialect

Some of the older inhabitants of this quiet village still speak *Pelhasque*, a local variation of the *Nissart* dialect of Nice.

Behind the **Gothic fountain**, under a house, two half-arches lean against a Roman pillar. The right leads to the rue Lascaris and towards the war memorial, where you'll find a superb **view**. The left opens onto **L'Arma**, the oldest part of the village.

The **Musée du Terroir** explores local customs through objects, furniture, tools and clothing donated by the village's inhabitants (⏱*open Sat–Sun 2–5pm;* ⊕*no charge;* ✆*04 93 91 71 71, town hall*).

Flanked by an elegant pyramid-shaped Lombard bell tower, the 12C **church** is made up of two coupled chapels. On the left upon entering is a retable, with 15 compartments made by Honoré Bertone in 1579. On the right is a representation of Peille as it looked in the Middle Ages. Ste-Anne is featured on a 14C fresco.

Via ferrata – *Park in the public car park at the entrance to the village and follow the signposts.*

⊷*0.5mi/800m. Allow 3.5hr. Admission* ⊕*€3€. Equipment hired on-site. Contact the Absinthe bar,* ✆ *04 93 79 95 75. To hire a guide, contact a professional mountain guide ("guide de haute montagne").*

This energetic hiking trail above the village of Peille crosses a series of secure footbridges and rope bridges.

▷ *Take CV 7 "route des Banquettes" to Col des Banquettes.*

This pretty, shaded panoramic route leading to the **Col des Banquettes** (2,440ft/744m) offers fine **views** over the Baie de Menton and the Mediterranean. ⊷*4hr round trip.* From the pass, there are a number of hiking trails leading to the Pointe Siricocca, a former watch tower perched above Ste-Agnès, with breathtaking **views** over the Menton coast and back country.

▷ *Return to Peille and back along the vallée du Paillon, then right on D 21.*

Gorges du Paillon★

The route crosses a lush, wooded ravine.

L'Escarène

Built at the junction of the road to the resort of Peïra-Cava and the beginning of hairpin bends leading up to Col de Braus, from 1591 to the 19C, this large town stretching along the bottom of the Paillon Valley was an important staging post on the Salt Road from Nice to Turin (*Route du Sel* – ⓒ*see SOSPEL p384*).

Église St-Pierre★

This 17C church, flanked by two chapels of the Black and White Penitents, is the work of the Niçois architect Guibert.

On the road to Col de Turini, the imposing mausoleum dedicated to the Ist Division France Libre, inaugurated in 1964 by General de Gaulle, commemorates the sacrifices and battles of the Liberation at the end of the Second World War.

▷ *Take D 2204 south to Col de Nice and turn right onto D 215.*

Berre-les-Alpes

This village is built on a charming site at an altitude of 2,215ft/675m. From the cemetery there is a **panorama**★ of the Pre-Alps of Nice and the sea.

▷ *Return downhill on the same road, bearing right onto D 615.*

The road wends its way through chestnut and olive groves.

Contes

Originally a Roman settlement, the village is built on a rocky promontory that dominates the vallée du Paillon de Contes like a ship's prow.

The south chapel of the church contains a remarkable altarpiece by an artist belonging to the Nice School (1525). The central panel representing Ste-Madeleine has disappeared but the **predella**★ illustrates her life.

Bordering Paillon (on D 15, in the direction of Coaraze) is a site with two mills: a 13C oil press still in use by the village (Dec–Mar), and a 14C iron forge, where large farming tools were made until 1958. You can visit the forge and a reconstruction of a 19C country kitchen (⏰open Dec–Oct Sat 9.30am–12.30pm, 2–5pm; ⊜2€; ℘04 93 79 19 17; www.ville-contes.fr).

▷ Take D 715 to La Grave; cross the Paillon and take D 815.

The road winds uphill through pines and olives above the Paillon, giving way to the rocky outcrop of Contes and Berre-des-Alpes.

Châteauneuf-Villevieille

This village on the site of a Ligurian settlement, later a Roman camp, overlooks the vallée du Paillon de Contes. The 11C Romanesque church, **Madone de Villevieille**, is decorated with festoons and Lombard bands. The interior was restored in the 17C with ceiling frescoes. Behind the high altar, a fine plaster altarpiece frames a 15C wooden statue of the Virgin and Child.

The deserted ruins of the medieval walls and towers (🚶1mi/2km, 30min round trip) contrast starkly with the rocky landscape. In the Middle Ages, the villagers hid here during attacks. From the top of the bluff there is a sweeping **panorama**★.

▷ Go back to D 15, which leads to Nice via the vallé du Paillon.

② VALLÉE DU VAR AND VALLÉE DE L'ESTERON
41mi/66km. Allow half a day.

▷ Leave Nice by the promenade des Anglais, which becomes promenade Corniglion-Molinier. Join the D 6007, then turn right towards Plan-du-Var.

The D 6202, which hugs the east bank of the Var, allows quick access to Nice's hinterland. In a landscape composed of flower beds and vegetable plots, vineyards and olive groves, the hill vil-

lages loom into view, one by one: on the west bank Gattières, Carros and Le Broc; on the east bank Aspremont and Castagniers at the foot of Mont Chauve, followed by St-Martin-du-Var and La Roquette-sur-Var. The **view**★ includes the snow-capped Alps on the horizon.

▷ Cross the river over pont Charles-Albert and take D 17 to Gilette.

The site of the village of Bonson, on an impressive rocky spur high above the river on the west bank, comes into view followed by Gilette, nestling in a cleft.

Gilette

🚶🚶 2.4mi/4km before Gilette, stop at the **Musée Lou Ferouil**★ to explore the tools and crafts of yesteryear (⏰open Tue–Sun 10–5.30pm; ⊜4€; ℘04 92 08 96 04; www.louferouil.fr).
From place de la Mairie follow the arrows up to the castle ruins for an impressive **view**★ of the corniche roads, the Var valley and the Pre-Alps of Nice.
There is a pleasant walk, bordered by acacias and plane trees, below the castle with fine **views** of the hill villages – Bonson and Tourette-du-Château – and of the Alps to the north.

▷ From Gilette take D 17 north up the Esteron valley; 1mi/2km beyond Vescous turn right onto a narrow road, which climbs to Vieux-Pierrefeu.

Vieux-Pierrefeu

Alt. 2,028ft/618m. The village is reserved for pedestrians. Austere and proud, Vieux-Pierrefeu is a handsome perched village with beautifully restored stone-work throughout. High above the Esteron Valley, this former Roman signalling post (Petra Igniaria) was a link in the chain that ran from Hadrian's Wall on the border between England and Scotland to Rome.
The church just down the road in Pierrefeu has been converted into a picture gallery called the **Musée "Hors du Temps"** (⏰open summer; contact the town hall; ⊜2€; ℘04 93 08 58 18). This small museum houses a

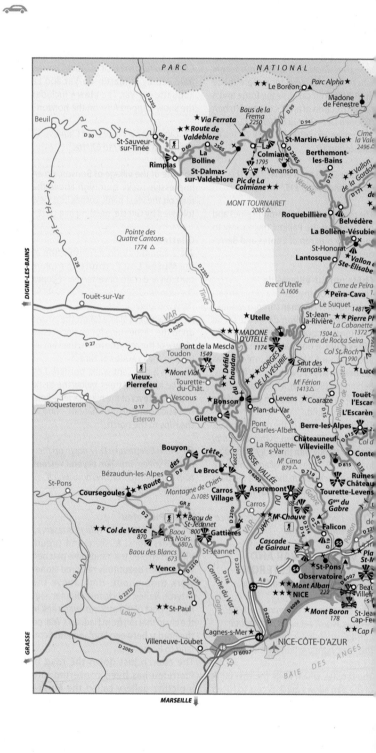

TORINO

CLAPIER
C^ode de Estrech
Fontanalbe
Casterino
★ Tende
★ La Brigue
2935 △
Baisse de Valmasque
△ 2872
Mt Bégo
Mt SACCAREL 2200 △
St-Dalmas-de-Tende
Levense
N.-D.-des-Fontaines ★★
Vallées des Merveilles
2685 △
ME DU DIABLE
Granile

MERCANTOUR
HAUTE VALLÉE DE LA ROYA
◆ Gorges de Bergue ★
l'Authion ★★
P^te des 3-Communes ★★ 2082
Fontan
Mon^t aux morts
★★ Gorges de Saorge
Saorge ★★
Cabanes Vieilles
la Giandola
le Turini
Vallée de Turini
Mt Mangiabo △1801
Roya
ITALIA
ulinet
N.-D.-de-la-Menour
879
Breil-s-Roya
la Bévéra
Cascade
Col du Perus
Col de Brouis ★
ges du iaon ★★
M^t 654 Agaisen △745
Col de Vescavo
Piène-Haute ★
us ★
St-Roch
Nervia
Sospel ★
Olivetta
Fort Suchet
642
Col St-Jean
Col de Castillon 707
ue de Braus
Forêt de Menton
Castillon
Viaduc du Caramel
GENOVA
Gorges Grillon
Col des Banquettes
Peille ★
Monti
★ Vallée du Carei
Roia
S 20
SAN REMO
GENOVA
Ste-Agnès
★ Castellar
Gorbio
59
A 10
eillon ★
Mont Agel 1110 △
Roquebrune-
Ventimiglia
S 1
St-Martin-de-Peille
MENTON ★★
Cap-Martin ★
N.-D.-de-Laghet
Cap Martin ★★
La Turbie
MONTE-CARLO ★★★
e ★★
MONACO ★★★
Cap-d'Ail

MER   MÉDITERRANÉE

N

ARRIÈRE-PAYS NIÇOIS

0   5 km

View of Bonson

unique collection of paintings on the theme of Genesis, with the work of 40 contemporary artists including Brayer, Carzou, Folon, Erni, Vicari, Villemont and Moretti. The drive down D 17 affords **views** of the Var valley, Bonson and La Roquette, perched on its rock.

Bonson★

Built on a remarkable **site**★ high on a rocky spur above the Var valley, Bonson offers an exceptional **view**★★ from the church terrace of the Vésubie springing from its gorges and meeting with the waters of the Var, the Défilé de Chaudan. This famous, wooded area was razed by a fire in 1994 that destroyed everything up to the edge of the village.

The **church** contains three beautiful *primitif* paintings from the Nice School. On the back wall there is a **retable of St Antony**, where the figure of Ste Gertrude, who was invoked against the plague, is identified by the great rats climbing up her shoulders. In the south aisle is a **retable of John the Baptist**, attributed to Antoine Bréa (the centre panel has been spoilt by overpainting). At the high altar, in a Renaissance frame, is a **retable of St Benedict**★, including the figure of Ste Agatha clutching her wounded breasts. Ask for the key at the town hall *(Mon–Fri 9am–noon, 3–5pm; ℘04 93 08 58 39; www.bonson.org).*

Mont Vial★

12.4mi/20km from Bonson.

▷ *Take D 27 west towards Puget-Théniers.*

The picturesque road twists and turns along the flank of the hill with attractive glimpses of Gilette. After Tourette-du-Château take the road going sharply down to the right, which winds to Le Vial ridge before reaching the summit (5,082ft/1,549m, *U-turns possible*). Those who have made the effort to climb up, will be rewarded by an impressive **panorama**★★.

▷ *Return to Bonson by the same route.*

The road loops down to pont Charles-Albert, giving beautiful **views**★ of the Var valley. Cross the bridge and turn left onto D 6102. North of Plan-du-Var cross the River Vésubie where it joins the Var. The road to the right climbs up the Gorges de la Vésubie (℘ *see Vallée de la VÉSUBIE p374).*

Défilé du Chaudan★★

The defile, named after the little village of Chaudan at its southern end, has been created by the Var, which has worn a deep, narrow and winding channel through the rocks. The road follows the course of the river in and out of every bend and through four tunnels.

At the northern end, at **pont de la Mes-cla**, the River Tinée flows into the Var.

▷ *Go back to Nice on D 6102.*

EXCURSIONS
Coaraze★
▷ *6mi/10km north of Contes on D 15.*
Heading up towards the Col St-Roch (3,248ft/990m), the stunning "route du soleil" skirts around a hill covered with olive trees. A small, tastefully-restored village, home to the artist Jean Cocteau in the 1950s, dominates the scene.
The **historic streets★** and long, vaulted passageways of this charming medieval bourg end in a series of small squares and fountains. Surrounded by cypress trees, the terrace garden affords **views** down the valley and over the Rocca Seira peak.
Walk through the old cemetery to the **St-Jean-Baptiste** church. The Baroque interior contrasts starkly with its plain bell tower and façade. The church has no fewer than 118 stuccowork angels and cherubs.
Notre-Dame-de-la-Pitié – *Return to the D 15 northwards, then take the small road on the left – Route de la Chapelle-bleue.* A former oratory dedicated to the Virgin Mary, it is also known as the "blue chapel" because the life of Christ is painted on the walls in monochrome blue (Ponce de Léon, 1962). Fine **view** of the village from the terrace.
Chapelle St-Sébastien – *Take D 15 south. After 1.2mi/2km turn right towards La Gardiola, route des Jouncas.* Nestled in the landscape, on the route de Nice, this chapel is dedicated to St Sebastian, invoked to protect against the plague. It is decorated with elegant frescoes dating from 1530, repainted in the 19C.

Levens
Perched at an altitude of 1,968ft/600m, the medieval village streets of Levens, lined with ancient houses and fountains, are a pleasant place to stroll.
Place de la République opens onto an attractive public garden, its shaded terraces overlooking the valley and the curved façade of the Baroque Chapelle

> ### Sundials of the rich and famous
> The alleyways of Coaraze are filled with sundials, many designed by celebrities. Jean Cocteau created *Les Lézards (The Lizards)*, Mona Cristi designed *La Chevauchée du Temps (Riding Time)*, while *Blue Time* is the work of Goetz. *Le Piton et sa Couronne en Vert et en or (The Peak and its Green and Gold Crown)* on place de l'église is by Spanish explorer Ponce de Léon.

des Pénitents-Blancs. In rue du Docteur-Faraud, the Chapelle des Pénitents-Noirs presents a fine collection of artworks, many displayed in the crypt. At the summit of the village, you'll find an **open-air swimming pool**.

▷ *Go up rue Masséna.*

Past the Masséna family home (1722), explore the surviving ramparts and the **Maison du Portal** (☉*open Sept–Jun Sat–Sun 2.30–5.30pm; Jul daily 2.30–6.30pm; Aug daily 10am–noon, 2.30–6.30pm; ⊘no charge; ℘04 93 79 85 84/71 00; www.lamaisonduportal.fr),* which houses the sculptures of Jean-Pierre Augier and temporary exhibitions. At place de la Liberté a vaulted passage-way leads to the heavily restored church.

▷ *Take the path on the left.*

The **view★** extends over the confluence of the Var and the Vésubie, and the Chei-ron and Mercantour massifs.

Duranus
▷ *5.2mi/8.5km from Levens on D 19 north.*
The road overlooks the deep Gorges de la Vésubie (☉*see Vallée de la VÉSUBIE p374)* from a great height, with a glimpse of the chapel of Madone d'Utelle *(left)* high in the mountains. Duranus, a pretty village surrounded by orchards and vineyards, was founded in 17C by the people of Rocca-Sparviero, a ruined village at Col St-Michel.

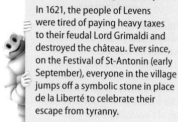

Celebrating Liberty

In 1621, the people of Levens were tired of paying heavy taxes to their feudal Lord Grimaldi and destroyed the château. Ever since, on the Festival of St-Antonin (early September), everyone in the village jumps off a symbolic stone in place de la Liberté to celebrate their escape from tyranny.

3hr round trip. Discover the remains of an ancient village deserted after an earthquake in the 17C, before returning to Duranus to explore the 19C **aqueduct**.

Saut des Français★★

Shortly after leaving Duranus. Information point selling guides and craft products (Jul–Aug 10.30am–6.30pm).

At the northern end of Duranus is Frenchmen's Leap, commemorating Republican soldiers who were hurled over the edge in 1793 by guerrillas from the Vésubie valley. Utelle and its chapel overlook the dizzying vertical drop.

ADDRESSES

STAY

Annexe Lou Pourtail – *Entrance at l'Auberge de la Madone, Peillon. 04 93 79 91 17. Closed early Oct–late Dec. 6 rooms. 14€. Restaurant* At the foot of the village, this old cottage inn is full of charm. Regional cooking. Rustic dining room and garden terrace.

La Vigneraie – *rte. St-Blaise, Levens. 04 93 79 77 60. Closed 9 Oct–11 Feb. 18 rooms. 8€. Restaurant* This family-run, country-style inn and restaurant is known for its generous home cooking and comfortable, if basic, rooms.

Chambre d'hôte Les Lys – *288 chemin des Meingarde, access via D 215 towards L'Escarène, Berre-les-Alpes. 04 93 91 81 09. www.les-lys.com. 3 rooms.* Situated in an annexe to a large property, the rooms afford

a **panorama** of the surrounding mountains. Vast garden with BBQ.

Chambre d'hôte les Cyprès – *289 rte de Châteauneuf, Contes. 04 93 62 58 77. www.lescypres.fr. 3 rooms.* 1920s Niçois house with ground-floor bedrooms. Sombre, refined décor. Breakfast served under a pergola or vine arbour.

Chambre d'hôte La Maïoun aux Oliviers – *360 rte des Mortissons, Pierrefeu. 04 97 02 12 81. www.maioun-aux-oliviers.com. 3 rooms.* La Maïoun aux Oliviers has fully-equipped, individually decorated rooms and suites surrounded by an olive garden.

EAT

La Voute – *42 r. centrale, Peille. 04 93 04 56 85. Closed evenings from 8.30 pm and Wed.* Central restaurant with a small rustic dining room that opens onto the Hôtel du Consul. House speciality: pizza pancakes.

La Fleur du Thym – *3 blvd. Charles Alunni, 06390 Contes. 04 93 79 47 33. www.lafleurdethym.fr. Closed mid-Aug, early Jan, Tue eve and Wed.* Decorated in yellow hues, this rustic Provence restaurant serves generous portions of regional cuisine.

La Capeline – *5.5mi/9km from Gilette by D 17, Toudon. 04 93 08 58 06. Open Mar–Oct, Sat–Sun Nov–Feb and closed Wed. Reservation required.* This small house in the vallée de l'Esteron serves a fresh, daily menu of regional dishes seasoned with homemade olive oil. Simple, rustic décor and shady terrace.

Le Mas Fleuri – *RD 19, Le Grand-Pré, Levens, close to the stadium. 04 93 79 70 35. www.masfleuri. com. Closed late Oct–mid-Nov. 8 rooms. 7€.* A refreshing and recently restored restaurant with a simple white dining room and shady terrace. The chef, a "champion de France du dessert", serves a traditional menu of Niçois dishes. Plain, rustic bedrooms on the upper floor.

Lucéram ★

Alpes Maritimes

The pretty village of Lucéram, perched dramatically on a steep rock below the Cime du Gros Braus, is known for its colourful roof tiles and an exceptionally rich collection of religious art.

VISIT
Medieval Village ★
▶ *On pl. Adrien-Barralis, follow the arrows to the church (église).*

A maze of stepped streets, Gothic houses and vaulted alleyways make up the medieval town. The church terrace affords **views** over Lucéram and beyond the hills to the sea.

Église Ste-Marguerite
Guided tour on request at the tourist office (⌘2€) or included in the village tour (⌘5€). ℘04 93 91 60 51.
The interior of this simple 15C church was remodelled in the 18C with elaborate plasterwork. The 15C **altarpieces**★★ are the most complete group attributed to the Nice School. In the south transept is the **altarpiece of St-Antoine** framed in Flamboyant Gothic panelling. Behind the high altar, the **altarpiece of Ste Margaret,** divided into 10 panels, is by Louis Bréa: around the central figure are Mary Magdalene *(bottom left)* and St Michael *(top left)*. Three fine altarpieces by the Bréa School are in the nave.

▶ **Population:** 1,228.
◔ **Michelin Map:** 341 F4.
▯ **Info:** Maison de Pays de Lucéram, pl. Adrien-Barralis. ℘04 93 91 60 51. www.luceram.com
◑ **Location** 14mi/21km northeast from Nice.
▯ **Parking:** Near the fire station and close to the post office.

The **treasury**★ comprises some remarkable pieces: a silver statuette of Ste Margaret (1500), a finely engraved 14C reliquary, a statue-reliquary of Ste Rosalie from Sicily, two candlesticks and an alabaster Virgin (16C). On the left of the entrance stands an unusual Baroque Pietà in painted wood and to the left of the chancel another one in plaster on cloth dating from the 13C.

▶ *Exit the church, go down to the right and walk up montée du Terron.*

This path leads to the **ramparts** (15C), of which a corner and a defensive tower remain.

Chapelle St-Grat
0.6mi/1km to the south on D 2566, turn left on leaving the village before the tunnel. Walk down the path.
This chapel is decorated with frescoes attributed to **Jean Baleison**. Beneath a

Lucéram

© Xavière Belon/Fotolia.com

Noël des Bergers★

Each year shepherds from the neighbouring mountains make their offering of lambs and fruit to the church to the strains of fife and tambourine music.

triple Gothic canopy are the *Virgin and Child*, who is holding a dove, St Grat bearing the head of John the Baptist and St Sebastian in elegant attire with an arrow in his hand.

Chapelle Notre-Dame-de-Bon-Cœur

1.3mi/2km northwest on D 2566, park on the left, then 15min on foot. Interior visible through the bars.
The frescoes, attributed to Jean Baleison, are interesting despite some shoddy repainting. In the porch are *Good and Bad Prayer* and the martyred St Sebastian. In the chapel are the *Adoration of the Shepherds*, the *Adoration of the Magi* and scenes illustrating the life of the Virgin.

Musée des Vieux Outils★

Guided tour on request at the tourist office. €2, or included in the village tour (€5). 04 93 78 46 50. www.musee-de-luceram.com.
Opened in 1998, this museum retraces the history of the village and its surrounding area. Set in the sumptuous St-Jean chapel, the collection includes tools for working the land, turning wood, mining arsenic, forging iron, and growing vines and olives. The walls are lined with black and white photographs of the village and its inhabitants, offering a glimpse of rural life before the arrival of mechanised tools. Don't miss the anti-wolf collar.

Musée de la Crèche★

Same opening times as the Musée des Vieux Outils. Open Dec–mid-Jan Tue–Sun.
Unique in the region, this museum on the village square houses between 150 and 200 items, each designed and donated by the village's inhabitants. The most impressive was made using 33,000 matchsticks. This magical museum contains crèches from around the world, with the oldest dating from 1948. The *santons* (clay figures) are made from a complete range of local materials: clay, porcelain, matchsticks, glass, wood, wool, fabric, wire and even chocolate.

ADDRESSES

EVENT

Circuit des Crèches – *Ask for information at the tourist office.* In December–January, over 400 nativity scenes (crèches) are displayed in the cellars and streets of Lucéram and Peïra Cava. A shepherd's procession and mass in Provençal take place on Christmas Eve.

Lucéram's Medieval History

Lucéram was divided into two distinct parts: the upper village, built on a steep rocky slope between ravines, and the lower village, a former passage on the **Salt Road**. Due to its exceptional defensive advantages, Lucéram has been home to a staggering range of inhabitants over the last 3,000 years, starting with the Ligurians, Celts and the Romans followed by the Franks, who each built residences and strongholds on the site. The comtes d'Anjou later built a **château** (13C), of which there are extensive remains to the south of the village. Another particular feature of Lucéram is its multitude of chapels belonging to brotherhoods. A stronghold of the Order of Malta and the Templars, Lucéram had seven such chapels outside the village. Just two remain today: the Chapelle St-Grat and the Chapelle Notre-Dame-de-Bon-Cœur.

Utelle★

Alpes Maritimes

This isolated village, lying at an altitude of 2,625ft/800m, projects like a balcony over the vallée de Vésubie. Once the most important town between Tinée and Vésubie, Utelle has preserved much of its original medieval character.

- **Population:** 685.
- **Michelin Map:** 341 E4; region map: p368–69.
- **Info:** Town Hall ℘04 93 03 17 01. www.vesubian.com.
- **Location:** Utelle is outside the gorges of the Vésubie valley (left at St-Jean-la-Rivière). Be cautious on the hairpin bends leading to the village.

SIGHTS
Église St-Véran★
This 14C church, altered in the 17C, has a surprising interior combining mountain austerity (groin vaulting and rounded arches resting on archaistic Romanesque columns and capitals) with elaborate Baroque details (stuccowork around and on the arches). It has an elegant Gothic porch with carved panels illustrating the legend of St Veranus in 12 tableaux.

A **carved wooden altarpiece**★ depicts scenes from the Passion. There is an altarpiece of the Annunciation (Nice School) above the first altar in the north aisle and a 13C Recumbent Christ below the altar in the south aisle.

Chapelle des Pénitents-Blancs
The chapel near the church contains a carved wooden altarpiece of the Descent from the Cross by Rubens and six 18C paintings.

EXCURSION
Madone d'Utelle Panorama★★★
⏵ *3.7mi/6km southwest.*
The sanctuary of the Madonna of Utelle, founded in 850 by Spanish sailors who had survived a storm, was rebuilt in 1806. Pilgrimages take place on 15 August and 8 September, and the interior contains a large number of ex-votos. A short distance from the chapel stands a viewing table (alt. 3,852ft/1,174m) covered by a dome. There is a breathtaking **panorama**★★★ over a wide expanse of the Alpes-Maritimes *département* and the Mediterranean.

Madone d'Utelle
© Nicolas Thibaut/Photononstop

ADDRESSES

ⴾ/EAT
⊜ **Le Bellevue** – *rte de la Madone.* ℘04 93 03 17 19. *Closed early Jan–early Feb and Wed.* On the outskirts of the village, perched on a ledge, this family restaurant is perfect for mountain enthusiasts. Clean rooms and swimming pool with **views** over the valleys. Simple cuisine prepared with vegetables from the garden.

⊜⊜ **L'Auberge Del Campo** – *rte d'Utelle, St-Jean-la-Rivière, 3mi/5km east of Utelle on D 132.* ℘04 93 03 13 12. ⴾ. *Reservation recommended eves.* This small inn with a bohemian atmosphere is built on the remains of a former sheepfold. Small dining with a terrace overlooking the Vésubie gorges. Provençal cuisine.

Vallée de la Vésubie★★

Alpes Maritimes

The pines of the upper Vésubie valley merge into a patchwork of terraced vines, olive trees and perched villages before sweeping down the slopes to the deep gorges and mountain torrents below.

🚗 DRIVING TOUR

Plan-du-Var to St-Martin-Vésubie
68mi/110km. About 5hr.

If you wish to stop and take a photograph, use one of the rare roadside parking areas. Stopping on these narrow passes can be very dangerous.

D 2565 follows the narrow, winding Gorges de la Vésubie★★★. In St-Jean-la-Rivière turn left onto D 32, which climbs towards Utelle.

La Madone d'Utelle★★★
See UTELLE p373.

Make a U-turn at St-Jean-la-Rivière and turn left onto D 2565.

Beyond St-Jean-la-Rivière, the valley squeezes between bluffs of rock, skirting the foothills of the Brec d'Utelle.

Lantosque
This tiny perched village has a canyoning **via ferrata** course *(2hr)*, which crosses the Gorges of Lantosque *(contact the Mairie for information, ☎04 93 03 00 02).*

Roquebillière
This little town has been rebuilt six times since the 6C due to rock falls and floods. After the last landslide in 1926, most of the villagers left their austere old houses and moved to the west bank, where the **Église St-Michel-du-Gast**, a church combining Romanesque and Gothic styles, has stood since the 15C.

- **Michelin Map:** 341 E4; local map: *see NICE.*
- **Info:** Pl. Félix-Faure, St-Martin-Vésubie. ☎04 93 03 21 28. www.vesubian.com. Syndicat d'initiative de Belvédère, r. Victor-Maurel. ☎04 93 03 51 66. www. mairie-belvedere.fr.
- **Location:** The Vésubie, an eastern tributary of the Var, is formed by two torrents: the Madone de Fenestre and the Boréon.
- **Timing:** Allow one day to discover the valley.

On leaving Roquebillière-Vieux turn right onto the road to Belvédère (D 171).

The picturesque road winds up the **Vallon de la Gordolasque★★** between Cime du Diable (Devil's Peak) and Cime de la Valette.

Belvédère
The **site★** of this charming village overlooks both the Gordolasque and the Vésubie. From the terrace behind the mairie (town hall) there is a **view★** over the downstream waters of the Vésubie, with Mont Férion and the forêt de Turini on the left , Mont Tournairet on the right and Roquebillière-Vieux below. The road (D 171) continues up the valley past massive rocks and tumbling waterfalls, including the **Cascade du Ray★** where the river divides into two branches.

Cascade de l'Estrech★
The road ends near a path (🥾 *0.6mi/1km of mountain track)* that leads to the beautiful Estrech waterfall flowing down from a **cirque★★** of snow-capped mountains. The surrounding area is teeming with mountain orchids, passerines, golden eagles and ibexes.

Return to D 2565; turn right on D 72.

© Wolfgang Stalb/iStockphoto.com

Reintroduction of Bearded Vultures

Driving through the gorges, you may be lucky enough to catch a glimpse of a **bearded vulture**. An endangered species in Europe, this majestic bird has a windspan of 9ft/2.8m. The biggest of all the Alpine birds, it has some very curious habits: alternating between gliding and steep dives, it surveys the sloping pastureland for the carcases of chamois or ewes before swooping down and lifting their bones (which can weigh up to 7lb/3kg) into the air. They then drop the bones onto the rocks below, shattering them into pieces. The vulture was once considered as useful to shepherds as sheepdogs are now.

Decimated in the 19C in the Alps, it survived in the Pyrenees and in Corsica. As part of a vast national programme to reintroduce them to the area, conservationists have been releasing the vultures into the Alps and the **Parc national du Mercantour** for the past twenty years.

Berthemont-les-Bains
This therapeutic spa has naturally sulphurous waters of 86°F/30°C used as long ago as Roman times. As the road climbs, the valley changes to a landscape of chestnuts, pines and green pastures which has earned the region around St-Martin-Vésubie the title of "Suisse Niçoise" (Nice's Switzerland).

ADDRESSES

STAY

Auberge du Bon Puits –
Le Suquet, 3.4mi/5.5km south of Lantosque towards Nice. ℰ04 93 03 17 65. Closed Dec–Easter, Tue except Jul–Aug. ⬚.
This roadside inn, with a small number of modest rooms, is built from local stone and stands on the banks of the Vésubie. The dining hall features an open fireplace and exposed beams. There is an ornamental park with ponies and a play area for children.

CALENDAR
Polenta festival –In early March, Belvédère plays host to a major festival devoted to polenta served with a generous helping of *daube*, a local beef or boar stew.

St-Martin-Vésubie★

Alpes Maritimes

St-Martin-Vésubie stretches out along a rocky cliff between the Boréon and Madone-de-Fenestre rivers. Surrounded by peaks and Alpine greenery, this popular summer mountaineering destination is known as the "Switzerland of Nice".

▶ **Population:** 1,300.
◔ **Michelin Map:** 341 E3; region map: pp368–69.
▤ **Info:** pl. Félix-Faure. ℘04 93 03 21 28. www.saintmartinvesubie.fr.
◉ **Location:** Located 44mi/71km north of Nice on the D 2565.
🅿 **Parking:** Park to the northwest of the entrance to the old town.

WALKING TOUR
▷ *Start under the plane trees on pl. Félix-Faure.*

Rue du Docteur-Cagnoli
A narrow street bordered by Gothic houses with handsome porches and lintels runs north–south through the town. Several 14C houses survived the fire of 1487 (Maison du Coiffeur).

Chapelle des Pénitents-Blancs
The chapel has a carved façade, a bulb-shaped bell tower and, below the altar, a recumbent Christ with cherubs holding instruments of the Passion.

▷ *From rue Dr-Cagnoli turn left into rue du Plan to pl. de la Frairie.*

Place de la Frairie
From the terrace overlooking Madone de Fenestre Torrent is a **view** of the gushing river and nearby mountains, Cime de la Palu and Cime du Piagu. The church is behind the square.

Church
This Roman building, beautifully decorated in the 17C, features a richly dressed 12C statue of the Madone de Fenestre. On the last Saturday in June, it is carried in procession to a mountain sanctuary (◔*see Excursions*), where it remains until September.
The second chapel's left-hand aisle houses two panels from an altarpiece attributed to Louis Bréa. From the terrace is a partial **view** of the Boréon valley and Venanson village.

EXCURSIONS
Venanson★
▷ *3mi/4.5km. Leave St-Martin-Vésubie by the Boréon bridge and take D 31 south.*

The village square, standing on a triangular rocky outcrop 3,819ft/1,164m high commands a good **view**★ of St-Martin and the Vésubie valley.

Chapelle St-Sébastien
🕓*Open on request at the restaurant La Bella Vista. ℘04 93 03 25 11.*
This 15C chapel is considered one of the most complete examples of Niçois art, with the interior covered in **frescoes**★ by Baleison. At the far end, beneath a Crucifixion, St Sebastian is pierced by arrows; on the side walls and the ceiling are scenes from the saint's life.

Parish church
Pl. de l'Eglise.
On the left of the entrance is a triptych of the *Virgin and Child*, flanked by *St John* and *St Petronella*. At the high altar a Baroque altarpiece (1645) of the Coronation of the Virgin features the donor.

Le Boréon★★
▷ *From St-Martin-Vésubie take D 2565 5mi/8km north up Le Boréon's west bank.*
The resort stands on a superb site (4,201ft/1,500m) on the southern edge of the Parc National du Mercantour by the **Cascade du Boréon**★, where the river drops 130ft/40m down a narrow gorge. Le Boréon is the starting place

A Mountaineering Pioneer on the Riviera

The Chevalier Victor de Cessole (1859–1940), a member of an old Nice family, took to climbing late in life when his doctor recommended exercise and fresh air. He enrolled in the new Club Alpin Français when already in his thirties and became a compulsive mountaineer, successively climbing the highest peaks in the Alpes-Maritimes (Mont Clapier and Mont Gélas) and setting several records in the Massif de l'Argentera.

De Cessole recommended walks, described in illustrated brochures, are forerunners of the guide books of today. His activities earned him the presidency of the Club Alpin Français, a position which he held for 40 years, and enabled him to inaugurate and organise the chain of mountain refuges. In 1901 he opened the Nice refuge above Madone de Fenestre. He initiated the first skiing competitions and is considered to be the founder – in spirit at least – of Beuil, the oldest resort in the area. His interest in nature led him to establish the first measures for the protection of wildlife in the region – the banning of the picking of *Saxifraga florulenta*, now the emblem of the Parc du Mercantour.

for forest walks, up to the high peaks and mountain lakes.

♦♦ Parc Alpha★

🕐 Open Jun–Aug 10am–7pm (last admission 4.30pm); Apr–May and Sep 10am–6pm (last admission 4.30pm); Jan–Mar and Oct Wed and Sun–Sun (daily school holidays) 10am–5pm (last admission 3.30pm). 🕐 Closed Nov–Dec (except school holidays, daily 10am–5pm, last admission 3.30pm). 🚌 10€ (4-12 yrs 8€). 🕿 04 93 02 33 69. www.alpha-loup.com.

At 4,900ft/1,500m altitude, this unique site has been created to help visitors learn more about the **Parc national du Mercantour**. The Parc Alpha, named after the dominant couple in wolf packs, aims to reconcile man with the environment and the wolf.

After crossing a nature preserve (Le Pas du Loup, a grandiose and refreshing pass surrounded by larches, pines and spruces), cross the Boréon to the Temps des Hommes, to watch a short audiovisual show presented by four key mountain professionals in the former cowshed.

After discussing the reintroduction of the wolf to the valley, return to the 29 acre/12ha park, half of which is reserved for three packs of wolves living in semi-

View around Le Boréon

© Nicolas Thibaut/Photononstop

The Return of the Wolf

In 1995 the presence of a pack of eight wolves *(Canis lupus)* was confirmed in the Parc du Mercantour. Constantly in search of new territory, these wolves had crossed from the Abruzzi in Central Italy, where the wolf population is estimated at more than 500. There were 19 in the Parc National du Mercantour in 2000 and 12 in 2002. The wolves suffer a bad reputation, so the Parc du Mercantour conducts a campaign of awareness and education with shepherds, who now pen flocks at night and use sheepdogs (the Pyrenean Patou) to prevent wolf attacks. It also teaches them more about this animal at the root of so many legends and stories. The wolf centre at Boréon will, perhaps, help to change the way these creatures are regarded and so help conserve them in their natural habitat.

liberty in vast enclosures (36 wolves in 2009). The large number of wolf cubs born here every year (between 6 and 7 per litter) is seen as evidence of the successful integration of these mammals into their new environment. Their health is monitored by a team of carers, while a group of scientists studies their behaviour.

Observation cabins in the Le Temps du Loup area allow you to observe these creatures in the wild. Visitors never have to wait long before the spell-binding show begins. Arrive at **feeding time** *(6 days out of 7, between 2.30pm and 3pm at the Maison des Soigneurs)* to watch them circle their food, before wolfing down huge pieces of beef, chicken, fish and rodents.

It is possible to drive east to the **Vacherie du Boréon** *(1.5mi/2.5km)* and admire the strange outline of the Cougourde. To the west, skirting the park, a 2.4mi/4km road crosses the **vallon de Salèse**.

Vallon de la Madone de Fenestre

7.4mi/12km east – about 30min. *From St-Martin, take avenue de Saravalle.*

The road climbs rapidly up the Madone valley between Cime du Piagu and Cime de la Palu, crossing and re-crossing the river. It ends in a rugged rock **cirque**★★ much appreciated by mountaineers. Caïre de la Madone, huge and pointed, rises nearby, and the slopes of **Cime du Gélas** (10,312ft/3,143m), covered

with frozen snow, dominate the northern horizon on the Italian border. The **Madone de Fenestre** chapel is a place of pilgrimage, which in summer houses the statue of Our Lady of Fenestre. In September it is returned to St-Martin-Vésubie in solemn procession.

HIKE
Via Ferrata du Baus de la Frema★

At the Col St-Martin, turn right opposite the mini-golf (sign "Via Ferrata"). Parking possible on the access slope. The Via Ferrata begins at the end of the car park. Open Jun–Sept. 4.50€. 04 93 23 25 90. www.colmiane.com.

Via Ferrata offers ideal facilities for anyone wishing to learn rock-climbing. The full course to the Baus de la Frema peak takes 4hr and includes a footbridge (115ft/35m long; 164ft/50m above ground level) and rope bridges.

DRIVING TOUR

Route de Valdeblore★★
18mi/29km. Allow 2.5hr.

North from St-Martin by D 256.

The road linking the valleys of the Tinée and the upper Vésubie passes through the Valdeblore district, a mountainous region of pastures and wooded slopes. Before the tunnel is a fine **view**★ over Vésubie valley and St-Martin.

La Colmiane
This ski resort in the Col St-Martin (alt. 4,921ft/1,500m) consists of chalets and hotels dotted among the pines.

○ *At Col St-Martin turn left onto a narrow road leading to the ski-lift.*

Pic de La Colmiane★★
⚡ *Ski-lift to the summit. Jul–Aug daily 10am–6pm (Sat–Sun only Jun and Sept, 10am–5.30pm); mid-Dec–end Feb 9am–7pm. Closed Mar–May, Oct–mid-Dec.* ⊙3€ round trip (summer), 4.50€ (winter). ☎04 93 02 83 54.
From the top is an immense **panorama**★★ south over the Vésubie valley and Turini forest; east over the Mercantour; north and west over the Baus de la Frema to Mont Mounier and Valdeblore.

St-Dalmas-de-Valdeblore
Stroll through the winding alleyways of this village before visiting the Romanesque **Ste-Croix church**, which features a pyramidal Alpine-style bell tower, stout buttresses and Lombard bands on the chevet. Above the high altar there is a polyptych by Guillaume Planeta of St Dalmas, St Roch and the Evangelists. In the north aisle is an altarpiece of St Francis attributed to André de Cella. Behind an altarpiece of the Rosary (17C) in the south apsidal chapel are the partial remains of some very old frescoes.

La Bolline
A pleasant summer resort at the heart of a light chestnut grove that contrasts sharply with the dark wood on the opposite slope.

○ *West of La Bolline turn right on D 66.*

Rimplas
The curious **site**★ of this village on the edge of a cliff (3,281ft/1,000m high) is striking. From the chapel, there is an extensive **view**★ of the Tinée valley, Bramafan valley and Valdeblore.
🚶 *2hr round trip.* A nice, easy trail leads down into **St-Sauveur-sur-Tinée** by the GR 5, northwest of the village.

🚲 *By road towards Valdeblore on D 2565, then La Tinée on D 2205, right for St-Saveur, left for Nice.*

ADDRESSES

🛏 STAY

🍴🍴 **La Châtaigneraie** – ☎04 93 03 21 22. www.raiberti.com. Closed Oct–mid-May. 🅿. 37 rooms. ⊒5€. Restaurant ⊖. Pleasant accommodation nestling in a peaceful park with pool and WiFi. Ideal for those who wish to go climbing or hiking in the Parc du Mercantour.

🍽 EAT

⊖ **Le Pic Assiette** – La Colmiane, Pic de La Colmiane. ☎06 21 01 63 68. Closed Nov. 📷. Reservation required. 1 room. ⊒. At 5,900ft/1,800m altitude, this restaurant has astounding mountain views. Ride up by chairlift in summer, and come down by mountain bike.

🍴🍴 **La Trappa** – 7 pl. du Marché, St-Martin Vésubie. ☎04 93 03 29 23. Closed late Oct-late Nov, Wed in Jul–Aug, Sun eve. and Mon. Niçois restaurant with a summer terrace overlooking a quiet pedestrian street.

🛒 SHOPPING

Markets – Tue, Sat and Sun on pl. du Marché *(summer season)*.

🏃 SPORT & LEISURE

Ski – Le Boréon has 18.6mi/30km of cross-country ski trails.

Luge d'été – Pic de La Colmiane. ☎04 93 02 83 54. www.colmiane.com. Jul–Aug: 10am–6pm; Jun and Sept: weekend 10am–6pm. Monorail sledge with chairlift ride 11€, descent only 7.50€ (carnet of 10 chairlift rides and sledge descent 80€) – children under 4.4ft/1.35m must be accompanied by an adult (10€ for 2).

Forêt de Turini★★

Alpes Maritimes

Bristling along the slopes between the Vésubie and Bévéra valleys, the Forêt de Turini is carpeted with fresh young maritime pines and oaks, rising to a dense thatch of maple, beech and spruce topped by a crown of bright green larches.

🚗 **DRIVING TOUR**

7 L'AUTHION★★
Round trip 11mi/18km from Col de Turini. Allow 45min.
The Authion road passes through magnificent mountain scenery.
🚫 *Roads blocked in winter.*

Monument aux Morts
The Authion Massif has twice been a backdrop to military action. In 1793 the Convention's troops fought here against the Austrians and Sardinians, and in April 1945 the DFL (Free French Forces) pushed back the German army. Panoramic **view**★ from the memorial. Continue along D 68, then right at the fork to Cabanes Vieilles military camp. The road runs through Alpine pastures with **views**★ of the Roya Valley.

▶ *Turn right by another monument onto a track and continue 547yd/500m.*

Pointe des Trois-Communes★★
At this altitude (6,830ft/2,082m) there is a marvellous **panorama**★★ of the peaks in the Mercantour and Nice Pre-Alps.

▶ *Return to D 68; at the war memorial take the road back to Col de Turini.*

7 VALLON DE STE-ÉLISABETH★
Round trip 11mi/18km from Col de Turini. Allow 1hr.
The road (D 70) winds northwest, cutting its way between the peaks of Calmette and Scoubayoun overlooking the Vésubie tributary.

⌖ **Michelin Map:** 341 F4; local map: *see NICE.*
▶ **Location:** Situated in the Nice hinterland 9.6mi/ 15.5km from Menton, the forest covers 1,350/3,500ha acres between the Vésubie and Bévéra valleys.
🕐 **Timing:** Allow one day for the Col de Braus tour.

Gorges de Ste-Élisabeth
This rugged gorge cuts a savage gash in the concertina-like folds in the rock.

▶ *Soon after the tunnel, stop at the Chapelle St-Honorat.*

St-Honorat Viewpoint★
The **view** extends from the terrace by the chapel over the perched village of Bollène, the Vésubie and the Mercantour peaks.

La Bollène-Vésubie
From this village at the foot of the Cime des Vallières, the road winds down the Vésubie Valley on D 2565 *(towards Nice).* The **Turini Camp-d'Argent** (5,577ft/1,700m) offers forest skiing. Return to Nice along the valley and D 2565.

7 COL DE BRAUS ROAD★★
Round trip 47mi/76km, leaving from Col de Turini. Allow one day.

The drive to Peïra-Cava passes through the thickest part of Turini forest.

Cime de Peïra-Cava★★
1mi/1.5km – plus 30min on foot round trip.
🚶 Panoramic **views**★★ of the Vésubie valley from the top.

Peïra-Cava★ *Alt. 4,757ft/1,450m.*
This summer resort and winter sports centre is perched on a ridge between the Vésubie and Bévéra valleys.

▶ *Beyond the village turn right into a car park, then walk 55yd/50m to a stairway on the left.*

La Bollène-Vésubie

J. Malburet/MICHELIN

Pierre Plate★★

This peak provides a **panoramic view**★★. Return downhill to D 2566 and in La Cabanette turn left onto D 21. The road descends through steep bends with magnificent **views**★.

◐ *D 21 continues to Lucéram.*

Lucéram★

See LUCÉRAM p371.
◐ *South of Lucéram D 2566 slopes into the Paillon valley to L'Escarène.*

L'Escarène

See NICE p364 1: *The Two Paillons.*
From L'Escarène D 2204 climbs northeast up the Braus Valley to Sospel.

Touët-de-l'Escarène

The road passes through this charming little village with a Baroque church.

Clue de Braus

The rift that opens up beyond Touët village is short, but impressive. From St-Laurent (hamlet) one can reach the Braus waterfall (🚶 *15min*). The D 2204 winds around 16 hairpin bends before climbing to **views**★ of the Nice observatory and Cap d'Antibes.

Col de Braus

Alt. 3,287ft/1,002m.
Beyond the pass the road descends through 18 bends offering extensive **views**★★ of the Bévéra valley. The road skirts Mont Barbonnet.

Col St-Jean

At Col St-Jean, between the dwellings on the left, an old army road leads to **Fort Suchet**, built 1883–86. ⏱*Open Jul–Aug, contact Sospel tourist office* 📞*04 93 23 25 90.*

Sospel★

⏱*See SOSPEL p382.*
The D 2566 climbs northwest through the forest up the **Bévéra valley**★. There is a beautiful waterfall on the right.

Gorges du Piaon★★

The *corniche* road runs beneath an overhang of rock high above the bed of the stream, strewn with huge boulders.

Chapelle Notre-Dame-de-la-Menour

An oratory marks the beginning of a path that provides **views** of the valley. The route passes through the charming village of Moulinet before returning through the forest to the Col de Turini.

ADDRESSES

🛏 STAY

🍽🍽 **Les Chamois** – *Turini (Col de).* 📞*04 93 91 58 31. www.hotel-les-chamois.com. 15 rooms.* Mountain-style restaurant with terrace. Pleasant accommodation; some with balconies.

Sospel★

Alpes Maritimes

Once the capital of the comté de Ventimiglia, this mountain village straddling the Bévéra river was a staging post on the Salt Road linking Turin, capital of the Kingdom of Sardinia, to the coast. Today its historic houses and olive groves, surrounded by high mountains, create a picturesque backdrop for hiking, canyoning and river rafting.

☙ WALKING TOUR

THE OLD TOWN★
A map of the village is available from the tourist office.

Right Bank
Place St-Michel is framed by a church and a run of arcaded houses. The oldest (Palais Ricci), to the right of the church, bears a plaque recording the stay of Pope Pius VII, exiled by Napoleon in 1809.

Église St-Michel
🕓 *Open daily 9am–noon, 2–5pm.*
At the time of the Great Schism this church was a cathedral. The Romanesque bell tower with Lombard bands flanks an imposing Baroque façade. The interior decor is pure Baroque: huge altarpieces, *trompe-l'oeil* frescoes and

- **Population:** 3,394.
- **Michelin Map:** 341 F4; region map: pp368–69.
- **Info:** Le Pont-Vieux, Sospel. ℰ04 93 04 15 80. www.sospel-tourisme.com. Vallées Roya-Bévéra. ℰ04 93 04 92 05. www.royabevera.com.
- **Location:** Sospel lies 12mi/19km north of Menton on narrow, winding roads.
- **Timing:** Allow half a day, with 1hr for Fort St-Roch.

gilding. In the north apsidal chapel the **Immaculate Virgin**★ is one of François Bréa's most accomplished works.

Old Streets
To the right of the parvis, large stairways lead to the ruins of a Carmelite convent, now almost hidden by vegetation. Carry on to reach the remains of some fortifications, including a huge 15C corner tower and, further on, a semicircular arched gateway. Go through this gateway and follow a stairway to **rue St-Pierre**, which runs on from the cathedral parvis. Note No 30, which has two ornate Renaissance windows and a Gothic ground floor with an ogival door.

Old bridge of Sospel

© Rémy Masseglia/Fotolia.com

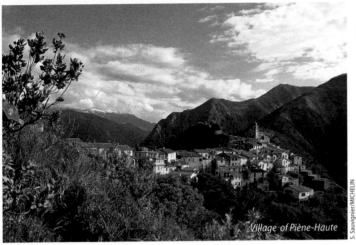

Village of Piène-Haute

S. Sauvignier/MICHELIN

The road, lined by arcades, leads to the square behind the *mairie* (town hall).

Old Bridge★
The toll tower on the 11C bridge, rebuilt after the Second World War, now houses the *Syndicat d'Initiative* (tourist office) and, in season, an information centre about the Mercantour National Park.

Left Bank
Cross the old cobblestone bridge to **place St-Nicolas**, with its old houses and 15C fountain, the oldest in the village. Rue de la République to the right once housed a host of small businesses and enormous cellars used by passing merchants as warehouses before they settled their toll at the bridge. The houses along this road feature beautifully carved stone lintels *(nos 14, 15, 23 and 51)*. The picturesque and narrow rue des Tisserands leads to the 17C Ste-Croix Chapel.

EXCURSIONS
Fort St-Roch★
◗ *0.6mi/1km south of the village, on D 2204 to Nice; turn right after the cemetery (signed).* ◷*Open Jul–Aug Tue–Sun 2–6pm; Apr–Jun and Sept Sat–Sun and public holidays 2–6pm.* ◷*5€.* ℘*04 93 04 00 70.*
This fort was part of the Alpine **Maginot Line** of fortifications built in the region during the 1930s. An underground town 164ft/50m deep, it could survive for up to three months without contact with the outside world. The tour covers the underground galleries, the kitchens, an electricity generating station, an operating block, the firing stations, a small cinema and artillery rooms, as well as the periscopes, which enabled the inhabitants to view their surroundings.

Piène-Haute via Col de Vescavo★
◗ *5.6mi/9km. Allow half a day.*
From Sospel take D 2204 east.
After 1mi/2km turn right onto a road signed "Piène-Olivetta". After 2.5mi/4km D 93 reaches Col de Vescavo (alt. 1,568ft/478m). The road then crosses the border to the Italian village of Olivetta.
Follow D 193 to the left.

The road continues to climb up to the charming little village of **Piène-Haute**, in solitary splendour on an outcrop 2,011ft/613m in altitude. The best place to park is on the esplanade at the entrance to the village.
Before setting off downhill on foot, admire the **view**★ of the old houses huddled side by side below the castle ruins. The church, on a rise, has a beautiful carved bell tower and an unusual red marble altarpiece. Above the village, by

383

Water over the bridge

Sospel toll bridge is one of the last fortified bridges in Europe. Originally lined with shops and homes, it was also used as an aqueduct to supply water to the left bank.

the castle ruins, are splendid **views** of the Roya valley.

HIKING TOURS
Botanical Trail

▶ *The path is below D 93 to the right towards the Olivetta frontier post. Go down the slope from the road towards the railway, then turn left under the bridge. A signpost near a ruin marks the start of the botanical footpath.*

🚶 *1.5hr on foot round trip.* This delightful footpath, marked with boards detailing the plants to be seen, goes through a wood of young oak trees, scrubland (which was once cultivated in terraces) and a holm oak wood.

Mont Agaisen

▶ *4.3mi/7km by car. From Sospel take the road beside the post office that climbs up the north bank of the Bévéra. After 1mi/1.5km, turn right and follow a road uphill towards Serres des Bérins.*

🚶 *1hr on foot round trip.* On entering the Bérins district, take the surfaced road on the right, heading south. After a short stretch through some woods, the old army road reaches the first small forts of the fortified complex of Mont-Agaisen (⛔ *closed to the public*). Leave the car in any free space along the road.

On the path that leads to the summit (alt. 2,444ft/745m) is the occasional casemate or firing turret. To the south at the edge of the summit is a large metal cross and a good **view** of the village, the Bévéra valley and Mont Barbonnet. There are other **viewpoints** on the summit, towards Col de Brouis and north towards the valley dominated by the bare peak of Mont Mangiabo (alt. 5,909ft/1,801m).

🚶 *3hr.* More experienced ramblers can opt for a variation on this excursion, leaving from the village and undertaking it entirely on foot. In this case, they should leave from the Groupe Scolaire overlooking the village and follow the path leading off to the right, marked *"GR 52 – Mont Agaisen"*.

The track merges with the GR 52 (red and white blazes) for about 0.6mi/1km. Turn left onto a surfaced road at the junction and follow it uphill for another half a mile or so until you reach the first military ruins and rejoin the itinerary described above.

DRIVING TOUR

9 COL DE BROUIS ROAD
21km/13mi. Allow about 1hr.
🕐 *See region map pp 360–61.*

This road is an extension of the Col de Braus Road (🕐 *see Forêt de TURINI p380*) towards Turin, formerly known as the "Salt Road".

▶ *From Sospel take D 2204 east.*

There is a **view** to the rear over Sospel guarded by the Fort du Barbonnet.

The Salt Road

Owing to its essential role in the preservation of meat and the tanning of hides, salt has always been of considerable interest to tradesmen. Provençal salt-works have supplied Piedmont since the Middle Ages. The salt was unloaded from sailing barges in Nice and transported by mule to Turin through the Col de Braus, Col de Brouis and Col de Tende via Sospel and Saorge. This strategic highway became known as the Salt Road (Route du Sel). Now embellished with works of modern art, it is still the main highway between the Riviera and Piedmont.

Col du Pérus

Alt. 2,146ft/654m. The road runs just above the deep Bassera ravine.

Col de Brouis★

Alt. 2,884ft/879m. This pass takes its name from the heather-like shrub that thrives in the area, known as brouis. The monument above the car park on the right commemorates the last French attack of April 1945 against the German forces, who had been driven back into the valleys. A broad **view** ★ opens up of the peaks on the far bank of the Roya. The road descends to La Giandola.

La Giandola

Attractive mountain hamlet with a Renaissance church tower.

⊙ *Return by the same itinerary; it is also possible to take a detour via Breil-sur-Roya (↪see BREIL-SUR-ROYA overleaf) or to return through the Vallée de la Roya to Saorge, 3mi/5km away (↪see SAORGE p387).*

ADDRESSES

🛏 STAY

⊜⊜**Chambre d'hôte Le Domaine du Paraîs** – *La Vasta Supérieure. ℘04 93 04 15 78. domaineduparais. monsite-orange.fr. 🗷. 3 rooms. 🖵.* This large mansion has retained many of its charms, including the original Tende stone sink and drainer in the kitchen.

⊜⊜**Chambre d'hôte Villa Amiel** – *ave. des Martyrs de la Résistance. ℘04 93 04 12 69. ww.villaamiel.com. By reservation mid-Nov–Feb. 🗷. 4 rooms. 🖵 5.50€.* Owned by an English couple passionate about hiking, this residence bordering a small stream has two upper bedrooms and two smaller, but charming rooms in an annexe building. Organic breakfasts.

⊜⊜🍽 **Hôtel des Étrangers** – *7 blvd. de Verdun. ℘04 93 04 00 09. www.sospel. net. Closed Nov–Mar. 27 rooms. 🖵8€. Restaurant ⊜⊜.* This unpretentious hotel-restaurant makes a great base for exploring the area. Swimming pool. Dishes prepared with fresh produce.

🍴 EAT

⊜⊜**Le St-Donat** – *quartier La Vasta. 1.8mi/3km NW via rte du Col de Turini. ℘ 04 93 04 14 94. Closed Nov and Mon–Tue except Jul–Aug. Reservation required in low season.* Situated in the Mas Fleuri campsite, this restaurant is open year round. The chef prepares all the dishes himself, including the pasta.

⊜⊜**Le Restaurant Le Bel-Aqua** – *Hôtel des Étrangers.* Regional cuisine prepared with market-fresh produce. Opt for the terrace overlooking the Bévéra in summer.

⊜⊜**Côté Cuisine** – *5 blvd. Jean-Médecin. ℘ 04 93 79 81 37. www. restaurant-cotecuisine.com. Closed Mon–Wed. Reservation recommended.* A former grocery opposite the bridge, this restaurant is run by a farming couple. Local cuisine prepared with organic or regional produce: homemade bread, pasta and farm olives.

🛍 SHOPPING

The village is known for its honey and its handcrafted objects made from olive wood.

Markets – Pl. Gianotti on Thu and pl. de la Cabraïa on Sun mornings (especially honey and goat's cheese). There is a market selling regional produce on St Michel's Day (29 September).

🏃 LEISURE ACTIVITIES

Canyoning – *℘04 93 04 15 80. www.sospel-tourisme.com ✉Contact the tourist office for details.* Canyoning is authorised between April and October on Monday, Wednesday, Friday and Sunday from 9am–5pm.

Hiking – A list of all the hiking paths starting from the village is available from the tourist office. There are also facilities for exploring the neighbouring countryside on horseback.

CALENDAR

Les Baroquiales festival d'art baroque – *www.sospel-tourisme.com.* First weekend in July. Baroque music concerts, street events, tastings.

Breil-sur-Roya
Alpes Maritimes

A popular spot for fishing, hiking and watersports, Breil lies below the summit of Mont Arpette (5,282ft/1,610m), astride the Roya river, just a few miles from the Italian border.

VISIT

The old village consists of picturesque streets shored up by ramparts and ancient gateways. The Renaissance **Chapelle Ste-Catherine**, which hosts regular art exhibitions, stands south of the parish church.

Sancta-Maria-in-Albis

Pl. Brancion. ⏰*Open daily 9am–noon, 3–6pm.* ✆*04 93 04 42 19.*
The vast 18C church with its carved doors (1719) and Baroque interior is adorned with an ornate 17C **organ loft** of gilded wood. An early **altarpiece** (1500) stands to the left of the chancel.

Écomusée du Haut-Pays

Gare de Breil. ⏰*Open Jun–Sept 2–6.30pm.* ✆*04 93 04 42 75.* ◉*3€.*
The old Breil train station has been transformed into a railway museum featuring an old steam train, a tramway trolley and working model trains.

PRACTICAL INFORMATION
TOURS

Self-Guided Tours – The tourist office provides a detailed map for exploring the village, as well as three hiking intineraries promising "fascinating and panoramic views".

TRANSPORT

Access by train: The Italian and French rail links from Nice and Ventimiglia towards Cuneo and Turin pass by the stations of Breil (Roya-Bévéra), Sospel and Tende.
A particularly scenic trip. 👥 In summer take the "Train des Merveilles", which has live commentary of the route ((⏰*see Planning Your Trip p32*).

▶ **Population:** 2,092.

◔ **Michelin Map:** 341 G4; region map: pp368–69.

▦ **Info:** Pl. Bianchéri. ✆04 93 04 99 76. www.breil-sur-roya.fr. Office du tourisme de la Vallée de la Roya. ✆04 93 04 92 05. www.royabevera.com.

◉ **Timing:** Breil is situated on the main road from Ventimiglia to Turin, via the Col de Tende pass, 14mi/23km from Sospel.

ADDRESSES

🛏 STAY

🛏 **Le Roya** – *Pl. Biancheri.*
✆*04 93 04 48 10. www.hoteleroya.com. 13 rooms.* ⊟*8€.* This hotel on the left bank of the Roya stands out because of its brightly coloured façade. Simple, unadorned rooms and spacious bathrooms. We recommend the rooms overlooking the mountain or the river.

🏃 LEISURE ACTIVITIES

A.E.T. Nature – *392 chemin du Foussa.* ✆*04 93 04 47 64. www.aetcanyoning. com. Open daily by reservation.*
This company organises hikes, *via ferrata*, rafting and a camping refuge for up to 20 *(reservations required)*.

Roya Évasion – *11 blvd Rouvrier.* ✆*04 93 04 91 46. www.royaevasion.com. Jul–Aug 9am–noon, 2–7pm; Apr–Jun and Sept–Oct Sat–Sun 9am–noon, 2–7pm.*
For canoeing, rafting, hiking and mountain biking excursions. Equipment for hire.

CALENDAR

A Stacada – *www.breil-sur-roya.fr.*
This four-yearly event (next 2013), held on the 3rd or 4th Sunday in July, celebrates the abolition of the *droit de seigneur* following a revolt by the inhabitants of Breil against a local tyrant in the 14C. Mock fighting and street chases ends in the *a stacada*, local patois for the "tying up" of the lord.

Saorge★★
Alpes Maritimes

Situated at the mouth of a gorge, between two rocky cliffs, Saorge clings to the steep slopes of a natural amphitheatre. For centuries, this extraordinary site was an invincible stronghold, protecting the valley, with its fortified castles,.

⌔ WALKING TOUR

THE OLD TOWN★
The town's stepped and vaulted streets lined with 15C houses fronted by sculpted lintels are spread over three levels, each with its own small square and fountain. Don't miss the terrace offering a beautiful **view**★ over the Gorges de la Roya.

Église St-Sauveur
The south nave of this 16C church has an 18C canvas depicting *Elijah with the Virgin and Child*, a fine Renaissance tabernacle, a 15C font beneath a painting by a local artist (1532) and a *Virgin* in gilded wood beneath a canopy (1708).

> ◗ *Leave from the southern end of the village, bearing right at the road fork.*

Madonna del Poggio
⚞ *Private property.*
The early Romanesque building has a soaring **belfry** with six rows of Lombard bands. This is the oldest religious building

- ▶ **Population:** 431.
- ⚙ **Michelin Map:** 341 G4; region map: pp368–69
- ℹ **Info:** Mairie (Town Hall). ℘04 93 04 51 23. www.saorge.fr.
- ◗ **Location:** Saorge is located 7mi/11.5km north of Breil-sur-Roya.
- P **Parking:** Park at the north entrance to the village.
- ◷ **Timing:** Allow 2hr for the village and one day for the gorges.

in the Roya valley. The journey back to the village offers a fine **view** of Saorge and its terraced olive groves.

> ◗ *Take a sharp right at the road fork towards the monastery.*

Couvent des Franciscains
◷*Open Wed–Mon May–Sept 10am–noon, 2–6pm; Feb–Apr and Oct 10am–noon, 2–5pm.* ⌔*Guided tours (1hr) 10.30am, 3pm.* ⚞5€. ℘04 93 04 55 55.
This 17C Franciscan convent, reinhabited by monks in 1969, is set among olive trees. The Italian Baroque-style church has a bell tower capped by a bulbous roof of coloured tiles. Small **cloisters** are decorated with paintings on pious themes. Splendid **view**★★ of Saorge and Roya Valley.

Couvent des Franciscains

© Nicolas Thibaut/Photononstop

INDEX

🚗 DRIVING TOUR

Saorge Gorges and Bergue Gorges
24mi/39km. Allow 4hr.
🗺 *See region map pp360–61.*

Breil-sur-Roya
🗺 *See BREIL-SUR-ROYA.*
▷ *Leave Breil-sur-Roya to the north by D 6204.*

The road to Col de Brouis (🗺*see SOSPEL p382*) forks off to the left.

La Giandola (🗺*See SOSPEL p382*).

Gorges de Saorge★★
The narrow road hugs the river's every curve beneath overhanging rocks. At the end of the gorges, there is a **view** between two rock cliffs of the stunning **setting**★★ of Saorge, built in curved tiers on a hillside clad in olive trees.

Gorges de Bergue★
Beyond Saorge and Fontan, the road ascends gorges cut through red schist

where the rock appears deeply coloured and foliated. The hamlet of **Granile** (🗺*see TENDE p391*) can be reached from here on a pleasant pathway. The valley widens out into the St-Dalmas-de-Tende Basin (🗺*see TENDE p391*).

ADDRESSES

🏠 STAY

⊜ **Berghe Chambre d'hôte Le Berghon** – *Hameau de Berghe Inférieur, 3.4mi/5.5km from Fontan on D 42.* ☎*04 93 04 54 65. www.leberghon. com. Reservation required in winter.* 🛏 *3 rooms.* ☕. This gîte in a tiny perched hamlet has three simple rooms. Pleasant hiking trails along the Céva mule track to the vallée des Merveille.

🍴 EAT

⊜⊜ **Le Bellevue** – *5 rue L.-Périssol.* ☎*04 93 04 51 37. Closed Mon eve, Tue.* Interrupt your tour of the covered alleys and settle in the yellow dining room. Panoramic **views** of the Roya Gorges.

La Brigue★

Alpes Maritimes

Part of Italy until 1947, La Brigue is a charming mountain village set amid vineyards in the Levense Valley, with views over Mont Bégo. The former domain of the Lascaris family, the village played an influential role in the Niçois *art primitif* movement.

🚶 WALKING TOUR

OLD VILLAGE

Topped with green schist roofs, the village's ancient houses cluster around the foot of the 14C chateau ruins. Some of the houses are built over arcades; others have carved lintels, often with a heraldic detail (*particularly rue de la République*). Place Vieille commands a fine **view** over Mont Bégo.

▸ **Population:** 630.
🗺 **Michelin Map:** 341 G3; region map: pp368–69
ℹ **Info:** 2 ave. du Général De-Gaulle. ☎04 93 79 09 34. www.labrigue.fr. Vallées Roya-Bévéra. ☎04 93 04 92 05. www.royabevera.com.
▷ **Location:** Located inland from Nice in the Roya valley. Arrive via St-Delmas-de-Tende, crossing the Roman bridge over the river, for the best **view** of Mont Bégo.
🕐 **Timing:** Allow 2–3hr to explore La Brigue and its sights.

Village of La Brigue

© Rémy Masseglia/Fotolia.com

To the right of the parish church stand two Penitents' Chapels: the 18C **Chapelle de l'Assomption** with its Baroque façade and graceful Genoese bell tower; and to the left the **Chapelle de l'Annonciation**, also Baroque, on a hexagonal plan, with a collection of ecclesiastical ornaments.

Collégiale St-Martin★

This parish church has a fine late 15C square Romanesque bell tower and a doorway framed in the Antique style (1576) with an older (1501) green schist lintel. The 17C organ was repaired in the 19C. The white marble font is crowned by a painted and gilded baldaquin. The church contains a remarkable collection of **Niçois** *primitif* **paintings★**. Chapels along the south aisle contain a Crucifixion with saints and donors comparable with Louis Bréa's in Cimiez, an altarpiece of St Martha recounting the legend of her arrival in Marseille on a boat, a rare realist painting by Bréa of the Sufferings of St Elmo, and a fine altarpiece of the **Adoration of the Child**, also by Bréa. On the north side, the first chapel contains a triptych by the Italian Fuzeri of **Our Lady of the Snows** (1507) with its 18C Baroque frame.

Local Trails

Ask for the maps from the tourist office.
The "Chemin des Oratoires" from La Brigue to St-Dalmas-de-Tende *(1hr).*
Nature Interpretation Trail between La Brigue and Notre-Dame-des-Fontaines *(1.5hr).*

EXCURSION
Chapelle Notre-Dame-des-Fontaines★★

 2.5mi/4km east on D 43.
 Open early May–early Nov 10am–noon, 2–5.30pm. Rest of the year by request at tourist office. 2€.

Set alone in the Mont Noir Valley near Mont Bégo and overlooking a mountain stream, the 14C chapel of Notre-Dame-des-Fontaines is built on the site of a former sanctuary dedicated to water, frequented as early as the 2C and 3C. It was succeeded by a small chapel, of which the 12C choir remains. Before the nave was raised in the 18C with seven clerestory windows, it was expanded to receive an extraordinary series of frescoes in 1492.

The frescoes★★★ – The chancel panels were discovered in 1950 under a coat of wash. They were painted in 1451 by **Jean Baleison**, master of the Gothic

Jesus Questioned by Pilate by Giovanni Canavesio

E. Bayer / MICHELIN

Painted Chapels of the Nice Hinterland

Scattered in the valleys of the Roya, the Paillon and the Basse-Tinée, many medieval chapels contain superb frescoes designed to teach the Scriptures:

- ◆ Coaraze, St-Sébastien
- ◆ Lucéram, Notre-Dame-de-Bon-Cœur and St-Grat
- ◆ Peillon, Pénitent Chapel
- ◆ St-Dalmas-Valdeblore Church
- ◆ Venanson, St-Sébastien

There are also several modern successors worthy of note: Matisse in Vence, Cocteau in Villefranche and Tobiasse in Le Cannet.

style. They depict the Four Evangelists (on the vault), the Resurrection of Christ and the Virgin's Assumption (on the walls), each painted in his light, delicate and graceful style. The nave (The Passion) and the inside of the façade (The Last Judgement) was decorated in the same period by the Renaissance Primitive **Giovanni Canavesio** (1420–early 16C), in a dramatic, realist and sombre Gothic-inspired style, revealing both a greater tension and a Renaissance sense of space and perspective. St. Peter is depicted brandishing a large knife and a scimitar during the arrest of Jesus; in the garden of olives, he sleeps lying down (not sitting) and during the denial, he is surprised in the process of warming the soles of his feet; when Jesus prepares to wash them, they remain strangely on the surface of the water. These anomalies may hide a secret pre-Reformation criticism of the papacy (represented by Peter), avid for political and temporal power (knife), attached to its physical comforts (warm feet) and unconcerned by the need for purification (symbolised by water).

ADDRESSES

🛏 STAY

🍽 **Hôtel Mirval** – *3 r. Ferrier – 4mi/6.5km SE of Tende on D 6204 and D43.* ℰ*04 93 04 63 71. www.lemirval. com. 18 rooms.* ⊇*8.50€* This late-19C mountain inn has functional rooms. The contemporary dining room and veranda overlooking the peaks serves simple regional cuisine.

HIKERS' REFUGE

🍽 **Le Pra-Réound** – *On D 43 outside the village after the Maison Adapeï.* ℰ*04 93 04 65 67. Closed late Nov–Feb. 6 rooms.* ⊉. ⊇*6€.* Hikers will appreciate this small refuge with motel-style rooms and terraces facing the peaks.

Tende★

Alpes Maritimes

Tende (alt. 2,677ft/816m) enjoys a breathtaking Alpine setting on the banks of the Roya, beneath the steep rockface of the Riba de Bernou. Along with St-Dalmas, Tende is an ideal starting point for trips to the Vallée des Merveilles (⚲*see Vallée des MERVEILLES overleaf*).

SIGHTS

Old Town★

Set in a maze of narrow streets, Tende's houses, many dating from the 15C, are built from local green and purple schist stone. Note the Renaissance bell-towers on the chapels of the Black and White Penitents. A 66ft/20m length of wall is all that is left of the mighty castle built by the Lascaris family and dismantled by the French in 1692. The site now affords a **view**★ over the village.

Collégiale Notre Dame-de-l'Assomption

This 15C collegiate church was built on the orders of Honoré Lascaris (comte de Tende) from green schist, except for the Lombard tower, which is capped with a small dome. The Renaissance-style doorway is flanked by two Doric columns resting on two lions. The inside is divided into three aisles by thick, green-schist columns; the Lascaris lords are buried here.

▶ **Population:** 2,025.
💧 **Michelin Map:** 341 G3; region map: pp368–69
🄸 **Info:** Ave. 16-Septembre-1947. ☎04 93 04 73 71. www.tendemerveilles.com. Vallées Roya-Bévéra. ☎04 93 04 92 05. www.royabevera.com.
◐ **Location:** The old town huddles below the château ruins on the left bank of the Roya river. Tende, full of dizzying switchbacks all the way up to its peak, was once part of the Old Salt Road to Cuneo and Turin.

👥🄸 Musée des Merveilles★

Ave. du 16-Septembre-1947, opposite the Customs Office. 💧◐Open Wed–Mon (daily Jul, Aug, Sept) May–mid-Oct 10am–6.30pm; mid-Oct–Apr 10am–5pm. ◐Closed 12–24 Mar, 13–25 Nov, public holidays. ◉2€. ☎04 93 04 32 50. www.museedesmerveilles.com.

This museum explores the history of the Vallée des Merveilles and its inhabitants through a series of relief maps and models outlining the local geological landscape. An archaeology section, which addresses the beliefs and daily lives of people in the Copper and Bronze Ages, includes castings of the famous *chef de tribus* stele, dioramas and

Tende

© Christian Goupi/age fotostock

Changing Borders

When the comté de Nice became part of France, the Italian King Victor-Emmanuel II managed to keep the upper Roya Valley for his hunting excursions. At the end of the Second World War, the peace treaty with Italy – confirmed on 12 October 1947 by a plebiscite – finally ended this situation and the upper valleys of the Roya, Tinée and Vésubie became part of France, thus naturally aligning the border along the waterways.

displays of objects discovered during local excavations. A final section explores the economic life of the region over the centuries.

EXCURSION
St-Dalmas-de-Tende
○ *3mi/5km south.*

This attractive resort, once the main frontier post on the road linking Nice to Cuneo, is a good jumping-off point for excursions into the Vallée des Merveilles, with facilities for cycling, riding, skiing and hiking.

La Brigue★
○ *4mi/6.5km southeast.*
○ *See La BRIGUE p388.*

Granile
○ *6mi/10km to the south. Head towards Casterino (D 91), turning left after 0.6mi/1km. After 3mi/5km, park just outside the village at Granile.*

This seemingly isolated village, surrounded by mountains, is lined with typical houses decorated with wooden balconies and stone slab roofs. There is an impressive **view** of the Gorges de la Roya.

○ *Return to St-Dalmas-de-Tende and continue up the valley.*

The apple trees in the meadows contrast with the rock-strewn olive groves in the regions around Sospel and Breil.

ADDRESSES

🛏 STAY

▱ **Le Prieuré** – *rue Jean Médecin, St-Dalmas, 2.5mi/4km south of Tende by N 204.* ℘*04 93 04 75 70. www.leprieure. org.Closed Mar. 24 rooms.* 🅿. ⬜ *8€. Restaurant*▱▱. Tastefully restored former priory with large, well-kept rooms decorated with locally-made furniture. The vaulted dining hall opens out onto a pleasant patio. Menu offers Mediterranean cuisine. Terrace overlooking Mont Bego.

▱ **Auberge du Mouton Dort** – *28 ave. des Martyr-de-la-Résistance, St-Dalmas-de-Tende, 2.4mi/4km south of Tende on D6204, above the train station.* ℘*04 93 79 18 08. www.lemoutondort.com. 7 rooms.* ⬜ *10€* This house, perched on a steep slope close to the Italian border, offers simple, well-appointed rooms with purpose-made wooden furniture. Meals in the small, simple restaurant attached to the inn.

🍴 EAT

▱ **Auberge Tendasque** – *65 ave. du 16-Septembre-1947.* ℘*04 93 04 62 26. Closed two weeks in Feb, Tue and Thu eves Jun–Oct.* This modest restaurant sits within walking distance of the fascinating Musée des Merveilles. Good Provençal cuisine; reasonable prices.

🏃 SPORT AND LEISURE

Lucien Bérenger – ℘*04 93 04 77 85. www.berengeraventures.com.* Professional mountain guides, abseiling, rock-climbing and canyoning.

Via Ferrata – Rope bridges and vertiginous canyon crossings using special mountain-climbing equipment. A demanding course *(5hr)*, you can opt for the shorter version *(2.5hr)*. *Map of the course and tickets available at the tourist office.* ⊚*3.50€ (children 12–18 years 1€).*

Ski – Fans of the slopes can find the nearest ski resorts across the Italian border at Limone *(accessible by train).* Cross-country skiing and snowshoeing can be found in Casterino. *For information, contact the tourist office.*

Vallée des Merveilles★★

Alpes Maritimes

Lying at the foot of **Mont Bégo** (alt. 9,423ft/2,872m) in a region of glacial lakes, valleys, moraines and rocky cirques dating from the Quaternary period, the Vallée des Merveilles is famous for its thousands of Bronze Age rock engravings.

Access Routes

There are two different ways of getting to the Vallée des Merveilles, although both involve a long hike:

▷ *Take the N 204 up the Roya Valley to St-Dalmas-de-Tende, then D 91 to Casterino and follow one of the footpaths:*

🚶 *3hr.* Lac des Mesches to the Arpette area and the Refuge des Merveilles.

🚶 *2.5hr.* Casterino refuge to the Fontanalbe refuge and the Fontanalbe district.

▷ *From Belvédère to St-Grat (⚙ see Vallée de la VÉSUBIE p374) and the footpath to Pas de l'Arpette.*

Over 373mi/600km of marked trails cover the area, including sections of the GR 5 and GR 52A trails, which circle the Mercantour National Park and cross through the Vallée des Merveilles. There are also trails which lead to Authion, Boréon and to the Madone de Fenestre (⚙ see Vallée de la VÉSUBI p374 and Forêt de TURINI p380). The engravings can be visited from June to September (⚙ see Practical Information for guided tour information).

A BIT OF HISTORY

The name Bégo is derived from an Indo-European root, which means the sacred mountain *(Be)*, inhabited by the bull-god *(Go)*. The region of Mont Bégo is an **open-air museum** comprising over 40,000 engravings.

⚙ **Michelin Map:** 341 F3/4.

▤ **Info:** Parc National du Mercantour, 23 rue d'Italie, Nice. ☎04 93 16 78 88. www.parc-mercantour.eu. Maison du Parc National à Tende. ☎04 93 04 67 00. www.tendemerveilles.com. Roya-Bevera Office du Tourisme. ☎04 93 04 92 05 www.royabevera.com.

▷ **Location:** The site known as the Vallée des Merveilles consists of seven distinct regions around Mont Bégo: the Vallée des Merveilles itself, which is the largest area; the Vallée de Fontan-albe, which is narrower; the Valmasque, Valaurette, Lac Sainte-Marie, Col du Sabion and Lac Vei del Bouc areas, which contain only a few scattered carvings.

⊚ **Don't Miss:** The Bronze Age engravings.

🕐 **Timing:** An overnight stay in a refuge is preferable for the Vallée des Merveilles.

Although the engravings were discovered and identified at the end of the 17C, it was not until 1897 that they were studied systematically by the British amateur archaeologist Clarence Bicknell. When the region became part of France in 1947, more intensive research was carried out by a team working under Henry de Lumley, which spent 30 years recording every engraving within an area of 30 acres/12ha.

Cut into the rockface worn smooth by glacial erosion 15,000 years ago, the linear engravings date from the Gallo-Roman period through the Middle Ages to the present day. The most interesting ones date back to the early Bronze Age (c. 2,800 BC–1,500 BC).

A stippling technique was used by juxtaposing tiny dots punched into the rockface with flint or quartz tools.

Vallée des Merveilles★★

Finding Your Bearings

The site consists of seven separate sectors radiating out from **Mont Bégo**: the largest site, the **Vallée des Merveilles**, is tucked between the Grand Capelet and Mont Bégo, and contains over half of the engravings; the smaller **Vallée de Fontanalbe** features around 40% of the engravings; lastly the Valmasque, Valaurette, Lac Ste-Marie, Col du Sabion and Lac Vei del Bouc sectors only contain rare, scattered engravings.

The Engravings

There are roughly 40,000 figurative engravings scattered over 3,700 rocks in the Vallée des Merveilles, at an altitude of 5,500 to 8,500ft/1,700 to 2,600m. Most of the figures are corniform, consisting of at least a body and a pair of horns (74%); the remaining engravings are made up of geometric figures, many divided into sections (15.8%), weapons, such as daggers, halberds and axes (8.1%), and anthropomorphic shapes, mainly divinities (2%). The corniform figures have a body (square, rectangular, round and triangular) and an appendage, such as a neck, head, eyes, tongue, hooves or tail. They are often linked by a yoke pulling a shaft attached to a swing plough guided by a small human form. The weapons have been particularly important in dating the site to the Copper and Bronze Ages since many similar objects have been found at nearby archaeological sites, such as triangular daggers fitted to handles and halberds with blades in the form of long perpendicular shafts. The anthropomorphic shapes are often depicted in groups of corniform figures, headless men with zigzag arms, or networked figures. These petroglyphs may correspond to a symbolic language and, along with Sumerian cuneiform (3,300 BC) and the Egyptian hieroglyphics of the Nile Valley (3,200 BC), they are possibly one of man's oldest forms of writing. The consistency of the engraving techniques and the iconographic themes suggest these figures were not produced by chance, but correspond to a conception of the world that was handed down from generation to generation through a graphic code.

Hiking at the Vallée des Merveilles

The Magic Mountain

The engravings reveal the preoc-
cupations of the Ligurian people
living in the lower valleys 4,800
to 3,500 years ago. The Ligurians
believed that Mont Bégo had
divine powers and the mountain
cult was devoted to the bull god,
who symbolised the power of
lightning and fertilising rain. Paying homage to the bull god would
have been particularly important
to these agricultural and pastoral
people, who hoped to ensure the
continuity of the rain, springs and

Engravings at Vallée des Merveilles

© Valery Trillaud/age fotostock

rivers that watered their crops. The ploughs and harnessed animals suggest
agriculture was practiced, while the crisscross patterns may represent parcels
of land. Although the more rare human figures have been given names –
Christ, the Chieftain, the Dancer, etc. – their exact meaning is far from clear.
Others are even more enigmatic, such as the Tree of Life at Fontanalbe. The
most famous engraving, the Wizard, shows what looks like a bearded man
with his hands above his head, his palms facing towards us and his fingers
spread wide. Although he looks as if he is casting a spell, this is, in fact, the
bull god brandishing lightning. Certain original engravings can be seen at
the **Musée des Merveilles in Tende** *(see p391).*

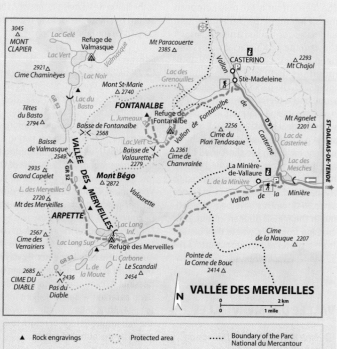

VALLÉE DES MERVEILLES

0   2 km
0   1 mile

N

▲ Rock engravings ∷ Protected area ⋯⋯ Boundary of the Parc National du Mercantour

Wolf at Parc National du Mercantour

The Mercantour National Park

Created in 1979, this 170,000 acre/ 68,500ha nature reserve spanning the Alpes-Maritimes and Haute-Provence regions was once part of the hunting grounds of the King of Italy. It is now twinned with the Parco Naturale delle Alpi Marittime, with which it shares a 20.5mi/33km border.

The Mercantour is the only European massif inhabited by three mountain ungulates, or hoofed animals, which thrive in the park's glacial valleys and deep gorges: chamois (over 9,000), mouflons (890) and Alpine ibexes (over 520). The park's medium-altitude woodland is teeming with stags, deer, hares, stoats and marmots. It also provides an ideal habitat for black grouse, snow partridges and numerous birds of prey, including the short-toed eagle and golden eagle. The bearded vulture has been successfully reintroduced to the park and, for the first time in France since 1942, wolves have begun breeding in the Massif du Mercantour after crossing from Italy, where they benefit from a protected environment (⟟see ST-MARTIN-VESUBIE p376).

◗◗ WALKS

VALLÉE DES MERVEILLES

◗ *6mi/10km north of St-Dalmas-de-Tende by D 91. Leave the car at Lac des Meshes.*

◪ *8hr round trip for strong walkers.*
Take the signposted footpath *(3hr on foot)* to the Refuge des Merveilles and then to Lac Long, the starting point for a guided tour of the Arpette area *(2hr round trip)*. It is possible to spend the night at the refuge *(reservation necessary)*, and then the following morning, walk up the Vallée des Merveilles as far as the Baisse de Valmasque *(about 2.5hr)*. Return by the same route to reach the car park in the late afternoon.

Fontanalbe

◗ *7.4mi/12km north of St-Dalmas-de-Tende by D 91. Park in Casterino.* ◪ *5hr. Easier walking than the first hike; ideal for families.*
Start south of Casterino by the information panel *(sign: Fontanalbe)*, taking the wooded path west and continuing to the refuge *(about 1hr)*. Bear left of the refuge building and continue to Lac Vert *(about 45min)*, the starting point for self-guided tours of the Sentier du Découverte *(1.5hr round trip)*.
For a guided tour of the engravings continue along the side of the lake to the guides' hut at **Lacs Jumeaux**. By staying overnight at the Fontanalbe refuge it is possible to climb the foothills of Mont Bégo as far as the Baisse de Fontanalbe (alt. 8,423ft/2,568m). Continue towards the Valmasque Refuge or return to Casterino by the outward route.

PRACTICAL INFORMATION

HIKING IN THE VALLÉE DES MERVEILLES

Important: these sites are situated at a high altitude (5,429-8,202ft/1,600-2,500m), so certain preparations are advisable: good physical stamina, mountain boots and warm clothing as protection against the cold and rain. Storms are frequent and sometimes violent, so it is wise to listen to the weather forecast. Study the route in advance on Map 1/25 000 – Vallée de la Roya – published by the Conseil Général des Alpes-Maritimes.

REGULATIONS AT THE SITES

Basic Guidelines: The main regulations are symbolised by the signs shown below *(don't walk on or touch the engravings or use iron-tipped hiking poles)*. Violations of these regulations, if detected by the official park guides, are punishable by heavy fines.

Visiting the Engravings: Although the Bronze Age rock engravings are protected for most of the year by a covering of snow, in recent years they have suffered considerable damage, inflicted intentionally or unintentionally by human visitors. To prevent such defacement the trustees and the officers of the Parc National du Mercantour have limited public access to the Arpette and Fontanalbe sectors only. Visitors may only enter these areas accompanied by the guides, who are on daily duty at the sites throughout the summer season.

For the Vallée des Merveilles – *Depart from the Refuge CAF des Merveilles. Jul–Aug daily 8am, 11am, 1pm, 3pm; Jun and Sept Fri–Mon 8am, 1pm.* ⬤*10€. www.vallee-merveilles.com.*

For the Vallée de Fontanalbe – *Open 8am from the Refuge de Fontanalbe, Jul– Aug daily 8am, 11am, 2pm; Jun and Sept Fri–Mon 8am, 11am, 2pm.* ⬤*10€. www.vallee-merveilles.com.*

Within the National Park

No domestic animals, no fires, no camping within an hour of the park boundaries and no disposing of waste within the boundaries. Refreshments and accommodation are available from the two refuges. Advance reservation highly recommended.

OFFICIAL GUIDES

Merveilles, Gravures & Découvertes *– 10 montée des Fleurs, Tende.* 𝄞*06 86 03 90 13 or 04 93 04 89 72.* Registered mountain guides approved by the Mercantour National Park for hikes and tours of the engravings.

Destination Merveilles *– 10 rue des Mesures, Villeneuve-Loubet.* 𝄞*04 93 73 09 07. www.voyages-randonnees.com.* Organises various outings and hiking tours in the Vallée des Merveilles.

Association des Guides, Accompagnateurs et Amis des Alpes Méridionales *– St-Martin-Vésubie.* 𝄞*04 93 03 26 60.* Guides specialising in the Vallée des Merveilles.

REFUGES

Refuge de Fontanalbe – 𝄞*04 93 04 89 19. Closed Oct-May - by reservation mid-Jun-Sep.* Accommodation and snacks available on-site. Reserve well in advance in season.

Refuge des Merveilles – 𝄞*04 93 04 64 64. www.cafresa.org (online reservations). Open mid-Jun–Sept; off season* 𝄞*04 93 04 88 90 or 06 27 00 59 44.* Accommodation and half-board on-site. Advanced reservation required.

INDEX

INDEX

INDEX

INDEX

INDEX

INDEX

Z

W

Walking Tours

INDEX

MAPS AND PLANS

MAP LEGEND

	Sight	Seaside resort	Winter sports resort	Spa
Highly recommended	★★★	≏≏≏	✳✳✳	♱♱♱
Recommended	★★	≏≏	✳✳	♱♱
Interesting	★	≏	✳	♱

Additional symbols

🛈	Tourist information
═══ ═══	Motorway or other primary route
❶ ❶	Junction: complete, limited
↔ ═══	Pedestrian street
ɪ═════ɪ	Unsuitable for traffic, street subject to restrictions
▭▭▭ - - - -	Steps – Footpath
🚆 🚆	Train station – Auto-train station
🚌 🚌	Coach (bus) station
·——·——	Tram
⌾	Metro, underground
P R	Park-and-Ride
♿	Access for the disabled
✉	Post office
☎	Telephone
✉	Covered market
·⚔·	Barracks
△	Drawbridge
⊌	Quarry
✗	Mine
B F	Car ferry (river or lake)
⛴	Ferry service: cars and passengers
⛴	Foot passengers only
③	Access route number common to Michelin maps and town plans
Bert (R.)...	Main shopping street
AZ B	Map co-ordinates

Selected monuments and sights

◉ ⇨	Tour - Departure point
🏛 ✝	Catholic church
🏛 ✝	Protestant church, other temple
✡ ☪ 🕍	Synagogue - Mosque
▰	Building
■	Statue, small building
✝	Calvary, wayside cross
◎	Fountain
●—■	Rampart - Tower - Gate
⋈	Château, castle, historic house
∴	Ruins
◡	Dam
✿	Factory, power plant
✩	Fort
∩	Cave
▱	Troglodyte dwelling
⌂	Prehistoric site
▼	Viewing table
₩	Viewpoint
▲	Other place of interest

Abbreviations

A	Agricultural office (Chambre d'agriculture)
C	Chamber of Commerce (Chambre de commerce)
H	Town hall (Hôtel de ville)
J	Law courts (Palais de justice)
M	Museum (Musée)
P	Local authority offices (Préfecture, sous-préfecture)
POL.	Police station (Police)
🛡	Police station (Gendarmerie)
T	Theatre (Théâtre)
U	University (Université)

Sports and recreation

🏇	Racecourse
⛸	Skating rink
≋ 🏊	Outdoor, indoor swimming pool
🎥	Multiplex Cinema
⛵	Marina, sailing centre
⛺	Trail refuge hut
□━■━■━□	Cable cars, gondolas
□+++++++□	Funicular, rack railway
🚂	Tourist train
◆	Recreation area, park
🎿	Theme, amusement park
⚚	Wildlife park, zoo
✿	Gardens, park, arboretum
🕊	Bird sanctuary, aviary
🚶	Walking tour, footpath
🙂	Of special interest to children

COMPANION PUBLICATIONS

REGIONAL AND LOCAL MAPS

To make the most of your journey, travel with Michelin maps at a scale of 1:200 000: **Regional maps nos 513, 518 and 519** and the new local maps, which are illustrated on the map of France below.

MAPS OF FRANCE

And remember to travel with the latest edition of the **map of France no 721**, which gives an overall view of the region of the Châteaux of the Loire, and the main access roads which connect it to the rest of France. The entire country is mapped at a 1:1 000 000 scale and clearly shows the main road network. Convenient Atlas formats (spiral, hard cover and "mini") are also available.

INTERNET

Michelin is pleased to offer a route-planning service on the Internet: **www.travel.viamichelin.com www.viamichelin.com** Choose the shortest route, a route without tolls, or the Michelin recommended route to your destination; you can also access information about hotels and restaurants from *The Red Guide*, and tourists sites from *The Green Guide*. There are a number of useful maps and plans in the guide, listed in the table of contents.

YOU ALREADY KNOW THE GREEN GUIDE, NOW FIND OUT ABOUT THE MICHELIN GROUP

A better way forward

The Michelin Adventure

It all started with rubber balls! This was the product made by a small company based in Clermont-Ferrand that André and Edouard Michelin inherited, back in 1880. The brothers quickly saw the potential for a new means of transport and their first success was the invention of detachable pneumatic tires for bicycles. However, the automobile was to provide the greatest scope for their creative talents. Throughout the 20th century, Michelin never ceased developing and creating ever more reliable and high-performance tires, not only for vehicles ranging from trucks to F1 but also for underground transit systems and airplanes.

From early on, Michelin provided its customers with tools and services to facilitate mobility and make traveling a more pleasurable and more frequent experience. As early as 1900, the Michelin Guide supplied motorists with a host of useful information related to vehicle maintenance, accommodation and restaurants, and was to become a benchmark for good food. At the same time, the Travel Information Bureau offered travelers personalised tips and itineraries.

The publication of the first collection of roadmaps, in 1910, was an instant hit! In 1926, the first regional guide to France was published, devoted to the principal sites of Brittany, and before long each region of France had its own Green Guide. The collection was later extended to more far-flung destinations, including New York in 1968 and Taiwan in 2011.

In the 21st century, with the growth of digital technology, the challenge for Michelin maps and guides is to continue to develop alongside the company's tire activities. Now, as before, Michelin is committed to improving the mobility of travelers.

MICHELIN TODAY

WORLD NUMBER ONE TIRE MANUFACTURER

- 70 production sites in 18 countries
- 111,000 employees from all cultures and on every continent
- 6,000 people employed in research and development

Moving
for a world

Moving forward means developing tires with better road grip and shorter braking distances, whatever the state of the road.

CORRECT TIRE PRESSURE

RIGHT PRESSURE

- Safety
- Longevity
- Optimum fuel consumption

-0,5 bar

- Durability reduced by 20% (- 8,000 km)

-1 bar

- Risk of blowouts
- Increased fuel consumption
- Longer braking distances on wet surfaces

forward together
where mobility is safer

It also involves helping motorists take care of their safety and their tires. To do so, Michelin organises "Fill Up With Air" campaigns all over the world to remind us that correct tire pressure is vital.

WEAR

DETECTING TIRE WEAR

The legal minimum depth of tire tread is 1.6mm. Tire manufacturers equip their tires with tread wear indicators, which are small blocks of rubber moulded into the base of the main grooves at a depth of 1.6mm.

Tires are the only point of contact between the vehicle and road.

The photo below shows the actual contact zone.

NEW TIRE

WORN TIRE
(1,6 mm tread)

If the tread depth is less than 1.6mm, tires are considered to be worn and dangerous on wet surfaces.

Moving forward
means sustainable mobility

By 2050, Michelin aims to cut the quantity of raw materials used in its tire manufacturing process by half and to have developed renewable energy in its facilities. The design of MICHELIN tires has already saved billions of litres of fuel and, by extension, billions of tons of CO_2.

Similarly, Michelin prints its maps and guides on paper produced from sustainably managed forests and is diversifying its publishing media by offering digital solutions to make traveling easier, more fuel efficient and more enjoyable!

The group's whole-hearted commitment to eco-design on a daily basis is demonstrated by ISO 14001 certification.

Like you, Michelin is committed to preserving our planet.

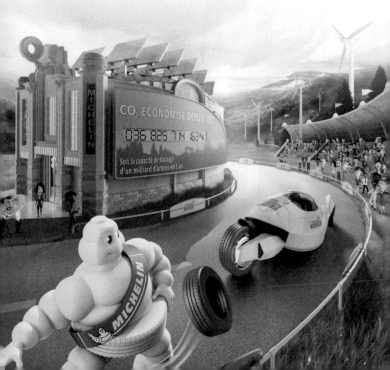

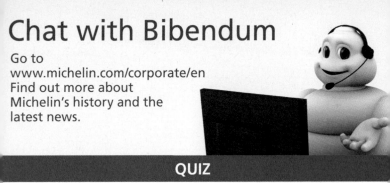

Chat with Bibendum

Go to
www.michelin.com/corporate/en
Find out more about
Michelin's history and the
latest news.

QUIZ

Michelin develops tires for all types of vehicles.
See if you can match the right tire with the right vehicle...

Solution : A-6 / B-4 / C-2 / D-1 / E-3 / F-7 / G-5

Michelin Apa Publications Ltd

58 Borough High Street, London SE1 1XF, United Kingdom

No part of this publication may be reproduced in any form
without the prior permission of the publisher.

© 2012 Michelin Apa Publications Ltd
ISBN 978-1-907099-55-7
Printed: December 2011
Printed and bound in Germany